HAPPENSTANCE

LESTER FISHER

authorHOUSE®

AuthorHouse™
1663 Liberty Drive
Bloomington, IN 47403
www.authorhouse.com
Phone: 833-262-8899

Published by AuthorHouse   09/03/2021

ISBN: 978-1-6655-3600-4 (sc)
ISBN: 978-1-6655-3599-1 (hc)
ISBN: 978-1-6655-3598-4 (e)

Library of Congress Control Number: 2021917387

Print information available on the last page.

Unless otherwise indicated, all scripture quotations are from The Holy Bible,
English Standard Version® (ESV®). Copyright ©2001 by Crossway Bibles, a
division of Good News Publishers. Used by permission. All rights reserved.

Scripture quotations marked NLT are taken from the Holy Bible, New Living
Translation, copyright © 1996, 2004, 2007. Used by permission of Tyndale House
Publishers, Inc. Carol Stream, Illinois 60188. All rights reserved. Website

Scripture quotations marked NIV are taken from the Holy Bible, New International
Version®. NIV®. Copyright © 1973, 1978, 1984 by International Bible Society.
Used by permission of Zondervan. All rights reserved. [Biblica]

This book is printed on acid-free paper.

PREFACE

I AM WRITING THESE BOOKS as a kind of "hard drive" dump of my life. I am trying to be as honest as I can, but like any hard drive, there are corrupted areas of the memory. In fact, the writing of this memoir is precautionary or, perhaps, prophylactic. Who knows when the hard drive will crash or start developing irreparable glitches. I figure I have learned at least a few useful things in my life. However, my physical condition is such that I probably won't have the opportunity to put some of those "invaluable" skills to work. Pilot said *quod scripsi scripsi*; I say *quod facio facio*. Meaning I have probably done about as much as I will be able to do. At the risk of being too pedantic, I will resort to the old saying; "If you can't do, teach; but if you can't teach, write!" Well, I have done, and I have taught, so now I write.

Returning to the computer theme, I am so impressed with the technological world we live in that I have liberally borrowed from it. Of course, I am not enamored of everything about the computer age, but it is an unmistakable boon to those wishing to write a book. I must confess that I have relied very heavily on Wikipedia.com. My first reason is that I am egalitarian; I think everyone should benefit from the internet like everyone benefited from the invention of the book. Guttenberg himself tried to control it, just like the monks had tried to control access to the hand written manuscripts before him.

My second reason for resorting to Wikipedia is because it is the perfect format. If I wanted to bring up a subject with which I think my readers are not familiar, why should I have to introduce the whole concept when Wikipedia does it so concisely? Every entry starts with a brief explanation, almost a definition, of the topic. If you need to go into greater detail, Wikipedia will usually have the current information. Maybe it is not absolutely verified like *Encyclopedia Britannica*; but have you ever read a 50 year old copy of these scholarly tomes? You will usually find a few outrageous fallacies within their hallowed pages. That is the nature of human knowledge, imperfect. At least with Wikipedia, you have people checking and correcting the information all the time. Besides, for the personal memoir of one insignificant individual, the world will not end if there is a mistake. Life is full of mistakes, and the ivory towered universities which are so disdainful of the Wikipedia, are themselves not above reproach.

At the risk of belaboring the point, this is a personal peeve of mine. I had an employer who jumped all over me for citing Wikipedia on a table of Pollinators of Agricultural Crops. Fine, but so far, that scientist has only been willing to provide a very small table of the pollination requirements of a very few crops that are grown in my State of Hawaii. Nor have I found comprehensive volume that covers such pollinator relationships in detail for a large range of agricultural crops. On the other hand, the knowledgeable people who wrote the table of crop pollinators for Wikipedia have gone to as many sources as they could find to build the table:

https://en.wikipedia.org/wiki/List_of_crop_plants_pollinated_by_bees

Of course all the information in the table is not verified to the absolute detail of experimentation. What Wikipedia does is take whatever information is known and what is not certain, is referenced to the source. What else this pollinator table does is save the average grower, who wants to know about his/her crop, the trouble of trying to track down the available information. If he/she wants to delve further into it, *ma·zel tov*! But if he/she just wants to know if the crop can produce without honeybees, at least Wikipedia has may have the answer Enough said on that topic.

This book does not follow a strictly chronological order. There is an element of free association. More accurately, there is the evolution of the thought process that led to this memoir. In the beginning I introduce you to the circumstance of the offspring of three generations of my seed and as many as four generations of the seed of my wives (of whom there were three). Then I go back to the generations before me and proceed forward in time through my life, with occasional excursions into the present. Some of the past is documented; some of it is purely from memory, as imperfect as that may be. I am at once trying to demonstrate how random it all was and yet, how predictable some of the outcomes of my actions and the actions of others have been. I won't say the sins of the father are visited on the sons, but I will say that parental input can profoundly affect output, sometimes for better and sometimes for worse.

I also hope the reader will not object to the many footnotes regarding so many things that have occurred during my lifetime, and a few that occurred long before I was born. You can gloss over them if you just want a quick read, and in the e-book version these footnotes will largely be embedded as links to the URL where they originated. Nevertheless, I think there are fascinating tidbits of information that I either knew before I wrote, or discovered in the process of writing, *Mea Culpa!* For example, I knew almost nothing about my step-father's experience in WWII. Using the information on his certificate of life membership in the Sixteenth Armored Division Association, I was able to find a trove of interesting and humorous information about the 64th Armored Infantry Battalion during their stay in Czechoslovakia.

I am a scientist of sorts, and find the natural world fascinating. You will find a lot of references to biological issues that I consider important. If it doesn't fascinate you, you need not read the footnotes to understand the text.

ACKNOWLEDGEMENTS

FIRST I WANT TO THANK my dear wife, Gretchen, who has been so patient and supportive through this whole process. It was she who preserved much of the information about our lives together, and she is most talented in the area of grammar and proper English. I also want to thank my son, James Kevin, and daughter. Colleen Malia, for not saying: "Are you crazy, Dad?" They have been supportive, even though they have both declined to read the memoir before it was completely finished. They have waited a long while. I also would like to acknowledge my dear Step-mother, Elizabeth Klungness (7/25/1924 - 9/21/2015), who kindly agreed to edit this book. She had been an editor and writer for many of her 91 years, and was still willing to help a neophyte.

CONTENTS

CHAPTER 1

Happenstance?

His shoots shall spread out; his beauty shall be
like the olive, and his fragrance like Lebanon.[1]
English Standard Version (2001) Hosea 14:8

MY LIFE IS COMING TO a point where I must do some soul-searching.
I need to determine what useful thing(s) I can do with my remaining time
on earth. As in the movie *Alfie*, the questions of life are, "In the end, is **Alfie**
happy, and above all, what's it all about, then?"[2] These are two very difficult
questions. Am I happy? And what <u>is</u> it all about? Is there a plan? Is there
a reason? Is there meaning? Or is it all just Happenstance? Unbeknownst
to me, just before I wrote this, a paper was published on the theory of
happenstance.[3] It pretty much reflects my life. Is that happenstance or
what?

Now it is two days after Christmas 2008. I am with Gretchen, my
first love and now, finally, my third wife. I have spent most of our free
time watching television except when we went to dinner with friends. On
Friday, after work, we went to a movie with the same couple. The movie
was *Marley and Me*, which puts some perspective on life. Even though it
was a dog's life, it pointed out the importance of commitment on the part
of the dog to the family… and I suppose the reverse. Our lives have been
like that also. It's all about family, but we are here in Hawaii, and the family
is all thousands of miles away, on what we islanders nostalgically call "the
mainland". Gretchen's daughter-in-law, Brandy, just gave birth to the newest
member of the family, Rylen Cooper, 8 lbs. 4 oz., 21 inches. He was born
in Portland, Oregon, on one of the coldest, snowiest winters, in over forty

years. The family brought Rylen home on Christmas Eve. All's well, except for the fact that the new parents don't have jobs, and we just had to give them money to cover two months' mortgage payments so that, hopefully, they will not lose their townhouse.

Gretchen and I have both been fortunate to have stay employed, and so has Brandy's father. He and her mother have been there for the whole delivery. While it is bitter sweet for Gretchen to have missed the birth of both grandchildren, we feel very fortunate in this time and place, since so many people are losing their jobs in America as a whole. Times are uncertain in 2008… we are perilously close to a recession the magnitude of the Great Depression of 1929. We can only hope that the incoming administration of Barack H. Obama will save us from international collapse. I actually had to retire from the federal government where I worked for 8 years (with an additional two years of service in the Peace Corps). And Gretchen was cut back to three days per week at the law firm that employs her. Fortunately, my boss at the USDA went to bat for me and managed to get me re-hired at the University of Hawaii, working on the Varroa mite eradication project in Hilo. This is on the Big Island of Hawaii where we live. Gretchen was also able to get two days' work with another lawyer, named Sandy. She was a member of the law office for which Gretchen has worked since she married me and moved to Hawaii. Sandy left the firm to take a job as a judge several years ago, and had since retired and gone back into private practice.[4] Sandy was not able to employ Gretchen full-time but the extra hours help us make ends meet, and give Gretchen some diversity in her job, which had become quite routine. My return to working with honeybees has also been a new challenge for me, especially given my age (sixty) and arthritic condition. They say bee stings are good for arthritis… Lord, I hope that is true!

These are the mundane facts, but the circumstances, the strange chain of events that led us to where we are now, are begging me to contemplate. They are all part of what, at times, seems a random sequence of happenstance. Yet how different our lives, and the lives of many others, would be if they had not happened. There would not have been a Rylen Cooper (at least not *this* Rylen Cooper), since his father, Cameron Peer, would not exist. Just as my son, James, born of an African mother of the Taita tribe of Kenya, would not be here in America to witness the inauguration of the first African American President of the United States. Barack Obama himself was the son of a Kenyan father and a Caucasian mother from our State of Hawaii. Nor would there be James's daughter, Taita, named for her grandmother's tribe, and Gretchen's granddaughter, Kayla (five), to be the two firstborn of that next generation. Nor would my now seventeen-year-old daughter be born to my second wife, Mary, who married me at graduate school. When I returned to UC Davis to pursue a master's degree, it led to the breakup of my marriage to James' mother, Charity. Later my daughter's mother left me to marry one of her employees, whom, by the way, I believed to have been my friend. Nor would their son, Daniel, have been born a developmentally disabled child. Six children, all born of this strange sequence of events that started when Gretchen and I were in high school.

I was in a Franciscan minor seminary, and she was the student body historian of the local high school in our hometown. How then did I, the potential future priest, meet Gretchen, eventually my last wife of three? Our fathers worked at the post office together, and her father asked my stepfather if he wanted to bring our family to a musical comedy, for which Gretchen's father was buying tickets. It was a simple request that would lead to such a long sequence of events and consequences.

Actually I should set the record straight since the reader will have long since been lost in the confusion if I do not explain. I met Gretchen when I was fifteen. Going to musical plays became a regular summertime activity of the Klungness and the Huffhines families. To be frank my lanky six foot two inch self was somewhat smitten with the perky, five-foot two, fifteen-year-old blond, when first she flitted down the stairs of the house her father had built. Nor was my mother unaware of the spark. In those high school years, she was more than willing to present this potential incendiary in my path to test the mettle of my vocation. She went so far as to bring Gretchen to Visiting Days at the seminary during the school year. This happened whenever we were planning an outing to some play or concert. I think she enjoyed Gretchen's company and liked mothering her, since she had to give away her only daughters for adoption. But I am sure she was not unaware of the obvious chemistry between her surrogate daughter and her also-illegitimate son. In our junior and senior years during summer vacation, Gretchen and I often went on dates together; all innocently, of course. The rationalization was that it is better to test the waters to be surer of one's intentions when embarking on such a permanent decision as the priesthood. By the time I had entered college, my mother had given up the concept of grandchildren and resigned herself to the fact that I was on the road to the Franciscan priesthood. To this day, I hope that my decision to leave the seminary and become engaged to Gretchen was not affected by the very strong influence of my mother.... if so, the influence obviously had the reverse effect of my mother's intentions. Of course, there was plenty of communication going on between Gretchen and me before the fateful decision was made. The late Fr. Benedict, the Dean of Students at San Luis Rey seminary, could have attested to our communication because he was reading and commenting. This included spelling corrections and advice, in my letters to and from Gretchen. Like a teacher grading papers he would fit his precise script in the margins in bold red. She likes to remember that Fr. Ben once wrote, "You didn't answer her question. She deserves an honest answer".

I have to beg some tolerance from you, the reader, at this point. As you may have noticed, my thoughts are rather free flowing as I gather the threads of history from my mind. In this first chapter, you may find the linkages confusing, and the connections thin. Try to understand that dredging up a life from 60 years of synapses is not always an orderly stream of consciousness. I can promise one thing, I will try to make it entertaining.

Well, Gretchen got her answer in the winter of 1967. She had already enrolled in the University of Washington, but she was home on Christmas vacation when I came home from San Luis Rey for the last time. Unbeknownst to Gretchen, I had previously broached the subject with her father by asking if I could marry her,

There was already tension in my parents' little cottage on the Toutle River. But the sparks flew when I stayed out until 2 AM with Gretchen in my parents' only car. It was before cell phones, and my parents were worried sick. My dilemma was that Gretchen was bawling because she didn't want to go back to the University of Washington without me. Needless to say, she did. Equally obvious was the reaction of my parents.... perhaps a bit severe, but very effective.

The next day, my parents took me and my baggage to a boarding house in the mill district of the logging town built by R. A. Long (Longview). I am sure the boarding house was one of the first structures built in the 1920's, and some of its residents were probably some of the first workers hired at Long Bell mill. One could not call it a flop house, but then it was not an upscale retirement residence either. The price was certainly manageable, even though I had neither job nor transportation. After one week, I moved to a boarding house more in the center of town, about half way in between Lower Columbia College, where I enrolled, and Pietro's Pizza Parlor, where I had managed to land a job. Those were long cold walks in the wet winter of '67, but definitely character building and enhancing to the long lean look that I had acquired from the Spartan meals at the minor seminary. My only paid meal of the day was a $1.00 breakfast at the Longview Café. I took my dinner at Pietro's Pizza Parlor, where Jack Troupe would let each of the crew make his own "medium pizza" for their lunch break. Needless to say, these pizzas would more properly be called *montagna*. My toppings were often three cheeses, peperoni, sausage, salami, Canadian bacon, olives, sliced bell pepper and tomato, topped with pineapple. Definitely all the food groups! I think I ate all of one meal at the boarding house; I believe it was stuffed bell peppers. Because of my classes and work schedule, I could never make the meal hours at the boarding house again.

Eventually, the owner agreed to charge me only for the room. It was a little room, but it was clean and it was near the bathroom with shower down the hall. The second story window looked out on the bare branches of an apple tree, and my writing table looked out on the gray streets of the gray town of Longview with lingering odor of the several pulp mills that fired the engines of commerce in that berg. It was a nostalgic, painful, yet hopeful time for me. I had no diversions, so I resorted to writing things like:

> Shoo-splash round rubber wheels roll
> While reminiscing I squat sit
> Upon this chair within my niche
> And wondering, wish and watch below
> Wet wandering rubber wheels go.

> "I do dearly!" dread I say it,
> Heard by her who might waylay it.
> Yet 'tis true, nor can be altered;
> Hope, I do, it bloomed and altar-ed!

My fondest memory of that winter was when I was writing a letter to Gretchen one day. I realized that flower buds on the apple tree were beginning to break open. It was probably my most profound realization of the promise of spring in my lifetime. I might have actually penned a poem, but I have no idea whether it still exists. The memory, however, has never left me. I ran across something I had written in my freshman year at the major Seminary, which may reflect the feelings I felt at seeing the buds bursting:

> There's something in the new growth,
> That's greater that the full growth.
> The hope in sunlit new growth
> Is seven times profound.

6

Nature saw them kind and gentle
Her do I see might unsettled.
To them t'was beauty fair and bright.
To me 'n'august and powerful sight.

Later I wrote something in a similar vein:

Seasons
When silver dew upon the green grass glitters
When hoary frost the spires of sunlight splinters
When wet mist massed on weeping oak trees
trickle
When warm wind's breath through rocky
rapids ripples.

It really did represent a turning point for me. I had done reasonably well in my coursework at Lower Columbia College. I think by that time I had advanced to a job at the Weyerhaeuser plywood plant making a whopping $3 per hour. I had previously made a few cents more in my summer jobs at the pulp mill. I was scheming to get back to that mill for the summer, particularly because they offered overtime. The dehumanizing monotony of being a drier sheet-feeder definitely did not hold the "glamour and adventure" of being a Lime Kiln Helper. One might be called from one's regular rounds of cleaning stacks and mud spills, to help open a stack washer which had just been shut down. Or even more glorious, double-time pay for mining the lime rings out of the kiln that had been shut down for Independence Day weekend. Although the dust was hot, dry and caustic, it was far superior to hosing out a liquor tank where every drop of alkaline water dripping from your nor'wester could burn your skin.

I wrote a description of my pulp mill experience for a freshman English class at San Luis Rey Seminary. May I take the liberty to include it, since Fr. Benedict seemed to appreciate it enough to read it aloud in class?

Sounds of Summer

The contents of this composition may strike you as somewhat sensual, and indeed they are, because the theme, the topic, and the concern of this paper are the realm of sensible noise. As a sort of reaction against the attempt of this school to abolish all forms of clatter, I would like to lose myself, and you, in a short contemplation of the whole wonderfully various world of sound, especially the one which I will re-enter this summer.

[The composition included descriptions of the sound of the bus, and the woods, but I leave these out and proceed to the sounds of the mill]

The Mill

The digesters' whoosh shatters the hum and grind and clatter and clunk of the pulp log chipper with a rushing stream of steam. A hissing shroud of steam softens the factory's loud pounding roar. But it's still deafening thunder throbs with the rush of red blood, as I pass on my way to work.

At the door of the kiln room, the sputter of small valves give way to the sonorous symphony of intoning electrical drones set to the beat of laboriously slow rolling ovens of cylindrical brick.

From the rear comes the monotonous scrape of the slaker-trough rake; there where the gyro-pumps rhythm-less whir runs in on the strident clang of the grinding trunnions that work their way up, then hammer fall, bang!

Farther still, at the five hundred foot length of the kiln, the hollow roar of a draft-tunnel blower rattles its bolts on a rapid unbalanced vibration.

And at the extreme, screams of steam, sprayed on the white-hot walls of the liquor-solution furnace, reinforces this acoustical combat.

San Luis Rey Seminary 1966

Still these jobs paid the bills.... Gretchen was coming home for the summer... The campus was in bloom... hope for the future was in the very sun-warmed air. I was so inspired that spring that I wrote a poem to Gretchen,

To one so fair her will-wisp hair
Can greet gold sun without regret;
Nor blush, but billow bubbling joy
And belle bright blue-eyed beauty blessed.

Light heart that's heaven's helpless coal
Whose warmly tender radiant glow
Un-nights the God-light. Gretchen grow!

How Gret the wonders where God blows
Te, tinder-fire of all-in-compass kindled love.

If I had to give a musical background to this picture of my youth, I think it would have to be Dvorak's Slavonic Dances.

The wistful, hopeful reveries of youth often have to give way to the realities of life. The debate of the summer was whether I would follow my original plan of going to Washington State College to pursue agriculture, or meld into Gretchen's plan and attend the University of Washington. With me pursuing… oh, I don't know, maybe microbiology. Dr. Helms had made the subject seem quite palatable, albeit not within the genetic inclination of my Irish "sodbuster" heritage. Needless to say, Gretchen won! Fall quarter would find me lost in Padelford Hall trying to apply for my classes.

May I digress slightly to describe my emotional state at this juncture? Padelford was a very modern building; a confusing labyrinth that I am sure was designed to weed out the inferior mice that could not negotiate the maze. Needless to say, I ended up in the ladies' restroom. There were so many letters and numbers on the door that only three letters registered in my mind, "men". I only realized I had entered forbidden territory when a woman entered the rest room only to quickly dart out the door again upon seeing me there. This then explained why there were no urinals. Briefly I had thought that perhaps the educated male *intelligencia* were required to urinate while sitting down (which does, in fact, make microbiological sense since science has discovered how messy the process of vertical urination is).

Amazing to myself, I did actually manage to register at the University of Washington. And no, science has not yet convinced the male population to pee sitting down. Even though, as I had learned in later years, Gretchen's mother had convinced her husband to sit when relieving himself in the family bathroom. Considering that most wives cannot convince their husbands to put the toilet lid down, this power that Jana had over her husband, Bob, may have explained why they were married for 48 years. And they would have made 50 plus if he had not succumbed to Parkinson's disease. Which is another ironic twist of fate, because there was no one man who had more *joie de vivre* than Robert Huffhines.

My discussion with my advisor was equally daunting. Some child genius in the newly exploding field of genetic engineering, he was sure that I needed to quickly get "up to speed". So he enrolled me in classes of genetics, bacteriology, organic chemistry and algebra. One of the Teaching Assistants in Bacteriology Lab was herself only 17; the next generation of whiz kids in that department. With labs, I had a total of 24 classroom hours. This was a lot for liberal-arts major, whose chemistry background at the major seminary consisted largely of a study of the cosmology of Teilhard de Chardin. Needless to say, in addition to maintaining a job and a girlfriend, I got a 1.8 GPA that quarter. Interestingly, Gretchen did exceptionally well that quarter. Better than she had in previous quarters, when she was alone in the daunting world of higher education. Subsequently I changed departments to Botany, a gentile old school, and made sure to soften my science-class load each quarter with a philosophy class.

That summer I had also purchased, with all my overtime pay, my first car. Four hundred hard-earned dollars for a 1960 aqua blue Chevrolet Corvair. I was so proud of it, and it rode like a dream. There was a reason for that… the independent suspension, before they learned about torsion bars, allowed the wheels to splay in and out with every bump… thus efficiently wearing the tire into a round donut in record time. I quickly learned the price of mobility… in tires, ball joints, shocks, clutches and eventually a complete engine overhaul. The mechanic assured me, when he had finished the overhaul, that there were a number of pieces of metal and a small pyramid of nuts and bolts that were absolutely unnecessary to the performance of this aeronautic engineering marvel. Strangely enough, I did not have any major problems with the Corvair after that. If I had the good sense to have put it into storage when I left for the Peace Corps, I might have owned a valuable piece of automotive history. Instead I signed the Corvair over to a Christian half way house in Ballard. As it turned out, I received a subpoena from the Chicago Court while I was in Kenya, because the Corvair had been used in a crime. The Judge let me off the hook with my lame explanation of being half way around the world in Peace Corps at the time of the crime. I don't know if the registration of the car was ever changed. Maybe my blue baby died in the crime? I'll never know.

But I fear that I have digressed again. The Peace Corps gig requires considerable explanation, especially since it was such a seminal event to my relationship with Gretchen.

Rather than pursue the details of ancient history at this early juncture, let's return to the contemplation of the curious and unfathomable fact of where we find ourselves today. On New Year's Day 2009, my daughter (then 17) called to say that she had a marginally enjoyable time with her Facebook friend from Wisconsin. He had driven all the way to Maryland in rather inclement weather to bring in the New Year with her. Of course, when I had called New Year's Eve, only to find that her stepfather did not know where she was, and that her mother was still visiting her own mother in San Francisco, my 20th century brain (raised on "Father Knows Best"[5]) went wild! I maintained my sardonic calm while discussing with my alter ego and former friend (Colleen's stepfather). My forced composure was because my alarm at the way Colleen has been raised in Maryland has caused considerable consternation in previous worrisome incidents. In spite of my restrained demeanor, it must have started some wheels turning, because my daughter admitted, in her recent phone call that she was probably in serious trouble with her custodial parents. I tried lamely to explain that any parent would be concerned! A "web-cam pal" can have a lot of connotations in the 21st century. The Badger had taken a hotel room in Maryland (but, in fact, they ended up staying with Colleen's parents) of course, I did not know that at the time. This is coming from a 17 year old talking about a 20 year old that she only knew from a year-long conversation by web-cam. "O brave new world, that has such people in 't!" (*The Tempest* by William Shakespeare).

Interestingly, my impression was that Colleen was not as pleased with this Badger as she had hoped, and that she perhaps had learned lessons from her previous youthful romances. Perhaps the "Tao of Steve"[6] had sunk in after my repeated reference to the importance of maintaining objectivity (translation: playing hard to get). Of course, I speculated that the Badger may not have been as satisfied with his marathon trip to the heart beat of the country, particularly since they didn't even find a decent fireworks display... and by implication, it was not "party on" in Maryland. Of course, I am interpreting this all from Colleen's telephone tone of voice, and I will be the first to admit that I am not the most astute father in history. I may be deluding myself. Perhaps there will be the tearful phone call next week... you know, the "woe is me, will I ever find love?" conversation. At least there has not been the "Do you know what your daughter has done now?" phone call from my Ex. I think the latter has given up threatening to try to send Colleen to live with me if she doesn't straighten up and fly right. Not that I would be displeased to have Colleen come back to Hawaii to go to College. But Mary, her mother, has made Colleen what she is, and one thing she has become is determined to stay with her friends and her life in Maryland.

Maybe young people really are more mature at a younger age these days. Maybe they have to grow up sooner, because they certainly can't rely on their parents to teach them good sense. Lord knows, we have screwed up our lives enough, and the kids are generally the collateral damage. Yet, here they are, trying to struggle through life, just as we did. Somehow, if we look hard enough, we can see a pattern, a hope, a determination, a will to survive.

Albeit so, that survival instinct seems more tenuous in today's youth than we remember from our youth. We had our worries and our problems, but the prospects of life were not nearly as formidable as what young people face today. Maybe if we went back two or three generations to war time or depression, those young people may have had as much to be concerned about as our kids do. But they did not have the speed and the pressure and the technology that have made living so much more tenuous. I sometimes like to watch the old movies, because they let us peer into the trappings of a more innocent age. Of course, there have always been the Mr. Potter's of *It's a Wonderful Life*, but there was also the community and the connections that sustained the working class in spite of the difficult times. You knew your neighbors, and your boss might have been nice enough to keep you on the payroll in spite of the difficult times. My mother remembered that the logging company kept her father and the other employees on the payroll even when the demand for lumber was depressed. Then you managed the hard times by reducing the work hours, not firing all the unessential staff. Of course, many did lose their jobs, but I don't think it was as cold hearted as it is today. Or was it? There are a few bright lights, like FEDEX, whose management had, by this date of writing, determined to cut back hours, not employees. But in light of the financial crisis of 2008, and seeing that is largely the fault of greed in high places, it is not hard to understand that the young people wish they could just step out of this world and form a different world that moves to a different drum… a slower, more thought provoking, more civil beat…. that of a heart and not a machine.

Still, as a father, I have to pray that another unexpected addition to the generations of my seed is not conceived. It may happen, in due time, but hopefully with a good foundation and love. My daughter is beautiful (which reminds me I failed to take advantage of the New Year's Day sale of her lovely graduation pictures), but she does not realize just how much she makes me proud. She is also talented, and I fully expect that she will come around to realizing that her ability to create in pencil, ink and paint could make her future. She had received an inordinate amount of encouragement towards education, to which her reaction has been contrary. Still, I cannot let myself think that she will "not figure it out" and find her niche in this highly competitive, but talent-loving society.

Likewise, my son James, who has lived a much more challenging life than Colleen, is also finding his love of knowledge and books. He realizes that he is underutilized in his un-chosen profession, even though he is very skilled at what he does. He fights fire for the forest service, which he came to as a consequence of happenstance. The school of hard knocks, so to speak, and 10 years of fire fighting has only recently earned him a permanent seasonal position on the Olympic National Forest. But his supervisors have used his talent, his ability to work with and lead diverse and sometime devious personalities. And he is a good teacher. Master Sawyer at age 33, he wields the power of good training like he wields a 32 inch bar, always spiced with anecdotes from a life of unsought adventures. I would go into more details about my rather impressive son, but I reserve for him the right to tell his own story. And I think someday he will. He certainly has no trouble maintaining my attention when we have the rare opportunity to share a starlight evening and a beer. I think he has a similar bard-like effect on a lot of people he has encountered in his exploits.

I received another phone call this New Year's Eve. It lasted for 2 hours! We were waiting to go to the homecoming party of Mae Kaler, a Native American friend, who had been the daycare giver for my daughter, and, in my opinion, the person who had the most positive influence on my daughter's development. How different my daughter's life would have been if her mother had not taken her to Maryland. If, instead, she had let Colleen grow up in "Mae land" with a circle of friends and a community culture that has produced a generation of balanced, happy, hopeful young people with none of the angst of most of this urban generation. Those preschoolers are now respectively a veterinary professor at Cornell, a dolphin protector, an architect, a Natural Foods store manager, a US marine/cowboy (paniolo style), and more good things to come. And at the center of that loving community was, and still is Mae. I haven't even mentioned the many exchange students that she introduced to life in Hawaii. If I think about my limited sphere of influence on the lives of generations, by comparison, she is a tidal wave of the Great Spirit.

Still, this pre-party phone call was from the oldest son of my first wife. Edward was the son of Charity Mshoi and a father whom Ed never knew. He was not yet a teenager, living with his grandmother, when Charity came to work for me at the County Council Hotel and Dance Hall in Taita Hills. I had not been in Taita long when one of the women, who worked at the hotel, told me that she had a friend that wanted to take English lessons. She had 5 children and had no job except to help her mother farm their small plot of land. That land was the legacy of the Kiwinda family. Reverend Jeremiah Kiwinda was the famous link in this family, because he was the first African to be ordained to the Anglican priesthood, and had gone on to become the bishop of his people. Edward was regaling me, in this phone call, with stories of the family. One story was that Desmond Tutu, as well as many important Africans from all over the world had come to the funeral of his 104 year old grandmother. That was all because of the century of connections between the Kiwinda family and the development of Taita and Kenya, as a whole. Because the Taita people had influence throughout Kenya, being early converts to Christianity, they had proven themselves to be an agreeable and hard-working people who moved into important positions of government and education during and after independence from Britain.

What Edward was trying to tell me was this. The daring step that his mother had taken to fall in love with me, and later follow me to America and marry me, had itself had a profound impact on Taita. I was thinking only of the impact on the 5 children and one grandchild that I had somehow managed to bring to Washington State. He was talking about all the people in Taita who followed suit. Cousins, acquaintances and sometimes strangers who knew that uneducated Charity had gone to America; if she could make it, perhaps others could succeed outside Taita as well. Ed was calling from the home of a cousin who had followed their lead, came to Washington, found employment and was even able to buy a house. He was telling me of Africans who had gone to Europe and Russia, and elsewhere. This was rather a surprise to me. I have worried a lot about the 5 children and James' nephew, Teddy (more like James' brother than his nephew). This is because after Charity and I broke up, I really wasn't sure what was happening with the kids. As it turns out, Ed has done quite well in business, and the next oldest brother earned an accountant degree and is working at Sylvania Co. Ed's nephew, Teddy, had worked for years with Ross, Inc. but has recently enrolled in that US Army and is posted to Bahrain. His niece has worked as a missionary teacher in Kenya, but her mother, who was a trained nurse when she came to America, has left that profession, and married and gave birth to several more children. Charity's youngest daughter and her three children have struggled with the hardships of Hilltop life, as did my own son, James. Fortunately James has come out of the Afro-American enclave of Tacoma. In fact, only one of Charity's sons has not had financial success. But that son started with a physical disadvantage. When I met Charity he could not walk. Between his oldest sister's and my efforts, we managed to get Sam to a hospital and to a point where he could walk. Nevertheless he has remained partially disabled. Fortunately, he is apparently a fairly content individual now. He lives with his mother, and, according to Ed, has become like the philosopher of the family. I also think the other sons are also happy that he is there to help Charity (who has never remarried). The brothers all contribute what they can to supporting Charity and Sam. After all, this is the African way, and although life in America has strained the bonds of family, for the most part they have not broken completely. Charity, of course, remains the main glue that holds them with that mystical power of *Mau* ('mother' in the language of the Wadawida). That is one thing that can only be understood by living with the people of Africa.

So I come away, from the conversation with Ed, believing that perhaps it has all been for the good… or, at least, more good than bad. Speaking to my daughter again the day after New Year's, also confirms my sometimes tenuous belief that, somehow, things may work out for the better. She and her friend from Wisconsin were enjoying their trips through the museums of DC, and she sounded happier than she has for some time. I also called her mother, who confirmed that the Badger seems like a nice guy, although she also suspects that the friendship is just that. Not a thing to be feared, but an indication that there is a certain measure of maturity in my daughter who marches to the beat of her own proverbial drummer.

My son James also called, and made me feel very comfortable about the New Year. He had spent it with his daughter in the chalet of his firefighter-brother and his professor wife. James made it sound as though they all enjoyed themselves, even though my son faces financial difficulties and does not really have a home in which to lie his head or entertain his daughter. I guess the whole group went back to visit my granddaughter's grandmother, which in itself is a positive sign after the unsettled breakup between James and Tammy. Yes, perhaps things will work out… perhaps we have a future in this world. After all, we all have our health, we are all sensible people and we can weather the storms that are certain to come our way.

I see that I have covered a lot of territory and a lot of years in these few pages. There is much filling-in to be done. So, I am taking that advice that I have given my children for so many years, "write it down". Surprisingly, Gretchen's mother and my grandfather were journalists. No, not the type that work for newspapers. They were journalists in the old fashioned sense of those who kept a journal all of their lives. I only have a fragment of my grandfather's journal, although my aunt and cousins still have his logs that date back to before the First World War. Gretchen's mother's journals go back to, at least, her teen years and Gretchen does have those. Ironically, both journals are the most un-emotive and manner-of-factual record of their two lives. Jana's entry upon the day of Gretchen's birth was "Gretchen was born. She weighed 6 lb. 8 oz." My grandfather's journal always contained the weather and other mundane details, although he would record visits of and to people and places. The most emotive thing that I could find in the volumes of his journal (that I possess) is about me. I visited him just before departing for the Peace Corps. I was hitch hiking with two Christian acquaintances of mine ... we were headed to California, where I was planning to visit my mother for the last time before I went to Africa. Gretchen and I had ended our engagement, and I was getting very involved with the Pentecostal movement. My grandfather was not a religious man, but he was not an agnostic or an atheist. He was not inclined to attach himself to any religion although he generally respected the belief of others. However, in this instance, he wrote, "I think Mike is on the wrong track". He would never have said anything to me, of course, but given all the things that have happened since, perhaps he should have.

But such disclosiveness was not the way of either my grandfather or Gretchen's mother, Jana. In fact, if they might have had time to know each other, they probably would have liked each other. They were sort of kindred souls. Both were thoughtful, relatively quiet, slow to judge, but usually right-on with their judgments. Perhaps Gretchen and I would do well to go back to their rather dry journals, since they are both deceased.... we might find out some things we had missed in our youth.. Gretchen says her parents were both opposed to her first marriage (not to me), but had concluded it was better not to interfere, lest Gretchen might later blame them. Albeit, her father did go around before the wedding singing a most telling song from the musical *I Do! I Do!* The chorus was, "my daughter is marrying an idiot! How can she stoop so low?"

My Grandfather liked Gretchen, and it was probably his advice that brought me out of the seminary, although I am sure he would not have wanted to be responsible. As he said, "I don't give advice". When I asked him what he thought about my growing affection for Gretchen in my senior year of high school, he said "If you can't stand the heat, stay out of the kitchen".

I find myself delivering such tried-and-true proverbial jewels of wisdom to my children all the time. Although, at that time, I thought it was pretty cryptic "non-advice". I am sure his approval of Gretchen is also why he wrote that in his journal. I was off course (Gretchen and I had separated by then). He did not come to my first wedding to Charity, probably because his second wife, Eva, was in advancing stages of Alzheimer's disease. However, he and his last wife, Josephine (we called her Josie), did come to my second marriage to Mary. He gave no indication of displeasure with Mary, but he nearly died on the spot. The Unitarian Church we had rented was built with a one story meeting hall and a sanctuary with a high ceiling that was shaped like the inside of Noah's ark. The ceremony was delayed and the temperature was rising rapidly in the 100+ degree heat of the Central Valley. The sanctuary was cool, but the windows would not open in the meeting hall. So everyone was sweltering, and Pat, Mary's father, himself an alcoholic of many years, had busted open the many cases of Champagne. He was pouring glasses liberally. My grandfather had only tasted his first wine that spring, on the Princess Marguerite cruise to Victoria, Canada, where Josephine and he were celebrating their honeymoon. Being a jovial and loveable pair, the captain had insisted that they dine with him at every supper, and, of course, to refuse the wine would have been impolite. But this wedding to Mary was no cruise, and there was no water to drink, as the wedding caterers had not arrived. So my grandfather, in his late 80's, in a full suit, was trying to quench his thirst with Champagne, with near lethal consequences. But being of sturdy lumberjack stock, he managed to make it through the day.

My mother, on the other hand, was not so quiet, having had a few too many bubblies at the behest of Mary's father. She was rather obnoxious; if not to Mary, certainly to her parents, and particularly to my swarthy Best Man from Bangalore. When Jairus tried to deliver the toast, she kept interrupting him. Still, how can you expect to tell a young... well not so young... couple that they should call the whole thing off, when you really don't approve of this secular wedding to your once-to-be-priest son? Of course, Fr. Carl, the priest for whom my mother was the rectory housekeeper, and who had baptized both my mother and me, had the good sense to stay home that day!

Nevertheless, had it not been for my second marriage, there would not be a Colleen Malia, born on the Island of Kauai in December of 1991. And now she is a few months away from graduating from High School, and all ready to enroll in college. Although her mother moved her away from me when she was only five, I am probably more attached to her than to any of my children by birth and marriage. My son and I are becoming closer as he has matured, but our relationship had to heal the wound of a six year old child, who believed that he was abandoned by his father. Whereas, in the case of Colleen, I don't think she has ever thought that I had abandoned her. Perhaps as she becomes an adult, she will realize that I have been less than a pillar of support, but I think she knows that I love her. James, I believe, has forgiven me for not being there. Actually, I think James has some appreciation for the effort my second wife, Mary, and I made to bring him to Davis and expose him to the world of "educated white folk". He particularly appreciated the advice and interest of Mary's professor father, Pat Purcell. Colleen, on the other hand, always knew that she was wanted for summers in Hawaii, and it has only been in her late teens that she has found the concept of summers in Hawaii as an obstacle to her life and friendships in Maryland.

So that is a passing overview of my life. I think I have mentioned most of the critically important people in my life. Admittedly, from the reader's perspective, at this point, it is like looking at the pieces of a jigsaw puzzle that was just poured out on the table. As I said at the beginning of the chapter, happenstance describes my life. I suppose you could say that about anyone's life. Even a life as "directed" as our newly elected President Obama. Had his father not returned to Kenya, had his mother not moved to Indonesia, had he not applied to Harvard, had he not interned at the law firm where Michelle Vaughn Robinson worked, would he have become the President of the United States?

For example, I met a man in Kenya who was catching honeybee swarms in Taita Hills. He was a retired agriculture extension agent from Colorado who had been invited by the Near East Foundation to work on a grant in Mombasa. He turned down the first invitation he received, because his wife Mary said, "You just retired! Then why would you want to run off to a foreign country to work?" However, when the Foundation invited him again one year later, he told his wife, "Mary, we have been married for 40 years, but I am going to Kenya. You are welcome to come." And she did, and found useful work at the Coast Province. He built two rice irrigation schemes on the Tana River. He also decided that they didn't have enough honeybees to pollinate the fruit trees at the Mtwapa Coastal Research Station. That is why he was catching swarms in Taita Hills. If I had never met him at the public market in Wundanyi, I probably would have never become interested in honeybees. As it happened, I began to help the white haired powerhouse of a man, Floyde Moon, and that led to the development of a course for beekeepers in Taita. It is also what led to my attending Univ. of California at Davis, which had been recommended highly by Dr. Gordon Townsend, Chairman of the Bee Biology Department at the Univ. of Guelf, Canada. Because of my work with Mr. Moon, I volunteered to help Dr. M. V. Smith collect pollen samples for the Canadian International Development Agency (CIDA). Dr. Townsend headed the CIDA project and had sent Dr. Smith to Kenya to start a beekeeping development project.

I would probably have continued to help the project, but I received a draft notice from the military and had to leave Kenya. On my journey, returning from Kenya, I visited Dr. Townsend at Guelf, thinking that I might be re-enlisting to work for the Peace Corps at the Mtwapa Research station. When I failed my military induction physical, and tried to reenlist in the Peace Corps, I was not allowed to return to PC Kenya because the Nixon administration chopped the Peace Corps budget. So I did pursue apiculture studies at UC Davis, after I worked five months for a bee breeder in California. Eventually I obtained a master's degree in International Agricultural Development. My later employment took me into other areas of science, although I never got closer to "overseas" than Hawaii. Unfortunately, I did nothing with honeybees for the next 36 years. Now, at age 61, I am again working on a government project trying to stop the spread of varroa mites in the honeybee population of the Island of Hawaii. The strategy was to kill all the colonies of honeybees within a 5 mile radius of the spot where mites were first detected. Equally unfortunate, the first thing that I did on the project was to recommend that they stop using a micro-encapsulated pesticide to try to bait and kill the honeybee colonies infested with Varroa mite. As it turned out, my master's thesis topic was the digestion of pollen in the intestine of honeybees. This was consequential, because bees have an organ in their stomach called the proventriculus. It is basically a valve that moves in and out of the honey crop (the bee's stomach) and its function is to move pollen from the crop into the lower intestine of the bee. Microencapsulated pesticides are about the same size as small pollen grains, Therefore, instead of being regurgitated at the hive and passed around the colony, the pesticide was being concentrated in the bowels of the foraging bees. Of course, the foragers eventually died, but the poison did not have much impact on the colony itself. My apiculture training finally came into play thirty-five years later... killing bees. Was it pure happenstance? Unfortunately, I also discovered the mite infestation in four hives, outside the eradication zone radius of 5 miles. That may be the straw that broke the camel's back. The State Department of Agriculture decided to stop the eradication program. The opportunity to be the first people in the United States to stop the spread of Varroa mite disappeared in a puff of my smoker.

This is the story of my life... one serendipitous or unpropitious twist after another; to what end I will probably never know until I lie on my deathbed... if even then?

CHAPTER 2

The Family in Oregon

Then the Lord passed by in front of him
and proclaimed, "The Lord, the Lord God,
compassionate and gracious, slow to anger, and
abounding in loving kindness and truth; who
keeps loving kindness for thousands, who forgives
iniquity, transgression and sin; yet He will by no
means leave the guilty unpunished, visiting the
iniquity of fathers on the children and on the
grandchildren to the third and fourth generations.
English Standard Version (2001) Exodus 34:6-7

ONE CANNOT REALLY UNDERSTAND THE intricacy of any
human being without knowing something about how that person was born
and raised. Sometimes that requires knowing more about the family history
of the person. Therefore I start this narrative as far back as I can remember.
There are large holes in my knowledge because there were not that many
members of the family that were willing to speak freely, even if I had had
the time or the interest to ask. Like my grandfather's journal, his side of the
family was inclined to avoid lurid facts, of which there were a few, and most
of those revolved around my mother's history. Fortunately, one of my distant
cousins, Linda Huff, has collected a genealogy of my mother's side of the
family, which has proved a very useful resource. About all I have ever been
able to get out of my mother's half-sister is a confirmation of my mother's
maiden name and military service. Of course, I have the official documents,
but I only have my mother's revelations to know the hushed history that led
to my birth. But I will need to start with her birth.

My mother was Kathleen Viola Seely, the illegitimate daughter of Frances Whitlock. The Whitlocks were a pioneer family of Western Oregon, one of the offspring of which was James Whitlock. This James, who was born in Silverton, Oregon in the mid-1870s, homesteaded in Tumalo, Oregon, with his wife Catherine, a comely dark-haired woman of a short lineage of Irish immigrants. Ma Whitlock, as we called her, who was born in Grand Rapids, Michigan, could recall coming across the continent on the train, but she had inherited hand-me-downs that had come with relatives to Oregon by wagon train. For example, a Podmore Walker serving tray, which we still have. There was not much information about my great great grandmother's side of the family. According to the notes my mother wrote, I think my great grandmother was second generation Irish American, and her mother had married and buried 3 husbands, all Irish. In the East she was married to a McDermott who had a son named Fred and a daughter named Catherine Agnes (Ma Whitlock, who was born in 1879). My mother did not know who Ma's parents were, but my second cousin, Linda Huff, has Catherine's parents listed as John McDermott and Mary Ann McGrath in the family tree that Linda shared with me. Apparently John died and Mary Ann married Ma's stepfather, McGrath. After Mary Ann came west with Ma, she married Tom McDonald. I do not know whether they had five children named Anna, Grace, Gladys, Frank and Jack or whether he already had some or all of those children. I remember Gladys (who never married) and Jack (who did marry). In confirmation of Linda Huff's account, I recently had my genetics done, and I find at least 4 members of the McGrath family in America with whom I share DNA.

Dad, as we called James Whitlock, fathered 4 daughters and 2 sons with Catherine. James was the son of John H. Whitlock and Elizabeth Moser, who were pioneers in Silverton, Oregon, where they homesteaded on Abiqua Creek in 1852. James, who was born in 1876, married Catherine Agnes in January of 1898, and they had their first son, Lawrence, in Meacham, Umatilla County, Oregon in 1899. James worked as a bartender in Yacolt,

Washington, was in Multnomah County in 1901 and moved to La Pine in 1915, where he set the first stakes to mark the future site of the Shevlin-Hixon Company lumber mill. W. W. Woodbeck's Bend Directory of 1917 listed "James Whitlock, with wife Katherine [misspelled], daughters Frances and Eva, machinist [presumably for Shevlin-Hixon]." On December 7th 1921 James Whitlock homesteaded 160 acres on Tumalo Rd. in Deschutes, Oregon. My mother had been born to Frances in February of that same year. So my great grandfather became basically a farmer, but he was involved in politics, He ran for County Commissioner in 1930. According to my mother, James left much of the farm work to Ma. I think he was a stern father, based mostly on my mother's report of the conditions of her conception. One of his sons (Lawrence) became a police officer in Seattle; one worked in the mill in Bend (Vern), and stayed on the family property at 1312 Milwaukee St. in Bend, Oregon, where Dad and Ma had moved in 1950. This was so that he could look after Ma and Dad in their old age. That actually became necessary when Dad was within his sixth decade. He developed some condition that made it hard for him to work, and eventually he ended up sitting in his rocking chair for most of the time until he died in his eighties. I only remember him getting up and going to the garage once. When he arrived there, he stood at the door and stared with a plaintive look in his eye. Then, without entering the garage, which contained a treasure trove of 19th century home wares (including a console Edison phonograph, a copper bathing tub, a deluxe wood stove with warming cupboards and the like), he turned back to the house, and may never have gone that far again. All of those possessions, which were precious to me as a kid, were eventually carted off by my great aunt, Eva, and given to Goodwill Industries. I still remember a song from the thick old Edison record.

> Will she come from the East, will she come from the East, where the Broadway peaches grow,
> Will she come from the North, will she come from the North, from the land of ice and snow,

Or will she come from the heart of the West, there where the sun goes to rest,
Or will she come a trottin' from the land of cotton, from a way down south.[7]

Now I understand my great grandfather's (James) condition, because I have developed arthritis in many parts of my skeleton. So far, I refuse to let it confine me to a rocking chair. Eventually the police officer died of complications of alcoholism, and the faithful son, Vern Whitlock, having buried his parents and wife, found he had colon cancer, and thereafter killed himself with a shotgun.

The daughters of James and Catherine had quite varied futures. One went mad (Elizabeth), one became a spinster (Gladys), one buried a daughter and a husband, and then went off to high life in the city of Portland (Eva), and my grandmother got pregnant when she was a teenager (Frances), and was wed to a lumberjack. I also don't mention all the names of my great aunts and uncles because their children are still alive, and I don't want to offend anyone in the family. I will mention Eva, because after she buried her husband, daughter, and later her sister, she married that sister's husband (my step-grandfather). Ma Whitlock had all of these children in the span of 10 years between 1898 and 1908. What is more, she and James had apparently moved around a lot in those ten years, because between 1903 and 1908 they moved from Aurora City to Yacolt, Washington and then to Meacham, Oregon, before they homesteaded in Tumalo. Women had to be made of sterner stuff back then!

I will not mention my mother's biological father except to say that he was worthless to me, and I assume that it was probably a rape. However, rape was a very hard thing to prove in 1920. Dad Whitlock may have discovered the two of them in the act of conceiving my mother, although I am unsure of that detail. I do know that Dad Whitlock kicked Frances, his own daughter, all the way home. Perhaps that contributed to the premature birth of my mother. It was a traumatic event for the Whitlock family, and both the mother and the grandmother never related well to the child. Nevertheless, Ma Whitlock felt a great guilt for the shame that she bore for her daughter and granddaughter. So she overcompensated by raising the tiny baby by swaddling her in a shoebox behind the kitchen's wood stove. When Dad was in the hospital at the end of his life (he died June 26 1962), my mother went to stay with Ma to help her. They had some serious conversations. In one, Ma admitted that she had hated the unwanted grandchild. I think it hit my mother pretty hard, because she had always felt loved by her maternal grandparents. She used to stay with her grandparents all summers long as a child and teenager. I think Ma was trying to apologize for the guilt that she felt, but my mother had not yet come to terms with the fact that even her own mother had always been embarrassed by her. It was only ten days later that Ma Whitlock followed her husband to the grave on July 4, 1962. It was the last meaningful conversation that my mother had with the dear old Irish biddy that had practically raised her.

My mother, as I suggested, had a somewhat troubled childhood. Not so much that she lacked for anything physically or educationally. My grandfather was, by the time of her birth, doing well in the logging industry. He had started as a sheepherder in eastern Oregon, but after a year of doing battle with his mule[8] and losing Buck (the best, and the only, dog he ever owned), he moved on to being an ox driver on the skidders in central Oregon. In his day, logs were skidded out of the woods with a high wheel axle attached to a yoke of oxen or team of horses.

Logging with horses. US Forest Service photograph. In the public domain. http://www.trainweb.org/highdesertrails/shlco/loggingequipment.html

This part of my grandfather's story can only be surmised from stories he told me while I rode around with him to the logging sites that he supervised as Woods Manager for the McCloud River Lumber Company. He had come a long way from muleskinner, then oxen driver up the ranks to management. He was a bucker and a faller before he became crew foreman. A bucker cuts the branches off of a fallen tree and then cuts the logs into manageable lengths. At that time there were some massive timber around, so a manageable length might be as little as ten feet.

A PART OF ONE SUGAR PINE TREE

One sugar pine tree bucked and loaded onto six flatcars. U. S. Forest Service photo. In the public domain. http://www.trainweb.org/mccloudrails/History/History02.html

I think most of his career was after the invention of the chain saw in 1926, but he certainly knew how to pull a two-man saw. I know this because I used to watch him and my uncle buck up old snag trees for firewood. A two-man straight-cut saw has teeth two or three inches deep, and can tear through a log, especially an old dry snag, lickety-split. I would not be surprised if that expression might have been applied to cross-saw jargon because of the way the saw almost licks its way through the log.[9] It also created a grip that Meritt never lost. In his nineties, when I would try to shake hands with him, he would take hold of my fingers and squeeze like a vice grip. He took pride in getting the jump on me that way.

What was more amazing about my grandfather is that he was not a blood relative, although he was more of a father to my mother and a grandfather to me than we could have hoped. At a time when having children out of wedlock was a great embarrassment to my great grandparents; Meritt was a truly gentle man. Born on May 9th, 1896 in Alsea, Oregon to, Guy Allen Seely and we didn't know his mother's first name[10], but she was always called Grandma Spencer. She died when Meritt was a small child. Guy and his two daughters and one son homesteaded in eastern Oregon. I don't know if they moved from Alsea after she died or whether she died on the homestead.

Conditions were harsh on the high desert, and Guy and his young family saw some of the severest winters in Oregon history. Aunt Nina once told me the story that the winter was so severe on the windswept plane that Guy decided to send the family to stay with relatives in Portland. They traveled by train, but Nina said the weather was so cold that the water tenders all froze and the steam engine could not move for lack of water. Obviously they all survived, but as I said, they made folks of sterner stuff back then.

I really don't know if there were any warm feelings or courting between my grandmother and Meritt before the rape, because no one ever talked about it, including Meritt. But some time after it happened, Meritt offered my grandmother, Frances, his hand in marriage. My mother says this did not happen until she was 4 years old. I don't know what that must have meant in his circle of friends and associates, but apparently no one ever questioned it (including his own parents) and it had no negative effect on his career.

This was after Meritt had returned from his tour in the Merchant Marine on the this tanker,[11]
USS Georgia (BB-15)

Union Iron Works & Bethlehem San Francisco

Hull #129	H. C. Folger	Atlantic Refining	Tanker	7,100 Gross Tons	10,300 Displacement Tons	Delivered 1916

http://www.pier70sf.org/history/shipsBuilt/ShipsBuiltpreWW2.html

After enlistment in the US Navy he was deployed on a destroyer in World War I.

I know very little of that either, since I have not read the bulk of his journal, which resides with his daughter, Mary. He did tell me that he had been on the escort convoy that delivered Woodrow Wilson back from the Treaty of Versailles. The most memorable thing to Meritt was that they were waiting in the calm of a port in the Azores when they received the orders to meet the President's convoy. By the time they left port, there were violent seas and every sailor on the destroyer was overtaken by seasickness. Interesting how the most unpleasant experiences of our life are often what stick foremost in our memories. I don't know the name of the destroyer, but Meritt said it was one of the first destroyers sunk in World War II. This would have probably been at Pearl Harbor on Dec 7, 1941

> **USS *Greer* (DD–145),** commissioned 31 December 1918, was a *Wickes*-class destroyer in the United States Navy, the first ship named for Rear Admiral James A. Greer (1833–1904). In what became known as the "*Greer* incident," she became the first US Navy ship to fire on a German ship, three months before the United States officially entered World War II. The incident led President Franklin D. Roosevelt to issue what became known as his "shoot-on-sight" order. Many have disputed whether the *Greer* acted aggressively before shots were exchanged.
>
> *Greer's* shake down voyage took her to Azores, from which she rendezvoused with *George Washington*, carrying President Woodrow Wilson home from the Versailles Peace Conference, and escorted her to the United States. After exercises in coastal waters, *Greer* was assigned to Trepassy Bay, Newfoundland, for duties during a transatlantic flight by four Navy seaplanes, one of which, NC-4, safely completed the historic undertaking. After further training exercises and a European cruise, *Greer* was assigned to the Pacific Fleet, reaching San Francisco 18 November 1919. https://en.wikipedia.org/wiki/USS_Greer_(DD-145)

Now a few short years after his honorable discharge from the Navy, and having returned to the woods, he is offering to take on a wife who bore another man's child, my mother. They married on April 13, 1925. This was the middle of the Roaring Twenties, and the logging business was booming like the rest of the country. So economically this nuclear family had a chance, albeit the circumstances were quite unusual. Still, perhaps the respect that people in the company and the Bend and La Pine community had for Meritt gave respectability to my grandmother. He was a hero of the Great War, a gentleman and a sturdy lumberjack.

What I know about the life of Frances and Meritt in the 1920s is limited. I am constructing from the memories of my mother, and a few bits of information from my grandfather. My mother remembers that Meritt had a temper, but by the time I knew him, I never heard him raise is voice to anyone. I think he might have taken me to the woodshed once, but I don't remember it being painful. In fact, I think I appreciated being disciplined by him.

On the other hand, my mother had a great deal of affection for Meritt, but felt that she had been unfairly disciplined by her mother. The symbolic example of that relationship was the broken eardrum caused when Frances boxed my mothers' ears. The birth of her half-sister Mary, on Nov. 24 1926, probably strained the relationship further, and I know that my mother always believed that Meritt loved Mary unconditionally, but was, nevertheless, kind to his step-daughter. My mother was bright and I think kind of kept up a competition between her and her sister. She played the older sister part, but there was not a great deal of affection lost between the sisters. Mary once jabbed the point of a ski pole through my mother's leg, which my mother always took as the symbolic explanation of why the sisterly relationship was tense.

I don't know how stormy or peaceful my grandparents' relationship was initially, but they definitely grew to love each other. I know that because my grandfather was devastated when Frances died in 1956…. I paced around the house with him as he bawled like a child. I felt so bad that I could not do the same, but I think I was so stunned by Meritt's reaction to her death. I had never seen him cry. My grandmother was not a warm affectionate woman, but she had a good heart and was attentive to me, as a child. I don't know what the relationship of my grandmother to her first daughter was in the early years. Strict, I am sure, but how affectionate they were with each other, I cannot say. I know they loved each other in later years, and it was my mother that came to care for my grandmother, when she was in recovery from the varicose vein operation that caused an embolism that killed her.

Still I am sure there were some adjustments to make in those early years of the marriage. Meritt was a busy man, taking on increasing responsibility at work, playing fiddle at the Saturday camp dances, catcher on the camp baseball team. He played with a broken thumb on occasion. Meanwhile, Frances was learning to be mother to one and then two children. She eventually became, not just a fastidious homemaker, but bordering on fanatical. By the time I came to live with her, she used Lysol wherever she would go, baked fantastic cookies and cakes, used bluing in all of her whites, and polished incessantly. She had a certain embarrassment about the condition of her mother's house when they would visit Bend, but by then Ma was doing most of the work around the place, and getting old. Frances was always happy to visit Aunt Nina's house, because this sister of Meritt was the oldest and had learned early to keep a neat house. Nina was also a very talented artist and kept a garden of about one acre. Frances was not so approving of Aunt Cleo and Aunt Elfie, Meritt's other sisters, who were not very concerned about the "absolute cleanliness" of their homes. I think my mother was closest to Cleo. I don't know if she had stayed with Cleo and Larry Mack at some time, but Cleo was the more adventurous spirit of the two sisters.

So it was obvious that Frances took on the task of married life with a determination to make up for the mistake that she had made as a teenager. I suppose that is also why she was so strict with my mother and Mary. This was not unusual in those days, but as time would tell, something was missing, because my mother did not grow up to be a wise and restrained adult, even though she had the advantages of a good home and a sharp mind. In contrast, Mary married during WWII and stayed married to the same man until he died. The Smiths had their problems in the early years, but they worked them out. I have always wondered whether that security, of knowing she was loved, made Mary able to form that lasting commitment, whereas my mother's life was fraught with emotional issues.

I think the life in the La Pine Camp was kind of idyllic from the prospective of the 21st century. The young folk of the camp played together as children, competed in sports and convened for dances and events in high school. Many had friendships that continued on into their adult years. In fact, the company for which so many of them worked held an annual picnic, and these people kept that tradition for many years after the company sold out. The Shevlin-Hixon picnics were a family meeting place in my childhood and I think my parents attended their last picnic just before I started high school. My mother told me on which boy she had a crush and which one had a crush on her... although, at that time, she did not know it. In later years, Lee Maker told her that he would have married her in a heartbeat if she had given him any encouragement. She always just considered him a very good friend. How different her life might have been. I think Lee Maker became a stalwart in the Bend community.

There were hard times. The depression was the first, which Shevlin-Hixon survived and managed to keep the regular work force intact. I am sure there were layoffs, but my mother said the company tried to keep most of the staff employed enough to feed their families. I never heard that any of the young people from that camp had to go off to join the WPA or the CCCs. If anything, those programs were a godsend to the logging business because all of the construction at the National Parks, the Hoover Dam, etc. created a big demand for lumber.

What did take away the youth of La Pine was the Second World War. Vernon Smith and Spencer Farley, my mother's cousin, along with many of his fellows headed off to the Navy, others to the Army and Marines. Vernon became Mary Seely's husband. My mother never mentioned boys that had been lost in the war. Whether that was a stroke of luck or something which that generation did not talk about, I am not sure. It is possible that not as many of the young men from La Pine went to war compared to cities around the country. This is because lumber production was an essential war industry. You hear of Rosie the Riveter, but there was never a Linda the Lumberjack; to my knowledge. Most of the Forest industry jobs remained man's work. Anything made of concrete and steel starts with a wooden form or a model. In the case of the wooden PT boats, they became the machines of war. Of course, all those soldiers had to be housed and lumber was the construction material of choice. Even the Japanese internment camps were all wood. So, though times were tough, Americans were at work and wood was at war.

CHAPTER 3

The Logging Camps

Now therefore command that cedars of
Lebanon be cut for me. And my servants will
join your servants, and I will pay you for your
servants such wages as you set, for you know
that there is no one among us who knows
how to cut timber like the Sidonians. **English
Standard Version (2001) 1 Kings 5:6**

BY THE TIME MY GRANDFATHER came to Shevlin-Hixon Co.
Camp, he was a supervisor and remained so until the camp closed.

By 1947 operations were moved even farther south, to
Chemult. The actual camp was set up approximately 18 miles
southeast of Chemult.

By 1944 the figured sustained yield of the forests was downgraded
to only 82 million board feet per year. Clearly the sawmills were
rapidly running out of trees to cut, and something had to be done to
correct the problem before it became more of a crisis. The end result
was that Shevlin-Hixon elected to sell out to Brooks-Scanlon [B-S].
The transaction became effective in November 1950, and the S-H
sawmill was promptly closed, with the last load of lumber shipped
from the facility leaving four months later. The end of an era was
at hand…. Those employees that could stay on with B-S did, but
many more were forced to leave, with at least some traveling south to
take jobs with the McCloud River Lumber Company operations in
McCloud, CA, which had been closely affiliated with Shevlin-Hixon
for many years prior to the closure of the Bend mill.
http://www.trainweb.org/highdeserttrails/shlco.html.

35

My grandfather was one of those who moved to McCloud River Lumber Co. His first assignment was to Camp Pondosa, where he was second in command under Bobby Vaughn's grandfather, who was Camp Superintendent. I was living with my grandparents before they moved to Camp Pondosa, and many of my formative memories come from that little self-contained beehive. The adults were bustling all around us, going on about their daily labors, while my friends and I diverted ourselves with games. Bobby was my friend, and we played many hours in the woods and area around the logging camp. As I remember it (probably inaccurately) we could go anywhere within the circle of track that went around the camp… except of course the base yard where trucks and equipment were moving around. We could tell if a train was coming by putting our ear to the rail… and they were not moving fast on that circular rail, so I guess the parents didn't worry about us getting hurt. There was a "playhouse" in the woods which was basically a rectangle defined by 4 poles, but many a family scene was acted out there by the girls and boys from the school. The school house was right across the road from our house in camp.

School house in Camp Pondosa (Reproduced by permission from the Eastman's Originals Collection, Department of Special Collections, General Library, University of California, Davis) http://ulibimage.ucdavis.edu/speccoll/east01/full/T-1337.jpg

Sometimes I would go into the school and the teacher would let me occupy an empty desk until recess. It is so rewarding to have found these pictures on the world wide web of places of interest to me, and which no longer exist except in the archives of Univ. of Calif. Davis. Another happenstance of life, the place where I graduated from university preserves my logging camp history.

I took my son James to Camp Pondosa one summer when he was 8 or 9. We were traveling back from Davis, California, to Washington. This was at the end of his summer spent with my second wife, Mary, and me. The strange new living situation in Davis, away from his mother and siblings, had made him reticent. This trip was our first time to spend one-on-one time together. All that was left of the logging camp was the general store and office

Hall and general store and office in Camp Pondosa (Reproduced by permission from the Eastman's Originals Collection, Department of Special Collections, General Library, University of California, Davis) http://ulibimage.ucdavis.edu/speccoll/east01/full/D-311.jpg

as well as one house that my grandfather rented. I know it was his house, because three sequoias that bordered the garage (since demolished) still stood. I was amazed how small the house was, not unlike these pictured.

Houses in Camp Pondosa (Reproduced by permission from the Eastman's Originals Collection, Department of Special Collections, General Library, University of California, Davis) http://ulibimage.ucdavis.edu/speccoll/east01/full/T-1338.jpg

It was just the shell of the place, but there was one cupboard drawer remaining. I admit that I stole it and installed it under the work bench in my mother's home in Napavine WA., after James and I arrived there. It was just a bit of nostalgia to remind us of the days in the logging camps. Although Pondosa still exists, it is now a large gravel-covered base yard for heavy equipment. It no longer hears the squeals of children and the dinner bell of the cookhouse or the music of the camp dances in the hall next to the general store.

That house was the scene of many memories. Such as bears knocking down the back fence to get at the watermelon rinds in the garbage cans. Also, we would go to the pigsty to watch the bears eat pig slop out of the boiling pots (still simmering in the outdoor wood stove). The cookhouse kept the pigs well-fed on leftovers from the lumberjacks' meals. Local folks would drive to the pigsty in the evening; surround it with headlights lit as if to illuminate a stage. The bears would peek out from behind the shed, and then would bravely come out in the spotlights to perform their ritual act of consuming much-favored pig slop. I don't know where the bears went in the daytime, but our parents never seemed to worry about us running into 'bar', or coyotes, or mountain lions, for that matter. In retrospect, I would probably have been more worried about my children tangling with a porcupine or a skunk. But those were freewheeling days, when parents were not on constant guard about the whereabouts of their urchins.

Less dramatic activities that we children pursued were going to the cookhouse to try to get the cook to give us cookies, and picking up cereal-box "surprises" from the old lady down the block. I think she was the teacher, or a retired former teacher. She must have eaten lots of cereal or Cracker Jacks because she always seemed to have a ring or a top or tiny comic strip to pass out.

We did some stupid things too… like any kid would. We would sneak into the bunkhouses to see how lumberjacks live.

Bunk houses at Camp Pondosa (Reproduced by permission from the Eastman's Originals Collection, Department of Special Collections, General Library, University of California, Davis) http://ulibimage.ucdavis.edu/speccoll/east01/full/D-322.jpg

One was built of discarded railroad ties burrowed into the bank of the railroad bed. No one ever locked their door in camp. We never stole anything because we knew we would be in trouble with my straight laced grandmother. Climbing on the Caboose was a major no-no. Later, when we moved to McCloud, we would receive detention for that latter offence.

The worst thing that happened to me in Pondosa was an incident that occurred while some of the older kids (probably less than 8 years) were building a clubhouse. I was inside the construction and stuck my head out the low door. At just that moment, the kid who was sawing lumber off the roof dropped the saw instead of the board. It cut deep into my cheek which shocked me to silence. The older kids saw the blood and ran me home, and my grandmother, horrified, drove me to McCloud at once. The doctor sewed me up, but he was on some kind of 'juice'. So he put me out with ether and only put 7 stitches where there should have been twice that many. When I got home, I barfed my guts out, because of the ether. I have that facial scar to this very day.

There was also a dark-haired girl in our little group of friends. I won't give her name, first, because I am not sure if I remember it correctly, and second, because I am not sure if she would like being mentioned in this account. Our games were innocent, but like so many children, we had to play show-me-yours-and-I-will-show-you-mine. In later years, she asked my cousin about me, and he gave me her email address. I wrote, but she never wrote back. I was, of course, kind of sweet on her, but so was Bobby Vaughn. I don't know much about what happened to either of them, except that the girl still lives in the area, and Bob Vaughn moved to Dunsmuir, CA, with his single mother. Our lives were idyllic in Pondosa, although they were probably not so for our parents; raising a family was challenging in a lumber camp, even for management. My grandmother adopted a fastidious schedule to combat the constant dust and wood smoke in our tiny company house. Nevertheless, I think we all survived, and had a mostly carefree early childhood.

No, that is not entirely true. While my grandparents were very good to me, I greatly missed my mother. Bobby probably missed his mother also.

It's not easy for a young woman to be pregnant and have a child and then find work and hire help to take care of the child. It certainly was harder in the 1950's. I believe that my mother tried to keep me as she was working, but it proved too difficult. One woman she hired to watch me proved to be some kind of a problem, which I never understood. I think my mother said she had a fondness for the bottle, and I am not meaning baby bottle. I do know that many years later I was diagnosed with a deviated septum in my nose. That was caused by a playground swing that hit me in the nose when I was still very small. So obviously, there was some inattention, but who was responsible for this accident I was never told. Something caused my mother to decide to follow the dictates of her social milieu and take me to live with my grandparents. This was probably not easy for any of the adults involved, but it probably was a wise decision as far as I was concerned, because I dearly needed the calm, fatherly influence of my grandfather, and the dutiful attention of my grandmother. Still, the heart of a 4-year-old boy yearns for his mother. I remember the day she left on the train from Dunsmuir, and I remember the subsequent letters and the promises that Meritt would read to me. My mother had promised to bring a rocking horse, before one of her visits. Instead, she showed up with a cardboard cutout of a horse that you hang over your shoulders and run around, pretending you are the horse and rider. I think it was supposed to be the Long Ranger's horse Silver. I was very, very upset. I wouldn't play with it and I pouted the whole time she was with us in Pondosa. Later I used the paper horse as if it was the most wonderful thing ever. But my mother never saw that. She just knew that she was unable to provide what I needed, or thought I needed.

When I was 5 or 6, she had a fairly good year of earnings, and was determined to make up for past inadequacies. That Christmas, she bought me and my two cousins sleeping bags, skis, two sets of toy soldiers and space men. I am sure it was a big hit on her pocket book, but I also know she was determined to make up for her absence. Not that anything ever really could. But, as I said before, I was in good hands with my grandparents.

CHAPTER 4

My Mother's Life

"Whoever causes one of these little ones who
believe to stumble, it would be better for him if,
with a heavy millstone hung around his neck, he
had been cast into the sea."
English Standard Version (©2001) Mark 9:42

LET US PICK UP ON the saga of my mother's life, because I have
not described how great the changes that occurred in her transition to
adulthood. I have mentioned that she was the dutiful older sister, and
probably always the more driven -- not so much by circumstances as by the
need to gain favor with her mother. She was an excellent student, received
the citizenship trophy and graduated from high school magna cum laud.
She was valedictorian of her high school class, of which there were seven
students graduating. Kay, as she was called then, was awarded a scholarship
to pursue bacteriology at the University of Oregon. Of course, her parents
were much in favor of her going to college in Oregon, rather than be lost in
the working world. They probably had reason to worry. Although, by that
point in time, I have no evidence that she had done anything that would
cause them to suspect that she would do aught but excel. That was a tragic
and fateful decision for my mother. She followed the dictates of her parents,
went off to college, and essentially turned her life from success to chaos.

At Oregon State University (OSU, although she later said it was Oregon
State College), she was one of the few, if not the only, female student in
Chemistry. The Chemistry professors at that time were not an open-minded

lot. They were very critical of her, and, as she described it, were defiant of her right to be there... "[she was] taking jobs from young men".

An explanation is in order about the history of the **Oregon State College**. It is one of the 72 land grant colleges initiated during the Administration of Abraham Lincoln,

> **Land-grant universities** (also called **land-grant colleges** or **land grant institutions**) are institutions of higher education in the United States designated by each state to receive the benefits of the Morrill Acts of 1862 and 1890. http://en.wikipedia.org/wiki/ Land_grant_college

My interest in the history of Oregon State is that it is the first contact my side of the family had with higher education as far back as at least four generations. In addition, it provided connection to the professions that the members of our family have pursued, namely agriculture and forestry. Sadly, even in the current generation, I, my half-sister, and my son are the only members of the family that have degrees higher than secondary school. I think my Cousin Ralph's son, Eric, pursued college, but I don't know if he obtained a degree. Therefore it is important to me to document the connection this family has to the fundamental building block of this modern nation. That cornerstone was the Land Grant College system that was initiated in the middle of a divisive Civil War under the leadership of arguably one of our most far sighted presidents.

> The university's roots date back to 1856 when **Corvallis Academy,** the area's first community school for primary and preparatory education, was founded in 1858; the school's name was changed to **Corvallis College** and formally incorporated by members of the Freemasons. The school offered its first college-level curriculum in 1865, under the administration of the Methodist Episcopal Church, South. On August 22, 1868, official Articles of Incorporation were filed for Corvallis College. October 27, 1868, is known as OSU Charter Day, the day that the Oregon Legislative Assembly

designated Corvallis College as the Agricultural College of the state of Oregon and the recipient of Land Grant fund income. As part of this designation, the college was required to comply with the requirements set forth in the First Morrill Act. The name was changed to **Corvallis State Agricultural College** and was then authorized to grant the Bachelor of Arts, Bachelor of Science, and Master of Arts degrees. The first graduating class was in 1870, granting Bachelor of Arts degrees. http://en.wikipedia.org/wiki/ Oregon State University

1890 the college became known as Oregon Agricultural College (OAC). It remained under that name until 1927.

1927 marked yet another name change, this time to Oregon State Agricultural College. The Oregon Unification Bill passed by the Legislative Assembly in 1929 placed the school under the oversight of the newly formed Oregon State Board of Higher Education. Doctoral education was first provided in 1935 with the conferral of four Doctor of Philosophy degrees. This year also saw the creation of the first summer session. The growing diversity in degree programs offered led to another name change in 1937, when the college became **Oregon State College.**
The university's current title, **Oregon State University,** was adopted on March 6, 1961, by a legislative act signed into law by Governor Mark Hatfield. http://en.wikipedia.org/wiki/Oregon State University

So my mother did attend what later became Oregon State University. Kathleen roomed with two other women, one of whom she kept in touch with for the rest of her life. I have a picture of the three of them somewhere, but suffice it to say, I knew only one of the women. Leona Cameron became a Certified Public Accountant, married, and lived, for many years, on Park Street in Portland, Oregon. After her husband, Doug, died she took to traveling the world over, and the last communication received from her was about her trip to Easter Island (Rapa Nui). I am not sure what happened to the other woman, but I will use this one friend (whom I named) to contrast with my mother's troubled life.

Apparently, my mother was so intimidated by the Chemistry Dept. that she stopped attending classes, but stayed in Corvallis to enjoy the college life. I have never tried to go back and talk to her roommate (if she is still alive), but I assume that it was not a period of restrained behavior on my mother's part. By the same token, it was not a long period, because I think she came home to La Pine within the same year. She had stopped attending classes, but had been inspired by a professor to write. She was honored for a paper she had written in some publication that gained her the attention of Herb Caen. He was a Columnist for the San Francisco Chronicle (note that I have not corroborated any of this at this time, because Herb Caen died on February 1st 1997. Coincidentally, that is my birth date fifty years prior). She told me that during her first year at OSC, Herb Caen had invited her to come to San Francisco to work on the staff of the Chronicle. At the same time, her parents got wind of the fact that she was not attending class, and rather than let her go off to what they considered the "City of Gomorra", they forced her to go to Seattle and stay with her Uncle Laurence, who was a cop. This decision missed the mark considerably, for instead of encouraging her creativity, her uncle's treatment only made her more rebellious.

She did not enter the Army until October of 1944, so there were five years between OSU and the Women's' Army Corps. Of course, it was a tumultuous time because the Second World War was already fully engaged in Europe, and the United States was engulfed in the war by the fateful attack on Pearl Harbor, December 7, 1941. What she was doing during those years I was never told. I assume she was working, but she never talked much about those years. On the other hand, her military discharge shed some light on those years. From January 1941 to November of 1942, she worked as a clerk typist for Crawford Construction Company in Bend, Oregon. I assume she may have lived with Uncle Vern and Elma during that time, because I know she did not drive, so she could not have lived out of town on the homestead in Tumalo.

She had some adventures along the way. She had entered the Women Accepted for Voluntary Emergency Service (WAVES) in 1942, but she was discharged for medical reason. She had obviously made a good impression with her fellow WAVES because she had a letter signed by all her fellows. It reads as follows:

> To Seaman Seeley: You know how we feel about you, so words would be superfluous. The Platoon. Sec 31.

The term "Seaman" was not a concession to gender equality in the Navy, but rather was a chauvinism reflecting the fact that the Navy not only could not allow a rank designation for these 'volunteers', but had no intention of ever letting them become a part of the august naval tradition. A few of the "seamen" – although they were all actually women – mentioned their places of origin in her farewell letter from them. They were from Denver Colorado; Whitewater, Wisconsin; Memphis, Tennessee; Salem, Massachusetts; Napa, Idaho; Warrenton, Virginia; and Madison, New Jersey. Those fifty-seven signatures probably represented the broadest spectrum of women that Kay had met in her sheltered life in the "Oregon Territory". Of course, Oregon was a state, but it was definitely "the edge of America" at that time.

From February of 1943 to April of 1944 she worked for Pacific Telephone in Portland, Oregon. So obviously she had migrated to the big city, but I also assume that she may have been living with one of Meritt's three sisters. Cleo Mack and her husband lived on Skyline Drive, so that would have been too far from work. Likewise, I think Nina Farley and her husband were already living near Cleo on Skyline. I know Grandpa Seely had a small restaurant near the train station in downtown Portland, but I am pretty sure she did not live with him. By the time I knew Grandpa Seely, he was living in a house on Skyline nearest Nina. Elfie Shire and her husband lived in Forest Grove. At least there would have been bus service from there to downtown Portland, so Kay might have lived with them. It was fairly unusual for a young woman to live on her own recognizance then, and when they did, it would have been in a boarding house with fairly strict policies. So, she did not get into any trouble during that period (or so I thought). Where she was between April and October 1944, I don't know, but I assumed she must have gone home to La Pine to be with her family before she entered the Army on October 15th.

The second time she enlisted, she joined the Women's Army Corps (WAC). She chose the WAC instead of the WAVES because she had been taken on board a submarine by a sailor she had met (no details were ever given. He was not her relative, because her cousin, Spencer Farley and brother-in-law, Vernon Smith, did not serve as submariners, although they were both seamen). The submarine only dove to the bottom of the harbor, but it was excruciatingly painful for my mother because of her broken eardrum. That discouraged her from applying for the WAVES a second time, in spite of the fact that there was a maritime tradition in the family. WAVES were not allowed to serve on submarines until this century. Probably WAVES were transported by submarine in some military engagements, but I guess my mother realized that she had issues with water, because of her ear.

Once she entered the WAC, her life changed dramatically. After one and a half months of basic training at Ft. Hood, Texas, and an extremely short marriage to Melvin M. Fisher whom she met in the Army, and who was from Oklahoma City, Oklahoma. She was transferred to Barnes Hospital in Vancouver, Washington. The reason I even learned about Melvin is that his name appears on my birth certificate, but that was in 1947, and she had already been transferred to Oregon in early 1945. He was not my biological father, as my mother explained in later years.

I found this information on the internet that describes a document, which formed the Army Force School. In particular, in section 5, it describes the WAC training program.

> **Armored Force School History** .5 linear Feet
> Materials, mostly General Orders and letters, drawn from Post Adjutant General's historical files concerning the establishment and organization of the Armored Force and Armored School, 1940-1944.
> Section 5: Mimeographed Orders; General Orders #33, HQ The Armored School,
> SUBJ: Attachment of WAC Detachment to Training Group TAS, 30 August 1943
> http://www.generalpatton.org/education/collections/Armored_Force_School_History.pdf

In AFS School, Kathleen Viola Seely was trained in El Paso Texas for eight weeks. She studied anatomy, physiology, *materia medica*, emergency medical treatment, and ward procedures. This gave her certification as a Surgical Technician, and she graduated at the rank of Private. She was then promoted to Staff Sergeant and served as a Quartermaster Supply Technician for four months. Later she spent seven months as a Medical Supply Clerk. She was Honorably Discharged from the Army at Camp Beal California on July 14th 1946.

Those are the paper records, but the story behind is much more colorful. What really happened was that she saw a lot of pain and suffering. She particularly remembered the soldier that had his private parts blown away, and another who had lost most of his buttocks to a grenade in his back pocket (it discharged as he crawled through a hedgerow, which pulled the pin). She told me about the use of maggots to clean the surgical wounds. She also relayed sadness when soldiers who had made it back from Europe or the Pacific Islands, died under her care. Her recollections generated sympathy in my tender grade-school mind, both for her and the soldiers. The official record describes her duties as, dryly, "inventoried and kept records of all company property. Supervised the duties of 2 supply clerks. For 2 weeks was acting first sergeant, handling all company administration." I think that description was fairly sanitized, because she seemed to have had a lot more interaction with wounded soldiers than the record would indicate. I think the demands on the hospital staff were great, and duties were probably blurred to meet the demands of the influx. I know that she felt good about her part in the war, and efforts to comfort the brave lads who had offered up their bodies on the front lines.

As a curious little aside, when my Uncle Vern learned that I had been transferred to what we call the Big Island (the largest island in the Hawaii chain); he related that he had spent time there in the Navy. I suggested that they come to visit. His comment was that he had not enjoyed his time on our island, and intended never to return. Hmmmmm!

My mother also told me that she was given very brief instructions on driving a Jeep during her tour of duty in the WAC. This was when she was at Madigan Hospital at Fort Lewis, Washington. On one occasion, she accidentally drove onto a firing range. Apparently the incident freaked her out so much that either she refused to drive thereafter, or the base commander restricted her from motor pool. This remained true until she was in her late sixties, when it became absolutely necessary for her to learn to drive a car.

She became a close friend with a WAC named Katherine Bornholt, whose parents lived in Kelso, Washington, about forty-five miles from Barnes Military Hospital. Apparently, they took their leave together, and, on occasion, visited Katherine's parents. My mother liked August and Mrs. Bornholt, whom we always called Mrs. B. Later in Kay's life, my stepfather received a transfer to the post office in Kelso's sister city, Longview. Therefore, we move to Kelso, and rented a house next to the Bornholts, Katherine's parents. By then, Katherine and her husband, Mr. Northness, had a dairy farm in Longview. I think the Bornholts provided a home away from home for my mother, and were, in many ways, more accepting of her than her own mother had been. That is so often the case with some mothers and daughters, but by the time she met Mrs. B, Kay was already gaining confidence and a sense of importance in the Military.

Although my mother had considered herself an ugly duckling in high school, she had molted into a swan by the time she entered the WAC. The uniform and it's responsibilities granted her poise and dignity. When she was at Barnes, there is a newspaper clipping with her in the court of Miss Flame 1946. They were all in uniform, so this was likely an event of the WAC, but obviously she had beaten all the competition, except one. Curiously, Kay did not save the accompanying article or the picture caption. Does this mean she did not want to remember the names of her fellow winners? We will never know.

One of Kay's promotion letters is contained in her scrapbook.

> Sept. 1 1945
> Subject: Promotion of enlisted Woman.
> To: Commanding Officer, 76th WAC Detachment, Barnes Gen
>   Hospital, Vancouver Wn. [as Washington was abbreviated
>   then]
>
> 1. Technician fifth grade Kathleen V. Seely, A-907694. 76th
>   WAC Detachment, is hereby recommended to Technical 4th
>   Grade,
> 2. Technician fifth grade Seely was assigned to this department
>   on or about 16 May 1945 as a clerk. Since that time, she has
>   been under my close observation and my direct supervision
>   and has displayed a noted willingness to cooperate with her
>   fellow workers and to perform her duties efficiently without
>   question or delay. This enlisted worker has never been late to
>   work or absent without leave since she was assigned to this
>   department.
> 3. Technician Seely is capable of performing the duties assigned
>   her at this office and it is firmly believed that this enlisted
>   woman is deserving of the above mentioned promotion. It is

further requested that she be permitted to remain on duty at
this office.

L. B. Ottaway

WOJG USA

C. O. Det. Of Patients

Her chevron is visible in two pictures of my mother. One of the
photographs shows her with a chevron that had three hat-bars on top and
one semicircular bar on the bottom with nothing in between, the insignia
of a Staff Sergeant. The other had three hat-bars on top, nothing on the
bottom and a 'T' in the space under the bars. I saw a picture of this chevron
on a website, but I could not make out the title under it. I assume it was some
indication of technical grade. She was proud of her accomplishment, where
she was promoted from private to staff sergeant in twenty-two months.

I think the Army had fairly strict policies about hospital staff
fraternizing with the patients. This was understandable, given the fact
that the wounded soldiers were vulnerable and certainly grateful to the
WAC nurses. Not a good environment for the development of a meaningful
romantic relationship. However, at the same time, the nurses were
vulnerable and undoubtedly hurting. Very young women were trying to
deal with new and powerful emotions, and did not have a lot of recourse
to support them in their confusion. So naturally it is not surprising that a
WAC might turn to her supervisor, and that the comforting and emotional
support would turn into more. Such was the case with my mother. She
fell in love with a non-commissioned officer on the base. He was married,
and therefore, not within his rights to take advantage of the emotions of
a younger woman. However, he did, and I am the result. Amongst my
mother's memorabilia there is a Barnes Hospital publication where his
name, Ottoway, is mentioned. He also signed her promotion letter (above).
I have never had any interest in finding out more about him, and my mother
obviously did not want to be an obstacle to his marriage, because a rapid
transfer and honorable discharge was arranged for her.

I did find this document from the family archives of the Church of the Latter Day Saints.

Lester OTTAWAY
> Birth Date: 30 May 1918
> Death Date: 20 Jul 2007
> Social Security Number: 544-03-8122
> State or Territory Where Number Was Issued: Oregon

> **Death Residence Localities**
>> ZIP Code: 89104
>>   Las Vegas,
>> Localities: Clark,
>>   Nevada

http://www.familysearch.org/eng/search/frameset_search.asp?PAGE=/eng/search/ancestorsearchresults.asp

Although this does not list his middle initial, I had entered that initial in the search criteria. And the death residence and birth date matches that of another obituary record that I found for a Lester B. Ottaway. I didn't realize that I had been named after him; I always thought I was named for my great uncle Lester who married the French war bride Jenny. So my birth certificate name, Lester Fisher, was a fabrication of my biological father's first name and my mother's first husband's last name. Lester Ottoway wrote recommendations for Kay, so that when I was one month old she was able to take a job at an X-ray clinic in Bend, Oregon. That is where she met Dr. Howarth, a radiologist.

Kathleen started to work for Dr. Howarth after I was born, but by February of 1947 she was giving birth to me. Apparently she remained in Portland, Oregon during the pregnancy, because that is where I was born. Where she stayed and who supported her I really don't know. But after Dr. Howarth began to work with her, he took her under his wing. From what my mother described, Dr. Howarth basically took my mother with her infant into his life and family.

Mom was still pretty vulnerable when she went to work for Dr. Howarth, because she fell for a superior once again. She trained as an X-ray technician under Dr. Howarth, and she must have been a quick study, because he became very dependent on her... not just for professional service either. She started babysitting for his two daughters, and going on "business" trips with him. That is why she had pictures of the two of them in the snow in the Three Sisters ski resort area. Sometimes she almost seemed to brag about their relationship, but she never gave specific details. She described Dr. Howarth's relationship with his wife as devoid of affection. Mrs. Howarth ignored his relationship with my mother, being more interested in her own social life than his emotional satisfaction. But Howarth and his wife remained married, possibly more because of his love for his daughters than for the relationship with his wife. In later years, my mother knew that Dr. Howarth was still practicing in the Northwest but had the good sense not to try to contact him. I know that she never forgot him. As with Lester Ottoway, she took nothing, but stepped out of Dr. Howarth's life, and left them to their wives and children. Was that a lack of self-worth on her part, or the mores of a highly chauvinistic society?

I suppose this could all be a fabrication of my mother's skewed memory of her complicated situation or of my inattentive listening. It eventually clarified in her agitated mind that it was not going to work. This perfect concubine status, which she believed she possessed with Dr. Howarth must have become strained. Alternatively, her conscience was getting the best of her, because she told me that she attempted suicide with a razor. They say cutting one's wrists is the least likely method to successfully kill oneself. In fact, one might wonder if the act is not more of a cry for help, than an attempt to end it all. I think she was telling me the truth about the attempted suicide, but considering that there were no visible scars on her wrists, it is more likely that she took an overdose of pills.

In any event, it certainly ended the relationship with Dr. Howarth. This was a level of exposure that he could not sustain in his growing importance in the medical milieu of the city of Salem. Dr. Howarth saw to my mother's medical treatment, but called for my grandfather to come take her and the infant home to La Pine, although by then Meritt had already been transferred to Chemult. My mother's discharge papers listed her home address as "Forty-eight Shevlin Oregon". Her story is that she went back to work in Bend, which is the closest hospital to Camp Shevlin. She had to have surgery in Bend for complications of the delivery of me.

I have no personal memory of Dr. Howarth's family, or any of the circumstances by which we came to Shevlin-Hixon. There are two five by seven inch photographs of "Dr'.s daughters", labeled Jeanie and Ann, in my mother's photo album, but that is the only record of her time with them.

Now there is a gray area here in which I am not sure what happened after she left Dr. Howarth. I do have one cryptic piece of documentation, a letter of recommendation from "your student" to "Harry". It was written on November fourth, 1949, and I am going to include it, not for its absolute veracity (I cannot even confirm that it was written by Dr. Howarth) but because of what can be interpreted from between the lines:

> Dear Harry --
>
> You will, sometime in the latter part of this month, be approached by a young lady with reference to the possibility of employment in San Francisco. She has been employed in our office and in one of the Salem hospitals during the greater part of the last two years. Though she is not as yet a registered technician, she is, I believe, fully capable of passing the Registry examination. Her name, by the way, is Mrs. Kay Fisher.
>
> Her employment in our office was terminated by a severe illness which necessitated her return to her home in Bend, Oregon, for a long convalescence. The surgical correction of a chocolate cyst of the ovary has not only "cured" that illness but has apparently relieved her of previous periodic incapacitation. She subsequently accepted employment with Dr. Charles Donley in Bend, which terminated within the past few days for various reasons which she can best express to you in person.

Mrs. Fisher has a good general knowledge of Radiological Office procedure, and can type reports accurately and rapidly from direct dictation at the typewriter, as well as from dictating equipment (we use the Soundscriber in our Office). She does not, to my knowledge, use shorthand. I have found her serviced particularly useful in collating material and writing, re-writing, and re-rewriting material for publication. Mrs. Fisher is, I believe, an unusually intelligent and adaptable person, and one who learns easily and rapidly to do unaccustomed tasks. One feature of her personality which I have enjoyed, but which many might find less agreeable, is a certain independence of spirit which I believe you will sense when you talk to her.

Mrs. Fisher is the sole support of her 3 year old son, Michael, and in view of her religious convictions there is no possibility of her remarriage: one of the commonest causes of attrition of Radiological ancillary personnel is thus inoperable in her case.

I hope that you can assist Mrs. Fisher in finding suitable employment for her talents in San Francisco.

As ever, your student –

Therefore, I surmise from this letter that my mother had a medical problem, and that my birth in 1947 was prior to her employment with Dr. Howarth. I know that during my birth she had postpartum bleeding that was life-threatening, but may also have been responsible for her subsequent health problems. I can also conclude that she worked in Bend (that is pretty clear in the letter), and that she probably accepted the job in San Francisco after she was laid off from Dr. Donley's office. Where I was during all of this, I am not sure.

I do have memories of that camp of the Shevlin-Hixon Co. Surely I was too small to remember anything at the time we moved back to the camp, but the memories that I have there usually do not involve my mother. So I assume that once she recovered, she must have gone back to work, I think she must have gotten a job as an X-ray technician in Bend, Oregon. She certainly knew the Mother Superior at the hospital there well. This I know, because when I was older, we always visited this competent nun each time we would come to Bend to visit Ma and Dad Whitlock. I am remembering that this nun, Sr. Mary Magdalene, was involved in the care I received at the Bend Hospital when I contracted meningitis. So this must have occurred sometime before I moved in with my grandparents, and would probably only have been possible if my mother had worked at the Bend Hospital. It was a Catholic hospital and so was probably precursor to the current St. Charles Hospital, which is no longer run by the Catholic Church. That hospital was staffed by the Sisters of St. Joseph, which is the same order that operated St. Rose Elementary School, where I later attended grade school in Longview, Washington.

Neither my grandmother nor my mother was a practicing Catholic, but my great grandmother had been. When she was a young woman, she had a discouraging experience with a priest in Bend (I don't know the details). She never attended Mass again. He was still the pastor there when she died. I don't know if she even was offered the last rites, but they would not give her a funeral Mass, just a graveside service. I wonder if priests realized what profound effect they had on those parishioners of bygone eras. Most Catholics today are far less awed by the authority of the clergy, even though the doctrine has not changed. Because of the influence of people like Sister Mary Magdalene, and probably out of curiosity about why her mother was so opposed to Catholicism, my mother eventually drifted into the "one true church" and took me with her at the ripe old age of seven.

I hope the reader will let me return to Shevlin-Hixon camp. These are the things I remember. There was a cook/butcher/baker for the camp whose name was Severt. I think he was a friend of my Grandfather, because long after the camp closed, Meritt would visit Severt when he was in Bend. They would chat over a cup of coffee at the Pine Tree Tavern, while I listened from my seat at the counter. Sometimes my attention would drift to the lake outside the tavern and I would watch people feeding the ducks. There is a picture of me in a chef's hat and apron, which I was told was given to me by Severt. He was a very slender, unassuming man, and why he sticks in my memory I am not sure, but he was very nice to me.

I remember riding on a bulldozer with my Grandfather. He had borrowed it to clear the snow and repair the road to our company house. I was a rather bashful boy, and I suppose it scared me a little bit, but I think Meritt thought I needed some "manly" experience at the ripe old age of 3 or 4. Or maybe he was assigned to babysit me, I don't know. More likely, if Meritt took me to do anything, it was probably because he wanted to show me something. This was true even when I was eight. Meritt always enjoyed taking me to the woods with him when I would visit McCloud in the summers. This was after I moved to Washington with my parents. In camp, I didn't see a lot of Meritt except in the evenings. He was a busy man in Shevlin-Hixon, but that was in the day that "the Company" felt an obligation to let a man have his family close at hand. I do remember his planting a garden with me one spring, but I ate the carrots when they were still tiny. I also remember going hunting with him on the weekends. He would say, "Do you have the salt shaker?" I would confirm that it was in the glove compartment. Then he would say, "When we spot a deer, be very quiet, then take the salt shaker and go sprinkle it on the deer's tail." I actually believed that by sprinkling the salt on its tail, the deer would stand quietly so Meritt could shoot it. I don't think he ever bagged a deer while I was with him; I am sure I would have remembered. I do remember mince pie made with venison.

My Grandmother did not work outside the home, so she was my full-time guardian. I remember there was a St. Bernard that used to hang out with me and the other kids in camp. I don't know whose dog she was but she was gentle enough to ride. I also remember we used to play in the snow, and then we would go in the neighbor's house to warm our feet. The woman would place a shoe box on the open oven door, put two chairs up to the woodstove, and have us place our feet on the shoe box so that the radiant heat would warm our sopping wet socks and feet. If I am not mistaken, that might have been Goldie Kundinger. I seem to remember that she would make us snacks, because she did not have children at home then.

The houses in camp were small, and they were portable. I remember being so amazed when they came to haul the house away. The porch folded up and covered the entrance. The house was built on skids, which they used to push it down to the flat cars on the railroad track that ran through the camp. Then the bulldozer would push the house up the ramps and onto the flat car. My grandfather actually had two houses. I remember sleeping in the second house in the same bed with my great grandmother, who was visiting for Christmas. There was a potbelly stove in the middle of the room, but the fire would go out during the night. I remember being awakened by the sound of Ma snoring and realizing that it was too cold to get up and go out to the outhouse. So, conveniently, there was a little porcelain pot under the bed, which Ma showed me how to use. Oh, the floor was cold! The outhouses in camp were fancy, two-holers with shiny wooden seats and lids (funny that I have wooden seats on all the toilets in my current home. There are just some things on which technology cannot improve.). There was the ever-present smell of swamp gas and Lysol. When we moved to Pondosa and had flushing toilets, I used to have nightmares about being sucked down the swirling watery vortex of those new-fangled contraptions.

My nightmares paled in comparison to the reality of horrific outhouse conditions, as was introduced to my high school biology class. The teacher, Friar Merric was a young priest in his first year at St. Francis Seminary. He liked to try to bring humorous facts into the study of biology. One day he read us a passage about the mortality rate in the United States caused by the brown recluse, *Loxosceles reclus*. Apparently the mortality was highest amongst men in the period of history when outhouses were the norm. After the advent of the flush toilet, the mortality rate became similar in men and women. The scientific issue here is what could have been the possible cause of the change? Clue: *L. reclus* tended to build its web in the orifice of the sump (i.e. just under the toilet seat), because that is where the flies enter to lay their eggs.

It is ironic how few things the mind of a child retains into adulthood, although I am sure the information is still all there; it just cannot be accessed. I do remember going to the movie theater in Gilchrist.

> Gilchrist was the last lumber company town in Oregon. The town was founded in 1938 by the family-owned Gilchrist Timber Company, with Frank and Mary Gilchrist as the owners and town founders. The mill moved there from Jasper County, Mississippi, in search of lumber and lower taxes, building a dam on the Little Deschutes River to create the mill pond. http://en.wikipedia.org/wiki/Gilchrist,_Oregon

In 1939, Gilchrist School was built by the Public Works Administration. I don't know if the look of the town followed the log-cabin design of the school, but the whole town was thematic. It was not unlike current day strip malls, where all the buildings are the same design and color. To a small child, it was kind of a gingerbread town. I don't remember any of the movies, but the town stuck in my head. Unlike other logging camps, Gilchrist survives to this day, although the mill and company have long since closed down for lack of timber. The Gilchrist primary school still had two-hundred and thirty-eight students as of 2006.

In Shevlin-Hixon there was a general store, and the owner of that store is clear in my memory, both from the candy she always gave me, and from the Shevlin-Hixon reunion picnics. She was known, and, I think, loved by everyone. Her name was Florence. She would peer at me over the rim of her thick glasses as she handed me a pack of Beeman's gum, free of charge!

I think my grandparents' closest friends were the Kundingers. I believe Joe and Goldie lived very close to us in Shevlin-Hixon. I am not sure, but I think Joe might have been a sawyer or a saw sharpener. Meritt and he would cut firewood together and hunt together. Goldie and my grandmother, Frances, were together much of the time. They shopped together, and did projects together. We would all go picking huckleberries together. Joe and Goldie later bought a farm in the irrigated Deschutes River Valley and spent their days raising potatoes. We visited them there with Meritt and with my mother and step-dad. They were salt-of-the-earth folk. Joe was about the same size as my grandfather and, I am sure, just as strong. I don't know if Goldie had another name, but I am sure she was named that for her blond hair, which changed to silver over the years. I remember her as always smiling. They were a good-natured couple, which is probably why Meritt liked them so much. Sadly, Joe was killed by a car. He and Goldie had hit a deer on the road, and while Joe was trying to tow the carcass off the road, a vehicle came along and hit him. I don't think Joe and Goldie had children, but I know Goldie never remarried.

Meritt and Frances also were close friends with a family that had their passion described in their name. They were Art and Pearl Rockeye, and while their son Richard was on the La Pine basketball team, their favorite sport was rock collecting. As I recall, Art was a machinist, and he had built his own rock tumblers and polishers. The first geode I ever saw Art had cut himself, the inside shimmering and iridescent blue. My mother mentions him as among the many boys she kissed in high school. I do remember going on a trip to the obsidian outcropping with the Rockeyes and my grandparents. I recall being underwhelmed by the pile of black glass that the rock hounds so favored.

I did not keep up with the families from camp after we moved to Washington State. My mother kept in touch with her classmate Hope, Lee Maker and to some degree, with Ray and Lois Gumpert. They were a couple from S-H camp who went on to buy land around Bend and raise sheep. Their daughter was a Miss Oregon contestant the year that we visited them. She had an Austin Healy Sprite sports car, and it was a thrill for a kid just reaching puberty to be "toured" in a sports car with a "beauty queen". Bobby Gumpert showed me the farm that day, and how much dirt gets trapped in the wool of a sheep. Then, that evening, we drove to the local drive-in theater and sat on the hill outside the parking lot, and watched the movie *sans* sound. It was a clear star-lit night in Eastern Oregon, which I will never forget. I suppose I could phone the number that I found on 411.com for the Gumperts, but maybe it is best to leave that past alone. I am dealing with my memories and sonder; to delve into current realities would be far too expansive. We meet so many people in a lifetime, and they all have their lifetimes, and before you know it, you have the whole world in front of you.

To summarize, the seminal events in the life of this little berg of a logging camp that interact with my life were as follows:

1947
Logging town of Shevlin moves from Stage Station area to Sugar Pine Mountain area seven miles south of Chemult.

1950
September 2, 1950 - Shevlin-Hixon Picnic held at Shevlin Park with 1200 to 1500 people in attendance. It was the first Shevlin-Hixon picnic since 1930. But not the last.
November 21, 1950 - Shevlin-Hixon sells out to Brooks-Scanlon.

1952
Logging town of Shevlin makes final move from south of Chemult to the Timbers area seven miles north of Gilchrist. http://www.fs.fed.us/r6/centraloregon/about/history-1950

By 1952 Meritt and Frances and I had already moved on to California, and others had scattered on their chosen paths, except the Rockeyes. Meritt and Art both went to work for the McCloud River Lumber Company. It would behoove us all to contemplate how fleeting life really is. This whole community had come together, lived their joint lives, and dispersed in the short span of five years. The amazing thing is that friendships were formed that went on for years after. This was helped by the efforts that individuals made to organize the annual Shevlin-Hixon picnics after the company sold out. In today's world, we might live in a community for fifteen or twenty years, and hardly be missed when we leave or pass on. I am reminded of the closeness of the community in Shevlin-Hixon when I consider the lifestyle of my current home in Hawaii. Of course, I am *haole*, (Hawaiian for "without breath" foreigner) so I am not an integral part of their community. Some of these families have multiple generations of relatives that have lived on this very island, in this very town, for decades. For example, there are so many De Luz that they just assume they are all related. I once asked a Japanese-Portuguese coworker, who was preparing for a family event, how many would be attending. She said matter-of-factly "six hundred". My cousins have a similar experience in Mt. Shasta, even though our families are relatively small. Although they had moved away and lived in the Bay Area for many years, now that they have come back to Northern California, they meet people every day that they went to school with in McCloud. My wife, for that matter, logs onto the Longview Daily News website every day to check the obituaries and learn what is happening to the town and people with whom she grew up. Alas, I have no such link. I guess that is why I strain to recall the people and experiences of my youth. My aunt Mary is still alive, but it would be awkward to suddenly descend upon her with a thousand questions about the past. Maybe I am afraid of what I might hear.

Sometime in this sequence of tumultuous events that hover around the end of the war, I moved to San Francisco with my mother, where we were living with Aunt Mary and Uncle Vern. By then Vernon had been discharged from the Navy. After a brief stint as a cable car brakeman, he began his career as a steel worker. I remember riding on his cable car, but I was never shown his steel worksites, which consisted of the construction of most of the freeway system in the Bay area. He had worked on the East Bay viaduct, which collapsed in the Loma Prieta earthquake of 1989 (of which construction Uncle Vernon had never fully approved). The Smiths had already had their two children, Ralph and Vernon Jr. In fact Ralph and I are close to the same age, although he was a year behind me in school. Vernie, as we called Vern Jr., was a year or two older. I guess they had accommodated my mother and me so that my mother could work while Mary took care of us kids.

I had an uncanny experience in the 1980s in San Francisco. My not-yet-wife Mary and I were visiting her friend Meredith. When I walked into her duplex, *deja vou* struck me immediately. It took me a while to realize that the structure was exactly the same design as the place we lived with my cousins in the Castro District. There was a long hallway down one side of the house, and on that hallway there were two doors; one was what they used to call a water closet, which is a room with just a toilet and a sink. The old-fashioned wide baseboards and trim were darkened with varnish and age. Although Meredith, the artist, had painted the place with bright mauve, the memories were welling up within me. Now, I don't assume it was the same duplex; surely many were built in that design, but it could have been the neighborhood. There was a stairway leading up to her flat, as there was in the place we lived in the '50s. I had remembered it to be a much higher staircase, but that was from the perspective of a child. I remember that the Smith's place had a back yard, which was accessed from a porch and stairway off the kitchen. I think we played there most of the time. We had a little fire engine that you sat on and pushed with your feet. I also remember that I had a choo-choo train meal server... the train held a bowl (the coal tender) and a cup (the smoke stack) and I think the fork was the engineer and the spoon was the coalman. Bad memories welled up, too. I used to hate it when my Uncle Vern would lift me up by the heels and then pretend to drop me. I don't know whether I was already a *bona fide* scaredy cat or whether that contributed to the syndrome. Perhaps it was simply the indignity of it all. I never liked carnival rides, and it wasn't until my ten-year-old son took me on the Salt and Pepper Shaker that I experienced rotating in three directions at once. Actually, I think it was a Ferris wheel where the cage rolled as you went around the great circle. One could control the roll, but my son threw the steering wheel all the way to the left, and we rapidly rolled for the duration of the ride.

I clearly remember my cousin Ralph getting hold of his dad's razor and coming out of the bathroom with blood all over his face... this was a foreshadowing of his subsequent youth. He was always up to something he should not have been. I also remember riding on the ferry, and taking the streetcar over the Bay Bridge to Oakland. At one time, the street cars ran everywhere in San Francisco, until General Motors and Goodyear bought up the public transportation and dismantled them to promote bus lines and highways; more roads, more cars, more busses, more tires. I think my last memory might have been leaving San Francisco with my grandparents. It stuck in my mind because, while we were passing by Richmond, there was a huge fuel storage tank on fire, with a massive column of black smoke billowing into the sky. Whatever it takes to keep the American juggernaut rolling, you know?

Now, my memories of San Francisco are clouded by the things my mother has told me since. I assume that the reason I was leaving San Francisco was because my mother had become pregnant again. She apparently liked to spend time at Vesuvio's, and in later years she told me that she had an affair with an Italian piano player, Lawrence "Larry" V. Vannucci (1918 to 1993). The fruit of this union was my half-sister, Martha, who was adopted by friends of the family, the Chaneys. Here again, what an impact parents and grandparents have on their children when they attempt to mitigate the embarrassment or the burden of the perfectly natural act of conceiving and bearing a child. My mother says my grandparents insisted that she give up the child for adoption. Whether that is the entire truth, or whether she was complicit in not wanting to interrupt her career (hence returning me to my grandparents) I will never know. I do know that she always regretted it. In later years she kept trying to establish a relationship with Martha, even using me to attempt to trick Martha into meeting her. Martha steadfastly refused, and there never was a reunion. I did meet with my half-sister on several occasions, initially because my grandfather thought we should know each other, and later she came to Hawaii after my mother died, to meet her half-sister-in-law, Gretchen, and her niece, Colleen. Prior to that I had only met her once when I was about seven at my grandfather's house in McCloud. Mom told me I would be meeting my sister, and I tried to talk to young Martha about it in the yard where we were sent to play, while the adults had a private discussion inside. I don't know if she had even been told that she had a brother.

Although half-sister and I have lost touch; I don't know why. There is no doubt of our relationship; we look very much alike in our complexion and features; my mother's genes were strong. Martha went on to receive her master's degree and have a successful career, first as a career consultant, and now as an employee of Nike in the Netherlands. She wrote a book on how to find your career in life, and I guess she has found hers. But life with the Chaney's was not all roses and peppermint. She told me that her adoptive father abused her, although I do not know the details. She grew up and found that her sexual proclivity was to women, and has had at least one long-term relationship, although I don't know anything about her now.

Meritt learned to golf with Martha and her partner... after all, he was only in his eighties! I think it was probably good for Martha to have that relationship with Meritt and his last wife, Josie. They were lovely and humorous people. Since both of her adoptive parents had passed, I think Martha needed some family humor at that point in her life. After our mother died, Meritt hoped that Martha would want to get to know her sibling better, and Martha did make an initial effort. Before Gretchen and I were married, the met in Portland, and when Martha has a back operation, Gretchen offered to stay with her to help her recover. When I visited Gretchen in Portland with Colleen, Martha came to dinner at Gretchen's apartment. Then, after Gretchen and I were married, Martha came to Hawaii, and stayed with us for a week. I have only recently discovered that Martha has written a second book under her pen name Marti Chaney[12].

Since I don't remember the move to Camp Pondosa, I assume I was not with my grandparents at the time. When I came there from San Francisco, it was to the little house in the camp. And, as I said before, it was not a boring life. In the summer, we would go to Bear Creek, which was not far from camp, but had all the amenities of a natural amusement park.

Engine 25 crossing the Bear Creek bridge. (With permission of the Jeff Moore Collection.)

There was a railroad trestle running over the creek. The teenagers probably dove off it when no one was around. We humored ourselves by placing rolls of caps on the rail, which would pop when the train ran over them. But the locals had also built a diving platform at the place where the water got wide and deep. I remember my grandfather swimming across the water with me on his back. I don't think I could even swim then, but he instructed me to hold on tight and away we went. He was a strong swimmer with a big barrel chest, and a whole lot of body hair… the hair on his head was already in remission at that time. I think Frances convinced him that he shouldn't be swimming with me, because I did not learn to swim at Bear Creek. Downstream from the pool there was an area where the banks widened and the water became shallow. This was where the little children played. I remember the bank being muddy and very slippery. Once, after my mother moved to McCloud and married my stepfather, James, we went camping on Bear Creek. I remember they went swimming in their underwear on a moonlight night. Let me just say that was a slippery affair! One time my mother was visiting Camp Pondosa and we went to Bear Creek. She and grandmother were sitting on the bank upstream from the railroad bridge. The water was more rapid at that point, so when a little girl slipped into the water, my mother jumped in to pull her out. She could only side stroke because she had to keep the water out of her broken eardrum. But she managed. It gave me a start to realize that both children and adults are vulnerable in the water. I don't know if I had previously realized it, since we spent so much time wading around in the water there at Bear Creek.

Of course, Bear Creek was only available in the summer, but in that part of the Siskiyou Mountains summers seemed endless. I remember we sometimes took road trips up to Castle Crags. Again, by the happenstance of life, my son spent one or two summers camping in the woods with a crew of young fire recruits in the Lassen National Forest and in view of the Castle Crags. This was when he was with the Bureau of Land Management Hot Shot crew based in Susanville, Eagle Lake District.

We would generally go to McCloud for groceries and dry goods. But, on occasion, we would go on to Mt. Shasta. I would play on a little old steam engine that was at the gas station on the edge of town. I don't remember that we ate out much, but I do remember winding up the day at the Mt. Shasta drive-in theater. It was a lovely spot on a hillside that looked out on the valley ascending to the mountains. I checked Google maps to be sure I was not imagining that you could see the shining spires of Castle Crags in the distance as the sun set to the west. The smell of Manzanita and the sound of the crickets dominated while waiting for the show to start. I don't know if we lasted through a whole movie. Meritt had built a platform behind the front seats of the Plymouth; which turned the whole back seat into a bed. Blankets had been provided and it was only a matter of how long we could stay awake.

One winter the snow got up to the eaves of the little house in Pondosa. There is a picture of me standing on the snow pile. I remember that the railroad snowplows were deployed out of Camp Pondosa and the engine watering tanks had huge icicles hanging from the spout. I don't know how they kept them from freezing solid, thus bringing the steam engines to a halt. I know my grandfather would take me around with him to the engine repair shop sometimes. It was not a roundhouse in Pondosa, but they could bring steam engines in to have basic maintenance done to them. Meritt would also take me to the cookhouse for lunch or sometimes breakfast.

Cookhouse in Camp Pondosa (Reproduced by permission from the Eastman's Originals Collection, Department of Special Collections, General Library, University of California, Davis) http://ulibimage.ucdavis.edu/speccoll/east01/full/T-1340.jpg

I was always amazed at how loud that experience was, with several hundred loggers and camp workers clattering their large porcelain cups and bowls and by the silverware striking cacophonously. There was not a lot of talk at first, because they were all "starving" and dove into their food with gusto. I can't remember if they lined up to be served, or whether the cooks brought the food to the table. I think the latter, because I seem to remember the serving bowls being passed to my grandfather and me. There were so many such bowls on the table that they did not need to be passed far. Whatever the case, it was very efficient, because the clientele did not have to wait for their food to be served. I do remember the food was very good, and especially the pies. Maybe that is where I developed my love of peach pie. The whole process would start with the noon whistle, and I think the back-to-work whistle was no more than a half hour later. There also may have been crew shifts during the busy season, such that the loggers would have to finish and file out efficiently so that the next sitting could be accomplished with haste. I don't know why Meritt would take me into the kitchen before or after the meal. Perhaps he was merely killing time chatting with the cooks, but more likely he needed to deal with the cooks about the provisions and numbers of diners they would be feeding from day to day. It was a heady experience for a young lad.

The cook in his kitchen at Camp Pondosa. (Reproduced by permission from the Eastman's Originals Collection, Department of Special Collections, General Library, University of California, Davis) http://ulibimage.ucdavis.edu/speccoll/east01/full/T-1336.jpg

CHAPTER 5

McCloud

And I will provide a place for my people Israel
and will plant them so that they can have a
home of their own and no longer be disturbed.
Wicked people will not oppress them anymore,
as they did at the beginning. English Standard
Version (2001) <u>2 Samuel 7:9-11</u>

THE MCCLOUD RIVER LUMBER CO. has been mentioned along
the way, but McCloud is the name of a town in Northern California about
ten miles from the town of Mt. Shasta (on Hwy 99, now Interstate 5). Both
towns sit at the foot of Mount Shasta, which is no mere mountain.

> **Mount Shasta** (*Úytaahkoo* in Karuk or "White Mountain") is
> located in Siskiyou County and at 14,179 feet (4,322 m) is the second
> highest peak in the Cascades and the fifth highest in California.
> Mount Shasta has an estimated volume of 85 cubic miles (350 km³)
> which makes it the most voluminous stratovolcano in the Cascade
> Volcanic Arc. <u>http://en.wikipedia.org/wiki/Mount_Shasta</u>

Before we moved to Washington State, I had no concept of the direction
'north'. North was Mt. Shasta… you didn't have to guess. There it was
looming over you, all white in winter, capped in white during the summer,
but always there, always massive, and always comforting. You never had to
look through the forest to see the mountain; it would tower over even the
tallest trees. Sometimes it would be shrouded in clouds; that could be a little
unnerving, but you always knew it was there, dominating the landscape,
governing the weather and our lives. It is not the least bit difficult for me to

understand how the indigenous people could have considered the mountain a Great Spirit, or god.

> Naturalist and author John Muir said of Shasta:
> "When I first caught sight of it over the braided folds of the Sacramento Valley, I was fifty miles away and afoot, alone and weary. Yet all my blood turned to wine, and I have not been weary since."
> Theodore Roosevelt said:
> "I consider the evening twilight on Mt. Shasta one of the grandest sights I have ever witnessed."
> http://en.wikipedia.org/wiki/Mount_Shasta

The Hawaiian people have a similar reverence for their mountain, especially those who reside on the principle island, and the first island colonized by the sea voyagers from Tahiti. Like the Karuk, they named their mountain "White Mountain" or *Mauna Kea*. But unlike the nine tribes living in the shadow of Mt. Shasta, they were the only people present that could name the mountain. Unlike its sister mountain *Mauna Loa* (the long mountain), *Mauna Kea* is peaceful and cold at the summit. The former has been an active volcano for the entire history of the Hawaiian people, and therefore more deserving of respect and even fear. Whereas *Mauna Kea* was a very spiritual place, where the Hawaiians went in summer to shape stone adzes and perform religious rites. Mount Shasta also could be feared, if the Native Americans had known or remembered in their stories, because it is an active volcano capable of eruption at any time. *Mauna Kea*, has been long dormant, willing to let *Mauna Loa* and its offspring, Kilauea, play the pyrotechnics. Mount Shasta, though inactive, has a pattern of erupting about every six-hundred years, and it has been two-hundred years since the last eruption. My cousins still live on the slopes of Mt. Shasta, but I don't think any of us fear the worst. My father lost his house on the Toutle River, Washington, to the furious eruption and pyroclastic flow of Mt. Saint Helens. So our family has a traditional relationship with the volcanoes, and, even though I live less than twenty miles from a river of actively flowing, flaming hot lava, I have a sense of calm that only the child of the mountains could have. Call it blissful ignorance if you will, but I cannot.

My relationship to the mountains has always been more pragmatic. While I enjoy observing them from afar, I seldom ventured there, and if I did it was for some purpose -- usually work -- to measure trees, or place honeybee hives. In regards to mountain climbing and similar suicidal sports, don't get me started. During the time that I worked at the Seattle laboratory on Harbor Island, an experienced climber and scientist at Weyerhaeuser Company took another young scientist and his wife up Mt. Rainier. The three of them were never seen again. Once, the boyfriend of a fellow classmate of my wife Mary asked us to attend a slide show of his ascent of El Capitan in Yosemite National Park. He projected the rock climb on the ceiling of their Berkeley apartment, as we all sprawled on the floor. Had I not been supine, I probably would have lost my cookies! I get a tingly sensation in my feet when I stand on the edge of a cliff, and these guys were sleeping in hammocks dangling from pitons on the face of that imposing precipice. Now my daughter has learned to rock climb and repel down cliffs. Ah, the irony of life!

Once, I hiked the Glenwood trail out to the base of the Pu`u O`o vent of the Kilauea volcano, but at the base of the enlarging mount a sign warned of potential danger. There was actually a skull and crossed bones printed on the sign; I guess the park service wanted people to take the hint. So my hiking partner (another Mike) and I decided that discretion was the better part of valor, and waited for our bolder compatriot to get his share of adventure breaking through the crust of A`a lava, bloodying his ankles. What amazed me the most was a Labrador that accompanied another party of young studs to the rim of the caldera. Easy for the lads, but they had shoes. The dog must have had sore feet at the end of a day of running over what amounts to glass shard. I think the Hawaiian named that lava A'a because it hurts!

My last hike to the Pu`u O'o was in 1998, when a party of us hiked out to the Na Po'o Po'o trail. It was twelve miles to the overlook where you could see below a line of fresh black Pahoehoe lava. A split in the ground had exposed a fissure, and for several days had sent up a curtain of fiery lava. About four miles on down the trail, there was a campsite where some rangers, visiting from Yellowstone, had been sleeping, when the lava burst forth. They wanted to stay for the show, but the park service insisted they vacate. By the time we arrived, the curtain had sealed over and a new vent had broken out on the southern slope of the Pu`u O`o caldera. The rest of the party hiked out to the campgrounds and got some great video of the boiling caldron. I could see it all from the overlook where I sat and waited. That was the last long hike I ever took, because by the time we had hiked out to the road, my back was killing me. As I found out later it was the first impact of the stenosis that affects me all the time now. The hike did not cause the injury, but genetics was gradually impacting my spinal column and taking away my freedom of movement.

My son, on the other hand, seems more spiritually connected to the mountain experience. He seems to relish the trips to the high lakes, and needs the rejuvenation that it provides. I remember very cold, wet days taking tree diameters in the Cascades. Although the honeybees were placed in the mountains in the summer, my trips to the mountain locations were mostly at night, to scout for bears and to move the hives. Not that the rolling Cascades were not majestic at dusk, but I was no John Muir. I remember going to the timberline when we were kids to try out our new skis, but I never learned to do it well. In later years, when I would go to the ski resorts with my second wife, I was bothered by the disrespectful sea of humanity that swarmed in from the cities to the slopes in winter. Camping in California's Big Sur was like living in a town of "rude nicks". Although I admit I did not join the bike trip through the forest to the sea, instead I opted to be the driver commissioned to meet the party at the base of the trail. I did do one fifteen-mile hike from Eagle Creek to Multnomah Falls, Oregon, when I was in the seminary. It was mostly downhill through a soft bed of fir needles and towering old growth Douglas fir, Western Red Cedar, Hemlock and under-story Maple. It was magnificent! The only other time I spent so long in the old growth forest was when I was doing a plant inventory on the Kalama River in the Gifford Pinchot Forest in Southwestern Washington. The inventory was being taken before the whole forest was to be clear-cut. I still can't believe how nonchalantly we measured and sampled with this cathedral of beauty towering over our heads. I think my son, because he has seen more than three-hundred forests in the caldron of flaming destruction, has been more vigilant than me to appreciate the beauty of one of the last great forests on earth.

Returning to McCloud and living at the base of Shasta. My grandfather moved into McCloud when he was promoted to be Woods Manager for the entire McCloud River Lumber Company forest operation. This gave him a small office in corporate headquarters, and a great big two story, five bedroom, two-bath house with a quarter acre of yard, a woodshed and garage. Compare that to a small two-bedroom house in camp. When Frances (my grandmother) would throw a women's canasta party; there was barely room to move around the fold-up card tables. In contrast, at the big house in McCloud there was a very large living room, a sumptuous dining area, and a sunroom along half the side of the house, and a covered L shaped porch along the side and front of the house. My cousins, the neighbor kids and I used to love to play pirate ship on the two hanging porch swing that could hold six "mates" at a time.

The big house was only a block or two from the corporate office, and the garage where Meritt kept his company car. So Meritt would rise at five every morning, put on his green Eisenhower jacket and pants with suspenders, make himself two over-easy eggs toast and coffee, don his fedora, and walk down to work. Life was good for my grandparents at the big house, and by association, was good for me.

I didn't really know what Meritt did at work until my mother and step-dad moved me to Longview, Washington. During the first two summers after that, I would visit Meritt and his second wife, Eva. Although I didn't go with him every day, when I wanted to, I could ride with him on his job. He would check into the office and then head to the McCloud Mill.

Flatcars of logs delivered to the **McCloud mill pond.** (With permission of the Jeff Moore Collection)

We would visit the millpond and talk to the steam donkey operator

Donkey steam loader, similar to the one used at the McCloud Mill pond. They were moved from one job site to another on flatcars. (With permission of the Jeff Moore Collection). http://www.trainweb.org/mccloudrails/LumberCompany/donkeyloaders.html

to find out how many carloads of logs had been unloaded the previous day, and what the backlog of inventory was that day. The objective was to make sure there were enough board feet being brought into the pond to feed the mill with a constant supply of saw logs. If the mill was down for equipment failure, he needed to know that so he could adjust the forest cut accordingly. To speed up the log dumping, Meritt eventually designed an un-loader. His invention would pick up an entire carload of logs and dump it into the pond. The company engineer got the patent and the glory, but I know Meritt designed it, because he built a model in the woodshed and showed me how it operated.

After he had the lay of the land at the mill site, he would head out to the various logging operations. Often we would stop at the facilities at

73

Pondosa camp, where the camp superintendent would bring him up to date on the operations. I used to be very embarrassed to go into the staff room with Meritt, because I was just reaching puberty, and the staff room was plastered from wall to wall with Playboy centerfolds. If we reached Pondosa around lunch time, we would stay and eat in the cookhouse. If we were early, we might catch that meal on the way back. I don't remember stopping for lunch in Burney Falls or elsewhere, so I guess we took a lunch on those days. I do, however, remember eating at the cookhouse. That was some really good eating; hearty stews, pork chops, and warm pies. Everyone knew Meritt because he had supervised operations in Pondosa before the move to McCloud.

The logging operation at that time was still largely oriented around the rail line and the big steam loader. This loader was built to travel on the tracks to the worksite (called spurs), then it was jacked up straddling the tracks so that empty flat cars could be pushed under it, and then loaded with logs. This was a much more efficient way to load cars than the donkey loaders which needed to be positioned along the side of the tracks. The logs were then skidded up to the loader with a bulldozer and loaded one at a time.

Large steam loader (upper right of frame). (With permission of Trainweb. org) http://www.trainweb.org/mccloudrails/LumberCompany/Landing.html

Of course, steam was eventually replaced by diesel loaders and logging trucks, but a large portion of the western forests were logged off and loaded with the track-straddling steam loader. And these were no "fence poles"; many logs were so large they had to be loaded one per flatcar. This was a hot job for the loader operator. Meritt used to take me up to the control deck to talk with the loader operators. It was loud and hot, and the sweat glistened off the skin of the burly man, whose arms were thickened by the constant motion of operating the big levers that wound the pull cables and rotated the rig back and forth, one log at a time. It was a man's world and the lumberjacks were tough.

After checking the several logging spurs, and making sure that everything was running smoothly, Meritt would turn the company car back to the long road home. Sometimes we would be eighty or so miles out from McCloud. Other times, if he was not too busy, he would head off into the woods so I could get a little taste of "cross-country". Actually, what I didn't realize then is that he was taking shortcuts. He knew all the old logging roads, because he had probably been on the crew that cleared the timber for those roads. By then there were saplings growing in the middle of the road, but they were young enough that we could drive right over them. You never knew what you might encounter on one of those old logging roads. Deer and bear were prevalent but you might also see squirrels, raccoons (which are normally nocturnal), and the occasional porcupine.

After returning to McCloud, Meritt would drive along the road behind the mill, which ran along the railroad tracks. This is where the carloads of logs would come into the mill site, and Meritt would be calculating board footage by sizing up the carloads that were standing there waiting to be dumped into the pond. This was a mental exercise for Meritt. He had only finished eighth grade, but he had learned math well. This is why they paid him a good salary. He never even took out a notepad, but he would go from the mill to the company office and write down his observations, which became the production records for the company operations. Nowadays it would probably take a team of computer-equipped technicians to keep the records that came out of Meritt's head.

In my lifetime, I only met one other man who had my grandfather's skill with numbers. He was a wholesale grocer in Centralia, Washington. He kept all of his books in his head. I know that because my stepfather's last wife audited him for the Internal Revenue Service. This happened more than once, but each time they would cancel the audit. The only records for the business were the receipt books that he kept of every transaction down to the last bag of flour and the last canister of tea. That would take too many man-hours to review. I used to buy groceries from this wholesaler, and I swear he could add a list of twenty-five numbers in two seconds flat. Mr. Sorenson also played the fiddle and/or (I can't remember exactly which) sang in a barbershop quartet. These were the skills that were required for success in the businesses of the late nineteenth and early twentieth century. They were probably the same skills that were essential in ancient times. The brain was still the most powerful tool in human society.

So math is why Meritt was transferred to McCloud, and that is how we came to live there. Those years left memorable impressions in my head, like the first time in the year that you would wake up to snow. I would look out the upstairs bedroom window and see that the pines and the firs were all white. A jolt of excitement would go through me, anticipating moonlight sledding on Parachino Hill, snowball fights, and building snowmen. After I started attending school, snow meant days off from school, and since I was not terribly fond of school, freedom!

In front of the house in McCloud there was a wooden sidewalk that ran along the row of company houses that were provided for the management-level people. For example, the house on the north (Mt. Shasta) side of the big house was the elementary school principal's house. At that time, Mr. James Hogin was the Principal of McCloud Elementary School. He or his family apparently bought the house when the company sold the town, because it is now a bed and breakfast DBA the Hogin House. At the end of the sidewalk nearest the company offices was the General Manager's home. This was a beautiful place with a porch all the way round, with polished log banisters and brownish red paint that made it look like it belonged in the shaded yard surrounded by beautiful old firs and pines. The manager's wife and elderly mother (I think she was in her nineties) would invite the neighborhood children in from time to time. I remember the interior to have lots of varnished wood, and a big poolroom… we didn't really go deeper into the magnificent interior of the house. She would use baked enticements to lure us in; I guess she just liked to have chattering kids around.

The wooden sidewalk represented a more genteel time. It was a time when the sound of leather shoes and bicycle tires metered out the resonance of the boardwalk. The company had made this concession to civility, while placing the auto lane (Lawndale Court) behind the row of houses. Thus the entire front lawn and property was a playground for the children, with trees to climb, bushes to shelter us for hide-and-seek, a gradual incline to roll our bodies down, and honeysuckle to savor. There was even a spooky, enclosed area under the house that was a great venue for play, albeit a haven for spiders as well, with an ever-present pool of hot water created by the steam-radiator discharge pipe. In the summer, some of the kids liked to catch grasshoppers, boil them in the steamy water, and eat them. That never appealed to me... neither the killing nor the consumption.

We ate sweet peas (genus *Lathyrus*) in the summer by the pods full. Growing wild in northern California, Sweet peas are on every list of California's poisonous wild plants. When consumed, in quantity they can cause mental impairment in children. I don't think we ever even got stomachaches from eating them, although I cannot speak to any impairment. Why did we have this wild source of "nutrition"? Because, beyond the mown and manicured lawn in front of the Big house, there was an open field of several unkempt acres. It extended all the way down to the railroad tracks in the middle of town, and, according to Google maps, it is still there, undeveloped. When my cousins and I were little, we were allowed to play in that field, as long as we did not go near the railroad. So, as in Camp Pondosa, we were not what you would call confined. We once had to chew on our socks as a punishment for getting them so dirty in the big field. Otherwise, we were as free as wildebeests on the Serengeti.

I don't remember the names of all the kids that lived on the hill on

Lawndale Court, but the one I remember the most was Rick McGiff. I don't know if we started playing together as soon as my grandparents moved to McCloud, or if it was only after my mother came and took a job as X-ray technician at the McCloud Hospital. Dr. McGiff took over as principal physician for the town and lived in a house above the hospital. The hospital was just up the hill from Lawndale Court, so Rick and I could visit each other most days. At the end of Lawndale was the house of the company engineer, Mr. Willis, who had a son, named Marshall. Marshall had a great old golden retriever who used to accompany us on all of our adventures. So not only did we have the whole territory below the Big House to play, but we had the manicured turf of the hospital grounds. One problem, we had to be quiet... which was hard!

Behind the hospital there was a large ravine where a small creek flowed most of the year but dried up between middle to late summer. As we got a little older, this area at the base of Parachino Hill was a favorite hangout (our winter playground as well). Cool water ran though this lovely little valley, and it was a great place for imagination. Catching lizards, chasing Monarch butterflies, chewing on stocks of succulent grass, and all the other things that young kids do when released to roam the valleys and the hills like Tom and Huck.

Coming from Mt. Shasta, the main street into McCloud was Colombero St. Lawndale Court ran into Colombero, and on the other side of Colombero there was Edgewood Court. Off Edgewood Court there was Oak St., which ran along the hill in front of Susie Colombero's house. I think her father, or his father, was high up in the company, because that street was named after the family. The Muma's lived on Edgewood, because Mrs. Muma was a nurse at the hospital. Their daughters, Sylvia Muma and her sister, as well as my cousins, and Rick, Marshall and the other unnamed kids from the right side of the tracks used to play together. Edgewood went up a steep hill, so we boys ventured to build soapbox derby cars to ride down it. Mine crashed but didn't burn anything but my pride.

I liked Susie a lot, and even invited her to dinner at the big house. I forget if my mother was living with us by then or whether it was my Grandmother who made it a very formal affair. She set the table in the big dining room, and made me dress up for the occasion. But I was in competition with the Doctor's son, who was a black-haired blue- eyed Mick... how could I compete? I think we were about five, maybe six.

Our small world in the echelons of society in McCloud expanded gradually. We children may have been better acquainted than some of our parents. Susie's parents were more protective of her, and she was not allowed to roam the neighborhood with us. I think mainly it was the boys who did the major exploring. As I said, there were limits, and mostly they were to stay west of the railroad tracks. I never thought about this before, but the tracks were kind of the typical demarcation zone that existed between the well-to-do and the working class in a lot of American towns. Colombero Road was a kind of mini-demarcation between the management class and the skilled worker class. Mr. Colombero was some kind of clerk. Mr. Muma was also a semi-professional person. My future stepfather's Uncle Louis, who lived on Edgewood next to the Muma's, was a Bookkeeper. Sylvia's mother, Sybil, the nurse, became a good friend of my mother when she went to work at the McCloud Hospital.

Just as an example of the kind of mischief we boys could get into, I once broke into my big fat pink piggy bank with a coiled porcelain tail. Then I talked Rick McGiff into joining me on trip down to the General Store, which was just across the railroad tracks below the company offices. I think we were violating two rules: 1) theft, and 2) passing over the boundaries. On the way, I was bragging to Rick how I had busted my piggy bank, but Sybil Muma was passing by and heard us talking. We went on to the Pharmacy where I bought a rubber pirate sword with the money. Perhaps I had some change left, which we used to buy a treat at the soda fountain in the Pharmacy which was in the corner of the General Store. This building still stands DBA McCloud Mercantile B&B and White Mountain soda fountain.

McCloud Mercantile B & B and White Mountain Soda Fountain. (Reproduced with permission of the McCloud Chamber of Commerce) http://www.mccloudchamber. com/lodging.html

Well, as luck and the grapevine would have it; my mother grilled me about whence the sword had come. Sybil Muma had already informed her, but my mother did not let on that she already knew. She asked me where I got the sword. I knew I was on the hot seat, so I claimed that it was on loan from Rick… nice guy, that Rick. So, she told me to give it back to Rick. Of course, he wanted nothing to do with it. Consequently I got, what they call in Hawaii, lickins! But that was not the most painful part. My mother bent the rubber sword in two, and threw it in a waste paper basket in the upstairs bathroom. Now that basket was only dumped if it filled up, and it rarely did. So there the sword sat for months. I used to beg to retrieve it, but I was steadfastly denied the pleasure. It was a powerful lesson about the importance of not lying… or stealing, for that matter.

In 1953 my mother came to visit us at the big house, because her mother was going in the hospital to have surgery for her varicose veins. The surgery was successful, but the recovery was lethal. My grandmother had already come home from the hospital and my mother was helping to care for her. Apparently an embolism stopped her heart, and she died. My grandfather was devastated. I think I previously mentioned pacing around the living room with him crying. I don't think Meritt was at the house when she died, and my Aunt Mary was also not present. My mother was the only one who saw her die. My mother had the most medical training of anyone in the family, but in those days, there was not a lot one could do to intervene with a myocardial infarction. The hospital was close, but even so, minutes are crucial, and blood thinners were not yet in general use. Even cardio pulmonary resuscitation, as we know it today, did not exist. When the heart stopped, it was usually the end.

My mother agreed to stay with Meritt, to help him over the funeral and mourning period. She had probably left her job in Yreka to do this, and apparently was able to get the X-ray technician job in McCloud rather quickly. I remember those evenings with Meritt. I appreciated them a great deal. We would sit in the dining nook listening to the radio, with Meritt drumming his fingers on the table to the beat of the music. Both my grandmother and my mother hated Meritt's percussive habit, but I inherited the trait from some ancient Irish ancestors. I love to drum out the music on any surface available, the table, my dog and myself, which also drives my wife crazy. Sometimes we could even convince Meritt to bring out his fiddle that he seldom if ever played in the big house. He would play the "Golden Slipper", the "Kentucky Reel", and "Old Gray Mare", but his favorite tune was the "Tennessee Waltz". I don't know if it had held some romantic significance for him, but you could definitely see the nostalgia in his eyes, and feel it in the music. But after that day when Meritt and I paced the living room, I never saw him cry again. He was a calm and gentle man, who accepted life as it came. When I visited him when he was dying at age ninety-six, I broke into tears. He chided me and said, "no tears when my ship goes over".... And then he proceeded to tell me a long joke (which was something he seldom did). It was funny, too[13]!

The funeral was in Bend, Oregon, and, of course, the whole family was there, including Meritt's sister, Nina, and Uncle Burt. I don't remember if Cleo and Larry came, but Dad and Ma Whitlock were still alive, and Uncle Vern and Aunt Elma were there. Also Frances' sister, Eva, showed up in her fox fur throw and high heels and loud piercing voice. Somehow,

Meritt became suddenly very impressed with Aunt Eva, and it was not long before Meritt went off to marry his deceased wife's sister. My mother thought that was a disaster. Eva had been around for much of Kathleen's childhood, but Mom had been a good friend with Eva's only child, Ellen. She was a sickly child but Eva had no mercy. Eventually Ellen died, and her father George, Eva's husband, died soon after. In my mother's eyes, it was no accident. My mother's judgment on this matter might have been clouded by her love of Ellen, but I think everyone will agree that Eva was the kind of woman who tries men's souls... as she eventually did Meritt's. But at this time, Meritt was infatuated. My mother said it was disgusting to hear this prince of a man tell her "I am so grateful that a fine woman like Eva would consider marrying a common lumberjack like me."

We lived in the house with Eva for a short time, but it was quite obvious that Eva was not going to tolerate having us "under foot" for long. On one occasion my mother dated a Mexican man named Julio. I know Eva had a fit and fell in it. She was all over Meritt like an overcoat about his bastard daughter and grandson. Of course, knowing my mother's history, you can imagine that a "woman of appearances" like Eva, who had just married into McCloud River Lumber Company royalty (in her mind), would not like to be faced, in her "very own mansion", with the embarrassment of a prodigal step-daughter. Never mind that this whole life was inherited from her dead sister. Frances had worked hard to help Meritt get to his station in life, but never saw the fruits of her labor ripen.

One did not cross my Aunt Eva. Therefore it was inevitable that Meritt finally suggested to my mother that it was time for her to be on her own, and we moved across the railroad tracks to an upstairs apartment on Quincy Street, in the middle of the town of McCloud. At least one of those two story houses is still there, because it is advertised on the Internet as the Quincy house B&B.

The Quincy House in the 2000s. (Reproduced with permission of the McCloud Chamber of Commerce).

This was not the house, but probably was the house to the north of our apartment. The old lady who lived there was a very nice lady and always had a beautiful garden. Our apartment was plain, painted a dull green with crabapple trees along the side path but very little in the way of landscaping. We were upstairs, and the couple below was not very friendly. I was always being cautioned not to run across the floor or make too much noise. This was all very strange to me. In Meritt's big house, I had a very large room and was seldom corrected for making noise or for not cleaning up my room... at least until Eva came to stay. As I remember, at the apartment, I wasn't even allowed to make a lot of noise outside, because the downstairs neighbors would object.

Quincy Street was an entirely different world. There were lots of kids in the neighborhood, but it took me a while to get to know them. They were a very different culture than the kids on Lawndale Court. These were the sons of mill workers and lumberjacks. Some of the men were coarse and drank heavily. Some were struggling financially. I was so surprised when I went to the house of the Longs who lived across the street. I forget how many kids they had, but they were sleeping three to a bed. Nor did my friendships with the kids on Lawndale remain the same. After I started school we still goofed off together. Rick and I used to get in trouble for horsing around in Mrs. Anderson's third grade class. But the relationships were not the same. They were up there, and we were down here "across the tracks".

There was one equalizing factor in McCloud that brought all the kids together. In fact it was probably the best feature of the town. Not that we lacked for things to do, but the swimming pool (open from Noon to four every summer day) was a godsend for the hot summers. On a visit to

McCloud years later, I was deeply depressed to see the pool in disrepair. A corral containing of thousands of soda cans was erected in front of the pool. It was there to try to raise money to restore the pool to its former glory (which, by the way, never happened). This we saw when my son James and I drove through McCloud when he was ten. This was almost as disheartening to me as the fate of the Waikiki Natatorium War Memorial was to the older residents of Honolulu. If you ever watched Hawaii Five O, you know the Natatorium, because it was frequently the scene of various criminal activities, clandestine meetings and generally a good place to film.[14] The Friends of the Natatorium have been trying to save the old derelict for many years, but there still is no resolution. I cannot imagine living in McCloud without a swimming pool, but residents still do.

In my childhood, the pool was a center of activity. Even before we could swim we would go and spend the afternoon in the kiddy pool. Sun screen? What was that? I remember I got a goofy looking snorkel mask that had an orange view panel and two breathing tubes. They looked like the antenna of a large bug with one big orange eye. The other kids laughed at me, but it was that mask that gave me the nerve to venture under the water. Then I swam away from the edge of the kiddy pool, then eventually into the adult pool. I was always afraid of the deepest end where the suction plate drew water out of the pool and into the filter plant. I guess some kid had told me stories of people being trapped by the suction because they came to close to that inlet. Otherwise, we learned to swim pretty much on our own. The parents didn't even accompany us to the pool. There were lifeguards and everyone considered the town safe enough to have kids walking off to the pool every day.

Of course, kids will be kids, and I remember the bullies. I only got in a fight once, and I think my cousins helped me escape. Sometime after Mom and I moved to Quincy, St. Uncle Vern and Aunt Mary had moved up from the Bay Area, with cousins Ralph and Vernie. Since Mom was on call at the hospital, and Mary was not working, I spent a lot of time with them.

Their house was only a block from the swimming pool, so we would always go there together and spend the sultry afternoons.

The pool was a center of activity for adults as well. Every summer there was an aquacade and the precision swimming was very impressive to me (not to mention the pretty girls). As I remember it, the team was mostly or entirely girls/women, but it looked so impressive at night from the bleachers with the underwater lighting beneath the incredibly star speckled sky of this mountain oasis of "culcha".

The pool was not the only place that we young whippersnappers were allowed to wander. In fact, it soon became possible to roam in little bands all over the town and surrounding area. Some days it was down to the golf course, the far side of which intersected a marshy area that was created by the soda springs[15]. The fishing was good there, so we would ride our bikes with our fishing gear over our shoulders. The soda springs smelled kind of funny, but was bubbly cold and refreshing. Even our parents would bring down jugs with lemon juice and sugar to make bubbly lemonade.

Other days we would wander over to the ballpark. Yes, McCloud had its very own baseball league, basketball league too. Usually there was no one at the Ball Park, so we would write on the bleachers, and play various and sundry games. In front of the bleachers was a slough, and once we played "Guadalcanal" in the muck. It is a wonder we didn't all come down with dysentery or worse! That only happened once... our folks were royally pissed!

Our territory expanded as we got to know more kids. A big increase in my circle of friends came after my mother married my step-father, James G. Klungness. I will talk more about that later, but suffice it to say that he had a very large extended family. He had two sisters, and each of them had had a passel of kids. Ann had eight, and Betty two. Not to mention that James had been married to Nancy long enough to have four children. The oldest was Mary, then Terri, and then Kim and the youngest was Stevie. Nancy had been injured when Kim was trapped under a car that had fallen off a jack.

Nancy picked the 1950's sedan up by herself. This one was an incredible feat even for a strong man, much less a frail woman. Kim was left unable to walk. Why James and Nancy divorced, I don't really know, but Nancy suffered from back trouble due to her Herculean feat. So I immediately acquired ten cousins and four step-siblings.

The cousins all lived about three blocks up Quincy Street. Well, I don't actually remember where they all lived, but they were usually hanging out at Aunt Ann's. She was a college graduate, but I don't think I ever knew her to work outside the home. Her husband Mr. Glenn was a lush, but he did work. Susie was the oldest daughter of Betty, and sort of surrogate mother to the whole tribe. She was a very pretty girl, and I was quite flattered when she decided to teach me how to spell Klungness. I regret that I cannot remember the names of all those kids. I remember Peggy whom, I understand, no longer lives in McCloud. It was a rough and tumble bunch, because the parents were often distracted by "the brew". My mother said the reason we moved out of McCloud was to get away from Nancy and from the drinking within James' family.

Knowing all these kids on Quincy Street also lead to knowing almost every kid on the street. There was Rodney, who had a great dog, a boxer, and whose mother was a free spirit from Australia. I was so shocked when the whole troop of kids was called to the open bathroom door to receive instructions from his mother... from the throne, so to speak. Not that my mother was a prude about nudity, but that did not include all the kids in the neighborhood. On the same street, the son of the Episcopalian Pastor lived across from my cousins. He and I actually were pretty good friends. We were both a little shyer and less rowdy than the rest. Unfortunately his dog bit one of the kids and had to be put in quarantine; I don't think it was diagnosed as rabid.

This expansion of our universe led to even farther expeditions. My dad's former family lived almost on the eastern edge of town on E. Minnesota Ave, heading toward Burney Falls. I remember that someone on Minnesota had a TV, and we would go to watch Hopalong Cassidy, followed by The Cisco Kid. Others lived way past Hoo Hoo Park to the northeast, on Shasta Ave., which was almost to the Mill site on the northern side of town. Soon we were wandering onto the outer edge of the mill site, doing incredibly intelligent things like chewing chunks of roofing tar from a storehouse where supplies were kept. The way we were always sampling the bounty of the land, one would think our parents never fed us. Pine pitch and green apples were other delicacies. Chokecherries, tiny little wild strawberries, and even some huckleberries grew near town. The latter were usually picked over (huckleberry pie is nothing short of food for the gods). We would probably have drowned in the millpond except for the fact that there was usually lots of activity there. We were afraid to be spotted where we knew we were not supposed to be. To my knowledge, none of us ever got injured, sick or lost. We were often tawny, grubby and late, but never the worse for wear.

Not to say we didn't try to get in trouble, my cousin Ralph especially. He had a proclivity to try to ride the horses at the Riding Club. I don't know how many times the attendant chased us out of the corral. We had heard that he used buckshot, but none of us were ever caught in his sight. Halloween is usually the time for mischief, but I guess we were still too young to partake in the mayhem. I remember one year I was dressed up as Woody the Woodpecker, but that is all I remember. I think there was usually some activity at the grade school on Halloween night. Speaking of which, the school was a social equalizer, because it was the only one, and all the kids from the east and west side of the tracks went to that school together.

Childhood friendships are ephemeral, though tragically overlooked by the parents. I wonder why parents don't seem to consider childhood friendships as crucial as the demands of their own lives. Take my friendships with Bobby Vaughn and the one girl in our play group. Essentially, moving to McCloud erased those connections. I very seldom saw them again, and at this stage of my life, know virtually nothing about them. The same is true of the close friendship that Rick McGiff and I had had when I lived on Lawndale Ct. We goofed off in grade school together, but we were not in the same social class, even though we were in the same classroom. After I moved to Longview, Washington, with my parents, I would return to visit Meritt, I didn't spend much time with Rick. The last time we met was one year at Camp Blanchett in the Puget Sound. Dr. McGiff was Catholic, and somehow he and my mother had communicated about the diocesan summer camp that I had attended the previous year. Dr. McGiff decided to bring Rick to camp; he rented a plane and flew Rick up himself (Navy Pilot in WWII). I think he actually brought Rick to our house, from whence we took him to Camp. At Camp, Rick and I quickly took separate paths. We were both in Nisqually cabin, but he was obviously more in-tune with the other boys. I was becoming less confident, more moody, and apparently not as much fun to hang with. That only added to my insecurities. I managed to have a decent time that second year at camp, but I didn't want to go again after that.

What I am trying to point out is that the friendships that children form in their impressionable years have an impact on them. The way parents put their own priorities ahead of those of the children can also have permanent impacts on the young ones. I see this in my own daughter. Until she was five, she was raised in Hawaii, and mostly in one community with one circle of friends. Then her mother, Mary, moved her to Maryland... and then moved her four subsequent times. Each time friendships that had been formed were interrupted. They were not always broken, but it is a lot different to live in the neighborhood with other kids, and having to have the parents arrange for sleepovers from across metropolitan boundaries. Colleen put her foot down in High School. Although she was miserable at Atholton High, she categorically refused to enroll in any other school.

At least the young people have Facebook and other social networks so they write to their friends. But face-to-face communication is the holy grail of social development, and networking will never substitute for it. Consequently, like me, my daughter is shy and somewhat socially inept, particularly among strangers. I have had years to practice public speaking and performing in a work environment, but I am still lousy at small talk, and I am more comfortable by myself than in a crowd. My daughter doesn't yet have the advantage of years, and her insecurities are sometimes disabling.

My wife Gretchen, on the other hand, was raised from childhood to college in the same community, and has attended every R. A. Long High School reunion except this year. After college and moving to San Francisco, she returned to her home town, learned her profession from a family friend, and married and had a child in that town. She reads the Longview Daily newspaper on the Internet, and still knows what many of her classmates are doing. She knows whose parents have died and who divorced, and who has been happily married all these years. In particular, she has one friend, Sherry, who has been her best friend since they were eight. Gretchen is not an assertive person, but she is very comfortable in a social situation, even among total strangers.

On the other hand, I really don't have a place I call home. Home is where I am. I would be no more comfortable in Longview than I would be in McCloud. I lived in Seattle, Longview, Centralia and Tenino, Washington; Springdale, Bend, Shevlin, Oregon; Taita Hills, Kenya; McCloud, San Francisco, Oceanside, Davis and Oakland, California. My longest time in one place (seventeen years) has been Mt. View Hawaii, although I lived in Maui and Kauai before Hurricane Iniki drove us from Kauai to Hilo, Hawaii. This is the American way of life. We move with our jobs, schooling, relationships, and happenstance. If we have children, the children are, for all intent and purposes, part of the baggage.

Even tight little communities like McCloud are not immune from the fluxing nature of American society. The cohesive unit of McCloud was the economic model of the 19th and early 20th century, the company town. That was what brought the community together, that is what provided the infrastructure, and important parts of the social milieu. When the family-owned company gave way to the large corporation, the social structure changed dramatically. When U. S. Plywood bought the McCloud River Lumber Company, they sold off the city of McCloud.

> U. S. Plywood survived until 1967 when it was merged with Champion Papers Inc. to form U.S. Plywood-Champion Papers Inc. (known as Ply-Champ for short). By the early 1970's the name changed again, this time to Champion International Corp. The various name changes had almost no effect on operations in McCloud.
>
> http://www.trainweb.org/mccloudrails/History/History06.html

Some of the labor force retained their job temporarily, but they had to buy their house or move. Later, the lumber company continued to decline or change hands, so many of the people in McCloud moved away. What was once the primary source of income in the town, now became the great uncertainty in the community. The McCloud River Railroad survived longer than the timber industry.

> The railroad celebrated 100 years of existence in 1997 and 10 years as an independent railroad in 2002. The future is reasonably secure as long as the Sierra Pacific mill in Burney remains open and shipping by rail, and SPI has access to enough private land that it is not as dependent on Federal timber sales as other companies are. Closure of the mill or any other catastrophic event could kill the railroad easily. The passenger business remains strong, but should freight operations cease it may not be able to support much more than the McCloud-Mt. Shasta City segment in the long run. Several hundred GE Capital owned boxcars continue to be stored on the railroad, producing small amounts of revenue from storage fees. The railroad continues to search for additional revenue sources; talks are on-going with potential freight shippers, including bottled water facilities interested in locating in McCloud. The McCloud shops has built several custom cars, including one

that is used to lay fiber optic cable alongside railroad rights-of-way and a group of six cars stored in McCloud that can be used to transport wreck-damaged freight cars. Special freight moves are also handled when offered, such as sawmill equipment from the scrapped Big Valley Lumber Company Bieber mill that was shipped out on flatcars in early 2002. The railroad continues to live on the edge, and economic winds could easily blow the company either direction. Only time will tell. http://www.trainweb.org/mccloudrails/History/History08.html

Time did tell, and the railroad finally shut down, after a being bought by an excursion train business, but that is another story.

The town of McCloud changed when MRLC was bought out by the paper company; every aspect of infrastructure that had once depended on the company now became large uncertainties. The hospital eventually was sold off and turned into a bed and breakfast facility. The very steam plant that provided heat to every house in the town disappeared. The shingle crew that spent every summer re-roofing all the buildings and houses in the town disbanded. Even the general store that had provided all of the needs of the citizens --on credit-- folded. The latter is also now a bed and breakfast. Most homeowners have since re-roofed with metal, which greatly reduces the fire hazard in a woodstove town. Cousin Peggy and her husband became the emergency medical technicians to get people to the hospital in Mt. Shasta. In the days of the Company, my stepfather was one of the volunteer ambulance drivers, as well as a volunteer fireman with the all-volunteer department. Fortunately for those residents who remained or who moved into the town seeking new opportunities, the romantic look of the town combined with the Mount Shasta skiing and fishing tourism, has kept the town alive and restored it to something like its former affluence. Whether the current McCloud has the cohesion that the company town had, I really cannot say. The Internet indicates there are a number of annual events for the tourists. In our day, the events were for the locals. When my step-dad's town team played an exhibition basketball game with the Redheads, it was for the enjoyment of the families and students of Coach, and my dad, the postman, and the other gangly local boys. The Redheads were a professional women's team that rivaled the Globe Trotters in skill if not in reputation. The team was in existence from 1936 to 1986, but there is still a website (allamericanredheads.com) and YouTube video of the Redheads playing exhibition games with male non-professional teams. http://www.youtube.com/watch?v=OkP-aBWJwUE

My stepfather had been involved in any number of comical exhibitions over the years, because he was perfect for the part: six-foot seven inches, flaming red hair, freckles over nearly every inch of his body. In the game with the Redheads, they tore up the town team. Several of the guys were over six feet, and some of the Redheads were quite short. Their favorite ploy was to dribble between the legs of the guys. When the guys would play one-on-one, one of the Redheads would take the ball and start dribbling wildly around the court, with her shadow in pursuit. Then she would pass the ball off but she would continue verily running around in and out of the other players with her guard in pursuit. This was a very effective distraction for the players and the crowd as the ball handler went in for the basket. When the town team adopted the zone strategy, the Redheads would gang up on the center nearly boxing him in the center of the key, all the while passing the ball around him like sputnik circling earth. I swear I probably laughed harder at seeing James Klungness be so harassed than at any other time in my youth.

On another occasion my stepfather... oh let's just stop the formality; he was the only man I ever called my dad, and I am going to refer to him as such from here on. The town of McCloud put on a variety show every year, and one year Dad was in it. He was six foot seven inches and the Coach six foot four inches. There were also two short hairy-legged guys all dressed up as Can-can dancers. And they did the Can-can; frilly skirts twirling high in front of their hairy be-gartered legs. That too brought down the house with laughter, but I still think the Redheads were funnier... and prettier too!

I would say that there were conspiracies that lead to my mother and my dad getting hitched. Of course, with James Klungness being one of only two postal clerks in town, it was inevitable that he and my mother would meet. Apparently they enjoyed chatting, because it was not too long before they started dating. I think if I looked into it deeply, I might not like what I see. My mother and I were baptized in December of 1954. This was after my mother had taken instructions from Fr. Carl Wellman at St. Joseph's Catholic rectory. What I would not understand for many years is that Fr. Carl was falling in love with my mother. He admits as much in a letter to my dad at the time of the breakup of the marriage between Kathleen and James, fifteen years later. My mother was giddy as a schoolgirl about Fr. Carl, but obviously was concerned that having just become Catholic, she was about to commit mortal sin by dragging Fr. Carl out of the priesthood. This she could not reconcile with her position in the community and her conscience. So she was probably looking to get into a marriage before she did something stupid. James was available, having recently divorced Nancy. Fr. Carl was fit to be tied about the whole thing, and as he says in his letter, did everything he could to stop the marriage between Kathleen and James. I might delve into all the complications of this relationship in volume two, but for now, let us stick with the circumstances in McCloud.

At age seven, I was oblivious to all of this. My part of the conspiracy is that I was pushing my mother very hard into the marriage. I told her it was perfect. He had red hair like me, he was tall, which I would be, and I needed a dad. My father's last wife, Elizabeth, recently told me that James was thinking more about having me as a son than he was about having my mother for a wife. Of course, she was biased. Elizabeth had observed that I probably did the same thing, when I got involved with my first wife. She had two older offspring, and three young children, with whom I was smitten. I don't think Kathleen and James dated very long, because I think the marriage occurred before the Justice of the Peace in McCloud in 1955. I cannot find the marriage certificate and the divorce certificate mentions a marriage in 1965. This is because the whole thing became very complicated after we moved to Washington. You see, Nancy and James were divorced in a court in Reno, Nevada. I am not sure whether California recognized the divorce, but the state of Washington most certainly did not. Therefore a lot of complicated legal issues had to be resolved before James and Kathleen were legally married in 1965, the year I graduated from high school.

Oblivious of the future ramifications, this small family unit was formed. I seem to remember that Meritt and Eva put on a reception for them. I think Meritt was relieved to have my mother married, and he liked my dad. I am sure Eva was driven by the need to bury the scandal that was my mother, so she could move in "polite society". For the next three years, all seemed well to me. I started kindergarten in McCloud, and continued up to third grade. Both my kindergarten teacher, and my first grade teacher were old women; schoolmarms of the type you read in old books. I don't remember the name of my kindergarten teacher, but I have record of my first grade. Myrtle Farnham was my teacher, and my situation got progressively worse over the year. I maintained a B average in most subjects except math and penmanship, which went to C in the last two quarters. But the deportment declined steadily from B to B- to C- the last two quarters. I got straight 'no' for "makes good use of time". Notwithstanding the influence of Miss Farnham, my nemesis was my second grade teacher, Dorothy Lambert. She gave me straight "yes" in all thirty-six of my behavioral evaluations, and only one B- in Deportment. She gave me almost all B's in my subjects with straight A's in "developing skills in handiwork" Even my math scores improved from B to B+ in the last two quarters. So why was she my nemesis? It was because she liked me, and she made school easy for me, which made me lazy. I don't think I necessarily deserved it. When she sent a large pile of unfinished school work home with me, I shoved it in a snow bank. These papers didn't surface until the snow melted. Our downstairs neighbors on Quincy St. were so "kind" as to deliver them to my mother. Lickins! Most of all, Mrs. Lambert didn't prepare me for my 3rd grade teacher, Alice Anderson.

Mrs. Anderson was tough, and she did not suffer fools. She gave me straight "no" in both "makes good use of time" and "exercises self-control". I don't think either Rick McGiff or I got our mouths washed out with soap, but we were often reprimanded for drawing stick pictures in class. They were depictions of battle scenes from the movies we saw at the local theater on Saturdays. She did give me straight A's in Memory work and music, but it was a mixed bag in several other subjects. I got 8 C's in 2nd quarter, only 4 C's in 3rd quarter, but 5 C's in 4th quarter. I will give Mrs. Anderson credit; she did take her job seriously. Without her influence, I don't think I would have been prepared for 4th grade. Mr. Monroe taught me at Wallace School in Kelso, Washington, and Sister Caroline finished my 4th grade education when I entered St. Rose Catholic School.

I was Lester Fisher on all my report cards from McCloud Elementary School, but James Klungness signed as my guardian on my report card for the 1st, 2nd and 3rd quarters of my 3rd grade class. My mother signed as Kay Klungness on the last quarter of my 2nd grade report card. It is pleasant to have those records and to remember the feeling of having a dad to sign my report card, and attend the open house. I painted a poster of the steam loader for the 3rd grade open house, and I remember my dad and Meritt were impressed that I was able to depict it in such detail.

Over the McCloud years my world continued to expand. We did not have television in our house, but we had radio, and programs like "The Lone Ranger" opened my mind to adventure and history. We also had the town theater, where we kids would go most every Saturday for the serials. There were space programs that were of lesser quality than "Buck Rogers," but we watched them just the same. One of my favorite serials was "Rin Tin Tin," which opened our eyes to duty and loyalty to the troop. Certain movies would come on an annual basis to the theater, like *Wizard of Oz* at Halloween, and Disney's *Peter Pan*, which was always a memorable event. These provided the grist for our imaginations and the games we played. We were also exposed, by default, to the news of the world. *Movietone News* was still the main window of the nation on the images of the world at large. I don't remember details but I know I felt secure in the knowledge that a stout, balding President Eisenhower seemed very much like my grandfather. The Movietone newsreel, the serial adventure, and the cartoon preceded every movie. Customers got a lot for their twenty-five cents. And you could stay for multiple showings. I remember my mother and I sat through two matinee showings of a Liberace movie called *Sincerely Yours* and then she went back that evening for more. She was a real sucker for a tearjerker and especially with a piano man.

Some movies had a great impact on me as well. The haunting song from *The High and the Mighty* still sticks in my head, and recalls the feeling of empathy with the young boy that was flying solo with the capable crew of the DC3. Only the calm determination of the captain (John Wayne) got the crippled plane home from Hawaii to San Francisco. I think the first science fiction movie I ever saw was *It Came from Outer Space*. That was really scary... I don't think I slept soundly for three days... maybe weeks. There were sometimes live performances at the Saturday Matinees. Vaudeville had already died, but local folks tried to resuscitate it. In all, the theater was an important venue in our young lives.

Having a dad was a big addition to my sphere of experience. He and my mother took up fishing, so I used to go with them. We would stay out on the McCloud River until after dark, watching the mosquitoes on the water bringing the fish up to feed. Fly-fishing was their sport, and the succulent rainbow trout was their reward. We usually did not camp out, but I had my first taste of coffee on the evening fishing trips. When we did camp out at Bear Creek or elsewhere, I distinctly remember the pure pleasure of trout cooked in butter and corn meal on an open campfire. We had movies of some of these adventures, but I have never been able to get Peggy Glenn (now Bennett) to part with the reels so we could transfer them to digital media.

My dad even arranged for me to go on my first airplane ride in a Piper Cub that belonged to a friend of his. Although James never flew, he had an appreciation for the air technology that had developed mostly during his lifetime. In WWII he was unable to enter the air corps because he was too big to sit in the cockpit of a fighter.

Instead he served with the Sixteenth Armored Division (64th Armored Infantry Battalion). They claimed to be "the Third Army Spearhead first into Czechoslovakia".

In fact, I knew virtually nothing about my dad's war experience. He was very involved in the American Legion and marched in the Veterans' Day parade every year. And of course we kids played war games and saw heroic war movies at the McCloud Theater, and later in TV reruns. But it took a search of Wikipedia to finally elucidate for me my dad's part in the War. It was a great revelation to me to learn where Lanky. red-headed, freckle-faced Jim Klungness had spent those years, and to realize why he was able to come home alive, despite having been attached to the very 64th Battalion that fought the "battle of the bulge".

Paraphrasing the Wikipedia account:

The division activated July 15, 1943 at Camp Chaffee in Arkansas. They sailed from the New York February 5, 1945.The 16th Armored Division docked in France between April11 and 17, 1945, and were processed into the Theater. The division was assigned to Third US Army on April 17, 1945, entering Germany on April 19, 1945, they relieved the Seventy First Infantry Division at Nuremberg on April 28, 1945. The Twenty Third Cavalry Reconnaissance Squadron engaged in combat from the Isar River to Wasserburg with the Eighty Sixth Infantry Division. The 23rd crossed the Isar River at Granek, April 30, 1945 and advanced to Indorf, where they seize small villages. They were driving toward Wasserburg, meeting slight resistance, when ordered to return to Nuremberg. The division mission was to provide security and training at Nuremberg, Germany, until May 5, 1045. When the 23rd Cavalry Squadron arrived at Nuremberg, May 4, 1945, it reverted to the Sixteenth Armored Division and proceeded to Waidhaus, Germany, May 5, 1945. The division was then assigned to V Corps, and attacked through the lines of the Ninety Seventh Infantry Division on May 6, 1945, with Combat Command B (CCB) making the main effort. They advanced along the Bor-Pilsen Road and attacked Pilsen, which was designed to capture the Skoda Munitions Plant, Czechoslovakia, on the same day. CCR advanced through Pilsen to assigned high ground east of the city. The capture of the city, famous for beer and munitions, marked the deepest point of American penetration into Czechoslovakia. The division was at Stříbro, Czechoslovakia on VJ Day, and returned to New York to be inactivated at Camp Kilmer in New Jersey on October 15, 1945. http://en.wikipedia. org/wiki/16th_Armored_Division_(United_States)#History

I also found excerpts from their Division newspaper known as the *16th Armadillo*. This was a particularly interesting article about how the newspaper got its name.

SERGEANT WINS RIVIERA FURLOUGH FOR NAMING DIVISION NEWSPAPER

BASEBALL PITCHER IS VERY SURPRISED WHEN TOLD OF SELECTION

"Well, I'll be damned", was the exclamation made by Sgt. Orville Williams, D Co, 16th Tank Battalion, when he was informed that he was the winner of the contest to name the Division newspaper entitling him to a 7-day vacation at the Riviera.

Sgt. Williams, who is 26 years old, hails from Portland, Oregon where he pitched for the Portland Beavers in the Pacific Coast League during 1938, 1939 and 1940. At present he is on special duty with the Division baseball team trying out for a berth on the pitching staff.

For two years prior to his induction into the army in 1942 he was employed at the Oregon Shipyards in Portland, operated by Henry Kaiser. From 1942 until December 1944 he served as a draftsman in the Air Corps at which time he was transferred to the infantry. Sent overseas on April 1 this year as a replacement, Williams joined the Division at Mainz. His job in the 16th Tank has been that of loader on a light tank. He was stationed at Foster and Randolph fields while with the Air Corps.

When asked why he had suggested the name Armadillo for the paper, Sgt. Williams said he had seen a lot of the little animals by that name while he was stationed in Texas and that they always reminded him of miniature tanks with their covering of "armor". Because of that resemblance he felt that the name Armadillo would be very representative for an Armored Division newspaper.

The judges who selected the name took into consideration the fact that the name is representative and at the same time is not a name used by some other publication. While all of the suggestions received were good, quite a number were names that are being used by other newspapers and magazines.

Sgt. Williams is postponing his trip to the Riviera until he learns whether or not he has succeeded in becoming a member of the Division baseball team.

Here are some other humorous notes from the *16th Armadillo:*

64th AIB's B Co Builds Homes In Valley To Avoid Tenting

Home isn't what you make it – it's what Co. B of the 64th Armored Infantry Battalion makes it. The boys got together when the 16th Armored Division moved into Czechoslovakia's Sudetenland and decided that this bivouacking in mere tents was strictly for the birds. A couple of Big Time Operators were culled from the outfit and the fun began.

The BTO's found a sawmill nearby with piles of newly sliced lumber neatly piled near it. The entire company was summoned and the house-building program was in full swing. Some of the boys went in for just plain home building. Others got more elaborate and erected little cottages, complete with shelves, places and pegs to hang duffel, stands for shaving and washing and other little items. There was no hot and cold running water or inbuilt latrine but the places began to shape up nicely.

STREAM IN VALLEY

A nice little stream that would make a trout fisherman drool flows in the little valley in which the company has made its homes. The houses are arranged neatly by the numbers and there is a great deal of fish-frying and beer-drinking in leisure time. The stream, incidentally, acts as an excellent cooler for the suds.

One of the fancier chateaux belongs to Tech. Sgt. Roy Nutt, of Sunbury, O. Nutt's Tepee C. P. is a model of efficiency. A telephone completes the elaborate layout. Sgt. Nutt explains that a platoon leader has to set an example for the men.

SHOWERS SET UP

Showers have been fixed up in one large building and the mess hall is so nicely erected that one native has offered a fancy price for it when the boys move out. The folks around the neighborhood are frankly curious about the American housing program. They walk by on the road above the valley, looking down at the array of homes covered by shelter halves and other waterproofing, materials. Some of the Sudeten kids are bolder and come down to gape as Pvt. Nicholas J. Witkovasky, of 756-A Union St., Brooklyn, gives out on the harmonica.

The boys are going to hate to move out.

http://www.lonesentry.com/newspapers/16th-armored/index.html

My dad said the closest he ever got to a German during the Famous Battle of the Bulge was when a Messerschmitt flew over his caravan. That, and "the Pilsner beer was good" was all he ever said about his part in the Great War.

Although I do remember his saying that he ate a lot of cherry cordials during the troop ship voyages. Apparently, everyone else was getting sea sick, so iron-constitution Big Jim kindly rescued them from their candy, which had been given to everyone at departure. He did earn a Bronze Star, and since he never said anything about it, I have to include this definition of the Bronze Star and to whom it is issued.

> The Bronze Star Medal was established by Executive Order 9419, 4 February 1944 (superseded by Executive Order 11046, 24 August 1962, as amended by Executive Order 13286, 28 February 2003).
>
> The Bronze Star Medal is awarded to any person who meets specific qualifications:
>
> While serving in any capacity in or with the Army of the United States after 6 December 1941, distinguished himself or herself by heroic or meritorious achievement or service, not involving participation in aerial flight, in connection with military operations against an armed enemy; or while participating in aerial flight prior to the establishment of the Air Force as separate from the army; or while engaged in military operations involving conflict with an opposing armed force in which the United States is not a belligerent party. The acts of heroism are of a lesser degree than required for the award of the Silver Star. The acts of merit or acts of valor must be less than that required for the Legion of Merit but must nevertheless have been meritorious and accomplished with distinction. The Bronze Star Medal is awarded only to service members in combat who are receiving imminent danger pay. http://en.wikipedia.org/wiki/Bronze_Star_Medal

I will venture a short explanation here. The separation of flight-from ground-combat with regard to eligibility for the bronze star was not made until the Air Force was distinguished from the Army Air Corps. This would have included countless service men and women who flew supply, reconnaissance, airborne rescue, covert insertion, and the airborne paratrooper divisions (e. g. the 82nd and the 101st Ariborne in the D-Day Invasion). That bit about the "opposing armed force in which the United States is not a belligerent party" were situations like the Flying Tigers, recruited and volunteer squadrons in China before Pearl Harbor and the declaration of War with Japan. At that time the military was very egalitarian in issuing the bronze star.

Big Jim would have liked to have been eligible for an Air Medal, but since he never made it to flight school because he was too tall at 6 ft. 7 in. He always had a fascination with aircraft. Every time an air show would come to whatever town we lived near, he would take me to it. We once saw a man fall to his death in a little gyrocopter at the airfield in Kelso, Washington. The guy was performing stunts, and it looked like he summersaulted the tiny craft, which caused the blades to snap off. But that did not deter us from the love of flight. We were there when the first Boeing 707 jet airliner landed and took off from the Portland International Airport. I don't know if my dad was able to visit the Smithsonian Air History Museum when he and his last wife were "Winnebago-ing" around the US after he retired. I know he would have been as impressed with it as I was when I had a two-day layover in Washington DC while I was in transit to my Peace Corps assignment.

Back in McCloud, there wasn't much flight activity. The small airport accommodated a few private and company planes, but there was no flight school or other way for my dad to advance his love of flight. Back from the war, he went right to work in the Post Office, in which he remained a federal employee for thirty-three years. The media portrays the WWII vets as the greatest generation. I think it is more appropriate to call them the long-suffering generation. There was a stoic acceptance of life in those people that I know were from that war. I guess they learned at a young age that things could always be worse.

I really do owe a lot to my dad. He taught me how to ride a bike. He coached my Little League team. He tried to interest me in golf. He did everything that a good father would do. In the end, I was probably a disappointment to him, at least in the realm of sport. He also wanted to support my flight training when I was in high school, but I refused (good thing, because if I had a pilot's license, I probably would have been drafted into Vietnam). But the one thing I did take from him was the ability to work, and for that I am eternally grateful.

One thing that McCloud did every year was Fiesta. These days they call it Lumberjack Fiesta to interest the tourist, but in my childhood it was just Fiesta, and it was strictly for the local clientele. It involved a parade. The cavemen would come from Yreka (the town's police force, I believe), but most of the floats and bands were local. The fire department was always in the parade, so my dad was always involved. I remember one year my parents dressed me up as Sad Sack[16], with my mother's oversized Eisenhower jacket, garrison cap askew, pack hanging low on my back, dragging a rifle behind me. I followed the fire engine and was the last in the parade. This conceit won a prize.

The Fiesta also included a carnival that usually had some small rides. They did not subscribe to the big carnival circuit companies. Rather they had local rides. There was a small train that had been hand built from a company speeder. There was probably a Shetland horse ride, although I don't remember it. There was a fishing pond and coin toss and all those usual games. All locally run by McCloud residents. One of the more popular things was the Dunker, where participants threw baseballs at a target paddle. If the ball hit the paddle, it would release a lever holding up a seat on which a local dignitary was sitting. Not a bad deal for the person on the hot seat because the temperature in July could often be in the 90's. This was not one of those carnivals where there is a big fence around it and you have to pay to get in. This was open field, enter at will, buy your coupons and play all day; and we did. We would go to the Fiesta in the morning and stay till lunch. Later, we would go back in the afternoon or evening. We played the games if we had coupons: otherwise we just played on the grounds. It is a wonder there were not more problems, but somehow the kids knew to behave themselves to a point. Perhaps the older high school kids would get into mischief, but even that was not really serious stuff. Pregnancies in high school were pretty uncommon. There was nothing like gangs in today's sense of the word, and if there were any drugs, they were really very clandestine. Of course, beer was the intoxicant of choice, and if there were any brawling, that would have probably been the cause. As I remember it, there was only one police officer in McCloud, and he had a reputation. You didn't push him too hard, because he knew how to push back!

About the worst thing I was aware of while I was in McCloud was that the teenage boys were wearing their pants way down on their hips. Funny how what goes around comes around. Every time I see a teenager trying to keep his pants from falling off his butt, I think of McCloud. Word was that Coach or one of the other teachers, if he saw a young hoodlum with his pants down around his groin, would come up behind the kid and yank his pants down. That was an effective technique. Apparently those guys were not ready to "let it all hang out". This was before the days of positive reinforcement and time out. The rule of thumb on child rearing was "spare the rod, spoil the child". I am sure this was taken to excess in some cases, but it generally led to a more orderly society, where you could let your young kids roam the town without having to fear for their lives.

So Fiesta, like everything else in McCloud, was open season… in a good sense. The feeling of being confined, or limited, or bored, did not exist for us. If nothing else was going on, we would spend the twilight hours riding our bikes around the grade school grounds. I guess we would take a spill every now and then, but no one I knew ever had to go to the hospital, or broke a leg. Even my first real experience on a bike was a liberating affair. I had been given a bike with training wheels a year or two before, I did not adapt well. My cousins, Ralph and Vern, received bikes at the same time (my grandfather's or my mother's gift, I believe), and they took to it like ducks to water. I could ride up and down the board sidewalk with the training wheels, but I was afraid to take them off. After my dad married my mom, he must have felt it important for me to be able to ride. By then, my first bike had been somehow "redeployed". I think it was a smaller size, maybe 24 inch. So my dad bought me a big 26-inch Murray with balloon tires and a metal canister between the seat and handlebars, which contained a battery and a button for a horn. It even had an on-board headlamp. It was "top of the line" for that time. It was a very heavy bike, which style went out of fashion for many years and is only now enjoying a comeback.

The best part this new transportation was that it came with instruction… the unwritten kind. My dad took me out on Quincy St. and said, "Get on". He pointed me down the street and pushed the bike forward until I was pedaling. Then he let me go, which was fine until I realized I did not know how to stop. So here I was rolling down the road shouting "How do I stop!", and my six foot seven father running down the street behind me hollering "Pedal backwards!" I finally heard him and attempted to back pedal. Amazingly it worked, but there was also the issue of balancing a heavy bike as it came to a stop. As I remember it, I took a spill. But there were two lessons in one brief flight. I could balance a bike without training wheels, and falling over on a bike that is standing still was not a catastrophe. Furthermore, this was my ticket to many flights of adventure that would have previously required slogging along like a foot soldier. Now we were ace pilots. Because of the many war movies (in actuality, propaganda films of the war years) we were steeped in the lore of those man-eagles, whose lives were tested in the clouds. Rick McGiff's father had been one of them, Pacific theater, torpedo bomber pilot.

Photograph of **Dr. John McGiff** standing next to his Torpedo bomber in WWII. (Photo graciously provided by his son Richard McGiff.)

So Rick was the leader of the squadron, so to speak. We would have dogfights at the school playground. I used my horn like gun trigger until the horn's dying battery gave off a sound not unlike a sputtering machine gun. In retrospect, I am still amazed that we never had any bloody accidents.

While we are on dangerous childhood pursuits, I should mention again our proclivity for everything railroad. My grandfather gave me an American

Flier train set on my fourth birthday when we were still at Camp Pondosa. The first time I ran it myself; it jumped the tracks and threw off blue sparks. After that I was scared to death of it until after we moved to McCloud. Meritt had mounted the track on a four by eight foot piece of plywood, and we had it set up in my bedroom in the big house. I suppose it was probably my friends who convinced me to start using it again, and we played with it on any rainy day that we could not roam the countryside. Later, the fascination with trains led Marshall Willis and me to climb on a caboose that was sitting on the two-way tracks behind the Railroad office building. I don't think we even got caught, but our folks found out somehow. Now that was serious! Of all the far-flung places we were allowed to roam, the railroad cars were categorically and unconditionally off limits. If my memory serves me correctly, I think I was grounded, which was, of course, a fate worse than death. However, given that the rail yard below the big house was a busy place, and cars would be moved at any time without warning, the grounding may have forestalled my demise.

One of the most exciting things we did on the railroad was the opening of the Burney line. McCloud River Railroad Company (MRRC) had grown to the point that they needed to hook up to the State rail lines including the Southern Pacific and Great Northern. This was accomplished by the laying of the Burney line.

> The biggest job in completing the new line lay in getting the railroad across Lake Britton, which was created by the Pit 3 dam. The construction of the bridge was contracted out, but the rest of the construction job was completed with the railroad's own forces. The new line was completed in early summer of 1955, and official opening ceremonies took place on 3 July 1955. Three special trains ran to Burney that day, with one of the road's last operating steam locomotive at the front of one of them. One entire trainload of railfans came from the Bay Area on a special train for the event. The last tie on the new extension was made of redwood and was provided by the Arcata & Mad River Railroad, which at

the time was the oldest continually operated railroad in the state of California. Four special spikes, two silver and two gold, were used to secure the rails into the final spike. Three of the spikes were provided by the railroad club responsible for chartering the special train, while the fourth was provided by the town of Burney. http://www.trainweb.org/mccloudrails/History/History05.html

My whole family was there for the event except Eva. That included Meritt, Uncle Vern, Aunt Mary, my cousins, my step-cousins, etc, etc. We boarded the Burney Falls train, with old Number 25 (see picture) in the lead, at about 7 AM the day before the fourth of July.

#25 Steam Engine decked out for the **Gold Spike ceremony** celebrating the completion of the Burney Line connecting Southern Pacific to McCloud River Railroad. (Reproduced with permission of the Heritage Junction Museum of McCloud, California.)

There were old passenger cars, and gondolas fitted with seats. We all chose the gondola so we could get a clear view of everything. This proved to be a good choice, because there were a number of "surprises". Some were planned, like the staged robbery, for which we had a full view. Others were not planned. As we were approaching Lake Britton, Ol' 25 was feeling the pressure of being shoved along by two disrespectful young diesel engines. As if to say, "I'll fix your little red wagon", the steamer jumped the tracks. The view of the lake was lovely, and it was early enough in the day as not to be unbearably hot. We watched the water skiers on Lake Pit while we waited.

Nevertheless, it took a couple of hours to get the old workhorse back on the tracks. I didn't realize it then but there was some drama when #25 started to rebuild her head of steam. You see, the diesel engineers couldn't risk pushing #25 off the tracks again, so they had put their locomotives in neutral and let #25 get the ball rolling. Now, that steam engine had probably pulled far bigger loads in her day, notwithstanding the massive locomotives behind her. So this was not a challenge for her. But watching a steam locomotive come to life is thing of wonder. It's noisy, and huff and puff, with pistons hissing, and wheel carriage coupling rods groaning. As the engineer lies on the throttle, the engine rears up almost like a Clydesdale. The large drive wheels spin and the coalman opens the sand shoot to put grit between the wheels and the rail. When the wheels grab the traction, there is a clanging of the couplings between the cars all the way down the line. Then ever so slowly, inertia gives way to motion and the whole line of cars begins to roll while the steam engine is straining at every rivet. All the while, the cadence of the chug chug chug redoubles. It was a proud moment for the old steam engine and her crew. I think a cheer went up from the passengers. Sadly, it was also the passing of an age.

It actually wasn't the end of the line for #25. If you follow the history of the MRRC (http://www.trainweb.org/mccloudrails/History/History08.html) #25 will pop up time and time again. She spent time as an excursion train, some rest time in a Museum, back on the rail for events and excursions, being finally retired by another restored steam engine #19. Her last run was on Presidents' Day weekend of 2001. I could not find out when #25 was first put in service, but she was well over 50 years old. They don't build them like that anymore.

The golden spike ceremony was impressive; although I didn't believe the spike was real gold (it was actually redwood). There was a large crowd of people that came, and marked this momentous occasion, the likes of which had been seen many time during the building of the western railways, but would not be seen again much in the future.

Steam engines on a dry and sweltering summer's day in the Siskiyous could be a prescription for forest fire. I couldn't say how often they were responsible, but there was no shortage of forest fires in northern California. It seems that when man makes an all-out assault on Mother Nature, she has her ways of striking back. It is fitting that the seeds of our destruction are usually carried in our own pocket. A carelessly discarded cigarette, the spark from a chain saw, a poorly prepared camp fire; these were all common causes of forest conflagration. Of course, Smokey the Bear was already posted on roadsides saying, "Only you can prevent forest fires". And the Forest Service was doing a pretty good job of not letting fires get entirely out of hand, thus adding to the buildup of fuel in the clear cut patches of forest. Before the white man, the Native Americans had carefully burned off the underbrush under stands of tall fire-resistant sugar and Ponderosa pine. Now the Manzanita (*Arctostaphylus nevadensis* and *A. patula*), snow brush (*Ceanothus velutinus*), bitterbrush (*Purshia tridentata*) and tan oak (*Lithocarpus densiflora ssp echinoides*) sprawl over the barren hillsides and choke the pine saplings. Only the squat and rugged jack pine seems to be able to fight its way through the thick shrubbery. And all of this is oil and wax-laden tinder for raging fires that lap up the standing forest around them.

To the point, some vary noteworthy scientists have argued for the preservation of the last vestigial stands of original Siskiyou forest by declaring them national monuments. Because of the ever-deteriorating condition in the post-logging forest, some of the largest fires in history have occurred in this very forest. The Biscuit Fire in 2002 burned over half million acres.

I remember two fires that occurred near McCloud. My grandfather and my Uncle Vern may have fought both of them. One was on Highway 89 between McCloud to Pondosa. I actually remember passing through that one. The other was on the road to Mt. Shasta just outside of McCloud. Living next to a forest can be hazardous, now more than ever.

In the wintertime the biggest hazard was snow, particularly for vehicles on the road. My grandmother and I were driving to Mt. Shasta one day in the 1951 Plymouth, when she hit an icy patch on one of the curves. I remember tumbling over and over again with the seat cushion falling on us each time we rolled. We ended up at the bottom of hill about a 30 foot high.

The car was upside down, but we managed to get the door open and climb out of the car. We were both intact. Soon a fellow traveler was hollering at us from the roadway above. He had seen us go over, and stopped to pick us up and take us back to McCloud. It was like that back then. Everyone looked out for each other. Nowadays, you might, if you are very civic minded, report an accident to the police with your cell phone. Back then, you knew that a person in trouble needed your help.

The Good Samaritan dropped us at the hospital, and the doctor (who had sewn up my face back in Pondosa) checked us for injuries. We were ok, but I had bit my tongue, so the doctor gave me some tiny pink pills. I will lay you a wager that it was a placebo, but at the time it made me feel very important. That same week we went to Dunsmuir to see the poor old Plymouth in dry dock. Weeks later it was back with a new coat of paint and as good as new. Contrasting vehicles then and vehicles now, a couple of years ago I rear-ended a small pickup in my Mazda Tribute. The pickup had no damage, and the Tribute had sustained a little damage to the grill. The insurance company totaled it; they paid blue book, but I was definitely not ready to part with my little SUV. It illustrates another difference between the 50's and now. Then things were repairable, recyclable, and reusable; now things are irreparable, disposable and replaceable, sometimes even people.

Speaking of things repairable, after my mother married James, she had a medical issue that put her in the hospital, and she had to undergo surgery. I assume this may have been further complication from the previous surgery to remove the chocolate cysts from her ovary in Bend. There was a new, young, and cocky doctor at the McCloud hospital, Dr. Jamison. He became her attending physician and surgeon. He was a graduate of Loma Linda Medical School in California. My mother awoke from the surgery only to find out that Dr. Jamison had performed an unauthorized hysterectomy on her. She didn't have long to adjust to her barren status, because three days later she had to go in for surgery again. This time Dr. McGiff performed the exploratory surgery to see what was causing her feverish reaction to the previous surgery. Well, it became very clear when he opened my mother up… there were three yards of gauze left in her abdominal cavity! Needless to say, my mother held a very low opinion of Loma Linda for the rest of her life. She was lucky that she recovered, but she suffered from what she called "adhesions"[17] for the rest of her life. I make note of these physical ailments that plagued my mother because they may have been contributing factors to other problems she had over the course of her life. One cannot be excused for everything because of something that happened years before. However, influenced by the painful irritations that now limit my life, I am more tolerant of others who may be silently suffering the pain of experiential or congenital damage to the marvelous system that is the human body.

My mother recovered well enough to return to work, but I am not sure for how long she was reemployed. There is no one left to ask. I don't remember having her home after she recovered, but I do remember going to the X-ray lab with my mother when she was on call. I suppose she needed to take me because she did not have anyone to babysit. Or maybe it was when I was older (third grade?). I would be in the darkroom as she developed film; sucking in the hypo, watching the illuminated dial of the timer, running the rinse bath water. I ended up doing much the same thing when I became a microscopist for Weyerhaeuser Co. and later, while I was doing microscopy contracts at UC Davis. Of course, in McCloud, Mom would always make me go behind the lead shield when she was operating the X-ray beam. I think she got pretty good at her job, but for some unexplained reason, McCloud was the last place she got a chance to practice the hard-won skills she had developed. I don't know how much my dad influenced that but I do know that later, after we moved to Longview she did continue to work. She was employed at St. John's Hospital typing reports for the Pathologist and other doctors on staff. She also started taking courses at Lower Columbia College to become a medical transcriptionist. I don't think my dad was too happy about her working and going to school. I guess it was still a pride thing for men…they were supposed to be the breadwinners.

For whatever reasons, it was not long before we moved from McCloud. As my mother mentioned, some family issues had started to cause problems for our young family. My mother had been without income during her convalescence, but what was irritating her most was the influence of my dad's sisters and his ex-wife, Nancy. She did not mention Madge, my dad's mother, who was the town librarian, and a bit of a heavy drinker herself. Of course, mother-in-law issues are always blamed for marital discord but in this case you had haughty Aunt Eva and a meddling Margaret Klungness... It was time to leave!

It was probably unfortunate for James' children when we left Longview, because they grew distant from their father in spite of the efforts that he and my mother made to have them visit us in Washington. Although his girls did come to his bedside in 1980 at the time of their Dad's hospitalization and eventual death, after his death there was little contact with Mary, Terry, Steve, (Kim had already died). When James was hospitalized for colon cancer surgery, complications led to his being placed on a ventilator. He was generally unresponsive during most of that time, and we were not really sure that he was still conscious. Elizabeth, his last wife, was convinced that she should try to continue his treatment and worked very hard to get him transferred to a clinic that specialized in getting patients off of the ventilator. At one point, several months into his treatment, he was taken off the ventilator, and Mary and Terry were able to visit him at that time. They were able to have a final conversation, but soon after he relapsed and eventually succumbed to organ failure. Gretchen and I had come to his bedside at the first hospital in Yuma, Arizona. At that time, when he was unresponsive, we felt that it was probably kindest to let him go peacefully. Whether the six months of suffering was helpful to either Dad or to Elizabeth, I cannot say, but at least his daughters had the chance to speak to him one last time.

I regret that I did not have the chance to talk to my dad at the end of his life. I don't know what either of us would have said. I certainly would have like to let him know that I appreciated him. When we were alone in the ICU, I did talk to him, and relate my appreciation of him, and the wish that I could help him at the juncture. I will never know if he heard me.

I don't remember much about the departure from McCloud. There are many experiences while we lived in McCloud which I have not related. But the chapter is long, and this is a good time to transition. Even though I leave McCloud with fond memories, now and then I wonder how life would have been if I had grown up there. It was part of a time warp when the world revolved around a little town and the company that ran it. Forgive me if I flash back to McCloud in subsequent chapters. It retrospect, one appreciates the confluence of people, experience and events that make a life. There is always a twinge of regret for the loss of contact with my friends and the town, but then I realize how different my life would have been. Who is to say which is better? Happenstance, that's all it is, happenstance.

CHAPTER 6

The Move to Longview

By the rivers of Babylon, There we sat down,
yea, we wept, when we remembered Zion.
Upon the willows in the midst there of we
hanged up our harps.
For there they that led us captive required of us
songs, And they that wasted us required of us
mirth, saying, sing us one of the songs of Zion.
Psalm 137:1-3American Standard Version

THERE WAS, MOST PROBABLY, A cold rain drizzling when we entered Kelso, Washington... The slightly putrid smell of Longview Fibre and other pulp mills hung in the air, and the day was very gray. I don't actually remember the arrival, but the law of averages would have recommended this description. Now don't get me wrong; the Pacific Northwest is beautiful with its majestic forests and expansive vistas along the mighty Columbia River. I am sure that Lewis and Clark were in awe, and Meriwether Lewis is quoted as having exclaimed at their arrival at the mouth of the Columbia in November of 1805 "Ocian in view O! The Joy!" However, after building and living at Fort Clatsop, their joy subsided. They also wrote in their journal things like this:

December 16, 1805
"The Winds violent. Trees falling in every derection, Whorl winds, with gusts of Hail & Thunder, this kind of weather lasted all day. Certainly one of the worst days that ever was"... -Captain William Clark.

March 23, 1806

"At this place we had wintered and remained from the 7th of Decr. To this day and lived as well as we had any right to expect, and we can say we were never one day without 3 meals of some kind a day, either pore Elk meat or roots, notwithstanding the repeated fall of rain which has fallen almost constantly..." -Captain William Clark http://www.epinions.com/review/park-Parks-All-OR-Fort_Clatsop_National_Memorial/content_150536097412

Now Fort Clatsop is at the Coast of Oregon near what is now Astoria, and granted the precipitation at the coast is a bit more extreme than inland. But the Twin Cities, Longview and Kelso, are on the first major bend of the Columbia a little over 50 miles from the Ocean as the crow flies. This means there is not but the Columbia Gorge to protect the cities from the ocean weather. And with all that water, and forest and offshore flow, the environment can be very damp in the winter, and none too dry in the summer, extending up to about August. Temperatures have been known to reach 105° F. in the late summer, but the winter temperatures hover in between 30 and 40° F. most of the time, and rise to a "blistering" 50° in early summer (that's Fahrenheit not centigrade). It really isn't that there is so much rain; the average annual rainfall is around 60 inches (compare that to my current home in Hawaii where we get over 200 inches per year). The difference is that, in Hawaii it may rain for a day or at most a week, and then the sun comes out. In McCloud, the sun shines on the winter snow as well as the summer. Storms would come and go. But between the Cascade Range and the Coastal Range moisture and clouds hang for months on end. The rain seldom falls heavily; it just always falls... but gently. Drizzle best describes it, the Land of Drizzle. Aberdeen, Washington, at the mouth of the Chehalis River, actually markets the stuff as canned "liquid sunshine". There is a short story by Ray Bradbury, called "The Long Rain" published in *Planet Stories* in 1950. The first paragraph reads as follows:

The rain continued. It was a hard rain, a perpetual rain, a sweating and steaming rain; it was a mizzle, a downpour, a fountain, a whipping at the eyes, an undertow at the ankles; it was a rain to drown all rains and the memory of rains. It came by the pound and the ton, it hacked at the jungle and cut the trees like scissors and shaved the grass and tunneled the soil and molted the bushes. It shrank men's hands into the hands of wrinkled apes; it rained a solid glassy rain, and it never stopped. http://en.wikipedia.org/wiki/The_Long_Rain

Believe me; that story sounded very familiar to me when I read it at age 12. Sometimes I wonder if Ray Bradbury was in the Northwest when he wrote it. And you can bet I love the ballad learned at Ivar's Acres of Clams restaurant in Seattle. It is attributed to a pioneer (a prospector turned north) who homesteaded in the Puget Sound. The first recorded reference to this song was in the Olympia, Washington newspaper, the *Washington Standard* in April 1877.

Old Settler's Song version 2

…So, rolling my grub in my blanket
I left all my tools on the ground
I started one morning to shank it
For the country they call Puget Sound

Arriving flat broke in midwinter
I found it enveloped in fog
And covered all over with timber
Thick as hair on the back of a dog

When I looked on the prospects so gloomy
The tears trickled over my face
And I thought that my travels had brought me
To the end of the jumping-off place

I staked me a claim in the forest
And sat myself down to hard toil

For two years I chopped and I struggled
But I never got down to the soil

I tried to get out of the country
But poverty forced me to stay
Until I became an old settler
Then nothing could drive me away

And now that I'm used to the climate
I think that if a man ever found
A place to live easy and happy
That Eden is on Puget Sound

No longer the slave of ambition
I laugh at the world and its shams
As I think of my pleasant condition
Surrounded by acres of clams.
http://www.mudcat.org/@displaysong.
cfm?SongID=4436

The sentiment expressed by the prospector, especially the verse about the "prospects so gloomy" touched a chord with me when I heard it. I had that feeling when we arrived in Kelso for the first time. To this day, when I think of Kelso, I feel the damn damp and dreary pall of my year there. Of course it is not true... Kelso is actually a popular town, but I just can't shake the effect it had on me as a kid.

Although I don't know the exact date we moved, I think it was the late summer or fall of 1956. I don't remember if I started 4th grade at Wallace School at the beginning of the semester or was a week or two late. I think the latter, because I think I remember being introduced to the class which was already in session. But I will discuss school later.

As I think I may have mentioned, my folks had rented a small house next to the family home of the Bornholts in west Kelso. I will say that August, Mr. B., had done a fine job of landscaping the quarter acre yard of their two-story house, and in fair weather it was a very pleasant garden in which Mrs. B loved to putter. But in winter the sidewalks were slippery with algae and black mold. The fruit trees were naked and the annuals were brown and dead in their beds. Their house was, however, warmed by a central furnace and the slightly sweet smell of pipe tobacco hung in the air[18].

In contrast, the house we rented was cold and small. It was what, in the Northwest, is often called a shotgun house; meaning, if you shot a gun at the front door, the buckshot would go straight out the back door. The oil heating stove was in the front corner of the living room, and getting the heat to the bedrooms and the kitchen in the back was a trick. Because the bedrooms were small, many of my toys and other household items had to be stored in the broken down garage next to the house. It was the first time I realized that mold will actually grow on things if you don't keep the humidity down. Fat chance of that in the Land of Drizzle!

The Bornholts were good neighbors, and shared their home and their television with us. That TV was a life saver, because we did not have one, and I had no friends, even after I started school. The Mickey Mouse Club, Jiminy Cricket, and The Hardy Boys were my small black and white window on life. I can still recite the Mouseketeer song, and Jiminy Cricket's song, "Look in the Encyclopedia, e_n_c_y_c_l_o_p_e_d_i_a!". I did have my dog, Boy. Sorry I didn't mention him in McCloud, because that is where he was adopted. I had never had my own pet, and when Boy --who looked like the dog in the Disney movie, "Old Yeller" -- wandered into our life; it was the beginning of my lifelong love of canines. He was not a particularly bright dog, but he was a lover. He'd lick your face all over while his stiff yellow tail was knocking down anything within reach. Dainty he was not, and used to roaming the streets, he was. In those days people didn't fuss much about dogs loose in the neighborhood, as long as they were not dangerous. So Boy was my playmate, my protector, my bed warmer, and my pal.

Mr. and Mrs. B were pretty important friends to my parents, too, especially my mother. Like me, she was adrift in a new world. While Dad was off getting his Yacolts straight from his Skoocumchucks, trying to fit in as a cog in the machine of the Longview Post Office, my mother was adapting to being a dutiful housewife. She had been demoted to domestic chores in a tiny little house with a dog and a kid. I don't remember her spending afternoons with Mrs. B., but I became a regular at the TV. My folks did go to the Bornholts every Saturday night for "Lawrence Welk", "Gunsmoke" and "Northwest Wrestling". The atmosphere was usually calm through the first two programs, but Wrestling really got the Bornholts' blood pressure up. I don't know if what was going on in the TV was a vicarious bleed valve for the suppressed anger that had built up over the years. It was funny to see that sweet old lady egging Tony Born on to even greater feats of atrocity; or was it the other way round. Tony was the villain. Maybe she was cheering on his adversaries. I was never quite sure.

Mr. B was a stubborn German. For example, he never believed that people landed on the moon. I don't think he ever saw *Capricorn One*, but that is exactly what he believed; that the whole landing was staged. My mother always said that an Irish woman shouldn't marry a German; I assume the Bornholts were her reference. But Mr. and Mrs. B were married many, many years before she buried him. This was not one of those cases where the partner follows the other to the grave, because she lived for quite a few years after Mr. B. died… and was quite content, I might add.

The Bornholts had an old dog named Biddy; she was a squat little mutt of some kind, probably terrier and maybe dachshund, black and white and almost as round as she was long. I remember that first Christmas my folks made a very large bowl of Tom and Jerry mix, and, uncharacteristically, had spiked it with rum before we went over to the Bornholts. I guess they were planning to really tie one on in the spirit of the occasion. We entered by the enclosed back porch, but there was a step up at the door of the kitchen. My mother tripped and the bowl of boozed eggwhites went flying. Guess who tied one on that night? I swear that little bitty dog lapped up that whole bowl which was damn near her volume (mostly air, but boozy). Funniest thing I had ever seen an animal do to that point in my life. It was a miracle she survived, but she held her liquor like a man 10 times her size. She could barely navigate the floor, but she managed to find a corner and collapse into it sound asleep.

The Bornholts daughter, Kat, and her husband lived outside of Longview. They had two daughters that were close to my age. They ran a dairy farm on the far side of Mt. Solo. From the Google Map it looks like the farm has been turned into a housing subdivision, but in the late 50's Mt. Solo Road was definitely out in the country. I think I had my first horse ride at that farm. It wasn't much of a ride, because the mare knew that I didn't know what to do, so she just went about her business of grazing. It was an interesting experience feeding the calves. You have to start them sucking on your fingers, and then transfer their mouth to the bucket's nipple. There is nothing softer than the tongue of a calf.

I do remember that Elvis had just burst onto the scene when we were visiting the Northness family, the girls were ecstatic that they had a 45 RPM of "You ain't Nothin' but a Hound Dog". We did not spend a lot of time at the Northness farm, though, because dairy life is very demanding, and they didn't have much time for socializing. Kat and my mother had been good friends in the WAC, but their lives had become very different. I think my mother's idea that she would have a readymade friend in Kat was not realized. They kept in touch, but they were not close. Mom was probably closer to Mrs. B. and continued to visit her until the end of her life. I always enjoyed going with her to visit Mrs. B, because she very often served us fresh apple pie with lemon raisin sauce… heavenly!

My Dad, having been raised in a small town, probably adapted to the Northwest quicker than either of us, although it was a big change for him as well. I think he had the distraction of trying to transition from a small post office where he and the Postmaster were the only staff, to a large post office where there were round-the-clock crews of 10 or more clerks. That is not including the daytime postal delivery people. In McCloud he had done everything, right down to carrying the cash to the bank (he had a berretta that he carried for those deliveries). In Longview he started at the bottom of the heap, and that meant being a bicycle letter carrier. If you have ever seen the old mail bikes, they were kind of short, with a small wheel in front to accommodate an oversized basket of mail. Can you imagine this six foot 7 inch, freckle faced, red headed man on one of those bikes? It gives new meaning to the word incongruent. Gretchen's first husband Norvin, who worked at the Longview post office in later years, was the last bicycle carrier in the United States. It was on the national news. He insisted on remaining in that position for his whole career, and retired not long after they made him give up his bike. My dad was perfectly happy to give up his bike!

James Klungness was always well accepted among his male peers. Although there were some differences with the other staff at the Longview PO, Jim was not a disagreeable sort. I think it was a little hard on his pride to go from being the best known man in town, to being just one of the mail carriers. He eventually did work his way back up to clerk, and then sometime substituting at the public window (which he enjoyed). It was not like him to be vain, but when his hair was turning grey, he convinced my mother to dye his hair with what I think was henna. Now that was a sight to see, bright, bright orange! He was working at the front counter with Gretchen's father who was already almost snow white. Naturally, henna does not come out of hair; it has to grow out. I hope that didn't hurt his chances when he ran for postmaster in Castle Rock, but he did not get the position after 30 years of service. Of course, Bob Huffhines did not get the position of postmaster in Longview either, even though he had served as acting postmaster for almost three years. Politics were not in either man's favor. Later, in 1968, my dad applied for a supervisory position. Sadly, he did not get that job either.

My dad had the last laugh, though. The Post Office had a reduction in force, and let postal employees, whose age and years of service added up to 80, retire. He had 33 years and was only 55 year old. He lived another 25 years. Bob, on the other hand, worked for the post office for 40 years, and died when he was 70, so he only had 8 years to enjoy his retirement, and for part of that he was suffering from Parkinson's disease. Bob was fortunate in that he had a very full life while he was working. He was a great enthusiast and was involved in all kinds of civic activities like becoming President of the Kiwanis Club and the American Cancer Society He was also a member of the Elks Club. He left the Elks Club when they refused to accept non-white members. He also organized groups to attend Washington and Oregon theater events, etc. After he retired, he took cooking classes at the community college, and began holding benefit breakfasts to raise money for the Kiwanis.

My dad's work life was a bit more somber. In order to make ends, meet he started a second job as a newspaper rural-route deliveryman. He would get off of the swing shift at the post office and then drive the fifty mile route, seven days a week, 365 days a year. On Sundays we had to remove the seats from the Volkswagen sedan, just to have enough room for the thick Sunday edition of *The Oregonian*. At Christmas he would take all the overtime the PO would offer; I can't ever remember spending a Christmas Eve or Day with him. When Bob retired, he and Jana had saved enough money to take a trip to Europe and Russia. Good thing, because they didn't know how little time they had left together. James, on the other hand, lived an entire other life after he retired. But that would take another chapter in another book to explain.

For me, the biggest transition to the Northwest was attending school at Wallace Elementary. As I said, I don't remember the details very well, except that I was introduced to the class on my first day by Mr. Monroe. This was my first male teacher, and it was a whole new experience. He was a good teacher, but he was not a humorous man. Things were very serious in his classes, and I started a week late. There was no funny business, no talking and passing stick figure drawings back and forth. Of course, I had no one to pass notes with, anyway. I didn't know anyone there, and it took me quite a while to get to the point where I had someone to talk to at recess.

Mr. Monroe gave spelling tests frequently; to me it seemed like every day. In reality it was a dictionary familiarization test, because we were allowed to look up the words. But did you ever notice that, if you don't know how to spell a word, it is a lot harder to look it up in a dictionary? Not like the internet, where you can put in any old spelling, and it will suggest a correct spelling. I remember having to write sentences on the board a hundred times, and then I had to write another 100 after I got home. This was real work! But it was good preparation for Catholic School, where spelling bees were a way of life.

We did do some interesting things in Mr. Monroe's class, like weaving belts. I remember the Washington State History classes about the settlers trying to get their wagons across rivers and up steep mountain passes. It all sort of melded into the gloomy aspect my life had assumed. It was cold and wet going to school. At recess, the classes had to stay in the all-cement, covered basketball court because the playgrounds were all muddy. I remember the kids would play football on the school grounds after school, and get covered with cold wet mud from head to toe. This was not my idea of fun, so I did not hang out with the neighborhood kids too much. There was one boy that befriended me, but I am embarrassed to say that I don't even remember his name. I do remember that he came from a very "working class" family, and he was never very clean. He always had dirt under his fingernails and tousled hair. He liked to go to the local junk dealers shop and buy little things like balsawood airplanes and strange mechanical devices. I suspect he may have grown up to be a mechanic or a machinist or maybe even an inventor. I really don't know what happened to him.

My other friend at Wallace lived in another neighborhood north of Wallace on First St., but we got interested in each other because of chemistry. No, we were too young for that kind of chemistry. I am talking about chemicals. She had a chemistry set and so did I. So show and tell for us was, you show me your disappearing ink and I will show you my litmus paper. Her name was Becky, and I remember going to her house and she came to mine. But we didn't have that long to get acquainted, because I moved in the middle of the school year. I never saw Becky again. In the grand scheme of things, kids are very low on the priority list.

What else can I say about Kelso? I know we had to be quiet all mornings when I was not at school. Dad had two weekdays off, and so he had to sleep until mid-day on the weekends. My mother did not drive, so even when the old '51 Ford was home, we had to wait for Dad to get up before we could go anyplace. I don't even remember going shopping. A few times we would go to the Kelso Theater for an evening movie, but generally we spend a lot of time at home in Kelso. I guess it was a little boring, but I busied myself with various solo activities and my dog.

But then my dog was killed. Some teenagers would drive down 7th street and when a dog would chase the car, they would open the door and hit the dog in the head. That is what happened to Boy; he had no evidence of injury, but had probably suffered a concussion and died by the side of the road. The younger neighborhood kids came to our house and led us to the place where he lay dead. That was a real shock to my worldview. We brought his body home and buried him in the back yard. I made a little marker for the grave.

My folks realized that I was taking Boy's death pretty hard, so they quickly arranged to get another dog. She was a small blonde dog; we called her Lassie because she looked like a diminutive version of the canine movie star. I don't really remember if she was just a puppy or whether she was a miniature collie or Sheltie. She was a sweet little dog, but shy. Not the burly boisterous dog that I was used to, but I liked her. My Mom especially liked the concept of a small beautiful dog about the house. In later years she got another blonde puppy that was a cross between a Dachshund and a Spaniel; I am sure it was because she reminded her of Lassie.

Lassie's fate was even more tragic than Boys. At least he had had a good life full of fun and adventure. Lassie was very timid about even going outside. So when we would let her out in the back yard to do her business, we didn't think about the possibility of her wandering off. But she did. We desperately searched for her for several days. I think it was about a week before someone told us that they thought she might be at the pound. I don't know if it was a City pound or an actually Humane Society facility. When we got her back she didn't seem right, and she became progressively more listless. Finally we took her to the veterinarian only to learn that she had contracted hepatitis. I am not sure if my folks had her euthanized or whether she had just succumbed to the debilitating disease. It was quite a while before we attempted to get another dog. Meanwhile I faced that cold and the school crowd with ever growing ambiguity. I wasn't really fitting in, and my one link to the communal feelings of McCloud, Boy, had been taken from me by some belligerent boys. I don't know when the movie, *Old Yeller*, came out, but it brought a flood of emotion when I watched it.

That winter was a tough one, but Spring brought some relief. Not only were the warmer weather and the welcome sun playing their part, but we were getting ready to move. My folks had secured a loan of $9000.00 to buy a large, old, baby-blue house in the Longview subdivision of Columbia Valley Gardens. The two-story house had been built in the 1920s on a quarter acre of land, like most of the neighboring houses on Pennsylvania St. The entire upstairs was divided into four small bedrooms along a long hallway. The ground floor had a substantial kitchen with a pantry, a fairly large dining area, and a modest living room. The back side of the ground floor had one more bedroom and the only bathroom. After the little rental in Kelso, this house gave us room to spread out. In addition there was an outbuilding attached to the house. A garage was bordered by a laundry room, and a room which became the shop. Behind that there were two more rooms and a big yard with about 1/16 acres of raspberries. On the right side of the house, the neighbors had planted a row of apple and cherry trees, which, by then, had grown taller than the two story house. There was also an early variety of apple in the back yard called a "Transparent", and a little concord grape arbor along the side of the yard. We were moving into what was almost a little farm, which someone had lovingly nurtured for years. The apple trees were prolific, the cherries were succulent, and the raspberries were my very first source of income.

Spring in the Northwest, whenever it comes, is a very peasant affair. Bob Huffhines used to revel in the occasion by reciting this refrain: "Spring has sprung, the grass is riz, I wonder where the flowers is?" It sometimes breaks out in February with early blooming cherries and crocus and daffodils. But that is a precarious event because the weather can turn bad and kill everything in bloom. More typically those early bloomers come out in April or May. The green is what is most impressive after a long grey winter. Everything is a bright green, almost chartreuse color, except for the yellow daffodils, the blue crocus, and the white and pink blossoms of apple and cherry trees. Living in Hawaii, as I do now, you tend to forget how magical it is to have the whole world come alive with green. Here in Hawaii the transition from season to season is almost imperceptible; green is around you all the time. And when I was in McCloud, I did not notice the absence of green so much, because there were evergreen trees everywhere. But in Longview most of the vegetation is angiosperm with a few gymnosperm thrown in for decoration. I was really impacted, dare I say overwhelmed, by the beauty of the transition from the dead of winter to the glory of spring. I think my heavy heart was lifted by that and the prospect of a new home. Perhaps Kelso might not have felt so glum, if we had arrived there in the spring.

There was so much room in this house that we didn't really have furniture for it, so there was a long period of trying to get sofas and an imitation "Lazyboy" for my dad, and the usual compliment of items. It was several years before we had three beds in the house, and I was sleeping on a kind of day bed that would now be called Danish modern but then was just cheap furniture. We had so much room in the dining area that my Dad agreed to take an old pedal organ that had been acquired by Uncle Larry and Aunt Cleo. Larry had not found the time to restore it so my Dad said he would try. The organ was red and ornate, but didn't work very well after my Dad managed to assemble it. The foot pedals did operate the bellows, but it was never tuned properly. Nevertheless we tried to plunk out some simple tunes. I don't know what the folks did with that when they later moved to the Toutle River, but it was definitely an eyesore in the house on Pennsylvania Ave. I remember our best purchase was a Ben Franklin style oil stove for the living room. We spent many hours standing or sitting around, or on, that stove, trying to take off the morning chill. We couldn't really afford to crank it up enough to heat the whole house, but it did, fortunately, provide heat to the upstairs bedrooms (heat rises). The kitchen, on the other side of the house was usually heated by the stove, and the heat from that range rose through a vent into my bedroom. We eventually purchased a little black and white TV, but when Dad's mother, Madge, came to visit, she was not satisfied with the little set. So she took Dad to Manchester's Appliances and picked out a big console color TV. They got a good price on it, because the wooden console had been slightly damaged, but the TV was in good working order. The broadcast stations were not; most programs were not yet in color and the ones that were would be very hard to adjust to anything approaching realistic color.

My mother said that TV was the beginning of the end of family civility. Before you know it, we were eating on TV trays, and dinner conversations were conducted during the one-minute commercials. However, the TV was the cause of Bob Huffhines and my Dad becoming well acquainted. We had the only color TV around, and Bob and his daughter Gretchen liked to come out to our house on Sunday nights to watch "Bonanza."

My life started expanding again in Columbia Valley Gardens at 3014 Pennsylvania Ave. The whole concept of having a big yard with fruit to eat was a new experience for me. In McCloud, I used to consume the little green crab apples that grew by the apartment. But here the fruit was cornucopian. In the great quarter acre expanse, I was practically able to take over the two back rooms of the out-building. These became at various times my kitchen (with discarded pots and pans), my laboratory (with my chemistry set and child's microscope), my hospital (doing surgery on my teddy bear), my news room (with the child's printing press) and many other incarnations of a fertile young mind. Actually, Dad tried to keep the shop to himself and his tools, but to no avail. I was always going in there making a mess carving wooden airplanes and building strange contraptions. These were useful times for my mental development; because I did go on to have a creative mind. In later years, I developed a technique for freeze sectioning tissue, as well as several devices for trapping, and sequestering fruit flies[19].

This was not done all in solitude either, because there were several boys my age right in the immediate neighborhood. Ironically, there were no girls. Mike Ray and his brother lived to one side of us, and the Shafer boy was two houses the other direction. Bobby, the kid I played with the most, lived across the street from the Shafer's. He and I were good friends until they move across town. I used to go stay with him at their new house, until one day his folks took us to a rodeo. On the way, his mom was bad mouthing our immediate neighbor, and I spoke up and said something like "you shouldn't talk that way about people when you don't know all the facts". Bad idea! I say that because I was *persona non grata* at Bobby's house thereafter. My first lesson in how the truth can be painful for the listener and the teller.

Mike Ray, his little brother and I played together a lot, but Mike was a bit temperamental. His Dad could be a mean son of a gun, and Mike was always getting in trouble because of things his brother had done. So they were often grounded. This meant that we could stand at the unfenced border of our properties, but he could neither come into my territory, nor I in his. When we were allowed to play at my place, we had some wild games. My folks were pretty lenient about the back yard, until they started planting a big garden and eventually fruit trees. So up to that time we built foxholes and forts, and ships out of boxes and saw horses, etc. Army was the primary game, even to the point of playing night raiders. I remember that on summer nights the mosquito abatement trucks would come through the neighborhood with foggers. We all had war surplus gas masks (sans filter canisters, of course), and we would run through the fog as if we were on the battlefield in a gas attack. To this day, I thank my lucky stars that DDT, for all of its negative impact on birds, was actually one of the least toxic pesticides as far as humans were concerned. The later substitutes, like lindane, were far more carcinogenic. By the way, although lindane was banned for use in agriculture in 2006, it is still used, by prescription, as a treatment for body lice. DDT, which was developed in WWII for use in delousing, would have been the far better choice. Nevertheless, we seemed to have survived our war games, both internationally an in our own back yards.

Unfortunately, Mike Ray went into the service during the Vietnam War, and was one of the few persons I know who was killed in combat (Gretchen photographed his name on the Vietnam War Memorial).

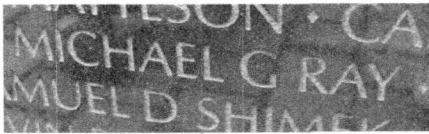

Michael Ray was my next door neighbor, but was killed in Vietnam. (Photo provided courtesy of Gretchen Klungness.)

Another boy in the neighborhood was Craig Tillotson. He lived across the street from us, and he was also an only child. But his parents were strict, so he didn't get as much opportunity to play with us as the other boys did. I remember one time Craig was with us on a hike out to the hill we called the Rock of Gibraltar (which it resembled). It was beyond the slough on Pacific Way, and it was on the property of Swanson's dairy farm (which appears to still be there, viewing the satellite map on Google). We had all taken our BB guns because it was initially supposed to be a "hunting trip". But, having been steeped in "the art of warfare", we decided to split up into two groups and play soldier on the slopes of Gibraltar. And we were having a really great time until somebody scored a hit on Craig's forehead about 1 inch from his eye. Needless to say, Craig was not happy!. We managed to get things under control, but that was the end of those games.

Although Craig surprised us, it was not without precedent. His father had a legendary temper, and that is part of the reason we did not play with him so much. Once the son left his bicycle in the driveway, and his dad hit it when he drove up to the house after a long day at the pulp mill. Vergil got so upset that he literally tore the frame of the bike apart with his bare hands. But he was a good dad and he would take his son hunting and fishing on their outboard motor boat.

I worked with Craig's father at the Weyerhaeuser Pulp Mill in Longview, where he was a foreman. I liked him but his temper did him in at the job as well. He once fired a man for sleeping on the job while tons of Kraft stock was overflowing from the washers he operated. The man filed a grievance and got his job back within six months, with back pay. Virgil and Betty, Craig's parents moved on to a job as an apartment manager in Vallejo, California. This happened when I was in the Seminary, and so I lost touch with Craig, but his parents and my parents remained friends. When the Tillotsons moved back to Washington and purchase a house in Vader, I would sometimes take my mother over to visit Betty and Virgil. After Virgil died, my mother and I still kept in touch with Betty, and she once visited us in Hawaii. She and a friend had taken a Hawaiian cruise on what was basically a spruced up WWII troop ship (actually they used a lot of Koa wood, not spruce, to refurbish the old rust bucket). She later said the best part of the cruise was the afternoon she and her friend spent with my mother and me. We went to Akatsuka's Orchid Nursery, and the Volcanoes National Park and we ate at the Volcano Golf Course. I guess it was more relaxing than the tour bus rides at every port of call.

Betty and Virgil were good folk -- salt of the earth people -- and Craig has been successful in his life because of them. He came to Hawaii frequently to work on Trident Submarines for the engineering firm that employed him. We talked on the phone several time during his visits, but we never were able to manage to get together on the same island. I sometimes regret that I have lost touch with so many people that I have known in my life, but the days of youth were not within our control, and that thread of human contact is fragile. Many things can break it, and often do. My mother was better at keeping in contact with people than I have been. There were a lot of other people from Longview with whom I have lost contact. As I said, Gretchen does better at keeping track of the old Longview crowd that she knew. But then she lived there off and on for more years of her life than I did.

CHAPTER 7

The Catholics

Now I say to you that you are Peter (which means 'rock'), and upon this rock I will build my church, and all the powers of hell will not conquer it. **New Living Translation (©2007)** Matthew 16:18

THE NEXT GREAT TRANSITION IN my life was the transfer to the Catholic School in Longview, Washington. This not only impacted my education, but also my circle of friends and my view of the world. St Rose de Viterbo Catholic Church was, for all intent and purposes, the product of Fr. Patrick Mulligan. Although Catholic roots go back to 1850 in the Longview area, the first church was built by the Franciscans (Ah, the irony that I would attend a Franciscan Seminary even though there had not been a Franciscan in Longview for many years!).

St. Rose's first church was constructed in 1928 for $17,500 under founding pastor Franciscan Father Leonard Bose. The 98-by-40-foot wood framed building seated 350 worshippers and served the parish until the current church opened in 1959 at a cost of $397,000.

Father Mulligan a driving force

The Franciscans relinquished the parish in 1941, marking the start of the 33-year pastorate of Father Patrick Mulligan.

"He was a driving force," recalled former principal Purcell, a graduate of St. Rose School and now an assistant superintendent in the archdiocese's Catholic Schools Department. "He was a very engaging Irishman," she said, "and as a kid the thing I remember was he'd do magic tricks on the playground. There are probably people in the parish who'd say he talked about money a lot, but I think that's probably why he was able to build the school and (new) church and do all that. He was the parish identity for a long time."

St. Rose School, founded in 1950, has become an integral part of the Longview community. Staffed by the Sisters of St. Joseph of Peace for a good part of its history, it quickly went from a K-6 to a K-8 school, with enrollment peaking at 400. In the 1970s, however, the middle school grades were dropped. And by 1989 the K-5 school was down to just 118 students. There was "serious conversation about closing the school," Purcell said.

http://www.seattlearch.org/FormationAndEducation/ Progress/062009/StRoseViterboParish06-11-09.htm

According to the above website [since taken down], St. Rose School is alive and well, and all of that would probably not have been possible without Fr. Mulligan. He was a Mick through and through, right from the old country, brogue and as thick as steel-cut porridge. The bit about the magic tricks was true, although we were all on to his technique. His sermons were soporific, but they certainly were effective for raising money. I mean, whoever heard of Catholics tithing in the 20th Century? When I arrived at St. Rose, Fr. Mulligan already had his 10 year plan proceeding on a five year schedule. Granted he built the school first, to his credit. But he was determined to get the main church, with its Celtic golden altarpieces from Ireland, and statuary from Italy, built so he could retire in peace.

I was transferring from Wallace to St Rose in the spring quarter. Sr. Caroline was the 4th grade teacher. She was young and sweet, but she was a real challenge to me scholastically. Sister Margaret Wood was principal then (1955-59); she was tall and regal. Of course, the kids were far ahead of me, and I had not even caught up to the public school system at Wallace. Being a new kid in a private school in the middle of the year is not something I would recommend for my children or my children's children. I felt awkward, stupid, and third class. My Dad would drive me to school before I got my bike. While other kids were arriving in big cars, some even in Mercedes (the lawyer's and doctor's sons), I was arriving in a rust bucket, puke-green 51' Ford… this was already 1958! My Dad eventually painted the Ford… with a brush… all black. You couldn't have picked a better color to show the brush marks, but it did slow down the rust![20]

The school uniforms were a source of embarrassment too. The theory of uniforms is that it eliminates the status differences between students based on dress. Wrong! For my parents the uniforms (blue sweater, blue dress shirts and salt and pepper cords) were expensive. So, my mother's solution was to buy the clothes oversized so I wouldn't grow out of them too fast. Although this was acutely embarrassing, I think it did me one great favor. It drove any semblance of vanity out of me for the rest of my life.

Gretchen's parents were also very frugal on the post office wages, but they had a better solution. Bob Huffhines learned to sew, and made all of Gretchen's dresses. My mother sewed things for me when I was in high school, but it was truly fortunate that I was in an all boy's school by that time. Really! …leopard skin pajama tops with bright yellow bottoms? Or what do you think about seersucker, striped salmon pink shirts, and a red, reversible vest with green plaid lining? I think she was, subliminally or otherwise, trying to reinforce my complete lack of vanity. Even when I had started my professional career at Weyerhaeuser Co., she was still at it. She thought I needed a suit, so she found a green tweed suit that had green arrowed slits for the pockets; I looked like a professional leprechaun…so, typical of me, I wore it to a professional meeting in Vancouver BC. Gretchen wonders how I ever got as far as I did in my profession, but I always say "It's not the clothes, it's the man." Now that I live in Hawaii, I have not owned a suit or a tie in years.

I suppose the 4th graders at St. Rose didn't know what to do with this country bumpkin from the woods. I was getting to the point where I was really embarrassed around the girls, but the guys at the Catholic school were all about the basketball court and the playfield. Some of them were already quite talented, and I was clumsy; so much for sports! The irony is that in recent years I had my genes evaluated by 23andMe.com. Turns out I have a marker on the ACTN3 gene which produces the alpha-actinin-3 protein. This is a common result for elite power athletes! It certainly passed me by. My son is very athletic (but he won't take the genetic test to find out if he has the gene).

I tended to gravitate to the more fringy boys like Greg Firth and Mike Momberg. John Polis was Mr. Polish among the St. Rose crowd. He was smart, talented (he could play a mean accordion) and he was athletic… short but fast! Nevertheless, in spite of his good reputation among the kids, he was open minded enough to join me on walks home from school. He lived about half way to Columbia Valley Gardens. Once I got a bike, it was a little more difficult to walk with him. Nevertheless, since he had been open minded enough to walk with me, I continued to walk with him until we reached his house.

I don't know if it was John who got me into the Altar Boys, but I remember he was the one that instructed me in the rubrics. Friction with some of the rowdier lads began to develop because of the Altar Boys. The roster was competitive, and Jerry Reynolds and Frank Peterson didn't much like me getting opportunities that they were missing. John and I took the job with a measure of responsibility, while Jerry and Frank were always goofing off, trying to get at the sacristy wine, etc. Herb Karnofski and Jan Karnoski were also altar boys. Jan was a cousin of Herb, but he was one of the ultra-cool kids; good at sports, blonde, facile with the "chicks", in grade school no less. In high school Jan ended up being an item with Gretchen's best friend Sherry (she was a cheer leader). Herb was a more reserved fellow, with good reason. His mother was a nurse and his dad was a heavy-drinking longshoreman. He had three younger brothers, and was largely responsible for them on a daily basis. Consequently he was also a serious minded Altar Boy, and we began to get along.

I forget whether Lyle Shabram was at St. Rose when I started, but he was another St. Rose kid that lived in Columbia Valley Gardens. We also became pretty good friends, but I don't remember exactly how. I am not sure if he was an altar boy. His dad was an inventor[21], and on more than one occasion he took Lyle and me to his workshop down by the Cowlitz River. It was full of old washing machines (which he used for parts) and large cement rollers on which he had installed heating coil. This was used to cut out gloves and bags from a moving sheet of plastic. The key to his invention was that he had figured out how to make the bags and gloves with a lip that was offset, so it would be easy to open. To this day I do not understand how he did it. He had also invented a process like Polaroid, but that company beat him to the patent. His obituary indicates what a great inventor and father he was.

The Shabrams had 8 kids and were straining to send their kids (Lyle had an older sister and a bunch of younger brothers) to Catholic school. My folks used to invite Lyle to do things with me, like going to movies, and picnics and such, but I used to go to Lyle's house a lot. There was always something going on at Lyle's house; you really didn't have to go anywhere. The Shabrams moved away from Longview when I was in seventh grade I believe. His dad was offered a job at Rexall Co. in their research division (they wanted to buy his patent). That summer after they moved, Lyle's folks invited me to visit them in Walnut Creek, California. That was the reason I didn't visit McCloud that year. I think I stayed a couple of weeks, because the whole Shabram family went to Disneyland and took me with them. We had a great time, and it was the only time I ever saw Disneyland. They had a huge station wagon and a tiny little Fiat. It was quite a trip. I think one of Mr. Shabram's corny jokes kind of summed up the trip. While passing by Hillsboro on the El Camino Real, he asked, "What did the tree say to the gardener." As the eucalyptus trees along the highway flashed by us, he answered "You clipped us!" Inventor jokes; you had to be there.

Just out of curiosity I looked up the Shabrams on the internet. It turns out Lyle Jr. followed in his dad's footsteps; in fact, they have joint patents on some items. Lyle Jr. has his own patent on a mechanical capo that can selectively depress individual strings to create chords. He also invented a collapsing table trademarked as Spiderlegs, and other related inventions. He operates his own company in Carmel CA.

My mother also liked Herb Karnofski. She knew his mother, because she had started to work at the hospital as a medical transcriptionist. She also knew that Herb didn't have a lot of opportunity to just have fun, so she would invite him along for things that we were doing as well. And he would come over to our house quite often. I would go to his house occasionally, but I was pretty uncomfortable there. It was a whole different bunch of kids and adults than I was used to. It wasn't all welcoming and friendly like the Shabram's home. I guess it was Lyle's mother that made his house so inviting; whereas Herb's mother was usually not home, and often his father was. Not that Herb Senior ever did anything bad to us, but maybe it was just Herb's mannerism when his dad was around that made me think something wasn't right. Also, at other times Herb's mother had to sleep in the daytime because she did shift work, so it was easier for him to come to our house. I think he liked my mother, and it gave him some time to be a kid when he came to our house; although Herb was an old soul even when he was a kid. Herb kept in touch with my mother, and the last time she saw him, he came to Hawaii. My mother was living with me after she had an operation to drain a brain hematoma in the late 1990s.

All of these friendships developed over time. I was still pretty isolated when I was in Sr. Caroline's class. At the end of the school year, I went to stay with Meritt and Eva for part of the summer, so I didn't make a lot of friends in Longview that summer. I have mentioned the visits to Meritt before. It was probably good that my folks arranged that because it made the transition to the Northwest a little easier. Meritt was a very important influence in my life, and I think the trips to the woods with him made me feel like a person. Everyone respected Meritt greatly and just being close to that was, in its self, elevating. The days that I didn't go with him were not so elevating. Eva had a real knack for making me feel inferior. It was like she was always suspecting me of something. I didn't get into any trouble that summer, but it almost seemed like she was expecting me to screw up. I spent a lot of the time trying to stay away from her. In her favor, she was a good cook. Her waffles were very light… not surprising since she would fold whipped cream into the batter. I still use that trick if I want to impress guests. It's ironic that all I really remember from the trip to McCloud was my trips with Meritt to visit the logging sites. I think I did visit the old crowd, but not that much. Rick McGiff was not often available and I don't think Eva would let me wander down to Quincy St. to hang out with the old gang there.

The next year at St. Rose was a big change. Sr. Caroline was gone (transferred). I did not mention that, while we lived in Kelso, my folks had enrolled me in Catechism class at St. Mary's Church. My instructor was a nun from St. Rose whose name was Ignatius Loyola. Now, Saint Ignatius was a male saint and the founder of the Jesuit Order. I did not realize this nun had taken a male name, until I had her for my teacher in 5th grade at St. Rose. She was an ex-WAC, and a very substantial woman, both mentally and physically. And she certainly knew how to keep the troops in line. There was the dodge ball line, the spelling bee line, the minuet line (mandatory dance, ugh!), and there was the "sight line". The latter requires explanation. You see, Sr. Ignatius must have played softball in the WAC. She kept her keys tucked under her bib, so they would be handy in case there was out-of-line behavior in the classroom. I have personal knowledge! When I was whispering to the neighboring student, the keys would thump me on the chest. She was a very good aim. Never poked an eye out, or caused any bruises. She was a deadeye; in the chest every time up to 30 feet. It works with my dogs, and it works with students as well. She was equally intolerant of aberrant behavior in the playground. Once Jerry Reynolds and I were "duking it out" in the playground and I was not holding my own, so to speak. Sr. Ignatius grabbed Jerry by the front of his shirt and whacked him upside the head… more than once. I guess Jerry and I were both on the carpet (in detention), but Sr. Ignatius came near getting booted out the door. She managed to defend herself against the parents, because there was no question that the fight was uncalled for and was initiated by Jerry. Needless to say, Jerry did not bother me after that incident.

The summer after 5th grade, I think I went to McCloud again, but it might have been later in the summer. Early that summer, I think I worked in the strawberry field. Mom and Dad had taken me briefly to pick berries for a Finish family the first summer we were living at Pennsylvania Ave. That was really challenging, but my mother stayed with me and picked her share of berries. I think I probably didn't pick much. I can't remember if Dad delivered us to the farm in the morning and then picked us up when he got of work, or whether we were only there for part of the day. I am sure I was not a very good picker, but the Finns seemed to appreciate my mother's picking. I am sure it was hard work for her, too, because she had not done that kind of work for years. She may have helped Ma Whitlock pick raspberries when she was spending summers on their farm in Tumalo. It's fitting that I should start my work life in a berry field, because berries would play a part throughout my life.

Just to put it in perspective, I am going to list briefly all the times I have interacted with berries. When I was a kid in Pondosa, we used to go picking huckleberries. Next I earned money picking the raspberries at our house in Longview... Next I picked strawberries for Highland Berry Farm (which is still in business, at least as a U-pick farm). Next I was picking wild blackberries and red huckleberries on the Toutle River for my mother to can. Then we went U-Picking when I was at University of Washington. Next I was identifying wild species of Northwest berries in Dr. Hitchcock's Taxonomy of Northwest Plants. Then I was trying to encourage Wadavida farmers to plant the blackcap raspberries that some settlers had left at the stone house that was being used as a pre-school in Taita Hills, Kenya. Next, I was picking wild berries of all kind (elderberries, blackberries, red huckleberries) in Tenino, Washington, to try to keep my family fed. We also planted strawberries and raspberries. Next I was managing a raspberry farm in Puyallup Washington; the second year I was tilling under the raspberries and replacing them with blueberries. Then I did a microscopy project on raspberries for a scientist at the Washington State Agriculture Experiment Station at Puyallup. Then I was studying pollination ecology at UC Davis, while working in fruit and nut crop research. Then I was Garden Manager for the Married Student Housing complex in Berkeley; I sold my plot of loganberries, boysenberries, raspberries and strawberries for $100 when I left for Hawaii. Then, on visits to the Northwest, I was cultivating and planting a raspberry patch for my mother in Napavine, Washington. But out here in Hawaii there are not many berries. There is a very rare native raspberry, and there are some invasive blackberries and thimbleberries, but none in quantity. I have worked with fruit crops growers, including one who grows strawberries at 3000 ft. elevation in Waimea and one who grows red raspberries at 700 ft. in Pahala. I have a friend who raises a small patch of the same black cap raspberries here in Hawaii that was growing at the settler's house in Taita. The friend's farm is in Wa`a Wa`a near sea level; I was so surprised to see a heavy crop of lovely berries at sea level in the sub-tropics. I have some weedy blackberries in my yard at 2000 ft. elevation, but they bear tiny yellow fruit and the birds eat the berries and the bugs eat the leaves. So I planted mulberries along one border of my property. We harvest mulberries in some years, but I miss the Northwest fruit! I forgot to mention that my grandfather was experimenting with berry cross-pollinating when he had a plot of berries in Salem Oregon. And of course my great grandparents raised raspberries to sell. So that is a lot of interaction with berries for one family!

After the last summer visit to McCloud, on the trip back, Eva got really mad at me. She was criticizing someone, and for the second time in my life, I criticized the criticizer. Again I say, that is not a very good idea. Usually the people who take great pleasure in bad mouthing others end up having absolutely no tolerance for being criticized. When you made Eva mad, you better wear earplugs because her voice was devastating to the fine hairs of the auditory canal. I am sure Meritt cringed the minute I opened my mouth. After all, when Eva was doing her usual diatribe, it was just a dull roar, and you could kind of ignore it. I am sure Meritt had perfected the art by then. However, if you crossed her, you better be prepared… and I was not. I think that is probably why I was not invited back to a McCloud trip after sixth grade. In fact, the whole family saw less and less of Meritt after that. Although Eva would let Meritt visit his daughter and the Smith family often. In later years, there were fifty miles between us and Meritt, but it was 300 miles to Mary and Vernon's house in Mt. Shasta.

I probably should not judge Eva too harshly, because she eventually developed Alzheimer's disease, and it really is not certain when it started. Meritt had a hard number of years with her, and the hardest were the early stages of the disease. Later, as she became more incapacitated, she was easier to control, but at the earlier stages she would do things like telling the neighbors that my grandfather had a gun and was going to kill her. After Meritt retired, he and Eva moved to the Keizer subdivision in Salem, Oregon, so they were more proximate to our home, but we only visited them a few times. I remember how proud Meritt was of his berry patch (he probably had 1/8 of an acre at Salem) in which he was cross-breeding varieties. Their house was flooded out in the 1964 flood[22], and Eva insisted that they move to a senior community called King City in Tigard, Oregon. There he only had a small area to grow things. It was in Tigard that Eva really started to go down the slippery slope of dementia, so Meritt's world got very small during those years. He planted an apple tree at Tigard, and never has there been an apple tree so lovingly nurtured and pruned. After Eva died in her 80's, he continued to nurture that tree. That tree was instrumental in facilitating the next, and very happy, last marriage of his life. She was a widow who lived across the street from him. He was trying to think up some excuse for introducing himself, and finally decided apple pie would do the trick. Lame excuses like, "I have so many apples I have to have help using them up", prevailed. Finally he invited her to a rodeo. She was from Alberta, Canada, so rodeos or whatever they call them (Calgary Stampede, I think) were familiar from her childhood. One thing led to another and they were soon on their honeymoon on the Princess Marguerite, dining with the captain on their way up the Strait of Juan de Fuca to Alaska. He was 83, and drank his first glass of wine on that trip. I tell all of this here, just to point out how our lives change with time. Although Eva restricted our access to Meritt, he lived on to have a happy final marriage, and our whole family benefited from seeing how happy and humorous Josephine and he were together. Here is an example: they always played two rounds of cribbage every evening, and Jo always beat him. Until one night, Meritt won the first round. Jo wanted to play the second, but he refused to ever play cribbage with her again. He wasn't mad, but he was so determined to beat her (after being skunked for several years) that when he did finally win, he was satisfied!

I think I either met the Olson Brothers at the berry field or they invited me to try berry picking. Kris was actually a year ahead of me at St. Rose, but somehow we got acquainted and hung out together. Like Lyle, he also was from a family with 8 kids. His oldest brother Dave was an upper class student at St. Rose, and was always around. He had a deformed arm, but he could do amazing things with the stump that extended only a short way from his elbow. He could tie fishing gear just by using his stump like an opposing thumb. He raised worms for sale and used them to fish in the slough, Lake Sacajawea, and the Columbia River. I never understood how he could skewer a wiggling worm with one hand. I liked to spend time at the Olsen house, too, because, like the Shabram's house, there was always something going on. We all had bikes by then, so we traveled a lot of places in and outside the neighborhood. St Rose was on a street that ran along Lake Sacajawea, so the whole lake came into our extended territory. Also Mt. Solo was an easy day trip. We never tried to climb the power line towers on top of the Mount, but I think the Olsons were tempted.

Dave Olson had a paper route and Kris would sometimes talk me into going with him when he substituted for his brother. That got me interested, and when the kid, who picked up papers at the same drop site as Dave, wanted a substitute, I got the job. Eventually I took over that kid's route. In fact, I think I traded my heavy Murray for his stripped down bike with high handle bars. That was a mistake as I will explain.

By the time I took over the paper route, I was riding my bike to school. The school was three miles from my home in Columbia Valley Gardens, but the paper route, although it was 6 miles long, ended closer to Lake Sacajawea. That means it was closer to St. Rose than to home. Therefore, my routine became, rise at 5 AM, make breakfast, and hike up hill almost 2000 ft.(or so it seemed) on Cascade Way to where the newspaper drop box was at the top of the hill at the corner of Madrone Dr. From there it was generally downhill on Cascade, but there were several side streets that were either uphill or downhill from Cascade. So I would have to ride or walk my bike up and down those side streets. When I got to the bottom of Cascade Way I was at Pacific Highway, and usually went from there straight to school. This means I would usually arrive at school early unless I got a late start. On those late days, if I was lucky, my dad would take me on the route and then drive me home. From there I had to take my bike to school. One time my dad offered to drive me on the route, but he was out of gas. So I rode my bike about a mile to the gas station on Pacific Hwy, carrying a 1 gallon gas can. On the way home, the can got caught between my knee and the handle bar, so I went down, and broke a chip off my front tooth. It hurt like hell, particularly if I opened my mouth to the cold air; but we still had to get the papers delivered and I had to get to school. I think we did go to the dentist a day or so later, but he said the pain would go away, and there wasn't much use to spend the money it would take to create porcelain prosthetic. I have that cracked tooth to this day. Like the scar on my cheek, it adds to my "tough guy" look. I always thought of myself as kind of a wimp, but in retrospect, I guess I was actually a pretty tough kid.

I remember towards the end of my newspaper career, I was having more and more trouble with my "cool" bike. Finally, I was rolling down the Cascade when I realized that back peddling was not slowing me down. The brakes drum was totally shot. I managed to get stopped, at the cost of several layers of shoe leather. I threw the bike on into the bushes on the side of the road and walked the additional two miles to school. I never went back to recover that pile of junk. For all I know, it might still be rusting away in the bushes. From the Google Satellite map it is clear that the Cascade Way is more covered with vegetation than it was back then.

Occasionally I would have to yield the road to a skunk. Cascade Way was then and is now an upscale area, which made the paper job worth the sweat. Christmas bonuses were good on what we affectionately nicknamed "Nob Hill". Of course, in those days you had to collect the money yourself. Some people were really good about paying their monthly bill, to the point that I never even met some of them. Those good customers would leave the check in the paper box. On the other hand, some people were nearly impossible. They would make you come back two and three times: "I don't have any money today", "Can you come back when my husband is home", "Can you make change for a hundred dollar bill"... yeah, likely story! But I guess that is how I learned to be respectful when I wanted to just scream. And you can be sure that if I forgot to deliver a paper, the loudest complaints would come from those households from which it was hardest to collect payment. Good training for government service.

I don't remember meeting Kris or Dave at the paper drop box after I took over the other route. They might have beaten me to the drop, or more likely, Kris did not take over that route when Dave got another job. I really don't remember. Kris went to high school the year before I did, so we didn't see as much of each other that year, and after I left for the Seminary, we only got together once my freshman summer. That was a fateful meeting, but I will deal with that escapade later. There was already friction developing between us. Dave, Kris, I think Mike Momberg, and myself went on a camping trip on the

Coweman River. It was a great spot to camp, and that day on the river was very pleasant. But the next morning, Kris and I got into a fight about something. We were barefooted, and we backed into an area of low vegetation, under which was a plethora of large black slugs. Both of our feet got covered with the thick slime. It literally took a few days to get that sludge off of our feet. I remember the slime more than I remember what we were fighting about.

I suppose I should deal with the summer camp issues at this point, since it was another significant "Catholic" event in my young life. I think the first year that I went to camp was probably the summer of my 5th grade year. I am not really sure about that. Camp Blanchet was one of two diocesan Catholic Youth Organization camps for Catholic boys (girls too, but in separate sessions). It was run by Gordy, Fr. Marquist and the seminarians from the diocesan seminary in Kent WA. The camp itself was out of Gig Harbor in the Puget Sound. I have tried to find it on the internet, but the only camp that is still operating is Don Bosco. Cabrini and Hamilton were two camps that came later, but it looks like Don Bosco is the only one left; at least the only one that still advertises camping sessions. On the CYO Seattle Diocese Facebook account, one entry was by a fellow who attended Blanchet in 1972, so it must have been around that long. It is kind of disappointing to know that the camp folded. As I remember it there were a lot of "itty bitty campers" who worked hard to build that camp.

The staging area for the camp was a boat dock at Gig Harbor. A WWII landing craft was waiting at the shore. The Walrus, as she was called, had a song in its honor: (to the tune of the "Sinking of the Titanic" song)

Oh they built the good ship Walrus, and when they were through
Gordy said this ship the water ne'er go through.
Fr. Marquist raised his hand, said this ship will never land.
Oh it was sad when the great ship went down.

Oh it was sad, mighty sad,
Oh it was sad, mighty sad,

It was sad when the great ship went down,
Counselors and guides, itty bitty campers lost their lives
It was sad when the great ship went down.

The campers would file onto the open loading ramp, the seminarians would load up the luggage, and off we would go to Camp Blanchet. The camp was built on the shore of an island (I cannot determine which but there is a small island is directly west of Gig Harbor called Raft Island). All Saints Retreat Center is on the East side of Raft Island, and from Google Map it looks suspiciously like the land formation that was the site of Camp Blanchet). Although the island is developed with neighborhoods and even a University of Washington Campus, in 1958 there was not much on the island except Blanchet. There were bunk houses and a community bathroom and a large mess hall, much like the one at Camp Pondosa. I think we had 10 campers to a bunkhouse, and a counselor. The residence of a bunkhouse formed a tribe, and competition between the tribes was encouraged in the form of work parties and sports events. I think I was in Nisqually both years that I attended camp. Being naturally shy, I was quite awkward in forming friendships at the lodge. But the emphasis was on teamwork, so eventually you began to feel part of a team. I remember the first year; one of the major projects was to dismantle a very large boat house for building materials to construct buildings at the camp. By the time our group got there, they were already taking up floorboards, as the superstructure had already been salvaged. The floor was built over a series of logs that were easily 5 ft. in diameter and the whole thing was probably 30 by 90 ft. It might have been a dance hall or a restaurant; it was too big for a house. The "houseboat" must have been built at a time when they were hauling those great logs out of the Northwest forests. We would trek down to the shore, load up with board, and haul them up the hill to the camp.

I don't remember if we pulled Scotch broom that first year, but we surely wore ourselves out on the broom the second year. That was a chore! Later in life I learned from an old logger that the proper way to root up a Scotch broom is with a Pulaski[23]. It is a special tool with a sharp blade about a foot long… but narrow and strong. The old logger must have made his own, because unlike the commercial version of the Pulaski (which has an axe on one side and the digging blade opposite the axe), his just had the digger. You cut deep down to the root and then you lever it out with the tool handle. At Camp Blanchet we did it the hard way.

I guess I should first explain about Scotch Broom[24] in the Pacific Northwest. Scotch Broom as the name implies is an invasive species, and has done remarkably well since its incursion. Particularly in logged or burned over forest, the copious quantity of leguminous seed rapidly invades. It has an attractive spathe of yellow flowers which, in recent years, turn the hillside to yellow gold in mid-summer. So Scotch broom was the enemy and we were the defending army; but in the absence of the proper tool, we resorted to medieval tactics to defeat the invading horde. As many campers as could get a grip on an individual broom plant at one time, would pull in unison to try to dislodged the tough fibrous root. Add to this backbreaking task, the added incentive of beating the other tribes in square feet of broom cleared, we were feeling the strain. One might imagine it as a group of serfs launching the battering ram against the castle gate. Similar to the sailors on a four-master hauling up the rigging while singing "heave haul awaaay, we'll heave and haul together. Heave haul awaaay, we'll haul away Joe". It seemed like these work parties were always in the afternoon, on sunny days with the sweat rolling off our brows. I learned something about teamwork on those parties.

There were fun activities, too. There was a craft session every day, where we wove belts, poured and painted plaster molds, made rosaries, and I even made a copper engraving. We also had regular exercise and swim training. At the end of the session there were water competitions for different swimming strokes, relay races, and the greased watermelon chase. Believe me when I say, it is almost as hard to hold onto a greased watermelon as a greased pig. I had known how to "just swim" before that, but I learned the Australian crawl, side stroke, butterfly and backstroke at camp. Every night we would have a campfire, with songs and skits.

Near the end of a session we would have an over-two-night camp out. The first year we took the Walrus out to Oyster Bay. Looking at the bay on the Goggle satellite image, it is apparent that it is a long distance from Camp Blanchet, and I remember the ride on the Walrus to be very long; such that when we arrived at our destination, we had a slight case of sea-legs. That is, when you walk you kind of roll, and when you sit quietly your surroundings seems to sway. The other thing I learned at Oyster Bay is how prolific Mother Nature is in the sheltered waters of the Puget Sound. There were copious quantities of star fish, sand dollar urchins and jelly fish (fortunately sans tentacles at that life stage). There was such a plethora of sea urchins that their dead shells, called sand dollars, dominated the bay floor. At our camp site, we had row boats so we could go out on the shallow bay. At one point another camper and I started filling the boat with starfish and sand dollars. We eventually had to turn the boat over to keep it from sinking under the weight of our "haul". I guess we were pretending to be fishermen, but unfortunately there was not much of food value in that bay (or at least anything that we had the gear to catch). I don't know if I would have recognized if there were oysters there or not. Probably they were over-harvested years before.

The next year the camp out was in an area that I cannot recall. I think we had to hike to that site, so I guess it was on the far side of the island from Camp Blanchet. One thing that camp site did have was clams; butter clams, mostly. I remember being horrified that the kids would set their clams next to the hot coals of the fire, and as soon as the shell popped opened they would slurp the slimy innards into their mouths, sand and all. Since then, I never have developed a taste for semi-raw seafood. On that outing, we did get to take a Walrus ride across the sound to Penrose Point State Park which was only about 3 miles away from Camp Blanchet. So it was basically an overnight trip, where we slept around the campfire on the beach at the Park. If you have never been to the Puget Sound, you probably cannot imagine how fortunate we were to have the opportunity to enjoy this beautiful area of Mother Earth, before the area was pock marked with civilization. It is still beautiful, but at night the city lights diminish the brightness of the stars. Back then, on a clear night, you could see millions of stars. I suppose that may have contributed to the sale of Camp Blanchet. It was no longer the outdoor experience that it had been. I'm glad my folks chose Blanchet instead of Bosco. I had many opportunities to do forest camping in my life, but Camp Blanchet was the only time that I experienced the unique habitat of shoreline. Although, one day in the future I would work for a Limnologist. Interestingly, years later my son was stationed on the Puget Sound at Hoodsport, although he has currently taken assignment elsewhere, He hopes to someday get back to the Puget Sound and the Olympic Forest.

I will say that the first year's camping experience was probably good for me. I didn't really relate very well to the campers, and I was not a favorite of the staff. I guess I was just too shy. I don't remember the names of anyone but Gordy, the manager, and Fr. Marquist. I can't even picture any of their faces. The second year, I was more hopeful of fitting in because Rick McGiff was coming up from McCloud. My parents had been in communication with Dr. McGiff, and he was intent on giving this rustic experience to his son. I don't know if the McGiffs had already moved to Carmel, California by then, or whether Rick was still in McCloud. I was just happy because I figured it would be easier to have a buddy at camp. However, it didn't turn out that way.

Rick immediately fit right into the tribe and their activities in general, so much so that he kind of ignored me. Of course, we had not spent any time together since McCloud and both of us had changed. So, in some ways the second year was less satisfying that the first. Rick and I were in the Nisqually lodge, but my concept of having a "buddy" was dashed. Frankly, Rick and I subsequently lost touch completely, and it is only as I write this that I tried to locate Rick on the internet. Sure enough, a "Richard McGiff" popped up on Facebook, and you could hardly mistake the face. I sent him a message, but I have not had a reply. If it is not Rick, but a son, the genes are very strong, because he looks exactly like Rick.[25] In fact, the picture has him wearing a coonskin cap (complete with tail); just like the caps we had when we were kids. Fess Parker, playing Davy Crockett, was a favorite vicarious hero of our youth. Ah youth! Where did it go?

Moving on, my sixth grade experience was entirely different than 5th. It is amazing how a teacher can influence the life of two score and eight youngsters (48/class). Sr. Ignatius' style was forceful, regimenting and bold. My next teacher was Sr. Aurelia. She was so entirely different from Sr. Ignatius. Just the names tell much of the story. Sr. A was slight of build, blanch white skin (what you could see ringed the bib), and almost otherworldly in her mannerisms. It is amazing that she was able to keep control of our rowdy bunch, but she had a saintliness about her that greatly intimidated the impish voices in our heads, and rather encouraged the little angel on our shoulders. I don't even remember outbursts from Frank or Jerry that year. In short, she was a spiritual force with which to be reckoned. Only one other person had that effect on me in my life, and that was Fr. Kevin, the Rector of St. Francis Seminary. Rector is a good name for it, because people like Fr. Kevin and Sr. Aurelia made you take stalk of yourself, and set yourself right. I imagine it might be a little like the effect that Mother Teresa had on people. I mean, how could you cross her?

I don't remember many details of sixth grade. I think it was so orderly that it was almost forgettable; nothing shocking or exciting ever happened. My only vivid experience occurred when I was sick. I had been out of school for a few days, and my dad, thinking I was better, had brought me to school to pick up homework. Horror of horrors, I threw up on Sr. Aurelia's shoes. Literally! I vomited as we stood there, and when I got back from the bathroom, typically, she had already cleaned up the mess. Talk about scarring a young mind! It was like there were no anomalies in Sr. Aurelia's universe...she never mentioned it again. Neither did I! Academically, I think it was a good year, although I have none of my St. Rose school records to prove it. It wasn't a terribly successful year socially. Of course, boy-girl interactions are always difficult at that age, but I was beginning to feel particularly dorky before the word was invented in 1960. I did have my circle of friends outside school, but things were still tough at St. Rose. I did not feel part of one big happy family, no matter how kind Sr. Aurelia was. We didn't have the pressure of sport that year as we did in Sr. Ignatius' class. This is because they had begun to build the new church and the old one had been torn down that summer. That meant the gymnasium, which to me had been a place of ambivalence, was now the substitute parish church. It would still be used for ceremonies and performances, but it was no longer available for gym class or sports.

I don't know whether my first year of Little League baseball had been the summer before 6th grade or happened after that school year. My father was the catalyst and had even become the assistant coach for the team. I remember the tryouts were at Columbia Valley Garden School right down the street from our house; so some of the kids already knew that I was not an athletic wonder. I don't think I was picked until near the end of the selections; which, in itself was an embarrassment. And the season proceeded from bad to worse. Dad tried hard to develop my throwing arm and teach me to bat, but it was definitely an uphill battle. I became and outfielder (mostly right field). And I don't think that I ever threw home a fly ball in time to stop a runner. Also I cannot remember ever hitting a fly ball, although I did get on base a few times. I was bored and mortified most of the season. That was my only season of Little League. At least I learned enough to be chosen as first baseman for intramural baseball when I went to the seminary.

My basketball career was even more spectacular in its failure. I did get on the team in 5th grade, when we still had a gym. I was playing center in my first big intermural game at the YMCA, when I unexpectedly received the ball. Ah, my moment of glory. I could barely dribble, but I managed to dribble all the way down the court. No whistles from the referees or the audience. I was amazed how fast I was because I had left all opposition guards behind. I took my stance, I shot, and it went straight into the basket! One problem, it was the opposition's basket! Needless to say, I did not make the team the next year.

By then my self-image was either being impacted by my increasing weight or my spectacular failures were affecting my eating habits. My dad was very stoic about all of this. He did the best he could to interest me in the world of sports. His favorite was golf, and when we lived in McCloud, he took me to the links several times. But he could tell I was not interested. So he tried to interest me in other sports, but I think he finally realized that, not only was I not getting interested, but every failure was making me more disinterested. I give him credit; he did not badger me, or give me the silent treatment. He himself had to withdraw from his love of golf, because my mother thought it was too expensive. He would play occasionally, but between working two jobs, and keeping the family fed, about the only opportunity he had to play golf was the annual Post Office golf match. There, he was up against Dick Price, who was himself a semi-pro, and would often take annual leave to go to golf tournaments. James had a powerful drive, but what always killed him was the putting. They sometimes refer to it as "choking up", and it was his Achilles heel on the golf course. I regret that he was not able to see me play sports in high school, because he certainly never had that pleasure of fatherhood, i.e. seeing his son do well in competition. I will talk about that more when I get to St. Francis Seminary.

In spite of my lack of success in the sports arena, Dad always took me to arenas of other kinds. When the circus would come to town, we were there. When the Navy band came to town, we were front and center. When the Harlem Globe Trotters came to town, we were courtside. When the air shows were held in Kelso or Vancouver, we were looking skyward at the aerial display. And every Fourth of July, we were always there for the fireworks at Sacajawea Park. I remember that Dad took me to see Jimmy Durante and Anita Bryant at the Portland Coliseum. That was a memorable performance of a consummate old vaudevillian. We went as a family to see Leonard Bernstein conduct the New York Philharmonic at the Portland Cow Palace (before the Coliseum was built). As far away as we were from the podium, we could still see the ripples of motion in the conductor's tuxedo. I had never seen a man so completely throw himself into his work. And as I mentioned before, we went to see the first Boeing 707 land at the Portland Airport. Also, in 1957 we watched the USS Nautilus[26] during its "Home Run" exercised on the Pacific Coast. During that voyage the Nautilus passed under the Lewis and Clark Bridge[27], and we were on it… taking movies, I think. Dad also took me to see the Portland Beavers play a few times (now that was truly boring for me, but he enjoyed it.). We never did go down to Portland to watch the Rose Parade, but several times we went as a family to see the Ice Capades at the Portland Coliseum. I think he took me to see a hockey game once (now that was interesting… you really have to pay attention to keep track of the puck.). In short, James did his best to be a good father to me. My only regret is that we did not grow closer as I got older. He probably never knew how much I appreciate him until now.

Seventh grade was a different story as well. Sr. Virgil was a young teacher… probably first year. She was more fun, but had problems with her student charges. I mean, give the woman credit. Seventh graders are notorious. To have thrown her into a seventh grade class of fouty-eight students was like throwing her in a lion's den. As the song we used to sing at Camp Blanchet went:

> Daniel was a dentist, he wouldn't obey the king.
> The king said he wouldn't stand for such a thing.
> So he threw him in a manhole with lions down beneath,
> But Daniel was a dentist so he pulled the lions' teeth.
> https://www.lyricsmode.com/lyrics/c/children/adam_was_a_gardener.html

I have to say, it was kind of like that for Sr. Virgil. It took her a while to get her "tooth extractions techniques" down, but she eventually brought some order to the seething horde. Remember, we were the peak of the baby boomer generation. Schools were budging at the seams everywhere. Being young and enthusiastic was in Sr. Virgil's favor. Being young and enthusiastic was also her greatest weakness. It was not uncommon for the class to lead her off track onto a topic of interest that was not exactly 'in the syllabus'. I remember distinctly when she had to explain sex in religion class. If I remember correctly, she did a pretty credible job. She had obviously been raised with boys, because she knew how to call out the guys about being goofy. I think at one point she actually said: "Oh, stop giggling girls, and pay attention. You're going to need to know this." Actually Sr. Virgil was so real about all of this, that I wonder if she made it through the Vatican Council years, or, like so many other religious with brains, left the order and had a couple of kids of her own.

Sister Virgil gave me my first "big public speaking" opportunity. I was very interested in science, so I was given the chance to give a presentation on the physics of flight. I can still see myself running across the front of the classroom with a large piece of construction paper folded into a wing, to prove that air moves faster over the upper surface, thus reducing the pressure on the upper side of the wing, thereby causing lift. And I really have not shut up since. We have a joke around my house. Quoting the Ducks Breath Mystery Theater[28], whenever I am expounding on science, my wife will say "he has a master's degree, in Science!" which can be interpreted to mean, he is full of hot air... and I don't mean steam. At any rate, that "lecture" cemented my reputation as the geekiest guy in St. Rose, and started to turn the tide from me. My fellow students started to get the idea that I might actually be smart or something. Ultra-cool guys like Bob Bordeaux actually started letting me into his entourage, although that actually had painful overtones. For some reason Bob thought it was great sport to bring me to the floor with a titty grab. I thought it was weird, but at least I was part of the group. Bob lived near Pennsylvania Ave. and in seventh grade I was actually able to go to his house, and ride around with him and his sister in her 1950 Ford. What a young person will do for acceptance. They would actually take me on the 'cruise route' to Capt'n Yoby's hamburger joint. Best halibut fish and chips ever! Cruising was a phenomenon of the time, where all the teenagers who had 'wheels' would drive on a frequented route through the town, ending at the "burger joint". This was better, A and W was on the route, and Arby's had the meat, but Capt'n Yoby's had the fish!

By Seventh grade the class hierarchy had become well established. At the top of the heap were Mark Minthorn and Marilyn Pepin (who later married and divorced), Kit Mullen (who graduated from Univ. of Washington), Bob Bordeaux (who stayed in Longview, married and worked at the mill), and Jan Karnoski (who graduated from college and ended up the owner of a sporting goods store). Pat Purcell and Rick O'Connell and a few other guys were in this group (I don't know what happened to them). There was also a group of girls that ranked up there, like Shirley Lessard and Veryl Perrot (both of whom married and stayed in the Twin Cities area). There was a new girl, Suzanne, who was very pretty (don't know what happened to her). Larry Lefebvre was popular, but he was kind of a bad boy, part "the Fonz" and part Johnny Zuko. He tended to hang out with Frank and Jerry off the St. Rose campus. Mike Momberg, Greg Firth, and I were still on the fringes socially. John Polis was still in the top group scholastically, but because he was short, his basketball prowess was not helping him stay at the top. By that time, playing the accordion was strictly square (John graduated from the Univ. of Washington, served a tour in the Navy, became a sports commentator, public relations person for the American Soccer team, and is now public relations spokesperson for an animal adoption program in Utah). There are others whom I have forgotten, but I am confident that they have all gone on to their own respective and respectable lives. I ran into a St. Rose classmate, Veryl Perrot, at a Foodland supermarket in Kauai, Hawaii (where I was living in the early 1990s). She recognized me right off; I was kind of embarrassed and finally showed my ignorance by guessing that she was Mary Ellen Garvey. I don't know whatever happened to Mary Ellen but her brother, John Garvey, was Gretchen's classmate in high school. Veryl was, of course, vacationing with her family in Kauai at the time. Now that was <u>pure</u> happenstance.

I think it was Sr. Virgil who proposed that we have a seventh grade barn dance. By then, I think she has a supporter amongst the clergy. Fr. Dooley had arrived on the St. Rose scene, and more of a Harold Hill[29] you might never find. That wily salesman passed himself off as a professor of music to sell the town of Gary, Indiana, band instruments for a marching band. My reason for comparing the priest to *The Music Man* will become clearer when I discuss our eighth grade escapades. But Fr. Dooley was definitely in support of a dance for the budding teenagers of St. Rose.

The dance was held at the farm of the aforementioned Swanson family, who had a large barn on Pacific Way. A great deal of preparation went into this dance, which was being touted as the Harbor Lights Ball. We built and painted a large image of a light house, and decorations included streamers, and balloons, and I seem to remember one of those spinning balls that reflect spots of light all over the room. There was no live band, but someone had a good record player and everyone had been practicing there steps to American Bandstand[30]; except me, of course. It was, in the immortal words of Yogi Berra, "*deja vu* all over again" for me. I did not dance, just as I had not danced at the summer dances that were held at Monticello Junior High the summer before. Those Saturday dances had a live local band that played the best music, like "Speedy Gonzalez," "Tequila" and the like. We shy boys were line up on one side of the gym floor while the shy girls were huddled at the other side, giggling amongst themselves. Gretchen was at those junior high dances, although I did not know her then; but she was actually out on the dance floor… always! She had the good fortune to be in a dance troupe, called the Junior Folklanders, which, if she ever was shy, hoofed it right out of her. I, on the other hand, dutifully trekked down to the dances that summer, and the Harbor Lights Ball, too, but I and my awkward friends spent the time gawking. Oh, how we so often limit our experiences in our youth; and spend the rest of our lives trying to make up for it!

I think the music was part of what was drawing me to the dances. I had been listening to records on my folks' stereo hi- fi, which they had bought soon after we moved to Longview. Before that I had been listening to old 78 records that I played on my dad's aged Brunswick wind-up portable record player. Strange recording like, "It's in the Book", and "Grandma's Lye Soap." There was also an Al Jolson recording of "Sonny Boy" ("There's a Rainbow 'round my Shoulder" was on the flip side). After we got the stereo player, we started collecting whatever 33 1/3 records we could afford, mostly purchased at the eighty-eight Cent Store for three dollars an album; several anthology type albums, things like *Songs of the Thirties*, and *Sousa's Greatest Hits*. We did score a Harry Belafonte album, with songs like "Day'o", "Matilda" and "There's Only One Like Me". Also, we were bringing home albums from the library; lots of show tunes and some classical albums. I really didn't start collecting 45s until I got to Seminary, and started playing in a band. But I liked listening to the band at the Junior High, and I was particularly interested in the drums. Strong beats were a very dominate part of the Rock and Roll of the time. I started pestering my parents for a set of drums. Granted they bought me bongos first; and that went well with Harry Belafonte, but I wanted real drums. So sometime between seventh and eighth grade my folks bought me a snare drum, a cymbal and a bass drum. It was not the full Monte, but my folks really were not in a position to do more. At first, I would not play in front of anyone, particularly not my classmates. But I practiced with the records and began to get the rhythms down.

I also was developing an interest in art. I was doing fairly well in Sr. Virgil's class. She was working on perspective and depth in landscape drawing. I was good at that, and I was particularly good at drawing sailing ships. I also tried my luck at drawing vehicles including dabbling in building plastic models, but I was not very good at that. I also watched a television series called John Gnegy's "Learn to Draw"[31]. I remember doing fairly well on the landscapes and the dog, but not very well on the human head. He was really pretty helpful, in that he taught you how to use charcoal, to blend it into shading, and to use it to outline the drawing before filling in the details. I probably should have kept up with drawing; I might have gotten pretty good at it. My daughter shows considerable talent in art, particularly human figures and portraiture. My son, like me, dabbled in drawing when he was young, but he too has let his life push aside such artistic pursuits. He is more inclined towards the literary arts, and I think he might have some very interesting tales to tell if he ever has the time to do it.

All of this behavioral transition corresponded with increasing responsibility at St. Rose. The advantage of an eight year elementary school is the fact that the upperclassmen begin to be given jobs and are expected to set examples for the younger children. Myself, I was in charge of some part of the safety patrol, helping the younger students cross the highway in front of the school. I was also chosen as movie projectionist... I guess because of my interest in science. I guess it was the beginning of my 'technical career'. There is a certain prowess that one attains when one can overcome the stoppage of the projector, and restore the vicarious world of the cinema. Changing reels was to be expected, but the shorter the interludes, the better you were liked. And if the projector stopped and the heat of the lamp began to burn the film; you could hear the audience gasp at the growing Rochette blot on screen.... until you, the projectionist, saved the film from utter destruction. Of course, we were mostly showing educational short films, but kids love the escape from the boredom of class, and consequently, they appreciate the skill of the projectionist. Later in life I saw the Italian movie "Cinema Paradiso," and it made me more aware of the power of the celluloid.

I was beginning to understand that acceptance is about usefulness. If you aren't useful, what good are ya? Even the class clown is useful... he/she makes people laugh. And that is useful. People need to laugh; in fact, we pay big bucks in this culture to people who have the ability to make us laugh. So I was beginning to understand that I needed to start building my skills. Projectionist was one simple skill. Perhaps music, in my case drums, could be helpful. And the paper route and the berry picking were beginning to pay dividends as well; particularly the paper route. Not only could I earn money, but I was getting in shape, slimming down, starting to think about physical prowess.

Of course, I had no previous experience to make me think of myself as being athletic, but I was developing some endurance. About the time I was going into eighth grade, a series of articles appeared in the Oregonian, complete with illustrations. A woman named Lilia had started a series called Lilia's Yoga[32]. Each week there would be one or two black and white photograph of Lilia in a Yoga posture with brief explanation. It didn't hurt that the woman was quite attractive (and still is after all these years). I began to take considerable interest, and actually started checking books on yoga out of the library. Back then, books on yoga were not full of lithe and graceful bodies, but rather hairy gurus with boney bodies and long beards. You know… the real thing! Had I never seen the photographs of Lilia, I am sure I would never have become interested. But I tried to do the poses, and I tried to absorb the diet… except the yogurt. I bought a quart of plain yogurt, but I never finished it. I did develop a strong liking for vegetables, and in my Peace Corps experience, a near craving for Indian food. We have one little restaurant in my current home town, that I feel personally responsible to keep in business. Akmal's closed once, and I was crestfallen. When they opened six months later in a more cost-effective location, I vowed to keep their vindaloo and raita (which is made with plain yogurt) as part of my weekly diet.

I regret that I did not keep up with the yoga after I got bogged down with the stresses and strains of life. But I will say that yoga served me well in my younger life, and probably has given me endurance that I would not have had without it. I think the meditation was particularly helpful in learning

LESTER FISHER

to focus my mind, such that when I need to, I can shut it down. I can still make my heart rate drop at the doctor's office just by focusing. Because I left yoga behind and have since developed osteoarthritis and gained too much weight, I don't believe I could take up yoga again. I did buy a video of yoga for old people... yeah, that's a laugh. If these people on the video are old, I must be a mummy. They do show some useful postures like the "old dog" and the "dead bug". Nevertheless, I know it is a powerful discipline for the mind and the body.

I don't remember very well the transition into the eighth grade.... But I remember very distinctly the transition to Sr. Anna Mary Brown, principal from 1959 to 1967. Now all the nuns were interesting women in their own right, but Sr. Anna Mary was probably the most engaging teacher I had up to that point in time. She was from northern Alberta, Canada; I think Peace River, although I am not sure. As I learned over my life, Canadians, and particularly the Canadians from the far North, are a unique breed. Josephine, whom I have mentioned in conjunction with my grandfather, was a similar personality to Sr. Anna Mary. There was nothing affected about them. You knew from the minute you met them that you were dealing with the real person, not some persona for their position in life. I want to call both of those women salty, but I don't mean in the vulgar sense. I mean like salt, that gives flavor to food, they gave flavor to life.

After Meritt died and Jo had finally come to the point where her family thought it necessary to put her in an adult care facility, Gretchen and I visited her about the time that we were preparing to marry. The staff of the facility was convinced that Jo was mentally missing. Although it was true that she was not able to form her words. I was not convinced she was that out of it. Nevertheless, even I was surprised what happened next. Gretchen told Jo that we were going to get married. Jo, with a distinct twinkle in her eye, said directly to Gretchen, as clear as can be, "Are you sure you know what you're doing?" We had a good laugh about that one, and my suspicions were confirmed that Jo's family was not paying close enough attention to her, or they would know that the lights were still on under that shock of snowy white hair.

Sr. Anna Mary could get that twinkle in her eye as well. I think it is that moment when the individual is mentally stepping back from the situation at hand in order to assess. Then that realization of the comical irony of life hits them and they begin to formulate their humorous response. Sr. Anna Mary's favorite expression was, "T'ink!" She wasn't addressing Tinker Bell; she was trying to get her student's attention. If you "t'ink" about it, it is a much more effective exhortation than "Think!" The digraph 'Th' softens the impact; the 'T' sound is much stronger. If 't'ink' is a colloquial expression for 'think' I am sure Sr. Anna Mary was purposeful in retaining the colloquialism. And I have never forgotten it; because that is the impact it had, it made you, well, think! Not just regurgitate, but think about for what it is you were studying; you future, for one thing. She made it apparent that learning a little algebra, however odious, might be a useful thing in future.

We have discussed how difficult seventh graders could be, but the juvenile brain does not advance greatly in one year. Plus, eighth graders in an eight-year elementary school get cocky. They begin to believe that they are "all that". Sr. Anna Mary was very effective in dispelling that notion. She was a short woman, not at all regal like her predecessor, Sr. Margaret. Nevertheless, she was not above collaring some of the rowdy lads, albeit some of them were strapping tall by then. I was 5 ft. 11 inch, and I think Larry Lefebvre was probably already 6 ft. I don't think Sr. Anna Mary ever grabbed an eight-grader by the ear, but she didn't have to… she already had your attention!

Oddly enough, this woman from Peace River (which is really out in the sticks) liked baseball, so at World Series time, first the radio and then the television came into the classroom. At that time, it was quite technologically progressive of Sr. Anna Mary. I think we were able to get two hours of class in before the broadcast began. I guess she figured it was part of our education. In fact, she relied heavily on the available technology to get information over to us. She was an advocate of the Bell Laboratory series of television program on science: "Our Mr. Sun"[33], "Hemo the Magnificent", "The Strange Case of the Cosmic Rays" etc. These were 'assigned viewing'; which was a new concept in education. We would watch them on Sunday or Saturday night, and were required to write a report on each program. Such forward thinking uses of the newly ubiquitous media of television was a powerful eye opener for our young minds. When I was studying plant physiology at UC Davis the scientists had just figured out the photosynthetic pathway... only to discover that there were actually two, C3 and C4. I remember thinking of the image of the little chef "Photosynthesis" going behind his secret curtain to produce sugar from sunlight and air. It was all very mysterious back then. Now there are at least five identified photosynthetic pathways[34] and those are only the light induced pathways for producing carbohydrates from carbon dioxide. We didn't even know there was a whole world of animals at the bottom of the sea that get their energy from the sulfur spewing from the black smokers.[35] But I would probably never have entered this world of science without the inspiration of people like Sr. Anna Mary and Frank Capra's intelligent and engaging approach to science.

While I had a great interest in science in eighth grade, outside influences were affecting my future. Between Fr. Mulligan, Fr. Dooley, and the nuns, there was a lot of effort to interest us in the "sacred professions." I think it might have been Rick O'Connell's mother that got the word out that St. Francis Seminary in Troutdale, Oregon, was having an open house. I don't know what her connection would have been, unless she was hoping to get Rick on the seminary track (like most Catholic mothers with a lot of kids, at least one was expected to become a priest or nun). They had the same kind of open house for the Diocesan Seminary in Kent, and I vaguely remember seeing the campus, but I don't know if it was on an open house excursion. I can tell you quite frankly, that diocesan seminary did not interest me in the slightest. It was a big stone affair, something like Hogwarts in the Harry Potter series.

In contrast, the Franciscan seminary was on an old dairy farm. It had an attractive Spanish style house that served as the staff quarters, the refectory, and classrooms for the upper classes. The student dormitory was a converted milking barn. Cleverly, when the Franciscans modified it, they put heat tubing in the poop gutters[36] and cemented the whole thing over. It was a great idea, because it was by far the more comfortable building. When you put your bare feet on the floor in the morning, the floor was warm. But I am jumping ahead of myself here. So I will stick to the description of seminary visitation days.

A visit to St. Francis was arranged, and probably two carloads of eighth graders from St. Rose went to the open house. The student body was still small (thirty-five students in 1959), and everyone seemed quite friendly... not at all intimidating like the Diocesan seminary. Herb Karnofski, Brian LeTourneau, and Rick O'Connell were there for sure, but I think Jan, John, Pat Purcell and other notables were with us. We were served a nice lunch and ball games were played... I believe it was in the spring and probably the game was baseball. There was also a recreation room in the barn next to the old milking barn. There was a pool table and an old upright piano where freshman Charlie Biegler and Fr. Mario Cimmarusti were dueling. Both were phenomenal. Charlie would play a song that Fr. Mario did not know, and then Fr. Mario would play it. He would then do the same thing to Charlie, who would sit down and play music he had never heard before. Charlie later went on to be a professional musician. I liked all this; priest playing music with students, free and easy interaction, friendly sports competition, and an idyllic pastoral campus. There was also a big new building under construction, so there would be plenty of room to take in the thirty three students that would become my freshman class.

But before that would be possible, I had to pass eighth grade, and my folks would have to figure out how they were going to come up with the tuition. Of course, they had been paying tuition at the St. Rose, but the quarterly tuition for St. Francis was $400 and that was an entire month's paycheck for my dad. This was not going to be easy. Plus, the pressure was on to raise the money for that big new church at St. Rose. Also, my folks would have to apply for my admission, and we did not know how strict their criteria were for taking students.

Fr. Dooley was in full stride by this time and the success of the barn dance had given him an idea of how to raise some money for the church. About January he had proposed that the eighth grade put on a school play, actually more of a musical. He apparently had previously had some experience at this sort of thing, and before you know it he had a script. It was based around the song "Molly Malone" but borrowed music heavily from *My Fair Lady*, and perhaps some other musicals which I cannot remember. By the time he had started tryouts; my voice had stopped cracking, and actually was settling in to the lower ranges. For that reason, I think, I was chosen for the vocal ensemble, and that also involved being part of the crowd, on stage. I can't remember if the part involved any dancing, but I guess you could call it acting…sort of, but without any lines. Of course, all the best looking and smartest kids were chosen for the lead parts.

At first the practices were more like choir practice. Actually, in retrospect, I think I must have been in the church choir as well, because I remember being in the old church's choir loft. Maybe I am imagining that; maybe we just sat in the choir loft when there were overflow crowds at Sunday mass. I think the old church had been dismantled by the time Fr. Dooley was organizing the play. We practiced in the school gym/church/meeting hall/theater. I was rather enjoying it. Fr. Dooley was very upbeat and could engender interest in the group; and we started to sound pretty good. When we moved to onstage rehearsals, it was a bit more awkward. We had to interact with the girls during scenes, and chit chat during the lulls. I won't say I was any good at it, but some of the guys were more than skilled. I mean Fr. Dooley had to keep an eye out for some of the pairs because there were curtains to hide behind. Finally we made it through, no one got pregnant, and the big performance was on the horizon.

I won't say I have any clear memory of the performance or even if we performed it more than once. I will say that I think "we broke a leg". I think the audience liked Fr. Dooley's production very well, and we all got plenty of applause. I say that was my introduction to the theater, but I forgot my big début in, I believe, second grade. I can't remember if I was the toothbrush or the washcloth, but I can remember our big line was a Ben Franklin quote: "early to bed and early to rise, makes a man healthy, wealthy and wise." I think that was as deeply imbedded in my psyche as the image of the cavity army attacking the Tooth Castle. Although the shiny tooth paste men came to the rescue, I had nightmares about it for weeks. I wonder if Pepsodent (or whichever company produced that short film) realized what impact it would have on a young child. Even the Claymation film *The Munchers*[37] was not nearly as scary, although, typical, Claymation films were very accurate.

So, my acting career up to eight grade was definitely limited. I guess you really can't include things like home movies and church events, like first communion. Speaking of church ceremonies, the next one in line at the St. Rose was Confirmation. Of course, unless you are not Catholic, in a Catholic school, Confirmation is practically mandatory. Mark Minthorn was not "of the faith" so he skated out of the affair, but the rest of us went *en masse* to have the bishop smite us with his miter. All very ceremonial, of course, but we did have to take a pledge not to let the dreaded fruit of the vine (or the barley brew) cross our lips before our 21st birthday. I cannot say how many of my classmate fulfilled that pledge, but I did. I'm not bragging; I was living under a major threat. My mother said that if I was to drink or smoke, I was to do it right at home in front of her. I mean, talk about a game stopper! Of course, it didn't hurt that I went right in to seminary the next year. Inebriating beverages were not encouraged among the troops… but that is another story, "truth or consequences" that I hope I don't forget to tell.

And then, lest I forget the most important ceremony of my young life, I graduated from eighth grade. We had another senior dance before day of the grand event. Believe it or not, I actually danced with a girl. Actually I danced with more than one, but it was a whirlwind in my mind… which apparently had erased all memory. All I can remember is the wide skirts with petticoats that were in style at the time. Lest you be misled to think I had become a bon vivant… let me dispel that notion. I think the dances were two and the conversations were very limited.

I did feel fairly well dressed at my graduation. As I remember it, my blazer looked very much like the one Mark Minthorn was wearing (although I am sure his was much more expensive). And I was no longer the pudgy kid. Although I certainly did not think of myself as attractive with my facial scar, weak chin and crooked teeth, if I kept my mouth shut, I cut a clean line. Like all graduates in history, I had a certain feeling of pride. At once, you have certain camaraderie with the class of which you never really felt a part, and at the same time a nostalgia that this tribe of our youth was disbanding.

Before the fateful day, I had started to become a little more emboldened in my personality. I was hanging out more with Mike Momberg and less with Herb Karnofski. Mike's mother was very nice, but his father was a Panzer. Literally, he had been in the battle of the budge in the German tank corps that caused the bulge. He was captured and sent to an internment camp in the USA. By the time I met him, he was a naturalized citizen, I think. Ironically, my dad and Mike's father discussed the war at an open house or something. We were not privy to the conversation, but as I said before, my dad did not talk about the war to us.

On one occasion, I was feeling rather vain about my newly developed prowess on the bongos, and Mike Momberg wanted to go downtown, ostensibly to check out the chicks (although that part was a total flop!). So we dressed up in what we believed to be "beatnik" garb. Jeans, T-shirts (mine had more of a split neck and, across it, broad black and green stripes, white deck shoes, and I was carrying my bongo drums. We had both applied some black coloring to our face to simulate beards. I don't know what we used, but in retrospect, it looked incredibly stupid. So we went to town this way, snapping the finger on one hand, and doing the hipster walk. I am sure most of the people that saw us, thought we were "nutz", but some people were amused and some people kind of played along with expressions like "Cool daddio" and "Dig the beat". I don't think I had ever even heard a really beatnik rap or cool jazz composition. I think the inspiration for all this was actually Maynard G. Krebbs of the "Dobie Gillis" show. Which reminds me, how come they never show "Dobie Gillis" reruns? Those were critically formative programs from the late '50s. As Gretchen, who knew Mike Momberg in high school, put it; "If I had seen you two coming I would have run the other way.... screaming!" She did confirm that Mike was "too cool" in high school. I guess I can blame part of this aberrant behavior on Fr. Dooley, since the musical had put us in a "thespian mode".

At the epitome of new found boldness, I asked my parents if I could put on a party for the eighth grade class. They agreed, and the party actually materialized. The whole class did not attend (which is a good thing, since the house was not that large), but I was surprised and impressed at who did come: Kit Mullen, for whom I secretly had a "thing", Marilyn Pepin (who was a close friend of Kit), Bob Bordeaux, Jan Karnoski and Herb Karnofski. I am not sure if Mike Momberg came. Maybe Brian LeTourneau came. I can't really remember who all came, but it was a big deal! I do remember that. I even played my drums a little, but that did not attract much attention. What did attract attention was Bob Bordeaux doing the titty grab on me... at my own party in front of all the cool girls for god's sake! That humiliation was what I remember most about the one and only party that I ever threw in grade school.

CHAPTER 8

The Franciscan

9 is it too small a thing for you that the God of
Israel has separated you from the congregation
of Israel, to bring you near to himself, to do
service in the tabernacle of the LORD and to
stand before the congregation to minister to
them, 10 and that he has brought you near him,
and all your brothers the sons of Levi with you?
**English Standard Version (©2001) Numbers
16:9-10**

I DON'T REMEMBER WHAT I did the summer before I went to
the Seminary. I do remember that we had a party at Millersylvania Park
either right after graduation or soon thereafter. The weather was gorgeous.
Millersylvania Park is south of Olympia, Washington, on Interstate 5. It is a
lovely clear lake surrounded by groves of evergreen trees where the camping
areas and picnic tables are, and there is also a boat dock where one can rent
prams and canoes for the day. And that is what we did, practically all day
long, except when food was being served. I remember getting nasty sunburn
out there lounging on the boat. Again, if there were much interaction with
the girls, I was not privy to it. After all, I was contemplating the priesthood,
you know? Still, I don't mind saying the girls looked pretty attractive in their
swimsuits instead of their school uniforms. Of course, there were not any
yellow polka-dot bikinis among good Catholic girls. But the song would
have been out there on the radio, and the culture was definitely changing.

I don't even remember if I had a boat to myself, or whether I rented
it with other guys. Probably the latter, but my memory of it is like a

soliloquy... just me and the lake. I am sure that was not true, but oddly, that is all I can remember. I have always enjoyed rowing, and this was the perfect opportunity to hone my skill at it. I had my first experience of rowing on that outing at Oyster Bay when I was at Camp Blanchet. Maybe the other guys in the boat decided to hang out with the fairer sex, and abandoned me to my nautical pursuits. I was just happy not to have to be embarrassed about being fat, but able to show my "finely tuned body" in a swim suit (yeah, that's a laugh, or at least that is what I thought at the time). It did feel good to be able to power those legs (made strong by bike riding and the arms made strong by toting newspapers), to propel the small boat through the water with as much force as I could muster. Ironic that here I was staying clear of the girls because I was preparing for the priesthood, but in later years I would take my 6 kids to Millersylvania Lake to experience boating.

This is becoming kind of a free-association trip down faded memory lane. Speaking of the yellow polka-dot bikini, it reminds me that we must have gone to Collier Park in Oregon that summer for the Shevlin-Hixon Reunion. It was being held in Collier Park instead of Bend, because so many of the former residence of the camp had moved south when the company closed. The reason I remember that is because Vernie, who was two years older than Ralph and I, was all agog about the "Yellow Polka-dot Bikini" that Brian Hyland had brought to the airways that summer. Transistor radios were starting to appear everywhere, and every time it would come onto the radio at the picnic, Vernie would stop dead in his tracks to listen. The Smiths, at that time, were living in the Bay Area (Hayward to be exact), and they were therefore very hip kids. Vernie was a bit of a muscle nut, pumping iron, and building his prowess with the ladies, ducktail hairdo, "Blue Suede Shoes" and all. Ralph, on the other hand, was building his reputation as a sportsman, particularly a baseball player. He was also not shy around the ladies. He had done very well at little league, and was a favored candidate for the teams at Hayward

High when he enrolled. I remember I was very impressed, dismayed, and dumbfounded how different they were after moving back to the cosmopolitan life of the San Francisco Bay.

I don't remember much else about the picnic, although I do have memories of the unique group of people that were the former employees of Shevlin-Hixon. I have previously described what I could remember of those people. I do remember that it was a reassuring feeling to know that the cradle of my mother's youth still existed in these people, and they welcomed us as old friends would.

I am not sure if I went back to Hayward with Mary and Vernon and their sons that summer, but at some point I stayed with them in Hayward. At that time they lived on a steep hill, and I remember we would hang out on the curb of a summer's evening with the other girls and guys in Ralph's neighborhood. This was a peculiar experience for me, because, whereas in McCloud we had been like an extended family, I realized that my world and their world were entirely different now.

What else I did that summer, I cannot remember. It became a very busy time preparing for my departure. There was a long list of requirements. I think I had to have some teeth work done. All of the clothing I took had to be tagged, and there was a specific list of what had to be available to me for the school year. All much regimented, but my parents were very dutiful about providing me with what I needed.

As it turned out, I was not the only St. Rose student who went to St. Francis Seminary that fall. Herb Karnofski (who had been a good friend), and Brian LeTourneau were also enrolled. I seem to remember that Rick O'Connell may have enrolled, but dropped out quickly, either before school started or soon after. Thus, I was not alone in this entirely new environment, but it was just that, an entirely other world. We were given sophomore guides to get us oriented, and our parents were able to join us in the milking barn as we unloaded our gear and took the first lay of the land. But departure time was at the evening refectory bell, and we all entered what had been the living room and dining room of the old farm house, to partake of our first meal.

Original farm house and first classroom, refectory, kitchen, laundry and staff quarters of St. Francis Seminary. (Photo provided courtesy of Richard Hopp.)

I forget how we were assigned to tables, but each table had 6 students and a table head, who was an upper classman. I think this was the first year that there were actually four separate classes. The seniors were a short haired, 1950s breed of young men. They had been born the year before WWII ended. Sterner stuff than we were used to in St. Rose. Joe Biegler, from Spokane Washington, tough captain of the Spartans, skier, cool, collected, slow to speak, but everyone hung on his every word, which is why he was senior class president for the first 3 quarters. Vince Richey, also of St. Pascal's Parish in Spokane, elegant, aloof, captain of the Trojans and the Skibrüders, wrestled the senior class presidency away from Joe in the last semester. Richardson, McNicholas and Miller were the three seniors who were least memorable to me, although all of them had performed well in their own right as sportsmen, actors, scholastics and artists. Within a class of six, every man has a chance to excel at something. But the very names of the intramural sports teams belie the mindset, Spartans and Trojan.

The last member of the senior class of 1960-61 was the most memorable of all. His yearbook testimonial says it all:

> Bruce Timothy McDaniels, Sacred Heart Parish, Winlock Washington, has filled our years at the seminary with laughter and happiness. His fun-loving manner and good nature have helped us all look at the brighter side – especially when the winter cloud cover refused to lift. He was elected senior class secretary and in the same year was named first Third-Order prefect. His deep base

voice enriched our choir all the years that he was here. He worked on *The Franciscan* in his sophomore year and *Troubadour* his senior year, He was a member of the gun club for two years. A trick knee, acquired in his junior year, sidelined Tim for most sports; nevertheless he continued to be an ardent fan. *Troubador1960-61 St. Francis Seminary Yearbook*

I don't know who wrote that description of him, but it was spot on. Tim was the only senior that signed my yearbook, and he was a hell of a nice guy. During our initiation, Tim was the most merciful with his freshmen slaves, and I conspired with Herb and others to buy Tim during Senior Slave Day (a fund raiser for the Third Order). Jumping ahead, our class was merciless on the freshmen who followed us, and some were pretty brutal with their senior slaves. But how could we be tough on our slave, ol' Tim... at one point he begged us to give him a hard assignment because he thought he would look wimpy amongst his peers.

Back to the moment of the first day at St. Francis, we were sitting at our tables, knowing nothing of what goes on in a seminary. As we stood for the blessing, we wondered what to expect of our respective table heads. The seniors that year were all respectable and respectful guys. They were strict but they were fair. The juniors, on the other hand, had a few deviant apples in the barrel. McCay, Greenfield and McCollum were decent guys, but Valentine, Stiley and Straub all had mean streaks. They knew they would soon be top dogs, and they were out to assert their authority. This became apparent almost immediately in their positions as table heads. In fact, it is ironic how different the class of 1962 was from 1961. Those juniors were the first post war babies, and I always wondered if the stresses of post-war America gave rise to a different psyche than the stoic generations of the war years. Of course, some of their parents, like mine, had been in WWII, but things were changing rapidly in 1946 and 1947. Perhaps that influenced the temperament of all of us in those postwar generations.

After the blessing, the rules of the table were laid down with various "interpretations" depending on the table head. Each serving bowl was passed around the table after the table head had taken his share. Most table heads were wary of hoggishness in the underclassmen, and would call out anyone that was taking an inordinate portion of any dish. Some table heads were particularly cagey and would restrict each student to one spoonful per dish. If the food item were plentiful, he might pass the bowl around again for a second spoonful. If not, he would take the remainder of the bowl for himself. This was most likely to happen with desserts.

Other items of table etiquette were also being closely observed by the table heads. Boisterousness, goofiness, boorishness, and bravado were all frowned upon. I didn't say they were suppressed completely -- after all, this was high school – but the behaviors were subject to punishment if not curtailed. I learned very early on in my seminary career that almost every infraction of the rules supplied the labor that ran the well-oiled institution. Meaning, dish shift was highest on the list of approved punishments. The table head had only to report said behaviors to Fr. Claude to effect one's banishment from free time and serving on dish shift. Normally dish shift rotated from student to student, but the unrestrained among us provided delivery from dish shift for those more disciplined. Later in my freshman year, a comical incident occurred when Tim Daniels was my table head. He had involved us in a conspiracy to contrive a demonstration of his magical powers. He would wave his hands over the table only to have it mysteriously rise from the floor. Just as this impressive feat of psychokinesis had reached its apex, Fr. Claude appeared around the corner of the refectory. The table dropped to the ground with a loud crash; which piqued the curiosity of Fr. Claude who approached the table with a disapproving frown. Tim, recovering his composure, said "I want to report all of these clowns for dish shift."

After the first repast, what would become an all-too-familiar ritual began: soliloquies of the Dean of Discipline. Fr. Claude would take his position at the passageway between the two halves of the dining area. I believe there was a bell on the wall. The square-jawed, bespectacled father would straighten his cord, and then his cowl (grabbing the front of the bib in one hand and the tail of the cowl in the other hand to adjust it) and then he would clang the bell once. After the first night, silence would normally occur instantaneously, but on this our first night, we had to be suppressed by the upperclassmen. Fr. Claude would then proceed with a sometimes long, seldom short, always tedious list of announcements for the day. On this evening he needed to inform us neophytes of the rules of behavior in the free period after the meal. For example, how we were to occupy ourselves during the evening study hall, writing thank you letters to our parents (who had just left). The Dean stressed the necessity of being present at vespers at the precise hour of 9 PM, and the necessity of silence from vespers until after morning mass and breakfast. He also went into detail about the direct route we were to take to the dormitory; also the limited amount of time we were allowed to perform the evening ablutions before lights out at precisely 9:30 PM. He also made it perfectly clear that any recalcitrant who dared delay lights out or stirred after lights out (for any reason other than gastrointestinal distress), would spend his daylight free time at the industrial sink in the refectory. And so began my life at St. Francis Seminary.

I may be imagining some of the details of these first days at the seminary, but the routine I describe in the previous paragraph was, for all intent and purpose, immutable. Morning in the cow barn came with the truly startling blare of a fire alarm. It was a fire alarm, but there was no fire. Probably just as well that the alarm could practically shake you out of bed, because as the days wore on, waking up became harder and harder. At least the floor was warm (which was not the case when we moved to the new building the next year). On that first day, there was not a mad rush to the toilet and the sink. But later on, it became almost a contest. Who would be first in line, first dressed, first out the door? One fellow was particularly irritating about this habit. Richard Hopp greatly prided himself in being "ahead of the curve" (which he became in later life, as a lawyer). He was a tall lad with very big feet, and his slippers slapped against the floor with every step. This became an odious sound to us, the somnambulant, in the sonorous cavern of the new structure. There was no time to shower or make your bed before Mass. So with teeth brushed, face washed and hair combed, we hiked the 100 yards up to the chapel.

The chapel was in the new building right next to the classrooms. The building with its many windows and all concrete structure was not easily heated in the morning. So weekday Mass was a coat affair; ties were optional, except on Sunday. Who had time to tie a tie on a weekday?

Just out of curiosity, I Googled the old seminary, which is now the Springdale Job Corps Center named Dragon; all of the original buildings are still in place, although other buildings and parking lots have been added. I recognized the cross-shaped profile of the main building that was under construction when we arrived that fall. Even the old farm house and all the barns and milking shed are still standing. I guess the Job Corps never had money for a complete redo, thought they built a new dormatory. The trees are much bigger now; the tree in front of the milking barn door completely covers the attached building that had probably been converted from the milk processing room of the dairy. This building housed the Franciscan brothers and a couple of the priests.

There was a red-leafed tree (I don't know the species) that had been left in front of the classroom entrance at the end of the cross-shaped building. That tree is now enormous. It grows over the top of the two story building and is still completely red leafed.

Cross-shaped building that provided dormitories, classrooms, a chapel and gymnasium for St. Francis Seminary starting in the fall of 1961. The tree to the left, was not as tall as the building that year; now it towers over the structure. (Photo provided courtesy of Richard Hopp.)

The whole Seminary was on a cliff overlooking a large bend in the Sandy River. The freshmen class the year before we came had lost a student

175

over that cliff. His name was Loren Thomas Phelps, and his death had been a somber event in the short history of the school. It was perhaps a portent of "the glory that was Camelot". While it was a time of growth, expansion, high hopes and great successes, it was all too short lived, and ours was the second to the last class that St. Francis Seminary graduated before it was sold by the Franciscan Friars to the Job Corps. I just hope their trainees had as many good times as we did on that hallowed campus.

When Mass was over on the first day, we trekked the short distance over to the refectory, and partook of our first breakfast in silence. Of course, the natural instinct in a new situation with a lot of new classmates would have been to, as we say in Hawaii, "talk story". Instead, in the ineffable wisdom of the Pius the Tenth, he decreed that seminary life would oppose the secularization of the aspirant to the priesthood, and enforce certain rigid disciplines that would purify the mind and heart (loosely paraphrased from his encyclical *E Supremi*). This included maintaining silence until after breakfast. Then what are you going to do with a bunch of restless teenagers when they cannot talk. Well, naturally, you read to them. So every breakfast except Sunday, if I remember rightly, we were read to during breakfast. How that promoted spiritual growth I am not sure, because the books I remember were not particularly profound or spiritual. The only one I can remember by name was *The Loved One* by Evelyn Waugh. I think I remember it because of the sheer ironic nature of the upscale Angelinos compared to our more pragmatic Northwestern roots. I swear, I cannot remember what other "great books' were read to us to fill our furtive minds; not even the chapters that I was assigned to read in my senior year. Because that is how it was done; the upperclassmen were assigned to read. I seem to remember one other book that was read in refectory, Herman Melville's *Moby Dick*. You would think the "audio books" would have made more of an impression on our young minds. I suspect at some point we were read Ugolino Brunforte's *The Little Flowers of St. Francis*. Perhaps the intention was to instill literature subliminally.

After breakfast, Fr. Claude would perform his ritual, and assign the dish shift crews, work crews, announce scheduled events and dismiss us for a brief moment of "freedom". During the time after breakfast and before class, we were expected to make our beds, prepare any materials for class, and/or speak. As we soon discovered, laundry was to be in the basket before Wednesday. The bottom sheet was to be removed each week, and another placed. This was complicated for teenagers, because it means you had to live with one week-old sheet all the time. That wouldn't be a problem for me now, but we were growing boys… in the complete absence of girls, even seminarians have wet dreams, and it was embarrassing as hell! Since the laundry only came back once a week, if you didn't have enough changes of pajamas and close, you were screwed. We were beginning to learn the meaning of regimentation.

I have mentioned some of the priest and Brother Conrad in previous chapters: but until we started having classes, we did not have many interactions with the faculty. Oh, one of the young priests in the rectory by the milk barn would come in to turn the lights out at night. The first year that would have been Fr. Alberic Smith. Now a better likeness of Ichabod Crane you could not find. He was a slender man with a large Adam's apple and large ears. He wore wire rim spectacles, and because of his jet black hair, in spite of being closely shaven all the time, he still looked like he had 4 o'clock shadow. He was a nice enough fellow, but he was a new teacher and not exceptionally interesting. Of course, it didn't help that he was saddled with all the math and science classes. He taught freshman algebra, but he also taught Franciscan History, which actually <u>was</u> interesting.

Now, probably the most dynamic teacher that year was Fr. Mario Cimmarusti. We had religion class with Fr. Mario, and a more detailed, dare I say earthy, presentation of the life of Christ I have never seen since. We relied pretty heavily on the Gospel of Luke because, having been a physician, Luke went into important physical details about Christ's passion. For example, Luke mentions that blood and water came out of Jesus' chest when he was lanced by the Roman soldier in order to finish him off before the Sabbath sunrise. Well, there was a whole class just on that subject. It turns out the water was actually pericardial fluid that had been induced by the stress of the torture and crucifixion. The reason why Christ did not die sooner, and needed to be terminated, is that crucifixion is a very slow and painful death caused, in the end, by asphyxia. It was not the bleeding hands and wrists (although we went into great detail on the positioning of the nails) that would have killed Jesus, but rather fatigue. The basis of crucifixion is that the position makes it impossible to breathe unless one can lift one's torso with the legs.

I am going to digress here, to the time of writing, and make a political statement. You, the reader, should know that I may do this from time to time to illustrated the ironic and haphazard nature of my current world. My reaction to these events will reflect the impact that my upbringing has had on my interpretation of these events. The first example follows.

I was so flabbergasted at the news media when they were describing the "accidental death" of detainees in Iraq:

> Abdel Jabbar al-Kubaisi, a onetime opposition figure who rallied to Saddam's regime shortly before the 2003 invasion, said that during his 16 months in custody, three former Saddam officials had died under questioning, although he had not faced physical torture…
>
> He named the three detainees he said had died under interrogation as former prime minister Hamzeh al-Zubaidi, former Baath party official Adel al-Duri, and former intelligence commander Waddah al-Sheikh. http://www.democraticunderground.com/discuss/duboard.php?az=view_all&address=102x2010721

Throughout the months that this was discussed and pandered in the media, no one ever mentioned that the position in which the detainees were held constituted crucifixion. They were tied to the bars of a window with their arms stretched above and behind their backs. That is crucifixion; all that would be required to kill them was that they be fatigued to the point that they could no longer raise their bodies up to breathe. I know that water boarding was the suspected cause of their deaths, but can you imagine what hue and cry would come forth from the Muslim community if anyone had ever suspected that the Americans were literally crucifying Iraqis? Hell, I learned that when I was 15… in Fr. Mario's class.

Mario's class was fun. He would get so excited about his teaching that he would sometimes swing between two desks. Now that is a site to see; a friar minor swinging back and forth like a big brown bell. And when he was ready to "get into it' on the black board, he would shove the sleeves of his habit up to his shoulders to expose his arms covered with black hair. It looked like he was about to have a fight with the figure in his imagination. He also had a nervous habit of twirling his cincture cord with the three large knots like a beat cop twirling his baton. I don't think he every hit anyone with his cord, but I cannot swear to that. I do remember him rapping the cincture on students' desks when he wanted to make a point.

The details of the life of Christ that we studied were in keeping with the trend toward demythologizing the Bible. What he was trying to do was give us a very real understanding of the times, the brutality, the unlikelihood that such a religion could survive in a Romano centric world. It was by far the least "religious" religion class I ever took. What it proved to be was good fact-centered history of a pivotal juncture for mankind. Ironically, it was the *Pax Romana* that made it possible for Christianity to spread throughout the Mediterranean.

Fr. Mario also taught us English, and he was the choir director for the Seminary. He never emphasized public performances, although we did do a Christmas concert for the families and he would direct the choir for Open House and other ceremonies for the public at opportune times. He was very good at Gregorian chant, which in our freshmen year was the bulk of our liturgical music. This was before the Vatican Council that was convened by Pope John XXIII between 1962 and 1965. Fr. Mario brought me into the choir in the winter quarter of 1961, and I am grateful, because I greatly enjoyed Gregorian chant.

We were branching out into modern liturgical music like that of Carl Neilson's "Peace Prayer of St. Francis", but the bulk of the liturgy was in Latin and the music was Chant. We had not yet started bringing folk singing to the sanctuary, or adopting good old Protestant standards like "Onward, Christian Soldiers". I think the blend of male voices in the pure sounds of the Chant is still a moving experience, and it is perhaps why, in spite of everything from polyphony to atonality, Gregorian chant is still performed and enjoyed. Every evening, at the final prayer, we would sing *"Tota Pulcra es O Maria, et macula originalis non est in te"* (fourth century antiphon for the feast of the Immaculate Conception). I am quite sorry that I have lost my little Gregorian chant book, but I certainly have not forgotten it all. I can still sing an ominous chorus of *Dies Irae, dies Illa, solvet secum in favela*! In recent years I was attending a Christmas party for Gretchen's law firm and they were doing the Hawaiian version of" The Twelve Days of Christmas". Each person had been assigned one of the verses, and when I belted mine out in a deeply resounding Gregorian tone, everyone was startled. Then a chuckle went 'round the room as the tension subsided. Who knew?

Fr. Kevin was our Latin teacher for all three years. *Puer et puella ambulant in silvia.* I have mentioned the character of this man, but I have not described the teacher. He was quite serious and at the same time very matter of fact about the subject. It was a subject we had to learn and we better get to it! Having never been exposed to any language but English, this was a challenge, not only for me, but for most of us. At least the sound was familiar because most of us had been altar boys. Fr. Kevin's teaching method was strictly traditional, heavy on the rote memorization and grammar. I suppose this method has its supporters to this day, but it is a good way of assuring that a language, that is already dead, stays that way. The very act of translating each word, one by one, insures that the mental circuitry that develops will be more of a dictionary than a language experience. I learned this in Peace Corps training after 6 years of Latin, 4 years of Spanish and one year of Greek, I can read, write or understand none of these languages as well as I can Kiswahili. After only one month of high intensity language training (HILT) I could converse. What does HILT mean? It means the teacher talks to you in the language you want to learn... just as if you were in a foreign country. You have reference books, and it is helpful if the teacher is good at pantomime, but basically you learn by ear and by actions. Fr. Mel tried to have us do "conversational" Latin when we were sophomores, resorting to things like cross-word puzzles and various other games. Unfortunately, we had already been hard wired, and he faced an uphill battle to tear us away from out English-Latin mental dictionaries, whether mental or in print. But I will cover this subject more when I get to Fr. Claude.

Fr. Kevin had the thankless task of bringing us from infant babble to adult speech in Latin in one year. I would say he was successful. By the end of the year we could put together a complete Latin sentence and translate too... usually with a dictionary at hand. At least we understood the archaic structure of the language: the declension, the conjugations, the word order, the genders, the importance of making the gender of nouns correspond with the adjectives, etc. I thought it was all quite complicated until we moved to Greek, and then, in Peace Corps, I learned Kiswahili, where the whole sentence has to match the alliterative structure of the subject (e.g. *Kijiko kikubwa kinatumiwa kwa kula chakula.* tran. A big spoon is used to eat food.). You could carry that image to the first year Latin. It was like spoon feeding us with a ladle. Of course, it didn't hurt that we had Latin class six days per week. What none of us realized at the time was how important Latin would be to our understanding of other languages, our religion, and the structure of our civilization in general. Fr. Kevin held the keys. He also was a paragon of virtue and the focal point of the seminary's survival.

At the time we started class, Fr. Claude was one of three language instructors, but we did not have him for class in the freshman year. His duties, besides riding herd on the whole rowdy bunch, were instruction of the upper classmen. He taught Greek and Spanish. He was actually fluent in Spanish, as also was Fr. Mario who taught sophomore Spanish. Fr. Claude 'taught' outside of the classroom. He also often supervised study halls, which during the week were silent, but on the weekend, when we were supposed to be writing our weekly letters to our parents, he was also disk jockey. This was music that he approved and it was piped into all of the classrooms. I know all of the western songs by heart: "Tumbling Tumbleweed", "Don't Fence Me In", "Cool Water", "Yellow Rose of Texas"... I think you get the drift. I never realized until recently that Fr. Claude might have been from Northern California (there are some cowpokes up thar!) because he had a brother in Redding and a sister in Yreka. I do know that he was a tough character in the seminary. He was probably chosen for Dean of Discipline because there was nothing an itty bitty seminarian could do that he had not already done in his day. He would come in and out of the classroom during study hour. He would sit at the desk and read or work on paper work, but it would appear that he was being constantly called away. In fact, on many occasions, he was using that ploy to spy on us. Although the classrooms were lighted by large wall to wall windows in the daytime, at night the reflection from the ceiling lights would conceal any activity outside the classroom. It took us a long time to realize that he would just stand outside the classroom and take notes like a detective behind the one-way mirror at the lineup room. Then, at the appropriate (most compromising) moment, he would enter the classroom and call students to stand out for sleeping or talking or just acting "nutz". Standing out was meant literally... sometimes for the whole 2 hour study hall. At first there might be 10 or more standing at the blackboard; later only the most recalcitrant suffered the ignominy. I admit, I was a slow learner.

By the middle of that year Fr. Christian Mondor had arrived from Junipero Serra High School in Salem...and the seminary would never be the same again! Gretchen likes to call him the Casting Director's idea of a priest. He had entered the seminary later in life, so, as I may already have discussed, had lived "on the outside." He once showed us pictures of him in his bathing suit and barrel chest at "Muscle Beach" in Los Angeles. He was an avid skier. If he didn't start the Skibrüders, he was their strongest supporter on the faculty.

Fr. Christian Mondor with three members of the **Skibrüders** on the slopes of Mt. Hood. Left to right: Bob Scholze, Bill Meyer, Fr. Christian and Phil Sowa. (Photo provided courtesy of Bob Scholze.)

Fr. Chris, as we called him, also climbed Mt. Hood with one of the Brothers. He said the brother saved his life because Chris slipped off the ice ridge at the top of Mt. Hood, but Brother Peter had the presence of mind to dig his pick axe into the ice, thus breaking the fall, which would have killed both of them.

Fr. Chris was probably supposed to be our English teacher, but had decided that more important than English was the ability to read... fast. So he started the quarter with all the latest technology in Speed Reading Science. After all, John F. Kennedy, the young new President of the USA, was purported to read 4000 words per minute. And Fr. Chris was not wrong; that was a very important skill to develop. I am very auditory, so I never did achieve the reading prowess that my wife enjoys, but there is no question that the class helped me read faster and smarter. I think several of the students graduated with reading speeds over 1000 wpm; I think my fastest recorded speed was 800, but I learned how to skim-read for important details, and that has been an invaluable tool all my life.

Fr. Chris also emphasized useful tools like library research. Before he arrived, it took an act of Congress to get to the Municipal Library in the city, and usually only upper classmen were allowed to roam the earthy streets of Portland. They were really earthy then, too. The Burnside was classic skid row[38], and only a few blocks from the City Library and Powell's Books[39]. Fr. Chris started assigning the freshmen library research assignments and was able to arrange transportation for willing participants to partake of the world of learning in books. I think sometimes we were delivered to Troutdale where we could catch City Transit busses into the downtown area. I think we called from the library before returning and gave our proposed bus and ETA (you youngsters will not remember a time when you had to find a public telephone to be able to do something so simple). And you had to have not spent your change at Powell's Coffee Room. Worse yet, we could not copy the text we needed. Xerox[40] was too new and too expensive for general use).

Fr. Chris also took over the course in public speaking, which was required seminary training. If I remember correctly, the freshmen classes were more oriented to debate. There may have been some oral reading of literature. I also remember there was some encouragement to try different forms of writing, including poetry. I am sure there were some original compositions, but the one I remember most clearly was Mike Theboult's couplet gem: "Old friends are friends to their ends." Ok, maybe it was a haiku (?), couplet (?), or free form? He did get razed about that "couplet" most unmercifully, but as I live, and age, his poem seems truer every year. I tried my hand at poetry but, I must admit, without success that year. Perhaps I needed experience to be able to wax poetic.

I do remember reading *Black Like Me*[41]. That was at once disturbing and life altering. I wrote a book report, and got a good grade on it, but I had never previously been exposed to the real situation of the African Americans. They weren't even called blacks then, but I lived in an area where the blacks were few and far between. I can't think of anyone of African American heritage whom I knew personally up to that point. Of course, the news media was already covering the Civil Rights movement, but what I had heard prior to the seminary was limited. Also, in the seminary, radio and TV were virtually *verboten*. A canonical proscription against newspapers in the seminary was still in effect. One of the first things a lot of students did when they got to the library in Portland or Powell's was to go to the newspaper reading room. So for me to read this story of a white man chemically darkening his skin, and traveling through the South as a black man was like peeling away the scales from my eyes. Of course, I was outraged. After all, my ancestors had been treated with discrimination when they got off the boat from Ireland, and they were the same color and spoke the same language (well, almost). The Irish immigrants were initially portrayed as near baboons. Yet they had risen to a position of respectability in American society as police officers, crew foremen, soldiers and priests. Nevertheless, in the 1950s, the Irish themselves were among the very segregationist that were keeping their heel on the necks of the blacks. These were descendants of Africans, who had, in many cases, arrived a century or two before the Irish diaspora caused by the Great Potato Famine. I could see that there was a great injustice here, and one that I needed to oppose.

This is how the year of regimentation and learning began. After classes, everyone had assigned chores every day. There was a laundry crew, the refectory crew, the grounds crew, the bathroom crew, and the rest. As freshmen, we were assigned to upperclassmen as needed. The upperclassmen, over time, took on certain permanent assignments depending on their skills and interests. So they knew the proverbial ropes, and it was their duty to instruct the neophytes in proper execution of the tasks at hand. I remember that the cross shaped building which was still under construction was in need of work that the contractors were not scheduled to do. One job was painting the entire completed section of the building (even though we occupied the lower western wing for classes). Our older T-shirts and pants became quite colorful that year. There was also a continuous war in progress on the "Eastern Front". The long driveway into the seminary was lined with blackberry vines, and if you are from the Northwest, you know that blackberries and Scotch Broom would take over the country if allowed. So the platoons of freshmen would march out to do battle with the dreaded vine. It was great for the soul. If you had unresolved issues, you could take it out on the blackberries, hacking and chopping your way to mental stability.

Some did not survive all this regimentation and by mid-year our numbers had dwindled. Some were declared unfit by the Faculty, but others were unimpressed with the demands of seminary life.

Not for lack of sport, I might add. Sports were a mandatory part of the ecclesiastical development of character. The whole school was divided into two camps, the Trojans and the Spartans. The names could have been more original: the Rooks and the Knights; the Crusaders and the Templars. Instead the illusion of ancient pagan military conflict was perpetuated in a modern, Christian, non-combatant competition.) Each season brought a new sport, but all were enlisted, unless excused by a doctor's order. Tryouts were used to determine who would be Varsity, Junior Varsity, and what was euphemistically called Intermediate division. The latter was more often ignominiously referred to as Pee Wee league. Needless to say, as ungainly as I was, I began my sports career as an Intermediate. Hey, I was already over 6 ft.; "who you calling a Pee Wee?" We were not allowed to play standard football, because the school did not have any equipment. But seriously, you think flag football is safe? Good that you did not play for St. Francis! In my sophomore year they tried to start a soccer league, but between the shin splits, osteomyelitis, and ski injuries, the insurance company threatened to cancel the school policy altogether. Needless to say, soccer was dropped, but in spite of donated wooden skies and sloppily repaired bindings, the Skibrüders had to survive!

Thrills and Spills

By Ed Vachal in *St Francis Herald* vol 2 no. 3, April 1963

On March 19th the crisp air and shining slopes of Mt. Hood were disturbed by 18 eager skiers from St. Francis Seminary. The vanguard was led by 2 avid and experienced seniors, Pat Buckley and Ernie Ghezzi, and not so experienced crippled Junior (myself) and likewise crippled freshman, Lee Meyer. Our ability as skiers was not exactly equal to the icy slopes, to say the least!

The freshmen stayed at Timberline Lodge with Fr. Christian who was teaching them the fundamentals, i.e. snowplow, plow-turn, stopping, (a very important factor in skiing). Later in the afternoon Fr. Christian escorted the freshmen down the Grade Trail to Government Camp. Incidentally, Leo and I enjoyed the thrilling Glad ride, compliments of the efficient Mt. Hood Ski Patrol.

I forget how many times a week we played sports. I think there were practice sessions on some afternoons after class, but the games were played on Saturday afternoons after morning classes and chores. We had a free afternoon every Wednesday, on which students could leave the campus. I don't remember the captains scheduling practices on those afternoons. Free time was precious. Football was replaced with basketball as the weather became too wet to slog through the mud in the outdoor field. The unfinished half of the cross-shaped building was used as the basketball gymnasium because the proposed second floor, on that wing, was not yet built.

The gymnasium, which was intended to be converted into two floors, still remains as a gymnasium with cement floor in the current Sprindale Job Corps Center. (Photo provided courtesy of Richard Hopp.)

The floors were polished cement, so we had to wear sneakers and even then it was slippery. Cleaning the gym floor was an important job; lives depended on it. We used a compound that is something like sawdust, treated with some oily substance. If the sweepers left those particles behind, it was like booby trapping the court. I think Joe Beigler was my coach the first year. Ernie Ghezzi was our captain the next year; he was only a junior, but it was clear he "had it all".

Just an aside here, speaking of the difficult floor and Ernie Ghezzi's prowess. In my junior year, the Varsity team played the fathers on Parent Visiting Day. My Dad (6 ft. 7 inch) had been a good center in his high school days, so he joined the team. It was a tight game, but Ernie Ghezzi,

Bill Valentine and George Matter were able to hold the dads at bay, and won the day. My dad paid dearly for that game; first time to play basketball in how many years (maybe since the Redheads)? He already had a bad back because he threw me in a snow bank when I was a kid. After that game, I think he had to wear a back brace for months.

Following basketball season, the spring brought the all-American game, baseball. Spring can be a beautiful time of year, but showers were not out of the question. In the tradition of baseball, games were frequently rained out, to the point that it was difficult to complete the season's playoffs to determine the winning league. Not to mention that the season was broken up by the Easter Break and the traditional week-long camp out at Camp Howard on the drainage of the Bull Run Reservoir.

After the games on Saturday, we again had the option of liberty, but we had to be back to the seminary for dinner, followed by study hall. Outings on Saturday were often *en masse*. Things like games with other schools (seems like we played Serra High in Salem once every year); hiking expeditions to Multnomah Falls, Rooster Rock State Park, Larch Mountain, even as far as the fish ladders on Bonneville Dam. Believe it or not, we even went all the way to Winlock, Washington, to participate in a religious conference at St Mary's all-girl high school at Cowlitz Prairie (the site of St. Francis Xavier Church, the first Franciscan Mission in the Pacific Northwest). Whoa! That was a heady affair. I will tell more when I write about the Troubadours).

Therefore, because the Saturday "free days" were often commandeered by the management, Wednesday afternoon was really our only day for solo outings. I think our first trip was to Dabney State Park just outside of Troutdale at the mouth of the Sandy River. That time we walked, but by Christmas Ed Vachal and I had agreed that we would bring our bikes for the Winter session; which we did, and which earned us the reputation of being the most freewheeling and the most often late for dinner. It was 13.2 miles, round trip to Gresham, but it was a heavy peddle; even if the return trip was downhill to Troutdale, from there it was uphill to Springdale and St. Francis.

Parents were allowed to visit on the first or last Sunday of the month (can't remember which), and I quickly earned the reputation of being a late returnee from those outings with my parents. All in all, I was beginning to establish a pattern and that was causing me to become a very experienced dishwasher. I forget whether it was my junior or senior year when Fr. Claude, having to check me in late from another parental outing, said "No more excuses, Klungness". He would never accept one after that.

In the first year I started become pretty good friends with Charlie Biegler. He was a funny guy, and a very talented musician. I think I brought my drums to the Seminary after Christmas, and we started the Freetime Five. It started with Charlie and me and Bob Flieschman, then Larry Hiller joined, and Phil Mothersbaugh, who played the guitar. By the time of our first student body performance, Fr. Christian had joined with his newly acquired 4 string banjo and Jim Nelson had agreed to pluck the cello that had probably been lying around in the music room for years. We were billed as the Freetime Five Plus Two. I think we did instrumentals of "You Are My Sunshine" and I can't remember what else. That group was ill fated, because by my sophomore year, Charlie (who would have been a junior), Bob and Jim were gone. Like I said, seminarians dropped like flies; it was like being in the army in wartime. Father Chris was still interested in keeping a music group together, but he was leaning toward the latest rage, folk music. Larry Hiller dropped out, and my drums were not of interest to a folk group. Phil Muthersbaugh was essential and Ernie Ghezzi, Terri Wenzel and Larry Landry were doing their own solo thing. I had forgotten that there is a picture of those three in the yearbook in my sophomore year showing them playing for an eighth grade class of visiting prospective seminarians. Ironically, Larry Landry is playing Fr. Christian's four string banjo. That's ok, Fr. Chris was moving on to the 5 string, and Larry impressed him with his deep delving into the world of *Folklander* Magazine and Bob Dylan styling. By a magnanimous concession of Fr. Christian (I believe) I was allowed to drag the cello to practice in Fr. Christian's quarters. I didn't know how to play the cello, but they let me try. Well, I knew if I was going to retain my position in what would become the Troubadours, I needed a bigger voice. Now that was a problem because I could not sing while playing an instrument. My folks came to my rescue by buying me an upright bass that Christmas (in fact there is a picture of me with my bass in the annual. I was playing outside, so it must have been spring). So Ernie and Terry and Mothersbaugh and Chris formed the quartet and I provided the bass backup. For some songs requiring percussion, Ernie would take over at the bass, while I played the snare drum. Later I quickly learned to mouth-trombone for those interludes. Ernie also sometimes played those drums.

Fr. Christian had this all figured out. He knew he was going to lose Terry, who was senior that year, and, as it turned out, Mothersbaugh had left that summer as well. The ranks of the Troubadours kept shifting, but their popularity was "meteoric". So Ernie, Larry and Chris and I carried it into my junior year, and Dan Van Dyke and Kurt Seippel filled out the quartet in my senior year. Handsome Dan was a late bloomer musically speaking, but he became very popular on the engagement circuit, and Kurt was an underclassman who helped carry the Troubadour tradition into the last graduating class of St. Francis Seminary. He was joined by Dan Skarry and Arlin Roler as documented in 1964 to 1966 yearbook (on which I was the 1965 Editor); they were performing at a Christmas Party with Fr. Chris and his five string. Over those years Fr. Christian had arranged for us to play Longview, Spokane, Newport (Oregon), Cowlitz Prairie; Seattle, and points in between. I always suspected that the good Father was well aware of the publicity benefits, not to mention the contributions the Troubadours brought into the coffers. When the Troubadours played the Longview Kiwanis Talent Contest (and won), it was at Gretchen's high school, R. A. Long. She remarks that, "all the girls in the audience were aghast at the complete waste of manhood". Similar feelings were relayed at St. Mary's High School, and Serra High, etc. etc. etc. Fr. Chris had also arranged to bring Mike Russo and Ron Brentano to perform for the seminarians and for several Gas Light Sing Alongs, which were full and fun fundraisers for the seminar. He also brought Eddie Peabody, with whom he became good friends, and who gave Chris one beautiful, mother-of-pearl inlaid, five string banjo. I don't know if the two 45 records that we cut made a big contribution to the school, but there were darn few records left after the sales were done. In fact recently, Fr. Christian lamented to me that he could not find any copies of the first record, but I was able to provide it. It wasn't a runaway success like Soeur Sourire[42], but look at the competition we were up against: The Brothers Four, the Kingston Trio and Peter Paul and Mary (and I don't have to footnote those groups!).

I think the most memorable performance that the Troubadours did was for the Poor Clair Cloister in Spokane, Washington. I suppose they thought it was a great treat for them, who live in complete isolation and observe silence 24-7. *Au contraire*, the pleasure was all ours. When they opened the screen that normally hides the sisters from view and from viewing their visitors, there were giggles of joy. I had never, up to then, seen a happier group of women, and have never since. Even the old curmudgeonly skeptic that I am now remembers that day and recalls that those women had an inner beauty and peace that one seldom, if ever, sees in life. It was truly an honor for us, and we all felt very privileged to have had that blessed opportunity.

On that trip to Spokane, we played one of our largest audiences to that point in time. One the way back from the gig, Fr. Christian was apparently feeling more cocky than usual. It was a beautiful moonlight night along the Columbia River, so he decided to "navigate by the stars". I don't know how long we drove without headlights, but there were no other cars on the road, and we were all feeling bold. You know, you have to break a rule once in a while, even if you are a Catholic Priest. Maybe the Poor Clairs were praying for our safety! Or as Kathrine Hepburn said "If you obey all the rules, you miss all the fun."

I think Herb was a little taken aback by my aberrant behavior. He did not write in my first year annual, but in the second year he wrote this:

> ...A friend in need is a friend indeed. But you! Who could be yours? You can never trust you when I _try_ to get to sleep. I never goof around, and most of all, I am the most mature person in our class. Got to go now, my mud pies are finished baking. Herb

He was being facetious, of course, but it probably was true... he was the most mature person in our class. I guess that is kind of what came between us, I was a goof off, and he was perfect. I'll bet I had more fun.

Charlie Biegler was a nut too, although he had to behave himself because his older brother was student body president. He was at once a sort of Joe E. Brown character and Harpo Marks. He would make funny expressions, sometimes sounding like Donald Duck, and other times he would do something that few others in the world can. He could roll one eye way off to the side while looking straight at you with the other. That was most peculiar, and he definitely did it for effect. It makes you wonder what his brain saw when he did that. Similar to what a chameleon can do with its independently rotating eyes. But Charlie was a good musician. There is a comical picture in the yearbook of Ernesto, Carlos and Guillermo, the Mexican Trio, playing for sophomore Classnight. That was Ernie Ghezzi, Charlie and Bill Valentine, but you can bet it was Charlie's idea. Chuckles, as we called him, befriended me early in the first year, which in itself was unusual for a sophomore and a freshman. I was really kind of disappointed when Charlie did not show up the next year. I don't remember whether he knew at the end of his sophomore year that he would be leaving, and told me. Perhaps he just said goodbye in an unusual way that I did not understand, until he did not show up the next year. I have tried to look up Charlie a number of times in my life, but I have never found him. There was a Joseph A. Beegle (Charlie's brother) who was a teacher in the Spokane Public School System, but I could never find an address or contact number.

One of my partners in crime was Ed Loughrey. Ed was a large fellow, taller than me and substantially built. He was a Tacoma city boy who had a proclivity to mischief, like me. He was loud and boisterous, and imaginative. I made some serious money off of Ed, because he was always asking me to give him massages (I guess he was always overdoing it on the ball field or the hikes or whatever). My response would be "put your money where your mouth is". I guess that sort of got our banter off to a good start. And I guess he liked the massages. I don't know, maybe he got high on the Absorbine Junior ointment.

Probably the stupidest thing we did, which earned us a passel of dish shifts, was in the dormitory after evening prayers. I need to set up the scene. As the cross-shaped building was being competed, the freshmen had been moved up to the second floor dormitory on the north side of the southeast wing. I remember the seniors put on their play "Twelve Angry Men" in the Milking Shed Dormitory that winter quarter. Outside the dorm in the center of the building there was a hallway. The whole end of the dormitory was spanned by a chest-high glass window, looking onto a hallway. Across the hall from the dormitory was Fr. Claude's quarters. So, if you kept a lookout peeled, you could see Claude's comings and goings. At the other end of the dormitory was a fire escape with a full sized metal staircase. The door was not locked and we could use that escape in the daytime, but it never occurred to us pea-brained freshmen that Fr. Claude would ever have occasion to use that fire escape. Why? The noise of one climbing that staircase would reverberate throughout the dorm. But we sorely underestimated the cunning of Claude "Clouseau".

On this cold winter's night as we were preparing for bed, the effect of the day's meals was to enhance the normally prolific gastronomy of Ed's intestines. Not wanting to suffer gastric distress, and at the same time wanting to make the best of a comical moment, Ed was bending over, making the motions of a battleship's cannon being brought to bear on the hull of an unsuspecting bark (that would be me) and letting fly with volleys of noxious gas. Although Fr. Claude, from his imaginary crow's nest on the stairs, deemed us partners in puerile crime, to this day, I consider myself to have been an innocent bystander.

Now, here is the irony, Ed did not return to St. Francis in my sophomore year. Again, I don't know if it was because the faculty asked him to leave, or did he decide on his own to abandon the "higher calling". If it was the former, why was I not also blackballed? If the latter, why didn't I know about it? Ed and Tim Hennessey (who was also from Tacoma) came to visit me in the summer of my junior year. Tim went through sophomore year with us, but dropped out before the junior year. By then I was working at the pulp mill and living on the Toutle River (which I will describe later). I was driving a 1953 Chevy panel van, and while I was at work, those two, and some of the seminarians from Longview (I am not sure who) went joy riding in my old truck. That visit was the last I ever saw of either Tim or Ed. (according to my mother's letter's, Ed went on to play football for the University of Washington.)

I may have already related the incident of staying out late with Pat Rogers the year before, which had led to the accident on my first day after getting my driver's license. I also don't remember seeing Pat again after that, except once I ran into him when he was working at the Longview Radio Station (actually that is not true; I had dinner at his folks' place before he went into VISTA). Brian LeTourneau and Herb Karnofski outlasted us all, and graduated from San Luis Rey, the seminary college. What has always puzzled me is how these decisions to quit the seminary were made, and why, after leaving, we did not maintain contact?

To my knowledge, there have only been three attempts to hold class reunion. The only one I was involved with was at Cowlitz Prairie… I don't even remember what year. Only Brian LeTourneau, Herb Karnofski, Joe Lauritzon, Ed Vachal, Steve Barnsuki and I came to that reunion, and Steve is the only one, out of all the classes of SFS who became a priest. Brothers Conrad and

Peter, and one of the other Priests came, and I was glad that I had that chance to see Brother Conrad again. In contrast, Gretchen has gone to 5 of her High School reunions, and approximately 40% of the class of 400 attended. It is odd to me that a tight-knit group at SFS that had developed such camaraderie simply slipped into obscurity once they left the seminary. I don't mean they have themselves not made their mark on the world, but there is no sharing of experience among the former students of St. Francis. At least that is my experience; perhaps others have made more of an effort to keep in touch.

Commander Phil Sowa, who, after St. Francis, entered the Navy and became a flight commander, contacted me in Davis when I doing my Master's degree there. Phil had always been fascinated with the hawks catching the updrafts at the edge of the cliff at SFS. I guess he became one. Anyway, he spent the evening and that night with Mary and me in Davis, but that was the last time that I saw him. Maybe I was too political about Reagan's little wars in Granada and North Africa. Although Phil could not discuss it at the time, he may well have been flying in those campaigns. Later my mother reported that her last contact with Phil's family was when he was transferred from Whidbey Island, Washington, to England. More recently, I have found evidence that he may have retired to his home town in Mt. Angel Oregon, but his telephone number is in the Silverton, OR directory. I am still trying to get in contact with him.

One old compatriot that I have tracked down is Joe Barreca. I will tell you more about Joe as we move through the years at the seminary, because there is a lot to tell. However, I found it ironic that, in my search, a picture turned up of Joe, with a full beard, standing in a pile of goat manure! Joe has also returned to the land, raising grapes, rockhounding and writing a blog for his rockhounders' website, Map Metrics[43] in Rice, Washington. He had tried to maintain contact with me a few times over the years, when he was building his underground house in Kettle, Washington, and working as a Land Assessor for Lewis County. At that time my life was a whirlwind and he got my address in Kapa`a, Hawaii, spelled all wrong, so we had not been in contact until just this last week. Joe has not lost his philosophical bent. I hope he will not mind me taking the liberty to include some of his *zeitgeist*:

> So I think of manure, not as the icon for everything that has gone wrong, but the essence of the way things work. Things come to life. They die. They get eaten. They turn into manure. They come back to life. It's the circle of life. It's living physical karma. What goes around comes around. With care, it gets better every step of the way. It could be the foundation of a whole philosophy of natural ethics, but I'm still working on that.

> Make no mistake. Manure is still teeming or steaming as the case may be, with life. Life doesn't just die, it changes into new kinds of life. Actually I think a lot of these microbes are inside of us keeping us, or at least the goats alive, which in turn keep us alive. Curiously, they benefit greatly from a little helping hand in getting mixed together, evening out the moisture, bringing in fresh air. So we have a symbiotic relationship. Sometimes you work the pile. Sometimes the pile works you. http://mapmet.com/page11004716.aspx

Joseph Barreca on his farm in Kettle, Washington. He tends his heritage grapes and writes his blog, among many other activities. (Photo provided courtesy of Joseph Barreca.) www.mapmet.com

That is Joe in a nutshell! When we were sophomores, Joe was keeping a journal of what he called "Claudisms" (humorous antidotes from the observation of Fr. Claud). I asked him if he still had that journal. He said it had been lost along the way through communes and underground comic strips, and working for "the man" and raising two daughters. It's funny how life just kind of carries us along. It _is_ all happenstance!

CHAPTER 9

On the Horns of a Dilemma

9 Rejoice, O young man, in your youth, and let
your heart cheer you in the days of your youth.
Walk in the ways of your heart and the sight
of your eyes. But know that for all these things
God will bring you into judgment.10 Remove
vexation from your heart, and put away pain
from your body, for youth and the dawn of life
are vanity. **English Standard Version (©2001)
Ecclesiastes 11:9-10**

THERE ARE MANY MORE THINGS that I could tell about the first
year at St. Francis. Just in case you have not figured it out yet, we often
referred to the seminary as SFS, you know, like the military jargon KISS
meaning "keep it simple, stupid". The problem that I am having is keeping
on the timeline -- you may have noticed. There is method to my madness,
but for the life of me I could not explain it. To understand it, you have to have
some understanding of how the human brain works. It is not a filing cabinet
(i.e. infancy to high school, bottom drawer, earliest memories first). No, the
mind is a series of synaptic connection. The stronger the initial impulse
that creates the connection, the more cross-linked it is to other synapses
in the grey matter. If the memory is reinforced, the synapses become even
more cross linked. They are just beginning to understand that the brain is
not just chemically altered by experience, but actually changes physically.
These patterns of cross-linked synapses affect the way memory is recalled.
If a familiar memory is recalled, it may light up a connection to an obscure
memory that had long been forgotten. Why only today, I was talking to Fr.

Chris on the phone and he mentioned an incident I had totally forgotten. We were talking about Fr. Mario, and Chris mentioned in passing that he had dressed as Aunt Jemima. Whoa! The image came flooding back to me. It was a Halloween costume party, I believe, but what was so funny was that absolutely no one could figure out who it was in the costume. I think we thought some woman had crashed the party. And Fr. Mario was not one to let such a delicious deceit be "de-cloaked" surreptitiously. Fr. Chris and I both laughed at the thought. My point is, if the story I relate does not flow as you would expect, just remember that you are studying the labyrinthine synapses of my mind. Perhaps one of my reasons for writing this book is just that, to rebuild old synapses. Recent research has revealed and video documented that there are cells in the brain that add myelin to new nerve synapses, and remove myelin from unused synapses. The ol' use it or lose it trope is actually true!

I don't want to leave the first year at SFS behind, because it so impacted my life. As I was saying in the last chapter, I wondered why some students would leave and others would stay. Usually the decisions came as a surprise; students we thought would surely stay, left, and students we most expected to leave, stayed. I think I understand a little bit the circumstances that led to Tim Hennessey's decision to leave at the end of his freshman year. Tim was a porky guy, and Tim McDaniels, who himself was no beanpole, razed freshman Tim, as did others. In the first yearbook, there is actually a picture of Tim McDaniels holding Tim Hennessey in the yearbook.

Tim McDaniel and Tim Hennessey, whom he is holding, are examples of what Brother Conrad's good cooking can do for you. (Photo by Fr. Claude Riffle from the SFS annual, *The Troubadour* Ed. L. M. Klungness)

Notwithstanding his girth, Tim was one of the most popular guys in our class; kind of our "Friar Tuck" character. Nevertheless, Tim Hennessey, on his own initiative, took it upon himself to lose the weight. He followed a miserable dietary routine that dropped his weight almost in half, I believe. Prior to the austere diet, Tim was jovial and fun loving. As the diet progressed you could see him getting more serious and less carefree. Then one day, Tim and I forget who else, were making candles for what reason I am not sure. An accident occurred that led to Tim being burned severely on his legs and, if I remember correctly, part of his hands as well. It took a long period of recovery, but he was not sent home. He was in the dormitory with our class throughout his recovery, but he stayed in bed for much of that time. Herb Karnofski was like a nurse to him, bringing him food and water, and even, as I remember it, helping to change his bandages. I don't remember a doctor coming into the seminary, although I assume they must have taken Tim out to the doctor from time to time. Tim did eventually recover, but I think his whole view of life had changed because of this traumatic incident following on the heels of such a drastic weight loss. I cannot remember if this all occurred before Easter and the trip to Camp Howard, but I remember that Tim was on that first camping excursion. Perhaps the accident happened later in the spring, which would mean Tim went home having just recovered from some drastic changes in his life. But again, I don't really know if Tim decided, on his own, not to return for the sophomore year, or whether the faculty had been involved. I certainly never needed to lose weight in my seminary years, but I think this incident made me more cautious about the concept of pushing one's body to the limits, whatever those limits might be.

As I mentioned, Herb had been a great help to Tim during his illness. Herb was a great help in many instances... he may well have been the most mature student in the class. So it grieved me to find out from Phil Sowa, whom I had only tracked down today, that Herb Karnofski had died of cancer fully two years before. He had only recently retired from Weyerhaeuser Company after 35 years of service. Herb and I had not kept in touch since my mother died in 1997, so to find out that he had died without my even knowing -- when Phil had attended his funeral -- was unnerving. Herb and I grew up together. We attended grade school, high school and the first two years of the major seminary together. Herb and I started working at Weyerhaeuser the same summer; me in the Pulp Mill and him in the Engineering Division. My job was to clean stacks and hose down spills. His job was to observe and calculate process efficiency. I think he claimed to have already saved the company $50,000 before we graduated from high school. After college I went on to Africa, and a plethora of jobs, returned to graduate school, and ended up in Hawaii. After college, Herb settled down and slogged it out at the Company for all those years. He was well known in the Longview community. Close friends with the owners of the Masthead Tavern, Herb moonlighted as their bouncer for years. I guess it was a diversion from the ponderous monotony of wood products. One year, when I was working for the Weyerhaeuser Forestry Research lab and living in Tenino, Herb asked me to deliver a bundle of plywood to the owner of the Masthead. My old '49 GMC was available and the price discounted. My mother and I visited Herb at his house once when I was visiting from Hawaii. He had a lovely house, a beautiful garden and a nice roommate. The rumor was that they were gay, but no one ever offered me any evidence that it was true, especially not Herb. I used to wonder about some of his close friends when we were at San Luis Rey (the major seminary college); but one of those guys is now a Franciscan priest in the same parish where Fr. Chris is stationed. I once visited Herb at Weyerhaeuser Hardwood Furniture Manufacturing plant in Longview (actually the wood used was Northwestern alder). I could see then that the job was wearing on him. But it also allowed him the freedom to travel, which he did extensively on his vacations. His obituary said he loved to come to Hawaii, although he only visited us once when my mother was alive. But to think that he had finally earned his freedom from the Company only to lose his life to cancer... that is heavy. He was a good man, who had helped put his brothers through college, helped his parents in their old age (both having died before him). Herb brought enjoyment to the patrons of the Masthead (including

Gretchen and her ex-husband). Perhaps the saying it true, the good <u>do</u> die young?

I want to ponder how we got interested in the careers that we pursued. In Herb's case, I think it was pretty much what life presented. I think he would have stayed in the priesthood, and been a darn good priest, even if he had been gay. I cannot say that Herb did not choose to leave the Order of Friars Minor (OFM, the official name of the Franciscans), but I suspect that some decision was made by the San Luis Rey faculty or the Order's Provincial. Did the decide to turn the whole class out? I know that Bill Halvorson stayed in the novitiate for several years with Fr. Anselmo, but he was the only one, and he left eventually. I don't know anything about how this all came about, but I suspect that Herb was not happy to leave the order. The happenstance, which then became the controlling influence in his life, was the fact that he had "done good" at Weyerhaeuser in 1962, and the Longview staff took Herb under their wing. Born under the clouds of Weyerhaeuser pollution, lived under same, died under same, except for one brief shining moment when we were the disciples of St. Francis.

On the other hand, I was a latecomer to religion. Baptized at the age of 7, I had a lot of catching up to do in order to make my first communion at St. Joseph's church in McCloud. Fr. Carl Willman was our Catechism instructor (he never let the parishioners take that duty away from him until he retired in 1980). It was exotic stuff to a boy raised in the woods, but I think the thing that captured my attention the most, was the visit of a White Father, in his all-white cassock, from Tanganyika. He came to conduct what the Catholics call a Retreat, and we attended most of it. This was truly exotic stuff; I mean deepest darkest Africa! Actually, his slide show didn't seem dark at all. Except for the black smiling faces, everything looked pretty bright and cheery, with colorful clothes, and colorful stories about the mothers letting their infants pee in the mud between the pews of the church, and beautiful wild animals, and sunshine most of the time. At one point during the homily at Mass, Fr. Paul began to babble. Everyone looked at him with puzzlement, but he seemed unaware that he had slipped into Swahili (the actual name of the Language is Kiswahili). Fr. Paul was from the mid-western USA, but by then, he had been in Africa for so long that English was no longer his native language… in fact, he was not even aware that he was not speaking English. This was cool!

Fr. Paul enlisted the parishioners in a funding project called the Jungle Bucks. My mother contributed $1 per month to the Jungle Bucks for the rest of her life, and Fr. Paul dutifully produced a newsletter with pictures and text of the progress that was being made at the Tabora Mission in what is now The Republic of Tanzania. My mother always wanted to visit Tanzania, but never got the chance. I ended up in Kenya, and had as part of my territory the town of Mwatate, which is the border town to Arusha, Tanzania. I never traveled to that country during my tour of duty. However, I did have the pleasure of traveling to Africa in 2008 for the International Entomology Conference in Durban, South Africa. Following the conference, I visited Tanzania, and I will talk about that visit later in the third book. I had a great admiration for Julius Nyerere, the first president of Tanzania. But I always wondered if it was Fr. Paul that put the bug in my brain to go to Africa. When Peace Corps invited me to Kenya, I didn't even know that it was right next to Tanzania and that they spoke Swahili in both countries. Ah, there's that old happenstance again! In fact, in my Peace Corps application I request to be posted in the Philippines (where the Franciscans had missions), India (whence the Peace Corps was expelled) or anywhere in South America (I spoke Spanish). Instead the Peace Corps invited me to Kenya, East Africa. Go figure.

So things that happen in one's youth can profoundly affect the choices you make in your future. Another influence on what Gretchen later called my "missionary zeal"[44] came in the form of a Franciscan priest who was our retreat master at Lent in my first year at SFS. He was an imposing man with a kindly face; I do not remember his name. He had been a missionary in the Philippines for many years and spiced his homilies with many antidotes from his experiences on the Island of Mindanao. His stories were so convincing that when I was applying for the Peace Corps, I did not choose Africa for a destination, but rather listed all of South America (because of my Spanish training), India and the Philippines. Of course, by the time I was selected, the Peace Corps had been kicked out of India, and I am not sure why I was not chosen for the Philippines[45]. Even more baffling is why they did not consider my six years of Spanish a good reason to send me to Spanish-speaking South America. Nope! Kenya... where the hell is Kenya? Happenstance? I am beginning to wonder. Nevertheless, I have no doubt that the Missionary from the Philippines had influenced my thinking as much as did Fr. Paul.

That first year at the seminary, I think I also read the *Utopia* by Thomas More. I did a very impressive book review on it and got an A. In conjunction with the Utopia, I had found a book about what might have been the source material for Thomas More, who himself wrote that he was told the story by a seaman named Hythloday.. The author of that thesis (whose name I can neither remember or find on the Internet) proposes that More did take the basic structure of the Utopian society from the account of Hythloday. He was describing a Central American civilization. The author points out that the land mass described in the Utopia resembles Japan more than any part of the Central American peninsula, but he also makes analogies to various aspects of Mayan culture which seem to be paralleled in the Utopia. Thus, I was already being influenced in my cultural thinking by idealistic, but practically-based, social structures[46].

I also went on to read a biography of Thomas More and a compendium of letters between the man and his daughter Margaret. It is ironic, when you read the vitriolic polemics that were exchanged between Thomas (who would not take the oath of succession from the Roman Church) and his long-time friend. Erasmus (who espoused the Protestant cause from Rotterdam). The latter was trying to get Thomas to relent as he awaited his execution in the Tower of London. Contrast that with the gentle loving letters to his daughter from the Tower of London. At the time he was waiting to be beheaded because he would not sign the Act of Supremacy of 1534, which separated the Church of England from the Catholic Church. One could not help but be swayed by the humanity of this very public man acting on his conscience in the interest of the society for which he had such high hope. While I Google these subjects in pursuit of that illusive author, it is profoundly clear that Thomas More (or Moore, as some prefer) has impacted western society far beyond any influence he had in his lifetime, even as Chancellor to the King of England.

While we cleaned toilets, conjugated Latin verbs, played flag football in the mud, and spent an inordinate amount of time in chapel, our minds were being broadened to a world of ideas. At the same time our command of the spoken language was being honed by Fr. Christian. He took a rather unconventional stand by combining the speech lectures of the freshmen and sophomore classes. Can you imagine the terror of a lowly freshman addressing an audience of skeptical sophomores? And they did <u>not</u> make it easy; their critiques were harsh, because they had been similarly grilled by their predecessors. I think more nerves were frayed at speech class than in final exams at the end of the year.

Nor was Fr. Christian archaic in his approach. There is a picture in the yearbook of Tim Hennessey addressing the class facing a microphone, taped to a music stand. Ye gods! Not only the ignominy of a public speech, but a recorded speech... to be replayed and rehashed. Sometimes you even were required to listen to yourself in review. Even the reel to reel tape recorder is visible in the picture. This was pretty advanced technology for a high school speech class in 1961. Didn't I mention that we were still making copies of text on a mimeograph machine[47]?

All of the priests were intent on building our vocabulary, and I forget whether it was Fr. Mario or Fr. Christian (or both) who was (were) constantly testing us on new words. Of course, studying Latin helps because there are practically two "English" languages. There are all the Celtic words that form the base of the language, and then there are all the Anglo-Saxon terms that were adopted from French, which is, of course Latin in its origin. Seth Lerer, Stanford professor of Philology, gives food words as an example. Bread is a Celtic word, *pain* is the French word from the Latin *panis*. This is different than the root for frying pan[48], which comes from the old English *panna*[49]. So, here's a brain teaser, what is the origin of pancake[50]? The 'cake' part, although originally Old Norse, is a lot closer to Old English. But the 'pan-' could be either 'bread-' or 'made in a pan-'. It is probably the latter, but by 1430 the Saxons had already invaded England; think about it. Lerer also gives the example of animals; we don't eat deer, chickens, cattle and pigs but rather venison, poultry, beef and pork. The latter are all derived from French words: *venesoun, pouletrie, boeuf* and *porc* (the latter is actually directly from the Latin *porcus*). I rest my case. Latin is the root of a very major part of the English language.

Now Fr. Benedict would argue, in his college English class, that the Celtic words were the most powerful, and tend not to sound pompous. But some need to be used sparingly for greatest effect… generally this is truest with regard to the four letter expletives. Think about it. A less offensive example would be "crap!". Even "damn!" is used way too much, and it isn't even a Celtic word (*L. Damnum*). I think Fr. Benedict reveled in reading The Miller's tail by Geoffrey Chaucer the effectiveness of "fuck!". He considered it a perfect example of the effective use of the Middle English language. Used sparingly off course!

At Easter, all the ordinary routine of seminary life came to a halt. Holy Week is a continuous progression of ever more involved liturgy culminating in the all night ceremonies of the Holy Saturday and Easter Morning. At exactly midnight the haunting strains of Gregorian hymn, "Alleluia", break the stillness of the night. After the long reading of the Passion on Good Friday, and the somber ceremonies of the divesting of the altar, the Easter morning ceremonies are very moving and uplifting. One could really get a feeling for the life of the medieval church, where the entire life of the community revolved around sacred ritual from the ringing of the Angelis, to the celebration of Sunday Mass. In a confusing and disjunct world where thousands of competing diversions vie for our attention, the memory of the calm and reassuring life of the cloister is comforting.

During the days on Easter week, classes were suspended, and work parties were formed. Work was done in silence, so it all feed into the meditative atmosphere that was probably first introduced by St. Benedict in 529 CE. But after all that religious ritual, young 20th century youth needed a break! The break was several days at Camp Howard. We would load up the old Volkswagen van with provisions and the White Elephant[51] with seminarians and off we would go the 30 miles up to the camp in the woods. As I said, Camp Howard was on the edge of a ravine which was the watershed and outflow from the Bull Run Reservoir. From Google Earth you cannot see the camp because it is so heavily wooded now, but it does still exist… I think it might be a Boy Scout Camp. SFS would rent the camp in the late winter because it was cheap and no self-respecting summer camp would be held in a damp, cold Northwest winter. But, you know, that was the charm of Camp Howard. All the cabins had little potbellied wood stoves, and sometimes we would get them so hot that the stove pipe would glow deep red right up to the roof plate. It is a wonder we didn't burn down the whole camp. There was a large hall and kitchen, where, if the rain was pouring, we would congregate. The basic routine of the seminary was preserved, in that Charlie Biegler was the bugler who would blow revelry at 6:30 AM. Mass would begin soon thereafter. Breakfast was served and dish shifts assigned (naturally). I will always remember the placard over the sink, paraphrasing Tennyson, "Ours is not to reason why, ours is just to wash and dry." But aside from the Mass, the meals, and convening at campfire circle on some evenings, we were pretty much on our own. No, I mean really! We could do whatever we wanted to do… it was near celestial in its simplicity. Some hiked, some parked around the potbelly playing cards, some read, some competed at chess (I think Joe Barreca started carving his chessmen that first year at camp) and some played music. I think Charlie had brought his accordion and Muthersbaugh brought his guitar. There was no room for my bass on the bus, so Barreca got the bright idea to build a washtub bass. It sounded pretty good, too. Apparently Joe is still playing washtub to this day (he emailed me a picture of him playing music with his friends up in Kettle Falls, Washington). I remember that "Mountain Dew" became our favorite song that year. Of course, we didn't have any brew to imbibe, but sometimes you just have to improvise. However, I will tell of some vintner experiments that we conducted when I get to junior year.

By the end of the week our clothes all reeked of smoke, our boots were wet and muddy, our bellies were sometimes in a state of revolt, but we were refreshed and not at all ready to return to civilization and seminary life. But, as the Bard would say, "that's the rub!" The inevitable came, and we packed up to return to SFS. Each year it was always a question whether the van, loaded beyond capacity, and the White Elephant loaded beyond its years, would make it up the last steep grade to Camp Howard. That was never a problem on the return. The van and the students were lightened by a week of roughing it, and it was all downhill from camp. Then the only issue was whether the brakes on The White Elephant would hold... obviously they did, or I would not be writing this.

Leaving SFS at the end of that first year was at once a joyous experience combined with a twinge of regret. It had been a tough haul, but it had changed us immeasurably. We were now part of a clan, a corps, a cohort, a troop. First, we were the largest freshman class in SFS's short history. Next, we were now inducted into the elite group of "our alma mater". Finally we were making our first step into the Order of Friars Minor (OFM). This was an old institution that started with Francis of Assisi in 1209 CE. Like the Benedictines, the Jesuits, the Dominicans, etc. the Franciscans have their own traditions and world view. I don't think we ever took a class in Franciscan theology, but we were certainly steeped in the tradition. There was much emphasis on reading J. K. Chesterton's *St. Francis of Assisi*. This

158 page book was to the Franciscan seminarian what The Double Helix by Watson and Crick would be to a biology student.

Chesterton tells the story of St. Francis in relatively modern terms (it was first published in 1928). It captures the fundamentally new philosophy of life that Giovanni Francesco di Bernardone brought, first to a small band of followers in the mountain community of Assisi. Soon Chiara Offreduccio (St. Clair) was captivated by the sincerity and poverty of this young mendicant. She begged to be including in the band of Christian beggars, but Francis arranged for her to reside at San Damiano church, which he had rebuilt. Other women joined her and lived out their cloistered life in that place. Later, some of the married faithful wished to join his idealistic lifestyle, so he formed the Third Order for lay families. Although Francis died when he was only 44, in 1226, he had brought a whole new wave of spirituality to the aging Catholic Church. Franciscan writers, mystics and holy men (like St.Thomas More) have made great contributions to Catholic theology and Christian life in general. Fr. Chris was just telling me that one of the graduates of SFS, who is now a professor at the Franciscan School of Theology in Berkeley, California, has translated and brought together all the works of the Franciscan writers like Bonaventure, Dun Scotus, etc. He has or is about to publish a compendium of these writings, which, according to Fr. Chris, have already brought a revival of the Franciscan spirit with the OFM. Although none of my class actually made it into the OFM, I'm sure some, like Herb, remained members of the Third Order, and the philosophical mindset of the Friars Minor has not faded from their memory.

Another perspective on Catholicism would be the words of the father of my ex-wife, "There is no such thing as a recovered Catholic". He himself was raised Catholic, although he punched a nun (his teacher) in the stomach when he was eight, un-enrolled himself from Catholic school, and became an agnostic. Nevertheless, he spent his life in social work trying to help recovering alcoholics.[52] What compelled him to do that altruism or Catholic guilt?

Previously, I was talking about the regret that I felt leaving SFS that first year. I was going back to the life I had before this close-knit band of brothers. It was a kind of lonely time. Although there were other seminarians in my home town, we did not meet much that summer. The other kids that I knew from St. Rose had moved on to high school and their new spheres of influence.

Basically I was alone most of the summer. I didn't have a job, and I had returned too late to go to the berry fields. So I enrolled in summer school at Monticello. I took French and Typing. It was a peculiar feeling, being a seminarian out in the world at large. Of course, I didn't know anyone in the classes, and it remained that way throughout the weeks that I attended class. I somehow felt obligated to distinguish myself, so I wore a long sleeve white shirt and tie every day. I guess I thought it would discourage fraternizing with the opposite sex, and I was absolutely correct about that! I might have passed for a Latter Day Saint (LDS) on a mission, but I didn't have a partner. We see the Mormon missionaries all the time all over Hawaii, and they are always dressed in black slacks and white shirt with black tie. They are also always in pairs. This approach has apparently been equally successful in island nations throughout the Pacific, and I believe it is one of the fastest growing churches throughout the developing countries of the world. The reason there are always only two LDS missionaries is because they have very strict policies[53], which I imagine to be very effective. I don't think I knew that when I was attending summer school, but I can confirm that I met zero persons of the opposite sex that summer. Well, I wasn't supposed to anyway, was I?

My French teacher was a stodgy man, probably in his 50s, who always wore a suit and tie, He had lived in France, although he was not a native speaker. I learned a little rudimentary French and he did emphasize a conversational approach. It was my first exposure to French and I do believe it is a most pleasant language to hear. The other night Agnès Varda was reflecting on her filmmaking career on the Public Broadcasting Station's program *Point of View*. The subtitles were small, and my eyes were tired, but I left the program on just to listen to the melodious *lengue Français*.

The typing class proved to be a boon in later years, but I was not keeping up very well. I would do some of the exercises, and I did learn where the fingers needed to be placed. However, when the teacher would put on music, so that we could type along to the music, I ended up just tapping out the beat, but producing nothing legible. This gives me the opportunity to relay a little known fact. When typewriters were first invented the keys were arranged in alphabetical order. That is logical, but when the typist began to get used to the position of the letters they began to type very quickly. The problem was that they were typing faster than the hammers would strike and retract. Since all the hammers were coming together at the same spot, they were jamming together, which damaged the typewriters. *Ergo*, the QWERTY keyboard[54] was invented to slow the typists down. You see, C. L. Sholes reasoned that if he put the most commonly used characters in the most awkward positions (i.e. those were hardest to operate with the fingers) that would slow down the typists. That is why 'a' is under the left little finger, and punctuation surrounds the right little finger. The letter 'e' is the most commonly used letter in the English language and it is awkwardly operated by the left middle finger. Wikipedia does not explain this design conceit, but if you think about it, the reason for using the QWERTY keyboard has disappeared. Computers do not have mechanical hammers, so why do we still configure the keyboard in this most difficult arrangement? The answer alludes to a very fundamental fault of human nature. We will call it 'the tyranny of habit'. It worked, everyone got used to using it, so there is no incentive to improve. If you ponder how widely this rule applies, you will understand why the human species has progressed so slowly over the millennia.

Pondering such "weighty issues", I would wander about town after class. I did not have a bicycle at the time, so I would walk from the Junior High to the Post Office (The J. high was half way between our house on

Pennsylvania and the post office where my dad worked). I am not sure exactly why I did this, although I think that I would sometimes go to lunch with my dad at the Safeway lunch counter near the post office. My classes ended in the morning, and I figured I didn't want to just go home and sit around. My dad must have been on day shift then, so I probably was able to ride home with him after work. The Post Office was across the central park from the city library, so I would go to the library and listen to records. Why? Who knows? Boredom, I guess. I didn't have money to spend. Maybe I was supposed to be looking for a job, but that was a daunting proposition, so that didn't happen. I probably could have gone swimming at the YWCA, but I didn't. All I can remember is that I spend a lot of time just wandering about town that summer. This did accomplish one thing; it was good exercise. I would probably walk 6 or 7 miles in a day.

My dad took over the rural paper route before I went to SFS, so he was still doing it that summer after my freshman year. I would go on the route with him, probably not every day, but at least every Sunday. After my classes ended, I think Dad was able to change to swing shift, so we would start the route when he got off at 11 PM. I supposed he picked me up at home when I would go with him on weekdays. That was part of the reason that I was making motions of wanting to get a job… so I wouldn't have to go on the route on weekdays. If I was in town for the evening for a movie, I would go back to the post office, and wait for Dad to get off shift. The paper route was about 50 miles, starting in Kelso; we would go up to Castle Rock and back on the west side of the Cowlitz River. My only incentive for going on the paper route was that I had gotten my driver's learning permit, and he would let me drive the easier parts of the route.

Somehow on those nights, Dad could pick up the San Francisco talk shows on the KGO AM radio. That was about the nearest thing to "intellectual" you could get in Longview. In the daytime, only the local station KLOG (Longview) and KXL (out of Portland) could be picked up on a good radio. There were not many Christian or Country radio stations in the Twin City area back then. KLOG was all the popular music like rock and roll, but KXL played "easy listening" music, which <u>wasn't</u> to a teenager. But KGO had all kind of topical material. There were liberals and conservatives. The callers could be real nut cases sometimes, but it was entertaining. Who knew the world out there could be so crazy. As I said, race was a pretty big topic. And there were a lot of rednecks and radicals calling into the station in San Francisco. So we listened while we went through the monotonous routine of delivering newspapers to the homes and newspaper bundles to the carriers.

Dad and I did not talk much. I don't know how he felt about things. We couldn't talk sports, and I guess he figured I had all my "growing up" conversations with my mother. I don't know what their understanding (or misunderstanding, as the case may be) about me was. It seemed like she was more or less the decider, although she would say that they agreed about things. More likely, he let her make the decisions. She was usually the one who punished me, and that sometimes got very physical (welts on my butt and such). I remember when I was about 10, she insisted that Dad should be the one to punish me. He did, but he didn't have the heart for it. I remember that particular "whipping" distinctly, not because it hurt. It was the only one he ever gave me. I was not a very disobedient youth, so the lickings subsided, but my Mom resorted to other techniques. For the second time I got involved with the toy of a neighbor kid. I think the toy got broken, so I was grounded… in my room… for a week… and on water and All Bran cereal. That's right, not even bread and water; <u>bran</u> and water… ugh!

It wasn't that Dad wouldn't talk to me, but our conversations were not comfortable. For example, when I was younger, if my Dad was getting ready to go somewhere, I would ask "where ya goin?". His response would invariably be, "Crazy, you want to go along?" I would go, but I was never sure where. It was on a "need to know" basis, I guess. I remember when Dad would get mad or cut himself or miss a turn, he would say "God!… bless America and all her ships at sea." I guess that kind of sums him up. He was a very internal person. I suspect his dad was very similar. I don't think they were close, either. I mean, maybe he did love me, but he never showed it. We never hugged… a handshake was about the only acknowledgement that I would receive. Of course, I was not an infant when he came into my life, but neither were my African kids. I tried to be affectionate with my kids, and my son James still hugs his Ol' Man.

Sometimes we would have brief exchanges about what was being said on the radio. Most of the time our discussions were practical: how to do the newspaper inserts, how to tie the bundles, how to arrange the bundles in the VW after the seats were removed. I got my driver's permit that summer, so he started teaching me to downshift on a hill, etc. At first, he couldn't handle driving with me when I was learning. His strategy was simple. He would take me out to the sand bar on the Columbia River, set up his fishing pole and chair, and hand me the keys. I drove all over the dyke that bordered the bar. I got into jams, almost rolled the VW over on the steep bank, and probably ground off a few gears. It was a good strategy; before the summer was over, I was driving him on the route.

I had attempted to drive one time before these training sessions with my Dad. Fr. Carl Willman was visiting from California, and he would take Dad to work so that we could use our car. One evening he offered to let me drive. I put the VW in reverse and tore out the driveway and across the street. I only managed to break within a fraction of an inch from our neighbor's mailbox. Needless to say, Fr. Carl did not offer again.

I remember another "driving' experience that I had that summer. [Do you see how the brain works… one synapse excites another nearly forgotten labyrinth.] My mother's friends, whom she knew when she worked in Eugene, Oregon, were visiting the husband's parents on their farm in Rosewood, Oregon. Bev and Gene had twin daughters who were, at that time probably 3 or 4 years old. So we drive down to visit with them. Gene's father asked me if I wanted to drive the tractor. Big opportunity! And so I did, for about an hour or so, by myself. Then the family came out and asked me if I wanted to take the girls around on the tractor. We got them situated (big responsibility now!) and the grandfather suggested that I take the girls up the hill. There was a long farm road that let up the pasture to a hill top probably beyond shouting distance away; which we did without incident. The girls were having a great time, and I was feeling very important. It had been a slow trip up the hillside, so when we got to the top of the hill, we saw a pickup truck coming behind us. I don't know if we had been gone so long that the folks were worried, or whether they just wanted an excuse to come up the hill as well. There nominal excuse was that grandpa wasn't sure if there was enough gas in the tractor to get us home. The view was well worth the trip. I forget whether I drove back alone or the girls insisted on returning on the tractor.

I beg your indulgence here to tell a bit about Bev and Gene Williams. Beverly was a knockout blonde with a personality that would not quit. I was fascinated with her from the time I was a toddler. I must have been weaned prematurely; because I was fixated on Bev's bosom; so much so that the adults continued to comment about it into my most embarrassing teenage years. Gene was an up-and-coming graduate student at Univ. of Oregon, who went on to be one of the founding computer engineers at a company that I will not name. He and Bev moved to Tujunga, California, and had three daughters while he became a mover and a shaker in the computer industry. A group of his fellow engineers had a falling out with the parent company, so the split off and formed another very successful computer company which is credited with building the first minicomputer.

When I was in college in Oceanside, CA. Gene and Bev invited me and Phil Sowa to visit their beautiful home in the foothills of Los Angeles. They also took us to Universal City. Gene wasn't actually around for that, but Bev and the girls made it a most enjoyable visit. I cannot remember if we stayed overnight, but it seems unlikely that we would have come the 90 miles from Oceanside for a one-day visit. It might have been when we were either going or coming from San Luis Rey for the school year. Gene and

Bev also came down to San Luis Rey on another occasion and took us out to dinner in Escondido. We were so fascinated with Gene's car because it has a gauge that showed how much fuel was being consumed at any point in time (I have never seen one since until my wife bought a Kia Rio. It gives us an instantaneous readout in mile/gallon). They looked like the perfect family, and we were very pleased to be so treated by them.

Unfortunately the pressures of corporate life led to the dissolution of Bev and Gene's marriage, but Bev married again, and lived an adventurous life with her second husband. They ran a business together, but for fun, they were Airstream buffs and they travelled all over the country with the club called the Airstreamers[55]. They stopped to see my mother several times on their trips through the Northwest. I was there for one of those visits and I was impressed with the life Bev had chosen. I don't know how Gene and the girls have fared, because I lost touch with Bev after my mother's death (primarily because I can't remember her married name). The failure of their marriage taught me that no matter how perfect things may seem in this society of appearances, you never know what is happening within the relationship. In the case of Bev and Gene, I know more, but I am not telling.

Whatever else happened that fateful first summer "on the outside" is lost in the fog of memory. You are probably wondering what the dilemma was to which this chapter's title alludes. What you need to know about the vocation to the priesthood, is that it is a perpetual dilemma. There I was, 15 years old, hormones raging, out in the "real" world with girls seeming to be every place you turn. I was doing my best to avoid contact but that was not easy. There were girls on TV, girls in the store, girls at the swimming pool, girls, girls, girls. Although the Elvis movie of that name was not released until November of 1962, the trend was already happening! My dilemma was to decide, at 15, whether I wanted to forgo any contact with the opposite sex, or whether I should keep my options open. I didn't think I had much in the way of options at the time, but it was a hypothetical question. I liked the camaraderie of the seminary, but I was convinced that I was missing something. Duh!

I spent a lot of confessional time on this subject. I had started masturbating sometime between my 8th and 10th year, but it was a source of great guilt, because the Catholic Church did not approve. I had managed to avoid the "deviant" practice at the seminary, but those afternoons at home left a lot of time for temptation. I think that was part of my reason for roaming the street, but this proved to be a two-edged sword. I didn't talk to the girls I met on the street, but that doesn't mean I didn't think about them. At one point I was going to confession at St. Mary's in Kelso, because I didn't like Fr. Mulligan as a confessor. His idea of the sacrament of shriving[56] was to say the absolution and pass out penance… usually a number of rosaries. Fr. Henry Buckman, pastor of St. Mary's. was a roly-poly, friendly sort of priest. One day he surprised me by asking me, in the confessional, to come back to the sacristy after confession. When I did so, he greeted me with a big hug, and held me for a minute or so. Then he asked me if I wanted to come to breakfast as the rectory. Which I did, and ate cornflakes with honey (first time for me, and it was good). I can't remember what we talked about, but it was all very mundane. I suppose, given the scandals that have wracked the Catholic Church, you might think this priest's actions were suspicious. However, while I did not understand exactly why he invited me, I think his intentions were innocent. He knew I was a seminarian struggling with temptation, and I think he thought I needed a hug.

CHAPTER 10

The Great Storm

6 Then the LORD answered Job out of the whirlwind and said:
7"Dress for action like a man; I will question you, and you make it known to me. **English Standard Version (2001) Job 40:6-7**

THE BEGINNING OF SOPHOMORE YEAR, as I have alluded, was both disturbing and welcoming. It was disturbing because of all the classmates who had not returned. It was welcoming because nothing else had changed. The same faculty was in place, although Fr. Dunstan Duffy was added after his 5th year of theology. Our dorm was on the southeast side of the building, but was essentially the same 29 beds and lockers, but there were only 22 sophomores to assign to them. The new freshman class was smaller than ours with only 13 students. Among them, Tony Searing and Pat Rogers were from Longview, WA. Pat may have come in as a sophomore, because he was in my 8th grade. The food had not changed; Brother Conrad Holland was on the job, but now he had some help from the new brother, Virgil Messinger.

Our new classroom shared a wall with our freshman classroom, but we were next to the growing library, and the room did not have the distraction of so many windows. Unfortunately I was assigned to a desk next to the only window that looked out of doors (didn't they know I had a tendency to stare out windows and daydream?). I remember that room very distinctly; many significant events happened in that room. Well, I mean significant events happened when we were in that room. Because of the available space, it was the room chosen when we were allowed to watch events on TV. Pope John the XXIII had been elected at that end of deadlock in the College of Cardinals. He was chosen as an interim Pope because he was old. But the first thing he did was convene a Vatican Council. This became a period of great changes in the Catholic Church, including letting us watch television… rarely. A rotating book rack with paperbacks was added to the library… and we were allowed to buy them! Fr. Claude even let us watch the seminal performance of the Beatles on "The Ed Sullivan Show." I am not sure if that was the first year that we were allowed to have movies, but we had several that year: *Shane, Seven Brides for Seven Brothers, Brigadoon* and others I do not remember. I guess Fr. Claude thought we needed to know about romantic relationships, even if we were not going to have any.

We started into the routine of the quarter quite normally. Fr. Kevin was still our Latin Teacher. Fr. Dunstan was our world history and religion teacher. Fr. Kevin must have substituted for Fr. Dunstan because I remember him teaching us religion in the sophomore classroom. We were getting into personal moral issues. I was surprised when Fr. Kevin was talking about sexual issues and purity, he blushed profusely. This is a man who slept on a board over the bathtub in the little bathroom off his office. I suspect he was what the Church calls a tender conscience[57].

Fr. Alberic still had us for math, specifically geometry. Fr. Christian had us for English and Speech, while Fr. Mario started introducing us to the Spanish speaking world. As part of their speech and drama classes, taught by Fr. Mario, the upperclassmen put on a play called "Brother Orchid" by Leo Brady[58]. But the freshmen got more laughs with their not-for-credit original play. One skit was Bill Meyer as 'Ben Casey' and Steve Weyer as 'Dr. Zorba' and Tom Freeman as 'Dr. Newcomb' performing a 'delicate' operation on Mark Chelowinski. Another skit was of 'Eliot Ness' (Kurt Seippel) and his 'boys' (Dan Zwicky and Marty Osterhous) get the drop on Marshall Dillon (Bob Fleischmann), Chester (Tony Searing) and Doc (Pat Rogers) and two native Americans (Jim Barshaw and Mark Chelowinski).

The seminary lost a lot of theatrical talent when all of those characters left the seminary. Meyer, Seippel and Searing did stick with it for the 4 years. So that left the sophomores to top all those performances with the classic comedy, "Great Caesar's Ghost" by W. D. Fisher[59]. Ironic as it may be, I, Lester M. Klungness, played the part of Caesar's Ghost. I think we had them rolling in the aisles. I would "appear" through the firewood closet in the fireplace that was located in the refectory. Not many in the audience knew that there was an exterior door to the closet so I could walk out the refectory door, and reappear from this 'secret' passage. My costume was a pair of shorts and a chain around my neck (I guess that was homage to Christmas Carol). I don't remember who directed this masterpiece, but I think it might have been speech class for Fr. Christian. It was seminal in 'perfecting' my skill and going for the laughs.

The first sign that the year was going to be earthshaking was the earthquake. I don't know what magnitude it was, but it put some major cracks in the walls of the brand new building. No one was hurt, nothing else was damaged, but it was a warning.

We did the usual things that sophomores do. It was our job to initiate the freshmen. It got kind of gory. There were pots of evil tasting noodles, mud, and mayhem. Probably the worst of it was the Kangaroo Court in which Joe Lauritzon was the prosecutor and, I believe, Brian LeTourneau was judge. The physics lab had acquired a hand-held high voltage generator, and they would use it like an interrogation probe. I was actually worried that one of the terrified, blindfolded freshmen would literally die of fright. The 50,000 volts, no matter how low the amperage, is a painful proposition. I was embarrassed by my own classmates. In later years I would read of the famous experiments of Milgram[60] in which he demonstrated that people will follow orders of authority figure to inflict pain on another person, even if it violates their deepest held beliefs. Even amongst seminarians, it was possible to witness the underlying cruelty that we inherited from the chimpanzees (Pan _troglodytes_) not peaceful bonobo (Pan _paniscus_).

For the first work party of the year, I was assigned Tom Freeman and Mark Chelowinski. They were a couple of characters. Chelowinski was particularly a cut up. Ironically, 'cholo' means a kind of troublemaker[61]. I tried my best to teach these guys the proper way to work and counseled them against following in my wayward footsteps (i.e. always getting assigned to dish shift). Nevertheless, they carried on, and both ended up getting kicked out of the seminary that year. It was the beginning of my roll as 'Klugy', the sophomore with a heart. I was just following in the footsteps of my mentor, Tim McDaniels. There is a picture of Freeman and Chelowinski standing in the sun, dressed like Mafiosi or *marero* with dark shades and black ties. Chelowinski has on a light colored blazer and Freeman has on a long-sleeved bright red shirt. This was their swan song as they moved onto the world at large. They were actually good natured kids, and I assume they probably went on to be responsible adults.

This was the year that the Troubadours were actually formed. I was at a loss without Charlie, but as I said, Fr. Christian was kind enough to invite me into the fledgling folk music group. I would dutifully haul the school cello up to Fr. Christian's quarters on the second floor of the old farm house. The group would convene, and I would try to pluck out the beat, as they experimented with new chord progressions. In the first half of the year, this was strictly an intramural sport. As we developed a little proficiency, we may have played for student body events, but Fr. Christian's sights were set higher. We started with simple songs from America's history. Meanwhile, Fr. Chris was honing his plectrum style on his new five string banjo. Muthersbaugh was the foundation guitar. Ernie Ghezzi was there for his voice, and, he would not like me to say it, for his good looks. From the beginning I was not in on the harmony. I can sing, and I was one of the bass voices holding up the ecclesiastical choir. However, I could not sing and play the instrument at the same time, and never had been able to do so since. When you learn an instrument entirely by ear, you have to listen closely to hear where the music is going. It is distracting to have to try to sing, too. Of course, hundreds of thousands of musicians do it every day, but this brain did not want to double track.

I have no documentation of who played in the first incarnation of the Troubadours. I don't think it was too long before Larry Landry joined in, and that is when we really started delving into the serious folk music. Forget all the rock and roll, forget the country music, forget the blues, we are talking Folk. These were not necessarily the songs that became part of our repertoire, but they felt very authentic. Joan Baez and Peter Paul and Mary (PPM) were starting to popularize some of them. "Where Have All the Flowers Gone"[62] was written by Pete Seager but it is based on an Ukranian folk song. Cumbaya was an old spiritual... and an extremely easy song to learn. "Barbara Allen" (also called the Rose and the Briar) was actually a song from the Elizabethan era[63]. About then the Brothers Four came out with "Froggy Went a Courting"[64]; which was also an old song from the South. We would throw in some traditional spirituals as well, and these were what we used at the first folk Mass. "Just a Closer Walk with Thee" was our favorite. "Amazing Grace" was right up there. I made endnotes on some of these songs because that was part of the mystique of being folk music buffs. It was a matter of pride to be historically accurate while enjoying the music.

Eventually we started adapting more modern compositions that were written by contemporary song writers like Bob Dylan, and some of PPMs material. "Hollis Brown" and "Puff, the Magic Dragon" were examples. Of course PPM's rabble rousers were borrowed from Woody Guthrie. 'If I Had a Hammer' and "This Land Is Your Land" became our standards. And we were trying to keep up scholastically at the same time. This didn't start to be a problem until we went on the road. On the one hand, having the opportunity to travel outside the cloistered walls was a good incentive to study fast and hard. On the other hand, it was also a diversion.

Up to October 12th, nothing eventful stands out in my memory. On that date in 1962, the wind began to blow very hard. Bill Halvorson and

I thought "Cool, let's go outside and lean into the wind." Which was all well and good until the fruit trees beside the pathway started falling over (literally uprooting). At first we were thinking, "Hey, this is really neat". But then huge branches started blowing by our heads, and we finally had the good sense to escape to the building. We continued to watch from the stairwell door, as more trees and debris and whole pieces of roofing were blowing around all over the place. Being at the top of the Sandy River Gorge at a bend in the river probably funneled the wind up and over the cliff. Just as the sun was beginning to set the lights went out. There was a mad scramble for the sacristy where they kept all the used-candle stubs. Everyone was issued a candle and the lighter wicks were passed from one trembling seminarian to the next. It wasn't that they were so scared, but the wind just whistled through every crack and cranny of cross-shaped building, making it very cold. The wind continued to blow through the night, but by morning it had subsided. I forget what Brother Conrad was able to conjure up to feed us that night, but in the morning he was already moving his wares out to the outdoor barbeque so he could whip us up some hotcakes. Old Marines are enterprising that way! What had hit us was what was later called the Columbus Day Storm[65].

It is fortunate that floor tile had not been laid in the cross-shaped building yet, because for the next week we were all wandering around with sacristy candles. The most traveled areas of the floor were completely covered with wax drippings... as were the desks, the window ledges, and the student lockers. That was a job cleaning up all that wax!

But the first job was to clear the debris off the roads and the grounds. That was where I got my first chain saw lessons. I think it might have been Br. Raymond that taught me. Up until this point I have not mentioned either Br. Raymond, the maintenance friar, or Mr. Albrecht, the carpenter, because they were behind the scenes, so to speak. But after Typhoon Freda, we all stood up and took notice of these two men who were so important to keeping the facilities running. Herb Karnofski came "into his own" as the *jardinier extraordinaire* after the hurricane. There was much landscaping to do. Of course, we all worked on the cleanup and clearing of the grounds, but Herb became the lead planter. I was a fair to middlin' grounds keeper myself, and after the storm I became the person of choice to do ground maintenance. I like to think it was because I was good at managing the freshmen, as well. Perhaps this was the start of my agricultural career?

We had a huge job cleaning all the blown down brush that had accumulated everywhere on the campus. The fallen fruit trees had to be sawed up into cord wood. There certainly was no shortage of wood for the cooking fire. The weather cleared up after the storm so the work was not as unpleasant as it would have been in the cold rain. It was nippy, but there was enough sun that the troops could work outside for a good part of the day. I don't remember exactly what we did with it all; I don't remember there being any burning piles. Perhaps we threw a lot of it in the gulch along the driveway leading to the seminary; you remember my mention of the place, blackberry heaven? I think it became a huge compost dump. When we had cleaned up the grounds, we went on to help a family that was a big contributor to the seminary.

That family was the Nordstrom family of the famed shoe dealership of that name. They had a beautiful log cabin mansion on the banks of the Sandy River. After we had cleared their yard in quick order, the family invited us in the house to see this delightful domicile. On entering the front door there was a very large living room with a very large fire place tiled with slate (as I remember). The banister that led upstairs to the bedrooms was a curved log that looked like a huge anaconda. At the end of the banister, nearest the ground floor, there was a large burl that looked like a serpents head. All of the light fixtures were made with two inch round limbs that had been sawn in half, barked and varnished, and then constructed like a small log cabin. The logs that made the walls were also debarked and varnished to a high gloss. The kitchen cupboards were also covered with the half round poles. In total, the effect was a home that was very cozy and warm, if sumptuous. It really had the flavor of the northwest and reminded me of the company manager's house in McCloud.

When the sun went down on the days after the storm, there wasn't much we could do by candle light. Nevertheless, seminarians had time to sit around and "bond". I do believe that the experience of the storm, and the week of working together brought us all into a more cohesive state. Funny how roughing it makes guys get along better. When everything is normal, guys get antsy. I've heard that there is a saying in the army: "If the troops ain't bitchin' som'n's wrong." I can believe that. When things get so bad that everybody hunkers down and shuts up, then you know the situation is desperate. This storm definitely did not leave us in a desperate situation. We were glad to be out of class. We were working our bodies in the daytime and our mouths at night. Perfect! And Fr. Claude couldn't even turn on the "fire alarm".

Actually, I can't remember how the Dean of Discipline did get us up in the morning; Charlie was no longer around to blow "Reveille"[66] and we did not have a church bell. Nevertheless, Mass went on by candlelight with all of us in attendance as faithfully as we frequented Br. Conrad's campfire meals. Physical work every day didn't seem so bad, but you didn't want to get too used to it. That is because we knew there would be some catching up to do when the power came on and things became routine again. Neither the new building nor the old ones were much worse for wear after the storm. There might have been a few ceramic tiles blown off the Spanish style roof of the old farmhouse, but Raymond and Mr. Albrecht took care of those details. Other than candlewax everywhere, and the absence of the orchard, you wouldn't know anything had happened. There were a few less trees in the compound, but we also brought in about 30 potted evergreens, and started planting them with a vengeance. That was perhaps a bit too true, because a significant portion of those trees did not survive. Now if Herb had planted them, I am sure they would have been fine, but my thumb was not quite green enough yet. Actually it had more to do with the fact that the taproots were bound by the hard soil in the small holes we had dug. That is when I learned that gymnosperms are very different than angiosperms. The former has a tap root like a carrot, if you break off the tap root the tree will not grow. Also, if the tap root encounters hardpan, the tree cannot grow. On the other hand, one of the adaptive advantages that an angiosperm has is that its roots can grow any which way. There is a lesson in there for life, I am sure.

After the storm the quasi monastic life continued unabated. Fr. Christian continued to pit the freshmen against the sophomores in speech class debates. But now we were the cocks of the walk, the know-it-alls. In retrospect I can see that the faculty had intended speech as character building curriculum. A daunting experience for freshmen, but a challenge for the sophomores as well. Can you imagine the ignominy of being bested by a couple of freshmen in a debate? I can't remember being defeated myself, but that may have more to do with my mind blocking out traumatic experiences than with reality. The yearbook shows Pat Rogers and Tony Searing taking on the experienced sophomore team of Ed Vachal and John Hanna. I seem to remember that the Longview freshmen held their own!

It seems as though there was a chink in the monastic armor that year. Strange things started to happen. For one, there was a Nuns' Day on which a whole flock of black and white robed women toured the seminary. And I have evidence that the Troubadours played for them (although I was not in the picture); Fr. Chris, Kurt Seippel and Phil Muthersbaugh are clearly seen serenading the women. Apparently I was either late or on dish shift. The celebration of Fr. Basil's Silver Jubilee was probably not an unheard of thing for a seminary, but then Russo and Brentano were invited in for the first Hootenanny... Shocking stuff! Then before you know it, the Third Order of St. Francis, Oregon Chapter, were filling the gym to capacity. Then there was Gambling Night, to raise money for the Franciscan Missionary Union. Why, we even went roller skating...at a roller rink... with people... even girls! What had the storm done to our peaceful cloister? Or maybe it was that folk group... playing for student assemblies, and nuns. Maybe there was a bigger storm brewing outside the seminary. Everything was changing; you couldn't stop it.

Christmas came fast that year, but you know, I don't remember a darn thing about it. We usually put on a Christmas performance for the families, but I don't remember what this year's celebration included. I remember Fr, Mario had us tuned up for *"Puer Natus in Bethlehem"* and "Little and Drummer Boy"; perhaps it was a musical history of Christmas?

All I remember about Christmas of 1962, after I got home, was that my folks had moved out on the Toutle River, and we spent the whole time periodically walking across the road to check the Toutle to make sure it wasn't passing flood stage. During the day, eighty-year old Floyd Munyon sat in his little wooden river shack with a pot belled stove fired up. He had his fishing pole and lure cast in the water. His son, Lawrence, would come down to check on him from time to time. That might have been the year that someone brought us an elk roast, and we cooked it in the fireplace with the Dutch oven[67] that my grandfather had given to my mother. As I remember, elk makes a mighty nice roast, although I have never tasted it since. Our little 24 ft. by 24 ft. cottage on the River was a lot cozier than the house on Pennsylvania street. They intended to sell the big house but had not found a buyer. They would not even find renters for it until my junior year at the seminary.

Typically, my mother had gone crazy with decorations for the tree. Now we lived out in the woods where you could cut your own Christmas tree. I went to my first Midnight Mass at St. Mary's in Castle Rock. It is a little town on the banks of the Cowlitz River at the place where the Spirit Lake Highway takes off from Interstate 5. Today, Gretchen's brother, who is only four years older than we are, is in a nursing home there in Castle Rock. This graduate of West Point and Harvard is incapacitated by the not so gradual loss of frontal lobe activity in his brain. This is another example of the irony of life (happenstance?). I don't really understand why my folks decided to move to the Toutle, but I am glad they did. My Father had been 6 miles from the post office, now he was 20 miles from work. I think my mother loved the life in the woods. It certainly wasn't an economic advantage for them, and my dad eventually lost the cottage to the eruption of Mt. St Helens in 1980. Nevertheless, I very much enjoyed the summers I spent living on the Toutle River.

When we returned to the seminary, I had my upright bass with me... that was my Christmas present. Believe me, it was a job squeezing it in the VW bug; which story I forgot to tell; i.e. how the family's second VW bug was acquired. I don't know that I got to play with the Troubadours right away. Of the five or six pictures of the Troubadours in the 1962 yearbook, only one shows my bass, and that was being played by Ernie Ghezzi. Never mind; I got my chance. As I said before, there is a full page picture of my bass with me practicing outdoors next to the seminary's newly acquired VW bug. That car would become the errand vehicle for the school, and in the following year I would be the first designated driver from our class.

That winter, while not the coldest we experienced at SFS, was replete with snow. Fr. Christian and the Skibrüders were off to Mt. Hood every chance they got. We mere pedants were confined to snowball fights -- dare I say, wars -- and igloo building. Spring came softly, and warm afternoons were not uncommon.

Spring brought Holy Week, and then Camp Howard. I have already described those consequent events in the previous year. Easter is so steeped in tradition that, even with the liturgical changes, activities were very similar to the previous year. We did learn a version of "The Prayer of St. Francis," which starts, "Lord, Make Me an Instrument of Your Peace". I have never been able to find this version on the internet to confirm the composer. This composition was fitting in its atonality, and the fact that the racial unrest and the Vietnam War were taking their toll on peace. The war was not yet horrible enough to elicit strong reaction amongst the citizenry, and was not forward in my memories. The Civil Rights protests were not so ignored. The novelty of Camp Howard had, however, worn a bit thin, and there were so many new and interesting things happening at the seminary, we were a little anxious to get back and see what would happen next.

That year, Fr. Christian was our English instructor, and not only did he make reading mandatory (biweekly book reports), but he made it easy, by providing paperbacks and helping us get to the library. Also, the school library was in the next room! I read probably more than I had before or since, including Dante's *Inferno, Confessions of St. Augustine, Portrait of Dorian Gray, I Promessi Sposi*, and others that I do not remember. We were not restricted from reading *To Kill a Mocking* Bird or *Catch 22*, but I was always a bit independent. Just because everyone else was reading those books didn't make them mandatory reading for me. The mental images from Dante, although dim, are still with me to this day. The forlorn lovers and suicides in the first ring of hell, and the corrupt popes in quagmire at the bottom ring of hell have permanently altered my concept of the degrees of inhumanity. *The Confessions* impressed me that a man in the 4th century would have much the same personal struggles that we still have in the 20th century. *Portrait of Dorian Gray*[68] was just kind of weird, but I needed to write a book report. *I Promessi Sposi*[69] probably had the most profound effect on me. It opened my eyes to the fact that we are all at the mercy of nature; at any time we could be thrown into a desperate life or death situation, in which, with regard to human behavior, all bets are off. I don't know if I read Sinclair Lewis' *Arrowsmith* in the sophomore year, but the book also deals with the random circumstances that can so profoundly change our lives[70]. As I remember, Arrowsmith's wife died because he had spilt a test tube of *Bacillus botulinum* in his lab, which contaminated a pack of cigarettes; from which his wife, Leora, later smoked. *Ironia est tropus per contrarium quod conatur ostendens*[71] (which I freely translate as meaning "irony is a bitter pill that confounds whatever endeavor is attempted").

I will perhaps end this chapter of my life with quotations from the yearbook. I had a page set aside for "Frosh", and here is some of what they said.

"Well I guess you are the only Troubadour from the original Free Time Five Plus Two. It's been nice knowing you. I guess you don't know yet but I won't be here next year. I got the word last Saturday from Fr. Kevin. Well, that's life." "Flash" [Bob Fleischmann]

"Klugy, this is a reminder to always be happy, because unless you are happy you'll get nowhere. Leo" [Leonard Rickey]

I have to diverge from my quotations to comment on Leo. Leo Rickey was a tall gangly fellow like me, and in many ways he was almost like a protégé to me, as I was to Tim McDaniels. I think he wondered why I was so cheerful and kind to lowly freshmen. His picture was neither in the group photo or the individual class photos. Nevertheless he made it to his next year at SFS, and was, elected president of his sophomore class while I was elected vice president of my sophomore and junior class. We met again at University of Washington. I was in my Jesus Freak[72] stage, and I think he was rather distainful of my decent into fundamentalism.

Some other freshmen quotes are significant to me.

"Way to go St. Francis, but Francis didn't get caught. Always, Kenemer "[Ken Latimer, does not appear in the yearbook until the next year]

"Klugy, you certainly do remind me of a 'MONSTER'. You always just dink around. Pee Wee Lee" [pint sized Lee Meier was also not in the group or class photos until the next year.]

"I was a freshman once too, ya know? Dan Skarry" [He was in all yearbooks from1962 to 1966]

"Klugy, you always have a cheerful spirit, and I hope some of it rubs off on me. I hope to see you next year, and best of luck. Tom Burchett" [He was in yearbook 1962 to 1965]

One of the seniors had some kind remarks for me too.

Mike, Old Partner, we've really had a blast this year, and I am going to be sad to miss you this [next] year. Your kindness, I am sure, you inherited from your parents (They're pretty neat). I gonna miss playing the blues with you but I'll remember you in my prayers, and you remember to do the same. Your partner Ernie [Gezzi. He graduated in 1964]

And one of my classmates who left SFS before our junior year wrote:

"Well old buddy, here is the end of another year. I am proud to say that I have been one of your classmates. Good luck in wherever you go, whatever you do, and 'whoever" you will be with. Keep of the terrific heat. Don't step on the ole Volks. For now, your buddy and fellow beat. Lar!" [Larry Hiller left SFS in 1963]

The latter was Larry Hiller; I doubt if he knew how prophetic his words would be. I don't know if we had talked about the opposite sex (probably), so the "whoever" probably had overtones of future relationships. I don't know if he meant to say "keep off" or "keep up" the heat; either way, I can interpret significance. We did crank up the heat folk singing, and there were plenty of times in my life where I have been on the hot seat... probably inadvertently turning up the flame. Larry encountered his hot seat in Vietnam. We visited him in Bremerton Naval Hospital in the late sixties. He had been shot and had multiple fractures in his leg. His biggest worry was that he would not heal up well enough so that he could return to Nam. He admitted that combat duty had taken hold of him like an addiction (although he did not use those terms). I remembered thinking how ironic it was that a Franciscan seminarian would be skilled in the art of war. As St Francis said "Let me be an instrument of your peace"; I guess there are many ways to interpret that. After all Francis himself went off to the war twice; first with the intention of being a famous soldier[73]. But he was struck down with illness which lead to his eventual conversion and the formation of the Lesser Brothers (*Fratres Minores*). The next time Francis went to North Africa, it was as a poor beggar intent on meeting the sultan to try to talk him into stopping the Holy War[74].

I have always opposed the wars to which we Americans seem inextricably drawn, but I do not fault those who, in good conscience, feel that war is sometimes necessary. Phil Sowa has been a pilot and a flight commander through Granada, Panama, Libya, Bosnia, 1st Gulf War, Iraq and, at least from a desk, Afghanistan. Am I going to accuse him of being a war monger? Hell, no! George W. Bush and that 'Dick" Cheney, yes, but those who fight the wars do not make them. Thank God, there are some men of conscience within the ranks of the military. War is such a welcoming place for evil to thrive, that without "a few good men" the armies and the world would devolve into chaos… and has done so more than once in history. I wish we could beat our swords into plowshares, but the species has not evolved to that point yet. Maybe genetic engineering's finest accomplishment will be to incorporate a little more Bonobo and less Chimpanzee into our genome[75]. *Pan (also Homo) paniscus* is the species name for the bonobo. *Pan troglodytes* is the name for chimps. I don't know if the scientists who named them realized how profoundly different these species were even though they share most of their genome with humans. The names say it all, i.e. the little bread [eaters] and the troglodytes.

When the sophomore year ended, I was heading home to a house far out in the country on the Toutle River. I was not sure that I would have a job, but I found one working on a farm about 2 miles up the Toutle River Road. It was the property of a local jippo logger. I tried to Google jippo, but all I got was family histories and quotes from novels. Even Wikipedia did not have an entry. I did find a jippo logging contract, but apparently the name is only used in logging circles. Mr. Conradi made his living doing logging contracts for Weyerhaeuser Co. He had a small crew and a limited amount of equipment, but it was enough to keep him and his wife, Annabelle, in a comfortable living in their hundred year old farm on 100 acres. They had originally purchased it from a retired sea captain, who had homesteaded the property. He had built two houses and accompanying barns and storage sheds nearly a century earlier. Subsequent to purchasing the property, the Conradis had built their dream house on a clearing by a bend in the Toutle river. That house had burned to the ground a number of years before I worked for them, so they had been forced to move back into the old farm house. Annabelle kept a few cattle, and occasionally a rescued fawn or young elk, The Fish and Wildlife staff had brought her the orphans because they knew she was good with them. Some of those animals or their offspring are still at the Seattle Zoo, where they were transferred when they got too big for Mrs. Conradi to handle. Mrs. Conradi also had her cats and a cocker spaniel that she loved dearly... so much so that she would heat her dog food on the stove. She was a somewhat eccentric woman, and prone to be doing 5 things at once. Therefore, more than once she had forgotten the dogfood on the stove. Consequently, the house always reeked of a most peculiar odor.

The occasion of my being hired was by way of Lawrence Munyon, our neighbor, who worked for the Conradies when they needed him. It was about haying time, and Annabelle had hired him to bring in the hay, and repair the fences so they could move cattle into the mown pasture. Lawrence himself was in a little better shape than I am now, but he was no strapping youth. Mrs. Conradi agreed that he needed the help for the task. So I was hired, and I probably learned about as much that summer as I had learned in previous 10 summers. First we baled, then we hauled and stacked, and then we went to work on the fences. I had never handled barbed wire, but Lawrence had years of experience. It was tiring work, but it was healthy, and Annabelle always insisted that I drink a quart of whole milk that she provided at every lunch. I guess she thought I was too skinny to be a really useful farm hand. "Ya got'a bulk up for that kind'o work." Lawrence only worked with me until the haying was done, then Annabelle kept me on for "chores" that Lawrence would not do. This included feeding the animals, scything the compound where the grass was growing out of control, and other one-time-only projects. The animals were mainly the few cows and one old Herford bull. I don't remember if she actually named him Ferdinand, but if not, that is how I thought of him. He was about as much like a bull as I am like a ballet dancer. You could walk right around him and feed him and hose him off, but you had to be careful about one thing. If you started to scratch him with a shovel or a stick, you better be near a gate or a door where you could escape. No, he wouldn't charge you; he would pin you. You know, up against a wall. Why? So you wouldn't stop scratching him… he loved his scratch.

The other jobs that Annabelle wanted done were mostly clean up. She wanted to rent out the other house, but it had not been lived in for 50 years or more. It was a very sturdy old house, built with 2x4s that were actually 2 by 4 inches, and siding and wallboard that was solid 1 inch thick Douglas fir, mostly clear grain. There was a lot of cedar in the house, too. I suspect the 2 to 3 ft. diameter blocks that the house rested on were old growth cedar, because that wood is so full of natural insecticidal resin that no self-respecting termite would touch the stuff. I would venture to say there are probably still people renting that house, or it has been sold, since I cleaned it up. And the round cuts of cedar log that supported the house may still be intact.

Fortunate for me that everyone figured cleaning up that house was a herculean task, because the hardest part for me was to avoid sitting down and read the newspapers pasted to the wall boards. They were from the previous century. I did while away[76] some time that way, sitting with piles of debris and rat droppings all around. Fortunately I did not contract any lung disease during the operation, but I did eventually get the house cleaned up well enough for them to paint it and rent it. Other jobs on the place were similar. Clearing a path to the tool shed, hauling off derelict equipment, and removing tussock grass from the more swampy pastures. One day she took me down to their former dream house which had burned down years before. It was a beautiful spot and I could see the nostalgia welling up in her eyes. The river stone fire place was still standing; the gentle shoosh from the nearby rapids, and the sound of birds were the only distractions. I can't remember exactly what it was that she had me do down in that peaceful place, but it must have caused them great pain when the whole area was literally buried under tons of lava mud from Mt. Saint Helen's eruption in 1980. I guess they had only one consolation, mainly, even if they had rebuilt the house, it would have just been swept away again. Am I getting monotonous in my reminding the reader of the happenstantial nature of life?

Now, before I go on to describe the other pleasant aspects of life that summer on the Toutle, I have a confession. My friends from St. Rose, Mike Momberg and Chris Olsen, asked if they could come out and visit me on the Toutle. My mother was game with that, so they came out to visit (I am not sure if it was one day, or whether they slept over one night. That Saturday we grabbed my single shot 22, and walked into the woods on a Weyerhaeuser logging road that was about half way to Conradi's from our house. I knew from previously hunting out on that road with Craig Tillotson, that there was a large beaver lake along that road. I had never been beyond the beaver lake, but they wanted to press on. Eventually we came to a clearing, where any idiot could determine that there had been recent logging. Not only that, but there wwere also an old 1955 GMC logging truck, and a box of fire tools. The fire tools box was locked, but the lads were feeling their Wheaties and busted into the tool box to see what they could find... amazing! There were axes, and Pulaskis. Fortunately there were no containers of hydrocarbons, or we might have been tempted to burn down the whole damn forest. Instead, my buddies decided that the old truck was a derelict and needed to be reduced to junk. So they proceeded to tear into the truck with the axes. They busted out all the windows and then started chopping holes in the hood. I was a little stunned, but I decided to shoot the tires with my 22, just to see what would happen. They eventually tired of this maniacal sport, and so we headed home.

On the way home, I was getting nervous... in my mind I was thinking, whose truck was it? What if someone comes asking my parents? What if we left footprints? So when we got home, while the lads were distracted by something outside, I took my mother aside and told her what had happened. I can't remember if she confronted the boys then, but they left soon after, and she proceeded to try to find out whose equipment it was. That meant contacting Weyerhaeuser, and she ended up getting Hugh Wickett, the Weyerhaeuser Pulp Mill manager. Well, he inquired, and it turned out to be Ted Conradi's jippo logging equipment. Great! So now I am getting paid by the wife of the man whose livelihood I am destroying.

Well, suffice it to say, the other parents were called to a conference with Hugh and Ted, and an agreement was worked out that the parents would share the cost equally. Each family paid about $1500; which was a lot of money for a man who only earns $400 a month. It turns out the only destructive act that I did, shooting the tires, had no effect. So my parents paid only because I had been so stupid as to lead these budding juvenile delinquents into the woods.

Both of the boys were madder than hell at me, and we did not have any more "outings" after that incident. They should have thanked me, because if we had not turned ourselves in, Weyerhaeuser would have brought in the police, and all three of us might have ended up in Juvie. Nor did they suffer any further consequences. It did not go on our records, and they were free to do their thing. I, on the other hand, damn near got kicked out of the seminary. I was only accepted back on probation. I never did see Mike Momberg again. Chris came to visit me one more time when he was in the Army. He was on home leave from the army, and he brought his fiancée out to meet my family. He had unpleasant tales of his job in Vietnam. It was to sit atop the military garbage trucks and knocked Vietnamese people off with his rifle butt. They were trying to scavenge what they could. The military logic was that the scavenger could be Vietcong trying to recover documents that might reveal the troop deployments. Most likely some of those people were poor Vietnamese that were just trying to survive. At least Chris came back alive, and probably has a parcel of kids now, but I bet he won't be telling his kids about his exploits in "Nam".

By the way, that aforementioned "hunting" trip with Craig should have, and eventually did, cure me of the sport. Craig was and is an upstanding person, and he was seriously trying to hunt for small animals or fowl. After trudging for several hours without seeing any game, we ended up in a wooded field between the Munyon's farmhouse and my folks' cottage. There was a small pine tree about 7 ft. high in which a whole flock of little, what we called, 'snowbirds' were roosting. They were probably *Dendroica nigrescens* or the Black-throated Grey Warbler.

Black-throated Grey Warbler. (Reproduced with permission of Graham Montgomery).

I am including a picture just to emphasize how senseless was what we did next. It still horrifies me to think that we stood around that tree for a several minutes shooting the little gray balls of fluff. We probably killed 8 or 10. Why they didn't fly away, I could not say, unless they were protecting a community of nests. Mrs. Munyon was also incredulous. Later she asked my mother if she knew "who were those juvenile delinquents who were shooting bird" in her yard. I think she knew it was me, but was too polite to say. I never again went hunting. I have shot domestic animals and I once downed a wounded deer that had wandered into our property in Tenino. My conscience is not pricked by that 3 point buck who looked me squarely in the eye as if to say: "I am done for now, please send me on my way". Since then, I only once obtained a hunting license or purposely hunted wild game.

There is one other sad fact that I will discuss here, although it happened a few years later. Lawrence Munyon, who had gotten me the summer job, and who helped my Dad put up four tree poles for a "diamond" antenna for our TV. Lawrence visited my folks regularly, brought firewood and was always there to help his parents or any neighbor. He died of cancer. I thought he was a tough old cowboy, who had worked hard all his life, but now I realize that he was already suffering from cancer when I worked with him. That is part of the reason he did not have a regular job, and stayed with his folks to take care of them. They were both in their eighties, and he was their only son, but he preceded both of them to the grave. I wrote a poem for his mother after he died. If I could find it, I would include it. Ah, there it is, in my college notebook:

In Memoriam Lawrentii

The blow:
> A slow spreading growth,
>> The sturdy, stooped, and stoic figure
>> Struggles under life's long load,
>>> His sacrifice unknown.

He raised the branchless tree
> That brought the far off light,

A diamond wire of life,
> That bears man's common plight
> To both our in-rooms sight.

He shouldered wood
> That should have been our common chore.

A debt we owe,
> That warms with fire's glow
> The hands and hearts of those,

Who thanklessly have loved him more,
> When his life was worn
>> Beyond another man's concern,

When gratitude expressed
> Can only mourn.

Now we can move on to some lighter topics. Let's start with the composition that I wrote in college, but which describes my sensations that first year I was on the Toutle.

A flow of gentle breeze, a background sound, a roar. The wind always blows. Although it's rarely ever wind, but water. The river's flow over

rocks, through holes. A constant sound that never comes or goes…
except when I walk around the bend. Then the water tends toward
the rustled trees, and these two flows blend. But when I come back,
it sounds like the track of a log truck far off down the road, hauling a
full load home. So real is it that instinct makes me tread the crushed
rock trench beside the asphalt bed. It shakes the woods; they watch.
I hear the blown oak groan. These are the sounds of home.

As I think I said previously, we lived right next to the Toutle River.
We were not on the banks but we were just across the road. Just before the
Toutle reached our house it went from being two streams around a central
island to being one wide, fairly shallow and slow moving stretch of water.
That was in the summertime. There was a bit of rapids on the far side of the
little island and not on the near side. There were little bits of beach along the
road side of the river. The water was always cold, probably between 65-70
°F. So in the early summer it wasn't too bad for swimming. However, about
July the glaciers on Mt. St. Helens would add a lot of glacial melt to the
Toutle. Then the water was more challenging; probably in the high 50's or
low 60's. They say you can't spend too long in 55 °F water without getting
hypothermic. Well, it was a short swim over to the island; on a sunny day
you could thaw out before you had to swim back. It was part of my daily
routine. It was not as much fun on overcast days – which are many in the
Pacific Northwest -- because you could not warm up before you had to swim
back. On those days swimming was more of a constitutional than a sport.

I failed to mention my good old dog, Sox. I had gotten him when we
lived in Longview, and, although the dogs ran pretty freely around the
neighborhood there, Sox was in seventh heaven when he came to the Toutle.
The day Sox and I first met, I was asleep in my upstairs bed which faced the
driveway. The sound of a postal semi-truck entering our driveway woke me
up. I thought it was strange that such a big truck was parking at our house,
but I was tired and went straight back to sleep. A little later, I awoke to a
warm sensation on my ear. A wee little, white and brown puppy was licking
and chewing on my ear. That was the beginning of a beautiful friendship.

His face was half white and half blackish-brown with a touch of tan, and his feet were white such that he looked like he was wearing socks. He had a white tip at the end of his tail, and long soft fur that was mostly blackish-brown on top and white on the bottom. We think he might have been part Australian Shepard, and his intelligence supported that theory. The truck driver said he came from a cross with a Boxer. But, other than the almost brindle multicolored coat, you could not see Boxer in him. He looked and acted like a Shepherd, and that was the glory of being on the Toutle. He was always out 'herding' something, mostly deer, of which there were many. The deer eventually were the cause of his demise; a buck, trying to defend his family, gored Sox in the rear. The injury did not kill Sox, and he lived a couple of years after that; but the wound never properly healed, and my folks finally thought it was more merciful to put him down. I was with him when he went peacefully to sleep on the Vet's table.

Like Boy, we did have some good years with Sox! He was not neutered, so he would occasionally wander off for the whole day. One day, one of my Dad's fellow employees (who lived 3 miles up the Toutle River Rd) told my Dad he had better come up and collect his 'property'. Turns out, their little Fox Terrier had had a puppy that had almost the same markings as Sox. I guess he had "got busy", as they say. Because she had a white tipped tail, we called her Tippy; and father and daughter had several good years together, too. There was no mistaking whose pup she was, either. They both had long soft fur, and they were well matched in brains and agility. The one difference was that Sox was a confident watch dog, but he would make friends with strangers very quickly. Tippy was very shy and would hide out from strangers until she was absolutely sure they were ok. When she came out of her shell, so to speak, she was very sweet with visitors. A true lap dog she was!

Sox actually saved my mother's life after they moved out on the Toutle. There was a damper in the fireplace, which we frequently closed at night. We did this so the wind would not howl through the house, taking all the heat with it. One night my mother closed the damper, thinking the fire had long since been snuffed out. But she was mistaken. In the middle of the night, she awoke to the sound of Sox woofing at her in that plaintive way dogs do when they want to tell you something. She suddenly realized that she had a raging headache and was having hard time breathing. Then she realized that the house was full of smoke; much longer in that house, they would both have been asphyxiated. She managed to craw to the door and they both vacated the house. Some dogs might have just tried to claw their way out at the door, but Sox seemed more concerned about my mom than his own safety.

My mother loved it out on the Toutle. Since she could not drive, she was there a lot of the time. A lot of women would have been bored, but don't forget that my mother was born in a logging camp and spent her summers riding horseback on the Tumalo farm of her grandparents. She loved having salal berries (*Gaultheria shallon*) and evergreen blackberries for her "garden". Being in amongst the evergreen pine and Douglas fir, where the chipmunks and the crows were sounding off all day, was just her "cup o' tea".

I too enjoyed the seclusion of the Toutle. Every weekday morning I would get up at six; eat my bowl of fruit with toast and coffee; pack my little lunch (if mother had not already made it); ride my bike the 3 miles to Conradi's. There I would work until noon, eat lunch and drink my quart of milk, work out my 8 hours, then ride my bike home. Usually I would take a dip in the Toutle (to save well water which was scarce in the summer). After cleaning up, I would eat dinner and maybe do some chores. In spite of Lawrence's diamond TV antenna, reception was lousy so I might listen to records and play my bass, but I don't remember reading anything that summer. It was not a whole lot different than being a monk. Of course I had my mother to talk to and Lawrence would come by and occasionally we would visit the Munyon's. Otherwise, only when we would go out on the weekends, would there be much interaction with people.

I had not abandoned my Dad on the paper route, but it was too complicated for me to work days and do the route at night. I did help him on Sundays. So the folks decided to let me work the weekend and pay rent for my room and board. The rent was set at $90 after my first paycheck from Annabelle. We all had plenty of incentive for me to work the weekend paper route, because I needed to get my license. And I finally did. I may not have already related the unfortunate accident after my first solo run on the paper route, but my license was not suspended, and I could drive without an adult driver to accompany me. This changed Mom's life too, because now we were not stranded on the Toutle. If we wanted to use the car to go to a movie or go shopping, we could go into town with Dad when he went to work. We would have to wait until he got off from work, that night, and then drive the route with him. This did not work out well with me during the week, because I had to get up to go to the farm in the morning, so if we did go to town with Dad it would usually be on Friday. He was usually off on Saturday (if I remember correctly) so I could go with him to do the Sunday paper route.

Being able to drive meant we could do other things that had not been previously "convenient". I have already explained that Bob Huffhines and his daughter had been coming to our house in Columbia Valley Gardens to watch "Bonanza." Since that was no longer possible (we had the color TV on the Toutle, but the reception was terrible), Bob suggested that we attend a musical in Portland together. Unlike my own daughter (by the time she was in high school, she never wants to do anything with her parents), I was willing, nay happy, to join the folks in any form of entertainment. We were not inundated with electronic diversion in those "ancient" times.

On August 3, 1962, we dressed for a special occasion as if we were going to church. We meet the Huffhines at their house on 21ˢᵗ Avenue in Longview. It was a tidy two story that Bob had built with his own hands. The living room was bright and friendly, although I won't say the bright red stuffed chairs went well with the brown couch. Otherwise, it was quite welcoming, and Jana Huffhines' demure, slightly southern expressions like "You all" (not Y'all), and Bob's rather poorly disguised Texas twang added to the feeling of southern hospitality. She was from Louisiana, and Bob was a Dallas boy. Of course, Gretchen, ever proper, made her appearance slightly after the formalities were exchanged. As I said, she came flitting down the stairwell in a bright golden dress. Her blonde hair quaffed, her smile bright, her blue eyes sparkling. It was all I could do to keep my seminarian wits about me. After the appropriate conversation, we retired to our little VW bug, and they went to their 1958 Chevrolet Bel Air in their garage.

While we were driving to Portland, I was quiet, I believe. I think my mother was trying to get some indication of what I thought of Gretchen, but I was holding my cards close to my chest. I imagine Gretchen wasn't thinking much about me, except that she was thinking what a waste… she had already been coached that I was a seminarian and probably off limits. Actually she knew quite a bit about me because, as I mentioned, she and her father would come to our house in CVG, to watch "Bonanza" on the color TV. However, she had not seen a picture of me. Gretchen admitted later, that she too was pondering me on that hour long trip to Portland. She was surprised that I did not seem at all like the image she had of a dower seminarian.

Bob, who was the organizer of these events, usually arranged to eat at a restaurant before the show. I thought it was the Country Kitchen in Portland, because Bob loved a steak with baked potato and salad with Roquefort dressing. I must admit, I was sold on that meal, too. The restaurant had a standing offer that if one person in the party could eat a 72 ounce steak, everyone else in the party would eat for free. We never attempted it. As it turns out, on that first outing with the Huffhines, the restaurant was not Country Kitchen, but Mr. Robert's, and we had dessert at Holland's after the show. These facts were duly recorded by Gretchen's mother, as were all the daily events of her life from 1927.

The show we saw was the Broadway road production of "My Fair Lady."

This was a momentous event in our young lives. It was all the wit of George Bernard Shaw, plumbing the comedic depths of the male/female relationship. Beautiful costumes, beautiful actors, beautiful music. Enjoyable company made the whole evening a memorable night. Although Gretchen and I had to scour Jana's diaries to recall the date and details of this memorable event. Jana had saved programs of the hundred or more plays that their family attended in her lifetime. She also wrote on the program who attended and where they ate. This particular program was missing, but Gretchen found the entry in Jana's diary.

As far as we can tell from Jana's notes, Gretchen and I did not see each other again until the following summer. Her notebooks also reminded us that the World's Fair was held in Seattle that year. Gretchen's parents went in June and September. My folks went after I returned to the seminary, because I went to the World's Fair by myself.

I had left work at the Conradies' somewhat before school started, so I could attend a Catholic Conference that was being held in the large hall that bordered on the World's Fair compound. I think that building had existed before the Seattle Center was built for the Fair. I forget whether I took the bus or train to Seattle, and I don't remember where I stayed. I do remember spending a significant amount of time at the Fair instead of the conference. I saw the Firebird, which was controlled completely by a single handle shift and was supposed to be powered by turbine. General Motors eventually produced a line of Pontiac Firebirds, but they had ordinary steering wheels, floor shift and piston engines. The exterior looked only slightly similar to the original at the Fair.

Pontiac Firebird concept turbine car was displayed at the 1962 World's Fair in Seattle, Washington (Poster source: Duke University digital collection) http://library.duke.edu/digitalcollections/images/adaccess/T/T29/T2931/T2931-lrg.jpeg

AT&T was demonstrating the video phone. That is a technology that Ma Bell never did adopt. Video teleconferencing exists in many forms, but the monolithic phone company was already a thing of the past before that technology became available to the public. IBM probably had a display, but I do not remember it. At that time computers were the interest of business moguls and the military. UNIVAC had a display of the "library of the future" which was a mainframe computer. I think the crowd was skeptical, but UNIVAC's prediction has come true, with the exception that it is not all centralized on one privately-owned computer. Steve Jobs and Bill Gates were only 7 years old, and Steve Wozniak was just about to hit his teens.

The modern art exhibit was my first taste of "abstract"... up close and personal. There were strange animated sculptures that were made out of almost anything. There were huge paintings that didn't look like much of anything; some were in shades of grey. I very much agree with the appellation given the art form, "abstract art." In some cases I would have questioned the use of the latter word in that phrase.

What I remember most about the World's Fair was the food and the waitresses! Such attractive... accents. I had Belgian waffles, Danish scones, and Mexican enchiladas (which to this day is my favorite Latin dish). I did not ride the Monorail or ascend the Space Needle in the Bubbleator because I didn't have much money with me, but I have been up the Space Needle since, and both monuments to progress continue to serve the Seattle Skyline. There was really too much to see in the short time I had. I obviously didn't take enough away from the Catholic Conference.

Apparently, President J. F. Kennedy was supposed to be scheduled to speak at the World's Fair:

> As it happened, the Cold War had an additional effect on the fair. President John F. Kennedy was supposed to attend the closing ceremony of the fair on October 21, 1962. He bowed out, pleading a "heavy cold"; it later became public that he was dealing with the Cuban Missile Crisis. http://en.wikipedia.org/wiki/Century_21_Exposition

That fact reminds me that it was not a peaceful time in the world, even though the Fair's theme tried to emphasize the hope for a peaceful and prosperous future because of the benefits of modern science. We're still working on that...

CHAPTER 11

Hail to the Chief!

> [28] So Christ, having been offered once to bear the sins of many, will appear a second time, not to deal with sin but to save those who are eagerly waiting for him. **English Standard Version (©2001) Hebrews 9:28**

IT HAS BEEN DIFFICULT TO incorporate all the significant events of the times in this brief review of my life. Consequently, I have chosen to withhold discussion of the age of Camelot until now, because the importance of it is so magnified by the "martyrdom" of our young "King Arthur". Let me begin with the election of John F. Kennedy. Fr. Carl Willman was visiting during the Democratic convention of 1960 (same time he let me drive the VW). He was a strong advocate for Adlai Stevenson, because this statesman, in the true sense of the word, had proved himself to be an intellectual tower over his peers. Nevertheless, my parents were swayed by the youthful charisma of John Kennedy. After all, Stevenson had previously lost an election to Ike. JFK, with his beautiful wife Jacqueline, were already assuming the vision of royalty. America had moved from success to success under the generalship of President Eisenhower.

Nevertheless, as respected as he was, Ike's second term was ending, and his Republican colleagues had chinks in their armor. Mostly the nation wanted a strong and positive leader to match the optimism that had permeated the country. The Democratic convention was a messy affair with all the smoke-filled rooms and behind-the-scenes horse trading that had molded the party. Nor was Kennedy the "St. John of Avalon"[77] that we made him out to be. There is one conceit in that appellation that fits well; like the Bard of Avalon, JFK had a mastery of the language and a J. B. Shaw-like sense of humor. He was sophisticated but not pretentious, ready to banter with the press whenever they were most anxious to pin him to the proverbial wall.

We rejoiced when John was elected, and there is no doubt in my mind that his inaugural address played a large part in my decision to apply for the Peace Corps. But the Cuban Missile Crisis was one example of how complex the man was. He did not banter when he made the presidential address to the nation:

> On Monday evening, October 22 at 7:00 p.m. EST, President Kennedy delivered a nation-wide televised address on all of the major networks announcing the discovery of the missiles.
>
> "It shall be the policy of this nation to regard any nuclear missile launched from Cuba against any nation in the Western Hemisphere as an attack on the United States, requiring a full retaliatory response upon the Soviet Union."
>
> Kennedy described the administration's plan:
>
> "To halt this offensive buildup, a strict quarantine on all offensive military equipment under shipment to Cuba is being initiated. All ships of any kind bound for Cuba from whatever nation and port will, if found to contain cargoes of offensive weapons, be turned back. This quarantine will be extended, if needed, to other types of cargo and carriers. We are not at this time, however, denying the necessities of life as the Soviets attempted to do in their Berlin blockade of 1948."
>
> During the speech a directive went out to all US forces worldwide placing them on DEFCON 3. http://en.wikipedia.org/wiki/Cuban_Missle_Crisis#Crisis_stalemated

It was actually John Scali of ABC News that went behind the scenes to diffuse the situation; which could have led us into nuclear war. One needs to remember that as young as John Kennedy seemed, he was 48 and had been the captain of a PT boat in WWII. I can't judge the wisdom of Kennedy's decision to follow the policies of Eisenhower and basically continue the cold war. He does assume the responsibility for getting us into Vietnam, although Lyndon Johnson bears the responsibility for the great escalation of the war. I will say this; Kennedy did a marvelous job of handling the press during that whole Cuban crisis. The entire nation was right with him, and he even managed to resort to humor in more than one press conference. Recently we learned that Soviet naval officer Vasili Arkhipov, the Brigade Chief of Staff on submarine B-59, refused to fire a nuclear missile during the Cuban Missile Crisis. This courageous action probably saved the world from World War III and nuclear disaster.[78]

There was no doubt that "King" John had won the hearts and minds of the average American, although he continued to have his detractors in high and loathsome places. I guess we will never really know who those detractors were, although the head of the FBI was no friend of the Kennedys. Jacqueline was certainly a benefit to his public persona. Although the National Endowment for the Arts was not established until 1965, her involvement with the arts was seminal to that organization. She was also a highly respected ambassador to the world. Had the public know that John was not a faithful husband; his fortunes would have plummeted like a shooting star. Why, even the styles of the day reflected Jackie's impact. My mother was so proud of her A-line dress (white with blue collar and blue stripe down the front.) She was going to wear it to a concert, but she had to cancel because she was stung by a wasp and her whole hand had swollen. Dad and I went with the Huffhines anyway to see Harry Belafonte in concert. My mother was so bummed; but I think we went again to see him another time.

The Kennedy Administration was struggling to meet its goals when I returned to SFS in the fall of 1963. The year began on a good note. The changes brought on by the Vatican Council were continuing under Pope

Paul VI, and it was looking to be an eventful year. John XXIII had fulfilled his dream to let fresh air in the Church before he died. Fr. Kevin summed it up in the SFS 1964-66 Yearbook in these words:

> To accomplish this [a firm commitment to the goals of physical, mental and spiritual development] in a restless age full of changes, a seminary must provide stability coupled with a sinewy suppleness that will allow it to flex and bend while fastened securely to the pillars of solid educative principles. It must strive to meet the challenge of the times that demand a sharp delineation of ideas, an updating of methods, a meaningful liturgy, a true spiritual formation while maintaining a shoulder-rubbing contact with the real world, a deeper understanding and acceptance of the human condition, and a better than average education.

I love the part about the "shoulder-rubbing contact with the real world"; we definitely had that. We even worked in the soup kitchen on Burnside. No use getting bogged down in the pedantic details when so many important things were happening in my junior year. However, for the sake of simplicity and my failing memory, I think I will follow the 1964-66 yearbooks in the order of events. Basically, the book combines the 1963-64, 1964-65 and 1965-66 years. I plead guilty to part of the delay. I was responsible for the yearbook lay-up in 1964-65, and took the draft home with me the summer of my junior year. I came up with the clever bit about using Brother Juniper cartoons for the section dividers (I hope somebody got permission to do that). I picked photos out of a pile of prints, that Fr. Claude had sent home with me, and wrote captions; but it was not finalized when I brought (or mailed) it back that year. Fr. Christian took the literary bull by the horns and finally pulled the beast together. I don't know who helped him finish, but most of the credited contributors were people from my class and the class after us. In a curious homage to happenstance, lay-up became an important function in several of my future jobs (microscopist, scientific writer, and publisher all of which require photo and text presentation).

One of the first events in the fall of 1963 was to welcome the new faculty, and the Troubadours were called to perform. Also Fr. Chris and Brother Peter (who played mandolin) did some strumming and plucking for the event. Music was rapidly becoming the theme of the year. Quick rundown: we had Fr. Mario for drama; Fr. Alberic for physics; Fr. Mel (new) for Latin; Fr. Claude for Spanish and Greek (can't believe they forgot to include Greek among his credits in the yearbook); Fr. Dunstan for Latin; Fr. Roland (new) for Religion and music (including choir); Fr. Meric (new) for Biology; but again, the busiest by far was Fr. Chris. We had him for American Literature and US History, but he was also still teaching Speech, Reading, Debate and Drama to other classes. Fr. Kevin was holding 'the fort' together, but he managed to teach 1st and 2nd year Latin.

I would like to go straight into all the fabulous plays that we produced, but I have to get a distasteful incident out of the way; I had to face Fr. Kevin. My future in the seminary was on the line. The vandalism incident had not come up for the first couple of weeks, so I had almost forgotten about it. But my parents had not, and they wanted to clear the air. Actually, the fact that I had turned us, the perpetrators, in to the authorities worked in my favor. Not only did Fr. Kevin allow me to go on probation, but Mr. Wicket wrote in his official reply "If Mike needs a job in the future, have him contact me". Fr. Kevin assured me that I would have to keep my nose cleaner and have some backbone in the face of temptation if I wanted to get "hired" by the OFM. Pheeeeeeeeeeeeeeeew!!!!!!

So if I had to pick the most enjoyable classes that year, it would be Fr. Chris for History and American Literature. If I had to pick the most peculiar, it would be Fr. Claude for Spanish and especially Greek. Spanish was taught in Spanish; that'll wake you up on a cold September morning. Greek was not taught in Greek but it was all Greek to us. Fr. Claude once got so frustrated trying to teach us the declensions of αηθωροσ (anthropos, trans. man), that he stood on the desk and began to beat out the rhythm: αηθρωπ**οσ**, αηθρωπ**ου**, αηθρωπ**ον**, αηθρωπ**οι**, αηθρωπ**ων**, αηθρωπ**ους**...

you get the idea. Oops! Left out the Dative: αηθρωπ**ω**, αηθρωπ**οις**. There is a picture of Fr. Claude in the yearbook with his glasses pushed catawampus on his head and his long fingers stretched irregularly over his face. That was his classic expression of frustration. I am so sorry that Joe lost his book of Claudisms; he had some doozies! We were in first year Greek, and we were reading Xenophon's Anabasis[79]. My guess is that they figured there was so much repetition in the book that it would be an "easy read"; I mean, Xenophon describes every excruciating detail, like how many *parasangeis* they marched each day. In case you wondered how I know the word (it means 'the distance an army could match without resting').

Spanish was equally challenging but a lot more fun. Fr. Claude would have us learn Mexican songs, read South American poets, and go to Mexican movies at a local theater in Portland. Some were silly vaccaro movies, but some were profound (e.g. The true life's story of Juana Gallo. A woman who rose to become one of the leaders of the Mexican revolution). Senior year was more of the same in Spanish, but one incident floored us. Fr. Claude came into the physics lab one morning and drew a "banana" on the blackboard. We were not going to study the physics of bananas, but the physics lab was the best place for Spanish because there was ample floor space to do skits and act out descriptive conversations in the tongue being taught.

Then Fr. Claude asked, "*¿Que es esso?* (What is this?)

Of course, we responded in unison: "*essa es una banana,*"

We should have known by the gender that this was a trick question.

"No, *eso es un plantano*" El Padre replied.

"No, *esa es una banana*" we retorted.

"*¡No!esO es un plantanO*" he insisted.

We were beginning to wonder if the good Father had slipped a cog, or worse yet, gone off the wagon. I am not suggesting he had a drinking problem; he just was not making sense to us. This discussion went on for the whole class. At first we thought he was trying to confuse us with a misuse of gender. Then we thought we had misinterpreted his drawing. Then we thought there must be some cryptic meaning. When we were totally at wits' end, he ended the class for the day.

Can you believe that he left the drawing on the board? And it was waiting for us the next day. We wracked our brains trying to figure out what Claude was up to. No one could. If the reader knows Spanish, you will consider us very foolish; but of course we had never seen a *plantano* and steeped as we were in translation, we were convinced there must be some plot afoot.

The next day the discussion started again. I forgot to mention that Fr. Claude had made the motions of peeling a banana the day before, which only added to our confusion. Today he started making slicing and stirring gestures… and we were totally mystified. Then he started motioning up and down as if he had a plunger in his hand, or maybe a weapon. Maybe he was beating someone with this banana-shaped weapon. Fr. Claude was milking this for all it was worth as he made the gesture of a *mestiza* pounding mash.

Finally, he told us,

"*eso plantano es un tipo de fruta que es usado como potato. No es dulce porque es llenos de almidón.*"

We were not sure of the Spanish word for starch (*almidón*), but we were beginning to get the point. It was something different than a banana, not sweet, more like a potato. We still didn't know exactly what a plantain was, but we were finally convinced that such a thing existed Fr. Claude brought some to class on another day; sure enough, plantain is a type of starch banana that is used for cooking.

This was a very wise exercise on Fr. Claude's part. As Americans, we are so used to "knowing" everything by its English name; we have a hard time stretching our minds around other concepts for a word, or another word for a concept. There was a valuable lesson in this seemingly futile exercise. I found out just how useful that was when I took High Intensity Language Training in the Peace Corps. Some of the student volunteers just could not stretch their thinking to interpret the actions of the instructor who was acting out the Swahili sentences that she/he was describing. In contrast, some of the instructors, who were actually agricultural officers (not teachers), could not figure out how to describe in gestures what they were voicing. This was so frustrating; unlike Fr. Claude, they would just repeat the word or phrase over and over again, hoping that somehow we would suddenly realize the meaning. Have you ever seen an American talking to a non-English speaking person, and increasing the volume of his/her voice to try to get the point across? It doesn't work that way. As children we learn to associate actions with words. We are not incapable of that when we become adults, but sometimes the instinct is suppressed by previous learning.

Regarding the meat of our education; U.S. History was <u>made</u> by Mondor. The projector got a lot of use that year. Fr. Chris was constantly bringing in documentaries and historical movies for us to watch. It got to the point that, for times sake, he had to assign the whole of the Series on World War II to be viewed as homework. The series was created by the military under the direction of Dwight Eisenhower; his introduction to the series can be seen on Youtube.com at:
http://www.youtube.com/watch?v=v7wxuCs5fxo

These documentaries were completed for the European war, when Eisenhower made that introductory clip. He mentions that the Pacific war, still in progress, would be similarly documented. Fr. Chris checked the entire series out of the library over the course of the year, such that by the time we got to WWII we all had a good concept of the progress of the war. Having been made by the Allied commander, it progressed like a War College documentary with battle footage, strategy, and animated maps showing the progress of the Allies in both theaters of war. This not only made Fr. Chris' job easier, but was teaching us to use available media to study and enhance our understanding of history. I still love to watch the History Channel go on about ancient battle strategies. You can almost imagine that Ken Burns[80], the modern day documentarian, must have had a teacher like Fr. Christian to inspire him to eat and drink history.

I really have been convinced, over the years of my life, that those who do not understand history are doomed to repeat it. How many times since WWII have we re-involved ourselves in conflicts that could have best been avoided by taking Dwight Eisenhower's advice? In particular, the part about the strength of working together as free peoples to thwart the potentates and dictators that seem to constantly arise from the rubble of a disenfranchised populace.

Fr. Chris continued to demand personal reflection on our reading in American Literature. Admittedly, Larry Landry spoofed him one time. He read and wrote a book report on a book named *Danny the Dinosaur*, actually a children's book, 20 pages max. Fr. Chris bought bait, hook, line, and sinker. He was impressed with Larry's psychological evaluation of the character dynamics. Larry finally confessed in order to save both of them the embarrassment of being asked to read the book report to the class.

Otherwise, the objective of getting the class to read extensively was a good thing. I'm sure there was some required reading, although I cannot remember what text we used; but I am sure we covered American literature well. I know that the college English Literature under Fr. Benedict had a large tome called The Norton Anthology. Chris tended to go more to the book or the essay. I remember we spent some time on Henry D. Thoreau's "On Waldon Pond." We must have covered American poetry fairly well, because I remember some I would have never known otherwise; we certainly did <u>not</u> read Walt Whitman at St. Rose. I found Emily Dickinson most interesting, and so did my young daughter in later years. And of course, who could forget "The Road Not Taken" by Robert Frost:

> I shall be telling this with a sigh
> Somewhere ages and ages hence:
> Two roads diverged in a wood, and I --
> I took the one less travelled by,

and that has made all the difference.
http://www.davidpbrown.co.uk/poetry/robert-frost.html

Robert Frost was the poet laureate at the time of Kennedy's Inauguration. Apparently he had composed the following poem for the event:

"... The glory of a next Augustan age
Of a power leading from its strength and pride,
Of young amibition eager to be tried,
Firm in our free beliefs without dismay,
In any game the nations want to play.
A golden age of poetry and power
Of which this noonday's the beginning hour."
http://www.orwelltoday.com/jfkinaugpoem.shtml

However, the sun briefly blinded Frost's 85 year old eyes and he could not read, so he resorted to reciting a poem more familiar, "The Gift Outright."[81] The words he did not read were at once prophetic and ominous. Kennedy's "young ambition" was tried by fire, but the Augustan age came, with all the failings of its ancient predecessor. The golden age, like Camelot, faded into history. In the final lyrics of the musical:

Don't let it be forgot
That once there was a spot
For one brief shining moment that was known
As Camelot. http://www.allmusicals.com/lyrics/camelot/finaleultimocamelotreprise.htm

I also read Arthur Miller's *The Crucible*, Jack London's *Call of the Wild*, John Steinbeck's *Of Mice and Men*, Herman Melville's *Moby Dick*, Ernest Hemmingway's *Old Man and the Sea* and many others. I think I can say I came out of Fr. Christian's Am. Lit. class with a much better understanding of our uniquely American contributions to the language.

Having set the stage, it leaves only to declare the mournful deed. On November 22nd 1963, the President of the United States was gunned down in Dallas, Texas. One hour after the assassination, SFS faculty and Students participated in a solemn requiem Mass with Fr. Christian as celebrant and Fr. Mario as choir master. Fr. Claude and Fr. Alberic were co-celebrants. After Mass the mood continued to be mournful, as we watched Walter Cronkite relay the events on our 21 inch black and white television. I don't remember how long the routine was interrupted, but no one felt much like ignoring the momentous calamity. I know that we watched Jack Ruby murder Lee Harvey Oswald. We watched the funeral procession, with John John saluting the casket. I think I probably got a more complete view of the historical events than I would have had if I had been elsewhere. For example, Gretchen saw the original reports, but then she went on a ski trip with Community Church Youth Fellowship. One of the advantages of the semi-contemplative life is this ability to concentrate on matters of importance. It was important for us to try to understand what was happening to the country and what our world would be like when or if we became priests. We knew little about Vice President Lyndon Johnson, and there was considerable suspicion that something sinister was afoot. That suspicion has never subsided completely, even though official accounts confirm that Oswald was a lone assassin. I don't know where I stand on that debate. I will say that President Johnson picked up the torch and was probably more effective that Kennedy in getting the civil rights legislation passed; and then went on to the Great Society, War on Poverty, and, unfortunately, the expansion of the Vietnam War. Like now, everything might have succeeded if we had not been bleeding off resources in a fruitless war. Dr. Patrick Purcell[82], who was intimately involved in the planning of the War on Poverty, was incensed when the funding began to dry up as the war budget ballooned.

Not to leave this chapter on such a heavy note, let me speak of my experiences as seminary chauffeur. Because I had gotten my license over the summer, and because my father had a VW bug, I guess the faculty felt I might be a safe bet to enlist as driver for the smaller errands, like trips to the library, etc. On our first major outing as a group, we were all going to see *Music Man* by Meredith Willson[83] produced by Beaverton High School theater group. I was carrying 3 or 4 students in the bug (tight squeeze). When we got into town I was a bit confused and turned down a one-way street. Surprisingly, we saw Fr. Kevin and the faculty in the VW van coming the other way. At first I thought "why are they going the wrong way?" WRONG! I was the one defying the law! Fr. Kevin did not bring it up at the performance, but I may have had a little "aside" with him on a later occasion. I did retain my driving privilege, and went on to achieve other feats, such as Yearbook Editor, Grounds Manager, Troubadour Bassman and Seminary *Bon Vivant*. I am. of course, being facetious, but these were all exposure to skills that would be handy to me over the course of my life.

CHAPTER 12

The Entertainers

⁸ Awake, my glory![b]
Awake, O harp and lyre!
I will awake the dawn!
⁹ I will give thanks to you, O Lord, among the peoples;
I will sing praises to you among the nations.
**English Standard Version (©2001) Psalm
57: 8-9**

OF MY SIX YEARS IN the seminary, 1963-65 were probably the most eventful years and the most fun. We were traveling with the Troubadours; we were acting in great plays; we attended symphonies (even the Boston Pops with Arthur Fiddler on tour); we participated in religious conferences with Mt. Angel Benedictine seminary, Sierra High School in Salem, St. Mary's High School in Cowlitz Prairie. We played intermural games with some of those same schools. We had ecumenical events with many faiths, and a grand convention of all the northwest chapters of the Third Order of St. Francis and local Franciscan parishes. The year culminated with the Silver Jubilee of the Dean of Discipline. Fr. Claude celebrated his Silver Jubilee in in the spring of 1964. Fr. Kevin, Fr. Claude and Fr. Christian were the co-celebrants of the solemn Mass, at which Herb Karnofski, Phil Gilday, Bob Sholze and Bill Halvorson served. Those lads couldn't sing with the silver-throated Choir. I say that tongue in cheek because, in fact, "some of them" could sing.

That reminds me that poor Herb would have loved to sing, but his voice kept cracking well into his high school years. Later, Herb was inducted into the San Luis Rey choir I know Phil Gilday could sing, because when Roy

Orbison released "Oh Pretty Woman"[84], Phil was singing it incessantly. Phil had the job of managing the Canteen (snack bar). He would go in the storage room (for audio visual equipment, etc.) which was also the Canteen; there he would play the 45 rpm of "Oh Pretty Woman" over and over and over again. He <u>loved</u> to do the growl. I know because I spent <u>a lot of time</u> listening with him. I don't know what excuse Bob and Bill had for not being in the choir. I think Bob was far more interested in sports, and Bill may just never have had enough sleep to belt it out with a clear voice. I'm telling stories on my classmates here. Halvorson was the wildest sleeper I ever knew. Not only did he talk in his sleep but he churned butter all night long. If you looked at his bunk in the morning, the bedding was always completely wound up into a pile, usually half on the floor. He was a smart guy and stayed in the OFM longer than any of us, but I guess his brain was just always working overtime, even at night. You know, Einstein claimed his greatest ideas came to him in his sleep.

That fall, there was an Indian summer, so we were able to go on outings to the Blue Lake swimming pool, Rooster Rock, and Multnomah Falls Park. There were also plenty of leaves to pick up that fall, so grounds duty was high on the priority list. Leo Ricky formed his Happiness Club of sophomores that fall. Each member had his own handle. Ricky was "Cardo", Bowder was "Wambat", Meier was "Lamb bone", Burchett was "T.B.", Bjorne Hansen was "Nardo", Barnufsky was "Noodle", Roler was "Troll", Hughes was "Ah-cha", Arnold was "Barnold", Wilson was "Gordo" and Hermens was "Hermes". I can't prove it but I always wondered if Ricky had taken his cue from me, who already had the handle "Klugy" and the reputation for being "a friendly guy", especially towards the underclassmen.

Under Fr. Mario's tutelage the sophomores put on some pretty impressive plays. *The Master of Patlan* was their first production. Done in the style of Molière, I am not sure if it was adapted (I could not find the title with Google). They did a credible job. There next play was *A Message From Kufu*, a comedy. I could not find out who wrote it from Google, but I found an interesting reference to Marlon Brando playing a part in that play[85]. So it exists, and as I remember it was very funny.

There was a Christmas pageant for the families in 1963, in which we all participated. At Christmas time in 1964, the juniors put on Dicken's *A Chritmas Carol*. Bill Halvorson was Scrooge and Herb Karnofski was Bob Marley's ghost. Fr. Chris made sure that it was spooky. It substituted for the pageant that had been put on every year for the families of the seminarians at Christmas.

The junior-senior play in 1964 was *The Million Dollar Saint*. It was performed in May for the support group called the Friends of St. Francis Seminary. I could only find one reference to this play on Google[86]. It was a funny play which pokes fun at the Jesuits and the Franciscans. St. Francis returns to a contemporary Jesuit University and converts the Quarterback (me) and the whole team to his "simple" life. This life did not include shoes. The critical scene was when the football team comes into the Dean's office barefooted. I pulled it off perfectly in rehearsal, so Fr. Mario, the director, didn't think it would be necessary to remind me to take my shoes off in that scene on opening night. Well, naturally, I marched into the Dean's office with my size 12 wingtips. The play came off well, but the audience had to exercise a little more willing suspension of disbelief than would have been necessary if I had done my job.

The following year, Fr. Christian, in keeping with the American Literature theme, directed the juniors and seniors in Herman Melville's play *Billy Budd*. Bob Sholze was perfect for Billy's part, and Barreca, Karnofski, Vachal, Halvorson and Bill Meyer were all members of the crew. I had a part, but I think my performance in *Million Dollar Saint* had affected by "acting career"; in Billy Budd, I was the Dansker, who has one line: "Right as rain, I'm a tellin' ya".

That was my last chance at theatrical fame, but I was still in the Troubadours. We were a busy bunch in both of those years. Since I can't remember the exact order of the Troubadour performances, I won't attempt to put them in order now. If Fr. Chris comes thorough with a timeline, I will revise it.

Probably the first engagements we had were fairly local. I remember Fr. Chris brought Brentano and Russo back to perform for the student body and to inspire the Troubadours; and that time they brought a bass man. For his own inspiration, Fr. Chris (5 string banjo) would invite Sid Wagner, a local professional banjo player, to play with him and Br. Peter (mandolin). More inspiration for the Troubadours, but more than that, these jam sessions lead to a funding method for SFS. Fr. Chris started organizing Gaslight Sing Alongs at the local Franciscan parishes. These soon became popular with our parents and many outside the seminary's sphere of influence. The Troubadours were not invited to those events (underage for events serving beer), but we had many other engagements, some of which were probably booked at the Gaslights.

To me, the most memorable Troubadour trips were the ones that took us out of town. Locally, it was quick trip after class, play, home to bed, and up for class in the morning. The out of town trips were real escape from SFS. I have already told you about the trip to Spokane, and the visit to the Poor Clairs. That was a real adventure which also including performing for the bishop in Spokane. We also made a trip to Seattle to play for a parish there. We had a large crowd, and I think we stayed overnight but I can't remember where. We also played for an assembly at Junipero Serra High School in Salem; that was a day trip, but we got a lot of adulation from the female student body. I don't remember if we played Mt. Angel... didn't want to make them jealous. The Third order convention at St. Mary's High School in Cowlitz Prairie was very memorable. Not only was it an all-girls school, but the SFS lads were having a two day discussion session with them. The girls took us on tour of their school. I remember the science experiment where they were showing a negative impact of rock music and a positive impact of Mozart on the growth of bean sprouts. Of course, we were a smash hit with the student body; I doubt if the Kingston Trio would have gotten a warmer reception.... Peter Paul and Mary, maybe. Tim McDaniel's sister was there, I believe. I wouldn't be surprised that she could recount the event if I could find her... or Tim himself[87].

The most interesting trip was to Newport on the Oregon Coast. We stayed overnight and we played at a restaurant right on the ocean (can't remember the name). Apparently there were some influential folks at that gig, or Fr. Kevin would probably not have agreed to such a distant trip. We had time to spend at the beach, and actually went swimming in the ocean in November. Also the next day we visited the Devil's Punch Bowl State Park, which is north of Newport but before Depot Bay. We were dressed in our suits (Troubadour uniform was black suit, red vest, black tie and red socks), but the whole group wanted to climb down into the punchbowl.

I was a bit apprehensive about it and decided to leave the reverie early. A bit later a very large wave came rolling in and the guys remaining in the punchbowl had to make a mad dash for higher ground. Kurt Seippel and Larry Landry actually got their suits wet, but luckily they made it out to play another gig.

The trips were often eventful, because SFS had acquired a Corvair van.

The **Greenbrier** carried the Troubadours all over the Northwest. Left to right: Klugy, Fr. Chris, Dan Van Dyke, Kurt Seippel and Larry Landry. (Photo provided courtesy of Rev. Christian Mondor)

It was called a Greenbrier, but the engine was the same air-cooled job that powered my little sedan. I am very familiar with that engine because, as I mentioned in Chapter 1, I had a Corvair. The engine of which had to be removed... three times. The particular problem with the van was not something that plagued my little aquamarine "dream car". In order to install the engine in the rear of the van, the engineers had been forced to divert the fan belt up and over the engine and around and back to the flywheel. I think the belt was easily 7 ft. or more laid out end to end. The problem was that this belt would often slip its moorings, so to speak. I would hate to count how many times we would lose power on the street, on the freeway, on the byways or highways of life. First we would have to push the van out of the road to some safe spot where we could unload; 3 guitars, banjo, bass, luggage, paraphernalia, memorabilia, and St Christopher's medal (which was placed as near the engine as possible to encourage the patron saint of travelers to intercede for us with regard to the power plant). Fr. Christian would then dutifully snake the fan belt back on its pulleys. That was quite difficult before we got smart enough to carry a long handled screw driver that would reach the hard places. Now mind you, the Greenbrier (and ours was actually green) was otherwise a very reliable vehicle. It took the Troubadours and Fr. Chris on countless journeys around the Northwest. Had Fr. Chris been driving the Greenbrier on the occasion of one fateful trip to the coast, he probably would not have ended up dangling precariously over the edge of an ocean cliff. The Chevy Nova was a later addition to the fleet, and Fr. Christian became far too familiar with that car. I am sure St. Christopher remembers working considerable overtime when Motorman Mondor took the wheel of the Nova. Suffice it to say that the Sandy River Rd. up to the Seminary was a winding road with several sharp curves. I am sure Fr. Chris shortened the distance by a mile when he drove that stretch; because he was not a great respecter of the center line. Perhaps I have revealed too much. Fr. Chris is still alive and well at 85, so either he was a devil of a good driver, or he had a protector (St. Christopher had not yet been demoted[88]).

The Troubadours even had a gig or two during summer break. I remember one time when I had to buy an extra seat on the Greyhound bus to get the bass from Castle Rock to Portland. I got a lot of remarks about that: "Who's your girlfriend?", "Is she pregnant?", "Didn't you know there's a size limit on luggage?", silly stuff like that.

Another quite significant gig for the Troubadours was arranged by Gretchen's father. He was President of the Longview Chapter of the

263

Kiwanis Club; which club held a talent contest every year. On April 10 1965, the Troubadours entered the contest as I think I have previously mentioned. We did not actually win the contest outright. I think the judges had mixed emotions about giving the prize to a group from out of town, but it was obvious that we had the audience support. To resolve the conflict the judges split the award between the Troubadours and a very talented young singer who was both local and vocal. R. A. Long High School auditorium was very large (it was built to accommodate its student body of over 400). That night, the house was nearly full. Jana Huffhines wrote an unusually long note (for her) about this event. In her most understated way, she comes nearer to describing it all better than I have in a whole paragraph:

> G[retchen] and Chris [Bowerman] went with Klungnesses to friend's [Brian LeTourneau's folks] for party for boys from St. Francis who played on program [Kiwanis Amateur Show]. At 12 [AM] they came by and played for us. Fine group, including Mike K[lungness].

You see, by this time, as I will explain later, Gretchen and I had become quite well acquainted, and her folks knew much about Fr. Chris and the Troubadours. Typical of our outings, there was always some family or group that would wine and dine us (sometimes literally) in the afore- or aftermath of the performances. In this case the LeTourneaus had rolled out the red carpet. I am sorry that Bob and Jana were not invited, but Fr. Christian was most gracious to have spent time with the Huffhines after fulfilling his obligatory stint with the LeTourneaus (who were significant contributors to SFS); especially since he was the one who would have to drive us the 70 miles back to Troutdale that night. But he was always up for a good time. And, of course, I was having way more fun than was legal… this was the home of the girl who would take me away from the Franciscans.

During 1963 to '65 the Troubadours remained the same musicians: Dan van Dyke (guitar), Larry Landry (guitar and comb), Kurt Seippel (guitar), Fr. Chris (Banjo) and me (bass and hand trombone, occasionally drum). We cut a 45 RPM in our junior year and another in our senior year. The first record was "Cumbaya" and "Old Bill" on the flip side. We cannot find any copies of this record, and both Fr. Chris and I would very much like to. The second record had "Ballad of the Carpenter" and "San Francisco Bay Blues" on the flip side. I have three copies of the original 45 rpm, and Fr. Christian has had it re-mastered onto a digital medium. In case there are any unresolved copyright issues which arise from this description, suffice it to say that the records were all sold for just enough money to cover the costs (according to Fr. Christian). There is only one picture of this group of Troubadours in any of the SFS yearbooks, but the caption reads: "This lively group spread the name of the Seminary over a big territory."

When we reluctantly departed the Troubadours, Fr. Christian was not daunted. Kurt was still with them, and he quickly brought Dan Scary, Arlin Roler and Dee Bowder into the fold. Although I wasn't there for it, word has it that they were a hot group, too! Fr. Chris and I are still wondering what happened to all of the Troubadours. I know that Ernie Ghezzi retired E9 from the navy; Dan van Dyke became a lawyer in his home town, McMinnville, OR; the rest, we do not know. I would like to know what happened to my first musician friend, and the guy who got me started with the Freetime Five, Charlie Beigler.[89, 90]

I recently received a collection of memorabilia from Bob Scholze. Bill Halverson told me Bob lived in Alaska and gave me an email address. Bob finally answered my email and has since sent me these items from SFS. Among them is a copy of the "St. Francis Herald. Volume 2 no. 3. April 12 1963 Editors: Pat Buckley and Larry Landry. pp. 5." In it, there were two articles about the music at SFS. Larry Landry wrote the first article:

Troubadours
by Larry Landry
"Perhaps the greatest effect of the folksong surge had been
the revival of the almost lost art of people making their own music.

(Irwin Silber:*Sing Out*). The discovery of the joy to be found in folk music has been discovered by almost ¼ of the student body who now play guitar, banjo, etc.

February 22 Ernie Ghezzi, Mike Klungness, Dan Van Dyke, Kurt Seippel, Larry Landry and Fr. Christian entertained members of the Third Order [of St. Francis] at St. Mary's Academy.

On March 9th, the Troubadours saw their biggest engagement, The Sheraton Hotel. There they entertained the ACCW [Archdiocesan Council of Catholic Women] with great success, even after a slow start, mostly due to nervousness. No matter who we sang for, though, we always have a good time – often more than the audience does – for the greatest enjoyment comes from make music ourselves.

I wrote the second article myself:

Franciscan Music
by Mike Klungness

"The playroom is jumpin', Charlie must be hammering out another hot one."

Charlie "Fingers" Biegler, piano player first class, nothing fancy, just a lot of jazz; and it was with him that home made music came into its own at St. Francis. That was around '60 when Fr. Christian was just picking up the banjo and "Had" Muthersbaugh hadn't yet laid his hand on a genuine guitar. Charlie was a real crowd drawer, and listening to him play was the common pastime.

But since then Fr. Christian has graduated from picking and plucking and Muthersbaugh is out knocking 'em dead with his Band to Beat the Beatles.

There were some others in this first stage of Franciscan Harmony. When the Freetime Five plus Two was formed (it was the hallmark with Fr. Chris and "Had") Bob Fleischmann and his squeeze box held a cornerstone membership in the year of FF+2; Bob has since come into his own as the composer of the swingingest piano instrumentals you've ever heard. I'm still banging holes in my beat-up snare drum; but a little bass slappin' on the side keeps me from driving the other musicians crazy. Larry Hiller, originally chief xylophonist of the FF+2 has been taken by the folk singing craze – he just got himself a new "guiddy" about a week ago, and he's been playing every day since he got it. As a matter of fact, the folksong bug is biting just about everybody around the old school. Why there are so many guitarist and banjos and whatnots lying around the music room that it is well-nigh impossible to find a place to sit.

Let's go down the list and see what their prospects are. Of the seniors there are Pat Buckley, Ernie Ghezzi and George Matter. Pat is the most proficient in the bunch, though George is arriving near Pat's very quickly. Ernie has a guitar but his Pilipino rhythm comes through best on a hot bass number. Among the Juniors, Larry Landry is "Mr. Music." With talent running out his ears, it's a good thing that St. Francis nabbed him before Pete Seeger came 'round. Then there is Dan Van Dyke, voice of an angel (but mischievous as the devil). There's no "nut" in his knuckles, though he and his music can keep me occupied for hours. Others in the junior class are Ed Vachal, creator of several jazz renditions, one of which is called the "The Swinger." Larry Hiller, who's pretty swinging himself, can sing for hours with his repertoire. Dick Hopp has his eye on classical Spanish guitar.

In the sophomore class, Kurt Seippel and Dan Skarry carry the Minstrel's burden. Kurt has been at it since he was knee-high to his brother, who taught him to play. Dan's a "chip off the old block" having been trained by his father.

All I can say about the freshmen is that they hold the future of music here at St. Francis, and the outlook is good.

And so went these "authoritative accounts" of the musical history of SFS. Ironically, of those still living, most still use those instruments that I listed.

I don't know whether I should discuss this here, but Gretchen just turned up my high school diploma and report cards from SFS from out of their cedar-chest grave. Turns out, Fr. Claude actually tried to teach us

Greek in our junior year. In the second semester of my sophomore year I was a model student. I got 4 B's and A's in World History and Geometry (of all things!). But I got Cs in Public Speaking and Spanish. We were, of course, rated for our "personality" as well. I got 4 (out of a possible 5) in everything except Courtesy and Fellow Students. The Fellow Student thing still mystifies me; and it remained 2 for my entire time at SFS. You know, as I read this, I am not sure if they were ranking from low to high or from high to low. Was '5' the worst score or the best? It makes a big difference, because if the latter, my "personality" declined considerably over the 4 years. However if 5 was the worst score, I really screwed up on Authority in the 2nd quarter of my junior year. Actually that is probably right, because that was probably the year Fr. Claude said "No more excuses, Klungness!" That report card also rated me 4 on Responsiveness. That interpretation of the scoring also retains my reputation as a nice guy. There had been improvement but over the years I didn't get a Personality score higher than 3, and most were 2s. Isn't it weird how we try to categorize everyone and everything? On the one hand, what does it really mean; but on the other hand how are you going to rank people so that you can decide who stays and who goes?

I did manage to get out of SFS with a 3.4 grade point average, and considering the quality of the education, I felt pretty good about that. There were no give-away grades in that institution! I do think I might have gotten better grades if I had not been part of the Troubadours, but that was a valuable part of my education too; it just didn't get graded on the report card. Fr. Christian was substituting for Fr. Kevin when my last report card came out. He gave me a B in Drama for my one line in *Billy Budd,* but he was no push-over in American Literature and American History; I got a B in both. I had done fairly well in science and math over the 4 years; even got 2 A's in biology. The A in Geometry really surprised me. Gretchen keeps saying how she doesn't know how she got through Geometry; now I can lord it over her, because I finally know that I got an A! Well, you have to take your 'credit' where you can; Gretchen had a lot higher grade point average than I did in high school.

Oh yes, about the golden girl; what was going on between Gretchen and me during this time? Thankfully Jana Huffhines had documented every encounter. You know about the first encounter in the summer of 1962. Well, since Gretchen has gone to the work of typing up her mother's journal, we might as well look it over.

> Sunday, June 2, 1963   Jim, Kay and Mike Klungness came over after mass (11:30) and we all went to Portland. Ate at Country Kitchen, visited Grotto (in rain, mostly), and after went to Civic Theatre – *Damn Yankees* - very good.

This was a very humorous look at temptation ("whatever Lola wants, Lola gets"); and in such pleasant company.

> Friday, August 16, 1963   G went with Klungnesses at 1[PM] to Portland to shop for Mike. Bob and I met them at Oyster House in Portland at 6:30. Ate there and saw "Irma La Douce" at Civic Theater. G rode home with Mike.

You may notice a theme developing here; every musical is somehow about romance and the relationship between men and women. First, Liza's plight in *My Fair Lady*, then Lola's wiles, then Irma, the free spirit. This was all very heady to youth in his and her prime. This was probably the first time Gretchen and I were alone in a car together, too… but, in case you were wondering, I was too "good" to engage in any hanky panky.

> Sunday, August 25, 1963   G left at 8am for Ashland with Gene Ellis and wife and Sherry Munden.

> We rode out to see where Klungnesses
> live.

I was already back at SFS, but I find it interesting that they decided to come to the Toutle and check out my parents' place. Of course, they were already friends, and it was a lovely drive out on the Toutle River. Still, I find it interesting that they would take the time.

> Sunday, November 3, 1963　Skipped church. G went. Mike Klungness came by about 12:30, and we all went to Klungnesses for early TG dinner. All took Mike back to seminary at 6. Stopped at Holland in Vancouver for pie.

Gretchen and I had both forgotten this trip. It seems the parents may have been intent on making sure that the two of us spent time together. I suppose Bob was curious about the seminary, but isn't it a little ironic that they would drive 30 miles north for Thanksgiving dinner and then approximately 100 miles down to Troutdale just to take a seminarian back to school? The Huffhines were not Catholics.

> Sunday, December 1, 1963　G went to Portland with Klungnesses to hear memorial concert for Kennedy.

I was touched to be able to share this solemn occasion with the Huffhines; I am grateful to Jana to have recorded this event that had faded into the dark halls of our collective memories.

> Monday, January 20, 1964　Bill (Koon) walked G home. Bob got off early and we went with Klungnesses to see "Sound of Music" in Portland. Ate at Prima Donna. Food not good, but show excellent.

Bill was the official rival for Gretchen's heart; that is, I was the one that was supposed to be out of contention. I guess I sort of believed that then, but I was just lying to my heart on that one. Why did they have to take us to "The Sound of Music" for God's sake; about a novice leaving her religious vocation for a Sea Captain with 6 kids?

Thursday, December 3, 1964   At 5 went with Jim and Kay Klungness (all 3 of us) to Statten Place in Vancouver for dinner and to Paramount for "My Fair Lady." Wonderful.

This was the movie version of the musical with Audrey Hepburn and Rex Harrison, pounding in the theme of the eternal and inescapable "battle" between the sexes. This was very memorable, and having read Pygmalion later, I realize that Shaw was drawing together all the most subtle nuances of the impact that attraction has on reason. And believe me; I was beginning to be very attracted, against all my mystical reasoning.

It is odd to me that Jana would not have mentioned Gretchen and me attending that movie. I was probably in seminary, but I distinctly remember going to that movie at the Paramount Theater.

Saturday, April 10, 1965   G and Chris (Bowerman) went with Klungnesses to friend's for party for boys from St. Francis who played on program (Kiwanis Amateur Show). At 12 they came by and played for us. Fine group, including Mike Klungness.

This you already know, but what you don't know is that Gretchen and I were already smitten with each other, and why it took so long to admit it, I don't know. Neither of us was being forced to these occasions against our wills. It was almost reminiscent of the old days, when families would discuss who was to marry whom, and then chaperone the couple to assure that all went well.

Sunday, May 2, 1965   Bob, G and I went to see "Sound of Music"
at Portland. Met Klungnesses there with
Mike and 2 friends. Boys had to go back to
Seminary, but Kay and Jim ate at Country
Kitchen with us.

I don't remember which "Sound of Music" this was, but probably the play with the road company. I doubt the seminarians would have paid the price of a live performance, so I guess my folks must have paid for their tickets. Gretchen remembers that Phil Gilday was one of the guys – kept up a "running commentary all through the movie!" George Matter was the other seminarian, a senior from Longview.

Apparently Bob Huffhines had requested the Troubadours to perform at a Longview Community Church Youth Group, but the circumstances are discussed in this letter I wrote to Gretchen,

> May, 5, 1965
> Dear Gretchen,
>
> It is with great regret that we inform you that the Troubadours will not be able to perform at your Church's youth group meeting, as I mentioned last Sunday. This was one audience we didn't want to miss, but things have a way of piling up at the end of the year (as you can well understand) and some of them had to be cancelled.
>
> Fr. Christian was impressed that your dad would drive all the way out to S.F.S. to make the request. As a matter of fact, when he realized that we would have to cut a few engagements, he was seriously considering giving the Longview appearance precedence over the request to play at Serra Catholic High School in Salem. As it turned out, both performances had to be called off.
>
> At any rate we would have loved to entertain your group; perhaps the opportunity will provide itself sometime this summer.
>
> Sunday was a most enjoyable day to say the least. Sound of Music was terrific, the company was first rate, and the weather was "almost" perfect. I have one objection which I have to admit I am in

part to blame for (misplaced preposition, terrible grammar!). That is, the fellas and I didn't see nearly enough of you and your folks. If I had not "faux pas-ed" by not inviting you to the Rod and Reel like I was supposed to, you could have, for one thing, partaken a little more fully of the Wit a la Gilday. I notice that you caught his most comical observations during the movie; let me say that you have not begun to tap the uproarious humor of Phil Gilday.

Well I wanted you to meet Phil and Bill Meyer, swell guy just not so vociferous as Phil. Guess, What time we did have together will have to suffice.

It goes without saying that I wanted the fellas to meet the Huffhines family. When you are fortunate enough to know wonderful people, there's no use hogging the privilege, I always say (though that's the first time I've said it).

Say, I better close this thing and get to bed! Tell your father thanks very much for inviting us to the Amateur show and trying to book us with the Youth Club. Tell your Mom happy mother's day, Tell your brother good luck in final exams. And good luck to you, plus God's abundant blessings on the whole Huffhines' Army.

Sincerely yours, Klugy

The next time we met is duly noted by Jana:

Saturday, May 29, 1965   G went to graduation of St. Francis Seminary with Klungnesses. They went to Pietro's after.

Graduation was a fine affair; my grandfather, my Aunt Nina, my folks, and Gretchen (the Huffhines' representative) were all attending. I don't remember too many details, except that we were supposed to wear all black suits for the event. Instead, the Troubadours all put black sox over our red ones, and had our red vests tucked under our coats, so that Fr. Claude would not suspect what we were about to do. It was our last act of independence. Just before we processed out onto the stage, we exposed our red sox and vests. Fr. Claude's only consolation was that the graduation pictures were all shot in black and white, so no hint of red appeared in them. That night at Pietro's was probably the closest thing to a date that Gretchen and I had. Of course, the folks were there, but it was loud and they were distracted. We were not; we were focused on each other.

CHAPTER 13

The Summer of our Discontent

Why do you stare at this young woman of Shulam,
as she moves so gracefully between two lines of dancers?
New Living Translation (©2007) Song of Solomon 6:13

THE HORNS OF THE DILEMMA were poking hard as we departed SFS for the summer and an uncertain future. On the one hand, I had not disgraced myself or my family by being kicked out of the minor seminary; and I was being offered the opportunity to continue to the major seminary. At the same time, my affection for Gretchen was growing stronger, and I was truly in a quandary about which path to take. At the time I would have thought the seminary to be "the one less traveled by", as Frost had written. Today I can say I don't know; I certainly did not take the well-trodden path in my days. Life might have been much straighter forward if I had stayed with the Franciscans. I am sure Fr. Christian would have mentored me well. But I fear to think what blunders I might have made. I believe it was at the time my mother died that Fr. Christian suggested I might want to consider coming back the Franciscans as a brother. I fear I was far too secularized to make that leap.

Because of concentrating on the journal of Jana Huffhines, and because the yearbook for my junior and senior year were combined, I skipped rather blithely over the summer between junior and senior year. Focusing entirely on the events with Gretchen, I neglected rather important details. Therefore, at this point I will recap some of those important events.

Mr. Wickett was true to his word, and he gave me a job at the Longview Pulp Mill the summer of my junior year. It was my first "real" job and I was quite nervous when I went to the Weyerhaeuser employment office. It took a couple of weeks to get the final word. As soon as we knew, my dad decided I needed transportation to get to work. We found and purchased a 1953 Chevy panel truck (actually more of a crew-hauler with seating for 9, and windows all along the sides). It cost about $250, as I recall, and was dull orange with brown spots of Rustoleum paint in all the rusty spots. Wow, first vehicle, and it was a truck! I felt about 100 ft. tall with my hard hat, my lunch pail, and my "ride".

My first day at work, I was trained by a Lutheran seminarian, who's name I cannot remember, even though we worked together at the Lime Kiln for a good 4 summers. He was older than me, and because we normally worked different shifts doing the same job, Lime Kiln Helper, we never got well acquainted. I got to know that machine operators much better, because they were my direct supervisors, and it was almost obligatory to spend some time chatting with them during their shifts. Their job was to monitor the operating kilns, liquor tanks, transfer pumps etc. They often had time on their hands. Whereas the Helper had a routine set of tasks to keep him busy between emergencies. Barring any unforeseen breakdowns or spills, those jobs needed to be accomplished within the 8 hour shift. Each operator was in charge of a certain division of the pulping process, and could call the lime kiln helper into his department to help with emergencies, or the overflow thereof, at any time. I mean that literally, I usually got called to the washers. This was because tons of brown stock pulp (i.e. what they use to make newspaper) had spilled out all over the floor and the sump below the machines. Just for clarity, in the Kraft process, raw lime is brought to the kiln; it is fired in the kiln, until it becomes anhydrous, which makes it a caustic. The lime is then fed into the slakers, where it is diluted with water, and all the lumpy lime rock is raked (or slaked) out of the mud that is produced. The caustic chemical in the mud (primarily sodium hydroxide) is water soluble and ends up in the liquid portion of the slurry. The water is then separated from the mud, and becomes what they call liquor. This is pumped to the 4-story digester tanks where the caustic is combined with woodchip, and then pressure cooked. The liquid (called liquor) is then pumped onto the washers, where it is sucked out of the mash (pulp) while clean water is sprayed on the washers to remove the remaining liquor. The pulp is then pumped on to the bleaching plant, where it is refined into various grades of pulp (e.g. newspaper and cardboard stock, and bleached craft which is used in everything from toilet paper to white stationary). The used liquor, which is full of wood resin, is pumped to the steam plant and sprayed onto the white-hot walls of the furnace as I described in the first chapter. The steam plant provided much of the energy that runs the mill.

George Cussics and Floyde (I don't remember his surname) were usually the operators that I was with most of the time. Over the operators was a foreman who had responsibility for the whole chain of production from lime to bleached stock. Craig Tillotson's dad, Virgil, was my foreman sometimes but usually it was George Slatter. Mr. Slatter was a deliberate man of few words; he kind of reminded me of Meritt. There is a lot I would say about these men, but I don't know what has happened to them all. Suffice it to say, I learned a lot about life from the Weyerhaeuser folks. George Cussics had been a self-employed jeweler, but eventually found the security of a company paycheck more palatable than the uncertainty of business in the face of electric watches. Although the job was probably below his capabilities, the necessities of life had put him in this position. He was trying to get to retirement with a pension. I think he assuaged his conscience by being a union shop steward; which job he took very seriously. The first summer I was there, the union prevented the startup of the mill after the July 4th weekend on account of the water fountains. Water was life to the lime kiln workers; without water and saline tablets, a worker could quickly succumb to heat prostration. The issue was that liquor would back up in the water lines when they shut the pump system down for the holidays. Cussics could prove, just by shaking the water cooler, that those fountains were full of green mud. This taught me something about why we have unions. The company didn't care that there was caustic mud in the fountain. As long as it had settled, it probably didn't present a risk to those drinking from the fountain. The point was, none of us knew what was in that muddy water, neither the company nor the union. Noxious chemicals like chromium, cadmium, arsenic, mercury, lead, etc. could all be present in that lime that was quarried from the ground and sent directly to the mill. Granted that chromium and cadmium are human micronutrients, they are both high toxic over a minimum molarity required for enzyme activity. This is the point; it takes damn little mercury to do damage to your nervous system. The fact that Dr. Veach, my dentist, would give all of us kids a penny with a drop of mercury on it, so we could "turn a penny into a dime", only reinforces the ignorance of even the most educated people of that generation. Can you imagine how much volatile mercury was in Dr. Veach's office after years of turning pennies into dimes? Both Dr. Veach and his father, who had started the dental practice, died relatively young. Even lowly lead, which was used in thousands of things since it was first smelted by the ancient Egyptians[91], can cause retardation and poor mental function. There is a theory that one of the causes of the Roman Empire's decline was the lead pipe that fed every patrician household in the city of Rome. For the better part of the 20th century, America's fuel consuming culture was pumping tons of lead in to the very air we breathe. So if shop steward Cussics wanted to prevent Weyerhaeuser Co. from earning one day's income from the pulp mill so that the workers could drink clean water, then I say more power to him!

There is always danger in any industrial process. Pulp mills are no exception. Twice in the time I worked at Weyerhaeuser, men were overcome with chlorine fumes in the bleach plant. I heard tales of men falling into the slacker vat. No major digester explosions ever occurred at the Longview mill, because they had a relatively good safety record. But who knows if the men I knew came down with white lung just as they were about to enjoy their retirement years. White lung, as you many have guessed, is the lime equivalent of miner's black lung. The body does not like breathing caustic chemicals for years on end.

To those great proponents of nuclear power, I say, when you can guarantee me that you can build a device that <u>absolutely cannot fail</u>, only then can you talk to me about nuclear power. Take the example of the British Petroleum deep well accident this year in the Gulf of Mexico. Crude oil is a natural, fairly benign product of the earth; and sealed away under the earth is hardly an environmental hazard. However, when you "accidentally" dump literally millions of barrels (not gallons; 55 gallons to the barrel; more than two men can lift) of crude into the teaming oasis of life that is the Gulf of Mexico, observe how massive the destruction it can cause. Not to mention the additional damage to the global environment caused by the burning, dispersing, and sequestering of the crude. That will eventually all end up in the atmosphere as carbon dioxide or methane; the net result of which will be the ever increase rate of warming of the whole earth. Never mind... had they managed to suck all that oil out of the ground and process it into fuel, it would mostly have ended up in the atmosphere as fuel-burning byproducts anyway. Even plastics eventually break down and enter the carbon cycle. And maybe that is one man's argument for nuclear power; but I say the risk is just far too great. If a spill, or an explosion of the magnitude of the Deepwater Horizon[92] had occurred at a nuclear plant, we would not be looking at multiple years to decontaminate the whole Gulf of Mexico. Instead we would be looking at centuries to try to collect and contain the lethal radioactive material that would be literally spread abroad. They said on National Public Radio the other night that everything on earth can be dated as pre-cesium and post-cesium. Cesium does not occur naturally on earth; but the minute (in geological terms) that nuclear bombs were being exploded in the atmosphere, that led to contamination of the whole surface of the earth with cesium. A wealthy collector of antiquities was trying to prove that the wine he had bought actually did belong to Thomas Jefferson. The cesium test proved it was at least older than 1942.

I don't have that much faith in the inventions of man, or the consistency with which man uses them. I have left a valve open. I shorted out a pump motor because I went to sleep while I was washing around it with a fire hose. I dropped a hot pizza on the head of the parlor manager. By stroke of good fortune, the valve only released several gallons of honey. Miraculously I was not electrocuted at the water hose. because there was a backup pump to take over the load. The manager had a bowler derby on his head, or else he would have been severely burned. If man is involved, no matter how foolproof the plan, something can always go wrong. The incredible thing is that we so trust this lump of blood-fed gray matter, that we are willing to hurl ourselves down highways at breathtaking speeds within inches of others hurling themselves in the opposite direction. And all that saves us from utter destruction is the uncanny chance that the grey matter will not fail, the heart won't cease to pump, or the attention will not falter. Don't think about it too hard; it is enough to make one agoraphobic.

Where was I? Oh yes, so the Longview Pulp Mill became the center of my life for the next 3 or 4 summers. It is hard to turn down $2.87 per hour when you are a starving student. Eventually, I think it got up to a whopping $3.25 per hour! The advantage was that all the major repair work was done in the summer, among other maintenance tasks. On Fourth of July weekend, the lime kilns were shut down to have their rings (build-up of molten lime rock) remove. This meant overtime, and it was a life saver. After all, now I had the responsibility to keep the orange bomb supplied with fuel. Gas was only $0.36 a gallon, but the truck only got 10 miles per gallon (Toutle river was 50 miles R/T= $43.20/ month). Plus, the freedom that the truck afforded also increase the mileage used. There were other costs as well. Although there were only four (recorded) outings with Gretchen in the summer of 1963, transportation demands increase in the summer of 1964.

I had forgotten until reminded by Jana's journal and Gretchen, that my step-sister Terry had come to stay with us for part of that summer. She and I got along modestly, but we thought she might like some female companionship as well, so my mother invited Gretchen out to spend the night, as Jana recorded:

Monday, June 28, 1965   G went to Klungnesses to spend night.
[I think Jim's daughter Terri Klungness
was visiting. – ghk]

On finding this entry, Gretchen asked, "Where did we sleep?". Although the cottage was very small and had only one real bedroom, Dad had previously enclosed the front porch, and I had slept there the first summer. By the time Terry came, my folks had purchased a big tent (the kind you can stand up in), and Dad had constructed a platform in the woods behind our house. This was the perfect situation for me because I was working shiftwork, and the tent secluded me from the noise. I had only two problems out there: waking up and sleeping late. I am being facetious, but we solved the waking up problem with an old fashioned alarm clock, placed in a big metal pan. The alarm was the kind with two bells on the top and a clapper that beats back and forth between them. The metal pan improved the resonance considerably; but the contraption had to be far enough away that I could not turn it off without getting up. The other problem, sleeping late, was an issue with the chipmunks. You see they considered that I had invaded their territory, and, although they did not so much mind me being there, they did consider me an impediment to their daytime routine. They quickly learned that if they came down the tree to near the entrance to the tent, and then set to chattering, chances were good that I would wake up and go in the house. Thus, leaving them to their chores without me underfoot!

Had I been a bit more polite, I might have thought to accustom them to being fed, as Meritt fed his tree squirrel in McCloud. Perhaps then they would not have minded me being in their territory. My only excuse is that, like my grandfathers trained squirrel, they would have become overly dependent on me, and would fail to provide for themselves adequately in my absence. I always wonder what happened to Meritt's squirrel when he moved to Oregon.

The visit with Terry the night of the sleepover was short lived, because

Tuesday, June 29, 1965   G called to work so came home early
from Klungnesses.

It always amazed me how thorough Jana was. I assume that Gretchen's "work" meant at the Longview Daily News. She had gotten the job, on the assurance that she would be able to drive the Newspaper's VW bug to run layup around to the advertisers. Since she had not gotten her license, although she had taken drivers training, she needed a quick backup plan. She called her driving instructor who lent her his VW to practice. He gave her a quick refresher, which included learning to drive a stick shift! True to form, she learned with lightning speed and passed her test by the time she had to go back to work on Monday. So now she was the newspaper lady, who became a paralegal (at least it's all paper and ink), and I was the seminarian that became a scientist (the celestial to the mundane).

According to Jana's journal Terry and Gretchen and I did not get back together again. I don't remember if that was the case or not. I also don't remember when Terry went back to California. It seems like Terry and I and the folks must have done some things together, but the only recollection I have of her is right at the cottage on the Toutle. Of course I was working, and Dad was working, and Mom did not drive; so her options were pretty much limited to weekends and the occasional trip to town for a movie. Perhaps my shiftwork made that more possible, but I really don't remember. Gretchen says that she and Terry did get together, swimming and inner tube riding on the Toutle. I am prone to trust Gretchen's memory. She said that is when she became aware of Type I diabetes, because Terry was on insulin since childhood. I do know that Terry never came back... I hope we didn't bore her to death (figuratively, of course).

The next encounter with Gretchen came when we went to Portland over the Fourth of July weekend. I probably would have been working the holiday itself, so we probably arranged to go early. This is what Jana wrote:

Friday, July 2, 1965   G went to Portland at 9:15 with Klungnesses,
who met friends there at the zoo. Bob and
I joined them at Mr. C's Hippopotamus
at 6:30 for dinner. [Father Chris was there,
too], and then friends left and rest of us saw
"Stop the World" at Civic Theater.

I am not sure who we met at the zoo; my mother had a thing about Packy[93], whose birth we had followed closely in 1962. We saw Packy in person shortly after he was born. You could say Mom was a Packy groupie. I don't remember the circumstances of why Fr. Christian met us for dinner, but I vaguely remember it. I don't think he went to the musical with us. In fact, although I fear disputing anything that Jana wrote, I am wondering if I went to "Stop the World". My recollection is that the first time I saw that play I was with Gretchen at the Theater in the Round at the Univ. of Washington. Oh, how clouded the faint visions of history become! I just wonder if Fr. Christian met us to drag me away on some Troubadour engagement. It would not have been the first time.

This next entry is also not in my memory:

Saturday, July 17, 1965   Bob, G and I went with Klungnesses
to see "Gypsy" at Civic Theater. Ate at
Hoyt's. After at Totem Pole.

I have no recollection of seeing a stage production of "Gypsy", but I will concede this next entry, because I was becoming more and more prone to dream up excuses to visit Gretchen; the semblance of seminarian aloofness was all but erased.

Thursday, July 23, 1965   Bob was off in afternoon. I cleaned
house, etc. Mike K. came by to see us.

The previous visit had probably been a ploy to tender the following invitation:

Monday, August 2, 1965   G went to hear Belafonte in Portland
with Mike K. and cousins. [Kay and I
were going but cousins came.]

Now that was a performance to see! I saw Belefonte twice in my life, once with guest artist Mariam Makeba[94] and once with Odetta[95]. I think this occasion was with Makeba, one year after she had been denied citizenship in here own country, South Africa. The performance was very moving, particularly when Makeba sang in her native language; which contains a click sound that we had never heard the human voice do. Then there was always the very amusing sequence that Harry always did with his guest artist, "There's a Hole in the Bucket". The day before the concert, my mother had been stung by a wasp and her hand was so swollen she could not go to the concert; she was very disappointed, to say the least. I am not sure who the cousins were; they might have been some of her cousins who lived in Portland, children of Jana's brother in Portland. My mother was able to attend the Belefonte concert with Odetta; but I am not sure that Jana ever got another chance to see him. I heard Mariam Makeba one more time in San Francisco in the early 1980's. She was in concert with her husband Hugh Masekela (whom I saw again with Gretchen in Hilo in 2008). Both had been involved in the movement to free South Africa from Apartheid.

By this point, Gretchen and I were looking for every excuse we could to be together. So a few days later Gretchen brought her friend Chris Bowerman out to the Toutle to spend the afternoon.

Friday, August 6, 1965   Left kids on own [G spent afternoon at
Klungnesses with Chris] and drove to
Portland for anniversary.

My mother was working on a plan for a last party for the SFS senior graduates before they departed for San Luis Rey major seminary. I imagine she had asked Gretchen for assistance making preparations, sending invitations or whatever.

Sunday, August 15, 1965   All 3 went to Klungnesses at 1 for Seminary picnic – 41 there in all, including 3 priests. Bob and G swam, etc. Enjoyable day, home about 10:30pm.

Now doesn't that just sum it up? Jana was the original Twitterer (Tweeter), she could get a lot of information in a very few words. Although, like me, I think she would have thought people who would make such brief comments, in a media that everyone on earth could read, would themselves be "twits".

That party was enjoyable; the Troubadours played. We tried to get a newly built fire pit to heat up so we could roast hot dogs. Did you ever try building a fire in a 2 foot hole in the ground? It looked nice, but short of constructing a bellows, there was no way to get oxygen to the fire. Brilliant! We made do; probably boiled the hot dogs and fortunately there was a great deal of potato salad. In fact, we had potato salad for a week after the party, and still had to toss some of it for fear it would have spoiled by then.

It wasn't that all the seminarians came to the party, but those who did come had family in tow. By then my folks had formed some good friendships with the other parents because of the Gaslight Sing Alongs. And there was quite a large party of young people that went down to the Toutle Gorge to swim; and they were not all boys, there was Gretchen and Chris, and some of the seminarians' sisters. A few brave souls attempted to shoot the rapids on inner tubes, but I was not one of them. I already knew how many people had been drowned in undertows at the spot in the river. Fortunately, no one was injured. Years later, Gretchen admitted to me that she was peeking! I was wearing a boxer suit, and I always had a habit of squatting like a Yogi. Apparently, she was able to catch a glimps of my privates... naughty girl! But it was a warm August day, and everyone was cooled off by the frigid glacial melt, fed and happy.

Right after that party, it was time to depart for the major seminary; but our departure did not curtail the activities of Gretchen and her parents. The next entry in Jana's journal about their joint activities was about attending another play. It is important to note that these programs had become a significant part of our lives:

> Friday, September 3, 1965   We and Klungnesses ate at Bon Fire in Portland and saw Mary Martin in "Hello, Dolly" at auditorium.

That must have been a great experience for them. I think Bob and Jana saw *Hello Dolly* with Carol Channing years later; but Mary Martin[96] had a stage presence that was second to none. My three year old daughter watched a video of the televised version of Mary Martin in *Peter Pan* countless times. Now Colleen doesn't even remember it.

The folks were on a roll that year; 8 days later they went to another performance:

> Saturday, September 11, 1965   At 3 went to Portland with Klungnesses. Ate at Embers; Visited Pittock Mansion, saw "Mary, Mary" at Civic Theater and went to Gay Nineties and Roaring Twenties. Home at 3am. G spent night with Chris [Bowerman].

Fr. Chris was not one to shy away from a good time especially if music was involved:

> Sunday, October 10, 1965   All slept late. Ate light lunch. Bob and I took brief ride. Met Jim and Kay Klungness and Father Chris and Brother Peter at Kelso Elks for dinner and to hear Eddy Peabody, banjoist. Wonderful time. Father Chris invited to do duet with him.

Fr. Chris and Eddie Peabody[97] became pretty good friends, and he performed for some of Fr. Chris' programs. Eventually he gave Fr. Chris a beautiful banjo that was all inlaid with mother of pearl, and was a great treasure to Fr. Chris. Trouble is, he took that banjo with him wherever he went. One day Fr. Chris was at the beach and wanted to take a dip. So he locked the banjo in his trunk, and put the key in a magnetic box under the grill. Apparently someone had seen him do that and stole the banjo. He didn't see in again for years; but he recently told me that he was in a pawn shop in San Francisco, and saw his Peabody banjo. He explained to the pawnbroker, and somehow convinced him to return the banjo to him. Now what is the probability of that happening? It's enough to make a believer out of you, eh?

Nor did our folks abandon SFS after our class had departed for San Luis Rey:

Sunday, December 19, 1965	Bob worked part of day. Decorated tree, house. Kay K. came for lunch, and we went to program at Seminary in Troutdale when Jim got off.

Although Jana was not specific about what the program was, I suspect it might have been one of the Gaslight Sing Alongs. I know my folks would have invited them.

So that is all I have to say about SFS. Those were good years, and probably all too short lived. If I had it to do over again, I would not have picked any other high school. And, though it has been many years since I have had contact with anyone who shared those years, it will always remain a fond memory.

Nevertheless, this relationship with Gretchen was a big dilemma as I was preparing to go to the major seminary in California. At the beginning of that summer, nothing showed up in Jana's Journals, because she and

Bob Huffhines were in New York State attending the graduation of their son Bob Jr. from West Point. Gretchen's aunt, Marnie, uncle, Clell, Grandmother Frankie, and cousins were there for her graduation. It is an unfortunate law of physics that her mother could not record what she was not there to witness. The Klungnesses were not invited because there were a limited number of ticket for the families of the 400 graduates of R. A. Long that year (the baby boom). However, we did get together with Gretchen, and I had purchased an amethyst ring for her (her birth stone was actually garnet) and in the card I wrote "Of course, you know I wish this were a diamond, but you understand why it can't be." Gretchen had that ring in her possession until after we finally married in 1999. It was stolen from our home in 2007.

CHAPTER 14

The Mission Bells

Sing a new song to the Lord!
Sing his praises from the ends of the earth!
Sing, all you who sail the seas,
all you who live in distant coastlands.

Join in the chorus, you desert towns;
let the villages of Kedar rejoice!
Let the people of Sela sing for joy;
shout praises from the mountaintops!
**New Living Translation (©2007) Isaiah
42:10-11**

THE FIRST TIME I WENT to San Luis Rey (SLR), I went by bus. My folks could afford neither the money nor the time off work to take me to California. I remember the trip only for the tedium that Greyhound bus trips were in those days. Buses had never enjoyed the glamour that rail had in its heyday. I remembered fondly the trips I made with my grandparents on the Coast Starlighter or the Daylighter, particularly the dining car and the dome lounge. Every time I have had a chance in my life, I have taken the train on the west coast with my daughter and my granddaughter. Amtrak has preserved some of the grand old Station Terminals quite well.

Great Northern poster encouraging post-WWII travel. (Photo reproduced courtesy of Burllington Northern Santa Fe Railway) http://library.duke.edu/digitalcollections/images/adaccess/T/T29/T2931/T2931-lrg.jpeg

The bus system on the other hand, has declined steadily over the post-war years[98]. Where that was most apparent was in the rest-stops. Originally they were in upscale parts of cities and towns, but the companies had either opted to move into areas with lower overhead, or the cities had become ghettos in the very areas the bus terminals were. Where there had once been decent restaurants and facilities, now there were low-end cafes and poorly maintained rest rooms.

It was to this road I was committed in the fall of 1965. Of course, it was about as far from home as I had been in one trip, and it had its moments of interest for me. This was before Interstate 5 was completed, so the buses took Highway 99 which ran from the border of Canada to San Diego California. I remembered some of the towns and sights that I had seen on my trip to Disneyland with the Shabrams 10 years prior. I always took great fascination in the miles and miles of planted crops in the Central Valley; in the north valley olives, almonds, walnuts, safflower, milo, and corn. In those days there were no rice paddies north of Sacramento. By now the Sikhs have planted rice all the way to Winters, California. In the southern Central Valley, there were walnuts and almonds, oranges, avocados, grapes, pistachios, as well as tomatoes and other vegetable crops.

When I arrived in Oceanside, California, I was surprised to see so many soldiers. I didn't realize that Camp Pendleton was just outside of town, and many a young Marine was training there for Vietnam. I think the seminary sent a vehicle over to pick me up, although I might have taken a taxi. When we came upon the mission I was impressed with the simple white washed beauty of it. Sam Luis Rey was at once ancient and yet comfortably modern in amongst the subdivisions of Spanish style ranch houses. I must admit I don't remember the pool of reflection.

The Pool of Reflections in front of Mission San Luis Rey. (Photo reproduced courtesy of Irfan Nooruddin, Ph.D)

At that time the mission still border on agricultural land in the direction of Escondido, where thousands of acres of avocado and citrus were grown. The mission itself proved to be quite an agricultural oasis in the dry arroyos[99] of the valley. Besides being a seminary for the priests, it was a training school for the Franciscan brothers. There was a bakery, a working farm with pigs, milk cows, and crops. There was a cobbler shop. Where the seminarians had the soles of their tennis shoes replaced with tire tread. This was so they could play basketball on the asphalt court. There were also quite a variety of fruit crops, including a small orange grove, lemon trees, pineapple guava hedge, etc. The central quadrangle was planted with 200 year old pepper trees that the *padres* had brought with them from *España*. We were soon in the compound and I was being shown to a room in the dormitories which stretch around the courtyard compound. My room faced the courtyard, and I was, as were all freshmen, assigned to a sophomore roommate. There was not much time for chit chat with the other seminarians from SFS, because we were assigned to unpack and get squared away before assembly. Also, we would soon find out that the policy was "no talking in the dorms". I forgot whether the first assembly was for lunch or for dinner in the refectory, but the thunderous mission bells were not involved. While we were in line waiting to be served food, Fr. Benedict began a routine that for us would become extremely familiar. After ringing a small desk bell to get our attention, he explained some of the house rules, and then proceeded with the blessing. Only after the introduction, could we serve ourselves from the sumptuously-presented lunch or dinner. Be advised that this was also a culinary training school for the Brothers who would eventually feed the various friaries around the Province. Fr. Ben probably rang his bell several times during the chow line, advising against taking the peanut butter and other acne-inciting foods (which nevertheless were available at every meal). He advised against taking particularly sumptuous portions, or just acting in any way boorish or impolite. After all, we were training to be priests!

We all thoroughly enjoyed the meal, and I believe we were allowed to converse at lunch and dinner but not breakfast. There was some catching up to do with those SFS graduates who came from other cities. There were also the upperclassmen and recent St. Anthony Seminary[100] grads to meet. Most of the discussions took place in breaks and between classes in an area behind the classrooms and next to the orchard. Because that area was also the smoking area, the time that I spent there was often in the orchard stuffing myself with dead-ripe oranges right off the tree! No one objected because, what fruit was not harvested, just fell on the ground to rot. And the oranges ripened in the California sun were sooooo sweet!

It was strange not to be able to talk to your own roommate (whose name I cannot remember after living with him for 9 mo.; Palchek, I think); and he and I almost never hung out at the break area. This developed into a weird relationship, the more fastidious he became about the condition of our room, the more slovenly I became (within the allowable limits, of course, and they were pretty strict). I got paid back though when I was a sophomore. By then I had become fastidious to a fault, but my freshman roommate was more disorderly than I had been. At one point he was actually brewing wine (out of available fruit) under his desk. Well, maybe you could more properly say he was "experimenting". He tried oranges, and then Nopal cactus wine[101]. Then he tried to ferment potato; he had visions of distilling vodka. I left SLR in mid-sophomore year, so I don't know if he survived his first year. By the way, my roommate in the first year did not return for his junior year.

That reminds me of an event that I forgot to mention in the SFS years. It also had to do with winemaking... the "cursed" brew! When we were seniors, several wise guys – who will remain unnamed – took it upon themselves to turn the milking shed (which was by then the senior's dorm again) into a winery... more specifically the boiler room. They were most impressed with their success, and decided to sample one night after lights out. However, proving that no good deed goes unpunished, one in this band of outlaws had contracted mononucleosis over Christmas break. Well, as you might suspect, it soon became quite clear who had been sipping the fruit of the vine; because they all came down with mono. We had to try to quarantine them on one side of the dormitory so the rest of us would not suffer for their "sins"! Herb was at his disdainful best while administering the only treatment we had, hot soup and aspirin. The penitents did survive, and some actually went on to SLR College... I guess the faculty decided they had been sufficiently chastened. To this day, it remains a question, who vectored the mono, and how did he get it?

The first morning at SLR began at 6 AM with the ringing of the angelus; and I do mean ringing... in my head... for several minutes. The bell tower was on the far side of the compound, but I swear that the sound waves would descend on the quadrangle and ricochet around the covered verandas for several minutes. I could see the bell tower right out the window of our room. I rolled out of the top bunk and proceeded to the sink to brush my teeth. When I turned on the tap, the water literally foamed in the glass. It was undoubtedly the worst water that I had tasted in my first 18 years. It was probably the high mineral content of the water, because it was also very hard to wash the soap off your body when you showered. As Dorothy would say in the Wizard of Oz, "Toto, I've a feeling we're not in Kansas anymore."

We only went to the old Mission Church for Sunday Mass and special events. The chapel was at the back of the quadrangle and could be reached under the porticos rain or shine... like it ever actually rained there! Since it was Sunday, after Mass, we were instructed to follow the upper classmen to the refectory inside the inner compound (the old refectory). This smaller rectangle within the larger compound was basically the domain and quarters of the faculty and the brothers. The bakery was there and the main kitchen, which we had to file through to get to the dining area. This consisted of quaint long wooden tables much more reminiscent of the mission's roots. I don't know what I enjoyed most in that convivial place; the hot cornbread with fresh churned butter and Mapleine syrup, or the pastries fresh out of the bakery ovens. As a table server at the old refectory, you might go in the cold locker to get the freshly churned butter, and encounter the boar's head waiting to be taken by the Mexican field hands to make "?"[102]. Again the rule was silence except on Sunday. At the old refectory the entire faculty joined us for breakfast. Why they decided to have the underclassmen eat lunch and dinner in the new refectory with only Fr. Ben presiding, I am not sure. Maybe the baby boom effect caused overcrowding. Sometimes one other priest would join Fr. Ben so he would not go "stark raving mad"; actually I think he enjoyed eating alone. He could read (to himself usually, but once in a while he would read us a passage or an article in the news after he finished his repast). Fr. Ben also had his quarters in the dormitory, whereas the other priest lived in the inner compound. As you may already know, Fr. Ben was the dean of discipline. Most announcements and important information were relayed at the lunches and dinners. Fr. Valentine[103], the president of the college, might eat with Fr. Ben, when he wanted to make an announcement. Otherwise we did not hear from Fr. Val often... except in the end-of-year evaluation. Each student passed the gauntlet of being individually apprised of his fate by Fr. Val.

Now Fr. Ben was a bit scary at first. Out of an almost Barney Fife visage, and black horn-rimmed glasses, looked piercing intelligent eyes. And when he stared at you, you could feel the moisture boiling off your body. But in fact, Ben had a wry sense of humor and a highly developed sense of the ironic. Let me say frankly, there was no need for dish-shifts in Ben's regime. I don't think anyone dared fail in his estimation. Fr. Valentine, the president of the college, was cold and aloof, but Ben was truly engaging. Tough and intellectually demanding, but you really felt like he had a mission to raise the awareness of each and every one of us. Most of his philosophical soliloquies occurred at vespers and generally were about some event upcoming or recently transpired (placing it in perspective). One of his first such unofficial lectures was about reading material. Ever since, I have felt it almost criminal to read mundane things like Readers' Digest[104], or Look Magazine[105]. This guy expected us to read Harper's[106] or Atlantic Monthly[107], and enjoy them. And movie fare, which he determined, did <u>not</u> include musical comedy. Rather, he reserved only weighty and important films that would raise the level of our awareness. I cannot remember them all but I am sure that each one was a learning experience. *La Strada*[108] by Fellini comes to mind; and Ingmar Bergman films were common.

I must have been pretty impressed with the major seminary, if my early letters were any indication. If you are wondering how I come by letters from 45 years ago (whoa! I'm shocked myself.); Gretchen saved almost every letter I ever wrote to her. And I must apologize profusely; I never saved any of hers… well, maybe for a while. In the beginning, it would not have looked right for a future priest to be saving letters from his girlfriend. Then, as in later years, I had to travel light. Everything we owned went home every summer (on Greyhound?) and Peace Corps would only allow 90 lbs…. you get the idea? This is a woman who visited or lived in her home town in the house her father built most of her young life. Besides, if I had left her letters with my father, they would have been swept away by the eruption of Mount St. Helens; have I sufficiently justified my excuses? At any rate, this is how I described the major seminary in one of my first letters to Gretchen.

Sept. 12, 1965
Dear Miss Huff,

Had a little bit of writing time left (two hours to be exact), so I thought I might drop you a little note. It will be the third this weekend. And to think that there was some rumor that heavy correspondence was discouraged.

Grand colossal congratulations on your scholarship, Mademoiselle! Does this cut short your working career, or does that ever sensible German mentality still hold sway, *typisches Deutsch* and all that? Again, congratulations!

Something tells me one Bill Koon was or will be a mighty surprised fellow when he gets home. *Pues, así es la vida*, and now maybe he will settle down to those studies and use that brain of his.

Mom couldn't remember the name of the new lucky guy. I won't ask who, but you can bet that I am interested.

I won't even ask how you enjoyed "Hello Dolly", because I know that you most certainly did, and will probably go on for pages and pages about it anyway. And, of course, in this too I am very interested.

Now whatever else is new in your life, you will have to fill me in on if you have a chance to write.

It occurred to me that you might be interested in the what's and such of San Luis Rey. Magnificent, truly magnificent – and a new swimming pool to boot!

All that could be said would take a book, but at least I can give you the general picture now.

Verified as having the most perfect climate in the United States, San Luis Rey maintains a year-round average temperature of 70 degrees, with a gentle sea breeze to modify the constant sunshine. Do you remember the verse from "Camelot":

"The rain may never fall 'til after sundown"

So far perfectly applicable. But you are saying to yourself that you would rather have the abundance of green vegetation. True, the surrounding hills are pretty dry, but here at the mission, beautifully laid out gardens (because they are made and kept by ourselves) are adorned with plants that bloom as far up as Christmas and perhaps longer. True, there are strange and exotic strains of cactus and palms and junipers, etc. but all the more interesting.

"In short there's simply not a more congenial spot."

The mission itself is very old, very historic, and, although by far not the oldest of the missions, has a color and beauty all its own.

The college, although not fancy in many respects, is clean, well ordered, well-equipped and filled with a spirit of cooperative effort, school pride and the improvement of the individual.

Good God, how did I get off on that tangent? When Fr. Ben reads this, he'll think it's a bunch of bull (could be, could be).

Well, not much time left so this thing better come to a sudden halt. I will try and fill you in on the great Fathers and the terrific classes some other time. Until then take care of yourself; good luck in school; say hello to Chris for me (and Bill if you see him) and my best regards to your mom and dad. God bless all of you,

Wordily,

Mike

By the end of the month I had not changed my mind, but Gretchen and I were getting used to the concept of Fr. Ben reading all of our correspondence. My letters actually came back to me with red-lettered comments and spelling corrections.

Sept. 25, 1965

Dear Gretchen,

Consider yourself "in"; "in" with me for your precision promptness, and "in" with Fr. Benedict for your infallible spelling. You would get along well with Fr. Ben; "perfection, nothing but perfection" is his motto.

This letter is going to be short and sweet (hopefully) with the main purpose of letting you know that your letter did arrive and was happily received.

So you are on cloud nine over College (typical, very typical)? Mom sent The Daily News clipping with that priceless picture of you, but no mention was made of the courses you were advised to take. Are they the same ones you had lined up this summer (with the exception of ¿archeology?)?

Chris picked a lucrative and interesting subject if that is what she's really taking up, but somehow, you just don't seem to me the archeological type.

297

Bene, scribe (loqui) in lingua Galliarum, si tibi placet. It's good practice.

Never did hear the outcome of your dad's great fishing trip from my dad (could it be that the catch was too small to mention?).

Good for Bill in regards to him "hanging in there" and as for your Army, Air Force sympathies, I agree with Bill. By the way, Fr. Ben thinks Bob Dylan is a pseudo-folksinger; you're "in" I tell ya.

Delivered your messages to the gang, and they asked me to return their regards. Phil Gilday asked how it was that you remembered him. I was tempted to ask him how you could forget him after Sound of Music (the running commentary, remember?).

Everyone is getting along well here. Remember Ron Fisher (helped shuck corn); he's a lot of fun. Everyone kids him to death about just about everything, but he always responds with comic good nature, which is to say, he gets along really well. He's just one example of a so far first-rate, well-adjusted student body.

But more of that sort of thing in a few weeks. Right now this letter must end *de pronto*. Therefore, *au revoir*, Take care of yourself. God bless you and your family, and what is your comment on the World News?

Long windedly,
The Klog

Obviously the newness had not worn off at this point in time.

In general my impressions of SLR were favorable. I loved the fruit, I loved the swimming pool, I didn't spend much time on the basketball court (for some reason I remember volley ball as being mandatory), but I spent a lot of free time in the pool, particularly when we would have the Santa Ana winds[109]. I could never understand why or how the ball players could play ball in that oppressive wind. In 1965 the Los Angeles basin was heavily polluted, and the Santa Ana wind of the desert would bring all of it down to us. Your lungs burned all the time, and I took relief in the water; sometimes I would hold my head underwater just to escape momentarily from the noxious soup. The rest of the year the air was fine.

In our first trips out of the compound, we walked to the orchards in Escondido. Another day we walked out into the arroyo; we ran into soldiers that were on some kind of survival test. We don't know whether we were in Camp Pendleton, or those soldiers had wandered off base. I remember that Bob Sholze got into a cactus with long thorns that, for all intent and purpose, locked themselves into his skin. I remember we had great difficulty pulling the cactus branch off his arm. But the seminal trip was to Tootsie's. She was, I believe, a friend of the college, but she was a very eccentric woman. She had a large piece of property right next to the municipal sewage purification pond[110] about two miles from the mission. She had every kind of animal imaginable, and took in strays of all kinds. When an old cow or a horse would die, her Chicano workers would haul the carcass to one of the ravines and dump it there. Ergo, even the buzzards were well fed at Tootsie's.

In the science lab at the college, there was a skeleton of a horse. A previous generation of students had gone to Tootsie's, collected a rotting carcass, hauled it to the compound and boiled out the bones in the middle of the quadrangle. Apparently the smell was horrific, but the net result was a major contribution to a biology lab that was, shall we say, low budget. There was also a human skeleton in the storage room. That had been exhumed from much closer by, although I don't know by whom. It was the skeleton of one of the Native Americans that had died and been buried at the mission in colonial times. Some of the biology projects were less involved; we participated in the Audubon Society annual bird count between SLR and Tootsie's. The combination of the aeration pond and all the food, that Tootsie tossed out for her animal menagerie, made that area a hugely attractive stop-over on the annual migration routes of a number of species of birds.

I am trying to give some context to the atmosphere in which my intellectual awakening occurred. Liturgy was an important component of our lives at the seminary college. The liturgy was a work in progress, with many different incarnations. We even had ecumenical liturgy with such diverse Faiths as Greek Orthodox, Byzantine Rite, Lutheran, Anglican, Congregationalist and Baptist. I was taken into the choir in the first semester; as was Herb, finally! His voice had finally settled in at 1st bass and I was 2nd bass. This was most enjoyable. I think one of our first chorales was *Sicut Locutus Est* by J.S. Bach. Wonderful; and when you surround a choir with a full pipe organ in the resonant sanctuary of the Spanish mission church, you have a celestial experience. In fact, although it was primarily a parish church, people would come from all over the surrounding area, both Catholics and non-Catholics, to hear the SLR choir in concert and for Sunday Mass. The church was virtually overflowing at Easter for the SLR choir's rendition of the 'Halleluiah chorus' from Handel's *Messiah*. Eventually we did two concerts in Oceanside that year. Our most prestigious performance was a choral presentation as part of a dedication of a Junipero Serra statue at Balboa Park, San Diego. This ceremony was presided over by Stewart Udall.[111]

I don't have any records of my classes at SLR. All I can relate is what I remember. I recall Fr. Benedict's English class very well; very tough, tons of reading. I think my first assigned reading was *Samuel Pepys' Diary*.[112] I was completely confused by the style, but it was one of the first English memoirs in the format that I am using in this one. I chose as my own reading material Isaac Asimov's *The Intelligent Man's Guide to Science*. First I read *vol. 1. Physical*, then later, *vol. 2 Biological*. That was some of the clearest and most interesting information I had ever read. Much of our reading for class came from Norton's Anthology of English Literature. One required reading that influenced me was an essay of Bishop John Henry Newman. What I took away from that essay was this: real knowledge is to understand that you don't know. Think about that one. When you think you have it all figured out, you are probably just scratching the surface. That has certainly become clearer and clearer every day of my life.

Logic, taught by Fr. Geoffrey, seminal! Don't get me started. I was not the best student of logic, but now I am the most convinced. I really feel that what is going wrong with this country (Amurka[113]) is the influence of advertising on our thinking processes. Advertising is based on the sophist arguments.[114] Consequently, our young people, who are inundated with commercials and their specious arguments, begin to follow the "logic" that they are exposed to constantly. *Argumentum ad hominum*, what's that? The result has been a real dumbing down of the public. The ability to discriminate and recognize fallacious argument is at all-time low ebb in this society. I dare say, the "sod-buster" of a century ago had more understanding of logic than the college graduate today. They used to call it "common sense", "horse sense", the "I'm from Missouri mentality". "The more things change the more they stay the same"[115]. Some parts of our American educational system could be accused of charging money for education, and "providing wisdom only to those who can pay". SLR education could <u>not</u> be accused of that.

Fr. Patrick O'Connell taught us Chemistry 1 the first semester. We actually learned a little chemistry, and even had a lab where the upperclassmen tutored the experiments. The second semester of "chemistry" was actually a philosophical and theological treatise on Teilhard de Chardin. Interesting, but it did <u>not</u> prepare me well for my future required sequence of chemistry at the Univ. of Washington.

Fr. Geoffrey taught us Philosophy, starting at the beginning, well at least of Western philosophy. It was a good foundation: Socrates, Plato, Aristotle and beyond…

Fr. Valentine may have had us for Latin, but it was not memorable… so I don't. The next year Latin was taught by a Latin scholar with a PhD in Roman History. <u>She</u> was not only very interesting, she was a nun! I want to call her Sr. Gertrude, but I may have forgotten her actual name. I think she told us that she chose the name because Saint Gertrude[116] was a Latin scholar. Our Sister Professor was actually involved with research in the ruins of *chivitas Romae*, the city of Rome.

I remember that Spanish class was actually Mexican History Class *en Español*. I don't feel guilty about not remembering the Spanish American priest's name, because his classes were not memorable either. At least I did learn more about our nearest neighbor to the south than I had learned in 12 years of American education. We are all woefully uneducated about our neighbors to the North and the South, as my Canadian friend will testify.

I am truly embarrassed that I didn't remember the name of the Choir Director and instructor of the Music Appreciation class. I should have remembered him well, after all of those hours of practice and concerts and classes listening to all forms of western music. I found his surname in my letters to Gretchen; it was Fr. Warren. I remember doing my semester project on Modern Classical Music. It was assigned to me, but I am glad I was able to do it. I gained a great understanding of the modern age from that music course. I particularly liked Rimsky- Korsakov, Stravinsky, Copland and Bernstein. John Williams was just getting started scoring films at that time. You can have Schoenberg and the atonal school; definitely not my cup of tea. The music listening room had an album of the Chichester Psalms[117] by Leny Bernstein; I used to spend many evenings listening to that very moving piece of music. I particularly enjoyed the Psalm 23 from that work. In the process of inserting a footnote I found that you can view Leonard Bernstein conducting the 23rd Psalm. Unfortunately that performance is no longer available on YouTube.com. However the Psalm 23 is performed by another conductor at https://www.youtube.com/watch?v=qSIZ8RY8cGI. Not to say one cannot find Bernstein conducting the Chichester Psalms on YouTube[118]

Of course, in the midst of all this traditional study, there was constant exposure and discussion of themes within the Church. These were mostly of changing theology, but also heavy in spirituality. I discussed this in my next letter to Gretchen:

Oct. 30, 1965
Dear Gretchen,

It's time to sit down and answer your last letter. First of all I have to tell you how really wonderful it was to hear your views on the Pope's visit [Paul VI visited the USA in 1965] and most of all your faith in the "sameness" of religions. In all honesty, when you said "they can find some similarity", you made me very happy. In its own way, that remark gives meaning to what we are studying and to the goal that we seek. Ministers and priests can preach all day, but unless there are those who trust God and each other, what good does it do?

Your question was a real whopper. I thought about it for hours, and then wrote a reply previous to this letter. It never was sent, because Fr. Ben pointed out how very little consideration I had given to the question, and suggested that I discuss it with the other seminarians (he also pointed out his own views in the matter). We've knocked it around all over the place, but our conclusion is, by no means definite. There was an approximately 50-50 split in the general consensus.

But without further ado, here is my general conclusion, needing voluminous explanation which will have to wait till Christmas:

Common sense says that a person certainly cannot do anything he wants, no matter how much effort he puts into it.

But immediately there are two objections raised against this statement:

a. It's sure murder to the aspirations of any poor devil who has a great number of difficulties to overcome.
b. It deemphasizes the tremendous potential influences of an individual's will on a situation, and, what is more, the influence of God's will on a situation.

To believe that a person can accomplish anything he wants is to leave that person open to a great deal of disappointment when he runs across his first big obstacle. But then too, a person with a lot of drive can accomplish some pretty amazing things and knock over some seemingly immovable obstacles. And "nothing shall be impossible with God." (Luke 1:37).

Well, that is the general idea of my viewpoint (and that's all it is, just an unproven viewpoint).

Thor must be a sharp guy, certainly not too lacking in the upper story and apparently endowed with a fair portion of ambition. And from the way you talked in the letter before last, he must have treated you to a very enjoyable evening.

It is easy to imagine your brother "enjoying every minute of it", but I am dubious about his presidency [of the West Point student body]. Not that he lacks the ability, but the initials don't match up. If his middle initial is A, that would make him president B.A.H.

The folks had an indescribably good time at the [Eddy] Peabody Blow Out, but Mom did manage to write five pages about the whole enjoyable evening.

It is a good thing that your favorite prof is teaching a subject so related to journalistic avocation, but I am still confused about this geology kick. Do you plan on writing for *The Scientific American?* Seriously, is this part of your course requirements for a B. A., or do you have a special side-interest it rocks? (and by the way, did you get that A that you were hoping for?).

Things have really been jumping here. I don't know whether you realize it, but this is a time of big changes for seminarians and Catholics in general. Thursday there was a big open discussion about updating our Third Order and the seminary (very interesting). Yesterday we held the first in a series of world-problems discussions, and today the sophomores are taking part in a Young-Christian-Students" discussion of religious liberty. All these things are unprecedented in the history of San Luis Rey. This all may seem "old hat" to you, but you can be sure that, while there is much to be said in favor of seminaries, there are many areas where they are behind the times. I just wanted you to know how excited we are to be part of the 'great updating'. Perhaps you are finding comparable excitement in the great changes that are going on all over the place.

I have to close now. Again, thanks very much for writing. Best wishes to your folks, Chris, Thor, and take care of yourself. "May the Lord bless you and keep you... and may he give you peace." (St. Francis of Assisi)

Mike

As the letter indicates, things were changing; ideas were being thrown about; accepting the status quo was really no longer an option.

You will probably be asking yourself, who are all these fellows that I am referring to in the preceding letters. Please understand that, in spite of the attraction between us, Gretchen and I were both working under the delusion that we were friends and that I was going to be a celibate priest. So naturally she went on dates with other guys. Bill Koon was a classmate of Gretchen's, but he had gone into the Navy. The Navy and he did not mesh, so he was discharged for mental issues. As Gretchen explained it,

"Bill was my 'serious love interest' in high school – we got back together briefly after his discharge, but it was never serious again."

The "lucky guy" mentioned previously was Norvin Peer; he eventually married Gretchen. Thor was Gretchen's neighbor, and had always been popular with the girls in the neighborhood; but for that reason was not to become a love interest for Gretchen. The Israeli Kibbutz system found by trial and error, that if you raise children together, their relationship will always remain fraternal; it became necessary to have exchanges between kibbutzim so that their young people could form romantic attachments.

I have to admit my letters back then were a bit snarky, especially when remarking about her male friends. I though I was so much 'wiser' than all of them because I was a seminarian. Little did I know how far away from my simplistic beliefs that I would wonder throughout my life.

I was relieved to be inducted into the SLR choir, because I was not able to bring my bass to SLR, so choir was my only musical outlet. Music had become an important part of my life, to which many of the significant events of my teenage years were attached. The choir was a step up intellectually. We had done some "good stuff" at SFS, but now we were headed into new territory. I don't suppose I had had a great deal of exposure to J.S. Bach up until then, but I was completely hooked by the precision and elegance of the compositions we were signing. It was not all heavy "long hair" music. We did some modern compositions. Our Christmas Concert in the Theater in

Oceanside was a mixture of medieval, polyphonic, renaissance, baroque, and contemporary carols; e. g. the Gregorian chant "Ave Maria" (11th century), Palestrina (16th century), "The Boar's Head" and "Lo How a Rose Ere Blooming" (both late 16th Century), Halleluiah Chorus (18th Century) "Holy City" (19th Century), "Little Drummer Boy" (20th Century); and there were more songs in what constituted a history of Western Christmas music.

I don't exactly remember when our second Oceanside concert happened; all I remember is that we were in great demand and it sold out. That was mostly, contemporary music; like the Boston Pops but all *a capella*. I dare say we did a dreamy version of "Try to Remember", and our "Ghost Riders in the Sky" was positively spooky! I have to admit that I don't remember much else from our "Pops" concert except that we were wined and dined at the house of one of our hosts and the Coors beer was flowing freely… maybe that is why I can't remember? Ok, I admit it; I was a light weight when it came to drinking alcohol…one beer would have probably lit me up like a merry-go-round. I was trying to stick to the Confirmation pledge I signed at St. Rose. Oops! I might have slipped up there.

Most of the Northwest students did not go home for Thanksgiving; which I discuss in the next letter to Gretchen:

> Dec. 4, 1965
> Dear Gretchen,
>
> Methinks I owe you at least one letter in exchange for the two or three that your end of this correspondence usually produces. I admire your principles but I honestly "have no objection to" old news. It's all news to me.
>
> As for being late, it leaves all the more room for interesting things to happen between letters. Also it give one busy young lady a chance to catch up with herself, and removes one lax seminarian's excuse for setting aside the books too often. Wouldn't you agree that it's just as all around good deal?
>
> Now, that we are both excused for being late, thank you very much for your last letter.

From the sound of things you are just plain swamped with a very busy but also interesting list of activities. But then with you I guess that is to be expected, and if you survived four years of high school in that manner, you'll probably make it through college without ill effects too.

Happy belated Thanksgiving. Hope they didn't lay it on too thick at the Daily News. [she apparently worked for the newspaper that Thanksgiving vacation] We didn't have a very exciting Thanksgiving day (it rained), but then when I thought about you "slaving away" I felt like a second class dog for complaining.

To add to that, Thanksgiving evening was a regular jolly affair. We had a big feast with the Franciscan community. Fr. Kevin was down from SFS, and to top it off, we had thirty guys on dish shift.

Another "interesting occurrence" within the last two weeks: I suppose you know that my mom and dad were down to Old San Luis. I tell you, Gretchen; they were on cloud nine all the way down and all the way back (they sent letters from different points on the return trip). This was their first big vacation in three years. Mom will probably tell you how she cried for joy all during Mass, and that Bev and Gene and the girls came down from L.A., and that the folks stayed at their house for two days, and all the rest. 'Course you can imagine how surprised and happy I was; some of the other seminarians were just as glad to see them as I was too.

What else? We had a very interesting guest speaker last night; he is one of the new and rare breed in the Catholic Church today called lay theologians, and he lectured on St. Paul with occasional plugs for the lay theology movement. History, literature, chemistry and Latin reports are all due and it is time to start cramming for final exams. Where does all the time go?

This Norvin Peer sounds like a first class character. Just the names are enough to throw you, Norvin and Ardis [Norvin's sister]. I did some research on them [the names]; *non existunt in lenguis*. So he is a "car nut"; they are usually "nuts" about whatever they get interested in. Will have to meet this guy.

"It's vely honolable fo you to take Judo". One question,

¡ ¡ ¡Why!!!

I had better close this thing. Write when you <u>can</u>, take care of
yourself, and God bless the Huffhines.

Mike

One clarification, Gretchen was not planning to take Judo. She was
talking about Norvin taking Judo; I got confused. Gretchen took ballroom
dancing for her Physical Education credits at Lower Columbia College.
Another clarification, I think the trip that my mother and father made to
San Luis Rey turned my mother around. Prior to that trip, she had doubts
about me becoming a priest, and about her never having grandchildren. On
that trip she met Frs. Ben and O'Connell and even Valentine. She was wholly
taken in by Fr. Ben's wit (of course she had been reading his comments in my
letters to her), and she was most impressed with the other faculty. Whereas
she had always been duplicitous in her intentions regarding Gretchen, now
her mind was changed. Instead of presenting Gretchen to me at every turn, in
hopes that I might marry her, now she was convinced that I would be a priest.
It was beginning to be a heady honor for her and my dad. The ironic turns
that will transpire over her life regarding grandchildren are heartbreaking.

There is one member of the faculty that I have not mentioned yet,
because he did not teach class to the underclassmen. His name was Fr. Carol
Tageson[119], and he was the Psychologist on staff for SLR. Our dealings with
him in the freshmen year were for psychological evaluation and counseling.
I don't remember at what point in my freshmen year that he administered
the battery of psychological evaluations and aptitude tests; the latter was
interesting; the former was intimidating. Although I was concerned to be
one of the last students to finish the written psychological evaluation test,
apparently I did not raise any red flags and I was considered a safe bet to
continue. I think it was probably before Christmas, so that the faculty could
decide who would stay and who would go; because a number of students did
leave the seminary over the Christmas break. I did not!

I wrote a composition before Christmas that lead to considerable
embarrassment. It was written the same time that I wrote the sound

compositions about the lime kiln and the description of the sounds on the
Toutle River. Fr. Ben was impressed enough with those compositions to
read them aloud in English class. There was, however, another descriptive
composition which he read, and which I did <u>not</u> save. It was about traveling
home and the anticipation of seeing my mother again. He did not identify
me, although I am sure some of the seminarians, who had been to our
place on the Toutle, knew full well who had written the composition by
the description of the scene. It was the first time that I realized that the
relationship with my mother was unusually strong. I won't call it inordinate,
but I am sure there are those who did. I was embarrassed that Fr. Ben read
it aloud. Apparently he thought it was well written.

I think I was probably as anxious to see Gretchen as I was to see my
mother, even though there wasn't supposed to be anything going on between
me and *jungfrau typisches Deutsch*; purely platonic relationship, you know?

As it turns out, I have no recollection and there is no written record of
the first Christmas home from SLR. I am not ever sure that I went home;
but I cannot recall any other place I or my family might have gone for
Christmas in 1965. I am not even sure how I might have travelled. At some
point I did fly home on the new Boeing 707 jet liner. I guess it would have
had to be that Christmas, because, on that first summer break, five of us
traveled home in a 1955 Chevy. As I mentioned, I traveled home by bus the
Christmas of 1966. It may also have been the time when Phil Sowa and I
went to Bev and Gene's and they took us to Universal Studios. It would have
made sense to travel by jet because the Christmas break was not that long.
But as I said, there is no record of any of it; and the fact that Jana Huffhines
wrote nothing about me or my parents in that December of 1965, pretty
much confirms that Gretchen and I did not even meet over that holiday
(because Jana recorded everything else we did together). This seems strange,
but two things were happening: 1) Norvin was dating Gretchen frequently
then, and 2) I think my mother might have begun to be concerned about
the growing affection between Gretchen and me. I will neither accuse her of

purposely preventing any activities with the Huffhines, nor did she promote it in the winter of 1965. My mother said in a letter to Gretchen that Fr. Ben had turned the seminarians out at Christmas break that year. Some stayed with other seminarians in California, and some went to Mexico, but I know that I did not do that.

CHAPTER 15

The Mission

O my people, listen to my instructions.
Open your ears to what I am saying,
for I will speak to you in a parable.
I will teach you hidden lessons from our past –
stories we have heard and known,
stories our ancestors handed down to us.
We will not hide these truths from our children;
we will tell the next generation...
**New Living Translation (©2007) Psalm
78:1-4**

I ASKED GRETCHEN THIS MORNING if she felt like she was living
with the past. Her response was "Yes, and it makes me kind of nervous!"
As I flail about trying to find scraps of the past to paste in this montage of
my life, I have to ask myself, "Why am I doing this?" I was up too late last
night reading all of the letters I wrote to Gretchen up to the date I left the
seminary, and also some that my mother had written to her. Although the
winter of 1966 is still largely a mystery to me, the reason for my pursuit
is becoming a little clearer. I guess I am really trying to find out who I
was, and what happened between then and now to make me the person,
curmudgeonly old fart that I am now. I know one thing for sure about 1966:
the daily routine may have been set, but the mental activity was definitely
not! It was periods of much thought, much soul searching, and even some
radical thinking. How did my mother put it in a letter to Gretchen a year
later?

Sept. 30 1966 "I wish he could bring Stan Mazur along [for Christmas vacation] – I am sure you have heard of Stan Mazur. He's the Kook that Klug was going off to form a new group with [following the life of St. Francis]. And man does Klug blow-up if you are derisive about that.

 But enough of my problems. But – as a tip – don't urge him. If he feels he has to – he's apt to be sullen and edgy. He can be. Then Christmas is spoiled for everyone."

That would turn out to be prophetic on my mother's part, in which she played a large roll. Talk about your self-fulfilling prophecies! But we will come to that bye and bye. For now, let's just say I was undergoing a kind of "spiritual awakening" and at the same time a great emotional conflict internally.

I think Phil and I also took those newfangled jet aircraft back to L. A. on our return to San Luis Rey at the end of the Christmas vacation. Mission life resumed as previously described. There were no communications between Gretchen and me for the remainder of the school year... at least none that were saved. Jana recorded only two events that she and Bob shared with my Mom and Dad during the winter and spring of 1966 (It is so handy to have her journal to remind us).

Saturday, February 19, 1966: Kay and Jim K. ate hamburgers with us and we went to sing-along at Catholic School in Portland. G went to see plays at school with Norv.

Saturday, May 7, 1966: Bob worked in yard, etc. I did usual chores – went by office for blood donor. Left 5:30 for Portland with Jim and Kay. G went, too. Ate at Peppermill and saw "Finian's Rainbow" at Civic Theatre.

The winter semester proceeded at a rapid pace with ever increasing numbers of activities on top of the heavy course of study. The seminary was really opening up to the outside world, and a lot of that kind of activity is described in my letters to Gretchen in my sophomore year. Suffice it to say, we were being challenged to not just think, but, as Sister Anna Mary would have said, "TINK!"

I think Fr. Anselmo joined that faculty that winter. He was a very charismatic fellow, and was full of new ideas and a particularly social action kind of approaches to the Franciscan life. I think the last of our classmates from SFS to leave the Novitiate was Bill Halvorson. That was because he was heavily involved with social action under the mentorship of Fr. Anselmo. I was told that Bill remained a Brother for 3 years. I don't know what he was doing, but apparently it suited him. Now he lives in Portland and has a family, I am told.

I think Fr. Anselmo's views bordered on liberation theology[120]; after all it was the '60's! Although I was not writing letters in the winter and spring of 1966, I was keeping notes and commenting on things that I read. I won't bore you with the long winded details, but let me just say I was trying to reconcile the pure intention of St. Francis in the *The Little Flowers of St. Francis*[121] with the complex logic (?) of the 20th century. Chesterton brought the Franciscan concept into the 1900's, but it was no less radical. I was not alone in my pursuit. Many young people were trying to find their way back to a simpler, more peaceful way of living. This was the time of the flower children and "make love, not war". As the footnote mentions, the stories of St. Francis were both charming and humorous. It is often the case that humor embeds the thought more thoroughly in your mind that other "weightier" cogitations. It was clear to me that the Order of Friars Minor was a far cry from the band of happy beggars that was Francis' original intention. I'm not faulting the Franciscans because they do a lot of good; but the vow of poverty of the individual members certainly did not translate to a lifestyle in any way resembling poverty. I have already mentioned examples of Friars who did live very simple lives, like Br. Conrad and Fr. Kevin; but San Luis Rey was a more sumptuous life than we had seen at SFS. Let me relate my description of the last feast that I shared at SLR before Thanksgiving of 1966:

> As for dinner, it was not dinner, it was great grand orgy! First everyone had to just go through and look at the food layout: palm fronds and bay leaves, three layered fountain of punch, pineapple swans, a decorated tuna glaze that took three hours to mosaic together, a firing 3 foot volcano stuck all around with Cornish game hens; a 40 lb. Turkey. Ham, prime rib; 3 kinds of pie and 3 kinds of cake, 7 salads, rolls, potatoes, dressing, Rosé, Benedictine, port. If the Brother's had not treated this as their big gift to the community, it would have been completely disgraceful. Think of the starving Indians; it's almost unbelievable.

We were learning about the injustice and poverty in the world, but we were observing the life of the professional ecclesiastics in the richest country in the world.

Stan Mazur was a student that had come to SLR by way of St. Anthony's Seminary in Santa Barbara. We started discussing things we had studied or lectures in which we had participated, and found that we were having similar doubts about the life we were leading and the idea that was presented to us. We would often meet on the outer door of the quadrangle that led out of the dormitory. It was a place where we could talk, because we felt a little "separated" from the student body in our thinking. We were actually saying to ourselves, "will we ever really live like St. Francis and the early band of brothers in this institution." We had a lot of time to think about it; because there were a lot of periods of meditation, retreats and long religious ceremonies during which about all you could do was think. I was reading Thomas Merton, and Eric Fromm, and a lot of long biblical passages.

I was also doing something that borders on divining. It has been done by men of religion and mystics down through history, but it is a hell of a way to lead your life. I would flip the Bible open and read the passage that came up at random. Not only that but I recorded them and, in re-reading them, some – no, many – are uncanny in their relevance to the questions posed. There's nothing wrong with that, unless you are trying to decide what to do with your life and you are expecting the passage to tell you. Some would call it a way of discerning the will of God. I would now call it the preoccupation that men have to be able to look into the future. Countless systems of divination have been created by every culture known to man. The Catholic Church would consider it occult in most contexts, but countless times you will see it come up among the Saints and mystics of the Church, St. Francis included. Who's to say whether it is real or not, but I know for my part it had led to a lot of confusion over the years.

I had read the life of John XIII[122] and I particularly enjoyed the little book, *The Wit and Wisdom of Good Pope John* by Henri Fesquet. Angelo Giuseppe Roncalli was a practical and very human man who figured it was time to bring a "little fresh air" into the Church. When I had a layover in Rome on my way to the Kenya in 1969, I visited St. Peter's Basilica. I was struck by the bodies of the dozen or so popes that were on display, looking as if they were asleep in their glass sarcophagi. I had read the biography of the saintly Pius X… and there he was! I mention this because I did not see John XXIII (he had not yet been exhumed); but the picture of his body is on the internet, lying in his glass coffin in 2004. Wikipedia says the Church attributes the preservation to good embalming, but a lot of Catholics believe that the bodies of the Saints are indestructible. Makes you wonder; all the bodies of the lousy popes are not preserved, and I am sure their embalming techniques were just as good then as now, and some of those preserved popes go back centuries. Maybe the coffin is more high tech?… Hmmmmmmmmm! However I looked at it, it was as surprising to see this picture of this dearly loved pope as it was to see the dead popes in St. Peter's Basilica.[123]

What I am trying to say is that there is a chasm between faith and reason. By all accounts those of true faith can expect miracles, but the rational man finds this very hard to believe. To Stan and me, what we read in *The Little Flowers*, was abandonment to faith like Christ had asked the apostles:

> "And why worry about your clothing? Look at the lilies of the field and how they grow. They don't work or make their clothing, yet Solomon in all his glory was not dressed as beautifully as they are. And if God cares so wonderfully for wildflowers, those are here today and thrown into the fire tomorrow, he will certainly care for you. Why do you have so little faith?
>
> "So don't worry about these things, saying, 'What will we eat? What will we drink? What will we wear?' These things dominate the thoughts of unbelievers, but your heavenly Father already knows all your needs. Seek the Kingdom of God above all else, and live righteously, and he will give you everything you need. **New Living Translation (©2007) Matthew 6: 28-33**

Instead of taking this passage metaphorically, Giovanni Francesco di Bernardone took it literally; giving away all of his possessions including his clothes; he threw himself on the mercy of God and the generosity of his fellow human beings. Stan and I could not say, "that's nice, wasn't that a quaint idea for this early Renaissance youth". We were asking ourselves, did he really mean it, because there is no question that Francis practiced what he preached, which was as close to the teachings of Christ as he could get.

Although I have documentation of the whole process that Stan and I underwent, I really have no grounds to go into a large philosophical discussion of this premise of faith, because I never had the faith (or courage) to adopt it. Stan and I certainly considered it. By the middle of the spring quarter, we were definitely discussing the possibility of just leaving the Seminary and taking to the street; a bit more daunting task in the 20th century? Perhaps that is not true; St. Francis certainly didn't have soup kitchens and half-way houses to fall back on. Conversely, St. Francis lived in a rural age and was much more accustomed to living off the land than we could ever be today. Were 13th century peasants more generous that 20th century laborers? Who knows? Stan and I were not to be the ones to find out.

I discussed my dilemma with Fr. Carol, the psychologist, and his advice was that I was exhibiting paranoid tendencies[124]. Definition: deep feelings of insecurity compensated for by delusions of grandeur. But what if it really was a grand idea? I think his diagnosis was a bit severe, because I have never had delusions of grandeur; in general I have always been a pretty humble (or insecure) person. However, I have been influenced by grander ideas than perhaps I should have. Maybe I have tried too hard to make a difference in the world. I have not been very successful at it; but sometimes I tried. At this juncture in my young adult life, Stan and I decided <u>not</u> to try.

Instead, we knuckled under the authority of Holy Mother Church and its servants, the priests at SLR. We set aside our assiduous pursuit of the pure path of the gospel, and concentrated on passing our exams so we could go home to look for work and lead our ordinary lives until we could return to this heady institution of radical thought… just not too radical. I sometimes wonder…… By the way, did I mention that Fr. Tageson, Fr. Ben, Fr. O'Connell and Fr. Valentine all left the priesthood and the OFM?

This is bringing up some deep emotion as I write. Fr. Christian remained a priest, and once he asked me if I wanted to return to the brotherhood. I don't remember where that was in the complicated sequence of my life, but I did not feel I was unencumbered enough to consider his offer. I don't know if he was serious, but you can believe that I sometimes wonder what life would have been like if I had stayed with the OFM and become a troubadour for God. This is what my mother thought:

> May 3 1967 [in a letter to Gretchen at the Univ. of Washington]
> I don't suppose you will ever understand how disappointed we were, not until you have a son of 20 years who suddenly changes course after seemingly have found his niche. I still think that he would have been an excellent priest, a great Franciscan, and a

perfectly happy individual. But I guess he can find all that and more out here, if he really buckles down to it. However, it will take a lot of patience on your part [referring to Gretchen], and a lot of help and understanding.

Either way, there would have been a change of course. I suppose she would have had more regrets if I had actually taken to the streets as an itinerant beggar trying to convert the hippies to Christ, Franciscan style. Who knows? Stan and I might have been as sucked into the drug culture as the flower children were. As it turned out, Joe Barreca got closer to the counter culture than either Stan or I. It doesn't seem to have hurt him; he may be more Franciscan than either of us. I can't speak for Stan, because I have not been in touch with him since SLR. I heard that he went on to Novitiate, but, when the novice master suggested that he should take care of his carnal urges by masterbating, it was the last straw! He left the OFM, married and had a parcel of kids. I don't know if that is true, but that is what I was told. I will, of course, go into more of the details of my sordid history after the year of "great aspirations".

To continue with the ending of our freshman year, there is not much more to say. There is much more to say about the summer and the following year, because there are records of it. I will say that, in my notebook, I summarized the spiritual quest that we had undergone that winter and spring as follows:

> I have given by now as much, and as deep. a consideration as my limited vision will allow to the three vocations to which our lives are aimed and to the three manifestations of those vocations which life presents me with and toward which the Spirit draws me. They are:
>
> First, the gospel ideal, the faithful, loving, poor, and suffering servant;
>
> Second, the Franciscan priesthood (the service of God's Church in the rule and life of St. Francis as it is now and will be lived);

> Third, the Christian marriage (the communication in the
> fullest extent possible among human being of the protective love
> and Fatherhood of God).

Thereafter, my notebook contained mostly quotations from various spiritual and social readings and lectures that we attended.

After final exams we were doing our annual cleanup work awaiting the release date. Some of the bolder students participated in an effort to dislodge a crow's nest in the top of a 60 foot eucalyptus tree. After many various attempts, Frank Scheidler and Phil Sowa took upon themselves the dangerous feat of climbing the tree and removing the nest. Frank could not carry it down with him, so he was forced to drop it with the 4 young birds in it. Amazingly two of the young crows survived. We could not abandon them, and the brothers did not want them around, so Phil and I agreed to take them.

Three of the seminarians travelled home with Bob Scholze, because his uncle, who lived in Santa Monica, offered to give him a 1955 Chevy sedan. So four of us north westerners bused to the uncle's home, spent the night, and then loaded into the Chevy, birds included. We took the Coast Highway, Interstate 101, and saw a lot of beautiful scenery. We did not stop for any extended time, although I think we did layover in the Bay Area for a day. We would trade off driving, and stop only to eat, pee, and feed the birds. There is one picture of us at a beach. We were limited on time so we decided not to do the North Coast Highway, but rather head up the central valley of California on I5 (of which large sections had, by then, been constructed[125]). By the time we were driving up the Willamette Valley we were pretty tired, and the driver was trying to stay awake. All of a sudden, one of the tires blew out at 60 mph. You can believe that we all woke up instantly! The adrenaline was pumping big time. The driver managed to get us over to the central island, and by a stroke of good luck, the spare tire, although lacking tread did at least hold air. Soon, we reached Mt. Angel and drove to Phil Sowa's home.

Blowout on Interstate 5. L to R Jim Halverson, Frank Schiedler, Bob Scholze and me. (Photo provided courtesy of Bob Scholze)

The birds were separated, one went to Phil, and I took the other. Phil's crow lived a good life for several years. Phil let him fly fairly early in the captivity, and apparently it continued to come back to the Sowa's home after each flight (it must have imprinted on Phil). Eventually it stopped coming; which Phil assumed was because it was predated or shot. I forget how I got home from Bob Sholze's home in Tigard, Oregon, but you can bet my parents were surprised to be welcoming home a crow. We kept him tethered in the garage for the first week or so; my mother became quite attached to him. Since I started working at the pulp mill right away, she was home to feed him. Crows are very curious and interesting creatures to observe. I didn't like tethering him, but it never crossed my mind to prune his wings. So when the weekend came I went to work on an A frame cage for him. Unfortunately, I was short of materials, so I closed up one end of the cage with cardboard. It would have been fine, if it had not rained that night. The cardboard got soft and the crow was able to escape. We never saw him again. I hope his instincts were strong because his training was nil. I can only wish that he joined the congress of crows in town and lived in a happy band of black-feathered brothers. There was a very interesting program on NOVA this year about how crows are taught by their parents. They really are very clever birds!

My folks needed the Pennsylvania Street house painted, so that it could be sold, Because of my job, we agreed that I would move in there and prepare the house for painting in my free time. That turned out to be a less than perfect contract, because the amount of free time that I had was diminishing.

Jana reported that Gretchen and I began to see each other quite early in the summer:

Friday, June 17, 1966: Took Gretch by Pay n' Save to pick up camera for Bob for Father's Day. She gave it to him. Norv came over. Bob and I drove to Portland to get tickets to "Irma La Douce" for G and Mike.

The folks then went off to a post office conference:

Thursday, June 23, 1966: Picked up Jim and Kay at Mike's place and left at 5:30am. Ate breakfast at Dalles, got to Kennewick for P.O. Convention about 11. Went to cocktail lounge in Black Angus.

Friday, June 24, 1966: Meetings all day. Ladies' luncheon – buffet and dancing at night. Rainy weather.

I can't say that Gretchen and I didn't see each other over those three days, but I am certain we at least talked over the phone. Then our first "official" meeting came:

Saturday, June 25, 1966: When Ks were up early, had meeting, left about noon. Ate lunch first in Pasco. Drove to Portland. Ate at Top of Scott and saw "Irma La Douce." Mike brought G – they ate at Hippopotamus first. Mike rode home with us.

That was a memorable day. First I was escorting Gretchen entirely on my own, I was taking her out to dinner alone, and we went to a very "sexy" musical at the elegant old Oriental Theater. The production starred the very talented Juliet Prowse[126], whose lovely legs went on forever. Be still my heart!

Juliet Prowse. http://looseleaftigers.blogspot.com/2009/08/all-kings-women-juliet-prowse.html

No use trying to pretend that I remember any other details of that summer. I know I worked hard that summer, but the numbing work of the mill left nothing in my mind. The times with Gretchen were memorable. Our next encounter was a dinner with Herb at my folk's place on the Toutle:

> Wednesday, July 6, 1966:   G started full-time [at Daily News], 8:30 to 5:30. She went to Klungnesses for dinner with Mike and Herb Karnofski.

Although Jana did not make any entries until the next month, I am pretty sure Gretchen and I were communicating. That is because I remember spending a lot of time in the telephone booth at the Pulp mill. I guess Jana didn't think it appropriate to write down every time I called Gretchen. Our next big outing was *Dr. Zhivago*:

> Thursday, July 14, 1966:   G went to Portland to dinner and "Dr. Zhivago" with Mike K.

Well, of course that was a mover and a shaker. That is, it moved you to tears but it shook you at the core. Such unrequited love… even my son was greatly moved when he read *Zhivago*, and he is a Russian literature buff. Between all of these emotional highs, I would work, sleep, work, sleep, and work. After all, this is America. I like the Mennonite tradition which I think they borrowed from Judaism; when a young couple marries, the community provides them with accommodation for a year[127], and they are not heavily obligated to work. In some communities, I think they actually provide the couple with a house. There was one such house in Willows where I worked for Hill Apiaries. I wonder how important a part that plays in cementing their relationship, such that when the storm of life buffets them, they don't abandon ship.

Jana had very little to say about our next outing. She was not there but I am sure Gretchen told her all the details:

Sunday, July 17, 1966: G went to beach with Klungnesses – seminary party.

That was a fun day at Long Beach WA. Fr. Christian had learned to play Laura's theme[128] on the banjo. I was really surprised that Gretchen doesn't remember that because she sat and listened to him for the longest time. I am remiss in that I did not remember that my parents were with us. Fr. Christian had brought some other seminarians, and I am not sure who else. I am sure Herb and Brian were probably there. It was an unusually nice day for the Washington coast. Lazy day, running on the beach, water too cold to swim, but the sun was warm and relaxing. There was time to talk, listen to the banjo, and bask in the warm conversation.

The next outing was a curious one:

Saturday, July 30, 1966: G went to Weyerhaeuser picnic at Jantzen with Mike K. about 10. They went by seminary and changed clothes, met us and Kay and Jim at Country Kitchen for dinner, to see "Oliver" at Oriental. M and G went to Ferrell's after show – we came on home.

Gretchen and I went by ourselves to the Weyerhaeuser annual event. There were a lot of people from work, but there were few of those people with whom I would have associated. Craig Tillotson and his parents might have been there. I think we ran into Herb Karnofski thare, because he worked at the management office of the Weyerhaeuser mill complex. I don't remember any of that. Jantzen Beach was an amusement park with carnival rides, a roller coaster, a spooky house they called the "Fun House". Gretchen thinks we went on some rides, but I know we did not go on the roller coaster... neither of us would have had the nerve. So whatever rides we did try would have been the tamer ones. The Octopus comes to mind.

You need to know that I still was not clear in my mind whether I was going back to the seminary, and consequently the relationship between Gretchen and me was very old fashioned, kind of sweet, and definitely affectionate... but no physical contact! It was like having a chaperon that was invisible. Every smile, every brush of skin, every time we held hands was magical. I really think the modern generation has lost the beauty of courtship. I guess the best depiction of that tradition is acted out in "The Quiet Man".[129] John Wayne and Maureen O'Hara are courting with Barry Fitzgerald as the coach driver and chaperon. They are not allowed to even touch... but they sneak away and have a grand Hollywood kiss. Well, Gretchen and I did not break away.

What we did do was go out to St. Francis Seminary. I asked myself why we did that, but I guess it was probably because I still felt safer in the company of the Franciscans. Things were not as likely to get out of hand on a warm and sunny day in July. I don't remember who was there but possibly Fr. Chris was there, and surely Br. Conrad welcomed us. We dressed for the evening show, and went to the Country Kitchen, which was on the East side of Portland. You guessed it, steak and baked potato, salad with Roquefort dressing. The play that night was good, but did not have the romantic impact of *Zhivago* or *Irma le Douce*. Still, rounding out the evening with a decadent delight at Farrell's Ice Cream Parlor gave the day the feeling of a good old fashioned love affair. I don't remember if they had ice cream sodas, but I have always craved them ever since. Perhaps there was a mental association with this enjoyable night. On the Big Island, only one ice cream shop, in Kawaihae, still knows how to make a real chocolate ice cream soda.

As you might expect, not much paint scraping was getting done. I was living with a minimum of conveniences at the house on Pennsylvania St. I did have the folk's stereo phonograph, and I was still checking out folk albums and Dvorak's Slavonic Dances from the library. I was also learning to fend for myself, because I shopped and made my own meals. I did get some of the house scraped, but the folks came over and helped push the project along. I believe we started painting the baby blue house charcoal grey that summer.

It was already August and time was getting short. I had to make a decision about this ever growing closeness between Gretchen and me.

> Monday, August 1, 1966: G went swimming and ate with Mike and Ks. Met us at bus station at 10 to pick up Cosgroves [Gretchen's Uncle Tom and Aunt Lina, who was her grandmother's sister].

Sometime along this juncture Gretchen and I had time to talk seriously about "us". It is funny how a day at the water can bring out all kind of discussion that you might otherwise never have had.

> Tuesday, August 2, 1966: Hot day. Kept car and drove Cosgroves and Mom around town a bit. Mike K. and Bill K came by. Mike and G and Bob and Tom visited boat at port dock.

That pesky Bill Koon kept showing up to interfere with my evolving plan. Bob rescued us on that one. Bill did not want to visit any naval ships (having had his fill of the Navy) so that left us to help Bob entertain Tom. I vaguely remember boarding a ship at the Port of Longview, but my thoughts were not on military paraphernalia, my thoughts were about Gretchen's paraphernalia! It was getting harder to avoid such thoughts.

Sunday, August 14, 1966: [Gretchen had gone by train to Seattle on Friday afternoon to visit Sherry for the weekend.] Bob painted house all day. I dyed bedspread unsuccessfully. Picked up G at 9:30. Mike K. came to talk to Bob about his future with G, etc.

This was a seminal day, August 14. Jana's brief but factual statement does not reveal the breadth or depth of the conversation that I had with Bob. I basically asked him for Gretchen's hand in marriage. I explained that I would not be able to leave the seminary precipitously, but I was shooting for leaving at Christmas of that year. Bob was not a bit surprised; you can imagine that he had probably been planning for this day for several years preceding. I guess a father just wants his daughter to be happy, and he could see that Gretchen was happy with me; frustrated perhaps, but happy. If we had made it to marriage while he was alive, I don't think he would have been singing, "My daughter is marrying an idiot, how could she stoop so low." The last time that I saw Bob, was long after Gretchen and I had gone to our separate lives, and he was already severely affected by Parkinson's disease. Still he was cheerful and greeted me warmly. I think he did like me, and would have been happy if I had been his son in law. Unfortunately that was not to be in his lifetime.

We managed to squeeze in one more musical that summer:

Saturday, August 20, 1966: Bob and I left at 4 for Portland. Met Klungnesses and G at Il Travatore for dinner – saw "Funny Girl" at Oriental – refreshments at Totem Pole. Excellent show.

Although I remember nothing about the performance, it must have been good, because Jana was very sparing with the expletives; "excellent" would translate to "over the top" in any more emotional person's language.

I must have been spending a lot of time with Gretchen, to the point that Gretchen is only mentioned in Jana's journal when she is present.

But all good things must come to an end. It was a busy time because I would soon be leaving for school. I did not see Gretchen again that week, but:

Sunday, August 28, 1966:   Mike and G had stuff for dinner. They went to mass at 5:30 – came home and ate and then went to youth meeting at Christian Church in Castle Rock.

I think Gretchen knew by this point what my intentions were, and was trying to accommodate my religious convictions. We needed some time to talk also so I took her out to lunch:

Monday, August 29, 1966:   Mike took G to lunch.

This was the day before I was to return to SLR. I am sure there were some heartfelt discussions although I cannot, for the life of me, remember anything that was said.

Tuesday, August 30, 1966:   Bob and Mike picked up me and G (she got off work) at noon – drove to Portland Airport. (Jim K. couldn't get off.) Picked up Phil Sowa there and went to Lloyd Center – got G typewriter. Left Bob's suit for adjustment. Ate at Goldberg's – dropped boys at airport at 4 (they were returning to seminary).

I guess there is nothing to be added to that. Very matter of fact, Jana expresses what contained mountains of emotion. My folks could not see me off to the airport, although I am sure my mother was not happy. They did not know yet that I had told Bob that I was leaving the seminary. Why

Phil's parents had dropped him off so far ahead of schedule, I am not sure; or perhaps it was all prearranged. So this was our last day together with Gretchen before we would return to the challenge that was SLR.

Jana kept track of everything, including the events that happened after I had returned to the Seminary;

> Saturday, September 3, 1966: Went to Portland with Jim and Kay Klungness and George Matter to see "Fiddler on the Roof." Ate at the Riverboat Queen.

My first letter from SLR was the epitome of practical good intentions.

> August (I cannot tell a misrepresented truth),   Sept 4 1966
> Dear Gretchen,
>
> I would apologize for not phoning, but first I would have to explain to my parents why I had called them collect. If you know what I mean? [long distance phone calls were still expensive then.]
>
> A very special thanks to your father and mother for transporting and accommodating us so royally. It is a flavor which deserves a return.
>
> If you don't know how much I thank you for everything, then I could never explain.
>
> A little word of warning, though it may be presumptuous of me to think it necessary. Don't pay too much attention to me this fall and don't worry about whether I come home at Christmas or not. "Why?" (as you are sometimes want to say). Because the people you meet and the work you do now at school are far too important to your future to receive less that 100% attention.
>
> I tell you this because I know that I too must give 100 percent application to the job at hand and what the future holds for both of us will all come out in the meat grinder (as George affectionately dubbed our scholastic program)

Must close, Will tell you about trip and trap some other time, or ask my folks. God bless you and your folks in everything you do. Love, Mike

Probably the only honest statement in that whole letter was "Love, Mike". Gretchen remembers being most confused by the almost curt brevity of this first communication since the "summer of love" and expressed commitment. Part of my concern in writing that letter may have been my need to deceive Fr. Ben, because he was still reading the mail. I am sure my intentions were good, and I was hoping to concentrate fully on my studies… after all, now I needed to be able to qualify to get into another college. The plaintive "Why?" that Gretchen had expressed more than once, was well justified. Here she had waited for me to make up my mind for 5 years, and now I was being a total dork; I was more concerned with "making good" than I was about reassuring Gretchen of my promise to her dad.

The next letter was an apology. It was full of erudite posturing, but it was obviously a response to the letter that Gretchen wrote (which unfortunately we no longer have). I begin with a poem of my own composition:

Sept 18, 1966

Lovely Lady, kind and dear,
 If my lateness rudely sears,
  Know whatever work I ought,
   You lead, light, my wholest thoughts.

Here come the intellectual conceits:

And my other excuse is that I wanted to finish *Objections to R. C.*[130] before responding.

Thank you for your provocative and enjoyable letter. For all its "incoherency", it has all the color of your conversations, That is, of a conglomeration of intuited gems of inspiration. Yes, I am teasing, but I mean it too, because there was much for meaningful meditation within the fancy lacework.

For instance the article about Lillian Smith[131] was a fiery wind. This lady has very definitely what the Germans call *Weltashuung* (world vision), and she is a member of Teilhard's *noosphere* or realm of consciousness, where men "rub their minds together, they become keener, brighter, more curious, more human."

I am trying to get you a copy of *Le Milieu Divin* by Teilhard de Chardin but *adhuc non possum.*

Also, the two books you mentioned come highly rated and for myself Bedoyere's[132] was very useful in synopsizing the problems facing the Church, which we study right now. The point is what did you think of the book? When I think about it, there must be hundreds of Catholic creeds which would be very difficult for anyone else to believe, "virgin birth' for instance.

As for the hymn by Faucett, it seems very meaningful, relevant and true. Certainly all religions are the same in their profession of the bond of human fellowship, of love. If they did not profess it they would be less than human. But let me ask a question: if all religions profess this same basic conviction, why is there so much difference of opinion, so much mutual objection, so much lack of fellowship among religious groups? Is it possible that, aside from barriers caused by petty human weaknesses, differences in creed themselves can create formidable obstacles to human fellowship, to love? For instance, if the very ground of one man's being is God Jesus Christ, and the root of another man's existence is Atman the Absolute or Allah the Just, where is the unifying foundation which supports love between Christians and Christians and Buddhists and Buddhists? Or are they all the same, God=Christ=Atman=Allah? They are not understood in the same way.

Back to the hymn, it is beautiful and it is tender. It reminds me forcibly of Donne's "Valediction Forbidding Mourning"[133]. [A copy of which I enclosed in this letter for Gretchen.]

Another statement which you made provoked some glimmer of thought also. Please bear with me while I sermonize. In your Look-strip you called advertising "a big sales pitch" and you said,

"With that attitude I might flunk out." Now I know that you were kidding and that you won't flunk out, but you're right, it is a "waste of money" and I detect that you sometimes consider it a rather useless avocation. May I offer a few encouraging words of your own selection:

"We can and must evolve to different and better human beings, not by withdrawing into ourselves, but by forcing ourselves right out into the crowd, by working with and changing the institution – government, church, business, school [and advertising or the others through advertising] – whose sole purpose should be to make each of us more human."

In short, advertising can be a noble profession, and if by it you can accomplish good, then "advertise all your life".

Now to the less abstract, but in many ways, more important concerns.

So you like the rooms and you're pleased with the courses and everything is squaring away like clockwork. As a matter of fact, I think the rooms are ingenious (though I wonder how you will reach the top bookshelf) [I have always had a bad habit of making "short people jokes"]. I think the courses sound stimulating (even logic which I know from limited experience), and I never doubted that you would be completely organized for the travel three weeks in advance. But one thing floored me, I was stunned to hear about the new shoes; let me guess, sandals or water moccasins? [The reader needs to know that Gretchen has an obsession with shoes to this very day]

Likewise, I am finding the studies extremely interesting this year, and have buckled down to them *con fuerte*. Which is why I am going to cut the many things I would have said short.

My parents were crazy about "Fiddler". I don't know [about] George [Matter]; I suspect he is a new man in many ways.

Apologies and best wished to Chris; I'm glad you got in touch with her again.

This will reach you the day before you leave, so may I conclude by saying thank you for all your good wishes and may this coming year be, in God's constant favor for you, the most fulfilling ever.

Love, Mike

PS: I do not expect you to write, as I think you know. But, of course, you also know that your letters are well appreciated when they come.

If you did not notice, I detect a first glimmer of doubt in the preceding discussion of religions. This will eventually lead me to an agnostic point of view, but at this point I was still deeply embedded in my Catholic faith. Gretchen, though steeped in Congregationalist (basically Presbyterian) tradition, was trying to be open minded about Catholicism.

Gretchen then also returned to the campus in Seattle, and our folks were left to their lives. I wrote a short letter to her after she arrived at Univ. of Washington, because I had received a greeting card from her.

September 23, 1966

Dear Gretchen,

Welcome to U. of W. Do I detect a minute undercurrent of excitement in your tone, or is it the recklessly irresponsible action of one completely overwhelmed by exhilarating enthusiasm? But, perhaps I mistake the card's origin. I can hardly believe that a lady of your propriety, so little given to emotional overflow, so un-impetuous, so bubble-less, could succumb to such an inexplicable URGE. But at last the light dawns; you must be some kind of a nut!

Thank you for the card and here is hoping that you are enjoying the getting-squared-away process, as I have not doubts you are. Who's your roommate?

Speaking of roommates, mine is quite a character. Last night sometime after supper, he was just showering up after a 32 mile bike-hike. The catch is that he was supposed to have been home in time for supper. A man after my own heart, although I think he had a better excuse (flat) than I would have had.

Good bye, take care of yourself, and God grant you all good things.

Con cariño,

Mike

P. S. I couldn't exactly describe it, but I've got to tell you about the funniest thing I have seen in a ____ of a long time. It had me laughing for exactly one hour and fifteen minutes straight. This seven foot, pop-eyed freshman named Gibson and I were talking at recreation last night about absolutely nothing. The conversation started out "have you ever wondered" and continued with that reoccurring theme "it kind of makes you wonder". The *modus operandi* was "a willing suspension of disbelief", that is, pure nonsense. But the funny part was not the ridiculous logic of the thing; it was the expression on Gibson's face. I wish you could imagine how wonderstruck that guy can look; "It kind of makes you wonder." I swear that we were both in stiches most of the time. Everybody else thought we had both cracked up.

There was a lot of tongue in cheek in that letter. Perhaps there was some excess in the humor that I related to Gretchen in the PS, but possibly it was a reaction to the previous year of overly intense delving into the deep philosophical issues... the most basic question being "what the hell am I going to do with my life". The laughter then was probably a realization that I was taking all this "wondering" entirely too seriously. Maybe it took a gawky freshman to point that out.

Communication with Gretchen began to be frequent and voluminous, in spite of my protestations about our need to concentrate on our studies.

Sept. 30, 1966

Dear Lady Fair,

Thank you from the bottom of my heart for the two very beautiful letters. And let me say that, if you ever refuse to send one of those gems, I will be unbearably smitten. And that's the truth.

Please pardon my delay in responding, because, though I am never disinclined to write you, you are right in saying that sometimes I must drop the letters in preference to the studies. Not that those studies are more important than you, but that they are more important because of you. So don't worry about making me waste time.

But I will give you the same admonition: first things first. Although I know that your good judgment (which pleases me greatly, about shoes and whatnot) will keep you on track.

I keep bringing this up, but, in regards to your attitude towards advertising; I forgot to mention the important point last time (I'm kinda dumb you know). It is that I admire your perception which can discern the weaknesses of advertising, but I openly praise the insight that lets you know or at least suspect the underlying value of the art...

Thanks for calling Mom, but I'm sure she was not disappointed with you for not contacting her sooner.

Yes it was nice of Norv's mom [Mrs. Peer] to call. As far as writing Norv goes, my opinion (for what it is worth) is that, if you think Norv knows how he stands with you, there is no reason why you can't be friends, despite that basic disagreement. If you do write him [at Fort Lewis], tell him to look up my Cousin, Ralph Smith, at [Fort] Lewis basic training. I think they would hit it off well together.

Your point about hiding meaning with poetic symbolization and about saying things straightforwardly, gave me a kind of "first look" at the nature of poetry. That is, good poetry expresses something in a poetic way, which could not be better said any other way. Bad poetry, on the other hand, just tries to say something differently. Does this bring us to a point of agreement or do you think there is still room to argue the point? But then when did we ever argue about anything?

You are very right: some things are very difficult to discuss in writing. If you do go to a Catholic information seminar, pick one which offers the best trained and educated and updated teachers, if you can find them. No, better yet attend different courses by different men, because in this time of reappraisal you are likely to run into defensive dogmatism from both liberals and conservatives. It is good to know both sides. One thing more, if somebody tells you something is an unquestionable doctrine of Catholic faith; don't believe it until you have heard it from at least three varying sources. "A word to the wise is sufficient", I guess.

Yes, you certainly do sound excited.

It also sounds like logic will be a bit more stupendous than you would have given it credit for before. But I must correct your logical fallacy of either *non cousa pro causa* or equivocation for declaring the "fun" to be [the result of the] combination of the T.A. and size of the quiz class. (Yes, I am trying to show off how much I don't know about logic).

It sounds like your roommate and you are going to be a couple of problem inmates; I'm really worried. And what kind of things did you run into without your glasses on?!

To make the beds, slide the top mattress ¾ off the bed; drape the sheets over and under the all side of the mattress; carefully slide back so that sheet folds under the mattress. Perfectly simple; all you need is two hours and a strong back.

Yes, you will probably miss your parents (and as your mom said in a letter they miss you), but you will soon get used to it. Your positive attitude towards the school and students in general shows a positive step in the right direction.

And so not to forget the poems: Cervantes had some very idealistic verbs to vocalize in that song. It must kind of grab you when you hear it sung. Kipling, while of course not profound, is loaded with wit in the original sense of the term. In return for your poetic *bona dona*, I offer you this psalm of song. I think this will mean something to you because I think we breathe a kindred spirit in the regard. If not; if you are not at times struck with wonder by the things that are, I know by your vibrancy that you are not far removed from it. [The poem that I sent was "Pied Beauty" by Gerard Manley Hopkins]

If you wonder what we are up to down here, I'll say, not much outside the very fascinating realm of biology, philosophy and Christian renewal; which tells you absolutely nothing? Seriously there are a couple of points of interest this week which I would like to tell you about.

Tuesday, we (20 sophomores) were inaugurated along with 100 Catholic high school students, into the procedures of this year's "High School of Religion" program. How does it sound? Two hour group sessions with 8 kids, 2 seminarians, and roving discussion leaders; meeting once every three weeks to discuss common problems and possible means of Christian social action.

Today Fr. Pat propositioned us with a field biology project to take a bird count on the San Luis Rey Valley, with the side purpose of helping the State Game Conservation Committee gather evidence for a grand showdown with the track-home business, who are trying to get building rights to all the *arollos* (or river valleys) of southern California. How's that for doing our duty? Almost as good a voting, I'd say; but I'm prejudiced.

Tomorrow we elect representatives to a big precedent-breaker in seminary history, our Student Advisory Council. Tah Dah!

I would also like you to know that my mother is recovering from the shock of my summer visit slowly but surely. Thank God!

That is all I have to say, and certainly it is enough. Before I close, thanks again for writing. It is a blessing to hear from you, and it is great to hear what you are up to (I have a trillion questions about UW but don't know where to start). Goodbye and may the God of Wonder bless you always.

Love, Mike

Again, you can see in this letter that, in spite of the enthusiasm that I had for the studies and social engagement in which we were participating, doubts about dogma were creeping into my thinking; which is why I advised Gretchen to be careful what she learned about the Catholic faith.

It was clear from my mother's letters of Oct. 6th and Nov. 1st 1966 that she did not know my intentions to leave the seminary. A comment she made in that letter on Nov. 1st seem to indicate that she suspected something, and Gretchen and my mother previously had a phone conversation. She said:

Can it be true that you didn't know? I thought that I frequently stated why I was taking you along – but you thought I was only teasing, didn't you?

Gretchen and I have wracked our brains about what she meant. If I had to guess, I would say she probably would say she was taking Gretchen along on seminary visits etc. to test the mettle of my vocation. She didn't want me to go into the priesthood without knowing anything about the opposite sex. Gretchen was pretty convinced that my mother was probably hoping that we would fall in love. Mom ended the letter by saying:

> I hope I said everything I should in the phone call, so I won't belabor the point.
>
> [Mom had talked to Bernard Letourneau who had visited SLR]
>
> He says all of the lads are much happier this year at S.L.R.C. The new privileges and getting out more make it a lot easier to take I guess.
>
> Mike wrote that he and Dan van Dyke and Dan Scary were going to play background for the choir's rendition of Kumbaya at the 11:30 Mass last Sunday. So you know things have changed!
>
> Jim went to St. Francis for the Father-Son Barbercue last Sat. Fr. Chris was not around (he usually isn't weekends) Fr. Claude coyly asked if Mike was at home…
>
> Gee, I can hardly wait till May's Mother and Son Brunch… Fr. Ben is always up from San Luis to speak to the mothers of the upper classmen. I had to miss it last year – but not this next one…

Unfortunately that was not to be. As you can see, being a seminarian's parent had started to become an important part of their social life. It was true that we seminarians were much happier with life at San Luis, and I was glad to have my bass again (although I have no idea how we ever got it down there, and back. In retrospect, I believe I was able to get them to put it in the luggage compartment of the big express busses.). But the relationship between Gretchen and me was not diminished by all the exciting events of my sophomore year. I was also living a vicarious life at the University of Washington through Gretchen, as is evident from my next letter.

Oct.4, 1966
Dear Gretchen,

> Feel so darn great tonight, I just got to let you in on it.
>
> Today was the feast of St. Francis; a holiday and happy time of year. You probably don't remember Jim Doll, but if you do, he came

to the Mission yesterday. It was great to talk to the old man and he looked real great too. [Jim left the Franciscans after his senior year at SFS. He had broken his kneecap in a roller-skating accident, and had to have extensive surgery to repair the kneecap.]

Also yesterday evening we had a provocative little movie called *Diary of a Country Priest*[134]; which got me started on a two hour walking meditation just crammed with tremendous little insights (?). You, of course, were the subject of some consideration.

Today, after sleeping on those enlightening and enjoyable thoughts, we had a tremendous little Mass with the grade school kids and parishioners. Then, after the wild Laymen-Frat baseball game, we took an exhilarating long hike over Tootsie's hill. And then, after the very sumptuous, un-Franciscan banquet, we had a very rousing little hootenanny by the lighted pool under the balmy stars. If you can decipher my meaning, the hootenanny ended up in such a way that not all heads were left above water. Anyway, it was a heck of a lot of fun.

So as not to encumber you with my reveries, I'll close. But here is hoping that your week was as enjoyable as mine, and that I may share a little of my happiness with you.

Con cariño,

Mike

In the same envelope:

Oct. 8, 1966

Dear Gret,

Received your very welcome letter. And managed to "wade" through the soap suds quite satisfactorily. Not only that, I was very much entertained; Things seem to be getting wilder and wilder in Haggett with every passing day. Apparently dorm life is the same wherever you go (e.g. the six o'clock angelus bells were unexpectedly discontinued as of this morning. Results: a half hour of extra sleep rudely interrupted by Fr. Anselmo and ten minutes of complete and total chaos before chapel.)

My folks received your letter and were very happy to hear from you. The classes sound extremely interesting, well sized, and of quality. Recounting, what happened to the other communication course and French?

The logic problems are in symbolic logic, so I have an excuse for not attempting them in that we are now studying linguistics and scholastic logic.

Some questions: how is Mr. Koon? More satisfied with S. U. [Seattle University]? (By the way, don't be too hard on the fringies. You can never tell in which one may beat the heart of Gandhi or Francis or, would you believe, Jesus Christ [as we do]?). Have you joined Folk dancing yet? Are you getting your exercise in general, not counting up and down fire escape, and to and from Laundromats? Did you see the Air Force game that you mentioned? Have you traveled far from Haggett and have you been to Seattle?

The articles you sent were very interesting; they show the amount of action and idea that is in the wind. Have you run into much serious discussion at Haggett? For that matter is Haggett mostly undergraduate and serving the nearest departments of study, or does it serve the whole school graduates and undergraduates? Have you come in contact with any of the social programs mentioned in the article, S.T.A.Y., Y.M.C.A., V.I.S.T.A., etc.? If so, what do you think of them, effective or not? The article mentions informal discussion sessions for the pre-majors. How available are the profs out of class? Do you ever see them leading informal chats or joining in student activities?

Your roommate sounds like quite a character. What year is she in and what is her major? If I am not being too inquisitive? The other young ladies whom you have mentioned sound like first class nuts. You haven't mentioned any of the men from Haggett. Are you not impressed with the male intelligentsia, and are not some of them from Longview?

None of these questions necessitate answers, but it any of them interests you, please answer them. I am very much interested in whatever you have to say about the "university of a thousand years".

Herb was asking about you the other day and said to be sure to send his best regards.

The weather sounds scrumptious up there. Here swimming is, of course, still very much in, but an occasional midnight shower has begun to put a green tinge back in the golden hills. Don't tell Nancy that; it would make her homesick. Also don't tell her about the smoggy clouds of depression which has swept southern Cal. In reaction to the World Series. But to tell her that we are beginning to appreciate the golden desert, and even L.A. has its spots of genuine beauty and interest.

On October 11th I sent Gretchen a post card of the mission with a note:

Gretchen, have an article that I would very much like you to read. I'm not sure you will agree with the article but it will certainly challenge you to think. It is in *Critic*, Joel Wells Ed. Oct. Nov. 1965. The article is "The Other Side of Dispair" by Thomas Merton. If you can't find it, I will type it for you; it is that good. Mike

I have received a total shock in searching for the source material of this article of Thomas Merton[135]. I had read a significant amount of Merton's work, and found him very helpful in resolving internal conflict. Imagine my surprise to learn that there was speculation that Thomas Merton may have committed suicide. If the reader is not familiar with Catholicism, the Church considers suicide the only unforgivable sin. Dante's first ring of hell is populated with the souls of unfortunates like archetypal Romeo and Juliet[136] who made the irrevocable decision to cut themselves off from the mercy of God. I guess I was not the only one having a crisis of faith. If I had taken to the ascetic life, I wonder what would have happened to me. It is important to note here that Francis of Assisi, although never accused of killing himself, led such a harsh and ascetic life that he died at age 44. The barbaric medical practices that he underwent probably helped end his life, but had he not denied himself so much, would his body have been able to resist the illness that killed him? And if that were the case, would he have become the immortal patron of peace and abandonment to God? Or is it true that "the good die young"?

Only one letter that I wrote to my parents still exists. How Gretchen came to have it I am not sure, but it might have been exchanged in the meeting that Gretchen had with my mother on Nov. 23rd, as was noted by Jana:

> Wednesday, November 23, 1966: G drove up to see Kay Klungness. Had long talk with her

Only Jana and my mother would have known for sure, because Gretchen does not remember. The letter to my folks was the reason my mother suspected that I would leave SLR:

> Oct. 14, 1966
> Dear Mom and Dad,
>
> It is an amazing and wonderful thing how the human person can love what it dislikes. It is a thing so seemingly contradictory that it becomes almost impossibility to human nature. There must be something more than natural, more than human in it. In hoping for the best even for the worst.
>
> About Meritt, Mom, you are as critical of yourself as I am of me, maybe more so. He is not trying to cut you, or give you hell, or punish you. He is trying, as a man, to do what he thinks is best in a very inhumane situation. He not only respects and loves you (and grows more so by your consistency), but he needs you. He needs someone who will understand his predicament and put up with it as best as they can. I know this from what he said when he was up.
>
> I was just thinking what that trip up must have been like for him. At home all he gets is strained relations and pettiness, when he goes to the Smith's it can't be a heck of a lot better, and now us, too. I wonder when was the last time that Meritt had a good talk with a friend who wasn't all hot and bothered; who could prove by his manner that life is worth it? Anybody would

become a little less than himself in such straights. So, next time he comes up, if he does, let's pretend like life and other people <u>are</u> worth it; that, as you say, the sun comes up and the trees are green and there are birds and dogs and deer, and warmth and kindness. "For it is in giving that we receive." Who knows, he may want to come back!

The trip to the beach sounded relaxing and enjoyable. I'm glad you could make it.

Yes, Mom, I could be a happy, very happy priest. But, as a matter of fact, I could be a happy anything; when I get my beams straight, I'm just not the depressible type. So the decision comes down to choosing one vocation and willing to make the best of it. When I was 2 months a lowly sophomore in high school, I promised myself, after an almost all night meditation, that the priesthood would be my vocation except for two occurrences: 1) that I would prove unfit for the job, 2) that God would manifest his will in the particular love of another person. And if you think that is compromising a higher ideal, read the life of St. Thomas More, or *Thomas Merton's No Man is an Island* on vocation, or a really great book by a man called Eric Fromm, *The Art of Loving*.

Afternoon

Big open house going on today, things are at a lull, I have done as much work as I am able, and now I'm recuperating. We met some very likeable people today, had a big picnic lunch, sang, enjoyed ourselves, and became thoroughly exhausted. Two objections were that the entertainment was not well planned, and that not enough of the faculty mixed in, nor did the families mix well as they should have. In general it was very successful and beneficial.

I thought of you both and was going to send regards by way of Mrs. LeTournaeu, but I forgot, At any rate, you know that I wish you could have been here, but let it suffice to relate the happiness of the occasion by this letter. (Incidentally, I think Phil Sowa had some visitors; relatives from L. A. I'm glad.)

Well, better wind her up. Take care of yourselves, and know
that God loves you and blesses you, and so do I.

Love,

The Prodigal

If the first part of this letter was confusing to the reader, I should explain
that my grandfather had made a trip to the Toutle, by himself, to talk to all
of us. He did not want to tell us over the phone or by mail that Eva wanted
him to stay away from us. I don't know if he knew at that point that she
was progressing into Alzheimer's disease, but she was becoming increasingly
irrational. In typical fashion he assumed the responsibility of keeping the
peace, and in his judgment, the best way to do that was to keep my mother
away from Eva. She really could become extremely irrational when ticked
off about anything. Meritt was trying to let us, and in particular my mother,
know that he was not personally rejecting us, but was trying to protect us,
and himself, from Eva's wrath. Of course, my mother was incensed about that
because she had seen Eva manipulate every situation to her advantage. To her
death bed, my mother believed that Eva had driven her daughter Ellen and
her husband George to the grave. She was afraid that Eva would do the same
to Meritt. But Meritt was a tough old lumberjack, and he had the last laugh
(his marriage to Josephine, wife #three, was a very happy one). He suffered a
lot (and alone) for many years as Eva declined into dementia. Eventually, she
got almost catatonic, so we were able to have some interaction with Meritt
after she passed from being able to respond consciously. It is a terrible disease,
which can wreak havoc on any family. I feel that Meritt sacrificed himself to
shield us from the impact, and I hope he got his reward in this life, and, _if_
there is an afterlife, there too. When Meritt was on his deathbed with colon
cancer, if I have not already told this story, I broke into tears. He said, "No
tears when my ship passes over", and then he proceeded to tell me a joke. It
is one of those stories that can be dragged out to any length; it was about an
old spinster, who was getting on in years, so the local pastor and the church
council decided to pay her a visit.

> All the typical formalities ensued, with tea and cookies. After she
> sat down to talk, the pastor breeched the subject: "Do you ever
> think about the hereafter?" The old woman responded affirmatively.
> She said, "First thing when I wake up in the morning, I go in the
> bathroom and think about the hereafter. Then when I go down
> to the kitchen, I think about the hereafter..." [and this goes on in
> similar manner for several iterations]. Finally she said, "And then I
> go into the pantry, and I think to myself, "What am I here after?""

Five minutes after my tearful outburst, I was laughing with Meritt.
Prince of a guy, the earth has seldom seen a better man.

The other part of the previous letter was my declaration to my mother
that I had finally decided to leave the seminary, although I did not say it
exactly. That is why I signed the letter, "the Prodigal". The trip that Merit
came to visit us was also the occasion of a private conversation that I had
with Meritt. I told him what my intentions were with Gretchen, but I
admitted that I was still having internal conflict about it. He said to me:

> I don't like to give advice, and so I won't. What I will say is this, if
> you can't stand the heat, stay out of the kitchen.

These were significant words for me; the prospect of a life of celibacy
suddenly seemed, not only daunting, but actually dangerous. I thought of
the story in the Little Flowers of St. Francis, about the brother who was
having carnal temptations. It is skillfully portrayed in one of two movies,
"Francesco, giullare di Dio"[137] or Brother Sun, Sister Moon.[138] Francis catches
the brother staring through a window at a large breasted maid working in
a bakery. He understands the brother's conflict, and counsels him to leave
the friars and join a lay band of followers; which Francis did establish as
the Third Order. I realized that I was probably like that brother, in need of
more than purely spiritual love.

CHAPTER 16

Ab patina decumbo in flamma
(Out of the frying pan into the fire)

> For a time is coming when people will no longer listen to sound and wholesome teaching. They will follow their own desires and will look for teachers who will tell them whatever their itching ears want to hear. They will reject the truth and chase after myths.
>
> But you should keep a clear mind in every situation. Don't be afraid of suffering for the Lord. Work at telling others the Good News, and fully carry out the ministry God has given you.
> **New Living Translation (©2007) Second Timothy 3 to 5**

IT WAS THE LAST WEEK in October when the decision came to a full blown conclusion. I was trying to be glib in my letter to Gretchen on October 29th, but the letter turns to the serious. This is because events were advancing rapidly to a close, as indicated by Jana's notations:

Wednesday, November 23, 1966:   G drove up to see Kay Klungness. Had long talk with her.

Sunday, November 27, 1966:   Kay K. called G re call she'd had from Father Ben. Kay very unhappy with Mike.

Isn't it ironic that it would be all about my mother?

October 29, 1966
Dear Gretchen,

Greetings from the great Pumpkin, and may all our Halloween broomstick excursions be (or have been) "sincere" and enjoyable. Now tell me that you did not watch the Halloween Peanuts show, and I will think you very untrue to your archetype. By the way, thank you from the entirety of this gang and myself for the DeVoe House's offer of that amazing and symbolic piece of printed word, "But we Love You Charlie Brown". We certainly would not refuse your thoughtful offer, and we always appreciate good humor. And, of course, we all love Charlie Brown.

Halvorson was here a minute ago to impart some words of wisdom, but he left to hear a radio in a nearby parked car. But thank God, we are blessed, he has returned, and his wisdom is ever with him:

"." [Halvorson's comment]

Are you not overawed, and does not your heart become replete with satisfaction as such moments of profound insight?

To tell the truth, I have been making slow progress with this letter. We are spending a free afternoon at this park called Live Oak. We were given instructions not to wander afield, and the bikes and the ball diamonds are taken, and the kids chased us off the merry-go-round and the swings. Here we have spent the afternoon, messing around generally, causing trouble, singing, talking playing cards, reading, and in one very oddball case, typing letters. The conglomeration of activities makes the pursuit of one a wee bit impossible, but it is infinitely interesting. Kreofski and Larry Warrenberg were sitting on the other bank of the stream a while back, when a swarm of little imps closed in upon them (cute as a button, especially one little toddler in red bloomers). But the last time I checked, the little tykes had dwindled away before a rather more advanced generation of youth, and not all of them were fellas either (thank God, and good berries). As you mentioned, it does the heart good to see people for a change, as a welcome change from the unusual experience of living head on head with a wild bunch of jerks.

This is getting funnier all the time. Brian and Larry just left to talk to some girls who were intently watching our choir perform, but before they could get there, the girls asked a couple of our clods if they could use the bikes and pealed off. They just returned with a crash landing. Now they have a good little discussion group going. Suddenly, Larry returns with the infinitely disconcerting news that the *idola feminina* had fallen to the status of "real dumb" sophomores. O various vanities! Such is the unfulfilled sex life of the species *Seminarianus*.

This ended my unfulfilled account of a very unusual day. One merely funny thing should be mentioned before moving on. Our 1936, straight six, super-coach, Little-Flower-Academy bus has the disconcerting habit of regurgitating un-burnt gas (backfires) at the breathtaking speed of 50 mph and over. This process has, as of today, received a maternal symbolism. It was estimated that the trip home laid 10 Volkswagens and 1 VW bus.

This page is what might aptly be called "running over" overly much. Talk about talking too much.

Enough prattle, now down to the serious business at hand. I received your letter within four days of sending my last one; I enjoyed every wonderful word of it; and for it I thank you from the bottom of my heart. As you said, it does discuss a disconcerting and confusing problem, and yes, I think I know exactly what is disturbing you (in a way, I am responsible, as I will explain).

I am very glad to hear that you made it home, and I am very much relieve to hear that you talked over this matter seriously with your parents. I hope that it was most profitable. Since receiving this letter, I have written a letter to your parents asking their evaluation of the situation as it stands now, and to explain this to them: my decision (which is not mine, as I will explain) is and always will be to leave the priestly vocation and take up a new one, on the condition that all the fact seem to indicate that such a motion would be as fulfilling and beneficial to you as I believe it would be for me. This then is why I told my mother to be honest with you, to voice her objections, because since I could not believe them or understand them, I could not express them for her. Whether she is right or wrong I do not know, and only honest discussion will prove her evaluation one way or the other. But do keep in mind in evaluation her opinion in you own mind: she still knows me fairly well; there are recent changes in my personality which she cannot comprehend, but as far as background goes, no one, not even you, know me as well as she does. The real question is, does she know me better than I do? Good Lord, I hope not.

For the fact that Mom's letter upset you I am honestly sorry: but for the frankness, with which you were prompted to handle the situation, I cannot honestly be sorry. It is hard to tell the truth, because I for one always wonder if it will help or hurt. But it does have to be done, or eventually it will hurt. (You can recognize those for platitudes, but, at present, it is all that I have to go by).

As far as Chris' disclosure is concerned, it was nice of her to give her opinion of our situation, but I don't for a moment credit her with a complete understanding of your mind in this regard. The only reason that I was inclined to believe her somewhat emotional evidence is because it seems to match my own incomplete evaluation. The fact is, Gretchen, I have still not heard you say it; I do not expect to hear you say it unless you think it necessary and you are darn good and ready to; and if you do say it, I do not expect you to say yea or nay, but only to make up your own mind as you will to. (I have freely made my decision; you have as much right to freely make yours.)

But as I said, I do not think it was or will be my decision, nor for that matter yours. If you remember Merton's words on the nature of love, you will know what I mean. The decision rests with, call it, the Ground of our being, and our respective decisions, to be good and productive of good, must be a reflection of that will which is the underlying and deepest Good of us all. I believe that we must reflect that will... in everything.

Attitude #2 It is good to navigate by lights on the horizon (Christmas), but don't let distant dazzling wonder overshadow present joys. And you don't seem to.

Attitute #3 What a party girl! But then neither calories nor friendship can be of harm… when taken in moderation.

We also take Copi word for word in logic, but you seem to have skipped part I, Language, as we will skip part III, Induction. Or did your prof. really rush you through two units of the stuff already? Good Lord, no wonder you are confused.

Agreed 100% that there is a lot to advertising; that it is extremely subtle; that, in fact, it can me almost a kind of brainwashing productive of either good or evil; and that the profession entails a lot of responsible judgment, and badly needs ethically responsible people. Ask your prof. how he would evaluate the book of a writer named Vance Packard, especially *The Hidden Persuaders*…

I cannot continue the letter; from this point, it gets far too preachy; it embarrasses me to think how much I thought that I knew. Gretchen was giving consideration to reading the Bible, and in her typical fashion, she intended to read it cover to cover. I was advising her against it, giving her all manner of "scholastic" mumbo jumbo, and even encouraging her to read the *Anchor Bible Series*.[139] For God's sake, there were probably 30 or 40 volumes already published at that time. I have it on good authority that Gretchen, although she may have taken all my pompous piety in stride, she did not often delve into the reading assignments she received from me. I know, shocking, isn't it?

Let's move on to a letter that was written soon after the former, but is a lot closer to reality.

Nov. 1, 1966
Good Evening Beautiful,

Do you mind if I pull your ear for a bit of this beautiful 97° evening? Writing a letter to you is about the only thing that can keep me awake after the all-day hike we took today; 97° F, isn't it ridiculous? Incidentally, the free day was Feast of All Saints; I'll bet you are beginning to wonder if we ever go to school around here. If so, this will kill you: tomorrow we are out of classes for a day of recollection (a handy thing to have right now).

Some of the guys tried for a monadnock[140] called Mt. Moro, which is 15 miles over dry hills and which our sophomore class reached last year. They didn't make it this time.

A sunny good morning to you, Bright Eyes.

Prepare yourself. I disown some of the statements in my last letter. I had a long and very fruitful talk with Ben last night; I was surprised. He said almost exactly what your father said, except that he was less cryptic, more aware of my situation, and had abundant evidence that what he said was true. I did not send the letter to your folks because I still did not have the one point to which your father objected straight. Thanks to Ben, I have it straight: my decision will not be a choice between you and the priesthood (which is what I had been telling myself), but between marriage and the priesthood. You just happened to be very helpful in pointing out to me that I have always favored marriage as much or more than the priesthood. But get this, would you: Ben says there is no reason to stall a decision; he says Christmas one way or the other. By way of exception, he says he would let me come back, but in the 10 years he has taught, no one in my situation ever has. Best of all, he says I am being honest with myself, and that is indispensible. (I think you would like Fr. Ben).

All this information should come to you, Gretchen, as a very welcome bit of news. If nothing else, it very definitely and rightly frees you from any responsibility for my decision, and from any obligation to me. Being a basically independent cuss, I intend to make a very independent decision. How that will affect you, I leave up to you to decide <u>independently</u>.

As for what my mother says to you, don't let it bother you in the least. As I suspected and Father pointed out, she is the one that is "all mixed up". Not at all hard to understand considering her situation and not to her discredit, she has an adjustment to make which will come soon enough.

With that clear, may I briefly finish my commentary on your last letter? We are agreed 100% that there is too much to say in a short letter, and yes, I wish to God we could just sit down and talk it out. Eng. Lit and Comm. Today sound very interesting; how about oceanography? Seventeen hours is heavy, but the lack of diversity may make it easier to concentrate on the subjects you are taking.

Fraternity party? Heavens! I am utterly scandalized; but you redeemed yourself by not tipping the bottle.

I was wondering when you were going to stop throwing money around like water, but it noticed that the wild Halloween card exactly made up for the quarter's worth of postage saved. Seriously, the cards are beautiful (and make tremendous bookmarks.) Haggett reminds me of the Top of the Hilton in Orange ("times are gettin' hard, boys").

You will be glad to have the Chef-Boyar-Bob home for Christmas, won't you?

Now just a short commentary on our activities, then I will let go of your ear.

Thursday we performed some folk music and *"Sicut Locutus Est"* with choir and instruments at the dedication of Cabrillo National Monument, San Diego (even made the local news). Afterword, we had a ____of a good time at University of San Diego eating, performing, and fooling around with the 90 seminarians there; a great bunch of guys.

Friday night we had a seminar on the ethics of law, by an unbelievably funny lawyer from San Diego.

Saturday, as you know, was spent at Live Oaks Park.

Sunday we pulled off another accompanied rendition of Kumbaya at high school Mass. That afternoon some of us went to the dedication of Oceanside Presbyterian; heard an amazing sermon. Tuesday, all day individual hikes, today retreat.

Other notes: The choir had started working on Handel's Halleluiah Chorus, wow?

Some of us are going to be able to take in a lecture in LA by Mister Modern Theology, Hans Küng. Today we are having a Byzantine rite Mass celebrated by our guest speaker (pretty wild).

Gretchen, *es toto*, and the bell just rang. God bless you beautiful.

Love,

Mike

Well, now it was crystal clear what to do next. Home at Christmas, into Lower Columbia Community College, get a job, not necessarily in that order. I would that it would have been that easy. It is amazing how much verbiage would be generated by the anticipation, the sexual tension, the pure frustration of waiting that last month and a half.

I frankly told Gretchen, while I write in the present, that I could not transcribe all the old letters, and that if she wanted any of it included, she would have to take over the transcription process. We'll see if she finds it important enough to share.

Nov. 25, 1966

Bon Dieu! You have never seen a more ghastly looking crew than this one this morning. 6:00 a.m. comes unbelievably early. As Dan said before Mass this morning, "the communion song will be a parody on 'Lord, I Am Blind.'" It goes like this: "Lord, I am tired. I wish I were in bed; help me to hold up my head."

At ten o'clock Wednesday morning, we had just gotten out of choir practice and were headed for the Wed. morning study hall. When we do have classes, we usually do not study therein (this morning we will probably all sleep; especially through Logic). Study Hall time is when the studying gets done, and when we learn the most. Our credit system is a standard accredited semester system. We are now carrying the standard 15 credit load; 2 units for Epic, 2 unit for Theology; 3 units from History of Ancient Philosophy, Logic, General Biology, and Latin. Chorale (varsity choir) is 1 unit; and Greek is an audited elective. Epic so far has been aesthetics and will now turn into epic genre, Iliad and Odyssey (your lit course will probably be much more thorough, but Ben knows his stuff and makes it very interesting). Theology is practically an open discussion course, but very informative, covering everything from liturgy to psychology (it is not accredited anywhere but in a Catholic University). Ancient Phil. covers Heraclites, Parmenides, Sophistic, Platonic, Aristotelian, Epicurean, and Stoic philosophy (Fr. Geoffrey is the very best teacher I have ever had, or probably ever will have. And yes, we had to study like the devil.) In logic, we are 2 chapters behind schedule on "Statements, Forms and Statements." Symbolic logic is much easier to understand than all the preceding material, but the complexity of the process of solving problems (mathematical) almost makes it difficult. Is your logic a two-credit course? If it is three credits, you must be taking the three units in Copi in minute detail. Does he have you work a lot of logistic problems? General biology is just that, too general. Fr. Pat covers some points well, but there is too much speculative and too little hard data. I am trying to make up my scientific knowledge deficit in side reading (but I'm not too sure where I stand.) Latin is Christian Patristic; I don't know where I stand there, and the sad thing is I don't much care. Latin takes up more study hall time than any other subject, but all the work does absolutely nothing towards increasing facility in the language. Oh, well. Sr. Gurty Joe is interesting (and unbelievably intelligent), but not much, and totally illogical. (That's not exactly true.) Choir is great (Warren is a first-rate director); and Greek . . . well, I haven't had much time for extra Greek classes.

Logic is confusing (especially for females!) and you did darn well to get a B. I too came out with a mid-term B, but the best could have been quite a bit harder.

In a way, I could say I don't exactly know how Herb and Brian and Phil are doing. We are too busy with studies to want to talk about them. As a result, there is not too much exchange of information about family situations and what not. We live here as a community and the subjects of concern are the affairs and concerns of the community. Private concerns and problems and even joys are shared only in so far as they have meaning for the community. I won't say this is good or bad, but it does work, and it keeps things running smoothly. I know this: Herb is giving steady attention to his studies and seems just about as well satisfied with this place as ever. Brian, as has been the case for a long time, is not sure that this is what he wants. He, too, is studying hard, living regularly, and is much relieved by the new attitude that pervades the place. (Oh, yes. Herb jokingly said he is having trouble hanging on to his faith. He says, "They say to hang on to the basic tenets, but so far they have knocked out every one.") Phil Sowa had been for quite some time having a difficult time reconciling his ideas with this club. It was causing him much bitterness and worry. I think now he is beginning to take things a little less hardly and therefore can tolerate the inconsistencies. Phil also is not sure that he could rather be a priest than a husband, but he is honest with himself, so that decision will come in due time. There are my opinions, and I may not have all the information.

I have not heard from P.G. [Phil Gilday], nor have I written him. This is not surprising, since most fellows don't much like to write letters. I don't much like to write other guys (except for a particular reason), and Phil violently detests writing letters in general. We will get in touch sometime if we happen to think of it; that will suit him and it will suit me.

Beth sounds like quite a character. Are all the girls who go to State nuts?

Fr. Ben discourages lots of home mail for the freshmen to teach them to stand on their own two feet and that they are no longer little boys under "Mommy's" wing. For seminarians, that is sometimes necessary, but Fr. Ben knows my situation and approves of our correspondence. Jim Palacek (passes out mail) used to wonder why all the letters from a girl, I imagine. But Jim's not too dumb (S.B. Pres.) and has sense enough to know that I know where I'm going.

In other words, write whenever you like. Ben doesn't approve us taking too much of our time writing out, however, so please understand if I fail to write at times or am not always too thorough.

Your descriptions of the activities of your friends, at WU are adept at giving insight into their various characters. My impression of Nancy is rather comical. Marv sounds like the right guy.

Will you be studying under Dr. Pellegrini?

Our concept of community down here is put to shame by your group. We try to get away from having to study n the same room together; you depend on it. Difference in temperament, no doubt.

I hope you have some Lawrence Welk records to go with your champagne parties. We certainly are able to produce mountain music to go with our mountain dew. (No, we are not all drunks. The fact is, one gallon of potato mash will produce about half a pint of vinegar alcohol, but it's the "spirit" of the thing, I guess.)

Concerning drinking parties, tell Sandy (if you think it right) that there is a very valid Christian witness involved here. The reason drinking is so "in" at parties nowadays is because anyone who has the self-restraint not to follow the crowd gets out of it. If more individualists took a more active part in community functions, the community might be inclined to take on a more responsible character. In theological terms it's called implanting the leaven of Christian virtue in the dough of society.

Evening 25th [November]

Dear Gretchen,

Please excuse this paper, but I'm in study hall and I just found out for certain cure that a certain wonderful somebody is the most honest, most imperturbable, most "herself" person in the whole God blessed world. Meritt, would that I had your perception to recognize a gem of a human being when I have lived so near her! Your mom is right, Gretchen. Not only are you a big girl but, Gretchen, you are a <u>woman</u> in the true sense of the term.

The reason I could not tell my mother (which was Fr. Ben's advice) that I am quitting is because of her and my background. The reason I could not explain this to you is because I didn't think you would be big enough to understand. I continually find out that I am underrating you; I was dead wrong, and I am sorry... I mean I'm glad I was wrong.

My mother's problem is this, and it is most definitely a psychological one (meaning she could not help it even if she wanted to) that because of her past experiences, she feels that she is very much a failure as human being (which, you know as well as I, is completely false). (Possibly this is an incorrect appraisal.) In view of this unworthiness that she feels, she long ago resolved that I would be the best thing she ever did, and eventually that came to mean that I would become a priest. Now certainly you will admit, more than others even, that she has made a very good and even better than usual contribution to the making of me into a full person. She will not admit it, and she feels that she is still completely responsible for me as a person. Now she is right in one way; like any human being, I am not perfect, and, in fact, in many ways (which you must eventually realize) I fall below standard. In another way, she is completely wrong; she is not responsible for me, and has not been since I started to think. But given this belief of hers and her estimation of herself, can you see how her whole value as a human being, in her eyes has hung on my becoming a priest? Does this hit anywhere close to your suspicions, or does it come as a surprise? If so, I hope you can understand what the problem is, and I know you will not hold it against my mother.

As for your being responsible, you are not. This is something which would have had to have been faced whether you had ever entered the situation or not. In one way, you are very helpful; you give me the courage to face up to the situation and to be honest with myself. Gretchen, I was never meant to be priest; I could have filled the role somewhat, but not willingly and not in a spirit of free choice. If that takes the wonderfulness out of the relation between us, I am very sorry. But a human relationship cannot be founded on a fiction, and I think you know it. The fact is, I want to be a husband and a father, and I love you. Whether I am capable of any of those three things remains to be proven.

Darn choir practice is going to keep me from finishing this tonight, but I'll sure give it a try.

"What happens to us now?" Bong! right over the head of me. Good question, if I knew which angle you were approaching from. You say you can see why we can't make the big commitment until the love has met the test of tie, so that must mean your question refers more to the course of action we must take for the next few years (talk about not knowing how you will react!) You said before that you have in mind to finish college and then go to San Francisco for a year to work; is that plan totally distasteful to you now? I hold you under no bond; you are free to do whatever you want. If you want to be under bond, I would say, I guess, do what your parents want? For me, the plan is somewhat tentative, somewhat set: one thing I must do is pick a University that I can get into, pay for, and get a good biological education in.

[not signed]

I was pretty hard on my mother in that letter, but in retrospect, I think it was a fair assessment, and probably Fr. Ben was clarifying those things in my mind. It is also quite clear that Gretchen and I had not fully considered all the consequences of my coming out of the seminary either. It is interesting that, although we modified our dreams while we were going to together; as soon as I went my "missionary" way to the Peace Corps, Gretchen headed to her "dream destination" of San Francisco.

November 28, 1966
Dear Gretchen,
Are you still speaking to me after that last letter? I think I may have made some pretty shattering remarks, but I will probably find out how you reacted with the next three days. Letters are hard to write and hard to understand; maybe I should have waited to tell you those things in person.

It has been a fairly regular weekend. I got all my application papers filled out, but still can't get hold of the Registrar to have him forward my transcripts. Choir practice this weekend has been long and fruitful, but we blew it at 10:30 Mass yesterday. Three members and the director, Fr. Warren, have laryngitis. Sunday morning and all afternoon was excavation day in the dorm. A hot water line busted so they had to take a jack hammer to the cement floor. The outcome: 2 floods, dust all over everything, a great pit in the floor, and no hot water.

November 29, 1966
Instead of going to night prayers tonight (Old Dick Hopp just moseyed on in to give my roommate's horn back to him. He tripped

over the pile of laundry, knocked off a precariously balanced stack of books, and almost discovered the still. Sometimes I exaggerate.) I finished off a biology article and then went out to scrounge up an extra book shelf in the barn. On the way back, I was taken aback by the clear sky and the bright moon, so I went up on the pasture hill to take a scenic view (it overlooks the entire mission to the west, and to the east it views the whole San Luis Rey Valley to the point where passed through the gorge into the ocean.

Now, as I said, I was struck by the moon, which set off a serious of reactions. When I came out of the dorm, I had thought I should make some attempt to recognize God's presence this evening. Given the evening, it was not hard. Here is an honest account of my reaction: first, I stare at the moon; that makes me start remembering Psalm passages; that reminds me of beautiful things; and immediately two things come to mind, God and Gretchen. Whether you believe that or not, you can believe this: I came away with an insight tonight. It has to do with the pessimistic, realistic attitude of my last letter, and this is how it goes:

There are three types of people and three ways of approaching, namely: like the dreamer, like the realist, and like the idealist. The dreamer is one who refuses to face reality; his is the least happy way of live. The realist makes himself face the painful, depressing facts of this life, and will not let himself by shaken by them; his is a happier existence. The idealist is one who faces the realities of this life head on but is not satisfied to be merely un-shockable. He looks for an underlying beauty and meaning coexistent with the hardships of living, and his is the happiest way of life. I do not apologize for trying to race reality in my last letter; I do apologizing for losing sight of the beauty in your life and in my life.

Enough. Tomorrow a lighter train of thought; I promise.

Sunday, Dec. 4, 1966

Fist, please forgive the crappy paper, but besides the fact that it is all that I have, it is the only thing round here thin enough for a 10-page letter.

Gretchen, 2 quadrillion things have happened this weekend; and besides, there are a zillion things I would like to talk to you about. This letter is not going to suffice!

A good place to start is with your picture: Blue Eyes, you look like a million … no, a billion dollars. Golden Mouthed Muses emblazon my speech! Your color is pure delicate radiance; your hair is !long! glistening golden silk of a most vivacious contour; your taste is impeccable; and your appearance is redundantly healthy. In short, you look great!! I like the new glasses, I think the dress is perfectly becoming (the colors of those are the liturgical season of Advent), and I love those golden locks. I could adulate *ad infinitum*, but oh, the wicked bond of time. No kidding, Gretchen. You are beautiful.

After Supper

If you could see me now, you would croak or laugh your head off. They have us all wrapped up in brown robes for the concert; mine is bound 3 sizes too big. Good Lord, I'm glad I met you; I'd hate to be wearing one of these for the rest of my life

There are a few minutes free before the concert, so how about it if I go through your letter point for point.

I'm really glad you had an enjoyable Thanksgiving, and so did I. I was thinking of you every minute. The Corvallis get-together sounds like it must have been a lot of fun. Talk about Nancy skipping classes. Congratulations on the Daily News job; I knew you could do it. I have no news of a Christmas job for myself, but I'm sure I can get one right after *Die Natalis*

Thanks for talking to Mom. Dad came down this weekend to get things straight; I'll tell you more about that later.

Post Performance

Have you ever tried to entertain 1600 people? It is quite a feat, and I think we did fairly well. Fr. Warren's biggest worry was the critics from 3 big San Diego papers, and music director of Mira Costa College, and the Doctor of Music from Palomar College. We weren't worried about our local critic because he has been plugging us all the way. We all enjoyed the workout immensely, and I certainly was a feather in our little cap.

Back to the beautiful letter of yours. And Heaven strike me down if I forget to tell you what a blessed joy and relief it was to hear the things you said in that letter. Gretchen, you're beautiful for a lot more important reasons that your good looks, you know. But I will have more to say about that, too.

Holy God, think of it; two weeks and a half till Christmas. We leave Luis here on the afternoon of December 21ˢᵗ. I'll be coming by Greyhound with the rest of the crew. Gretchen, can I level with you? I am going to leave it up to my parents whether they want to invite you to meet me at the depot. I'm grateful to you for wanting to welcome me home, and I would certainly appreciate it, but I know you can also understand that, not only for my sake but yours, too, The first thing I must do when I get home is make peace with my mother. That may mean meeting the folks along and talking things out. But rest assured; I know I could not put up with being in Longview for more than 18 hours (at maximum) without seeing you.

I was born nuttier than a peanut brittle bar, but that was sour pickles compared to the way I'm going nuts about you! It's super witchcraft; that's what it is.

A most omni-concordant and doxological gratuity for your bell-jingly Christmas felicitations. Merry Christmas to you, too.

Gretchen, tell you what, I have to go to bed now, so I will wrap this short piece up and send it to you, so that you won't be in suspense until Friday. But cross my heart, this will be followed up within three days with more detailed correspondence.

God love you, Gretchen, you're something else, something really special.

de profundis almae,
Love,
Mike, the Clod

[undated]

Read This First

Gretchen,

I just talked to Fr. Ben and got some new insights into the situation.

First of all, I am sending you the rest of this letter just because I don't want to throw it away. But be skeptical of it and critical. Lady, Father and my mother pointed out a couple of things that we should watch out for: for me, over-impetuosity; for you, over-enthusiasm. Girl, we both has good sense; let's use it.

Point one: careful of overestimating me, Gretchen; *e.g.*, you are by I.Q. smarter than I am; all the "wisdom" I propound is very definitely sophomoritis impressing gullible girls; you should certainly be able to tell by now that I am socially not too well adjusted; and to be associated with me in public will not always be exactly an honor. If you can admit these things, we're off to a fair start. I am as honest with you as possible. Do you then be honest to yourself about me.

Point two: What has happened between us is not exactly wonderful, it is very strange. To make it into something wonderful will take a long adjustment to the peculiarities of it.

Point three: Back to talking about "what shall we do." We shall play it cool, that's what. Take it slowly and critically. Yes, I am almost certain you could keep right on with your original plans (college, etc.), and I will make my plans as best I can.

In summary, I'm not exactly sure you know who I am, Gretchen, because no one that does know me can understand how you could think so much of me. No one disapproves, if you know what you're dealing with, but if they thought (or if I thought) I was deceiving you, then there would be great disapproval. Let us make an honest and valiant effort at Christmas to find out, one way or the other.

In conclusion, Ben says, if you and I approach this honestly and prudently, and granted that neither of us decides to break the friendship off (which is a justifiable thing), there is no reason in God's world why it couldn't someday work out. Be honest with yourself, and I in turn will be honest with you.

One thing still holds for the other part of this letter: you are a young woman, Gretchen, and a wonderful person to know and love.

God bless you,
Mike

Jana continued to succinctly record the family events over that holiday season.

Saturday, November 19, 1966:   Bob went to Jim and Kay's to watch Michigan – Notre Dame game in color TV.

Friday, December 2, 1966:   Bob said Jim K. flew down to California to try to convince Mike to go in military. [Bob did not actually come to SLR; she probably meant that Bob took Dad to the airport.]

I am not going to continue to burden the reader with my juvenile letter writing, but I will include the comments that I made about my Dad's visit to San Luis "to convince me to go in the army"... yeah, like that was <u>ever</u> going to happen given the way I felt about Vietnam. This is excerpted from a letter I wrote to Gretchen on December 5th 1966:

Now, about my Dad's visit. He came Friday afternoon; we talked 'til six. Saturday we bowled two lines, watched a ball game and talked. Sunday I showed him the plant here; we talked; he watched us fumble around a stage rehersal. He told me how things really were with Mom; I told him how things were with me. He talked to Fr. Ben for a good long session. We called Mom, she sounded good. Dad and I think we have this thing settled, but then we are the overly optimistic type at times. I, for one, think it will work out rather well.

Of course, Jana summed the plan up all very briefly:

Monday, December 5, 1966: Jim K. told Bob he talked to Mike at seminary (flew down). He plans to go to LCC.

There were a few more letters before leaving San Luis for the last time, but they were neither deep nor entertaining. The pressure of exams and extracurricular activities, as well as packing to leave permanently, consumed most of my time. There were probably some misgivings; it had been a totally different year, very alive, very thought provoking. I wondered how my classmate would fair in the coming winter semester. Would they make it, or would they lose their faith or their vocation. At one point Father Ben commented that Herb Karnofski might be the only north westerner that would survive to graduation. We all felt that way about Herb, but even he was having trouble hanging on to the tenants of the faith; as he said, they were knocking the pillars right out from under us.

I have often said, when asked about my faith, that I learned too much in the seminary. Of course, that is not entirely true. A few courses in rationalist philosophy at the University of Washington probably helped to nail the lid on the coffin; but a lot of issues did come up in the studies at SLR that would make any rational man wonder. It turns out that of those fellow SFS classmates that I have been able to contact, a bit less than half are still practicing Catholics. Not that they are all agnostic like myself; some have retained a deep spirituality: but the tenants of a ~2000 year old institution no longer hold the unquestionable authority that held sway for a good part of those ~2000 year.

I don't remember any of the details of my departure from SLR. I must not have loaded my bass onto the bus, even though, by then, we had determined that it would fit in the cargo hold under the passenger compartment. (Gretchen's collection of letters indicates that the bass did not follow me until sometime in mid-January.) I don't think I was traveling with any fellow seminarian, but I won't swear to that. My impression is that it was a very solitary, uneventful trip, and according to Jana's journal, it was really a one day trip, since we departed on the 21ˢᵗ of December:

> Thursday, December 22, 1966: Bill K. came by. Mike called
> from bus station. Bobby called
> re leaving Friday.

I have nothing to which I can refer to describe the arrival, and my memory is rather foggy about whether my folks did or did not let Gretchen attend. I don't know, but Jana's notes would suggest not. I suppose my Dad and Mother took me to the Toutle. It was good to see them, but I was, of course, dying to see Gretchen. I did go to visit the Huffhines the next day:

> Friday, December 23, 1966: Mike came over at noon. Had lunch
> with us. He and G went to town,
> then he shopped alone. We got
> call from Bobby in Portland. Left
> dinner for G and Mike and went
> after Bobby.

So, at last, alone with Gretchen, and finally officially able to enjoy all the intimate pleasures of courtship… this was 1966, and I was an ex-seminarian… don't let your mind run away with you, modern style. Let's just say we spent a lot of that evening on the living room couch. Gretchen had on a very soft and fuzzy sweater; which, believe it or not, stayed on the whole evening. But there was some surface exploration of an otherwise untouchable region of her lithe little torso. And, putting it as succinctly as her mother might have, if she had known, neither party was dissatisfied with the kissing!

Gretchen and Mike the New Years after he left the seminary for good. (Photo reproduced courtesy of Gretchen H. Klungness.)

I don't remember meeting Bob Jr. that night, so I suppose that Gretchen and I went out to town (perhaps a movie) before the Huffhines returned from Portland. I also had my folk's only means of transportation, the VW. After the movie, Gretchen and I got into an involved conversation about whether I would go to University of Washington. We had started to discuss this in our final letters, and I was already feeling the pressure:

> This was in a letter to Gretchen of Dec. 5 1966
> I'll bring my boxing gloves but can't we just discuss this Seattle kick peaceably? I was somewhat serious when I said that I would probably not be able to make it up [to UW] very often. You seem to have taken it well, but it is something for the Christmas Discussion Journal (C.D.J. for short) too.

> This was in a letter to Gretchen of Dec. 13 1966
> Yeah, Yeah; If I agree to two trips by the time vacation is over you'll have me committed to every weekend! What are you trying to do, probe me for soft spots? Alright already, I confess, I'll probably break down. Satisfied? Maybe I can get a weekend job, that'll save me. God save me, I am succumbing to the wiles of womanhood… and my own weakness.

So with that discussion already in progress, we got deeply involved in a plaintive pleading of her case wherein all the hugging and kissing and carrying on devolved into a sea of tears. It was 2 AM before we had the good sense to retire from the Triangle shopping center parking lot and head for home.

Of course, I did not arrive on the Toutle until 3 to 4 AM, and my mother was livid. As I mentioned before… well, I'll let Jana tell the story, rationally:

> Saturday, December 24, 1966: Mike got room at Broadway. G worked until about 1 or 2. Mike sent her dozen roses, came over later. He and Mom had hamburgers with us, and we all went to candlelight service and to Spencers for drinks, then G and M went to midnight mass.

It is hard to believe that my mother, who had been so anxious for me to come home, kicked me out of the house on Christmas Eve. I did not have transportation (my panel van had been in a big freeze and the block had ruptured, we sold it for $65). I did not have much money (the Broadway Hotel was only $25 per month, but that seemed like a lot). It was a cold rainy winter and I had to find a job before the Winter Quarter started at Lower Columbia College. I think I also said before that it was a rude awakening, but one that needed to occur; "you're not in sunny southern Cal. any more, Mike!"

I spent most of the Christmas vacation with the Huffhines. Christmas Eve was an enjoyable affair with the Huffhines and their relatives in Longview. I particularly enjoyed Gretchen's grandmother. I may be struck dead for using the term, but she was "plucky":

> Sunday, December 25, 1966: G picked Mike up at hotel and brought him over for breakfast. We all opened our gifts after. Spencers and Mom came for dinner at 4. Very nice day. G took Mike back after.

I don't know why Jana's refers to my bringing a suitcase to their house on the 26th.

Monday, December 26, 1966:   G worked until 1pm. Mike came
by and left suitcase – came back
around 3, folks picked him up
after dinner, and then later he
took G to show.

According to Jana's journal, it appears that my mother had softened a bit
by the second day after Christmas; perhaps she had realized that she had really
cut her nose off to spite her face as we say colloquially. I guess I left my Dad at
work, took Mom home to the Toutle, and then delivered the VW back to him.

Tuesday, December 27, 1966:   G had lunch with Jim, Kay and
Mike at Longview Restaurant
and then went to Toutle with
Mike and Kay. Came home at
10:30.

The Huffhines were most hospitable to me. Gretchen and I are asking
ourselves if we really went to the library the night of the 28th, or was that
the excuse we gave Jana to be alone.

Wednesday, December 28, 1966:   Mike came over about 4 –
ate with us. They [M and G]
went to library.

We were still on the romantic comedy kick, so, in spite of the tight
finances, we managed to take in a movie in Portland; we probably drove
Gretchen's 1955 Chevy station wagon (we called it the brown bomb, because
her dad had repainted it a *crème de café*).

Friday, December 30, 1966:   Mike and G went to Portland to see
"Gigi" at Off-B'dway.

I always will wonder what Jana meant in this next entry. What do you
suppose she thought the "etc." was?

367

Saturday, December 31, 1966:   G and Mike ate at Peterson's in Kelso, then road around, etc. G went to Klungnesses with Mike – spent the night there.

Gretchen and I just opened letters from this time period that Jana had written to Gretchen at UW. These were far more disclosive and gave a more reasoned perspective to what had occurred over this turbulent month.

I took Gretchen back to Univ. of Washington on January 1st. I did not have time to stop and meet all of Gretchen's friends although she did show me around the dorm and introduced me to whomever we met. I needed to get the VW back to my folks so Dad could get to work. I too was starting classes at LCC on the second of January, so there was not much time to think… although I did manage to write Gretchen…. a little every day. Of course, that is the only way I know what happened because I surely don't remember any of it.

I was well into my classes when I got my job at Pietro's Pizza Parlor on the 12th of January. The job paid $1.40 per hour and 1 pizza (made by the employee) on every shift. I think the pizza was more of a life saver than the wage. Jack Troup, the owner/manager was no Scrooge; he figured if you put in an honest "day's" work, you could have the small pizza any way you liked it. For one thing, the 'small' was what most pizzerias would call a 'medium' nowdays; and you could pile it high with condiments… well, maybe not to the ceiling. I liked the Canadian bacon, add hamburger or sausage, peppers tomatoes, pineapple, olives, onions and, of course, plenty of mozzarella. My breakfast was usually the Longview Restaurant's Lumberjack for $1.50, and my main meal was the pizza; that was all I needed for the day. Of course, I weighed about 145 or 150 lbs. then, all 6 ft. 2 in. of me.

I did not stay in the Broadway Hotel for long, basically because it was a real dive. But I managed to write some colorful description of it (most of which I had forgotten).

The place is kept warm, the food is good, and the showers are cold…

Now, about the people here. Both the women who cook are canonized saints; no kidding, they are very kind.

About half the residents are ancient. One, Old Dan, is totally blind and half deaf. Two are off their rocker. The little old lady, Mary, is funny; they give her a bad time about always being first in chow line. Of the younger men, 2 look rough. The rest are good natured working men of one sort or another. The youngest, relative to my age, are both crippled; I should find out their names. My big buddy is Uncle Bud, a vociferous old cuss who introduced me around, (told me the real charge for room and board), and got my first meal for me. He has many yarns to spin! Down the hall sits a soothsayer who is trying to convert me to re-incarnational intervention-ary (by miracle, medium, and witch) Deism. It's all very interesting!!!

By January 16th I had found another hotel that I mentioned early in this book. It was a boarding house really, but it was clean and more central to the locations I would have to frequent. Those were the college and the Pietro's Pizza Parlor. I described the Hudson Hotel this way:

> The Hudson is neat, clean, comfortable, there is a throw-rug on the floor, it costs exactly the same, except you don't have to pay for meals you don't eat, and the guys (no dames) here are much better heads (not as interesting, however). I'll have to go back to the Baltimore to visit now and then; it is a once in a lifetime experience.

Of course I did not go back; put the whole experience completely out of my mind until I read these old letters. When I was feeling particularly sorry for myself, I tried to relate to Gretchen little experiences that put it all in perspective:

> I thought I had it bad walking home in the rain today, until I met a little corker doing the same. Seems he is playing 7th grade basketball in Cascade [school], but his dad can't drive him to practice. He was

hoping his dad wouldn't make him quit because he has such a long walk to the gym. Spunky little character; cute too.

Another incident, which I will not quote, was the visit I paid to Kris Olson's wife and her roommate. They had invited me for dinner, while she was in the late stages of pregnancy, but Kris was serving on the garbage trucks in Dan Nang. I had only met her once or twice before he shipped out, but I guess she thought it would bring him a little closer to have an old friend of his at the dinner table. It made me realize that my plight was nothing compared with all the soldiers in Vietnam and their longsuffering wives at home.

While the war raged on in Vietnam, things were not going badly for me, or for Gretchen. I was doing pretty well in my classes at LCC, and keeping my head above water with work and finances. I was reconnecting with old friends, to the extent that I would be willing to socialize (not much). John Polis and I had a zoology class together, and other classmates from St Rose would stop and talk to me in "my" library cubicle, where I did most of my studying. Pat Rogers invited me over for dinner in January, and I had a good time with his family watching that now rarely seen TV. Pat invited me to his going away party, but I had to work. He was leaving to join VISTA. I don't think I ever knew where he was sent. Meanwhile Gretchen was doing well in her studies (not as well as she would have liked), but there were so many distractions in Haggett Hall; constant dramatics would be a good description.

Even my mother had mellowed about the whole thing. I kept telling Gretchen that there were no hard feelings, and that my folks still thought the world of her. I don't know if she was ever convinced. I knew my mother mellowed because she offered to put aside $50 per month to help out with school, and she even offered to do my laundry. That laundry offer was brought on by an incident at Pietro's. I had finally worked my way up from dish shift, through the back room jobs, and now I was put on the pizza maker crew. This was done in a display window so people could watch how pizzas are made. But when Jack caught a glimpse of the condition of my uniform, he sent me straight back to dish shift. It was not possible to wear the same uniform three days in a row without washing it; spaghetti sauce on white is just too obvious. Of course, it probably didn't help that I was probably the fastest dishwasher Jack had ever seen; all those years of punishments from Fr. Claude had prepared me... to be a permanent dish washer. Never mind, my days at Pietro's would be short lived, as Mr. Wickett was already plotting to find me a spot back at Weyerhaeuser. Don't ever let anyone tell you it is not good to have contacts in high places. One thing about Jack Troup, he never forgot his people. Every time I would come back to Peitro's to visit, he would serve up a complementary small pizza. To this day, I have not had pizza that was better than Jack's. He and his partner sold out to Campbell Soup Company, but the chain that ensued does not hold a candle to the original product.

Where I was going with that before I got side tracked, is that I was finding that I did not need my mother to do my laundry, and I don't remember ever asking her for the money. I was learning to take care of myself; I always wonder if my mother was a little nostalgic about that, because I really did not come back to the Toutle to stay with them for any extended time again. I visited, but not for long. The most time she had with me after that winter was when I got back from Kenya; I stayed at the Parish in Galt for a few weeks while I waited for my draft induction physical. When I was declared 4F[141], I eventually end up going to work for a beekeeper in Willows, California.

Gretchen made a few trips back to Longview that winter quarter, but I can find no evidence that I went to the UW. Although there were many people there that she wanted me to meet, I was just trying to learn to form my own social milieu. It was a skill I had not learned in the seminary, because the milieu came readymade. Besides, I thought it better for Gretchen to come home and spend time with her family, and mine, rather that put up with the constant mania of the dormitory. One of the elements of my milieu was the Hollow Lemon, a kind of hip joint thrown together out of an old soda fountain, and serving beverages and music. I think I may have played bass there, but I don't think we got anything very coherent going with the music. George Matter was a frequenter, and a girl from St. Rose named Barbara Demaree would frequently do things with us.

On one outing we went to Lewis and Clark College to hear Fr. Pat O'Connell who was a guest lecturer. He was always Dr. Pat O'Connell too, but now he had left the priesthood. This is what I wrote:

> We left the Student Center about 2:15 PM with dire predictions from Linda Torpa of an accident along the way. So I took it easy and we made it by 3:30 PM. We wandered around for a while; they have a beautiful campus, though they were constructing a magnificent library in the center.
>
> Oh yes, there were four of us, George, Linda, Barbara and *yo*; Sue Martin could not come. Barbara never saw any campus but L.C.C., and she was much impressed.
>
> At 4:00 PM we attended an hour lecture in the science hall at which Fr. Pat was guest lecturer. He didn't notice us in the front row until he got up to speak. He looked at me kind of absent mindedly and started to read his speech. Then it dawned on him! "Klugy, what are you doing here?" he said out loud as one of the profs was talking to him.
>
> It was a good but lofty lecture on Teilhard de Chardin; we were impressed but stupefied. The discussion question period afterward was wild. A number of the most vociferous and individualistic profs I have ever seen had a knock down drag out debate right there; hilarious. Some very vociferous students contributed their two cents too. We all enjoyed that tremendously.
>
> I said I wouldn't spend any money and I didn't except for gas. We packed a lunch of which we ate very little. This was because, after the lecture, we stayed to say hello to Fr. Pat. He was talking to a fella so the girl who arranged his engagement (and his room in the girls dorm!) came over and talked to us for a while. Cindy is from Southern Cal., Pasadena to be exact, and had been acquainted with

Fr. Pat. We ate dinner (lunch rather) at the student center with them, it was kind of goofy! But enjoyable.

After dinner we wandered around for a couple of hours until the ecumenical discussion session at 7:30 PM. I, for one, found it extremely interesting. Linda really added her two cents worth being a recently converted Nazarene. George kept bombing out questions, and even Barbara (who was in something entirely new) added a few apropos comments. Pat was great, just great. Cindy was eloquent. One exchange student had all the bearing and insight of a German Theologian. And ours was a relatively slow discussion.

We only got lost once, on the trip home, and we made it by 11:30. Oh there were a lot of mix ups, blunders, and faux pas on my part for the evening. And I think we were all rather uncomfortable at times (like at the student center. Because L.C. is socially elete, and we were not dressed or anything [lest that be misinterpreted, we were not dressed in our Sunday best]). But overall, I think it was a profitable evening, and in many ways enjoyable.

Come to think of it, that was my very last contact with any of the professors from San Luis Rey. I guess I saw Fr. Geoffery briefly at The Franciscan School of Theology when I went to play a gig with Fr. Christian in the 1980's. Otherwise, there was no contact with the faculty ever again. I talked to Fr. Alberic today (SFS science teacher); I had sent a message to him via a website of St. Anthony's Seminary, but I had no idea where he was. He replied by email and gave me a number to call. Within a half hour after he sent the email, we were on the phone discussing old times. Turns out, he had been assigned to San Luis Rey to teach science when Fr. O'Connell left the order. Fr. Alberic was also there at the time that San Luis Rey College closed. I will ask him what happened[142], if he is at liberty to tell. It is like part of one's history is erased if one's high school and college disappeared off the face of the earth. Ironically Gretchen and I met Fr. Geoffery's nephew when we were working as officers of the Democratic Party in Hilo HI. There is also, in Hilo, a fellow Democrat who attended Saint Anthony's minor seminary in Santa Barbara, and Fr. Mario was his dean of discipline. He confirmed for me the scandal that I will discuss later in the memoir. Were these two more instances of pure happenstance?

The upcoming chapters of my life would never be the same again, and only now I look back at this period of transition with fond memories and apprehensions. In the words of Charles Dickens[143],

> It was the best of times, it was the worst of times; it was the age of wisdom, it was the age of foolishness; it was the epoch of belief, it was the epoch of incredulity; it was the season of Light, it was the season of Darkness; it was the spring of hope, it was the winter of despair; we had everything before us, we had nothing before us.

CHAPTER 17

The Halls of Ivy

Now, regarding your question about food that has been offered to idols. Yes, we know that "we all have knowledge" about this issue. But while knowledge makes us feel important, it is love that strengthens the church. Anyone who claims to know all the answers doesn't really know very much. But the person who loves God is the one whom God recognizes.
New Living Translation (©2007) 1ˢᵗ Corinthians 8:1 & 2

THE PRESSURE FOR ME TO attend the hallowed halls of ivy remained high, even though I was having a good educational experience at Lower Columbia College. I was also learning a lot about getting along in the work-a-day world. I say in my letters to Gretchen that I really had to step up my game to work at Pietro's. Working in the Weyerhaeuser mill under union rules had made me soft. The pizza parlor was go, go, go, from the time you stepped in the door, until the time you left at night. Even Jack and the assistant managers were in high gear all the time. I remember Jack would have to take time to lock himself in "The Spice Room", where he kept his recipes. This was so he could mix up a batch of spices for the sauce or for the meat. I remember that when we would run out of pork sausage, Jack would go in the mixing room and concoct a blend of herbs that would turn ordinary hamburger into sausage.

Jack's business partner was not in Longview often, but when he arrived, he would do silly things like sweep up the cheese and meat that had fallen on the floor. Then he would go around offering to make our break-pizzas out of the scraps that had fallen on the floor. I guess he thought that would enhance the efficiency of the operation. Seems to me that Jack was the one who was enhancing efficiency, and keeping the secrets so well guarded that they were able to sell to Campbell's Inc. at the appropriate time. Now Pietro's is a chain up and down the west coast.

One particularly busy night the pizza trays were stacking up in the sink room at an incredible rate. I was, of course, called back to take up the slack on the dishwashing; which I did. However, when a call came in from the front register for more trays, I took it upon myself to deliver the goods. I had a stack of trays so high that I could not see over them; and I have long arms. They were heavy and hard to balance, but I managed to get them all the way to the cashier's counter. Whereupon, I lost control of the stack, the whole stack came crashing down with a cacophonous clatter. The poor cashier in front of me nearly died of a heart attack. I guess that blooper ranks right up there with the time that I had finally made it to the ovens (one of the critical and prestigious jobs). I seemed to be doing rather well, I thought, and was feeling a bit cocky that I had finally "made it". Pride cometh before the fall, or in this case, precipitateth the fall.... of the pizza that I was pulling out of the top oven, onto the bowler derby of the assistant manager, who was looking in the bottom oven. Need I say to whence I was banished? Ah! The things we remember.

The notable news of the letter of Feb. 15, 1966, was that my mother had recovered from her health problem and had decided to go back to work as a medical transcriptionist at St. John's Hospital. For my part, I had gotten a 3.33 grade average on midterms.

Unfortunately that descended to a 2.3 by the end of the quarter. Gretchen also got a 2.5 that quarter. It may be that the histrionics of the Klungness family were weighing heavily on our relationship. Alternatively I just might have been being bull-headed. Gretchen was having her problems with the dormitory life, and ever so much wanted me to move to Univ. of

Washington. On the other hand, in mid-quarter I applied to Washington State University, which had a far better agriculture program, which is what I wanted to pursue.

Add to that confusion, the fact that my parents were having their troubles at that time. My mother had been visited by Fr. Carl Willman the last summer that we lived in Longview, and she was looking to him for counseling. Things were not going well with my parents; they had both been excommunicated from the Catholic Church[144] and wanted to get back into its graces. The local parish priest in Castle Rock, Fr. Doyle, was advocating that they live as "brother and sister"; which was not a problem for my mother because she had already lost her attraction to my Dad. My Dad went along because he wanted to get right with the Church. Somehow, in her confused mind, she thought that if they moved to Davis, it would solve the problem. The logic was confusing; she thought she would be close enough to Fr. Carl to seek his advice (little did I know that advice was probably not all she was seeking). How does Davis come into the picture? Well, we knew that Davis had an excellent agriculture program, and she was thinking that if they moved there, I could go to Davis, and would become a resident and not have to pay out of state tuition.

So here is the dilemma I faced. I wanted to go to Washington State, Gretchen wanted me to attend U. W. and my mother was pushing for UC Davis. You can imagine how the infighting behind my back was going. Here is a classic remark from my letter to Gretchen right after April Fools' Day (appropriate, don't you think?)

> April 3, 1967
> ...Mrs. LeTourneau and my mother both say that women are born to badger and nag men into doing what they demand. I have one question to answer my own opinion of you in that regard: which would make you happier to know 1) that I came up [to visit] because I knew you wanted me to; 2) that I came up as much to see Philip as because I needed to see you and talk with you? Another question, why do <u>you</u> think I came up?

There are many other reasons why I can't go to the University [of Washington]. The first is, that is exactly what I yearn to do. If you know that "I don't think it is al all necessary to be always together" then you don't know at all.

...No I will not come to the University [of Washington]. Name me someone who thinks I should. Is it an indication that I don't care enough? God knows, it is hard enough to say no as it is. I have come this far and I will come no farther. I have preparations to make for the years ahead. God knows I must settle down to them.

Feeling particularly pressed, I presented Gretchen with a small ultimatum:

April 7, 1967

... I have come out of the seminary into a new life lived (God willing) for you and your children. Eventually I will have to demand some sign of your willingness to follow me away from family perhaps, away from home and family that has been your security up 'till now. This is the way of marriage.

I will go no further in marrying myself to your wishes (but that is not true for we still have much to give into each other before we will be living totally for each other).

This dispute raged on for months, mostly between my mother and me, and in letters between Gretchen and me. I don't want to make it sound like we spent all of our time fighting about it, but it was always in the background frustrating Gretchen, and bugging me. Our letters were full of platitudes and plaintive longings, even though Gretchen came to Longview on a number of weekends, and I was able to get to Seattle once in a while, because friends, like George Matter, would provide transportation.

My parents had taken a trip to California to visit family in McCloud. Then they visited the Tillotsons in Vallejo (where Virgil had taken a job managing an apartment complex). Subsequently they went on to visit Fr. Carl in Galt. Dad looked into transferring to Davis, but could not get a commitment from the Post Office. I guess they had some good times on the trip, but they were not happy with each other when they got back to Washington. As far as I was concerned, at least it took the pressure off about moving to Davis. Therefore I could concentrate on applying for schools in Washington State; of course, that included applying to the Univ. of Washington as well.

I tried to calm the discussion with these remarks:

> April [18] Sunday 1 AM.
> Dear Gretchen,
>
> Having acquired some degree of perspective again, I have some words of mature insight to elocute forthwith. In the trend of youthful behavior, I think we have all succumbed to the youthful pastime of self-created crisis to self-invented upset, because we are infatuated with the glimmer of bittersweet enjoyment that accompanies such a problematic existence. Maybe I think just for myself, but wouldn't you agree that half of our so called problems are imaginary? We are just having an excruciatingly good time exploring the trouble world. Kind of stupid, Huh?

What I did not understand until I re-read the whole collection of letters was this. The problem was that I was being pulled this way and that by people I love. I think Gretchen's parents thought I should just go be with Gretchen, although they were reluctant to intervene. In fact, I comment in the letters that I felt like Bob and Jana were both holding back. Theirs was probably the wiser tactic. Finally, I did what so often was the determining factor in my life, I left it to the circumstances that would transpire; at that time I would have called it "God's will". I told Gretchen that we would just have to wait and see what would come of it all.

The relationship between my mother and Gretchen went back and forth. I think it helped when I stopped trying to mediate between them. Gretchen backed off from communication with my mother, and she eventually got the point, and made overtures of mutual respect toward Gretchen. My mother really never had a problem with Gretchen; she loved Gretchen. Her problems were with me. She thought she was still responsible for my decisions, and needed to "guide" my life. I was, of course, perpetually resistant. After my folks returned from their trip to California, I wrote this:

> March 29, 1967 5 PM
>
> Peace again exists between you and I and my folks (my mother, I mean, Dad has always been on our side). Gretchen, There is much more that I must explain to you about my parents, though this is not the means of doing so. I thought I had no right to reveal the confidence of my parents. But I know now that between you and I there exist such a confidence already, that not to confide about the people we know would be like putting a barrier between one of us and the person whom we both know, but who is understood by only one of us.

In the same letter I reported that I had submitted my application to WSU, that my Dad had not been able to get a transfer to Davis, that I had gotten a 3.0 GPA for the quarter, and George Matter and I were planning a trip to Seattle. Ironically, the trip was on the weekend of April Fools' Day. We definitely succumbed to the occasion. It was awkward the first day, because Gretchen was bummed about her roommate, and I was having trouble negotiating with George. He was trying to get together with a woman friend whom I think had helped him during his stay in the hospital in Seattle. But George didn't want to leave Gretchen and me without transportation. He did contact the friend, and we did end up staying together the whole weekend. I was embarrassed how brazen Gretchen and I were. Sunday was a beautiful spring day, and the four of us went to the Arboretum to take in the sun. Gretchen and I devolved into a supine orgy of… you certainly could not call it petting; although we did keep our clothes on… barely. George and his friend sat beside us and talked.

What bothers me is that we were so wrapped up in our turbulent little world while the people around us were going through much more important issues than ours. It reminds me of the line from "Casablanca"[145]:

I'm no good at being noble, but it doesn't take much to see that the
problems of three little people don't amount to a hill of beans in
this crazy world.

I chided Gretchen in one letter, saying that we had not made efforts
to contact friends. Mike Ray, my former neighbor, was having trouble at
school, and not long after was drafted... and killed in Vietnam. Larry
Landry, fellow Troubadour at SFS, was working in a computer lab in
Saigon, presumably in the military, and honestly we have never been able
to find out anything about him since (Fr. Christian and I have tried). I
don't think he was killed, because I checked the Vietnam veteran records.
My cousin Ralph was having difficulty with his tour in Vietnam; he came
back to the states, but then went AWOL. I apparently spent quite a bit
of time with Kris's wife and her two daughters, but thankfully Kris did
come back alive, though emotionally scarred (now called post traumatic
stress disorder). George Matter himself was having a far more difficult life
than us. He had been involved in a motorcycle accident in which his leg
was burned on the exhaust pipe. It would seem to be a minor injury, but
he developed a gangrene infection in the hospital which soon got out of
control. The result was that he not only had to undergo one amputation,
but several. After almost a year in the St. John's Hospital in Longview and
the University of Washington Hospital, he had only the stump of his left
thigh. They were able to fit him with a prosthetic, but for an active guy like
George, that was a cumbersome and sometimes painful appendage. It didn't
slow him down too much though, and he was preparing to go to UW's pre-
med program at the same time I was applying for colleges. I mentioned in
a letter to Gretchen that, at one point, it looked like his $6,000 accident
settlement was not going to come through; which he needed for the tuition.
I think something finally worked out, because he did start at UW the next
fall. George graduated from UW, I believe. Like so many who have tried
to get into medical school without the important influence that come from
having a relative who is a doctor, he did not make it into medical school.

381

He became a teacher, and I heard was a whiz at wheel chair basketball. I have heard rumors of a drug problem in later years, but considering what he went through, I would not hold it against him. My point in writing this is to remind that we all can become very myopic about our little problems.

There are a number of people that I met and hung out with at Lower Columbia College and the Hollow Lemon. I am not going to name them, because, quite frankly, I had forgotten all about them. It made me question my own myopia. In February I was lamenting to Gretchen that I could not make friends (except George and John Polis). But the Hollow Lemon changed all that. There was a Japanese student, who didn't speak very good English, but we used to have long conversations to the wee hours. There were several Saudia Arabian exchange students that were always trying to get me to arrange blind dates with Gretchen's dorm mates. There was the all night talk/walk with Linda Torpa (mentioned previously at the Lewis and Clark lecture); we had to go in a Laundromat to get warm. And there was Sue Martin. She was a friend of George who had been very involved in getting the Hollow Lemon off the ground. She is the only one that I can almost envisage. She was a cute, tomboyish girl, with plenty of personality. I mentioned in the letters that she bought a motorcycle and was finally able to get up and running on it. But the fact that I can barely remember any of this and certainly would not recognize any of them in a yearbook, makes me wonder why the whole LCC experience receded into the depths of my memory.

The teachers at LCC I remember; at least the biology teachers, particularly Mr. Sneed (zoology) and Dr. Helms (bacteriology). Sneed was a funny duffer, who was always wearing a bow tie and losing his place in lecture and lab. Dr. Helms was a meticulous man in his appearance and in his teaching style. I don't remember my math teacher, and I only have a passing memory of my qualitative chemistry professor. Apparently, the impression the teachers made on me was reflected in the grades. I never had a good math teacher, but came closest too it at LCC. Unfortunately he did not save me in algebra. Nevertheless, it was specifically the improvement in my science grades at LCC that made it possible for me to get accepted at University of Washington. I don't remember if I ever even got a reply from Washington State, but UW responded very quickly, and by May 15th I was accepted.

May 15th was also the letter that reported to Gretchen that I had been hired at my Lim Kiln Helper job back at the Weyerhaeuser pulp mill. I had left Pietro's in the winter and started working at the Weyerhaeuser plywood plant. Now that was undoubtedly the very worst job I ever had in my life. It changed the course of my life. I spoke of this in the first chapter, but I did not describe what a dehumanizing job being a "dryer feeder" is. Just the name tells it all. You stand and feed veneer into a dryer for 8 hours. You can pee at breaks and lunch. If you need to be relieved, you have to flag down the foreman and have him stand in for you at the machine. Really, you are just a piece of the machinery. And, it didn't pay as well as Lime Kiln helper. I was feeling so cocky about my admission to UW and new job, that I started hinting, in my May 15th letter to Gretchen, what else I had done. I managed to keep it a secret until her next visit to Longview, but I wanted her to anticipate the surprise, so I mentioned it in several subsequent letters, without revealing what was the surprise. I had bought an aqua marine 1960 Chevrolet Corvair.[146] (It looked about like this one. If I had it today I would be a wealthy man.).

<32> **1960 Corvair.** (Photo reproduced courtesy of oldcarandtruckpictures.com http://oldcarandtruckpictures.com/Corvair/)

Now I had a job, wheels, admission to a major University, and a devoted girlfriend. What more could a young buck want? Driving into Seattle for the first time on Tuesday Sept 5th in my Corvair was like stepping into a new universe. There is a place on the freeway where you get a panoramic view of the south side of the City of Seattle with Mt. Rainier towering over it. Euphoria was propelling me. This was the day I went to find a place to live, which I did.

The summer had started off with the wedding of some fellow students from LCC, Dale and Cathy Witham; I was an usher for the wedding. We had shared some good laughs in bacteriology 101with Dr. Helms. Dale did rather well in spite of the fact that he was only attending the class to be with Cathy. Bacteriology wasn't his major; it was hers. The wedding was part of a pattern of domestic activities that continued throughout the summer. There were at least 5 wedding over the latter half of the year. I did not attend all the weddings with Gretchen, but she did attend Mass with me on every occasion (duly noted by Jana). The most of the summer free time was filled with mowing lawn for Bob Huffhines, occasionally cleaning house for my Dad, eating at the home of both parents. We were taking advantage of the good weather, by going swimming on the Toutle, or Ariel Lake. Sometimes we would picnic with the Huffhines. And, of course, all this was fitted in around our work schedules. Gretchen had a day job at the Longview Daily News and I was on shift work at Weyerhaeuser.

The first life changing event was the visit of Fr. Carl to the Toutle on July 20th.

This was a far more sinister event than I was even aware. He came and went fairly quickly, but he and my mother had made devious plans. We went on with our lives not suspecting any problem. I was a little surprised at the sexy swim suits my mother had purchased and the amount of time she spent basking in the sun. I chalked it up to her feeling better, because she had had a number of serious health bouts in the winter.

Meanwhile, Gretchen and I went about our new lives together as if we were an old married couple. We were having a good time. Gretchen invited me to go waterskiing on the Cowlitz River with Dave Spencer's family on Aug 9th. Dave was Gretchen's cousin, but he had been abandoned by his mother, Billie Frank Conrad. That led to his being raised by Gretchen's grandparents and her children. It was nice to be included in Dave's family gathering, since he was now a successful lawyer and could afford a boat!.

On August twenty-seventh 1967, Gretchen, I, and my folks went to a farewell dinner for Fr. Christian at St. Francis seminary. He had been transferred to Serra High School as Principal.[147] To tell the truth, I don't remember it, but Jana's journal never lies! We were also doing things with the seminarians when possible. We met up with Larry Warnberg when he came out of SLR. We spent time with Herb, such as ice skating at the Lloyds Center (Portland), and swimming in the Toutle.

Gretchen and I attended Lyle Shabram's wedding in Centralia September third. How that lad hooked up with a girl from Centralia, I am not exactly sure. It was a Catholic wedding through and through, and it was nice to see the family who had long since moved to Carmel, California.

I took my mother to the airport to fly to the East Coast to meet Fr. Carl on Wed. Sept 6th. How she pulled that off without anyone suspecting that she had something going with Fr. Carl, I don't know. Maybe I was just naive, or didn't want to believe the worst. I think my Dad already knew.

I took Gretchen to have her wisdom teeth pulled Friday Sept. 8. Bob and Jana had left on vacation, so I had to take care of the poor girl for the duration. It was not hard. She recovered quickly, and was back to work before the week was out. It was interesting, "playing house", but we were firmly committed to keeping it from devolving into "family life". In fact, Gretchen's description is colorful:

> "My recollection is that Mike drove me to Portland in the Corvair, and waited for me to have two wisdom teeth removed. Then he drove me home; picked up the pain medication; brought me home; made sure I took my pain medication and tucked me into bed in my room upstairs. My mother called to see how I was doing, and I told her on the upstair phone that I was ok, but in pain, and that Mike was downstairs "'puddling'around in the kitchen."

Needless to say the drugs had kicked in.

After my Mom got back from the east coast, she had some additional medical problems, so she went for medical tests on Sept 20th This was just a day before Huffhines took Gretchen back to UW for school. I drove up later so I could get some additional work days in before returning to school. The letters to Gretchen had, of course, ended at the beginning of the summer, from here on out we will be relying on old gray matter for the details. Not even Jana's journal will help much, since she only mentions events involving Gretchen. That did include a telephone conversation early in the fall quarter, in which Jana matter-of-factly states that Gretchen wants to [quit school and] work full time. A few days later, she records just as unemotionally that Gretchen had decided to stay in school. I'm sure she and Bob were relieved.

The place I had found to live in Seattle was a room and board situation in the home of a widowed English war bride, Mrs. French. I don't know if we ever knew her first name. She was hard of hearing so we always had to almost shout **"Mrs. French"** to get her attention. She was a Methodist, and had family in the city, but to be able to keep the house she took in three boarders. Chuck was an older man, a law student, who had come early and gotten the private room on the ground floor. Just as well, because I could not have afforded a private room. The loft that I shared with an engineering student from Medicine Hat, Canada, was roomy and sunny, due to strategically placed windows. Dave Humphreys turned out to be a good roommate. He was a studious fellow; to the point that Gretchen and I would try to get him out to socialize, sometimes successfully. I recently found Dave after low these many years (43 to be exact); he is happily married for 40 of those years, and has a son and a daughter. He graduated as a ceramic engineer and has never wanted for work since the company that paid for his tuition hired him right out of college. Nor is he anxious to retire. I have to be careful about telling stories on Dave; his wife, Marilyn, might not understand. One of those occasions on which we tried to "socialize" Dave, was with Gretchen's new roommate. Actually it was the occasion of my 21st birthday. We had gone to a nightclub in West Seattle that had go-go dancers. After we got back to Haggett Hall, Gretchen and I started our usual routine of heavy petting in the car. Not aware that Dave and the roommate, having had a bit to drink, were doing the same in the back seat. I forget exactly what broke it up, but I know Gretchen and I were laughing hysterically. Gretchen has letters that indicate that Dave and her roommate dated a few times, but obviously it did not work out. Dave was already committed to the girl from Medicine Hat. For all I know, it might have been Dave's only moment of carnal weakness.

At this point I need to step out of the narrative and recall again that I was the first member of my immediate family to advance to 3rd year college. None of my cousins, aunts, uncles, or grandparents had attended college, and my mother had withdrawn in her first year. She took college courses at LCC (including from Dr. Helms) but she did not complete her certification in medical transcription. She took shorthand, without a great deal of success. That skill has become such a dying art that Gretchen is probably the only legal secretary in Hilo who can still record and read shorthand.[148] Unquestionably, obtaining an education has become more and more essential to success in the American work force. Nevertheless, my family is living proof that the trend has been post WWII. My grandfather achieved a level of management in the McCloud River Lumber Company on an 8th grade education. Both Gretchen's father and mine, as well as my cousin Ralph got their post-secondary education in the Army. Cousin Vern went to work with his father in steel, and eventually succeeded in business. Why I was so determined to get a higher degree probably had to do with the nuns and the Franciscans.

I have discussed my experience registering at Padelford Hall; the confusion did not stop there. I had signed up for the Dept. of Microbiology, and was assigned a counselor whose name I have put out of my mind. He did me a disservice in that he took no account of my previous background or my economic status (I had to work). I guess bac-T, as we called it, was such a hot field that the counselor just assumed that all student would have to be red-hots. He set me up for 15 credit hours with 9 hours of laboratory. That was algebra (because I had gotten a D at LCC), genetics, bacteriology with lab, and organic chemistry with lab. That worked out to classes all day every weekday and I had to work to pay my board. Needless to say, I got a 1.8 GPA that quarter. The fact that Gretchen and I were together 72% of every free hour did not help. It did wonders for her; brought her grade point average right up that quarter. Thereafter, she sailed on to graduation. For me it was more of a Mount Everest assault!

The work was a job that I found on Harbor Island called Hardware Specialties Co.[149] Bob Unger and his father-in-law had one of the smartest management styles I ever encountered in my career. The testimony for this is that the company is still in business. Basically they are ship's chandlers; they strip all the useful equipment off of derelict ships and boats. I love the review that I included in footnote above; it was truly accurate; The wisdom of the management was that they divided the business up into various commodities: wire; hardware, etc. Each division had a person in charge. There were only 6 or 7 permanent staff, but each one was evaluated on the productivity of his section; the books were kept separately. At the end of the year, each section-head got a bonus based on the profit from his section. These guys worked 6 days a week, so Unger would take them all out to lunch on Saturday. One time it might be the local spaghetti shack; the next time it might be Bart's Wharf or Ivar's. (Both were very upscale). You can bet I was always there on Saturday, because it was usually the best meal I had to eat during the week. These guys were all very loyal, and I would not be surprised, if I went there today, I would find some of the same guys. They were there when I worked for Weyerhaeuser Research on Harbor Island in 1972-74.

I have to apologize; I didn't mean to knock Mrs. French's cooking. It was English plain, but it was healthy. I particularly liked the kidney pie. You wouldn't think it, but a six foot 2 inch 150 lbs. guy craves the protein and the carbs. I was not fond of the liverwurst sandwich every day, but there was also a peanut butter and jelly, so I survived. I did eat the liverwurst first, so the PBJ would take the taste out of my mouth. She didn't keep any snacks around the house, except three. In the cupboard she kept a jar of peanut butter, a jar sweet pickle relish and bread. Those became a study-time staple which I enjoy to this very day. After I left Mrs. French's, meals became more problematic.

I had a good lab partner in Bac-T, which was probably why I didn't flunk. Her name was Emily Du, and we became good friends over the years at UW. She was Chinese but she was raised in the Philippines, so she could cook wicked rice noodles as well as killer adobo (both were excellent). She was also very proficient in microbiology and went on to be a cracker-jack immunology tech. It didn't pay enough for her, so she took computer programming in night school and went on to be a programmer at a Seattle bank. She ended up marrying another programmer who she met at the Honeycomb Fellowship. We will get to that later.

So Gretchen was soaring, and I was crashing big time. I failed Algebra, withdrew from genetics and scraped through the other classes. If I hadn't gotten a B in chemistry lab, I probably would have quit. The C in Bac-T proved to me that it was not the field in which I wanted to major. So at the end of the quarter, I scampered over to the botany department, and got acquainted with their program. The bacteriology department was on the cutting edge, with 17 year old *wunderkind* that were extracting and sequencing DNA. In contrast, my newly chosen department was still a classical discipline. Botany was not totally descriptive, but they had not adopted the rigors of calculus and advanced biochemistry by then. Even genetics was not a requirement to graduate, although I did pass it in the fall quarter of '68. I also made sure that I had one philosophy class each quarter to offset the sciences. In the winter quarter, I stuck with mycology, organic chemistry (which started to make a little more sense to me), and Introduction to Philosophy (which boosted my grade point with an A).

Jana recorded that Gretchen took the train to Longview to attend Chris Bowerman's wedding on Oct 7th. Of course, I stayed, because my schedule was too tight with work and school. Bob and Jana brought Gretchen to UW on Oct 8th I met them at the dorm. I don't remember if Bob and Jana vacationed in Seattle, because they took Gretchen to see *Man of La Mancha* in Seattle on Oct. 14th. I didn't go because I probably could not afford the time or the price of the ticket. It could also be that the pressure to create opportunities for Gretchen and me to be together no longer existed. I am sure they probably asked me if I wanted to go to the play. I did have breakfast with Huffhines. After breakfast, they came to visit at Mrs. French's house. Oct 15th. I guess they wanted to see what kind of a Spartan life I was leading; I think they decided that I was living pretty well (but, of course, Jana would not record that kind of emotional information).

At Thanksgiving break, Gretchen and Dave rode to Longview with me in the Corvair. Jana noted that we had car trouble and Bob had to come pick us up, although she did not say where or what was wrong. Dave played golf with Dad on Thanksgiving Day and then we had dinner at Huffhines 23rd Nov. It was nice of the Huffhines to invite my Dad and Dave. As it turned out, my mother had already gone to live at the Parish in Galt with Fr. Carl, leaving my Dad to his own devices, as they say. I don't want to deal with all of that here; I am not sure that I will be able to bring myself to give what sordid details that I know, but I think it should probably be dealt with at the end of the memoir, when enough detail is available to better understand the context and the time. There are other unfortunate issues that I would probably consider in the same way, at the end or in another volume, when a little more understanding can be brought to bear on the foibles of mere mortals.

Nevertheless, I will let you know how Gretchen felt about my mother's actions. This is from a letter Gretchen sent to her mother:

Oct. 24th 1967
Mike hasn't heard from Kay since she wrote to tell him she
was staying at Fr. Carl's. Jim wrote and said she hasn't written

him either. That woman has definite mental problems. And I think she's really asking for trouble with this fiasco. I feel so sorry for poor Jim.... He really doesn't understand Kay (but then, who does?). Mike can do all right for himself, and Kay is asking for any trouble she has. But Jim is sort of a hopeless victim, isn't he?

Apparently the Corvair was repairable, because I went to Pietro's with Dave Gretchen and Dad on 24th. That evening we went to Bernard LeTourneau's Beauty Salon to see a movie made by the SFS seminarians. We returned to Seattle in the Corvair on the 25th. Dave mentioned this in his email of Aug. 6. 2010. I must admit that, had I not seen Jana's journal, I would not have recalled the Thanksgiving trip. I am amazed that Dave remembered it after 43 years. I am sure my dad enjoyed the diversion, and we needed a break too, in preparation for the end of quarter push to exams.

Near the end of the month Gretchen and I attended a party with many of the former seminarians who had drifted up to the Seattle area. Gretchen wrote:

> Oct 30, 1967
> Mike and I took Larry Warnberg and Dave (Mike's roommate) to Belleview last night to see Bob Scholze, an ex-seminarian friend of Mike's. He lives on a 53 ft. yacht at the Meydenburg Yacht Club. He gets free room and board in exchange for taking care of the boat. It's a beautiful boat and we had a very nice visit. Phil Gilday and his girlfriend were there too, and we all had a really great time. Bob is English major and a real nice guy.

Apparently we did have a good time, because not long after we did it again

> Nov. 13 1967
> Friday night after work Mike picked up Nancy and me and George Matter and we went to Belleview for a party at Bob Scholze's boat. There were about 8 people there not all coupled up, but just a "happy group", like it always is when ex-seminarians

get together. George took his guitar and banjo, and Leonard Ricky (another ex-St. Francis student) had his guitar too. We really had a good time. And Saturday I invited Leonard's date, Kathy McConaughey, over for lunch. She lived in McCarthy and had never been to Haggett.

Kathy did not stay with Leonard, but we saw a lot of her after that. She was quite involved with the Newman Center. The situation becomes very complicated later on due to roommates and drugs and her brother (this will come up later).

My most vivid memory of that Exam week was the Chemistry professor coming in to the class room (really it was more of a hall) and announcing the following bombshell in his menacing German accent [paraphrased]:

> We have 400 students in this class, and a few of them are genius material. I have written this exam to test their skills. Take 1.5 minutes per question. Don't panic, the test will be graded on the curve.

I couldn't believe he said "don't panic"; that only sent my heart to racing. Again, I think I was probably near the last group of students to turn in their tests when he called time. Thank God that he graded on the curve, because I was border line at best. The organic chemistry class in the winter quarter was much smaller and much more intuitive. I still got a C but I think I actually developed a basic understanding of how chemistry works… finally!

After exams, Gretchen went to Longview on the 19th of December. Of course, I stayed back to try to earn a little more money. I drove home on the 22nd. Gretchen and I spent the 23rd with my Dad. I am not sure what we did, but there was probably some last minute shopping. Dad came to Huffhines for Christmas dinner and Bob Junior's girlfriend Kathy was there for holiday. Bob and Cathy ended up getting married the next summer. She was a smart one, with whom Bob senior was very impressed. Bob had been a Republican and somewhat conservative (in the Eisenhower sense, not like the radical right wing that we have today). Kathy single handedly changed all that. By the election of 1972, Bob was voting for McGovern.[150] Over the years his haircut went from crew cut to long hair and side burns. During the National Bicentennial in 1976, he and my Dad both grew full red beards. Bob and Jana had been moving away from his Baptist and her Methodist roots by that time, and like all of us, they were swept into the new social order; liberal, socially conscious and opposed to the Vietnam War. By the end of the war in 1975, 2,594,000 US troops had served in Vietnam, 58,236 had been killed, 153,452 had been wounded and 1,740 were missing in action.[151] By this time the Vietnam War was dominating the news and on January 31st the Tet Offensive was started by the North Vietnamese.[152]

I went back to Seattle on the 26th of December, although I have no idea why (probably work). Jana records that I came back on the 30th. My Dad joined the Huffhines, Kathy, Gretchen and me at Dave Spencer's for Tom and Jerry drinks. Gretchen and I went to midnight mass in Kelso on Dec 30th. On New Year's Eve, Gretchen and I ate dinner with Bob and Jana (Bob Jr. and Cathy had left for home on the east coast). After dinner, Herb Karnofski came over to the Huffhines house and we played games until time for Mass.

It is downright weird to have so much detail about what we did that New Years, but have so little recollection of it. Yet some very significant things do not appear in her journal. For example, that Christmas Eve, I gave Gretchen her engagement ring after midnight Mass. Following Jana's notes so closely is bogging me down. It's like writing a research paper; I can hear her voice in the background saying: "Mike, please get this straight." I think Jana was so organized in her own life that she didn't want any confusion introduced by inaccurate memories. I guess that is why she kept the journals so meticulously. My grandfather was that way also. I guess life would be simplified if everyone thought that way; "just the facts, Ma'am".[153] I had to laugh when I plowed into Jana's 1968 journal; the first mention of Gretchen and I was that she had purchased birthday gifts: a clock radio and an alarm clock for Gretchen and me respectively. I guess Gretchen must have revealed that we were having a problem getting up in time for class?

The quarter started out quite normally. Except for the lousy weather, the classes were going well. The hardest part for me was driving down from Mrs. French's house to the massive parking lot by Lake Washington, and then hiking up to the center of campus in the rain, sleet or snow. It was probably a half mile to the Botany building; once I got there, all my classes were fairly close together. I have not described the campus at all, but it really is a quite impressive collection of old and relatively new buildings. Although it was not the original collection of campus building, the quadrangle of the college (called "the Quad"[154]) was an early development of all brick building, now totally covered in Ivy. Hence, the chapter head reference to the Halls of Ivy. At the end of the Quad, the Suzzalo Library is literally a cathedral to knowledge (very gothic, very scholastic).

Suzzalo Library at the University of Washington. (Photo reproduced with permission of the University of Washington Archive) http://upload. wikimedia.org/wikipedia/en/thumb/9/95/Suzzallo Library Across Red Square.jpg/220px

The Huskie Union Building (HUB) was the Student Union. Gretchen and I had a very enjoyable evening the last week of January attending the University Las Vegas Night at the HUB. I will let Gretchen describe it.

Jan. 28 1968

We went to Las Vegas Night – I really had a great time! Hugh Masekela[155], a jazz trumpeter was the featured entertainment – and he was fantastic. There was also a ragtime band from the Blue Banjo and a couple of rock-and-roll bands played in the Husky Den all evening. All the rooms in the HUB were gambling room of one kind or another – and we were all given $520 of play money as we came in. I played the roulette wheel a lot – came away with $1510, which isn't too bad. I think Los Vegas would be much more fun now since I could gamble etc. But then who could afford it if it were real money! Mike had a good time too, but he kept losing money. We danced a little and listened to the Blue Banjo band, saw a Greek belly dancer (Mike Liked that!) and generally had a really great time.

The fact of the matter is that I have always had bad luck, I steer away from any kind of gambling like the plague… except agriculture (which is a form of legalized gambling), and I never risked much money in that either. To be honest, I was a bit uncomfortable with all the fun we were having at the UW. Even the 'fun stuff" at SFS and SLR was for a higher purpose; raising money for the seminary, working with the youth organizations, "spreading the gospel". This stuff at the UW was all about us, the study was about us, the recreation was about us, the objective was to do the stuff that would let us live "happily ever after". Believe me when I say that. Just because I had come out of the seminary that did not mean I had given up all my ideals. I don't know if Gretchen ever really understood that.

It was ironic that Hugh Masekela was the lead act at Las Vegas Night, because he was himself in exile and working for the liberation of South Africa from apartheid. There was a lot of political activity brewing on campus, and we were completely oblivious. It would become far more overt before we finished college. I had no idea that my idealism would eventually put me in an African country that I could not even point out on a map.

The quarter started out more relaxed for me. I was taking philosophy with organic chemistry and Dr. Stumf's mycology course. I very much enjoyed the latter; especially since Dr. Stumf made sure there were always pastries and other goodies at class; he really knew how to keep the undergrads coming to class! The organic chemistry teacher was a lot more interesting too. I think he was Polish and had war stories to relate. Of course, I aced philosophy, so that indicated to me that I should use that strategy to get through my undergraduate program. And the strategy worked, too. I never got less than a B in philosophy except Studies in Continental Rationalism. My Catholic mind was coming around to rationalism slowly. I did get mostly B's and one A in my botany courses, but the other sciences were mostly C's. I hate to think how poorly I would have done if I had tried to take all science classes. Two ex-seminarians from SFS double-majored in psychology and sociology (They would later become my roommates). I should have taken a minor in philosophy but was too busy to discuss it with a counselor. The aforementioned departments were based in the Quad, which was noted for the cherry blossom displays in the spring[156].

The Quad (above) at University of Washington was constructed between 1915 and 1950. (Photo reproduced cowith permission of Daniel Seidman)

The department of Philosophy was in Savery Hall on the Quad, but some classes were based in Denny Hall[157], which, as the footnote indicates, was the original building on the current campus of UW.

Denny Hall was the original building one the current campus of UW, built of stone from the Tenino quarry. (Photo reproduced with permission of the University of Washington Archive)

Gretchen took Far East History there. The stone for it was quarried at Tenino, Washington, where I would live for almost 5 years. The quarry is now the Tenino Swimming Pool, but the water is so cold that no one ever goes there to swim. There's another one of those ironies of life.

Back to the chronological order of things *ala* Jana; Gretchen and I had our 21st birthday party together with Dave and Gretchen's roommate, as previously relayed. On Saturday, the 3rd of February, we drove to Longview in "old faithful" (speaking facetiously). On arrival, Bob promptly took Gretchen and me to the Washington State Liquor Store to get our identification cards. Purchasing liquor and even wine was strictly controlled in our traditional state, and blue laws[158] applied. Bars had to close at 2 AM, and the state liquor stores were closed on Sunday. Women were not allowed to sit at the bar, and they could not move their own drink from one table to another. "You've come a long way, Baby!"

After passing all the proscriptions, and being able to imbibe, the Huffhines and my father took Gretchen and me to the Elks Club for dinner and dancing to celebrate our birthday. Even though Jana woke up not feeling well, she went ahead and cooked a midday dinner for Gretchen and me so we could head back to Seattle at 3 PM. If there is a pattern here, it is that the Huffhines were very generous parents to both Gretchen and me. If we would have had the good sense to follow their encouraging lead, our lives would have turned out a whole lot differently.

My Dad came up to visit us at UW at the end of February, which Gretchen described in this letter:

> February 29 1968
>
> We had a nice weekend with Jim. The basketball game was good, and the Blue Banjo was tremendous. I'm really surprised that I like beer as well as I do, after all the nasty things I said about it all those times. Fortunately, I waited until I was 21 to realize that it wasn't that bad. (But I still like coke and milk better.) Mike bought a garter for me while we were there. It's a really funny thing.... A guy buys his date a garter, and the waiter comes to the table, takes the girl up on the stage, and puts the garter on her leg. The audience is yelling "Higher, Higher!" and it's a little embarrassing. But Dave bought Nancy one, too, and we got to go up together, so it wasn't bad.

To this day, Gretchen is a "cheap drunk"; meaning she drinks so little alcohol that it doesn't take much to get her "lit". We make a good pair, but, if we have been drinking, don't give us the keys!

I was beginning to get the hang of big university life about that winter quarter; and the results were a clean 3.0 GPA for the quarter; what a relief after the fiasco of the first semester. I was making plans to take a trip to California to see my mother. Gretchen had looked into airline tickets, but we decided we could not afford that. She was having misgivings about the trip, which were really a reflection of her parents' concerns.

> March 12, 1968
>
> I'm in a quandary still about going to California. I really do want to go, but I hate to make people upset and worried. Mike wants me to go with him, but if I go, I have to go on his conditions – as I suppose it should be. I think this all boils down to doing what Mike wants me to do or what you want me to do. As Mike's future wife I almost feel that his plans should come first. But I am still your daughter and I hate doing things you don't want me to do. But I suppose I ought to start making my own decisions without consulting everyone – and let the chips fall where they may.
>
> So I will probably wrestle with myself and my conflicting ideas and end up going with Mike – I don't suppose it'll be a lasting source of discussion if I do or don't go though.

Gretchen was half way through exams when she wrote the above. We had both done well in that quarter, and were ready for a relaxing trip. Of course, my intention in going to California was to get reoriented with my mother (read that, figure out what the hell was going on). The official reason for the trip was to have our engagement ring blessed by Fr. Carl; pretty ironic, huh? Like I said, my life has been a series of one happenstance after another, usually enmeshed in irony and convoluted with uncertainty.

According to Jana's journal, Gretchen and I arrived, from Seattle, back in Longview at 5:30 PM on the 16th of March. I went home and left Gretchen with her folks.

March 17, 1968

G slept 'till 10 AM, ate dinner with us. Mike came over at
about 5 PM, took her to church and Jim took them to dinner at
the Elks. G went to visit Mom in the afternoon.

Jana did not mention that we left for California the next day. There
is no record of what happened on the trip, so we will have to wing it from
memory here. It was obviously a whirlwind trip to in the little Corvair;
which at the time was running very well, and in spite of all the engineering
nightmares of the little air cooled wonder, was a very comfortable ride. I
remember thinking how smoothly it drove. It had a low center of gravity
and independent suspension (one of the engineering headaches), but it made
for a very smooth ride. It kind of gave us both a feeling of freedom being on
the open road, traveling through whole states, on our own.

When we arrived in Galt, we were greeted warmly by my mother,
but, in retrospect, there was probably some apprehension on Fr. Carl's
part. He had met Gretchen before on the Toutle, and, of course, he had
taught me catechism and baptized me. The pretext was that Mom had
taken over the job of housekeeper from Father's sister who had died the
previous year. Being the gullible guy that I am, I bought it. Gretchen was
more circumspect; she wanted to believe that it was on the up and up, but it
seemed peculiar to her. Her woman's intuition sensed that the relationship
was more like a man and a wife than priest and employee. There were no
overt signs of such a relationship, but it is hard to fool a woman. Apparently
the parish had accepted the concept, whether they believed it or not, I
can't say.

The irony was that my mother was certain that Gretchen and I were
already sleeping together, and had not made preparations for both of us to
sleep separately. We informed her otherwise, and I ended up on the rectory's
living room couch, while Gretchen slept in the small guest room which
adjoined Fr. Carl's office. Add to the ignominy of my mother's assumption,
the fact that the big concern of Gretchen's parents was that we might be

tempted to "procreate" on such an adventurous trip. I guess my mother was far more sophisticated on these matters of sexual liberation than I had ever known. All I knew was that she told me in grade school that if I ever got a girl pregnant out of wedlock that she would personally cut my nuts off!

I don't recall that we gave much discussion to the issue of my mother and my stepfather. I think we kind of skirted that subject like the Biblical leper. It's not like my mother could talk about how happy she was with Fr. Carl, nor could I ask why she broke up with my Dad. It was only after her death that I discovered the letters between her and Fr. Carl, and his letter to my Dad that I finally understood what had happened. I don't think we got around to having Fr. Carl bless our ring, either. If he did, the blessing did not take. In fact, I am not sure if the trip accomplished anything other than establish the kind of relationship we would have with my mother and Fr. Carl for the next sixteen years.

It was the custom of Fr. Carl to take Thursday off, and take my mother to Lodi for dinner. Gretchen remembers that we went to Lodi that Thursday March 23rd, and had dinner together with them. The reason that she remembers Lodi is because of the Credence Clearwater Revival song "Stuck in Lodi". She also remembers Galt and the whole Central California experience to be a trip she would not have wanted to make again soon. The flat valley had no appeal for her. I think my mother also regretted that she gave up the Toutle River for Galt, with freight trains roaring through town every few hours, stifling heat even in the spring time, and a chemical haze that hangs in the valley because of the inversion layer that holds in all the agricultural pollution.

I don't think we met any of the parishioners on that trip. We were not there on a Sunday, so I did not make Gretchen attend daily Mass. By then, I was pretty much out of the habit of daily Mass myself. As I said, I frankly don't remember what we did for the three days we were there. Fr. Carl would have been writing his sermon on Friday as we left to return to Washington. Fr. Carl's two strengths as a priest were that he took instruction of the young very seriously, and he was a very careful manager of parish funds. He actually kept two sets of books. At the same time as he was managing to keep the historic landmark St. Christopher's Catholic Church[159] from falling into ruins, he was keeping a separate account for a fund to build another church. Bishop Bell did not know this, and if he had, he would have taxed the parish more heavily. The bishop probably always wondered why all those successful Portuguese dairymen could not raise more money for their church. Well, as it turns out they did, much to "Bishop Ding-a-ling's" surprise. Fr. Carl retired from his pastorate in 1980, before St. Christopher's celebrated its 100th anniversary.

St. Christopher's Church, Galt. (Photo reproduced with permission from Dan Tarnasky, Historian/Archivist, Galt Area Historical Society.)

Without his pastoral stewardship, not only would St. Christopher's not have survived to become a historical landmark, but the parish would not have a new church, either. That church was built on land that Fr. Carl had clandestinely purchased for the parish. I guess it was his Pennsylvania Dutch upbringing?

The trip back was uneventful. We really didn't have time to stop to visit with anyone. I may have driven into McCloud so Gretchen could see where I was raised, but I don't think we visited anyone there. I remember some rather unsafe fondling on the trip back, but we managed not to have an accident. The weather was beautiful, and we were traveling with the windows down through Northern California and Ashland. Finally we stopped under a bridge in Washington State to do some exploratory biology before we would be with Gretchen's parents again. Yes, we were very old fashioned, and not willing to go past first… no, maybe second… possibly even third base; but no home runs on this trip. We definitely did have fun!

Jana kept the record:

> Friday March 22, 1968
> We went to dinner at Elks – acct my birthday. Got home 10:30 – found G and Mike had arrived 9:30 [PM]. G was in bed and left note to wake her up and I did. She reported good trip etc.

> Saturday March 23, 1968
> Bob had exam. Mike ate with us. They visited Kris and Marie Olson.

> Sunday March 24, 1968
> Mike had dinner with us. They left about 4:30 to go by Elks to see Jim, go to church, leave for Seattle.

That was our first spring break in which Gretchen and I spent almost the entire time together.

Now it was on to the new quarter, and for me it was a great quarter. I was taking the Philosophy of Science, History of Modern Philosophy, and Plant Classification. The philosophy classes were interesting, but the Taxonomy class was fascinating. Dr. C. Leo Hitchcock[160] was a very popular lecturer because his lectures were peppered and salted with information about the history of botanists who had explored the Pacific Northwest since the time of the British Territorial government. He himself and his assistant Charles Muhlick were responsible for the growth of the Univ. of Washington Herbarium to over a quarter of a million entries. Hitchcock's productive association with the famous botanist J. W. Thompson gave an authenticity to his absorbing discourses that I had seldom seen and may never again. I once wrote that Fr. Geoffery was the best teacher I ever had or would have. I was wrong; because Dr. Hitchcock was outstanding in his field (he did a lot of that, also). I was so impressed with the whole professional approach to education that I dedicated myself to getting an A in his class. I don't have the steel trap memory that it requires to be a cracker-jack botanist, but I loved every minute of learning to classify the entire botanical world. By the way, according to the website of the Burke Museum of Natural History and Culture, the Univ. of Washington Herbarium has estimated holdings of over 580,000 specimens include approximately 375,000 vascular plants, 80,000 mosses, 35,000 fungi, 23,000 algae, 16,000 hepatics, and 13,000 lichens.

On the 5th of May, Jana noted that her mother had been in the Americana Nursing Home for 20 days. It bothers me now to think how oblivious Gretchen and I were of her grandmother's advancing age. If ever there was a dutiful daughter, it was Jana Huffhines. She visited her mother in the nursing home almost every day that she remained alive. Bob visited Frankie often also, but Jana was stalwart. She did the same for Bob when he developed Parkinson's disease. She kept him home as long as she could and when he had to be put in assisted care, she was at his bedside at least once every day. Of course, she was a Red Cross employee, but that alone does not explain her devotion to her family. Gretchen did visit Frankie when she was in town, and I went with her once or twice, but it is clear that we did not have the respect for the elderly that Jana's generation had. Frankie never liked the nursing home, and tried to check herself out a few times. I remember thinking during one of the visits, "This is going to kill her." And it did.

The next time Gretchen and I visited Longview, we went on an outing with Bob and Jana.

> Sunday May 12 1968
> Mike came at 7, and we four drove to Clam Diggers' Breakfast at Ilwaco – big crowd, good breakfast, we drove on beach and came home on Oregon side, getting home about 12:30. We all went to see Mom [Frankie], had dinner at 3:15, kids left at 4.

On May 20th Gretchen met my lab partner Emily Du. She wrote this letter to her mother.

> May 20, 1968
> Mike and I went on a picnic with Emily Du, that little Chinese friend of Mike's from the Philippines -- we went to Golden Gardens

Park, which is on the Puget Sound and is really crummy, as far as we were concerned. I'm so used to places like Merwin Dam, etc, with clean grounds, etc. And this place is really awful…., The beach is really ugly and the facilities are bad. Needless to say, we didn't stay very long! Emily suggested driving to Tacoma to visit her "host family" so off we went. They are really tremendous people, and we stayed all afternoon and evening. Mr. Sheldon is the child welfare man at Shelton, and he places children in foster homes, counsels unwed mothers, etc. They even have a foster daughter living with them, in addition to their own boys (in high school) and a foreign student from Jordan. They are Catholics, and one of their daughters is in the Franciscan convent somewhere or another. Their home is fairly nice, and they have a large swimming pool in the back yard. We had a really nice visit, and they invited us all back someday when the sun is shining so that we can use their pool. We got back to Seattle about midnight – my roommates were beginning to think that maybe Mike and I eloped or something!!!

Sounds great. Both Vicki and Anne [roommates] are looking forward to meeting you, and they are very glad to be going out to dinner for a change.

I got and 'A' on my Shakespeare paper that I was working on at home the other weekend. Prof. Willeford commented on it in class – said it was one of the best papers on the clowns that he has read. He wants me to give it back to him for a while, because he wants to make a copy of it!!!! I was really pleased.

From most of the month of May, the Huffhines were preparing for the wedding of their son Bob to Kathy in early June. Bob and Kathy arrive on the morning of the 8th and Gretchen and I arrived in Longview at 11:30 AM. There was a whirlwind of activity that week, which culminated in a very nice wedding at Gebhertt Chapel of the Longview Community Church on Saturday June 15th. Gretchen was a bridesmaid (the dress had been altered by Bob), and I was an usher. The reception was at Henri's restaurant and it was a very jovial affair. It looked like the young couple had it all, brains, looks, and great prospects for the future. Bob became a lawyer for the Air Force Judge Advocate Corps, and Kathy became an English teacher at Boston College.

Before the summer break, Gretchen had been hired at Black Ball Freight Company, and, because she wanted to keep that job, she decided to stay in Seattle and attend summer school. I, on the other hand, returned to my job at Weyerhaeuser Pulp because I needed the money to continue to fund my education singlehandedly. Of course tuition was only $115 per quarter, but that was a lot to finance in addition to living expenses, books, car repairs, etc. in 1968. Gretchen and her Haggett Hall roommate, Nancy, had to find lodging since Haggett closed every summer. They found a little one-bedroom apartment at the back of a fraternity hall parking lot for a whopping $75 per month. I returned to my Dad's property on the Toutle... he didn't charge me rent, but I don't remember if I was still sleeping in the tent with the chipmunks. Gretchen wasn't very happy about this arrangement, but it was the best jobs that either of us could get, and we knew we would need the money to finish school so we could get married.

The communication between Gretchen and I declined substantially that summer. I don't really know why. I don't remember or have any records of anything exciting happening that summer. Before I had left Seattle, I had gone to the Naval Recruiter and taken the test for Officer's Candidate School. I remember thinking, why were they asking about what was the size of the community in which I was raised. I guess it had something to do with shipboard living, i.e. destroyer vs. aircraft carrier and the great difference in the number of crew members? At the same time I applied for the Peace Corps. Needless to say, the Naval Officers Corps did not contact me but, toward the end of the summer, the Peace Corps did.

Gretchen knew that I had applied for the Peace Corps. I went up to Seattle to see her after I received the invitation to Peace Corps. I had not replied yet, but I wanted to know whether Gretchen would be willing to go with me. I met her at her apartment in Greek Row. Nancy was not around, and we had the time to ourselves. I don't remember how long I waited until I told her, but the focal point of the day was the following conversation. I told her that I had received the invitation to Peace Corps in Kenya. I explained that there were three possibilities. I could turn down this offer, and wait for Gretchen to apply so that we could be assigned together, hopefully as a married couple. The second option was that I could take this assignment. That would mean that she, like so many wives and girlfriends of Vietnam soldiers, could wait two years for me. Or, the third choice would be for us to split up and go our separate ways. My memory is that she chose the latter that day. We both think she gave me back the ring that day (even though it is less clear in Jana's journals). I went back to Longview that day, but at some point between then and Labor Day I was in downtown Seattle, and was taking my keys out of my pocket when the ring fell on the pavement and rolled through a grate into a huge drain. It was so inaccessible that I didn't even try to recover the ring. Was that happenstance or bad judgement? It was odd that the platinum engagement ring with a small diamond was such an afterthought to me that I did not immediately place it in the box with the wedding band.

I have a letter that my Dad wrote to my mother about this time. Ironically, as Gretchen and I were breaking up just as the final nails were being nailed into the coffin of my parents' marriage. Dad wrote this letter to my mother:

Thursday evening, August 29, 1968
My Dear Kay,

I guess I'm way overdue in writing you, but then you know I'm not very good about writing letters.

It was good to see you and you appear to be well and happy. It is really too bad that we can't seem to communicate. As I told you before you left, I seem to go on the defensive every time we talk. I think it stems from the incurable inferiority complex I have. When you asked if I wanted you to come back, it took me by surprise. I fell that you don't want to come back, that is the reason I gave the

406

answer I did. And as long as you feel you don't want to come back we could never make it work. I do want you back, <u>but</u> only if you desire to come back. That and only then could we hope to work it out. Nuf said.

There will be another supervisor's exam held ...

(Oops out of typewriter paper)

So will try it once more. I was mailed a pamphlet a couple of weeks ago on what the contents of the exam will be and how to study for it so will bear down a little harder this time.

We are having an all Elks golf tournament in Raymond on Labor Day so will be taking off after work tomorrow and spending the whole weekend there. I went over a couple of weeks ago to make book on the course, and found they have a beautiful course there. The following weekend we start our club championship here as well as granddad tournament so will play them both. That will about wind up the season.

Last night (Wednesday) Bob Crosby and his Dixieland band played the Kelso Elks. He and his music are great. I even got out and did some shin kicking[dancing]. I had to leave early tho as I am working the early shift for three weeks.

I am planning on seeing an attorney for advice regarding legal separation, next week. I don't know what to expect, but will let you know what I learn.

Jean bought a new Buick last week and is it ever a beaut. I'd sure like to have the one she turned in, but it's just a little out of my class. I couldn't afford to drive it, let along buy it.

Mike is due home any minute so will close for now,

As ever,

Jim

He did buy Jean's trade-in Buick, and yes, he was dating Jean at that time.

Jana's journals track our activities, about which she knew, after that.

Friday Aug. 30 198
G called, re arrival Saturday morning.

Saturday Aug. 31, 1968
We met G's train at 11, Mike was waiting at house.

Sunday Sept. 1, 1968
Mike ate dinner with us – then went to work at 3. G visited
Sherry – brought her home to spend the night.

Monday Sept. 2, 1968 Labor Day. Mike ate with us at 3 PM, He
and G visited grandmother early. He went home fairly early in
evening. (we learned later that G gave him her ring back)

The truly ironic thing about this note is that it seems to reflect the
whole situation. Gretchen does not remember her parents discussing the
break-up with her. After all the effort they had put into the two of us, they
didn't try to talk either one of us out of our stubborn standoff. Because
Gretchen believed that was what it was; a spat, a disagreement which we
would get beyond. Perhaps her parents were torn, because they understood
that I was truly serious about going in the Peace Corps, but they were not
anxious to have me take their daughter half way around the world.

Tuesday Sept. 3, 1968
Mike took G back to Seattle.

Wed. Sept. 4, 1968
Mike called to see if we had seen anything of ring—he lost it!

I don't know why I did that, because I distinctly remember seeing the
ring roll out of my pocket and into the drain in Seattle. Memory is a funny
thing. I am sure I was not trying to deceive anyone…maybe I was lying to
myself. It is certain that Jana's account was factual.

Sat. Sept. 7, 1968
Decided on spur of moment after receiving letter from G to go help
her move to other apt. Called her and went. Got motel, she took us

to eat and to see "Prudence and the Pill" and "Guide to the Married Man" – our birthday present.

I think they were probably concerned about how Gretchen was feeling; being alone without even a roommate (Nancy had already left the little apartment to return to the dorms). Gretchen and I had worked out a deal to transfer the apartment to us for the fall quarter. We were Larry Warnberg, Tony Searing and myself. I have mentioned Larry before, but I have not said much about Tony. They were both SFS grads who were attending UW after they left SLR. We were all on tight budgets so we figured we could divide the $75 rent three ways. Gretchen left her parents' hideaway bed in the apartment, and I found a set of twin bed springs, and built a bunk bed around them. We all slept in the same bedroom, and Larry had his desk in the bedroom, and Tony and I used desks in the living room. It was a crazy semester, which I will relate after we consider the slow process of breaking-up with Gretchen.

> Sat. Sept. 14, 1968
> Bob picked G up at train at 11 AM... Mike came over at night for a while.

The fact that we had broken-up did not mean that Gretchen and I were not friends, and I still was willing to be there for her.

> Sunday Sept 15, 1968
> G visited Sherry briefly before dinner, Mike took her back to Seattle about 3:20 PM.

> Saturday Sept 21, 1968
> Bob [in his Postal Clerk capacity] gave Peace Corps exam in afternoon to Mike K.

Obviously I had accepted the assignment in Kenya, and the hiring was progressing. There were still a lot of hoops through which to jump, but the die had basically been cast.

Thursday Jan. 2, 1969
Bob took hour off and took G to train.

That night Gretchen called me, because she was very disconsolate about the fact that the whole plan for her future had been turned upside down. Her new roommates were both still out of town, and she way feeling very alone. I agreed to go over and console her. I stayed the night, and held her until she went to sleep. So basically, I slept at her house that night. She said it was a dilemma for her that she needed her friend, but I was that friend.

While Gretchen had spent most of the holiday at her new apartment, I had been brought into a new circle of friends by Emily Du. She was participating in a Christian group called the Honeycomb Fellowship. To this day I don't know what the ecclesiastical affiliation of the group was, because it was very oriented to being self-directed. The founders of the group were Tom Griffith, a counselor at Chief Sealth High School, Roy Gillette, a computer analyst for the City of Seattle, and a few others whom I do not remember. I remember Tom and Roy because they would both become important influences in my last year at the University, and also when I came back from Africa. But at the time, I was just one of the twenty or so young people that were drawn to the homey atmosphere of the Fellowship. It was usually held in Tom's home close to campus. Tom's wife Jean was a very motherly sort, having 5 kids by Tom already. They were the epitome of the kind of stability that I had not seen in my own family, and I was fascinated. But I tended to hang out with the younger members of the group, like Emily, and like another leprechaun-looking fellow, Bob White. Bob was a very social fellow within and beyond the Honeycomb Fellowship.

As it turned out, Bob had organized a skating party for the Honeycomb Fellowship at the newly completed Intramural Building (IB). The building was like heaven to the students of the UW. It had every type of indoor sports facility, including Olympic pool and basketball courts. The sauna and steam room were particularly nice. The skating was done on a basketball court, with rubber wheeled skates that would not damage the floor. Bob had a friend from Alabama who was on the UW Crew (shell rowing); but the irony of Hulet was that he was 6 feet 8 inches. He was so tall that he had trouble as a rower, because the crewman behind him would hit him in the back with every stroke. The solution to his problem was that he had to occupy the last position in the skull. Hulet was on work study, because, he was on scholarship. This was part of the UW's efforts to diversify the student body. Hulet was black. One of his work study duties was to be an usher at the roller rink nights. Everyone at the university was impressed with the IB and it was heavily frequentedby all including me.

The only problem with the IB was that it took out a lot of the parking spaces, but it didn't matter to me now because I was living about one block off campus, and as I remember, the Fraternity gave us parking space in their lot. It was like being advanced to a higher social stratum. Not really, we were still starving students, but the Fraternity was tolerant of us. We had to put up with quite a bit of chicanery from them. One day someone set off a tear gas bomb in front of the fraternity, but the gas all drifted down to our building. That was enough to convince me not to participate in any of the SDS[161] riots? Another time we had a party and the fraternity stole our keg from the porch. When we went to ask the frats, they denied it, even though they had about ten kegs lining the hallway of their fraternity. That will teach us to have a big party in a one bedroom apartment! The dumbest thing the fraternity did was during the aftermath of a heavy snow. They got on the roof of their 3 story building, and pelted passers buy with snowballs. Come on! If you are going to have a snowball fight, the opposition has to be able to throw back. Granted that they had limited ammunition, but have you ever tried to throw a snowball up 3 stories?

The Honeycomb was a friendly place to go for prayer groups and potlucks, but I had not thrown over the traces of my Catholic roots. So I participated in services at church of Blessed Sacrament, as Gretchen and I had the year before. The Newman Center and the Church were trying to encourage youth activities, so they were having a big dance at the parish hall. I got up the nerve to invite a tall red-headed student from the plant physiology class in which we were both enrolled. I am not going to mention her name, because she was a sister in one of the best sororities, and I am sure she graduated cum laude, and is probably a famous plant physiologist at some major university by now. Suffice it to say, she had a good time at the dance, and eventually invited me to a sorority function as her date; suits, formals, corsages, the works. There's even a Polaroid somewhere.

When our birthdays came round at the end of January, Gretchen and I decided to throw a party at her apartment. She made enchiladas and Bob White came to the party, along with a number of Gretchen's friends, my roommates, etc. After we ate and had some libation (you know Annie Greenspring[162] and Raspberry Ripple. For the upscale, Lancers, and of course Olympia and Rainier beer), we all decided to hike down to the IB to do the skate night. I will let Gretchen describe what happened from there.

> Jan. 26 1969
>
> I had a really fine birthday – Bobby and Kathy called Friday evening while the enchilada party was in progress. I thought it was really sweet of him to call! The party was fun; after dinner we went down to the intramural building to swim and roller skate, then came back here w/ a few extra people we encountered at the building. We sat around and sang, talked etc. for a while and then one of the guys who came from the intermural building started teaching us to, as he said, "really dance". He is a great dancer and the place was looking like a scene from the musical with everyone dancing together. It was really fun – everyone left about 2 AM. This "dancing instructor" wants to take me out next weekend to a dance in the HUB. His name is Hulet Gates, and he is from Birmingham, Alabama – and he's black. I'm not asking for your approval or disapproval, necessarily – just your opinion. I am aware of the problems inherent in interracial dating, but he is such a nice person and so interesting to talk to that I keep thinking [that] the problems will disappear (very unrealistic). Anyway, at least Seattle and especially the U district are pretty open about such things! He is on the Husky Rowing Crew and is a math

major – lives, naturally enough, in the Central Area of Seattle. You always said you'd caution me about the problems I would face dating a black and then let me do what I thought right. Well – now you have to play the roles from *Guess Who's Coming to Dinner?* (Except that I am not going to marry him, just date him!) and figure out whether or not you are or are not racially prejudiced. This all sound like some sort of defiant challenge, but I don't mean it to. You both have always been so good about people, and I really don't worry that you will disapprove of my dating Hu. I'm sure you will worry about the problems we will face, both from blacks and whites, but I wish you wouldn't. I'm 22 and I guess it's time I make some moves on my own. However, I suppose it would be wise not to mention this to Grandmother – can you imagine what she would say! Oh well – there's really no big deal, I guess – he just wants to take me to a dance. (I always said a good looking black was much more appealing to my tastes than an equally good looking white!!).

What Gretchen fails to mention, but later admitted, was that she spotted Hulet on the rink floor, and was so distracted that she crashed headlong into a wall. Little did she know that that relationship would hit her harder than the wall did. Happenstance strikes again! As it turned out, the Huffhines, who were both from the Deep South, were not prejudiced against Hulet, but Hulet never had the nerve to meet them. His loss, I would say.

Around Valentine's Day, I invited Gretchen to go to Las Vegas night, but I think her assessment of the evening is pretty accurate with regard to both the personal dynamic and the quality of the entertainment.

> Las Vegas Night was fun, but I felt like I was dating my brother. I went with Michael. We had a good enough time, but the evening was like a lesser repeat of last year. The only superb thing was the Pair Extraordinaire. They are two black guys, one on the bass and one who sings. They are fantastic showmen and are quite talented.

Obviously the spark had fizzled; Meanwhile I was getting more involved with a wider range of people through the fellowship and the church, the botany department and my roommates. This was a very broad group of people. Tony and Larry were hanging out with a bunch of people who were experimenting with drugs. The Honeycomb was mostly straight people, the red head was "upper-class", and the Blessed Sacrament crowd was the dukes' mix. The party at Gretchen's had been before the end of January, so when my birthday rolled around on February 1st we had a wild party at the little apartment. We had the whole keg (that ended up stolen), plenty of wine (contributed), moderate amounts of food which disappeared in the first half hour, and lots of music. Unofficially there were drugs also, although I didn't really know it... well, I knew that the smell in the air was pot. Gretchen came, but the only thing she remembers is that someone left her Hugh Masekela album on top of a lamp; which warped it into a bowl. I had invited the red head from the Botany Department, and she was a little overwhelmed. She lived a couple of blocks over in her mother's house, so I took her home a bit early. It was a crazy party, and when I came back, I began to realize that I didn't even know half the people that were there. The thing about a college campus is this. If the word is out that there is going to be a party, there are always plenty of people waiting to crash it. I distinctly remember going to bed while the party was still in full swing, and waking up, not long after, to what I thought was an earthquake. Actually it was a buddy of Tony's in the top bunk with a woman to whom he was giving the business. He was a big guy, so my primary concern was that my construction would hold, and they would not end up crashing down on me.

This took place before the red head invited me to her sorority gig, so I had not yet lost favor. But it was after we came home from the formal that Red and I got supine on her mother's living room couch. Just some heavy petting and fondling of the pectoral cornucopia, but that was not a good idea. She invited me to the house the next day... to meet her mother! I was politely given instructions to forget about dating big Red!

I guess I was looking for love in all the wrong places, but my next turn was a great frustration to Gretchen. Emily Du and the Honeycomb fellowship were moderate Christians, but some of us were beginning to be drawn to an Episcopal Church in the Ballard called St. Luke's.[163] Martha Patton, one of the students at the Honeycomb and I heard about St. Luke's at the Blessed Sacrament. There were two young Hippies that were trying to interest the Catholic youth in Pentecostalism or what would come to be called the charismatic movement. Jimmy Henderson and his friend (who was the son of a green grocer at the Pike Street Market) were playing music at the Mass. I offered to join them with my bass. Jimmy played the flute and his friend sang and played tambourine (I think). Martha and I started going to St. Luke's on some nights and Blessed Sacrament on Sundays.

When we first met Jimmy they were just playing along with the other musicians at Fr. Fulton's 5 PM Mass, which was the folk mass. The music group that was their when Jimmy and company arrived were playing folk songs like "Turn Turn Turn" and "Just a Closer Walk with Thee", but their favorite piece was "Hey, Jude". I know that doesn't sound very religious... more sensual if you listen to the words. But it is an amazing crowd mover, and the sing-alongs with this Beatles song became almost transcendental. This did not make Jimmy and friend happy. What we didn't realize is that they were trying to take over the music group and turn it into a more charismatic experience. They were also working very hard on Fr. Fulton to join the movement. Fr. Fulton was the elderly pastor of Blessed Sacrament, and a lovable kind man, who had been experiencing doubts of faith in his senior years. He knew the pastor at St. Luke's. Rev. Dennis Bennett[164], and was probably yearning for a spiritual awakening in himself and his parish.

I remember the night when Fr. Fulton turned the tide at Blessed Sacrament. In a sermon, he really opened up to the Pentecostal movement at Blessed Sacrament. It was too much for some of the band members, and by leaving, they gave over the control of the liturgical music to Jimmy. I continued to play music with the group at the church and traveled to various meetings with Jim and Martha and the other charismatics.

I would have done better in school that quarter if I had not been so involved with the religious movement. In the fall quarter, I had Plant Physiology, Genetics, Introduction to Social Ethics and Studies in Continental Rationalism. I got C's in everything except on B in Social Ethics.

The final step in the clearance for my induction into the Peace Corps was the security check. Gretchen was interviewed as a character witness. She describes it this way in a letter to her mother:

> March 18, 1969
> Some man – a James Anderson from the Civil Service something or other, called me today and made arrangements to meet me at the library this afternoon; he is running a security check on Michael for the Peace Corps. Boy if they run extensive checks like that on everybody it must keep a lot of people in business!

What she later admitted that she told the agent was that I had a tendency to proselytize ("too much religious zeal"). It was also quite irritating to Gretchen what was happening to me. In the same letter she lets fly with the complaints about me:

> I talked to Mike yesterday – that guy is really off his rocker! He had a slight accident with his car – ran into the back of a 1968 Fiat, which ran into a 1956 Thunderbird – and Mike's insurance is not paid up! He said that God was trying to tell him all week that he was going to have an accident; he got a ticket, had his car towed away, etc., and that was God's admonition to him, which he ignored! <u>So</u>, he had an accident! Also he isn't studying much for finals because "God will take care of him". Honestly, it is really difficult to talk much to him – he keeps interjecting "Praise God" whenever I say anything. I think I could say "I'm going to jump off a bridge" and Michael would say "Praise God". It's funny but

I really think he is cracking up. He says he isn't, though, on that, if he is, he's happier that way. I suppose if he is going to do crazy things, the kinds of things he'll do as a religious nut will be safer than some other kind of nut!

That accident was costly, before and after Peace Corps. I paid off the Fiat owner before I left, but I couldn't find the T-bird owner, so when I came back from Peace Corps my license was revoked for a year before I found and paid off the latter. What Gretchen didn't know then was that it was the religious fervor that caused the accident. A bunch of the Jesus freaks were riding back from St. Luke's with me; we were singing in tongues and praising God. I had stopped at a light, but the praying (with my eyes closed) distracted me from keeping my foot on the brake. Since I was stopped on a hill, I rolled into the back of the other cars. She wrote a letter to her mother in April with an equally disgusted assessment of my condition:

> April 12 1969
> I just finished reading *Native Son*, a book by Richard Wright that I borrowed for the guy who lives across the hall. It's pretty good, but quite depressing and hopeless. Mike called me just as I was finishing the book and launched into one of his sermons about God, etc. There certainly is a vast difference among people in the world – from the "anti-heroes" of *Native Son* to religious nuts like Michael and his friends! Mike refused to read *Native Son* because he sees no point in reading "hopeless" literature when there are such beautiful things to read in the Bible! I was disgusted at his speech, told him so quite bluntly, and have seen nothing of him since. (That was about a week ago) He has given up on me, I expect! (I hope)

Maybe God did take care of me that last winter quarter... with more than a little help from Gretchen. I was taking a full load of 20 credits. I was taking Plant Propagation from Mr. Muhlick, Dr. Hitchcock's associate. I was also taking Plant Mineral Nutrition and Plant Cytology with lab. Add to that five research credits in Botany and Introductory Psychology. I asked Gretchen to type up and deliver my research report to the Botany Professor who taught plant morphology as I was leaving for the Peace Corps. She was able to read my semi-Greek script and turned in the paper for credit. Otherwise I didn't do too badly (four B's and one C for the research project). Thank God! (?)

The beautiful thing was that my roommates had learned that we might be eligible for advanced placement credits because of our heavy language studies with the Franciscans. Sure enough, we were all awarded 19 advanced placement credits for Latin, Greek and Spanish; which meant that we were done! I did not have to enroll for the spring quarter. I was able to get a job as a lab assistant in the Plant Physiology lab that spring quarter, and I had a lot more time to hang out with my Charismatic friends. Martha and I spent a lot of time making the rounds of the prayer meetings, and Mass at Blessed Sacrament. She was not Catholic, but the Charismatics didn't care that much about denominations. To this day I don't know what denomination Jimmy and his friend were, but I was surprised to find out what had happened to them when I came back from the Peace Corps. I will write about that in the second volume of my memoir.

Martha took me to Whidbey Island before I left Seattle, so I could meet her parents. I don't really know what Martha thought about me; we were friends, certainly, but I don't know if she was getting serious about me. I certainly did not have any intention of getting into another relationship before going to Africa.

Gretchen tells of the time that Martha and I went to visit her in her one-bedroom apartment, to try to bring Jesus to her. She remembers that we were standing in the living room praying for her while she was in the bedroom packing to go home for the weekend. When she discovered our intentions, she said, "I can't stop you from praying for me, but I can stop you from doing it in my living room!" She politely (?) escorted us to the door, and sent us on our proverbial way. Fortunately, we did not follow Luke 9:5 "If anyone does not welcome you, shake the dust off your feet when you leave that town, as a testimony against them."

So, I made it through undergraduate school. I did not attend graduation, and in fact did not collect my bachelor's degree in Botany (awarded in 1970) until after I returned from Peace Corps. A lot of disturbing changes happened at the University of Washington, some for the better, some would ultimately prove to have been detrimental. One inevitable impact was growth. Gretchen and I visited the Greek Row area north of campus in 2013. Students were just arriving for the Fall sememster, and the narrow streets were completely jammed. The little apartment, that we had rented, on the back of the Farternity parking lot was still there but we did not even try to enter campus, because we knew that many of the beautiful open spaces on campus are now buildings. But what else can you do in this life but try to take your best shot and hope it is not aimed at your foot.

I recently decided to confirm that I was correct about the loss of open space at the UW Campus. As it turns out there still is a lot of open park-like space including the famous Quad, but there has been a lot of major construction in support of the "hard sciences". Huge buildings of computer science, and engineering were built. Most heart wrenching, my own department of Botany no longer exists:

> But on Feb. 1, after many months of planning and many more just wrestling with the idea, it finally came true. That was the date the Board of Regents authorized the departments of botany and zoology and the undergraduate biology program to merge into the new Department of Biology. https://www.washington.edu/news/2003/02/20/studying-all-life-new-department-combines-botany-zoology-biology/

They didn't even incorporate it into the Dept. of Environmental Science and Forest Resources, as they did at U. California, Berkeley. I am glad we did not go looking for my department, which was booted out by the Dept.

of Chemical Engineering. David Humphrey's old haunt. Isn't that just life for you? All the schools I have ever attended, with the possible exception of St. Rose, no longer exist. As happenstance would have it, sometimes I wonder if the whole of the civilized world is not just changing too quickly.

CHAPTER 18

The Solo Troubadour

"Take nothing for your journey," he instructed
them. "Don't take a walking stick, a traveler's
bag, food, money, or even a change of clothes.
Wherever you go, stay in the same house until
you leave town. And if a town refuses to welcome
you, shake its dust from your feet as you leave to
show that you have abandoned those people to
their fate." **New Living Translation (©2007)
Luke 9: 3-5**

AS I PREVIOUSLY STATED, WHEN I received the invitation from
the Peace Corps, I had no idea where Kenya was, other than that it was
in Africa. The one continent that I had not asked to go was ironically the
place I was to be sent. But in the immortal words of Alfred, Lord Tennyson,
"Ours is not to reason why, ours it just to do or die". Speaking of which,
Peace Corps was also a deferment from Vietnam! I was sure I would rather
fight bilharzia[165] and Tsetse fly than Vietcong.

Again, the events of the last month or two in Washington State are not
very clear to me, and there are no records to support my foggy memory. I
am sure that I made another trip to California before I left for Peace Corps
training. I believe Bob White and I hitchhiked to California together;
which was a feat in itself… but easier when you believe that you have "angels
watching over me, my Lord". I think we visited my grandfather in Tigard,
Oregon, but I cannot be certain of that. I do think that was when Meritt
wrote in his journal, "I think Mike is on the wrong track".

We managed to get a long lift from somewhere in Oregon practically right to the outskirts of Galt, California. I think we called my mother and Fr. Carl came to pick us up on the highway... I think. Doesn't really matter; the important thing is that we made it without ending up in a ditch. Luck of the Irish, I guess; I am Irish, Bob just looked like a leprechaun.

I do remember that Fr. Carl was pretty sure we had slipped a cog. I don't remember how long Bob stayed in the parish house in Galt. I think just long enough to eat and hit the road for Southern California. Never saw him again, so I have no idea if he ever made it where he was going. I stayed with my mother and Fr. Carl, and spent most of my time trying to convert them to Pentecostalism. Father could only take so much of it, so he escaped to his office to read his breviary, etc. My mother, on the other hand, had to listen to me pontificate. I sat on my haunches in a dining room chair, reading her Bible verses and assuring her that this was the true "way of the gospel". She probably wondered if I had suffered an emotional or mental relapse because of the break-up of the relationship with Gretchen. She knew what Fr. Tageson had said about my delusions of grandeur, but she did not say anything. This was unusual, not to get an argument out of her, because I had grown up arguing with her. I think she was just thankful that I had not left for Kenya without making the effort to see her. On the one hand, I am sure she was excited for me to be going to Africa, where she had dreamed of working with Fr. Heon in the Tabora mission. On the other hand, I think she had a lot of trepidation about me traveling so far away. She herself knew that she was experiencing heart problems, although she kept it from me, as she had when I was at San Luis Rey. It was actually more complicated than that: she had adhesions from the surgery in McCloud, which had caused hormonal imbalance issues, and she may have been in the early stages of diabetes although it was not diagnosed until much later. It was, in fact, her heart that eventually gave out, but that did not happen until she was 78.

Still, after a couple of days of "spiritual" haranguing, my mother and Fr. Carl had had about as much Jesus talk as they could take. I think I remember that she footed the bill to send me back to Washington by bus. I don't think I saw any of my other relatives on that trip, but I could not swear to it. I may have to correct that in future chapters, because I did visit my Aunt and Uncle when Ralph had returned from Vietnam. He was hiding out at the house of some friends, where I visited them and listened to the Grateful Dead while they smoked pot. But that was probably after I returned from Peace Corps.

Before I left for California, I had moved into Roy Gillette's basement as a temporary lodging until I would leave for the Peace Corps. Roy and Ruth were nice folks, religious, but not the preachy type. We Charismatics were a little over the top for them, but they were tolerant folks as well. Roy and I used to get up early, before he had to go to work. We would trek over to the covered swimming pool of a neighbor to swim,. It could be freezing but we would brave the elements; dry going there, and wet coming back. Roy had contracted polio when he was a kid, and I remember that he had difficulty swallowing. As it turns out, I just found him and Ruth in Loon Lake, Washington after 37 years. He has had several strokes and can no longer eat, due to complications from the polio. He can talk with some difficulty but we had a warm conversation over the phone., Even in the nursing home, he still feels his ministry is to make life a little more bearable for his fellows in the home. I have to respect him for that.

I know I spent some time at my Dad's house on the Toutle, when I came back from California. The reason I know that is because, I had taken my research project with me to Castle Rock, and I remember taking measurements on the growth of *Veronica filiformis*[166] roots in petri plates that I was holding on the sun porch. It was the report on that project that I had to rush to Gretchen. I delivered it to her where she worked in Miller Hall (the education department at the University of Washington), just before I left for Peace Corps training in Carolina.

Gretchen had also finished her degree a quarter early and had landed a job with Dr. Jarolimek, who was the Chair of the Department of Curriculum and Instruction. We often consider how different Gretchen's life would have been if she had kept that job as a Secretary II. Dr. Jarolimek was very fond of Gretchen and called her "Benny" (for Benedict Arnold) when she was preparing to leave for San Francisco. He sent Gretchen a Christmas card every year until 1999. If she had stayed at the University, she probably would have become an Administrative Assistant IV and retired with a full pension about the time when she was getting ready to come to Hawaii to marry me. Oh, the paradox of life, and the foolishness of youth!

I was in need of disposing of a lot of items that I had accumulated over the two years at UW. Most of my personal possessions, including a Hopalong Cassidy 1950 vintage cookie jar (which is now worth about $400), all went to a fellow I had met at the Fellowship. He was trying to get set up with a place to stay. I gave it all to him. My Corvair, as I previously mentioned, was turned over to a Christian half-way house for drug addicts, which Jimmy and I used to visit. The director of the house was supposed to have transferred the title, but before he was able, the Corvair was stolen and used in a crime in Chicago. Somehow, my Franciscan spirit of generosity would seem not to have seeded the fruition of good works. Had I kept and cared for the Corvair, it would now be worth somewhere between $2000 and $10,000.

I was only allowed to take 90 lbs. to Peace Corps, for which my Father had suggested a military issue duffle bag from the Bob's Surplus Store. You can bet I took my Bible, and some clothes, and not much else. For my graduation, my folks gave me a $70 wristwatch with jeweled bearings[167] (having worked with Mr. Cussics at the mill, I understood that the reason mechanical watches had jewel bearings was because they don't wear like metal on metal). It was the most expensive time piece I had ever owned. Most of the years I worked at the mill, I carried one of several $4 pocket watches in the pocket (which is provided for that purpose) in Levis' jeans. The wristwatch was probably one of the nicest gifts my folks had ever given me... with the exception of the bass, which has served me well for 49 years. Unfortunately the bass was one personal item that I could not take to Peace Corps. I left it with Roy Gillette, and he played it for the Honeycomb Fellowship for the years I was in Africa. When I came back and took my bass, Roy eventually found a refurbished wooden bass, and continued to play as long as he was able.

My personal effects and books which I could not carry ended up at my Dad's place on the Toutle. He had already built the addition to the Toutle cabin by that time. It was something he did not long after my mother left him. It included a bedroom that was half again as big as the whole of the original 24 by 24 foot house. To that was attached a bathroom with a bathtub/shower combo. It made the little cottage a lot more livable. I mentioned that he had also purchased a used Buick Riviera from a woman he was dating. He had joined the Elks in Kelso, and was becoming known as a kind of bon vivant. He loved to play golf, and in the evenings, he thoroughly enjoyed singing at the piano bar. He was apparently well liked by the members; so well liked that they elected him to the board of directors. I left for Kenya not having to worry that my Dad was suffering the loss of my mother.

I don't remember the flight to North Carolina, but I do remember the send-off that Martha, the Griffiths, the Gillettes, Emily Du and some other folks from Honeycomb gave me. All I was feeling was excitement, but I sensed that there was a little sadness in Martha's attempt to be cheerful. I did see Martha once after I came back from Kenya, but by then she had become heavily involved in a communal group at a black church in Seattle's Central District. She ended up marrying one of the white guys in that community, but I don't know what happened to her after that. Neither did Roy and Ruth, although they did, at least, remember her.

I do remember my arrival in Raleigh, NC. It was 3 AM, in the middle of a hot and muggy July. I had never been any place so humid. The airport was quiet with only the staff and an occasional passenger hanging around in the sweltering lobby. I asked the attendant at the ticket counter how I might get to town where Shaw University was located. The other attendants looked at me with a peculiar stare which I did not understand. You see, Shaw was, and still is, an all-black (then called "Negro") college in downtown Raleigh which is a Baptist institution. The attendant told me I could call a taxi, but I didn't think I wanted to spend my money for a taxi. So I went out of the small terminal to see if a taxi was even available. About then a large white Cadillac convertible with the top down pulled up in front of me. In it sat a very large man in a white suit and smoking a big stogie. For the life of me, I swear he looked like Boss Hogg on The Dukes of Hazard (although, that TV program did not air until 19 years later). He looked over at me and said "Where y'all goin'?" Well, you know I was up to date on the racial situation in the South – or so I thought – and I was not sure I wanted to tell this ominous looking man, who was driving around at 3 in the morning, that I was headed for a "Negro college". Nevertheless, I was young and gullible, so I told him that I needed to get to Shaw U. He looked me square in the eye and said "Shaaaww?" and then he said, "Git in!" Now I was beginning to be really worried, but I figured I didn't have much of an alternative by then, so I got in his Cadillac. Right off he started asking me questions, "What'chu want ta go over to Shaw fo'?" So I told him that I was coming for Peace Corps training, and that was our orientation spot. He seemed to accept that and continued his line of questioning. "Where ya from?", "How'd ya get interested in Peace Corps", etc. Bye and bye he pulled up alongside a collection of old buildings... that was a little spooky. Then he said "Yo' heer." I looked at him with a puzzled expression, and he replied "This is Shaw."[168] So I thanked the man, and unloaded my duffle bag from his boat of a car. He turned out to be a southern gentleman, and wished me well in my adventures.

Figure 37. One of the original buildings at **Shaw College**, founded in 1865, is the oldest historically black college of the south.

One of the original buildings at **Shaw College**, founded in 1865, is the oldest historically black college of the south. (Photo reproduced with permission of Keyunda R. Miller-McCollum, Ph.D. Director of Library Services Shaw University archive. CC BY-SA 3.0) https://en.wikipedia.org/wiki/Leonard_Hall_(Shaw_University)#/media/File:Tyler_Hall_Shaw_University.JPG

As I walked into what appeared to be the student center, people from the Peace Corps training program spotted me and took me to a bank of trailers that were serving as dormitory space for the campus. They gave me bedding (essentially just two sheets and a pillow with case), because that was all you needed to sleep in that heat. They told me what time the program would get underway in the morning, but they understood that I might need to sleep longer. As it turns out, I could hardly sleep, not just because of the newness of it all, but also because it was bloody hot. Within an hour my sheets were soaked with sweat.

For the next week, we took orientation classes at Shaw, because we were waiting for the campus of Kittrell College[169] to be prepared for the takeover by the Peace Corps training program. Shaw was actually in session, and black students were attending classes as we were occupying their campus. It was a very interesting experience for most of us, and particularly the night of the first moon landing[170]. Here we were, all the volunteers were white, half the PC staff was Kenyan, and the students from the college were entirely black. We were all huddled around a 20 inch black and white TV in the Recreation Center of an all-black college in the middle of the Deep South at the height of the civil rights movement. That college was founded in 1865 with the same sized endowment that opened Duke University in 1859. The latter has since grown into the College Triangle of the North Carolina State University, Duke, and College Park. Shaw University, on the other hand, is not much bigger than it was originally (less that 3000 students), and some of those first buildings still stand. Here we were, watching the first man step on the surface of the moon in a college that harkens back to the Civil War. Now is that ironic or just happenstance?

Kittrell College, the next stop on our journey, was and is even more iconoclastic. At the time we were there, it was still surviving as a 2-year black college. All of the buildings at Kittrell were the original 1886 structures. As the footnote indicates, Kittrell regressed in 1975 to a Job Corps center where young, probably mostly black, trainees learn the non-academic trades. Have we made progress, or is this all just happenstance? I can add Kittrell to the list of schools that I have attended that have since disappeared. You will recall, St. Francis Seminary has also become a Job Corps facility.

Don't get me wrong, I liked Kittrell. It was like living on an anti-bellum plantation. It was definitely rural, whereas Shaw had been quite urban. Raleigh was a big city even then, despite the fact that the sidewalks were "rolled up by 9 PM every night". Kittrell was ten miles or more from the little town of Henderson, NC. Looking at the satellite map, it isn't a whole lot more developed. The College itself is surrounded by woodland. I used to love to go walking on those muggy evenings and watch the fire flies do their light show to the accompaniment of crickets.

I must say, southern food is quite palatable, even dormitory food. I admit, it took some adjusting for a Yankee to have a big scoop of grits offered at every meal. Nevertheless, I learned to like them and they were a good preparation for Kenya, where corn meal cake is a way of life. The routine of the training program consisted of language classes every morning and cultural and other orientation classes in the afternoon. The latter consisted of geographic, agricultural, and medical information (e. g.about schistosomiasis, malaria, and other health hazards of living in East Africa).

The staff had set up a little "barn yard" and everyone was assigned to a turn at feeding the animals and milking the cow. One of the instructors formed a choir, so my bass voice got enlisted. Other recreational activities included some sports, and the "sports bar". The latter was called the Supa

Duka (freely translated, it means "super market"); which was really nothing more than a little shed where they sold beer and soda (I guess they must have had a refrigerator, but it would have been more "culturally appropriate" if the beverages were warm, because a "chilled" anything would be a rare treat in most parts of rural Kenya.

The Supa Duka is where George Gunkleman held sway regaling the troops with his tales of adventure in Brazil. He had done his first Peace Corps tour in that country at a time when conditions were not terribly stable. He was a large and burly man, full beard but sporting wire rim glasses. I don't know what his upbringing was, but he looked like he had been lifting hay bales in his youth. I guess a lot of the neophytes sort of considered him "extracurricular training". The 'suds' rather lubricated the lessons, as I recall.

The Supa Duka and the barnyard had all been recovered from the brambles by the PC Staff before training began. When each wave of trainees served their time in the milking barn, it was pretty easy to tell who had been on duty that day. Because the barn had been rescued from an overgrowth of vines and probably had been a habitat for any number of wild creatures, some of the fauna of that community remained; most notably the chiggers. I too served my time of scratching my ankles to a ruddy spotted glow from chigger bites. It was a good introduction to the kind of 6 and 8 legged critters we would face in Kenya.

There were some friendly local employees of the college with whom we enjoyed some palaver. The Peace Corps training staff were also, generally easy to talk with. Some could talk your ear off. I particularly remember Henson Nyange, who was a short little agriculture officer from Taita Hills in the Coast Province of Kenya. He was a very garrulous fellow who could imbibe with the best of them. How he managed to get through a morning of teaching after a night at the Supa Duka, I never understood, Nevertheless, he was definitely one of the best language teachers in the program. His rival was Nellie Mshila. Now she came by the skill naturally, because she was the daughter of the head of the Kenya National Radio. She was training as a communication major at a US College, and had done some acting as well. Henson was a surprise, because he, like the other agriculture officers, had never had any training in how to teach a language, especially by the High Intensity Language Training method (HILT). The basis of the HILT, in colloquial terms, is as follows: you throw the students in a room with an instructor for several hours a day. The instructor speaks only the language you are trying to learn, so the students just have to figure out what the instructor is trying to say. This is very effective if you have expressive people like Nellie and Henson, because they knew how to act out what they were describing. Some of the other instructors, particularly the Agriculture officers from Kenya, would just sit at the desk and recite the words to you over and over, with no gesturing and giving no clues as to what the words meant. Both Nellie and Henson had us in stitches (in the guffaw, guffaw sense) most of the time, trying every possible enactment that they could devise. If you think about it, that is how we learned our native language. There was another black instructor, who was a student actor, and I believe, American born, He was also good Kiswahili *Mwalimu* (teacher). Fortunately for everyone, the teachers rotated from classroom to classroom (or was it the other way round?). In either case, each student had the benefit of experiencing the teaching methods of the different *walimu* (teachers, pl.).

We were also being given instruction in cultural history, government, medical issues, and social etiquette. The agricultural training was relatively modest by comparison. This is where the other agricultural officers were most helpful, and little did we know that they were very involved in evaluating our performance. Near the end of home-country training, we were rated by the American and the African staff. A significant portion of the candidates were sent home. Of the remaining candidates, some had been voted against by the Kenyans, but the American staff decided to retain them. I am told that several of those individuals to whom the Kenyan's had objected, left the in-country portion of our training period during or soon after introduction to country. The Kenyans were aware of cultural issues that would be problematic for those individuals. One trainee, who was a graduate of an Ivy League institution, was slated to be assigned to the Ministry of Economic Planning. The Corps had high hopes for this fellow. Unfortunately, he had prepared for his journey by purchasing a lot of expensive equipment (cameras, etc.), but the airline lost his luggage in transit to Kenya. It disturbed him so greatly, that he quit the week he arrived in Kenya. There was also a married couple who voluntarily left during in country training; the Kenyans had suspected they might.

We who were selected to go to Kenya were relieved, although surprised at whom and how many left. The translocation to Kenya was an involved process, which consisted of three distinct stages, each of which took longer than one would expect. I think we had time to do some visiting Raleigh and Henderson before we left Kittrell College. As I said, the food impressed me; mmmm that southern fried chicken and chicken fried steak! I weighed all of 145 lbs at the time, so you can bet I was taking advantage of the dorm food as well as the allowance we were each provided for personal expenditures. Out last step of in-country training was being assigned to live with a rural family in North Carolina. I am told that some families lived in poverty conditions, with outhouses, and water drawn from a hand pump.

I am almost embarrassed to admit that Bill Berger and I were assigned to the Bullock Family. Mr. Bullock was the park ranger at Bullock Park on the North Carolina side of Lake Kerr. In addition, Mr. and Mrs. Bullock lived on Bullocksville Rd. Do you see a theme developing? Yes, the Bullocks were descendants of slaves that had been owned by the original plantation owner, Mr. Bullock. But our Mr. Bullock had achieved a position of relative status in the black community of the area. Not only was he the park ranger, but he also owned a vegetable sorting shed, where other black farmers would bring their produce (carrots and cucumbers mostly) to be sorted and graded for market. This was an additional source of income to their comfortable life.

The Bullocks owned a nice house which accommodated Bill and me quite comfortably. We would assist Mr. Bullock some when he had customers at the vegetable grading barn. Mostly we had 10 days of not much to do… except eat, and Mrs. Bullock liberally accommodated us in that regard. My god you have not tasted real southern cooking until you have tasted Mrs. Bullock's corn puddin'. Being young and foolish, I fed my face liberally without considering that I might get the recipe from Mrs. Bullock. To our good fortune years later, a dear friend of Gretchen's and mine, who was originally from North Carolina, gave us the recipe not too long before she was diagnosed with cancer, and died a short 3 months later. Sometimes the little pleasures in life seem all the dearer when the passing of a loved one reminds us how temporary is our lot.

Since Mr. Bullock had park duties on the weekends, Mrs. Bullock introduced us to her friends, and took us to the Sunday gathering at the local ball park; which, in itself, was a cultural "Brave New World" for Bill and me. We had never seen a social event that was so commonplace and yet so unique. It was commonplace to the local black community, because they gathered every weekend in the summer like this. Unique to us, because we were unused to see so many people who knew each other intimately and played ball, and ate and joked and bantered while the young folk from 4 to 14 were all line-dancing to "Popcorn", the latest single released by James Brown[171].

I met some people at the park who invited me to a soulful black church (not the one that the Bullocks attended) but more the gathering of the farmers and poor people of the community. Of course, I was game to try it, since I was missing my association with the charismatics. Bill, being Jewish, was not interested. The people, who invited me, picked me up at the Bullocks' house and took me to a small church somewhere in the vicinity. I had never experienced the traditional call-and-response style of the black clergy. I was moved that the people would call out in answer to most everything the pastor said. I do remember a plaintive rendition of the old spiritual:

Bye and bye, when the mornin' comes
When all the saints of God are gatherin' home
We'll tell the story of how we overcome,
And we'll understand it better bye and bye.[172]

It was obvious to me, from joining these people in song, that the Charismatic movement was not a new thing. That total involvement in the spirit and emotion of the service had been sustaining these long suffering people for two centuries. One can argue the rightness and wrongness of it, but when you are living in the middle of it, what harm if it gets you down the rocky road of life?

Lake Kerr, or an inlet thereof, bordered on Bullock Park which was not more than 200 yards from the Bullocks' home. So I would go down to the lake fairly frequently. My recollection was that Bill preferred to read. On my last visit to the lake, I left my watch on a park bench while I was taking a final swim. It was not until I had arrived back at Kittrell that I realized the watch was missing, and we were to leave for Washington, DC the next morning. Needless to say, someone in the former Bullock plantation was sporting a pretty nice watch. Some would have said I was carrying Franciscan-ism to the extreme; others would say I was exhibiting the early signs of a lifetime of forgetfulness. My daughter has that disease too! Whenever I suggest to Gretchen that I might be getting Alzheimer's, she quickly points out that I have been that forgetful "low these many years".

After we were returned to Kittrell, I made one last attempt to swim in the pond that passed for a swimming pool on campus. The water was a yellow green, but that is not what stopped me from indulging myself. The water was as warm as the air, such that it really was not refreshing to swim there.

The PC staff sponsored one last blowout shindig, which in Africa would be called a *sherehe*. It was to be as much like the Kenyan equivalent as we could make it. Nellie had trained the choir to perform "Mungu Ibariki Africa" (trans. God bless Africa), among other songs. The animals were to be slaughtered and roasted on open spits. I can't remember if the normally reserved agricultural officers did some kind of traditional performance. And then there was dancing to the wee hours.

The slaughtering of the animals was quite an affair. The Kenyans were adept at slaughtering the goats (a very common food source in Kenya), and the several farm boys in the group were not without skills in this area. George Gunkleman, on the other hand, was going to show us the proper way to slaughter a steer. The one we had was probably six months old, and not yet fully grown. So George's idea was to grab the steer by the neck and bop him in the head with a sledge hammer... which he did. Whereupon, the steer promptly let out a horrific "moooooooooo," and scrambled away as far as his legs could carry him. I seem to remember it taking nearly an hour to get the steer tied so it could be slaughtered. In later years I learned just how hard the forehead of a cow is. A colleague of mine tried to slaughter his steer by firing a 12 gage shot gun slug into the animal's forehead at point blank range. The same thing happened; the steer bolted, and had to be caught again to be slaughtered. After all the excitement, and when the food was served, I remember thinking how much tastier the goat was than the beef. To this day, I will not pass up an opportunity to eat barbequed goat or curry *ya mbuzi* (of goat or chevon).

An interesting aside: all of our European meat sources were given the French names by the Normans (e.g. beef from cow, poultry from chicken, pork from pig, and even mutton from sheep). Then why do you suppose it is that we don't have a French-derived name for goat meat? Well, actually we do have such a name for goat, although it is also sometimes called mutton (which is actually sheep). That name is chevon (from *chèvre*). I had never heard the word; I guess because goat is so uncommon in the Anglo-American diet. The Kenyans have no such affectations. Ngombe (cow) and mbuzi (goat) is the proper name whether on or off the hoof. If there is any confusion, the Kiswahili speaker will say *Nyama ya...* (meat of...).

I believe we started the journey from Kittrell the next day. We had a fleet of vans which took us to Washington, DC. We were then told that the flight arrangements to Kenya had not been completed, and that we would have a three-day layover in the Capital. We were given a stipend of spending money, but again I was not anxious to spend it all on a fancy, or not so fancy, hotel room. I did not stay with the group, but since we had arrived late in the day I did not have a lot of time to visit the museums. I ended up sleeping on a park bench that night, and went into the Washington Mall the next day. I visited the Aerospace Museum which was fascinating, and I may have hit other museums, although my memory is dim on that. What did strike me was the opulent grandeur of the government complex. I remember thinking that it was not unlike ancient Rome, and now we were beginning to conduct our affairs in the world like an imperial power. I was, in fact, somewhat dismayed, although I am sure the lack of sleep and fatigue from walking everywhere clouded my perspective as well.

I was walking by some street vendors in the afternoon when one of them called to me, and ask me who I was and what I was doing in Washington, D. C. It seemed like a friendly gesture, and I think he might have even offered me a hot dog (I guess I always looked hungry). We talked for a while, and then he said, "I have to close my stand and go home. Would you like to join me?" Seemed harmless enough, and so I did join him on his bus journey to his apartment complex in an area of DC that was obviously heavily inhabited by Middle Eastern folk. I was never quite sure what his nationality was, but he had a heavy accent. He told me his story and introduced me to his friends, but I don't remember any of it. I think we may have eaten at a local restaurant that served food from his country. Finally he asked me if I would like to spend the night. Again, I was not a suspicious person, and thought he was probably just being kind to a wayfarer. I certainly was not objecting to the concept of sleeping in a bed that night. So I agreed. When he took me to his room, I could see that the accommodations would be tight. He lived in what was essentially a bedroom with a bath. There was only one bed, but it was a double, so when he suggested that we both sleep in the bed, I thought maybe it was not unusual for two men to sleep in one bed according to his customs. I had read that it was very common place in Abraham Lincoln's time, and I knew that my neighbors in McCloud had slept several boys to a bed. So I agreed. I was so tired that I went to sleep almost immediately.

The next thing that I remember, I awoke to my host fondling my buttocks. What was more surprising was that I had a huge hard on. As soon as I realized what was happening I jumped up from the bed and into the bathroom which was on my side of the bed. When I sat on the toilet, I inadvertently ejaculated. This had been the one any only homosexual experience of my life, and I was quite disturbed about it. When I finally came out of the bathroom, my host apologized profusely, and asked me to go back to bed with promises that he would not do it again. And he did not.

When we arose the following morning, we went to eat at an all night diner. I offered to pay for the meal, but he would not have it. The conversation was much more strained, but he was very polite and guided me to the correct bus to get back to the center of town to meet the rest of the Peace Corps group. That incident would put a strange pallor over my whole experience of the capital city. Washington was synonymous with the war effort, fiasco, quagmire, and mistake. In my mind, I guess I was thinking *Tempest* and Aldus Huxley all together: "Oh brave new world with such people in it!"

Our next stop on the journey was New York City. Now that was a horse of a different color. The open avenues of greenery and bleached granite that was my general impression of Washington, gave way to towering sentinels of glass and stone, around which flowed a sea of confusing humanity. It was awe inspiring to drive over the bridge into Manhattan. Traffic blaring, yellow cab taxis weaving to and fro amongst the congestion. Again, we were ahead of the flight arrangements, so we would have to spend seven more days in this noisy bustling place. The staff delivered us to the Embassy Hotel, which is a haven for Foreign Service personnel and low level diplomats. I agreed to go in with seven or eight other guys on the price of a hotel room, because I did not know if I could get away with wandering the streets as I did in Washington, D. C. I might have slept the first night there. As it turned out, the prospect of sleeping in a room with a half dozen smelly, inebriated guys was not as appealing as the tide of humanity that was the streets of Manhattan in 1969.

Just walking down the street was kaleidoscopic. Suits, barefoot hippies, derelicts, Hassidics, street preachers, huckster, hawkers, blacks, whites, yellows, browns, blues-on-the-corner musicians all milling around, every one seeming to go nowhere but intent on going somewhere. The first miracle was the subway; for 10 cents you could go anywhere in the greater New York area. It was not pretty, but it was efficient. The second miracle was the street vendors, who were everywhere. I had never seen thick crust pizza; delightful! With fresh fruit, bread, vegetables, right on the street, you would not starve in Manhattan. I guess I did not see the impoverished side of the city... you probably could starve on the street there.

The next unique experience was a haircut. No electric clippers, just scissors flying around my head. Clip, clip, clip.. *Voilá*, done! I decided to buy some clothes that I thought I might need for Kenya. The haberdashery that I stepped into had everything I needed, and the prices were very reasonable. The denim shorts got me half way through my tour of duty in the African savanna. The socks did not last; I replaced them with some British product that lasted ten years.

I was already missing my bass, and needed some kind of musical outlet, so I stepped into one of those funky pawn shops that conjures up images of Rod Steiger in "The Pawnbroker" (although I did not see that movie until I returned from Kenya). I wasn't sure what kind of instrument to try. I looked at harmonicas; I had once owned an ocarina[173], a penny whistle would probably have been appropriate, but I wanted something more unique, and more bass. Then I saw it, the perfect instrument. The dealer told me it was a bass recorder[174], and I bought it... literally and figuratively. I say that because I was duped. What I actually bought was a tenor recorder. I decided I would take it with me as I wandered around the city, but it was too big to carry in a bag, so I purchased a leather bootlace and attached it to the recorder in such a way that I could carry it over my shoulder. This was fine, except that the police kept stopping me. I guess they thought it was some kind of weapon. When I explained and blew some notes, they left me alone. Actually, I met some pretty nice cops that way; I particularly remember an officer in Brooklyn who, after checking my "weapon" spent some time talking to me, asking about the Peace Corps, and explaining the layout of Brooklyn and various cultural facts of the place.

The rest of my recollections about New York are not going to be in any chronological order. They are just little vignettes of things that happened that I can still remember. I don't remember a lot of details like where or if I took showers, slept, ate, etc. But all of these incidents made an impression on me and have permanently influenced my recollections of the Big Apple.

In the early part of my stay, I tried getting a hamburger at a "greasy spoon". The waiter brought me a hamburger patty between the halves of a regular hamburger bun. That was it. So I looked at him with puzzlement and said

"Is that it?"

He kind of shouted back in that typical New York bravado,

"What? You said hamburger." (like the skit in Saturday Night Live[175]).

I said, "Is this all you get with a hamburger".

He said

"Whachu wan? Chu wan catsup, chu wan mustard, What?"

After a while, you realize that they are not being rude; that is just the way they talk in New York. And their concept of personal space ("my bubble") is much smaller than in the expansive western territories.

But there really wasn't much need to pay good money for a dry hamburger, because in every other respect the food in NYC is not only diverse and delicatessen-ish, but it is also damn good. With that being said, the only sit down meal that I can remember occurred just before I left NYC. I had been to Greenwich Village several times, and I had tried to look up the Franciscan parish there. The day I found the church, a priest was on the steps talking to a young blonde woman who seemed to be in some need of assistance. The priests apparently could not help her, so I took the liberty to ask her what she was doing in New York. The conversation began simply enough, but it ended up over dinner in a lovely little sidewalk café that served French food. It turns out that she had come from California to upstate New York to help her aunt who was ill and in need of a caregiver. But her aunt had died and so she spent what money she had taking care of probate and the dissolution of the estate. There was so little left, that when she arrived in New York City, she had only three dollars left to her name, and no contacts or relatives on the East Coast. We actually spent the whole evening together, and we talked about the Peace Corps and many other topics. I not only bought her dinner, but I paid $20 so she could stay at the YWCA for that night. Of course, I had to get back to the Embassy Hotel, because we were slated to leave of Kenya the next morning.

Here is the ironic part of that story. After I had been in Kenya for several months, I received a letter from this woman. We had not exchanged contact information, but she had tracked me down through the Peace Corps Office in Washington DC. She had enclosed $20 in repayment of the lodging I had spotted her, and she described her success in the Big Apple. She had landed a well-paid job, leased an apartment, and was generally enjoying life. She was very grateful for my small bit of assistance. I should have written back to her, but life was much too hectic at the time, and I have never heard from her again. Perhaps if she ever reads this she will track me down again to bring me up to date on her adventures. She will have already read mine.

Speaking again of Greenwich Village, it was, from my perspective, the most interesting part of NYC. Evenings were filled with all manner of people, wealthy and poor, straight and gay, actors and academics. This is because the Village is also the location of New York University, which basically surrounds Washington Square Park, the entrance to which is a great arch.[176]

In 1969 the entire park was teaming with people day and night. There is a central fountain, with grassy knoll surrounding it. There were hundreds of people there all the time, playing Frisbee, music, mime, mahjong, mayhem, and maybe even making love. In all, it was a glorious place to hang out and breathe humanity. The first night that I spent in the Village, I was befriended by a muscular man who assured me that he had been pugilists and would watch out for me. The problem was that he was so stoned or inebriated or drugged that he could hardly stand up himself. I expressed my gratitude for his concern, and we spread ourselves out on the lawn in front of the fountain and went to sleep. Because of my previous experience with the gentleman in Washington, DC, I woke up in the night, and moved away from the boxer. I found that a local church was open so I went in and continued my slumber on a pew. When I went back in the park the next morning, I did not see the boxer again.

The convenience of NYC is that where ever you are, at a moment's notice you can decide to be somewhere else. Just find a subway terminal and go. The next time I came back to the Washington Square Park, it was after dark, and there was a Hare Krishna group chanting and dancing around the great arch in the park. I stood and listened to them for quite a while. I was trying to reconcile in my mind why their form of worship was any different in its fundamentals than the Pentecostalism that I was still professing. I know some of my friends would have prayed for their "occult practices" to be thwarted… and suddenly the police were descending on us. You can't imagine the eerie feeling as blaring police sirens were closing in from the east, west and north through the long boulevard that was lined with trees and echoing apartment buildings. The Hare Krishna folks continued to chant as they wound their way out of the crowd like a serpent heading for its den. When the cops did arrive, the Krishnas were gone, and the cops were questioning everyone,

"What is going on here? Why the big crowd?"

I and my "zip gun" were not about to stay and explain, so I too wound my way out of the crowd and headed for my "den". I think I may have tried to play the Krishna chant on my recorder when I reached a quiet corner of the park.

The connections between India and the early Christians are an interesting speculation.[177] Although the belief in Krishna is much older than Christianity, the parallels between the story of Krishna and the gospel of Christ has not been ignored.[178]

The question for me has always been, if you tear away all the traditions (historical and mythical context of the religion), in the end, does it make the devotee more happy or peaceful or loving? I have known of Hare Krishna groups many times during my life. I think we even have one in Hilo or on the Big Island, which produced our current Congresswoman, Tulsi Gabbard. They are notable for their communal life (like the early Christian church). But then so are the Buddhists monks, and many other religious orders. I guess the key is, can you believe, but more so, if you believe, does it make the world a more peaceful place?

When you read about all the crime in the big cities, and you wonder if you are safe walking out your door, you probably wonder how in God's name I made it out of NYC alive. Well, I don't know who to thank for it, but I did survive New York. I spent quite a lot of time in Central Park, which, although not such a conflagration of humanity like the Village, was more of a pasture of people, like cattle munching their grass in the sun. Fortunately the weather was beautiful the whole time I was in NYC, and that tends to bring the folk out to Central Park. I don't have a lot of visual memory of it, probably because it blends into all the idyllic pastoral scenes that I have had the pleasure to peruse in my life. It's ironic that the park would have that impression on me, because it is surrounded by bustling cityscape. But that is the charm of Central Park; you can almost forget that you are in the midst of a great city, until you look up!

One evening, there was a concert in the park; Schaefer Music Festival with a ticket price of $2.00. It didn't make any difference that I did not buy a ticket; because I could hear it all perfectly well from outside of the crowded venue. I have always preferred that to being trapped in the crowd, blasted with amplified sound, and wishing for the nearest opportunity to escape. When my daughter was about 2 years old, her mother and I went to a Santana concert at Afook Civic Auditorium in Hilo. We had paid full price, but I walked in the auditorium as the band was already playing. It was so loud, that I did an about face, and walked right out the door with Colleen on my shoulders. Again, it didn't matter, because we could hear every bit of the concert at reasonable amplitude, and Colleen and I were able to dance to the music.

One of the lead groups at this Central Park Concert was Patti LaBelle and the Bluebells[179]; Saturday: August 23, 1969 (With Sam & Dave). I had remembered it was the Supremes[180], but their Central Park performance was not until Wednesday: August 12, 1970 (With The Meters). Now it might have been nice to see the Buebells, but I could hear the music perfectly well. I didn't feel that I had failed to get my "money's worth". At least now, with the Vidéotrons, you can be far away from the performance and still get an up-close- and-personal view of the performers. I just figured I was lucky to have heard Patti in person and I can always see "Diana Ross in Central Park" on YouTube[181].

That is about all I can remember about NYC. It was my first and last look at this iconic symbol of American affluence. Of course, we all saw much more of this great city in the aftermath of the 9/11/2001, but in summer 1969 the feeling of New York City was jubilance. Change was in the air, and there was anxious anticipation of what those changes would bring. It is ironic how the grand events of history play out on the world stage, media, and government, but the lives of individuals go on almost un-impacted by these events. Now that we have World News 24/7, we at least can learn what the main events were each day. Two hundred years ago, the common man didn't even know what had conspired to change his life until months and sometimes years later. I wondered, at the time of my departure from NYC, if the people I would meet in Kenya would be more or less oblivious to world events than were the New Yorkers.

I don't remember much about the flight to Kenya. We were chartered on a British Airways flight, so we were the only passengers. I remember there was an excess of drinking because the alcoholic beverages were all free. I didn't much appreciate the smoking section either, except that my recollection was that there were relatively few tobacco smokers in the Peace Corps group. That was not common amongst an average group of American youth at that time. There were pot smokers among the volunteers but it was not allowed on a government chartered flight. Our first stop was at Paris, but we were not allowed to debark. We looked at the Eifel Tower off in the distance of a gray morning. We all would have liked to have stayed longer.

Our next stop over was in Rome. We were given 12 hours to explore the Eternal City. We all took the same bus into Roma, over the dry summer planes of the Etruscan Garden of Eden. At least that was what it was in the time of the Etruscans. But it is now a far cry from the fertile land that it was. The Valley of Latinium is estimated to have been able to support 1000 people per square mile according to Carter and Dale 1955.[182] That may be an overestimation[183], but whatever the case, the soil around Rome no longer supports that kind production. In fact, the growing of grapes and olives was a concession to the deterioration of the soil around the whole Mediterranean region, because they can survive and produce on relatively poor soils.

Coming into Rome was definitely an eye opener. I just wish I had studied harder in Sister Gurtie's Latin class. A few things are easily recognizable like the Coliseum and St. Peter's Basilica, but there are amazingly ancient buildings and landmarks wherever you turn. There was no way to do Rome justice in 12 hours, so I stuck with the traditional haunts. Again, being an independent cuss, I did not stay with any of my confreres. Not knowing any Italian, I was winging it, but I managed all right. I was most impressed with the chocolate gelato that I bought from a street vendor just outside the

Coliseum, and that heightened my senses for the visual feast that was before me. As I mentioned before, I went to St. Peter's, and was impressed as much by the papal sarcophagi as I was by the artwork. I was still trying to reconcile in my head the palatial opulence of the Basilica with my knowledge of the practice of selling indulgences and the corruption of the Medici popes who promoted construction of this towering edifice. Neither the Franciscans nor the Charismatics put great store in such worldly glorification. I will say I was impressed with St. Peter's, but I was not edified.

On the other hand, the sleeping popes had a somewhat profound effect on me. Not that it changed the course of my life or anything so dramatic. Nevertheless, it came as close as anything I had previously experienced to providing some evidence of the belief which had been up to then, only faith. Of course, one can always find a scientific explanation of why these several popes had been preserved, when so many others decayed. But at that time, in the frame of mind that I had, it was quite convincing; particularly Pius the tenth, with whose life I was familiar.

Since the day was passing quickly, and I had not yet had a midday meal, I decided to look for a *ristauranti*. I did not have to wander far, because there are places to eat all over Rome. The place I found was in a small, whitewashed building. We have a little restaurant in Hilo that was opened by a man from Italy, and he had decorated his little café not unlike the one where I ate in Rome. The floor is cobble stone; the walls are plaster with an open beam ceiling. The entrance opens onto the street and there are vines around the doorway. It was cozy, small, almost like eating in a Mediterranean home. I don't remember what pasta I ordered, but I will never forget the taste of it. My Dad's good friends, the Sabarbos, had a restaurant in Weed, CA. The ravioli was hand made by the grandmother who barely spoke English. Somehow this *ristauranti in Roma was* better than Mama Sabarbo's. The best 7,000 lira I ever spent! I almost forgot the gelato that I purchased from a street vendor. This pasta and sauce was the most surprisingly delicious taste I think I had experienced to that point in my life.

Completely satisfied, I sauntered back to the bus stop in plenty of time to catch the airport shuttle. Because I was early, I had time to just wait and watch the local color. Just listening to the Italians yammering was enjoyable. No one ever accused the Italians of being tongue tied. I remember trying to sound out *"Arivaderchi Roma"* on my recorder. The other volunteers drifted back and we were off to the airport and our approach to the Dark Continent.

CHAPTER 19

Kuungana Kufanya Kusaidia Kenya
(Work together to help Kenya)

"Let us travel through your land. We will stay on
the main road and won't turn off into the fields
on either side. Sell us food to eat and water to
drink, and we will pay for it. All we want is
permission to pass through your land." The
descendants of Esau who live in Seir allowed
us to go through their country, and so did the
Moabites, who live in Ar.
**New Living Translation (©2007)
Deuteronomy 2:27-29**

THE FLIGHT WAS UNEVENTFUL, AND the weather was clear
so we could see the African Continent passing beneath us. Two things
impressed me: the vastness of it and the bareness. Hours passed and all
we could see was savanna with infrequent trees and tan sand (we were
too high to distinguish animal herds or small villages. I am not talking
about the dunes of the Sahara; I am talking about the Sudan, which blends
seamlessly in the planes of northern Kenya. It was a great relief to see the
green slopes of Mt. Kenya popping over the horizon; as we passed over
Marsabit Natural Reserve and then Namunyak Wildlife Conservation
Trust[184]. Of course none of us knew what we were seeing. After passing the
three peaks of Mt. Kenya,[185] the landscape changed dramatically. We were
observing the high plain on the eastern side of the Great Rift Valley. The
land is fertile and green and populated with small farms, large plantations
of coffee, tea, bananas, dairy farms, etc. The area was formerly known as

the White Highlands.[186] We were entering a nation that was only six years old, although the indigenous people had been there since long before the 16th century CE.[187] Now that is an irony of circumstances![188]

After we landed, we were greeted by the Peace Corps in-country staff, and escorted in a collection of vehicles to the Peace Corps Headquarters on Muindi Mbingu St. on the western edge of Jivanjee Park. There was an orientation, and then we were taken to lodging in the area. I thought it was called the Embassy, but neither of those names appears on Google Map. It was near the public market. For the two or three days that we were there, a young Kenyan befriended me and showed me around the local area. He took me to the public market which is called City Market in English, but I forgot if the lad referred to it as *Sokoni*. I still have a picture of the boy, but I have long since forgotten his name.

Fresh 'bowl' haircut with new Kitenge shirt which my young **Kikuyu friend** help me buy at the Sokoni. (Author's personal photograph)

The hotel came with breakfast which was tea, toast, egg and sliced fried tomatoes. Ugali[189] was optional, and meat was extra so I did not usually order bacon. At first I tended to stick to foods that I knew, but I soon became a devoté of the Indian Samosas. I bought a couple of kitenge shirts and got the worst haircut I had had in years. We were informed that the National Agricultural Fair was in progress; so since we were the Agriculture V group, the Director and staff took us to the fairgrounds. The only thing I can remember is ordering a foot-long hot dog with mustard. I didn't know that the mustard was the Chinese style which is loaded with horse radish. A hot dog is just not a hot dog with horseradish; but I was, as always, hungry, so I ate the whole thing.

The day we went to Embu to complete our training, we were advised about the different forms of transportation. Bus or taxi was most common.

Some areas were served by train (at that time, still mostly steam engines); Embu was not. I think we were taken by Peace Corps contracted taxis, which were of tourist quality. The local "taxis" were also called matatu[190], which at that time were mostly Peugeot sedans or station wagons. These were usually owned by the driver or his financier, and were often driven dangerously (hence the other explanation of the name matata, which in Kswahili means "trouble"). I took one to Nairobi from Embu, but I was glad that I was eventually assigned to a region where I could catch the train when I needed to go to Nairobi.

In Embu we were housed in a Farmers Training Center which was very near the Kenya Agricultural Research Institute (KARI), Embu branch. It was well equipped with running hot and cold water (something which would soon become a luxury). Embu is on the slopes of Mt. Kenya, so the mornings were brisk and the nights were cool. I was impressed with the natural surroundings, and judging from the Google satellite map, the whole area is still very agricultural with farm fields and orchards ringing the small city. I was particularly impressed with the African Tulip tree, which I had thought was a Jacaranda. For a "botanist" that was pretty far off mark. Jacaranda is a temperate deciduous species that bloom in delicate purple flowers; African tulip is a non-deciduous tropical species that sports huge whorls of orange flowers. African tulip is an invasive species here on the Big Island, but I must admit it puts on quite a show when it blooms. The highway passing the KARI was lined with old African Tulip trees.

The Training Center was comfortable, and the food was good. The British had cooks who were almost always local Africans or Asians. With the departure of many of the colonial officers, many of the cooks were left without work. We were almost instructed that we should hire these displaced workers when we went on assignment throughout Kenya. In keeping with this directive, the Peace Corps Training program had hired recommended local cooks from Embu, and they understood western cooking quite well. As I remember it, they did not even attempt to feed us

African cuisine, not even ugali. Perhaps it would have been better if they had. We had to learn sometime!

I don't remember whether we were sharing rooms, but I think we did, because I think Bill Berger and I were rooming together. East meets west, referring to him being a New York Jew, and me being an Irish Mick from the logging camps in Oregon. We got along pretty well, being both a bit different than most of the volunteers. Bill liked to read a lot and I liked to wander around the highways and byways reading my Bible and playing my recorder.

The instructors were mostly the same group that had taught us in North Carolina, so the language training continued unabated. The main difference was that now some of our other cultural and technical classes could be with Kenyan sources. We spent time with the instructors and students from KARI. We were also given instruction on motorbike operation. As part of our induction, they issued us Kenyan licenses on the US State Department authority, and that included permission to drive motorbikes. Once we had learned to drive, we were allowed to take the bikes out on short jaunts in the Embu area.

I mostly did my touring around the town on foot. I would meet students from the local high school on the road, and they were always anxious to speak English, while I was trying to use Kiswahili. Some students invited me to a local Anglican church, which I did attend several times. At the end of training, I actually got evaluated by the Peace Corps staff as having integrated within the local community better than most of my peers.

About half way through the in-country training we were distributed to local farm families, to live with them for ten days and participate in farm life, as the Kenyans lived it. I was assigned to a Kikuyu family in a village called Kithunguri. The father was the principal of the local grade school. He had several children including two teenage daughters. I got to know these daughters very well, because I helped them mound potatoes for days on end. The farm was a relatively large one by local standards, something like 10 hectares (about 20 acres). Typical of such small holder farms, they grew many of the things they needed right on the farm. They had a milk cow, several goats and chickens. Maize was crucial, potatoes were their cash crop, cassava was insurance against the failure of the rains, and plantains (starch bananas) were another source of carbohydrates. They also had a variety of small sweet banana that were heavenly. They were similar to the Hawaiian banana we call Apple or Candy banana. Apple refers to the fact that slightly under-ripe bananas can be baked in a pie and taste just like apple pie. Passion fruit had been introduced as a cash crop, but was actually more useful as a vitamin source, since a marketing system had not been developed. The principal was very receptive to the agriculture Extension Officers' suggestions for increasing the production of cash crops. This was urgent for him because he was paying school fees for his daughters and other children.

There source of water was a catchment cistern that was fed by rainfall on the roof of the buildings. They were very careful with the water for two reasons: 1) there was not much of it, and they had to be very judicious to make it last through the dry seasons; 2) the water was contaminated by airborne organisms and bird feces. I would get so thirsty doing hard manual labor in the fields all day that when I came back to the house, I was desperate for water. They warned me about drinking the un-boiled water, but I couldn't help but drink right from the tap. It was not until the last day on their farm that the practice caught up with me.

I tried my best to make a good impression by working hard to keep up with the young ladies in the potato field, but it was obvious that they had been doing this job since childhood. It was my first clear impression of how hard the women of Kenya work. They would joke and banter with me in English. Although these Kukuyu girls knew some Kiswahili[191], upcountry people are definitely not fluent in this language which was a trade language developed from dealing with the Arabs along the coast of Africa. We managed to get the entire field of potatoes mounded so that the tubers would develop in the soft loose soil. Mounding also reduces moisture loss by breaking up the capillary action by which water evaporates from soil. This was important because potatoes have a large water requirement, but once established, they put down deep roots that can extract water for a long time after the rainfall ceases. The major problem with potatoes in the tropics is *Phytophthora infestans* [192], so it is an advantage not to have rainfall in the later stages of tuber development. The moisture spreads the spores and mycelia.

Evenings were quiet, but it was interesting to observe that family interactions. They were not unlike those of any American family, minus all the technology. The mother of the children only spoke Kikuyu, so any time she wanted to communicate with me, the girls or the father had to translate. The father would ask me questions which I did not have the technological knowledge to answer. He finally gave up trying to get new information out of me. He spent time with his kids, assisting them with their homework, and advising them on how to succeed in school. By evening, the daughters were fully talked out, and I was usually half asleep by the time we finished the dinner. Mainly dinner consisted of Ugali and vegetable stew (there was usually a small amount of chicken or goat in the stew). They had kept a private room for me, but, of course, it was probably one (or more) of the children's room.

The family rooster seemed to prefer to take up his daybreak post right outside my bedroom window, so there was no worry that I would oversleep on any given day. The rooster's concept of daybreak preceded mine by a couple of hours. I was able to make it out of bed and to the breakfast table every day, such that they could not call me a shirker. I have to admit that I was so relieved that the last day was a Sunday, because I was already suffering the early stages of dysentery. When the Peace Corps vehicle picked me up, I was able to hold it until I got back to the Training Center, but then all hell broke loose. I think I did not make it to the dining commons for at least three days. We did not have a doctor on staff, so I didn't report my condition to the senior staff. I am sure they knew that I could be "plug-up" using the Peace Corps issued pills that contained opium. But the staff could not or would not offer this relief. Perhaps they felt we should learn how to deal with this common ailment. We had previously been instructed about the importance of eating only simple starches and liquids. The procedure worked, but it was extremely painful. After receiving an in-country assignment we had the salvation of a staff doctor that prescribed the antidiarrheal (opium) pills by the case. But I had learned a valuable lesson on that trip: be careful whence your water cometh.

Kiswahili class was going very well, and most of us were getting adjusted to the concept of living in a foreign country. Some volunteers started spending time in the local bars. Others were biding their time until they could get assigned. Others spent most of their time with their peers and the Peace Corps staff. I was not interested in maintaining close association with the staff, although I liked most of them well enough. I was intent on learning what I could about the place and the people.

Not long after we had been out on the farm assignments, we had a holiday. I talked to Bill about taking a trip up country to the place I had stayed. I forget where he was assigned, but he was game to see where I had been. So we took out a couple of Triumphs, and headed up the slopes of Mt. Kenya. I don't know how I found Kithunguri, although it was only about 10 miles from Embu as the sunbird flies. When we got to the farm of the principal, we found that the daughters were back in their secondary boarding school. The father showed us how to get there, so we went on to the school and managed to meet the daughters. They seemed quite pleased to see us. They were not able to show us around the school, but they were not in class because of the holiday. So we talked for some time. Then Bill and I headed back to the Training compound. I don't think I kept up a communications with the daughters. I think it was discussed, but I did not have time to correspond with family, much less short term acquaintances.

As our training was coming to a close, and decisions had been made about which trainees would leave country, the Peace Corps Agriculture

Program Director met with each of the future volunteers and suggested where we might be assigned. The volunteer, being just that, is not required to accept an assignment. Also, even after accepting an assignment, if the situation is not compatible, the volunteer can ask for reassignment or return home. This could occur a total of 3 times. If the volunteer rejected a third assignment, then the volunteer would be responsible to get him-/herself back to the USA.

When I met with the Director, he told me that they wanted me to go to a place in the Coast Province called Taita-Taveta District. I was to be a Youth Extension Officer, in the Ministry of Agriculture. He let me know that I was allowed to visit the assignment if I wanted to check it out. I asked him how I would do that. I can't remember if he said it would be totally at my expense, but for whatever reason, I did not feel comfortable to travel first class. So I took a matatu to Nairobi, and then I traveled by train to Voi, which is a town on the rail line in Taita-Taveta District. I wanted to be frugal, so I decided to buy a third class ticket for the trip to Voi. This proved to be very interesting, if not very comfortable. Third class is basically a box-car-like carriage with maybe three benches of seats. Everyone else sits on the floor or wherever. When I boarded the carriage, the first thing that caught my eye was a Maasai[193] lying on one of the benches clutching his spear close to his chest. I was not about to tell him to sit up so the women with babies could sit down. Instead I took up a position right under the water station. This was a ceramic urn with a push valve to draw the water. This was a wise decision on my part. Although the water urn was frequented often during the trip, the night was very warm, and there were probably 30 or 40 bodies in the carriage. My advantage was that as people drew their water, they would spill drops of water on my head, which kept me sufficiently cooled through the night.

The train arrived in Voi at 3 AM, so it was still dark, and I did not know where I needed to go. The station master finally directed me toward the Voi town center, as the place where I could get a bus to Wundanyi, the

District Headquarters. It was about a mile to the town, and I was not even aware that I could have run into elephants or baboons or, worst of all, plains buffalo. Well, oblivion is bliss, and I made it to town without incident. When I arrived there was a 1950 vintage tan bus, under which a light had been suspended. When I approached it, I realized that there was a man working under the bus. I called to ask if the bus would be leaving for Taita. He came out from under the buss on his mechanic's wheel board. I was surprised to see that this stocky man was wearing dress slacks and a white shirt. I thought, "What a strange custom." The man arose and handed me his wrist to shake so I would not get greasy. He explained that the bus needed repairs, and that he was hoping to have it fixed some time by the morning. I am not sure, but I think there was a local café open, and he pointed me to it. There is a national bus line that also comes through Voi in the night. Voi is 400 miles from Nairobi, and it is another 60 miles to Mombasa. There is also a bus that goes to Arusha, Tanzania. That takes it through Taveta town on the boarder of Tanzania. Voi is an important rest stop for the weary travelers heading to either destination. I think I ordered a samosa and a cup of tea, consumed them, and then found a bench to sleep on until daylight.

The bus was not repaired by daybreak but a crowd was gathering, and the conductor and the driver were working with the man I had met to try to get the bus rolling. Finally the task was complete; the gentleman washed his hands in some solvent and put on his suit jacket for the trip to Wundanyi. What I came to find out is that the gentleman was Jared Babu, the Treasurer of the County Council, and he had to get to an important meeting in Wundanyi, which is why he was single handedly fixing the bus in those wee hours of the morning! I would come to know Jared Babu much better in the future. Sometimes I think this bus incident was just one example of how he single handedly held the County Council, and by extension the District, together.

I would also find out later that this bus was called *Lukundu kwa Wose*. That means "love for everybody" in Kidawida, the language of the Wadavida

(Wataita) people. I would have many more encounters with *Lukundu*. Now you must understand, that, in order to keep your mind off the hazardous nature of a trip in *Lukundu*, they hired a conductor who was pure comedian. In the two years that I would spend in Taita, I never learned Kidawida, so I could never understand the banter of the conductor, but the humor was palpable. One time a drunken passenger had them stop the bus so he could urinate. He was too drunk to disembark, so he stood in the doorway and let fly. The conductor had the entire bus absolutely in stiches of laughter with his commentary on the *Mughosi wa Mlango* (commander of the doorway).

It was fascinating to watch the terrain crawl by as we wound our way up the hills to Wundanyi. I was sitting next to a man whose name was Washington. He said his parents had named him in honor of the famine aid that had come from the United States the year he was born. The heat and the smell of the bus were horrific, but the humanity was intriguing. The luggage, except for a few chickens, was carried mainly on top of the bus. Just loading it required two men, and when it was fully loaded the bus' center of gravity was raised considerably. Tricky on mountain roads, but that was not as questionable as the brakes. When the bus would reach a stop, the conductor would jump out and place blocks on the wheels so the bus would not roll away during debarkation. And did I mention that the roads were not paved? During rainy season, they were not roads, but stream beds. Fortunately my first trip to Taita Hills was in dry weather.

When we finally reached Wundanyi, it was already late in the afternoon. Jared Babu led me up to the County Council offices, and then pointed out the District Offices which were a little higher on the hill. I walked into the Agriculture office only to find that Patrick Katingumu, the District Agricultural Officer (DAO), was about to leave work for the day. Nevertheless, he invited me to his home for tea. It was one of the large houses built for the colonial officers, which Katingumu occupied by himself with his male domestic, since he was not married at the time. After we had talked briefly, he walked me through a valley that connected the officer's compound to the County Council hotel and restaurant, suggesting that I lodge there for the night, before I needed to take the return trip to Embu. He did not attempt to introduce me to any of the other officers who lived in a compound near his house (he could not call as there were no phones). That was the first taste of the formal relationship that I was to have with Katingumu. He was a responsible officer, and did his job well, later being promoted to higher levels in the Ministry; a member of the Kenya Coffee Board for Machakos in 2005. But, what I would come to find outs that the local people would called him a *Mzungu Mweusi*. That is, 'black white person', or 'black foreigner'. The British were noted for their aloofness during colonial times, and some of the young Kenyan officers thought it was their duty to carry on the tradition. I am not even sure what was tribal affiliation Katingumu. I assumed he was either Kikuyu or maybe Kamba (Machakos District).

The County Council Hotel and Restaurant (hereafter referred to as the CCH) was Spartan. The Council had built a dance hall with a kitchen attached, and probably later decided to build a few rooms for lodging, and a bath and toilet area. The bed was small, the bathwater was cold, and the food...well; that requires some explanation. The cook was one of those who had formally worked for the British, so he took pride in his knowledge of European cuisine. The problem was that they only served a couple of things at the county council. You could have beef with ugali, chapatti, or rice. That would be served with an 'appetizing' side of lettuce leaf (wilted in au jus). The chapatti was the thick African style. Whereas an Indian cook will roll out the chapatti 20 or 30 times, each time placing a layer of olive oil or gee on the flattened dough, the Africa will roll it out 5 or 6 times. The Indian chapatti (, it is called bhakri, I am told by our Pakistani restaurateur in Hilo). It is maybe $1/16^{th}$ inch thick and flakes apart easily, whereas the African Chapatti is perhaps ¼ to 3/8ths inch thick and barely flakes. Oh, and by the way, the beef is "grass fed" dry plains zebu cattle. The perennial question is, which is tougher, the cured hide of a zebu or the meat itself.

One adjusts, but it also explains why the Kenyans have such strong teeth. Nevertheless, the food did not lack nutritional value.

I did not meet any of the other officers or volunteers on that brief trip, but I met the local Taita people, and I was charmed. The cook at the CCH was quite proud to serve me the fruits of his labor over a hot wood stove, and Jenifer, the waitress was most pleasant. She was a large, jovial woman, who would also play a significant role in my life.

When I awoke in the morning, there was a gnarled old man chopping wood outside my door at the CCH. This man always had a hand-rolled cigarette in his mouth, and was almost as gnarled as the wood he collected. He would bring in the strangest collection of twisted branches to be chopped small enough to fit in the kitchen woodstove. He greeted me with the Kidawida saluation, *"Kwawuka?"* Of course, I did not know what he was saying, so I answered *"Jambo, Bwana"*. He was not satisfied. So he extended his hand to shake mine and put his other hand around my elbow and said *"Kwawuka?"* again. I answered *"Jambo sana"* and shook his hand back. This repeated several times, and then he gave up. What I learned later was that he was asking me "Are you up?". I was supposed to answer *"Nawuka"* (I'm up). Then he would say *"Kwa wuka mana?"* (Did you arise well?), and I was supposed to answer *"Nawuka mana."* (I rose well). Then he would say *"Kwa wuka mana putu?"* (Did you rise well, exactly?), and I was supposed to respond *"Nawuka mana putu."* or just *"Putu!"*. This would become a daily routine (almost a ritual) between him and me for the year that I would live at the CCH. I would find out on another occasion how important it is for a young person to exchange greetings with one's elders.

I had a breakfast of white bread (shipped in from Mombasa), and local eggs, with coffee made by putting scoops of Nestle's instant coffee in boiled milk. The latter was quite good and eye opening! Then I wandered over to the Town Center of Wundanyi which consisted of a loop road circling a public market, and surrounded by shops. Everything you could get in Taita Hills would be found here. Petrol, hardware, butcher shop, tailor, cobbler, bank, supply store (*duka*), etc. were all in the town center. There were an amazing collection of fruits and vegetables in the public market, and for unbelievably low prices. Of course, you had to haggle, but the Wadawida took great pride and enjoyment in their haggling. I remember it being explained to me later. Coming right out and stating the price (or anything else) very directly was not appreciated in Taita; nor, for that matter, the whole Coast Province. They used the expression "*kifimbo*". I could not find it in any of the on-line Kiswahili dictionaries, although one website defined it as 'a little branch' when used as a proper name. It might have been a Kidawida word, but it meant a little stretch, from reality, if you will. It was a playful way of making sure that the listener was paying attention. You were expected to understand that what was being said was not the whole truth and nothing but the truth. As I said, the Wadawida loved to barter.

And I loved what I was seeing in Taita. Wundanyi was at 3000 ft. elevation, so it was fertile and green and somewhat cooler than the surrounding savanna (which, by the way, was Tsavo Game Reserve). Wundanyi proper had a tree lined park with large soccer field, and a stream ran along the edge of the park. I liked it immediately, and decided that I would accept the assignment.

On the return trip to Nairobi, I splurged and bought a second class train ticket. This was much better; it purchased a seat in a sleeper compartment. You might have four other passengers assigned to your unit, but it was roomy and you could put down an upper or lower sleeper cot and stretch out if you so desired. The train is a genteel way to travel. You have time to observe the country you are passing through, and the rhythmic sound of the rolling stock striking the rail joints is very soporific. Kenya Railways was all built on narrow gage track so the maximum speed was about 35 mph. The passenger cars of that time were all wood construction, black leather upholstery, roomy bathrooms, and excellent dining facilities. The most enjoyable part of the trip was traveling through Amboseli National

Game Park[194], where you could see most of the plains animals while you ate breakfast.

I actually have a tape recording taken later in my tour of duty, on which I recorded a trip from Voi to Nairobi, where George Gunkleman and Dave (who was stationed in Nairobi) were traveling in the same compartment with me on the East African Railroad & Harbors (EARH) train. With the rumbling of the rails in the background I asked George to comment on rail travel. Keep in mind that George had already been living in the bush (veld) for some time, with an elephant's skull for a latrine, and boran cattle for company:

Me	"We are on the EARH which takes 24 hours to go 300 miles. Do you have any comments on the train?"
George	"No… I think, it's a pretty civilized way to travel… actually." [Said hesitatingly]
Me	"Is that all you have to say?"
George	"Well, I don't know… It's a bit slow…but quite civilized… unfortunately the bar has closed early tonight… and that curtailed probably the better part of the social evening. However… like I say… it's quite CIVILIZED… even though it does enforce a bit… of what I would refer to as early retirement. You have to go to bed at 9 o'clock or 10 o'clock. It's just hampering my social life… but other than that… it's quite nice. First class must be something phenomenal, but second class… I think… is quite a bit of luxury."
Me	"You say…it's civilized as compared with…?"
George	"Well, you know, just about other… all modes… Airlines these days are sooo…you know, hurried sort of a thing. You get… you get pushed through here and you get pushed through there. You know, some stewardess gives you some thrown together piece of airborne hodgepodge… she calls… well, a meal? On the train everything is much slower… but relaxed."
Me	"You can say that again!"

George   "Yes… well… a berth… be a berth what it may, it does have… you know… one does not compare a berth with a queen sized mattress…but aaah, but a berth does have its selling points! Relative to a tourist class CHAIR… in an airline..Huh? I mean chair… you know… relative size… there not the same thing we loth to sit in for luxury…you know? They expect a man to sit for hours in these things on the airlines… in what they call the blessing of a tourist fare… you know, economy class. The sort of thing… why it's no class at all!

And then we got into a discussion about who threw George's pillow on the floor and I said,

Me   "They almost threw it out the window."

George said "almost doesn't count [long pause]… Anyway, as I say, the train is quite nice."

Then George was off into a discussion of the discomforts of traveling the Tsavo in a Landrover. We discussed the vegetation and the elevation and debated about whether the animals we saw were Thompson's Gazelles, while the rhythmic rumble of the slow moving train climbed to the high plane of Kenya.

It might have been on this return trip from Taita to Nairobi that the Director invited some of the volunteers (that were also returning from their site visits) to come to his house for lunch and to see the Rift Valley. In retrospect, I believe he lived on the road where Baroness Karen von Blixen-Finecke[195] had lived. The Director's house was an old colonial one- story "mansion" that had an all thatched roof. A 55 gallon drum on a raised stone (or cinderblock) stand was the firebox where they could burn wood to heat their bath water. It was high enough that water would flow into the fixtures in the level house. I was always impressed with the ingenuity of the settlers, and the Director was enjoying the fruits of their labor. The Director and his wife were from Australia, so I think the life in Kenya was no stretch for them. And besides, the Kenyan staff builds the fires to heat the bathwater and cook their food.

After lunch, we walked out the road to the point where there was an overlook into the Rift Valley. You have probably seen that view in the movie *Out of Africa*.[196] The Valley is impressive in its sheer vastness. While we are on the subject of movies, if you saw "Ghost in the Darkness"[197], you have seen Taita Hills, which forms the backdrop (on location) for that movie. While we were walking back to the Director's house, we came upon a young Maasai warrior with full regalia and spear. Some in the party asked to photograph him. Now Maasai, and some of the other tribes, had the belief that having their picture taken would steal part of their soul. However, this young buck agreed to the request. After the pictures were taken, he demanded payment. Obviously he had lost his tribal superstitions and had become an 'entrepreneur'. Three of the volunteers from our group were assigned to Maasai Mara. Only one remained for the whole tour, and he was a priest on leave from the diocese of Chicago. Maasai have some strange customs about which I hope not to forget to tell you in later chapters.

The next day Bill and I departed for Embu, and the final stretch of our training program. Now I was getting anxious to get the training over and get on with the job. In my restlessness I was feeling guilty that I had not attempted to do any proselytizing among the Peace Corps trainees, so I thought I would try my luck on the unsuspecting local Embuites. I would play my recorder on the streets in the evening, and although most just looked at me like I was crazy, some people took an interest. One woman in particular (whose intentions – as I would later discover—were not spiritual) engaged me in extended conversation. She convinced me to buy her a beer at a local hotel, and while I was trying to talk to her about Jesus, convinced me to rent a hotel room with her. By that point, I was aware that she was a prostitute and that she had income in mind. But for me it became a contest; who would win the spirit or the flesh? It was a close contest, but I was able to get in a lot of spiritual discussion attempting to translate my King James gospels into Kiswahili which she barely understood. What a comedy! In the end, when she was almost sure she would have me, I pulled out my wallet, gave her 40 Kenya Shillings, hugged her and left. I am sure she was shocked.

Who knows, maybe it changed her whole life… I will never know because I never saw her again. What I realize now is that I was playing with fire, and would eventually get burned.

Very shortly after the "Jesus and the Prostitute" incident, we were called in for our final Kiswahili examination, and evaluations. I got a Foreign Service Institute rating of 3 out of 5 for my vocal Kiswahili (we were not tested on our written skill). Three was considered conversational. Four is professional and five is fluent. I think I did better than average for the training group, but that is not surprising, considering all the languages I had studied. Admittedly, Kiswahili is very different than any of those European languages, but I was rapidly developing a facility with the Bantu structure.

After the evaluations, about half of the original trainees remained, and we were ready to have our final induction orientation in Nairobi. It was a combination swearing in ceremony and party. We were all relieved to have made the grade, so to speak. Assignment of available vehicles were being made, with four wheel models going to volunteers that would be posted to the Northern Province, and the woman veterinarian who was assigned to the District of Lake Baringo.[198] I think her name might have been Gayle, and she was the subject of a Peace Corps documentary that I saw several years after I left Kenya. The motor bikes were all assigned, but some of us had to wait for a new order of Hondas (175 cc.) to arrive.

So without further ado, on a Saturday, I headed off to Taita on the train to Voi. Second class, of course (now our travel was covered by PC, as well all the expenses incurred). However, I don't think the DAO arranged transportation for me to be taken to Wundanyi, so I think I had to hoof it over to Voi with my 90 lbs of personal effects and take the bus to the Hills. The DAO had arranged for me to book a room at the CCH on a long term basis, so *Lukundu* dropped me at the CCH, and I got settled in before the week began.

The first day at work, who would be there to greet me but my Kiswahili instructor, Henson Nyange himself. It was nice to have a familiar smiling face among the all Kenyan staff of the District. I did not meet the Danish Volunteer on that day. The DAO assigned the acting 4K Advisor to take me under his wing and show me the program. Soon after independence, the youth program in the Ministry of Agriculture, had been patterned after the 4H program in the USA, where the four H's are Head, Heart, Hands, Health. Similarly, the four Ks are *Kuungana Kufanya Kusaidia Kenya*, which means 'Join together to work to help Kenya'. As an example of the limitations on development in countries like Kenya, the 4K Advisor was actually the graphics technician, who manually drew the maps, signs, and other documents needed in this low tech environment. Because land adjudication was in progress in Taita, there was a lot of demand on his services to document the newly divided parcels of property being created. In addition, his only mode of transportation was an ancient Triumph "one-banger", as we use to call it. Constructed on a sturdy frame, and having only one very large cylinder, this classic motor bike had served him well over the years (it was his personal possession). Whereas the Kiswahili name for motor bike is piki piki, the locals referred to his Triumph as tuku tuku, because of the deep throaty sound of the single cylinder engine.

At the meeting on my first day, I was also introduced to Karisa who was an officer who had been trained in Canada, and was most interested in discussing his time in the "North Country". He and I would have a mixed working relationship over the two years that I was in Taita. The District Officer, who is the principle administrator for the district government, was also trained in the west at Oklahoma State University, although I did not meet him until later. Henson and Karisa were principally involved in crops production. There was a livestock officer, but I seldom saw him. The bulk of the staff were Agricultural Assistants (AA), who were assigned all over the district and had no other form of transportation than muscle. A few AAs had bikes, but mostly they traveled on foot. The AAs were provided housing, if they desired to have it. None of the AAs were present for this first meeting with the greenhorn Peace Corps volunteer.

I will call the 4 K Advisor 'M' because, for the life of me, I cannot recall his name, although I think it might have been of the Madoka family. M took me around the local area of Wundanyi on the back of the Triumph for a couple of days before the rains began; after that motor bike transport was impossible. The local AA and the 4K leaders somehow got the message by the *Matunda* vine that we would meet them at a predestinated spot. [I am probably embellishing here; more likely we visited whomever we could find at home.] During his period of responsibility, M had documented the establishment of ~30 4K Clubs, but in recent years had not been able to serve the organization as well as he would have liked. The clubs, or *vyama*, had not fared so well without active support from the Agricultural staff except a few AAs who were intent on working with the children. Unfortunately, after the two days, the rains put a halt to traveling.

Besides settling into Wundanyi life, I spent the work days racking my brain to think how we were going to get the 4K movements back on an uphill climb. Talking with Karisa and Henson, they suggested that we might try to have a training session for 4K leaders at the Wundanyi Farmer's Training Center. So I put my mind to how we might go about doing that. I was dependent on the secretary at the Agriculture office to type up and mimeograph letters to the various AAs around the district, because, in the end, it would be the AAs that would make the contacts and invite the 4K leaders to Wundanyi. It seemed reasonable to try to have the training sometime later in the rainy season, because planting would be finished and the road conditions might have improved by the time the people would have to travel to Wundanyi. There are so many small details that need to be worked out when you are new in a country and new to the local staff. I was the low officer on the totem pole as far as office work was concerned, and I had to negotiate in as friendly a manner as possible. When you don't have a typewriter, and the secretary doesn't have time to type your documents, or she can't read your handwriting, or she doesn't like you, or whatever, it is hard to move ahead. And if you ask her to retype a document because of a mistake that <u>you</u> made in the original draft… well, you know you've got problems! I did finally talk the Peace Corps out of a manual typewriter, and then all the secretary had to do was mimeograph my documents, with mistakes and all. I have to give the typist credit though. Like manual typists the world over, they learn not to make mistakes! Otherwise they have to re-type the whole document, usually with several carbon copies.

So between M's transportation problems and my inexperience, things did not move very fast at first. M did take me to Werugha Valley when the weather cleared. Werugha is the vegetable growing center of Taita Hills, and supplied vegetables to Mombasa. Consequently they were concerned to have their children learn agriculture. So there was a concentration of 4K clubs in Werugha.

Not too long after I arrived in Taita, I received word that my Honda 175 had been shipped to Voi. I think I got a lift to go pick it up, and when they unloaded it at the train station, I was most impressed. It was blue and white with lots of chrome. I was looking good! I hopped on the bike and high tailed it over to Voi town. That's when I realized that the oil had been drained from the crankcase to ship it. Oops! I quickly added oil, but I will never know if my subsequent problems with the bike were related to that first mile *sans* oil.

The bike seemed to take the hills well, and you can bet I was proud when I came "putt putting" into Wundanyi town. The kids along the road were shouting *"Mzungu!"* and *"Piki piki!"* At that point in time, the only other motor bikes in town were M's and the Danish volunteer's. The Dane had been out of town when I arrived, so when he came back to town, he heard that I had arrived, and made a point to find out where I was staying and visited me at the CCH. His bike was an earlier model of 175, so we compared notes, so to speak. He had been having reliable performance from his machine, which was good to know. I think Bent Hansen (which was his name), invited me to have dinner at his house the first time we met. He had acquired a cook who was a truly talented fellow, and could really cook European style. I particularly remember his leeks in white sauce. Bent was a graduate of Horticulture from a Danish university, and he was assigned to increase vegetable and potato production in Taita Hills.

Another visitor who greeted me right after I moved into the CCH was Tom Wolf. He was a Peace Corps teacher at the Wundanyi secondary school, which was only a short walk from the CCH. This was my first major disappointment in Taita. Tom was a hot fingered blue grass guitarist, and I did not have my bass!*%#%& I still regret that; we could have taken the Hills by storm! Still it was very enjoyable to hear his strumming and wailing. "In the Pines" was a favorite. Tom had a teenaged Taita boy who worked for him, but they were also good friends. His name was Shako, and he and Tom would visit the CCH often. Tom sort of took on the duty of my Peace Corps mentor. PC teachers did not have vehicles, so I seem to remember that Tom used to hitch a ride with me from time to time, to visit areas that he either had not been to or wanted to go back. Tom was in the second year of his tour, so he left Taita about a year after I arrived.

Now that I had a bike it was not so hard to get around meeting the AAs and, through them, meeting the club leaders. The plans were forming up for the Adult 4 K Leaders Training Course. These were usually week long events where the Ministry of Agriculture housed and fed the participants for the duration. The DAO was supportive of the concept, or if he wasn't, he was feeling some pressure to support the Youth. So he agreed to foot the bill. I realized that I didn't have much experience to offer the leaders, but I made a determined effort to get as many of the agricultural staff as involved as time would allow. The District Officer gave the opening address, and the DAO had his part to say. I believe Karisa and Henson also taught a section on their crop areas. We tried to get as many AAs to come as possible, to encourage the exchange of information between them. The Home Economics extension staff people, who were all women, were also very helpful. I don't know, maybe I am imagining that the course was a lot more successful than it was in reality, but at least there had been a lot of hype about youth education, and I think it kind of got the ball rolling again. Some of the 4K leaders were also school teachers, and the Training Course certainly stimulated interest among the schools.

That interest at the primary and even the secondary level gave me the idea to do a series of lectures in the schools. In the first school term, my USPC performance report indicates that I conducted 22 lectures at various schools in the whole district.

M had made an effort to get me over to Taveta soon after I got my Honda. Taveta is a town built around an irrigation scheme on the border of Kenya closest to Arusha Tanzania. It is 60 miles from Taita Hills, and is inhabited by a tribal group that is closely related to the Wadawida, but they are called the Wataveta. The trip to Taveta was fun. Traveling across Tsavo Game Park, stopping to let Elephants pass, watching the herds of wildebeest, zebra, giraffe was exciting. The return trip was more akin to terrifying. Going to Taveta the murrum road surface was packed down, almost like concrete, and was easy to negotiate, even for a neophyte like me. But while we were in Taveta, the road surface was broken up by a road grader. That helps remove the built up "washboard", but the murrum[199] became powder. After a pleasant day with the Home Economics extension agent, the 4K leaders and members, we were late to hit the road back to Taita. Unfortunately, I was not experienced at riding in powder, so I verily crept back to Bura. M would go ahead of me, and then wait at the top of a hill on the road to see if I was behind him. This happened several times, but M was getting anxious to get home. So when we were pretty close to Bura and the road that leads up into the Hills, he waited for me one more time. When he spotted me in the distance, he took off and I didn't see him again until the next time I went to the Wundanyi office. It freaked me out a little, because it was getting dark and "there be wild beasts out there". Nevertheless, I made it to Bura and up the Hills. Ironically, it was the last time that M went on any 4K tours with me.

As we talk about the outer regions of the District, I need to discuss Sagalla Juu. It is a mountain range southeast of Voi which is inhabited

467

by another ethnic tribe, the WaSagalla, who are not closely related to the Wadawida but speak their own language, Kisagalla. I don't remember when I first reached Sagalla, but it was probably after I was issued a 4 wheel vehicle. I don't remember traveling there by motorbike. I might have been taken there in a Ministry of Agriculture vehicle, but I don't remember. The road was not good, but when you got to the mountain valley there was a whole community that lived there. It was not a trip that you could do in one day, but the great thing was that the Catholic Church had a rectory in Sagalla Juu, and they let me stay in their little house when I was visiting. It had a water catchment, a flush toilet, and was nicely furnished. That made it easier to make the trip. Since there was only one road into the valley, once you got there, all of the visiting had to be done on foot. I can see from Google Map that Sagalla has not changed that much over the years. There are obviously more houses, but the roads have been extended very little, and the access road is just as crooked as it ever was.

I liked the WaSagalla, and that is probably why, when I got a "Freedom From Hunger Grant" to purchase rabbit breeding stock, I worked with the 4K leader in Sagalla to receive some of the breed rabbits. In fact, I delivered them myself, shortly before I left Kenya for the last time.

I wrote a letter to Gretchen at the end of 1969. I am a little embarrassed at the effusiveness with which I described life in Taita Hills. I suppose I was trying to get in some digs at Gretchen for turning down the chance to travel around the world.

> Dec 19. 1969
> Dear Gretchen and Hugh,
>
> I am really sorry that my first two letters to you never reached you. I had some really interesting things to tell you about Africa and the culture over here. Now I'll have to write it all again.
>
> Thank you very much for your letter and for the greetings from Hugh and Judy and Dan (Of course I remember, how could I forget?). Please wish them the best of everything for this New Year. Believe it or not, I am very glad to hear from you; as Aunt Mary

put it "If friends don't write very often, it's a good indication that they don't expect anything to come in the way of their friendship." How's that for a pat excuse?

It's true that people really are that great over here. If you like the feeling of the American Black community, you would really dig its "ancestral heritage". And Taita is the epitome of good natured East African (really it has the reputation all over Africa of having the prettiest girls and the friendliest people of any tribe). They have been greatly westernized and Christianized of course, but they still have a very distinct, very warm mountain culture.

And, Oh God, are the girls beautiful. I'll send you some pictures, Hugh, it will literally blow you mind! Sorry Gretchen, but even you keep telling me that black is beautiful. That's not the half of it. The girls here are so docile, hardworking, and even tempered. Maybe the Lord doesn't have plans for me to go back to the seminary after all; but I hope I am not just rationalizing.

The country here is really something, too. Taita is a range of hills that rise out of the plains of Tsavo National Game Park, to 7000 ft. to a series of valleys and rocky peaks that have everything in common with Switzerland except the weather (some people say the Smokey Mountains or Scotland). In my time here I have been through Tsavo twice on my Honda 175 (piki piki) and to the beautiful white coast of the Indian Ocean (Mombasa) twice also.

The greatest thing about Africa is the most surprising relief from the American rat race, which everyone always talks about, but you just can't believe until you've tried it. Who ever heard of not locking your door at night or walking through the woods at night without fearing any trouble? There are practically no queers and criminals, and even the prison guards here don't have to carry weapons. The strangest things you will see here are the *wazi wazi* (these wild woods lunatics that run around making people laugh) and the denge [sugar cane brew] drunks.

You probably won't believe this but even babies her don't know how to cry. If a kid starts to cry they just laugh, bounce the kid around and whistle to him. Eventually he gets so that every time

he wants to cry, you just laugh at him and he'll start laughing too.
That's the God's truth (I'll send you a tape of it.)
Take care and God bless, and write again.

Love in Jesus,
Mike

In the winter of 1969, the 4 K leader training was a success and the teachers were getting used to having me visiting. We encouraged the school gardens, which in some areas already existed. So we were off to a good start. As we approached the end of the year, there were celebrations in Wundanyi. One of these was Kenya Independence Day, Dec 12th. There was much activity in the soccer field with dancers and drummers, and speeches, the works! I was much impressed by the Makonde.[200] They were a tribal group that had been distributed all over East Africa by the British, probably at the time they came under colonial rule in 1920. So there are small communities of Makonde in places like Taita-Taveta. What was so interesting about them was the dance that they did with carved wooden masks and some of the dancers were on stilts. I was very impressed.

Later in the evening I heard drums coming from an area beyond the public market in Wundanyi. I followed the sounds, until I came upon a traditional Taita drum and dance ceremony. The Taita (Wadawida) drumming is much more plodding than the complex finger movement of the Makonde. The Taita drums came in many shapes and some were large drums made from tree trunks. The heavy rhythmic pulse of the drums would send the dancer (mostly elderly ladies) into a trance-like state as they danced. It was a little spooky, but I liked the deep sound of the big drums and the way the drummer would slide his palm over the drum head to create a tonal shift.

The work schedule in the Coast Province was the kind of thing you see in movies about Central America. The hours are Four-two-two; four hours on, two hours off, two hours on. Siesta for lunch? Actually, I came to find out that it doesn't work that way. For the officers who could afford domestic staff, they could sleep from 12:30 to 2 PM. But for the average employee, that was definitely not the case. Few employees could even walk home for lunch, and if they had 2 hours, they would use the time to do things that work prevented them from doing, such as going to the market, sewing their own clothes, making tools and items that are needed domestically. I learned very quickly that you do not interrupt a secretary from her needle work during the two hour lunch break. The field staff did not keep the 4-2-2 schedule, because they usually had to walk an hour or more to get to their field sites. Then an approximately equal amount of time was spent returning from their work. I don't think there was a rule that they could not charge their travel time to the government, but six hours didn't give one enough time to accomplish the demands of the job. And when they did arrive home they had wood to gather, food to cook, dishes to wash, clothes to wash by hand, not to mention animals to feed and pasture and crops to cultivate. Marriage is much more of a necessity than a luxury for a working man in Kenya.

I soon realized that I couldn't do it. If I worked my full day, I didn't have time to do anything else but chores. At first, I ate exclusively at the CCH, which meant two meals a day of basically the same food every day. So I got a pressure stove and some utensils and started cooking for myself. I was trying to wash my own clothes in a bucket. Then I had to iron them with a device that needed to be heated on the pressure stove. And even just warming enough water on the pressure stove for a bucket-bath took time. If I wanted to do any reading, I had to fill the pressure lamp, pump it, light it (which often involves replacing the mantle), and then keep it pumped up for however many minutes it was needed. I couldn't throw my dishes in the dishwasher, and there definitely weren't any paper plates and plastic forks. We in the west are so spoiled by all the conveniences we have that make an 8 hour work day possible. Even then, more and more of us are eating out several times a week. So when Jennifer suggested that she knew a woman who needed a job to support her 4 children, I told her to ask this woman to meet me at the County Council. Now so far, I mentioned that most volunteers and locals had male domestics. But it did not seem strange to me to have a woman employee, because my own mother was housekeeper for a Catholic priest (in retrospect, not the best example). Jennifer was a friend of this woman, and apparently she thought I was trustworthy enough to recommend her friend to me.

When Charity Mshoi came for the job interview, I realized that her Kiswahili was a lot better than most people in Taita Hills. I asked her why. She explained that she had lived at the coast for several years (three of her children were fathered by an Mdawida who worked at Mombasa). So I suggested that perhaps she could be my Kiswahili instructor. She in turn said that she wanted to learn English. My Kiswahili got much better, her English, not so much. At first she came in the evenings so we could study after my work day, but I would often not be ready because I was doing my chores and trying to feed myself. Who had time for a one hour Kiswahili lesson? She suggested that she could come earlier and help me with cooking. One thing led to another, and in no time, she was doing my laundry, ironing, cooking, cleaning, and then I had some time left for Kiswahili/English lessons.

I knew that Charity had children and needed the money, so I paid her better than the going rate for domestic services. But I was curious about her family, and I kept asking her if I could meet them. So one day she brought her youngest son, Samuel Mzae.

Charity brought Sam to the County Council where I was living so I could meet her youngest, who could not walk. (Author's personal photograph)

He had been injured by an injection when he was an infant and his left leg had failed to develop properly, He was about 3 at the time, and was not walking. He was a cute little guy with a big smile if I could get him to quit turning his head away (shyness). I still didn't feel like I knew enough about the family, so I kept asking to meet them. She finally relented and one night she took me home to the homestead of her Father and Mother.

Although I did not know it at the time, the Mshoi farm is on the edge of the escarpment that boarders the eastern side of the Wundanyi Valley. If I were wandering there alone in the dark, I could easily have walked off the edge of a several hundred foot drop. In fact, the family's water source is a spring a short way down the side of the cliff. One wouldn't want to fetch water in an inebriated state! Some individuals had been known to take the plunge. The hike to Charity's home was about a mile, mostly uphill. The whole area consists of foot paths through the farms of the local land owners. It was the homeland of the famous Kiwinda family, to whom Charity's family was related. It was one of the first areas to be adjudicated into privately owned property. The feeling of traveling through a collection of mud houses with a flashlight in the dark was kind of eerie. I don't know why; I was probably safer than I would have been in New York or Seattle. There were no predatory animals at that elevation and population density. Small monkeys called *watima* inhabited the area, and contended with the human children who were sent to chase them out of the maize field in the daytime. But I didn't know that much about the area while I was passing through in the deep darkness, broken only by the flashlight and the dim light emitted from the open doorways of some houses.

When we walked in the door of Charity's family home, I was greeted by three pairs of white eyes, and dark faces that could barely be made out in the dim light of the candle. Charities father was seldom home, because he was a carpenter, and worked and lived with his son Wilson in Voi. Charity's mother was a short weathered woman with strong boney hands and piercing eyes. I always wonder if she had a premonition of what would happen. The conceit was that I walked Charity home to protect her in the dark, but we all knew that she was probably safer than I was. The children were disarmingly polite. Samba was the oldest, at that time about six years old. Mzae was between four or five years old. I was captivated; they were awfully cute. Let's just say, the next time there was a celebration at which the Makonde danced, Sammy was on my shoulders, trying hard to keep his head turned away from the scary dancers on stilts, but somehow he just couldn't help but look. When the dancer in the large mask lunged at Sammy, his eyes (which were eye to eye with the mask) were the size of silver dollars.

Life got quite a bit easier, thanks to Charity. I could devote more time to work, and there was much to do. Besides the school lectures, I had to visit with the AAs and do farm visits. I also needed to become familiar with the Chiefs; each area or sub-district had one. They were the law and the government at the most local level. They settled land disputes, appointed representatives to the county council, arrested the occasional drunk, and knew everything that went on in their jurisdiction. You really couldn't have and effective program without the support of the Chiefs. One day when I was heading over to Werugha Valley on my motor bike, I encountered the Chief from Werugha on the road. Soon after, the white haired Rev. Jeremiah Kiwinda came hiking up the hill at a healthy clip for this 80 year old man. A conversation ensued, which I was enjoying astride my bike, when all of a sudden the bike rolled backwards and into a 5 foot deep trench that the recent rains had eroded. I was extremely embarrassed to have the Chief and the Reverend helping me pull myself and my bike out of the ditch. I would like to have had the tape of the Kidawida that was going through the Reverend's head; but I can bet the translation would sound something like this: "Young whippersnapper! Can't get around without a piki piki, and then he can't even remember to keep the brake on when he is standing still." I think it was one of the few times that I met this patriarch of the community in person. He attended many events where I saw him, but that was the only time where I actually heard him speak.

One such event was the dedication of the government secondary school at Mwatate. It was to be named Kenyatta High School, and on that occasion, none other than Jomo Kenyatta himself was the featured speaker. And a rousing speech it was. Even I could understand the paced upcountry Swahili as his booming voice was punctuated with the wave of the fimbo (a horse-tail-cum-fly-whisk[201])

President Jomo Kenyatta **with his** *fimbo.* (Originally published in Somaliland Times.) http://www.somalilandtimes.net/sl/2005/225/19.shtml

Say what you will about the animosity between the tribes of Kenya, it was apparent to me that this man was highly revered by the populace of Taita-Hills, and people came from all over the District to see the First President of Kenya. When he finished his speech there was resounding applause and jubilant outcries from the huge crowd. I had my camera, but I didn't dare take pictures, as there were *askari* (policemen) closely watching the crowd.

Jeremiah Kiwinda had been involved in the establishment of another High School not far from Mwatate, a few years earlier. The Bura Girls' Secondary School was an Anglican facility on the old highway to Wundanyi. It was also the seat of the only Anglican church in Taita Hills. It was a large stone church built in the gothic style so favored by the Anglicans. When I first passed it, I was surprised to see such an impressive structure in the middle of the Bura rain forest. The school had a fine reputation, and I would come to know some of the teachers from that school. Bent Hansen would get to know one particularly well.

In my travels around the District, I was finding that there were some enterprising youth; with their *shambas* (gardens) they grew lots of different produce. There were also those who had animals. Goats and chickens were the most common. Goat and cattle were common sources of meat; chickens were so rare they were considered almost a delicacy. If a Mdawida (the singular of Wadawida) wanted to impress his guests, he would serve chicken. Even for weddings, beef was present, but poultry was a sign of affluence. This is probably because of the impact of Newcastle Disease[202], which devastated the otherwise common domestic fowl. What seemed to have no agricultural value was the rabbit. A number of the children kept them as pets, but my impression was that people did not eat them. Since we had been instructed how efficient small animals are in converting grass to protein, and because rabbits were not susceptible to Newcastle disease, I made it a point to try to encourage the use of rabbit as a protein source. Little did I know that after all the ensuing years, and having myself raised as many as 200 head of rabbit at one time, my last wife, Gretchen, would refuse to eat rabbit. But I should tell that story later; I am jumping ahead of myself.

The next program on the agenda was a training course for the 4K Members themselves. This would be more fun for me, but it would be a lot of work. First, we had to figure out how many young people we could accommodate, and then how they would be brought to the Wundanyi Farmer's Training Center WFTC). In most cases their parents brought them on foot, but for faraway places like Sagalla and Taveta, we had to arrange for government transportation. This we did with the DAO's approval. With the adults, all we had to do was provide them instruction in the daytime, but at night, they took care of themselves. Young people (there were girls and boys) need supervision even at night, so programs had to be arranged. Karisa and Henson were a big help with this, because Karisa was familiar with the concept of Summer Camp (maybe he had been a counselor at one in Canada). So we made arrangements for a big campfire. There was no place to have a fire at the WFTC, so I consulted the staff at the CCH, and they thought it was a good idea to have it in the open space around the CCH. I paid the old man ("Kwawuka") to cut extra firewood for the campfire, and Karisa prepared song sheets for the event. One I remember was *"Panya Watatu Vipovu"* (Three Blind Mice).

The WFTC had a cook staff, so the standard diet was routine. I had some additional surprises for the cook staff during the young peoples' program. I bought a collection of canning jars on a trip to Mombasa (must have had them shipped back to Voi by train). The WFTC staff had harvested a lot of tomatoes, so I showed them how to can them. I don't remember if the kids were able to observed the process because the kitchen was small.

Also I went around to the various 4K members who were raising rabbits and bought enough to feed the whole crowd. That was quite a crazy scene. The day that I was going to feed the 4K members rabbit, I had to slaughter them. At that time I knew nothing about how to slaughter a rabbit. So here I was, trying to cut their heads off with a butcher knife. Very messy and downright cruel; it would have been kinder to use a meat cleaver. I think the kids could hear the rabbits squealing. It was only later that I learned the meaning of a rabbit chop; i.e. a sharp blow to the back of the neck which breaks the rabbit's neck and kills them painlessly. With some help from the WFTC staff, we got through the ordeal, and skinned and quartered the rabbits. I then proceeded to cook the rabbits in a flour-gravy sort of stew. I don't suppose the kids had ever eaten anything like it before. I don't think I had the nerve to ask how much of it was actually consumed.

On the trip to Mombasa, I had also bought a large collection of vegetable seed, and Charity helped me plant a seedling nursery prior to the training. We had an area of ground cleared for demonstration of proper planting technique, which Bent Hansen supervised. I learned a lot from the demonstration myself; things like proper spacing, and methods of applying fertilizers.

The other officers also participated in the training, and I tried to show the kids how to properly keep their records and what was required to enter the Agricultural Show competitions. I must have trained them well because Taita won first place at the Coast Province that year, and 3rd place at the National Agricultural Show. But I will speak more about those shows later. The purpose of the training was to show the kids new approaches, and I think we succeeded. I even demonstrated canning of tomatoes. Storing food other than grain is not a common practice in the tropics. Whatever is not consumed or traded is fed to the animals or discarded. Meat and sometimes vegetables are jerked and dried. This requires little energy input other than the labor, and there is no expensive equipment involved. Canning is costly, in terms of firewood, and glass jars. Canning is also relatively unsafe without the proper equipment. The canned tomatoes came out fine, but I later tried to can beans at a similar training session in Taveta. It would have been fine, if I had had the good sense to can the beans <u>with</u> tomatoes. But I thought I could make a makeshift pressure cooker by putting a heavy truck-wheel hub on the lid of the canning pot. Fortunately, I checked the jars of beans before I left Taveta the next day. The bottles were full of bubbles. I had studied enough bacteriology to know that the pressure in the boiling pot had not been high enough to kill the *Clostridium botulinum* spores and they had started metabolizing the toxin. Had we not destroyed those beans, someone could have been killed by eating them. I had to marvel at the irony of it all. That same day someone showed me a harvest of honey that was to be used to make honey beer. It was not just honey; it was comb, pollen and bee larvae, because they harvest in the dark, and take whatever is in the half of the log hive. Actually, the honey beer ferments very quickly, and the reason is that the enzymes from the stomach of the larvae speed it along. Ironically, that concoction is quite drinkable, and not at all lethal, like the canned beans would have been!

When, in the course of the Youth Training, we came to the campfire, we marched the whole group from the WFTC to the CCH; a distance of maybe a mile. Then we gathered around the fire and began to sing songs and I can't remember if Karisa told stories. I think the kids were having a pretty good time until the District Officer and the DAO came walking up to our circle of young people. They took me and Karisa aside and told us that it was not appropriate to have young people out of the WFTC compound at night. I don't know what they were concerned about; we had supervising adults present. Maybe it was the association with the CCH. On nights when dances were being held, the CCH was the scene of drinking and "adult" behavior. But on this night there was nothing going on at the County Council restaurant or the dance hall. None of the junior officers could understand what the concern was. Nevertheless, the District Officer obviously had reservation so we had to shut down the campfire and march the kids back to the WFTC.

I think the 4K members enjoyed the week long course. They had been exposed to home economics, horticulture, animal husbandry, project management, and the agricultural officers themselves. Not many of these kids wanted to grow up to be farmers, although some undoubtedly would. Still they were able to see how agriculture could lead to professional government employment as well. And all the skills taught in 4K could be applied to other areas of their lives. Some of those kids went on to do some impressive projects, and that is part of the reason Taita won the Provincial and National Awards.

The AAs were a hard working lot in general, but some stood out in my mind. I remember the name of the AA from Mgange (Moses Mkalwe), and I remember Harrison Kimbio. Both of these men would have their careers affected by my presence; I hope they were happy where it took them, but I will probably never know. Harrison was an unusual looking Mdawida, because he had chocolate skin, slightly reddish hair, and green eyes. 'Kimbia' means 'to run' in Swahili, but that word described Harrison well. I can't exactly place his location (Ngerenyi I think), but it was down the hills from Wundanyi, so he had to do a lot of traveling up and down to get to the upper and lower portions of his territory. He was the kind of guy who was always ready to help and learn. He was also quite effective with the kids, and his 4K Clubs were among the most active. His association with me would eventually lead to his promotion into an entirely different field, but I will speak of that when we come to the honeybees. On the other hand, Moses ended up being assigned as the principle Youth Training Advisor when I was leaving Taita, but that is a complex story in itself.

Speaking of complex situations, the relationship between Charity and me was becoming just that. In our daily interactions and in our evening sessions of Kiswahili, I was becoming more impressed with her abilities, and her personality. All of my new friends knew her, because she was often present when they were around. In fact she cooked for them on occasion. Tom Wolf could see what a help she was to me, but I think he was concerned that something was going on. Bent, being a free thinking European, was quite matter of fact about Charity being my cook, although he wasn't sure why I wouldn't want one who cooked as well as his employee. Charity was not a very beautiful woman by African standards and certainly not by Taita standards (although she did have some serious booty). Taita had a reputation about its women. Obviously, Charity had been attractive to at least two men before me. She had her two oldest children by a Wakamba officer who was assigned to Voi. Edward, the oldest son disputes this, but doesn't know who his father was. Unfortunately, when the officer was posted back to Machakos (the homeland of the Wakamba) he married one of his own tribe. At the time I met Charity, her oldest daughter, Gertrude Tabu Mshoi was studying to be a nurse, and was living at a training hospital outside of Taita District. Charity's oldest son Edward Amon Mshoi was helping on the family farm, and was not attending school. He had been in and out of school but he did not like it; he was approaching his teens at the time. I think I was most impressed by Charity's resilience and spirit of determination. Here she was with minimal education (about 4th grade), 5 children to raise, and one of them was crippled. Yet she plowed ahead trying to earn what she could to keep the family going. As with many Wadavida she did this with a healthy dose of humor.

I certainly realized how dependent I had become on her assistance. Not just the chores, and such, but she was my window into the culture. She had many friends like Jennifer, and most people liked her. I was, of course, still clinging to my religious convictions, and would not have thought it appropriate to have anything but a respectful relationship with Charity. She was Anglican, like most of her family.

I was trying to find a church that I could attend, but there was no Catholic

Church in Wundanyi, and I was looking for something Charismatic. Such a church existed fairly close to Wundanyi on the main road out of Taita Hills. It was something like an Assembly of God Church and they practiced the whole Pentecostal experience, speaking in tongues, the music, the arm waving and the laying on of hands (for healing). I attended this Church a few times, but somehow it did not ring true to me. The trappings were all there, but the culture was somehow different. I guess it didn't seem as sincere. Maybe it was that I was not able to be taken into the community as completely as I had been a part of the movement in Seattle. Or perhaps I was right, and there was something superficial about it.

Sure enough, it turned out to be the pastor. It was discovered that he had been raping the young girl that he had hired to help his wife in their house. What was more shocking to me was that nothing happened to him. The whole scandal blew over and the pastor continued to lead that flock as if he were the voice of God. I think this rather profoundly impacted my faith in the Pentecostal experience. Of course, now I know that such "indiscretions" are common place all over the world. It seems the more high and mighty the servants of God become, the more precipitous their fall from grace. What I did not know was that I was about to take that fall myself.

Charity and I only had one textbook between us, so when we studied from the book, we were literally tete-a-tete. Having not had bodily contact with any woman since Gretchen, the proximity began to be titillating. I hate that word, but it is the perfect description of how a physical attraction can sneak up on you, when you least expect or seek it. I was also concerned for Charity having to travel home in the dark, and it seemed that she was leaving later and later each night. Finally one night it happened. I invited her to sit in my lap, we kissed and before you know it we were in bed. This was my first honest to goodness intercourse with a woman. Gretchen and I had had orgasms together, but not actual intercourse. It was for me at once a great relief, and yet waves of guilt came over me. I honestly promised God that night, that I would marry this woman. I asked her not to leave that night.

I think Jennifer was washing clothes in a bucket outside the rooms when Charity left the CCH that morning. I know Jennifer had been expecting this for a long time. As had Charity; I came to find out later that she had a physician install an intrauterine device the day after she started working for me. I guess Charity knew her limits. Obviously, I did not!

So this changed everything, now Charity was my mistress. It was not long before everyone knew it, including the Kiwinda family. I had been in the process of looking for a house that I could rent, so I could move out of the crowded confines of the CCH. One day a relative of Charity, who was himself a minister, approaching me in Wundanyi and said that he had a house to offer for rent. He described the location, and told me I could inspect the place at my leisure, because he had workmen that lived in the compound of that house. So first chance I got, I took my motorbike out to the Bura Ridge. The house was an unusual sight. It was a full scale ranch style house with metal roof and vaulted ceilings. It was perched right on the top of a long ridge and had an amazing view of the Tsavo game park on the one side (including the Sagalla Hills). The huge sisal plantations were also visible in the savanna. On the other side of the house Mt. Vuria and Mt. Susu were visible. There was a servants' quarter, and a mill where they kept a diesel powered grain grinding mill. This mill was open for rental in the daytime, where people would bring their maize to have it ground into cornmeal. If it had once been built by *wazungu* (whites), it had not been occupied by colonists for years. How it came to the possession of Charity's uncle, I don't know.

I was thrilled with the place, and the price was extremely reasonable. I recorded a tape to my mother where I described the view, and mentioned that there were crows with white collars, and the nearby rain forest reserve had pine trees on which grew a native orchid. Bent Hansen was most interested in those orchids. Before he took the Danish Volunteer position in Taita, he had received a job offer to work for an orchid nursery in Seattle, Washington (There is that irony of happenstance again). The workers at the house were also very interesting fellows; I had recorded their singing and a "concert' they performed for me on some 55 gallon drums. I also got a very loud and accurate recording of the *jogoo* (rooster); even though chickens were supposed to be difficult to rear, they always seemed to be right outside my window in every place that I slept. Actually, I may not have owned an alarm clock; who needs one when you have *majogoo* (plural of *jogoo*)? Until I listened to the tape, I had forgotten that that I could hear songs of a nursery school (within a mile of the house on Ngerenyi Juu). It was the homestead of the first Anglican missionary in Taita (probably 100 years old), built entirely of basalt stone, quarried from the volcanic cones that form the major peaks in Taita Hills. Apparently the basalt had hardened in the throat of the volcanoes that formed Taita Hills, but the hills were so old that the volcanoes had eroded away and left the basalt cores as the living testimony to their existence. This was most apparent in Mt. Iyale whose face jutted up hundreds of feet. The leeward slope of Iyale was more gradual and provided a Gibraltar-like plain, which was populated with farms and forest. Nevertheless, back on the Bura Ridge, this colonial farm house was alive with the sound of children chanting their numbers and singing. "*E macho macho sioni soini macho.*" (trans. E eyes eyes, I don't see, I don't see eyes.); the song was sung while the children covered their eyes. It was most rewarding to hear these songs that I had recorded, and to remember there smiling laughing eyes. I also was surprised to see black cap raspberries that the colonial priests had planted those many years before. I tried to propagate those in the next place I lived. I remarked in this tape that I was quickly forgetting everything about my life in America and was rapidly falling in love with Taita Hills and the Wadawida.

It was not that I was out of touch with the people I had known in America. In fact, I mention on the tape that, in addition to correspondence from my parents, I had received letters from Emily Du who was about to marry John Mattson. She was rooming with Barbie and Sheri. Barbie was in love with a guy named Mike, and rumor had it that Sheri was getting serious with George Matter. Martha Patton had reported a big increase in Bible study activity which seemed to indicate that there had begun a backlash to the extreme positions of the Yippies and SDS and Black Panthers the violence of which culminated in the Kent State incident.[203] In fact, I had received a box with 30 letters from the Honeycomb fellowship, some of whose authors I did not even know. On the same tape, I was trying to talk my mother into coming to Kenya (which at that time would have been $700 to 800 US), Tom Wolf had been visited by his brother and then both his parents. They all agreed that, in spite of taking tours all the way to Malindi on the northern coast of Kenya, the most enjoyable part of the trip was the time spent in Taita Hills.

My thought was that I could rent the house and bring Charity and her children to live there. What I didn't know was that this was a trap, and I stepped right into it. After I had agreed to lease the place, and when I was preparing to have Charity help me move into it, her uncle appeared, and informed me that I was not to take Charity with me. All along his plan was to disrupt the budding love affair between us. And it worked, for a time... but left a very bitter taste in my mouth (and my brain) about so called "Christians". I moved to and lived in the house on the ridge for a couple of months, but I was lonely and rebellious. You have to understand that this house was very isolated from the town, and there was no village nearby. Only the two workmen and whatever farmers would bring their maize to grind. The weather was stormy for part of the time that I was there, and the wind whistled through the rafters of that house in a most disquieting way.

During that time I had occasion to go to Mombasa because my motorbike was giving me problems. This required that I stay in Mombasa while the repairs were being done. I found an Asian- run hotel a little out of the center of Mombasa; it looked clean and had the standard breakfast, so I booked it for the nights that I would be there. The room was very open and airy. There was a sort of court onto which two (maybe more rooms) opened... in fact they were already open, because there were no actual doors. This court led to the bathing facilities and toilets. I thought it a bit strange at the time, because I was used to western style rooms where closing the door seals you off from everything outside the room. Not being the suspicious sort, I figured it was kind of a suite and that no one else had rented it, so the clerk rented the whole thing to me. I went to bed and rather promptly fell sleep.

When I awoke there was a woman in the court. She was taking a shower, and was obviously not the cleaning woman. At first I thought she didn't know I was there, because I could see everything she was doing. Only later did I realize that this was not an accident. From this point, the sequence of events becomes a little blurry in my mind. That is not a ploy to avoid description of what transpired; it is just a fact of my aging memory. Suffice it to say, she did know that I was there and when I got up to shower, she was obviously interested. So I spoke to her, and we began a brief conversation. I don't think she propositioned me or vice versa. I believe that she went about her business that day, washing and hanging her clothes to dry. I left to do my negotiations at the motorbike shop. It was not until that evening that I invited her to dinner. Her name was Cecilia. She was a Kikuyu from… perhaps it was Embu, which gave us a point of conversation. She was not an unattractive woman (which I found out later was an understatement… several Peace Corps volunteers had also been "attracted"). So we talked and we may have even danced; she definitely liked her Tusker (a local brand of beer). I had my share as well. The larger hotels in Mombasa, particularly those that catered to tourists, usually had good food and good live music.

When we walked back to the hotel, things got a little more touchy-feely, and by the time we got to our adjoining rooms, it was certain that only one bed would be used that night. Do I remember the details? I am afraid not… too much beer! I will say this; Cecilia did not treat me like a john. She even provided a condom. I think she realized that I was pretty much of an innocent abroad, and somehow that kept her interested. In fact, we spent the next couple of days together. I guess I realized that she was a prostitute, particularly when she had to have beer for breakfast. But I guess by then the missionary in me surfaced; I thought I would rescue her from her life. When the bike was repaired, I asked her if she would join me in Taita Hills. To which she agreed, and we took off for Taita on my Honda 175. I think we stopped in Voi to eat before we climbed up the Wundanyi Road, or maybe it was the Bura Road. I don't remember stopping in Wundanyi, perhaps because I was embarrassed to be seen by people I knew. I knew that we would have privacy out in Ngerenyi Juu (the house on the ridge).

I probably fixed dinner that night, but I did not have anything alcoholic at the house. She seemed to be doing ok when we went to bed, but I have vivid memory of that night. This young woman was already a severe alcoholic; in the middle of the night she began to have severe DTs. I had never seen a person in her condition; all I could do was hold her tightly as she literally shook all night long. I knew that there was no place I could go to get drink for her during the night, but in the morning I rushed to the nearest duka, and bought Tusker. I did not have a good way of securing it to my bike, so half the bottles fell and broke just as I was arriving at the house. Once she had consumed the remaining bottles of beer, she settled down. It was as if she had miraculously returned to normal. She asked me to take her back to Voi so that she could take the bus to Nairobi. I was heartbroken, not because I selfishly wanted to keep her with me, but because I realized that her days on this earth would be short. The words of the Simon and Garfunkel song ran through my brain:

> Cecilia you're breaking my heart
> You're shaking my confidence daily
> Oh, Cecilia, I'm down on my knees
> I'm begging you please to come home

I fed her, provided her with drink and gave her money for her trip. There was nothing else that I could do. I think I would have been willing to try, but I think she knew that it was a bigger human drama than I was prepared to deal with. I hope with all my heart that she got help with her alcoholism, but the odds of that are extremely slim.

Foolish me, to think that I could go around picking up women and that it would be a private thing between two people. The staff at the house at Ngerenyi Juu must have reported to the owner immediately. There was no telephone, and the owner almost never came to the house, but somehow the word got to him very quickly. So he made a surprise visit to the house, and told me that I could no longer rent the house, and would need to leave within the month. Whether he had intended to kick me out anyway, I will never know, but he certainly was not going to have his house used to shelter prostitutes. A very Christian attitude on his part, don't you think? I would come to find out over the years, that Christians are often unfamiliar with the kindness of Jesus toward a certain prostitute.

On the day after my birthday that year, I wrote another letter to Gretchen which alludes to my fall from grace.

> Feb. 2 1970
> Dear Gretchen, and Hulet if you are still hanging on.
>
> I belatedly remembered that you have a birthday somewhere around these dates, and I, for some unknown reason have decided to send you a weird birthday present. It is a genuine tourist item collected on the white tropical Indian beaches of exotic Mombasa. Just a taste of industrialized Africa. Next time maybe I can pick up something more Afro-natural, but this one was made by a brother....
>
> [this paragraph was questions about my degree and the completion of the research project Gretchen had typed for me.]
>
> Somehow being over here in the nitty gritty of real life situations make the intellectual charade seem so unreal and remote. But I probably won't be allowed to stay in Shangri-La forever, and I better make sure my return trip balloon doesn't get popped by a Wicked Witch.
>
> How is your cross-cultural experience coming along? Has the Black population of UW increased, or is tokenism winning out?

By the way, just exactly what are you doing these days? Are you teaching, studying, typing, trapping, or napping? Give my regards and the peace symbol to everybody that I should know. Also tell everyone that the world outside the good ol' gory US is really groovy.

Hang loose and don't get hung up. God it still great, but I am presently eating pea pods in the pig sties (if you know that parable).

Best to both of you,

Mike

The pea pods in the pig stys are, of course, a reference to the story of the Prodigal Son. I probably should have felt great remorse for the drumming I was getting from "Christians", but I didn't. In fact, having Charity's uncle surreptitiously kick me out of my lodging only strengthened my determination to get back together with Charity. I also mentioned in the tape that Charity and I had defied her Uncle, and that she had come to Ngerenyi Juu to cook for some guests of mine (who never arrived), and spent a night.

Therefore, I searched hard to find a place to stay, and ended up renting the house of a Police Officer who was assigned to Nakuru District. Himself being a Mdawida, he had built the 3 bedroom, one bath, brick house on 5 acres of adjudicated family land in Mgange, where he intended to return after retirement. But it was sitting idle, except for the lumber operation that his relatives were running out of the front yard of the property. This was a shame, because it was prime land also sitting idle, and it was located in a prominent place in Mgange where people passed by every day. The land adjudication was continuing out along the ridge that extends north from Mgange, but this was eroded, difficult land and was generally ending up being parceled out to those who had previously had little land rights. The Police Officer's house was a symbol of how the best land went to the wealthiest families in Taita. So I petitioned the Peace Corps to cover the higher rent, and I had intentions of turning the land into a demonstration farm.

The move took place in late March or early April, because on the tape to my mother on March 15th to 17th 1970, I mentioned that I had met with Fr. Paddy Cook at the Catholic Church in Mgange. We had had a frank discussion about my move to Mgange and my intentions to bring Charity and her *watoto* to live with me. I may have actually confessed to him and, although I don't remember it, he probably advised me to keep the relationship between Charity and myself on an employer/employee basis. I don't remember exactly how Fr. Pat became involved, but I seem to remember that it was he who set up the rental agreement, as the Police Officer was in Nakuru. He was certainly much more open minded about it than Alan Madoka (Charity's Uncle). I learned from listening to the tapes that Alan had been more concerned about the gossip than anything else, but Charity's family was, according to the tape, quite upset with me for caving in to Alan's assumed authority. The irony of this whole thing was that Charity's parents had refused to let her marry the Mkamba father of Gertrude because he was from another tribe. Not only had Charity had more children by another man, but now she was involved with a *Mzungu* that was from about the most distant tribe they could have ever imagined!

I was still just hoping that Charity would agree to come with her children to Mgange to live with me in the large house. I left word with Jennifer that I needed to get in touch with Charity, We met at the Wundanyi market one day. I invited her to have lunch at the CCH, and presented my plan. She agreed, but needed her mother and father's permission. I didn't know how that would work. It was one thing for an adult woman like Charity to take up residence with a Mzungu, but to release the children to this life took an act of faith on the part of Charity's parents. I suppose there was a bit of desperation in it all. The family certainly needed the infusion of financial support, because their situation was strained by Charity and the children. There was also another daughter, Charity's sister Priscilla, who was living with her infant son, Mawuganga, at Charity's parent's farm.[204] In the end, the parents agreed for the little children, Samba, Mzai and Sam, to come to

Mgange. Charity's mother wanted Edward to stay on with the family farm to help with the farm work. I don't know what the family felt about the uncle's intervention to try to prevent Charity from working for me. I know I would have been offended, if I were them. Of course, the circumstance was unusual, but one must remember, the family of Amon Mshoi (Charity's father) was eking out a living from the land and his carpentry. Whereas the uncle had been liberally compensated for his work in the Anglican church, which had made him able to purchase the house and maize mill at Ngerenyi Juu, in addition to his own family home.

Charity had more siblings. Her three brothers were Benson (who was a clerk for the denge[205] bar owned by the County Council), Samuel (who was a teacher at Iyale school and the father of 3 children himself), and Wilson (who was an apprentice carpenter who was working with his father at that time in Voi). All things considered the family of Amon Mshoi had done well by African standards in terms of attempting to educate their children and training them in the father's trade. But the rapidly growing family was strained by the limited land and resources and the limited education of the child bearing siblings.

I think Charity rode with me to Mgange on the *piki piki* to see the house and determine if it was suitable for the family. The owner of the house had furnished it with a bed or two, living room and dining room furniture. It had a separate kitchen with a wood stove with oven. Additionally, there was a screened food storage cupboard. I also had collected some resources. I had bought two twin beds from Tom Wolf when he left Taita, and several other useful items for homemaking. That included a kerosene refrigerator[206], which I could never get to work properly. Charity approved of the arrangement, although I don't think she would have objected to anything as long as she would be with me. Was it love? I don't know; she said it was. I realize that it was a godsend for Charity with regard to caring for her children, and I was entirely game for the task. We did keep the relationship platonic for the first several months that she and the children lived in Mgange. In fact, I began attending Mass at the Catholic Church which was nearby. The Irish priests that were there were nice enough about the whole thing and didn't seem to have any trouble with me having Charity as my housekeeper.

The children arrived with Charity on the bus a short time later. I remember the first night, after everyone had been assigned their beds etc. We sat down at the dining room table in the light of the pressure lamp, and all those eyes were looking at me with expectation. This was, after all, the first time they had been with me in my home at night.

Left to right: **Mzae, Samba and Samuel.** How could I not love these cuties? (Author's personal photo)

It was a whole new world for them, much different than the small family home, where everyone would huddle around the Charcoal burner (kijiko) and kerosene lamp to talk, study, etc.

This house was large and cold (on the windy slopes of north Taita). There was a fireplace, but it took wood which we had not yet gathered to get it warm enough to gather around a fire. And we only had two pressure lamps, so the rest of the house was dark and kind of spooky (for a young kid). I think they all wanted their mother to accompany them to the inside bathroom when they needed to use it. The concept of an inside toilet, in itself, was strange to them. They were used to an outhouse. Fortunately the toilet had a separate door, so they could have their private cubical for relieving themselves. I think one thing the kids adjusted too very quickly was the Paloma water heater.[207] It only provided water for hot showers, but this was a small miracle to the children. I was relieved to finally have a simple source of hot water myself!

For a time, after we had settled in, we would end up huddling around the kitchen stove, because that room was always warmer than the house. It was not until later that Charity talked me into buying the charcoal stoves that were called *kijiko*.[208] At that time in Kenya, the ceramic *kijiko* had not been developed, and the type use was manufactured by tinsmiths entirely out of recycled *madebe* (5 gallon kerosene cans). The advantage was that you could carry them around where you needed them for warmth. In the end it would prove to be a problem for Charity because they did produce an almost invisible smoke that darkened the brightly painted walls with soot.

The kids (whom I will hereafter call by the Kiswahili word for child *mtoto* pl. *watoto*) adjusted to the new home. The days were pleasant and there was ample yard for them to play. There were always adults around, because the carpenters who planed lumber for the owner worked there throughout the day when the weather allowed. Of course, Charity was there most of the time also. Sometimes she would hike over the Iyale/Wesu path to Wundanyi to see her family and pick up things from the public market. Oddly, Mgange didn't have much of a public market. There was an open air butcher, but the farmers did not bring much to the town center. There were a couple of bars, and a "grocery store" *duka*, but those didn't carry anything but the bare essentials. I arranged to have them order Kenya Creamery butter and cheese which was delivered in cans by a delivery truck that went around Taita Hills. But it was hard to get the store owner to keep it in stock. Mr. Shate, the store owner soon refused to keep the products in stock, so his competitor, who owned the restaurant and bar next door, agreed to order those products for me. I had only one occasion to deal with Mr. Shate after that. He had a lorry (large Bedford truck) that he leased and used to carry hides to Mombasa. Once I needed to take my motorbike to Mombasa. The crankcase seal around the shift lever had come loose and drained the oil out as I was climbing the Bura Road after a trip to Tavete. I will not tell the story here, but after I finish describing the new house, I will relate that very peculiar story.

Very soon after we moved in at Mgange, we started the farming project. We first cleared a garden behind the house, and I planted as many varieties of seeds as I had purchased for 600 KSh. I was able to establish Brussels sprouts, broccoli, beets, cucumbers, green peppers, celery and even artichoke. These were not found in Taita where the predominant vegetables are cabbage and tomatoes (varieties of which we also planted). These included Chinese and New Savoy cabbage, as well as climbing and bush varieties of tomatoes). I had seed left over to distribute to individuals who were willing to plant them.

I remember that Sam was crawling around in the dirt one day, when he ended up in a "highway" of *siafu* (which are a kind of army ant that is common in Kenya). We could not figure out why he was crying, until we came close enough to see the trail of ants under the grass. The big-headed soldiers had clamped onto his behind, and we had to do some "extractions". Poor guy, but I am afraid we had to laugh. His eyes had turned into saucers again, and he was whaling "SAFU!… SAFU!" (the Kiswahili term for these safari ants is *siafu*.)

It was clear to me that we had to do something about Sammy's dysfunctional leg. So we visited the local hospital several times and consulted with the resident Medical Assistant (who was also one of Charity's many relatives). They were not equipped to deal with the problem, but they suggested that he needed traction to lengthen his atrophied leg. Gertrude (Tabu, Charity's oldest child) was assigned to a hospital at the coast, and she was able to secure permission to put Sam in her hospital for treatment. So Gertrude visited us in Mgange, and we prepared for her to take Sam to the Coast hospital. It was the first time I had met Gertrude. She seemed like an intelligent woman and a rather attractive one at that. Charity was obviously quite proud of her first child, and first secondary school graduate among the nieces and nephews. Indeed she had gone on to graduate from nurses training school.

Sammy was gone about six months. We were only able to visit him at that Coast hospital once. I have a tape recording of that visit. I was making the tape to send to my mother. Charity prompted Sam to say

"Jambo nynanya, mimi ni mgonjua" (which means, Hello grandmother, I am sick). Of course, he was not sick; in fact he was in pretty good spirits. Sam was a trouper, in spite of being confined in a traction bed; he was obviously pleased to have his mother visit. They were feeding him during the tape and he was laughing and teasing with his mother. It is rather amazing that a young child like Sam could endure being penned up in a bed for so many weeks, but Sam's experience was all built around being in close contact with people. Someone always carried him where ever he would go, so I guess this was not so different. He was in a ward, so there was always something going on, and he had his sister to look after him. The staff treated him well because they all thought he was so cute. While we were there, the other nurses from Taita came by to check out who this tall Mzungu was; I could not understand the questions they asked Charity because they spoke Kidawida.

At one point Sammy made everyone laugh by calling someone *mjinga*; which means stupid. I can't make out from the tape (nor do I remember) who he was talking about, but he obviously had done it for effect. His mother jokingly said *"Kumbe, huna adabu?"* (So, no respect, eh?). A little while later, Sam began to ask to go home. I explained on the tape that he said that he wanted to wear his shoes. The conversation was interjected with joking and teasing, but it was hard for Charity to think of leaving him in traction much longer. A doctor arrived and talked to Charity and the group of nurses began to sing as the tape came to an end.

I don't think we took him out of traction that day; but when we did get Sam back to Mgange, he was in a cast and I had instruction to try to get him to walk. He was stubbornly resisting, so I had the carpenters build him a little wooden walker with wheels. He would refuse to use it, so I had to be forceful with him. I picked him up and stood him behind the walker and forced him to walk. He bawled the whole time for the first few days, but eventually got the idea that it gave him a little more freedom to move around, so he started using the walker on his own. By this point in time he realized that people were not always going to carry him around, and he was anxious to try to keep up with Samba and Mzae. So he improved. His leg was not perfect, and never would allow him to walk normally, but at least he could walk! In my arthritic condition, I have much more sympathy for him now than I did then. It is disconcerting when walking is actually painful, and the more you walk the more painful it becomes.

During this time the 4K program was expanding. Charity's brother, Samuel, was leading his students in a school garden project at the foot of Iyale, but the land they had to use was not good for gardening. I offered him a section of the Mgange property. It was a bit of a walk from the school (maybe 1 or 2 miles), but the soil was rich (having not been cultivated in several years) and Samuel wanted to plant a bag of soybeans that the Ministry of Agriculture had provided. Bent Hansen had already taken over half of the land for a potato demonstration plot and with the intention of producing seed potatoes for the farmers of Taita. He had hired two very hard working farmers, who cleared the 2.5 acres and terraced it. Then Bent hired them to plant and spray the crop, with the result that he had a beautiful crop of some tonnage on this pristine soil that had formerly been left to the weeds and lantana bushes. The farm was shaping up to be a very good demonstration.

The farm was more work than Charity and I could manage with my job and the care of her children, so I began to hire help for her to maintain the farm. We had a cultivating crew of about 8 people, and then retained four of them to tend and harvest the crops. We planted about an acre of Brussels sprouts. These were a great marvel to the people that passed by on the road. They had only ever seen cabbage, which is a staple crop for Kenyans. These Brussels sprouts grew as high as six feet tall, and produced not only the sprouts, but large leaves sometimes a foot in diameter. The workers on our farm, who were from the area with poor soil, began to ask if they could harvest the leaves and take them for food. Apparently they were quite edible, although a European farmer would have considered it an unproductive crop, because the energy was all going into the plant and not the sprouts. Still, we had sprouts to send to market. The Werugha cooperative took them reluctantly at first, not knowing where they could sell them in Mombasa. But very soon, they were demanding them. The Tourist hotels were so happy to see Brussels sprouts that they paid good money for them. We also raised broccoli, and that was even more in demand in Mombasa. We not only harvested the first head, but they so wanted the broccoli, that we continued to harvest the side shoots until they became as small a child's little finger... and still the market begged for them. Now days in America, these small broccoli stocks are called broccolini. I can't imagine what they would have paid for artichokes if I had ever been able to produce enough to sell. As it was, we enjoyed them ourselves.

We also raised green peppers and beets and carrots, and some celery. Tomatoes were, like cabbage, mandatory. We had so much cabbage that Charity had to show me how to dry it, and there was never a shortage of tomatoes. We bought some of Bent's seed potato, but not wanting to run the risk of disease, we did not continue to grow potatoes after that first crop.

Oh, I forgot about the peas. I had purchased a lot of pod-peas seed, and how the *watoto* loved to pick the peas and eat them in the field. This was all by way of demonstration. I don't think the DAO ever came to see what we had done, but I guarantee that a lot of people did, including the Chief at Mgange and Moses who was the AA for Mgange.

I will have to back track later about the other things that were going on in Taita and Taveta with regard to the 4K clubs etc. But while we are on the subject of the Mgange farm, I think I will just tell it all together. Once the farm was opened up, and the Iyale students were able to harvest their soybeans, I turned my attention to the issue of rabbits. I knew that there were a lot of rabbits in the homes of the 4K members, but I wanted to encourage them by giving them a market. So when I was in Mombasa again for motor bike repairs (which in itself, is a story I must tell), I checked a Mombasa butcher shop to find out if they had any interest in rabbits. They did! So I put out the word that I was buying rabbits, built holding cages for the rabbits, and began the marketing process. I will explain in more detail later. I was reminded by the tape recording that after finding a market, the Harambee School[209] in Taita had rabbits, and the Headmaster volunteered to participate in collecting rabbits from 4K members to sell in Mombasa. I can't say that that ever actually happened while I was in Taita, because later on I had to collect the rabbits in Mgange and get them to the coast myself. I tried to train an albino Mtaita to take on this marketing venture, but I am not sure if he succeeded either. I will discuss that in greater detail later in the story.

In addition, I got involved with honeybees and bee products like wax. I will need to explain that in more detail as well, but suffice it to say, at a certain time of year, the house in Mgange was the perfect spot for catching bee swarms. This was accomplished by building Greek top-bar hives.[210]

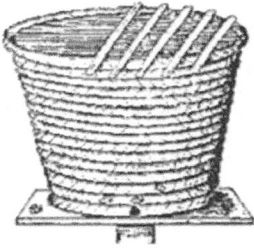

Ancient Greek top-bar hive. (Photo reproduced with permission of John Caldeira. President of the Figi Beekeepers Association. Originally published in *ABC and XYZ of Beekeeping* published by Root in the late 1800's) http://en.wikipedia.org/wiki/Top-bar_hive

We constructed hives, caught swarms and then sold them to interested beekeepers; even Jared Babu bought one for his farm. As the dry season would hit the Tsavo savanna, the honeybees would migrate up the hills to find late blooming forage. I tell this all in connection with the house and farm in Mgange, because it was the scene of a great increase in productivity for me and the 4K Clubs. Talk is cheap, but the best way to teach is by demonstration.

CHAPTER 20

Nyuki
(The honeybee)

My child, eat honey, for it is good,
and the honeycomb is sweet to the taste.
In the same way, wisdom is sweet to your soul.
If you find it, you will have a bright future,
and your hopes will not be cut short.
**New Living Translation (©2007) Proverbs
24:13-14**

PROGRESS WAS BEING MADE AROUND the vegetable farms of
Taita. I was in Wundanyi at the Petrol station across from the Public
Market, when a white Ford Bronco drove up. The appearance of a Ford was
such an unusual sight that I had to inquire. A tall white haired man with a
beat-up canvas hat got out on the driver's side, and a slight Arabian looking
man emerged from the passenger side. I introduced myself, and they did
the same. He was a retired Extension agent from Colorado named Floyd
Moon. I later learned Mr. Moon had lost his father as a boy, and put himself
through college raising honeybees. When he retired from the Extension
service, where he had been an agronomist, he received an invitation from
an international aid agency to come to Africa. I mentioned in a previous
chapter that Floyd had been invited to Kenya by the Near East Foundation
to do crops extension. Mary, his wife, said "Are you nuts? You just retired."
Knowing the obligations of the American husband, Floyd declined the
invitation. Fully a year later, he received another invitation from the Near
East Foundation, to assume an extension position at the Coast Province

of Kenya with objective: "Increase agricultural productivity in any way possible." This time he said to Mary, "we have been married for 40 years, but I am going to Kenya…. Are you coming?" She did. They lived in Mombasa for two or three years, and she also did public service work there.

The man with Mr. Moon was an agriculture technician, named Hassan Ali Hassan, who was assigned to assist Mr. Moon. They were both in Taita to deploy and collect swarm traps that they had placed in Taita in order to transport honeybees to the Coast Province. Mr. Moon had determined that there were not enough bees to pollinate the mango and cashew crops at the Mtwapa Orchard Crops Research Station. He was probably right that there were not enough honeybees at the coast, but the irony is that those two crops are not pollinated by honey bees! I suppose that information was not known then, but it has since been determined that those Anacardiaceae rely on a volatile floral odor that attracts carrion flies, not honeybees. The second irony is that Mr. Moon was attempting to breed those nasty African honeybees to the docile and productive European bees. Twelve years earlier W. E. Kerr[211] had conceived the same idea. The footnote rather understates the impact of Dr. Kerr's experiment gone awry. Millions of dollars are still being spent to try to stop Africanized bees from infesting the entire United States after having displaced European honeybees all over the sub-tropical and Mediterranean climates of South, Central, and North America. In the end, the Africanized bee may prove to be the better bee in terms of its resistance to varroa mite[212], but it has been a real learning curve for the beekeepers that had been accustomed to working with the docile European honeybees. Dr. Laidlaw (who was a honeybee geneticist at University of California, Davis) predicted that beekeepers would eventually be able to breed out the aggressive traits of the Africanized bee, and it would seem that that is beginning to happen low these ~50 years later. I can't say whether Mr. Moon's crosses of the two strains of bees lead to a more productive honeybee, but I can tell you that his crossed stock was not docile. Instead, the experimental colonies were strong and aggressive. It has never been reported in the literature that Mr. Moon's breeding crosses had an impact like the failed experiment of Kerr. This may be because no one has recognized that there are hybrid bees at the Coast, since the coastal bees were aggressive before the cross. The more likely situation is that the Africa genes probably drowned out the European genes. The African bees tended to dominate in the Americas even though, in the beginning, the vast numbers of drones were the European strain.

Mr. Moon was so impressive that I volunteered to help him. So he took me on his collection trip around the hills, and when it was time to retrieve the traps I went also. It was very successful. As I said, the bees would migrate up the hills during the dry season as nectar forage declined in the savanna. After that first swarm trap collection, I began to talk to Mr. Moon about holding a beekeeper training course. I assume that the DAO was skeptical when I brought up the idea; after all what do bees have to do with 4K members? I was prepared with the answer: I was already collecting *wishwa* from the watoto. *wishwa* is what is left after an African has chewed the comb of the honeybee to extract the honey, and pollen and larvae; what is left is a loosely compacted lump of wax and scale from the inside of old honeycomb cells.

Alternatively it could be the solids left over from brewing honey beer. The word itself means chaff, but *wishwa ya nyuki* (honeybee chaff in Kiswahili) or *wishwa wa choki* (honeybee in Kidawida) was known to the sons and daughters of the beekeepers. Most beekeepers in Taita were old men. Interest in the art of making hives (carved out of logs) had waned among young Kidawida. Although Patrick Katingumu was no more interested in bees that I was in paperwork, he reluctantly agreed to allow a training course for beekeepers to proceed at the WFTC.

I suspect Mr. Moon may have brought some pressure to bear on the DAO's decision. Floyd was on very good terms with the Provincial Agriculture Officer (PAO) in Mombasa, Moses Mukolwe. This was not so much for Floyd's work with bees, but because he had put in two irrigation systems on the Tana River and taught the people to raise rice. Grain staples were, at that time, a very high priority within the Department of Agriculture. Mr. Moon was also the subject of a 7 page article in *War on Hunger: A report of the Agency for International Development* (December 1970) titled "Pumps and Bees and a Man Named Moon". That article followed right after the article "Peace is a Grain of Wheat, the Story of Nobel Peace Prizewinner Norman Borlaug".[213] I think the PAO pretty much figured Mr. Moon should have carte blanche. Nevertheless, I noted on my tape recording that the written permission for the training course didn't arrive until it was over. First rule in former British colonies: you have to do what your supervisor tells you, but that doesn't mean you have to expedite the paperwork.

I'm sure that the DAO didn't think that I would get anyone to attend the course, but he didn't know that I had "ins" with the AAs. I think the staff that worked with the farmers knew that I was intent on doing things that would benefit the farmers and their children. I may have already met Michaeli Mwandighi. He was an older man, who lived near Mugange with his daughter's family, but he had traveled all over Tanzania and other parts of Kenya. He was very interested in helping keep the old ways alive. His name was significant. In Kidawida *nan digi* means 'forcefully' or 'with spirit.' "Bonya nan digi!" means "Do it!" or "Go for it!". The Kiswahili word 'Harambee' has a similar meaning; in Hawaii we would say "Gung Ho".[214] This was Michaeli Mwandighi. He was the only beekeeper I knew. He was not still able to keep bees, but he and the AAs were able to get the message to the beekeepers. Looking at the pictures, we had 17 beekeepers, and, with agricultural staff, 22 attendees in total.

The beekeeping class. Mr. Moon with field hat is center rear. I am to the left. Harrision Kimbio is second on the right from Mr. Moon and Hassan Ali Hassan is to his right. The names of the beekeepers I don't recall. (Author's personal photo)

I was already living in Mgange when the beekeeping course began. I note on the tape that Mr. Moon had come prepared as if he were going on a safari in the veld. He had tents and camp stoves and everything. When he saw the house, he was quite relieved to not have to unpack all the paraphernalia. He was comfortable in the guest room with Hassan.

The one exception was that he would not drink the water, unless boiled, or made into tea or coffee. I will say he was wise in that regard. I had assumed that the water we were getting from a municipal storage tank in Mgange Village was treated water or at least from a clean source. I had drunk the water in Wundanyi without boiling it, and had not experienced any diarrhea. What I found out later when I went up the road to Mwanda to the west of Mgange, was that the water came directly out of a stream that ran across the road to Mwanda, and that this stream was used by the locals to wash their clothes etc. It was not a particularly bad organism in the water; in fact, it did not seem to affect the Wadawida at all. Nevertheless, I was relieved to have a case of diarrhea pills always available for the Giardiasis. Mr. Moon had apparently learned his lesson previously, and suffered no ill effects on any of his trips to Taita Hills.

Mr. Moon did insist on his coffee in the morning, but once that was out of the way, he was always ready and rarin' to go. We were impressed to see so many beekeepers when we arrived the first day at the WFTC. Michaeli Mwandighi was there with them, also ready and rarin' (as was captured in a photograph during the course).

Mr. Moon had a Kiswahili text with instructions about beekeeping, but he did not have copies and no one in the Coast Province had ever even seen a Xerox machine. So he taught in English while Hassan translated into Kiswahili. In fact, Mr. Moon left the textbook with me, and I later incorporated it in the school lecture program. I believe it was an AA, who hailed from Mombasa (a native Kiswahili speaker), who read the text into my tape recorder. Then I could play it for the classes.

Mr. Moon was very methodical in his teaching style, probably developed over years in the Extension Service of Colorado State Univ.

He had graduated in 1929 from that college, and after some farming, and serving as a Captain in World War II, he joined the Texas Citrus Board. Later, he joined the Farm Home Administration in the Southwest, from which he retired. Nor were his lectures plodding; everyone in attendance was alert and inquisitive. I learned a tremendous amount myself, not only from the English portion of the lectures, but from the Kiswahili as well. It gave me the proper terms to use in Kiswahili to describe the life cycle, the function of the bees in pollination, the management techniques, the products and how they should be processed. It was very good background even for the course in Apiculture that I later took at Univ. of California Davis. The instructor of that course was the world renowned honeybee geneticist, Harry Laidlaw. The beekeepers seemed to understand the lectures as well; if they didn't, they did not hesitate to ask. Hassan was kept very busy during the course translating back and forth between Mr. Moon and the class.

On the third day of the course, we received word that the DAO wanted us to vacate the farmers training center, because something "more important" had come up. Mr. Moon was not happy about this, but he continued with his lecture on how bees swarm and migrate. He had placed a Langstroth hive[215] in the classroom which contained foundation wax sheets in the movable frames. Mr. Moon was explaining that a colony that is preparing to swarm will send out scout bees to look for a new home. They are particularly sensitive to the smell of beeswax, because it is an indicator that bees have occupied a spot previously. About that time, we started to see bees coming into the classroom thought the hog-wire windows. Mr. Moon explained that they were scout bees because of their search behavior and their non-aggressive posture. Some of the bees would find the hive, and then some apparent fighting would ensue. Floyd explained that it was probably because the scouts were from more than one colony, and were trying to chase off their competitors from the other colony. Then as quickly as they came, the scouts disappeared; we were left wondering if Mr. Moon had been "embellishing". Not so! At around 4 PM that afternoon, the swarm came. As J. E. Rosenthal, the author of the aforementioned article in *War on Hunger*, recorded Mr. Moon's retelling of the story:

> "As I was talking." he recalled recently, "about five or six bees flew in the window attracted by the beeswax. I said to the class, 'I think these bees are scout bees looking for a home.'
>
> "No sooner had I said that than there was a loud humming noise outside. It got louder. It was a whole swarm of bees on the way into the classroom.
>
> "The students in the class got nervous. I told them, 'Don't swat. Sit still. They won't hurt you if you don't hurt them. The bees are trying to locate the queen'
>
> "Sure enough, that's what they were doing, exactly as I had been saying in the lecture. The swarm flew in and settle on the queen in the demonstration hive. The students didn't make a sound. They didn't stir.
>
> "It was like a dream. Here I had been lecturing that this is what happens, then it actually happened, just the way I had been telling them. It was timed just perfectly. "You think Divine Power didn't have something to do with that?"

I had actually recorded what happened soon after the event, so I think my recollections are more accurate. It did actually take a while for the swarm to come to the classroom, and the queen did not land in the hive, but on the outside of the hive on the opposite side from the entrance. For a minute we thought they would not move into the hive; but soon the swarm began to lead the queen into the entrance. This process took long enough that every beekeeper there saw the queen as they gathered close around the hive. Their curiosity had overcome their fear. What you need to understand is that beekeeping in Kenya is really more like hive robbing. The beekeepers go in at night with a minimum of clothing, and a smoldering torch of grass. They enter one end of the hive, smoke it well and take about half the contents, and leave. The hope is that the queen will have moved to the other end of the hive; they are not concerned if they harvest brood, beesbread (pollen) or honey. None of the beekeepers had ever seen a queen bee before that day.

The more fortuitous thing about that event was that we left the bees in the hive in the classroom for the next two days of class. The result being that when the DAO came to see if we had vacated the classroom, he himself absconded very rapidly as soon as he realized there were live bees in the room. Mr. Moon was able to finish the course, and the beekeepers went home enlightened, and with no small amount of amusement. They also promptly told their friends and fellow beekeepers that *Bwana choki* was the man to know.

That evening we moved the hive from the classroom into the crux of a tree on the WFTC farm, and then went to Mwatate Animal Research Station, to collect a large hive that had been robbed repeatedly by some people in the area. Hassan thought this would be so easy that he did not put his bee suit on. Mr. Moon was fully dressed but when Hassan handed him the screen to seal the entrance to the hive, it was too wide. The bees began to boil out and Hassan probably got 200 stings before he got his suit on. I had my makeshift suit on, but Mr. Moon was kneeling at the hive trying to stop the bees with his gloved hands and without a smoker to calm the bees. I set to work trying to light the smoker, but it was the first time I had ever tried to do this. I finally got it lit and passed it to Mr. Moon, who, by then, was cursing at Hassan for bringing the wrong screen. When we finally got the hive sealed and loaded in the Bronco, tempers cooled a bit and we all had a good laugh... well, I am not sure if Hassan joined us in that levity. Mr. Moon and the bees had been very hard on him.

Heads up to the reader: I am going to abandon the chronological order of the memoir now, so that I can concentrate on the beekeeping development work. In the next chapter I will return to the approximately chronological order.

Later, we arranged a series of *mikutano* (meetings) with beekeepers in the lowlands around Taita Hills. Michaeli Mwandighi instigated this, and had me driving all over the savanna through sandy dry river beds and old abandoned Sisal plantations looking for beekeepers. By then I had obtained a Mini Moke (an Austin Healy built, small utility vehicle like a Jeep) from the Peace Corps. The reason for acquiring this vehicle I will explain later. Michaeli and a couple of other *wazee* (old men) traveled with us.

Later, at the arranged time and place, Mr. Moon then met us at the meetings that were convened in the bush. One of the beekeepers gave me a traditional log hive at one of those meetings. It was a skillful demonstration of workmanship. I wish I could have brought it from Kenya; but maybe it is full of bees by now. Those hives were certainly carved to last, and the wood they used was very hard, durable heartwood.

We collected other swarms in Taita before Mr. Moon left for America, and then later I delivered swarm traps to Mombasa for Hassan Ali Hassan, who had taken over Mr. Moon's duties. By that time, Hassan and I had become good enough friends that he had made the unusual gesture of inviting me to stay at his house. Hassan was a strict Moslem, and it was a real privilege to be invited into his home. Unlike the street dress of the Moslem women, the women were unveiled and normally dressed within the household. Hassan's wife was not only beautiful but she cooked exquisite food. I particularly enjoyed her curry with coconut milk rice. I believe they invited Charity to stay with us on another trip to Mombasa (I am not sure of that, but Charity had welcomed Hassan to Mgange, so I think it was reciprocity). Hassan had a very nice family with 2 lovely children. He had been successful in the Ministry in spite of his type 1 diabetes.

On the last trip to Mombasa to deliver swarm traps, after Mr. Moon had returned to the good ol' USA, I went to Mtwapa with Hassan. We were planning to install the swarms and check the hives that Mr. Moon had set up in a bee house that was designed after the plans of a South African beekeeper. This building reminded me of the shape of the Civil War ironclad, the Merrimac. The difference was that the cannon ports were actually the entrances to beehives. The hives were all inside the cinder block building which was kept cool by screen windows all the way around the building. The concept was that if one hive got out of control, the beekeepers inside the house would be protected from the other hives that might be roused to attack mode. The problem with the design is that you want to be damn sure there is no one passing anywhere near the building while you are working. That is why we headed out to work on the bees in the late afternoon, after the farm labor had gone home. Hassan installed the swarms in the remaining empty hives, then proceeded to the established hybrid hives. The bees in Mr. Moon's hybrid hives were nasty, but Hassan managed to harvest some honey before we decided that discretion was the better part of valor. Mtwapa is about 10 miles from Mombasa, but we noticed just after leaving the research station that the engine of the bronco was overheating. When we stopped and opened the hood, we immediately realized that the fan belt had broken. We had some bottled water with us, so we tried adding water to the radiator, but of course, that did not help much. At the 85 degree night temperature, the radiator could not cool the water without the fan. We limped along until we got to a petrol station (which was closed). We tried to find something to use to make a makeshift fan belt but we had nothing that would work. During all this time Hassan was suffering because he had not brought his insulin. He kept eating honey to keep from going into insulin shock; it probably saved his life. Finally a lorry drove up. I guess the driver had stopped to fill his water tank. We decided to beg for a ride to town. We left the Bronco at the Station with a note, and climbed in the back of the lorry. The driver dropped us at the Ministry of Agriculture, where I had left the Mini Moke; It was about midnight, so I was very relieved to get Hassan back to his home, so he could get his insulin.

After that I had a lot more respect for Hassan. I also understood why Mr. Moon had always complained about Hassan being useless during Ramadan. He was such a faithful Moslem that he kept the Ramadan all-day fast. You can imagine how difficult it was for Hassan to follow Mr. Moon around on his "all day all night expeditions". The Ministry had figured they would pawn Hassan off on the *Mzungu*. Instead, Hassan more that proved himself. In the USA today, the treatment Hassan received would have been grounds for a case under the Americans with Disability Act (1990). As it was, all he could do to support his family was to take the job that was assigned to him.

One of the volunteers from Ag V had been reassigned to the Canadian Beekeeping Development Project, sponsored by the Canadian International Development Agency. His job was to go around the country looking for information about beekeepers, bee-forage plants, and providing drums to collect honey for the Thika Salvation Army Farmers Training Center. Dr. G. F. Townsend had written the Kenya bee project and had contracted the Thika FTC for construction of Kenya Top-bar hives. I met with the PCV (can't remember his name now), and he gave me some honey barrels. He told me that Dr. M. V. Smith was coming to Kenya to study pollen and forage sources, and he suggested I should meet him. So I did. He set me up with slides and materials to do pollen sampling and mounting. I also traveled to Thika and saw the Kenya hive for myself.

When I got back to Taita I began attempting to construct Top-bar hives myself. Of course, I did not follow the first rule, "read the directions". I got the trapezoid design of the box, and the fact that the top bars provided the support for the comb. But what I did not realize was that there was a reason that the bars were not flat, but rather triangle shaped. So I purchased about 50 10 ft. lengths of finished lath. I thought this would be a cheap substitute for the triangular bars. Tom Wolf's friend Shako helped me built some boxes and we cut enough lath to cover the box. We painted a bit of hot beeswax on midline of the lath, and set it out to catch bees; which it did almost immediately. However, within a couple of weeks it was apparent, when we looked in the hives, that the bees had not built the comb along the length of the lath slats, but rather across them. This was no better than a log hive, although you could take off the slats individually by cutting the comb; it did defeat the purpose of having the bars as a way to extract and examine the comb.

Again, rather than go back to the instructions, I tried to overcome this problem by creating a raised bead of wax along the center for the length of the lath slats. This helped, because the bees would tend to start the comb on the bead of wax, but what I found out in Kenya, and then later doing experiments in California, was that the bees will build the comb in the direction they want. If the bees want the comb to wrap around, it will; if they want the comb to be cross braced, it will; and if they want it to circle like the comb in the trunk of a tree, it will. Remember, these are nature's engineers building with the lightest strongest structural design known to man. Old Reverend Langstroth had it right: if you want the bees to build comb the way you want them to, you have to provide them foundation wax and too little room to deviate from the pattern. The one thing that was true about the Greek top-bar hive is that bees will seldom attach comb to the top side of any surface that slopes 9 degrees or more.

The other relatively true thing about the Kenya top-bar hive design is the triangular shape of the bar. I learned this at UC Davis from a 100 year old hive built out of redwood by John Harbison.[216] The frames in the Harbison hive were built of 3/4 inch square redwood, but the horizontal bars were oriented to the frame with corner edge of the wood angled vertically (see diagram, end view).

Harbison comb frame (end view) was made from redwood; the cross-bars were turned 45° to vertical. (Author's personal drawing)

It is true that bees will tend to start their comb along the lowest edge of a stick or a branch or a rock. So the angled edge of the top-bar does promote the construction of comb in line with the top bar. Dr. Townsend remembered this when he designed the Kenya top-bar hive. The purported advantage of the Tanzanian beehive[217] is questionable to me, because even with a starter wax foundation, the bees will attach the comb to the vertical walls of the hive. Keeping the comb cut away from the walls would be time consuming, and in the end would probably be futile. After I returned to the USA, and worked at the Bee Biology Lab at Davis, I sent a design to Dr. Townsend that was a combination of the top-bar hive principle and the Langstroth design. Essentially, the brood chamber(s) would be standard Langstroth equipment, but the honey supers (boxes), build to the dimensions of the Langstroth hive, would have sloped sides (9°) on the short sides of the super. The honey supers would have top-bars, instead of frames, and the top-bars would be spaced with a metal spacer, so that the bees would be able to move up into another supper on top of the first. In other words, you would remove the need for Langstroth frames in any area where brood is not being laid. I should have published this concept, but it never caught on in the Kenya program. I did send the design to Dr. Townsend at U. Guelf. They were already too invested in the Kenya top-bar hive design. Dr. Townsend did eventually publish a set of designs for the Kenya Project, and in that article he mentions interchange of comb top-bar hive into Langstroth hive bodies.[218]

After our first "Taita hives" built out of one inch by twelve inch board, I realized the internal space of the hive was too small. So I went to a carpenter in Mwanda Juu; he claimed to be able to build the boxes out of 18 inch wide slabs of Silk Oak (*Grevillea robusta*), which the colonial foresters had planted widely in Taita, and were now approaching 2 foot diameter trunks. These trees had to be felled; the boards had to be cut with a two-man drag saw and the wood had to be cured. Then the wood had to be planed, sanded and only then could the hives be built. And a beautiful sight they were. I don't know why Silk Oak was so named, but the wood had a silky finish that is clear and almost grainless. Blindfolded, I guess you could mistake it for the touch of raw silk. According to my Description of Peace Corps service we built and sold 33 of these hives with bees in them. In addition I gave 32 lectures on beekeeping at the local schools, presented 5 beekeeping exhibits at agricultural shows, and initiated a survey which documented the high beekeeping potential of Taita District. Recently, in the course of writing the memoir, I discovered this document on the internet:

Honey for the people of Vuria

By J. Mwang'ombe (from the Eastern Arc
Mountain Information Source: 1999)

The Vuria Hill Self-Help Group is the name the environmental committee of Mgange Dawida has chosen for themselves. The residents of Mgange Dawida prioritized a Tree Nursery and Bee-Keeping project as the topmost project they wanted supported in this area. The tree nurseries raise indigenous tree seedlings for re-planting in forest gaps. This is a good example of a local community initiative for habitat restoration. The community hopes that, by replenishing and enriching the forest, they will have provided more forage for the bees to make honey from while restoring their forest to the original status. They also hope that this will increase the level of water in their streams and stop flush floods like the one that occurred during the El Nino rains resulting in death of two people.

The bee-keeping component of the project is an income generating activity. The honey thus produced will be marketed. The proceeds from the sale of honey will be used on community projects and also as a revolving fund to assist members start small businesses.

There are a total of six villages each with a tree nursery. Each of these has been supplied with bee-hives and the necessary honey-harvesting gear/equipment. The committee will be trained in appropriate honey harvesting techniques practically on the ground once the hives are ready for harvesting. Among the plant/ tree species being raised in the nurseries are;

+ Mngima (*Prunus africana*) used by the local community for construction.
+ Mwavwa (*Milletia oblata*) used in construction as posts, tool handles, acaricide and detergent made from the leaves. It is endemic to Taita hills forests.
+ Msuruwache (*Albizia gummifera*) used for fuelwood and as timber.

+ Ndido (*Maesa lanceolata*) used as fuelwood.
+ Shao (*Macaranga conglomerata*) endemic to Taita hills forests. It is among the most preferred as fuelwood.
+ Ngoche (*Lepidotrichilia volkensii*) used as fuelwood.
+ Mngorusa (*Polyscias stulhmanii*) used as fuelwood.

  It is clear from the above list that, the local people have chosen the type of trees carefully according to their needs.[219]

Can I conclude from this that I had an impact? Perhaps; there were certainly a lot of others involved. But had I not run into Floyd Moon in Wundanyi, and had Michaeli Mwandighi not taken us around to all the old beekeepers in Taita, the whole art of beekeeping might have been lost to the Wadawida People.

More recently I read an article about a project in the Tsavo savanna that fascinated me. Dr. Lucy King, MSci, DPhil., came up with the brilliant idea of using beehives to create elephant-proof barriers to protect the farms of Kenyans.[220] The sound of honeybees is very odious to elephants, because, if attacked, the bees go inside the trunk and mouth of the pachyderms. This can actually cause them to suffocate from the swelling of their airways. Dr. King decided to suspend the Kenya top bar hives in a barrier around the *shamba* (farm). Between each hive she stretched wire, so that if an elephant passed through, it would shake up the hives and cause them to go into attack mode. This is such a clever way to insure that the increasing population of lowland farmers will not precipitate a war on elephants. The elephants will quickly learn to avoid the farms, and the farmers will not want the elephants shot. This system is used in several African nations and India. The bonus is the increase in production of honey and wax.

What is more ironic, as I write this, I just saw a documentary last night called The Vanishing Honeybee. Say what you will about the anti-pesticide bias of the film, there is no question that honeybees, in the countries that practice so called "modern" agriculture, are dying off at alarming rates. Although it is still not definitive exactly what the cause of Colony Collapse

Disorder[221] is, several European countries have banned certain suspected systemic pesticides. The evidence is not yet definitive whether that will stop the decline of the honeybee in those countries. One thing is certain: the honeybee is under siege, and if the trend is not reversed, it may be that only the temperamental African bee will survive, and its best hope of survival is natural reserves like what is proposed for Taita Hills.

The irony for me is how much that fateful meeting with Mr. Moon altered the course of my life. That will become more apparent as I continue with the chronological recount of my life, but I have already mentioned that I was grateful for the opportunity to end my career trying to stop the spread of the varroa mite and the hive beetle on the Island of Hawaii.

At the end of his tour of duty Mr. Moon was tying up loose ends (he had to make an emergency trip to Tana River to repair the pumps on the irrigation schemes). Mary had already left for the USA, but the pumps had been supplied by USAID and therefore required American made parts, which did not arrive in a timely manner. While he was waiting, Floyde invited Charity and me to Mombasa to go deep sea fishing. I think we met him at the harbor and went straight to sea with the charter boat that he enjoyed renting. It was a beautiful day and a first such experience for both Charity and me. The captain put a line in for each of us; there might have been a bite or two, but the fishing was slow that day. Finally, after hours on the water, Charity's pole took a mighty dip; she started to grab it, but was too nervous to continue, so she passed the pole off to me. I was not really sure what to do, but I assumed you didn't want to pull so hard as to break the line. Mr. Moon adjusted the tension on the reel for me and talked me through the process of gradually reeling in the spirited fish. As it turned out, it was what he called a king fish, about 4 ft. long and all muscle. I think Mr. Moon was quite relieved that the boat did not get skunked. He would have liked to catch one himself, but this was not a new experience for him, and I think he was happy that he was able to show us this sport.

When we arrived at the harbor, we had previously arranged to spend the night at Mr. Moon's fine colonial home. There were rooms enough that Charity could have had her own room. Always before, when Mr. Moon came to Mgange, Charity slept in the room with the *watoto*. But he asked us if we wanted to sleep together or separately. We were surprised and thought it quite open minded for 63 year old American from the Southwest to offer us conjugal sleeping arrangements. Since we were, by that time, sleeping together, we opted to sleep in one room.

The next morning we awoke to the smell of coffee, and after we showered and dressed, Mr. Moon served us a very nice breakfast with the roe from what turned out to be a female king fish. It was tasty. Everything seemed quite cordial. After breakfast, Mr. Moon asked me to help with the dishes while Charity packed for the trip home. This was an excuse to take me aside and talk. As it turned out, the choice of sleeping arrangement was a test. And since I had failed, he felt it necessary to caution me about the problems of involvement with an African woman. I am sure that his intentions were sincere. He had nothing to gain or lose from this last lecture. He was genuinely worried about my future, and for that matter, Charity's. I am sure that he was almost as smitten with the *watoto* as I was, and he had seen us all in our home environment. But he was sincerely concerned that my future education and success in life would be impacted by the fateful decision to marry an African black, whether we ended up living in Africa or America. Of course, he was right, but times were changing and the impact was probably not as severe as he had imagined.

In fact, Mr. Moon wrote to me in the summer of 1971 to tell me that he and Mary had moved to the Pacific Northwest, Milton-Freewater, Oregon. And he kept in touch. He and Mary also went to Galt on their travels around the West Coast, and talked a long time to my mother and Father Carl about how difficult it would be for me to bring Charity and her children to the United States. I quote his letter on one of the tape recordings to my mother. He wrote "I hope you have considered the impact of this on your future. You are a young man with great potential".

When I left Kenya, Dr. Townsend invited me to visit University of Guelf, Ontario Canada; which I did. He was interested that I wanted to pursue the bee project in Kenya. I will discuss the circumstances of that later. Somehow he had been contacted by Mr. Moon, and informed of my personal situation. However, when I was not able to return to Kenya after my military induction physical, I applied to UC Davis. I don't know if it was happenstance, but Dr. Townsend visited Davis for a bee conference, and met with me. He encouraged me to continue my education but he strongly discouraged me from continuing the relationship with Charity.

Note to the reader. I am skipping ahead in time for the purpose of illustrating the involvement of Mr. Moon in my life, after I had joined Weyerhaeuser and brought Charity to Seattle, we went to Kennewick, Washington, to pick up a load of apples. The apples were from the farm belonging to the father of a young student from the Honeycomb Fellowship. The apples were not quite ripe enough to pick, so we had to wait. Since we were close to Milton-Freewater, Charity and I went to visit the Moons at their home. They greeted us very warmly, and Mr. Moon could not have been prouder of his garden and his one beehive.

After I took the job with the Weyerhaeuser Forestry Research unit and brought the family to Tenino, Washington, Floyd and Mary Moon visited our home on two occasions, ostensibly to pick blackberries, which we did. On the second visit, after Charity and I had lived there a couple of years and had our garden and chickens and rabbits and one turkey and one goat, we were having dinner with the Moons. Mary said to Floyd, "Now do you think they are going to make it?" He conceded that he had been skeptical, but it looked as if we were going to make it as a family. Of course, what was he going to say with Charity and the whole family sitting there? The irony is, in the end Floyd was right all along. I never saw Mr. Moon again; I am not sure whether Charity did, but if so, it would have been after I had gone off to finish my master's degree at Univ. of California. The Moons' adu;t children sent me an invitation to their parents' 50th wedding anniversary, but I did not have the resources to attend, and I guess I was too embarrassed to write anything for their family story. I guess I am trying to apologize for that with this story.

I have been trying to find out whether either Floyd or Mary is still alive, but I think I found pictures of their tombstones in Milton-Freewater. Floyd had put in 81 productive years on this earth, and Mary had lived "a life of dignified grace" for 97 years.

Floyd and Mary Moon will always be remembered as two "salt of the earth" Americans (photos reproduced with Permission of The USGenWeb Archives Project – Oregon MILTON-FREEWATER IOOF CEMETERY) http://www.usgwarchives.net/or/umatilla/photos/tombstones/miltonfreewater/milton-freewater-mo.htm

CHAPTER 21

Dikundane di diwose
(Blessings for everyone)

> "If you see that your neighbor's donkey or ox
> has collapsed on the road, do not look the other
> way. Go and help your neighbor get it back on
> its feet!
> **New Living Translation (©2007) Deuteronomy 22:4**

ON JUNE 1ST, 1970, BENT Hansen and I took a trip around Mt. Kenya. The Peace Corps apparently loaned me a Mini Moke, although I didn't remember that had happened so early in my tour. I believe the Moke was a temporary loan, until my Honda was repaired. Bent was reading the book by Isak Dinesen in the original Danish, and he wanted to see the country described in the book. I had not taken any long trips up to then, and, in fact, this would be my only "vacation" during my two year tour. We had hoped to catch the Wakamba Dancers in Thika (Machakos District), because they are famous for their strenuous and erotic dances. Unfortunately, when we reached Thika on Madaraka Day[222] we found out that the Wakamba dance troop was in Embu at the government celebrations there. It was too late to catch them but we went on to Embu and spent the night. I knew that area, but Bent had not seen it. The next day we went on to Meru, through the beautiful, tropical mountain rain forest with its large old trees and multiple streams. Through Kerindini and Chuka and all the way to Meru the road skirts the steeper slopes of Mt. Kenya. The road was windy and rough, but after Meru the road was paved and the land was at the same time dry and fertile. The Lewa Wildlife Conservancy on the north side of Mt. Kenya starts the arid Northern Territory. However, there are many substantial farms hugging the highway, until the land opens up to a large fertile plain that is fully developed in agriculture. This fertile plain extends from Muchiene to Timau, and, like most agricultural areas in the world, does not support any large cities or towns, even today. There are many people living in the area, but the development is distinctly rural rather than urban. Large wheat farms and other large scale agriculture had been introduced by the colonials. While people live all through the mountain region in small farms and homesteads, Nanyuki is the next population center to the NE of Mt. Kenya, and I think we spent the night there. Not that there was much happening in that little berg. Bent spent the evening reading.

The next day we passed right through Naro Moru, the District Headquarters, because our time was limited. We did stop at Kiganjo, the site of Kenya Cooperative Creameries. This was the source of my cheese and powdered milk (with cream still in it). I don't think we veered off to Kingongo and Nyeri because we didn't want to risk the lesser quality roads to Nairobi, so we went to the Makutano junction. We might have skirted Nairobi by taking the Garissa highway and hit the Mombasa highway at Kibwezi. I don't really remember, but it seems like we did spend some time going through the upcountry fruit orchards of the Machakos District. Bent may remember it differently. At the end of the trip, I think we were both convinced that we were stationed in one of the most interesting and beautiful areas of Kenya. Even the majesty of Mt. Kenya could not compete with looking from Mgange, across Tsavo, to the white capped peak of Mt. Kilimanjaro. Of course, neither of us climbed Mt. Kenya nor Kilimanjaro. I think Dennis Burkhart climbed Mt. Kenya, and Tom Wolf got altitude sickness on Kilimanjaro, which caused him to started tearing off his clothes. Mr. Moon had planned to climb Kilimanjaro with an oxygen bottle, but I can't remember if he made it.

On the tape recording I went into a tirade about how foolish the Kenyans were to send all their skilled Asian and British colonials away, and then they were begging expatriate experts to come in and help them run their large scale farms, many of which had been turned into cooperatives. What I didn't realize then was that the standing policy of the Kenyan government was that any person in Kenya at the time of independence had the right to claim Kenyan citizenship. In fact, they had seven years to claim citizenship. It might have been stipulated in the constitution. After independence, many colonials left immediately of their own accord, probably because they understood the animosity against them. Others stayed, but didn't want to give up their European citizenship, so they eventually had to leave. By way of example, there was an Indian family in Voi, the Patels, who were successful business owners. Only the father and mother were actually from India. All the sons and their families were born in Kenya. The father refused to take citizenship in Kenya so in the seventh year he was deported. Nevertheless, to his great surprise, all of his sons had secretly applied for citizenship. As a result, they inherited all the businesses. This was because the expatriates were only allowed to leave with a limited amount of the fruits of their years of labor. Listening to the tapes, I realize that I had a lot of youthful biases, some of which came to Kenya with me and some which I adopted from the expatriates while I was in Kenya.

I have not mentioned that there was a Peace Corps volunteer in Taveta. His name was Charles Howe, and he was from a previous agriculture group (Ag IV, I believe). He was assigned to Taveta to take care of the broken down irrigation scheme that was the life's blood of the Wataveta, but which had not had adequate maintenance since independence. Charles explained it this way: "There were also design deficiencies due to miscalculating the erodability of the soil and the effect on the static water table." Charles had been raised on a farm in Connecticut, so he knew the machinery of irrigation. With his degree, which was a bachelor of science in Agriculture majoring in Agricultural Engineering from the Univ. of Connecticut, he was perfect for the job. The Peace Corps and the Ministry of Agriculture were lucky to have him. The people absolutely loved him. He was just what they needed to organize the repairs of the irrigation system, because he knew well enough what needed to be done, and they soon learned to trust his judgment. Those who would not cooperate got the *kijicho* (evil eye) from Charles' supporters.

I met Charles when I first went to Taveta, but only briefly. The next time I went to Taveta I had intention to say overnight, and Charles offered me a place to stay. He was living in the relic of a German plantation farm house, which had been confiscated during World War I. General Smuts of the Imperial Forces routed the Germans at Taveta on March 11 1916. The grave of Robert King Holmes Burgess and other soldiers can be found in the Taveta Military Cemetery. The German Colonial Seat at Dar es Salaam, Tanzania (then Tanganyika) surrendered to British Forces on 3rd September 1916, after which the entirety of East Africa came under British rule.

Charles' place was comfortable enough except that there was a shortage of catchment water (Taveta is very dry) and the indoor plumbing had long since stopped functioning. Ironic that Charles, who had revived an entire irrigation scheme, was not able to fix the plumbing in his own lodging. As he put it, he had no motivation to do so. Charles was comfortable enough that he not only served out his 2 year tour, but returned for a second tour after I had left for America. I liked Charles, and he came to visit Charity and the family in Taita more than once. On his first trip, his intention was to climb Vuria with his older Honda 175, which he kept in good working order. He had been out in the flat land of the Tsavo savanna for so long that he longed for a "perspective view." We both started up the mountain road (built to service a radio tower), me with the shiny new 175 and him with the old workhorse. Well, he made it to the top, and my bike failed me half way up the mountain. There was something not quite right with it, because I did not weigh any more than Charles. Funny what running an engine a mile without oil can do to the compression. This venture happened twice, and both times I had to hike the last half of the hill. Charles didn't gloat, but he didn't offer to trade bikes for the climb, either.

Charles liked Charity and the *watoto*. Because he spoke fluent Kiswahili, he could converse with them, and they liked him, too. Charles, like Tom Wolf, left about half way through my tour of duty. However, he kept in touch by letters and at least one tape recording that we exchanged. When he returned to Taveta, I was already Stateside. At some point the communication broke off, and I don't know if I dropped the ball or him. But I have been trying to find him recently. I had forgotten that he lived in Goshen, Connecticut, but I recently located a number for a Charles B. Howe III in Goshen. I plan to call him tomorrow. The only other thing that I could find out about him was this article:

In This Hobby, Sometimes You Must Tread Lightly
By ROBERT HAMILTON
Published: September 9, 2001
The New York Times: NY/Region

Charles B. Howe of Goshen, who once edited a newsletter for the Connecticut Beekeeping Association and kept almost two dozen hives at one time, said there will probably be some backlash from the Franklin attack [a man who was killed by his own bees I surmised].

"But I think a lot of it will diminish with time because of education, and once it's not in front of people the issue will go away also" he said. "Most of the times, beekeepers are pretty innocuous. They're in a lot of places people will never see, their hives are moved in the middle of the night because the bees are quiet, and you put them out in the middle of the fields away from people, because you want your hives in places that are isolated so the bees are making honey, instead of guarding the hives."

He said he has slowly gotten out of the business because of another problem facing beekeepers: the return of the black bear to Connecticut.

"They were gone from the state for 200 years, but now they're coming back," Mr. Howe said. "They take the hives down and rip them to shreds. You won't find much left. They've been a bigger problem for me than the mites, because I can treat for the mites, but I can't do anything about the bears, because they're protected. And once a bear comes into a yard and finds a hive, they'll just keep raiding it until they're gone. I've had them in the back of my pickup truck and up on my porch."

Mr. Howe said he still keeps one hive.

"It's something that will grab a hold of you," he said. "They're very interesting insects. Their habits, their lifestyle. And it's calming, believe it or not, to work with a beehive -- perhaps because you have to be calm."

And I found this note about his civic activities.

> Goshen Good Neighbor Fund, Inc.
> Contact: C.B. Howe, President

I was not surprised about the civic organization, but I was a bit surprised about him being a beekeeper. In Kenya he had hired a local fellow to rob the bee colony that was lodged right over the sundeck in the wall of his Kenyan "plantation house". I was there the night the fellow was dancing around in his dungarees trying to avoid getting stung. I will have to ask him if he got the beekeeping bug in Kenya, or after he returned to Goshen the last time.[223]

When I returned from Taveta on my motorbike for the last time, I had almost finished the long climb to Mgange when I realized that my bike was really straining. I stopped to check the crankcase and found it extremely hot. Then I noticed that the gasket around the shift lever had come out and drained the oil... again! There was no starting the bike, so I had to push it the rest of the way home. The next day I tried to negotiate with Shate to see if I could ship the bike to Mombasa in his the lorry (truck). He agreed, but I thought he would say I could ride with the driver and his shotgun (alternate driver). There was certainly plenty of room in the cab, but Shate insisted that I would have to ride in the back of the lorry with the bike and the stack of dried cow hides. This honor was not free, either. I didn't really have a choice, so I paid cash. The lorry left a day or two later at 3 AM, and

I was on it. We traveled to Wundanyi to pick up more hides, and then we descended the main road (which at that time was under construction). Most of the way we traveled on the old road, but it was bumpy. There was no chance that I could sleep, so it was not until we hit the Mombasa highway that I dozed off. Suddenly, I was awakened by the violent swerving of the truck. The hides were slipping and sliding all over the bed, as was I! Fortunately we had secured the bike or I might have been crushed by it. When the truck came to a stop, I stood up and looked over the railing to see what had happened. To my surprise the driver was butchering a dik dik[224] that he had run down with the truck. Poor little ungulate!

Dik dik: a small African ungulate that was once very common, but has been hunted to low levels of population. (in the public domain CC BY-SA 3.0) https://en.wikipedia.org/wiki/Dik-dik

Of course, this was totally illegal, because the game animals were strictly protected. But the drivers were well prepared for all contingencies. They had a storage box built way up under the bed of the truck where the police would either not look, or would accept bribes to prevent them from having to soil their uniforms. I might have been inclined to turn the drivers in to the police to spite Shate, but I figured the drivers had families to feed, and I was sure Shate didn't pay them enough. Besides, he would just deny he knew anything about it, although I am sure he probably exacted his share of the carcass. You have probably already surmised that I did not like that man very much, but it would have been hypocritical of me to report him, because later, I was guilty of the same crime.

On the trip with Michael Mwandighi and the beekeepers he had recruited from around the lowlands of Taita, we were returning just after dark. That night a dik dik was blinded in our headlights. The old men were absolutely clamoring for me to run him down. Picture the scene: the road was completely wash-boarded, such that the whole vehicle was shaking violently as I sped to hit the innocent animal. The headlights too were bouncing around wildly so it was as confusing for me as it was for the poor dik dik. I kept hoping he would dart off the road so I would have an excuse to stop chasing him. No such luck; in his confusion he sealed his death warrant and I became a weapon of destruction at the hands of a blood thirsty mob of three… and in a government vehicle! However, this was Africa, and these were the descendants of a once mighty race of hunters. Also I have to admit that the small hind quarter of dik dik that was my share of the kill was well received by Charity and the family. It was a sweet treat that Charity had not tasted in many years. Besides, I had to admit, it was tasty…even better than *Mbuzi* (goat).

Returning to the bike which was delivered to the shop for repairs, this time it took weeks to repair, because the engine had to be overhauled completely. My motorcycling was getting expensive for the Peace Corps. I must have come back to Taita by train, because I have a tape that says I was walking to Wundanyi (about 5 miles) for a week or two. One day I was heading to Wundanyi with a lot of things on my mind because it was getting near the time for the County Agricultural show in Wundanyi, and there were a lot of preparations that need to be made. I was so distracted that I walked right past an old woman who was carrying a large bag of charcoal on her head. I thought nothing of it, until I heard in the distance behind me. *"Kwa wuka?"* When I did not respond and kept walking I heard it again, a bit louder this time: **"Kwa wuka?"** Finally it registered that she was calling to me. So I turned around and greeted her; *"Nawuka!"*. But she was not satisfied, so I walked back to where she was (a distance of 50 ft.) and greeted her again. She extended her hand and said; *"Kwa wuka mana?"* And I gave the traditional response: *"E Mao, nawuka mana!"* I shook her hand as she said again: *"kwa wuka mana putu?"* And I responded: *"Putu!"* Then she was happy and went on her way with the bundle that had been on her head the whole time. She was teaching me a lesson in *Heshima kwa wazee* (respect for one's elders).

This was about the middle of July, 1970, and the Agricultural Fair in Wundanyi was scheduled for August. I was trying to get support from the DAO, but he was very disrespectful. In one meeting I was the last to give my report, and he chided me because the report was too long. The next meeting, I gave a very short report (as he instructed), so then he chided me for not giving him enough information to decide if they should assign a staff person to the 4K. I was pissed, but I did not show it. Katingumu knew full well that the contract between Peace Corps and the Ministry of Agriculture was this: the Peace Corps volunteers would be replaced at the end of their tour with Kenyan staff.

At the next meeting, I was on the agenda, but the DAO tried to skip right over me and chose Henson to give his report instead. Without hesitation, I just jumped in and forced my report on the table. Fortunately, Henson Nyange made a joke out of it by feigning to be trying to speak over me. It could have gotten very tense except for Henson's playfulness. It was 6 PM before we got out of that meeting. I had vowed in my mind to put some pressure on Patrick Katingumu at a higher level. I was getting very discouraged at the lack of involvement of the officer-level staff, but I didn't want the DAO to assign one person to the 4K clubs because I knew that, as before, it would all fall on that one man. I wanted a commitment of support all the way up and down the line, including on the part of the parents, and schools (the schools had been the most cooperative, and I thought we should try to have a grant program for them). Even at the national level it looked like the Ministry of Agriculture was not putting support behind the Youth Training Program and the Peace Corps was actually considering pulling out of the 4K staffing. A few volunteers in that assignment had already left or chosen other assignments. I didn't want to give up, because I knew how hard some of the field staff had worked to promote the program. People like the Home Economics women and Harrison and Moses, and there were so many young people that were truly interested. So I redoubled my efforts, got my motorbike out of the garage, circulated to the local businesses to solicit prizes for the winning project entries, and made sure every student who wanted to enter the competition had a chance.

At the time of the show, we had our *kibanda* (covered displays) set up and there were actually more entries from 4K members than there were from the adult farmers. The DAO never came near the 4K display, although the area Chiefs and the District Officer did inspect them. The judging had to be done by the AAs because we could only get one officer (Karisa) to agree to judge the *watoto*. It was somehow beneath the others. When the prizes were being awarded to the adults' entries, none other than Patrick himself gave the prizes. He gave a *jembe* here, a tea pot there, all with great pomp and circumstance.

When it was apparent that no one else was going to award the 4K members their prizes, Karisa and I did the honors. Karisa remarked to me: "These prizes are much better than what they are giving the adults. How did you manage that?" I said that they were all donated prizes from the local businesses. There were tools like screwdrivers and hammers and a hand saw; most of these kids had never used any of these tools. There were also *pangas* (machetes); which was a tool that they all knew well how to use. There was also cloth for the girls, and some utensils, although I cannot remember them all now. It was an impressive support from the community businesses. And the projects that went to this Agricultural Fair went on to the Provincial show, which won Taita-Taveta District First Place in the Provence. It kind of put ol' Katingumu to shame, while at the same time bringing his District honors. Now he had to sit up and take notice.

Between my time in Mombasa and the next fateful event, Bent had a nasty spill on his Honda 175 while he was traveling to Mombasa. A dog ran out in the road; had Bent not been wearing his helmet, he would not have survived. The pavement had worn a hole through his helmet as he slid across the tarmac. He was in the hospital in Mombasa for some days, but

I did not even know that he had been injured. When he came back, having been informed of his ordeal, I went to visit him and apologize for not having come to see him in Mombasa. He understood, but we got to talking about motorbikes and the statistics. There was a rumor amongst the volunteers that most accidents happen at about 6 months after one starts riding a motorbike. At first you are cautious, but about six months in you get cocky and careless. I should have listened more closely, because I was already beyond my sixth month.

Sometime that fall, we had 4H members, who were touring from the USA, visit Kenya, including Taita Hills. They were winners of the USA national competition. We had found lodging for the young woman with a Taita family, but I agreed to take the young man at my house in Mgange. I say woman and man, but neither of them were more than about 20 years old, probably younger. I don't remember what the woman's background was but I found out that the guy was a farmer's son from the Midwest. I could imagine him having been raised on a combine, with his John Deere baseball cap, and Midwestern, no-nonsense attitude. They had already been in other provinces in Kenya for some time, so by this point he was kind of punchy. It was clear that the woman was having way more fun than he was. After their orientation with the Agriculture staff and District Officer, we departed for Mgange while the DAO's driver delivered her to the farm we had pre-arranged. When we arrived in Mgange, Charity fixed us a nice meal and retired to the kitchen with the kids, because "the ambassador" did not seem much interested in getting to know the "help" and her brood. Sure enough, he was "perdy" damn Midwestern. He and I spent the evening comparing notes, and from his prospective it all looked pretty grim. But little did either of us know that it was about to get a whole lot grimmer for us personally.

We arose early because we had to get to meetings in Wundanyi that morning. I was not aware that the other Taita bus, *Dikundane di diwose* (blessing for all), came to Mgange from Wundanyi that early in the morning. The local nickname for that bus was *mayai* (eggs), because it was painted a bright yellow with green trim. If I had named it, I would have called in "Green Eggs and Ham" (from Dr. Seuss). Believe me when I say that it looked like a giant egg when I came around a sharp corner in the road. There was the bus in the middle; to the left was a rock wall, and to the right was a cliff. I had visions of us becoming scrambled eggs at that moment. The only chance I had was to lay the bike down, with myself and my passenger. Fortunately the bus was barely moving or else it would have run right over us. We were probably going 20 mph, if that, but my head hit the bus and knocked me completely unconscious. The next I remember I was bouncing around in the back of the DAO's Land Rover with the two 4H ambassadors and Moses Mkolwe. Then I fainted again and did not wake up until the next day in the Voi hospital.

Unfortunately my passenger had not had such luck as to be knocked unconscious. He was wide awake as his leg broke in three fractures. He was awake through the entire excruciating trip to Voi. Everyone had been very concerned about whether I would sink into a coma, when, in actuality, it was he who had the more serious injuries. The woman 4H ambassador stayed with us at the hospital and tried to help relieve her fellow traveler's pain. Fortunately the Peace Corps contracted a twin engine private airplane to take all three of us to Nairobi. I don't think the Kenyan government would have been willing to do that for the 4H ambassadors. I was awake for the trip, and, in spite of the pain in my head, wrist and chest, I actually enjoyed the only aerial view I would have of the expansive savanna of Kenya. The plane was a twin engine Cessna 310B, which reminded me of Sky King[225] soaring over the plains of Texas.

We were delivered to the best expatriate hospital in Nairobi, rather than Kenyatta Government Hospital. Believe me when I say there was a great difference. They fixed my passenger up in a full leg cast and me with a wrist cast. There was nothing they could do for my broken clavicle, but they did monitor my brain for a while to be sure I did not have any residual hemorrhaging. As I said, it was a good thing the bus was not moving fast because we would have both been in much more serious condition. Still, my grumpy partner was in pain and not at all content about the situation. He was sure that he would never be able to climb on his combine again. Frankly, I don't know if he did recover full function of his leg, but it was certainly not for lack of good medical care. The hospital was excellent and the doctor was first rate. There was an army of Kenyan nurses and orderlies. They would offer you beverages every four hours (I got used to having Horlicks or Milo) and they would offer massages between each "tea" break. I'll bet no patient ever got a bed sore in that hospital. The meals were also excellent. While the "ambassador" grumbled, I marveled at how we were being treated. I generally turned down the massages. Not that the nurses were not lovely. Why, it was embarrassing! I began to feel this was not a worthy assignment for a Peace Corps volunteer. I don't know if my anxious anticipation of departing was the guilt of being treated so well. Or perhaps it was the guilt of having the ambassador reminding me every day that my driving might have screwed up his career. In any event, I reluctantly obtained my freedom, and commandeered a Mini Moke from the Peace Corps director (by now they were convinced that motorbikes and I were bad luck! The Mini Moke was an Austin Healy with a boxy body; it was open sides like a military jeep. They were two-wheel drive vehicles but they were in use all over Kenya for safaris. They had front wheel drive, which made them good for muddy roads.

I had come from Wundanyi with my Logan coat, so I thought I would be warm enough to make it through the game park at night. This was a 400 mile journey, after having been pampered in a hospital bed for 12 days. And a grueling journey it was. As soon as the cold air was whipping around my chest and my wrist, they began to ache mercilessly. But there was no alternative; I was committed to the journey and my only hope was to get it over with. I don't know how many times I had to stop for passing elephants (a major hazard on the roads of Kenya). I don't even think I stopped to eat. I just wanted to get home. When I finally reached the road to Wundanyi,

I had the option of taking the old, slow and winding road, or the new road bed that was under construction. I was sure the latter would be faster, so I struck out on it. It had rained the days before so that roadbed was a series of large puddles and disturbed ground. I was scared to death I was going to get stuck, so I just gunned the accelerator through the ominous looking spots in the road. I broke the bolts holding the trailing end of the metal plate under the engine. Thank God that plate was there, because I would surely have put a hole in the oil pan if it had not been protected by ¼ inch sheet of metal. And then I would have literally been up a creek without a paddle. But I made it to Wundanyi, then through the winding road around Mt. Iyale, and at long last home!

Charity was asleep when I arrived at 3 or so in the morning. She had not heard from me since the accident and the only information she had was what little that Moses heard around the Ministry of Agriculture, which was not much. I don't think she even knew if I had ever regained consciousness. She was doubly concerned what would happen to her and the kids if I died. So she was so happy to see me. All I wanted to do was crawl into bed. I was so cold that she got in bed with me, helped me put the liniment on my wrist and clavicle as I directed, and then hugged me as I dozed off to sleep.

I awoke in some serious pain, but it was nice to be at home again. I couldn't really report in to work (that was one of the advantages of there not being any phones in the whole town of Mgange). I needed time to get reoriented. This had been a big change in my daily routine, and the fact that I now had a passenger vehicle would change my job considerably. I laid low for a couple of days, getting caught up with 4K plans, checking on the progress of the gardens. There were workers to pay, crops to pick, etc. I checked in with Moses to see if any meetings were pending at Wundanyi.

I really couldn't sit still for too long. The first task was to get to the Ministry garage in Wundanyi to get the metal plate under the Moke fixed. I had to be careful with my wrist, because the doctor had indicated that the metatarsals that were broken could lead to problems in future if they did not heal properly. The doctor had removed the cast before I left Nairobi, so it was doubly important that I not overstress the fresh bone unions. I really can't say if I did a good job of protecting it, because I do have problems with my right wrist these days. As soon as I was able to crawl under the engine compartment and tie the plate up with some wire, I was ready to go.

The government garage was always backlogged, and I figured the vehicle needed to be checked out thoroughly after the beating I had given in climbing the new Wundanyi highway. So, after I checked in at the office, I hitched a ride with a government Land Rover that was headed to Mgange. That meant I would have to walk back to Wundanyi to retrieve the vehicle, but I was not in a great rush to get running around the Hills just yet.

I think the *watoto* enjoyed having me around the place, so we spent some time teaching them to sing songs in English, which were then recorded on the tapes to send to my mother. Around that time, one of the beekeepers, who had heard me say I wished I could buy a bow, brought me one with arrows. The workmanship of the bow and the arrows was exquisite. The basic design was that of an English long bow, made from a durable but flexible native wood. The arrows looked like they were fashioned from sticks, but I could not imagine what tree they used. Most of the vegetation in Kenya is gnarly and crooked, with only a few trees, like the silk wood introduced by the British, having long straight trunks. Even those did not have straight branches. Somehow the *fundi* (the craftsman) had known where to acquire straight sticks about 2 ft. in length. Why I needed the bow was for was the chicken hawks. We had chickens by then but they were free range. Therefore, they were live bait for the chicken hawks (I don't know what species, but they were impressive). There is not much you can do to discourage a hawk if he or she is set on dinner, but the bow helped. I never hit the hawk, but you know that he (or she) knew that s/he was being targeted; smart those raptors. I lost a few arrows shooting in the air, but the chickens survived.

Not long after the Provincial Agricultural Show, the National Show was coming up. Again the AA's and I managed to gather together a very impressive collection of entries. I had failed to read the notice that the exhibits were to be limited to 5 per District. I had a large cage that I had built to collect rabbits (about 4 by 4 by 3 ft.). We managed to get all of the exhibits in the cage, and delivered to Voi for shipment to Nairobi. The officers and farmers that had been invited to the Show traveled to Nairobi in government landrovers. The 4K members and the 4K Group leaders went up with them. I planned to travel by train, because I was back on my motor bike and I didn't want to do the Nairobi run again on a bike as I had previously. All went well; the people were delivered to the Fairgrounds and the officers picked up the displays at the train station. The judges inspected the entries and I think even Jomo Kenyatta came to the 4K pavilion, although I was not present for that event. When the awards were given, Taita-Taveta District had won Third Place in the Nation. The fact that I had brought too many entries was outweighed in the minds of the judges by the quality of the entries. I don't know if we would have done better if we had followed the rules. We were up against some very modern farm children from the White Highlands. They were Kikuyu but they had some impressive animals and crops.

Everyone in the Taita contingent was happy, but everyone was shocked when the prize turned out to be a one-bottom ox plow (*sans* ox). As we were breaking down the exhibit, I told Karisa that I would go to Peace Corps and ask for a vehicle to transport the plow back to Taita. But I asked him to wait so they could help me get the exhibits back to the train. Well, Karisa was in no mood to wait, so while I was negotiating with the Peace Corps, he loaded the exhibits, and the plow, and took off. How did he manage to get all of that in the Land Rovers? He left the two adult 4K leaders and three 4K members at the Fairgrounds; that's how!

When I got back to the Fairgrounds, it was already late in the afternoon, and the vehicle I had been issued was a step up from the Mini Moke. It was a VW Thing[226]; but it was still an open "jeep-like" vehicle and we would have to cross 400 miles of elephant territory in the dark.

Kurierwagen was manufactured by Volks Wagon, and is alternately known as Trekker in England and "The Thing" in America.(in the public domain CC BY-SA 3.0) http://www.thesamba.com/vw/forum/viewtopic.php?t=376382

This was not a good idea! The kids didn't even have any coats. I had to loan my coat to one of them. I don't remember if they shared it; the coat was certainly big enough. Now, the generation of Land Rover that Karisa was driving was not a comfortable vehicle. Nevertheless, the back end of a Thing was a darn site worse. I took a deep breath as I prepared to climb in the VW, which seemed filled to the brim with boney knees. I apologized profusely and began the journey to Taita Hills.

We made it through the Game Park without incident, although we did have to stop often enough for passing elephants. We were lucky that we did not encounter any heavy rain. There were some sprinkles, but these were just irritating; no one got soaked. As we headed up the Taita Hills, the air got colder, and the kids were shivering by the time we delivered them to their respective homes. I was shivering too, but at least I got my warm coat back to finish my trip to Mgange.

When I next went to the office complex in Wundanyi, I went straight to the District Officer. I complained that Karisa has put the 4K members at risk and should be reprimanded for not being more responsible for their safety. I was surprised at the DO's response. He said that he understood that this kind of behavior would not be condoned in the United States, which he knew, because he had received his PhD in the USA. "However", he went on, "things are different in Africa." He did not think it wise to reprimand Karisa. Shaming someone in that way is not done, especially an officer of the government. I accepted what he said when I was in his office, but later on I thought, "Now we know why we can't expect too much integrity from the government staff; they are not responsible for their actions."

As I said previously, having the Thing (or Trekker as the Brits called them) gave me a lot of freedom to cover more of the Taita hills. It has a higher frame so was easier to get up the furrowed, steep road to Sagalla. It was an interesting place, even more isolated than the Taita Hills. They had a school, and the Chief's office, and a couple of small *maduka* (pural of *duka*). That was about it. To tell the truth, I don't even know where they held church services because I don't think I ever saw a church building. Obviously the priest came for Mass, but I guess the Wasagalla could not raise enough money to put up an ecclesiastical edifice, although they did built the cabin where the priests and I overnighted. They were good farmers, although mostly traditional. To think they had survived in those hills for between 9 and 11 centuries.[227] There were not many source of water; in fact some of our PCV Ag V members were assigned to build a weir for the Wasagalla, which I am sure they greatly appreciated. Judging from Google Earth, there are many more homesteads in Sagalla now, but there is no sign of any major infrastructural development. Even the main road has the merciless hairpin turn half way up to the central valley; in a distance of about 6 miles from the Mombasa highway to the center of the valley you actually travel about 10 miles of winding mountain road. You realize, when you look at the satellite image, that Sagalla (Google calls it Sagala) is like a natural fortress. The valley is surrounded by forest covered ridges. It is easy to understand that an ancient people could become so isolated that they would develop their own language, and since the root of the language is different than the Wadawida, their ability to interact with the Wadawida was probably limited, maybe even hostile? All of the mountain tribes were at war with the Maasai, but they were apparently able to defend their high ground well. I have not been able to find the thesis of the Czechoslovakian graduate student that was studying the languages of the tribes in Taita-Taveta while I was there. She spent a lot of her time with Jeremiah Kiwinda, but I know that she went to Sagalla, and I believe Taveta as well. I hope she was able to finish her research because it was important anthropology, which is still being studied by scientists as far away as Japan.

I was told I could run into rhinoceros on the road to Sagalla, but I never did. Just thinking about that reminds me of the funny scene with the rhinoceros in "The Gods Must Be Crazy".[228] I did run across a snake on the way to Sagalla once; I have no idea if it was a black mamba, but I had previously seen people in Voi killing a mamba in their village cluster. In spite of the several hazardous fauna in Kenya, I was lucky not to have had a run-in with any of them. As I said before, I liked the Wasaghalla, and enjoyed "getting away" to their mountain retreat. It was well worth the bumpy ride.

While we are not too far beyond the discussion of the Agricultural Show, and the prize that we won, I should inform you of the plow's fate. I tried for several months to find someone who would allow the use of their animals (cows mostly; there are virtually no horses in East Africa because of the Tsetse fly) to try to put the plow to work. It was a lost cause. I don't know if the farmers feared that the plow would overtax their cows, or whether they just understood that the mountainous, terraced farms of Taita Hill were not well suited to an ox-drawn plow. Eventually, the plow was transported to the Provincial Office, and I believe that someone in the more expansive lowland farms was able to put it to use.

That does bring up the issue of appropriate technology, and I can give you a good example. There were two young men in Taita who made their living with a two-man saw.[229] I actually had occasion to hire them toward the end of my tour of duty to cut some lumber from trees on a property I had purchased for Charity. I believe these lads had also cut much of the lumber that was used to make the Kenya top-bar hives in Taita. They worked all over Taita Hills but their home was in the area of Mwanda and the forests on Vuria. The appropriate technology of which I speak, that would have been so appropriate for them, was a two-man chain saw that hung in the Farmer's Cooperative on the road to Wesu. Those two brawny men verily drooled every time they had occasion to visit the cooperative and admire this wondrous invention from across the seas. But the entire two years that I was in Taita, the saw hung in the Coop, and they sweated away, trading places periodically between the humid, steamy pit below the log and the sun-drenched perch above the log. In case you were wondering, they had to dig that pit (deeper than a man's grave) every time they had new logs to saw. They had no equipment to move the logs around, so the pit was usually dug where the tree fell. I had a great deal of respect for those hard working lumberjacks, this 4-fisted, 4-legged *kiwanda cha mbao* (lumber mill). In fact, I was sorely tempted by a Sikh business man to buy a portable sawmill. I met him at the CCH, and he told me that he was leaving East Africa, because he did not want to take citizenship. He wanted 10,000 Ksh.(then about $1400 US) for the machine. That is about the amount that I paid for the property and house for Charity. Maybe I made the wrong decision, but I was a Peace Corps Volunteer, not a Neo-colonialist. I hope that those brothers were able to buy that chain saw and prosper.

Somewhere along the middle of my tour of duty in Kenya, George Gunkleman was fired from the Bura Ranching Scheme (there were rumors of an illicit crop, but I can neither confirm nor deny them). To replace George, the Peace Corps sent in a real cowboy; his name was Jim Smith, and he was fresh off his dad's Texas ranch by way of one of the Texas agricultural colleges. This boy knew his beef cattle, but he was in a whole new world. And he wasn't eased into it like we were with 1.5 months of training stateside before ever coming to Kenya. He and his group took their entire training right in Mombasa, Kenya. Not only that, but the volunteers moved right in with families in that melting pot of many cultures. He came out with a functional command of Kiswahili (with a drawl of course: *Jaaambo, habaaari yaaako?*). He had a decidedly Texan attitude about the Kenyans too; but he was a hard working fellow, and knew his business well.

Conditions were a little harsh on Bura Ranch, so Jim didn't mind making the trip up the hill to Mgange from time to time for a little cool breeze and some good grub. One time we were having a party at my house, and Jim brought the meat... late. The party was already well underway; with some people already three sheets to the wind from drinking Bent's Everything-and-Pineapple-Juice concoction (he literally dumped all the booze in one pail and added pineapple juice). We were to the point where the African Catholic priest was making passes at the wife of Samuel (Charity's brother, the teacher, who was also at the party). Charity and I were on the porch catching some air and admiring the stars when a Land Rover drove up with one headlight aimed at those stars! As Jim was coming out of the Bura Ranch Road, a Kudu had jumped in front of his vehicle and smashed in the left bumper. So he came bearing a hind quarter of Kudu.[230]

Kudu from the Africaans koedoe, is a large species of antelope that tends to stay in thicket vegetation for camouflage. (in the public domain CC BY-SA 3.0) http://en.wikipedia.org/wiki/Kudu

Charity was, of course, thrilled. Having not imbibed as much as yours truly, she was in condition to undertake jerking the meat. The kitchen at the Mgange house was ideal for drying meat. For weeks we had dried Kudu to complement our *ugali na mboga* (the local staple of cabbage soup with cornmeal cake).

I noted on one of the tape recordings that I had taken Jim to Nairobi near the end of my tour, because he needed to sign documents transferring his father's ranch to him. I think his father had died, but I can't remember if he went home for the funeral. I mentioned on the tape that Jim had stayed with us in Taita while he was searching for a new job. He left the Bura ranch before my tour of duty was over, and before the end of his. He was hoping to get a job with the World Bank in livestock marketing. I don't know if I ever knew whether he got the job or not. I have tried to find Jim again in recent years. With a name like Jim Smith, that is an impossible task. I contacted one ranching family in Texas with the name Smith. That Jim turned out to have died at age 88, but his daughter was very nice about the whole thing. Jamie Smith very generously sent me her father's memoirs from WWII. I did not tell her that my father had left no personal record of his experience in WWII. It was a confirmation to me that even if the only people to every read this memoir was my own family, at least there would be a record.

On the subject of relatives, the Peace Corps policy was very good. If there was a serious illness or death in the family, the Corps would send the volunteer home with an open- ended invitation to return. Of course, they were also very responsible about volunteers who were injured or killed in service. We had one of our volunteers who contracted bone cancer, which was not properly diagnosed until near the end of our tour of duty. That was as much the volunteer's failure to recognize the symptoms up in the Turkana territory as it was the Peace Corps doctor's oversight. Once they knew, they gave him the best available medical attention in country until he shipped out. I thought surely he would not live long, but I talked to him after 2000. The Mayo Clinic could not cure his cancer, but he firmly believes God did. He explained his conversion experience, and then went on to relate that he has a business, a wife, and two children. I have to quote Shakespeare

> There are more things in heaven and earth, Horatio,
> Than are dreamt of in your philosophy.
> - Hamlet (1.5.167-8), Hamlet to Horatio

We did lose one volunteer in our group; which is noted in the Peace Corps Archives by these two records:

> **David Bogenschneider** of Beaver
> Dam, Wisc., died about November 18,
> 1970, while swimming alone, He was on
> vacation from his assignment as an ag
> Volunteer in Kenya, David was a graduate
> of Platteville State University.

David Bogenschneider Volunteer in Kenya has been missing for three weeks when his body is washed ashore in the Indian Ocean on Oct. 20, 1970. He had been on vacation with two other volunteers, but parted ways and went out on his own. "We don't know if he drowned or if there was some foul play involved," said his brother Larry. The Peace Corps rules his death an accidental drowning. [231]

Of course there were hazards living in Africa, but there were also hazards for our contemporaries living elsewhere. I am not just speaking of those in Vietnam; the home front was not all that safe, either. There were riots in progress in the big cities, and probably the most lethal hazards for my generation were drugs. In one way, we were kind of isolated from the big bad world in our little corner of "the Dark Continent." The Dayton Daily News did a bit of research on the Peace Corps' fallen in 2003. While there bulleted statements tended toward the melodramatic, it is a fairly accurate synopsis:

Bright lights of peace extinguished
Death in the Peace Corps, 1962-2003
Dayton Daily News

- Their mission is to spread peace by living and working in the developing world.
- But ever since President John F. Kennedy sent the first volunteers around the world more than 40 years ago, the cause of peace has had a tragic side-effect.
- Since 1961, about 170,000 volunteers have served in the Peace Corps, and 250 have died, about one every other month.
- The largest number, nearly 100, died in motor vehicle crashes.
- Others were stricken with heart or asthma attacks, strokes or illnesses such as malaria and even rabies.
- One was gunned down by a sniper, another trampled by an elephant.
- Twenty-eight reportedly drowned.

- At least 20 were murdered, and nearly as many took their own lives.
- Alcohol was linked to dozens of deaths — one of every six.
- Some deaths have never been explained, remaining mysteries to this day. In other deaths, families were given little information or weren't told the truth.
- Although the volunteers died from myriad causes, more than 180 of them had a common link. Each was younger than 30.
- Part of the legacy of the Peace Corps is the volunteer who never made it home. Some of those stories are told below...[232]

If you calculate the mortality <u>accurately</u>, that is only 0.427 deaths per month; that comes out to an attrition rate of 0.00147%; which, in my opinion, is pretty respectable for an agency that sends people to every corner of the earth. The author(s) of this article were really fishing when they made the comment about the "common link". For a good part of those years, Peace Corps was only sending young people; I wouldn't be surprised if the mortality rate is higher now that retired seniors are going into voluntary service. I know, from my visit to Tanzania in 2008, that they no longer allow Peace Corps volunteers to drive motor vehicles in that country (probably with good reason; the traffic is atrocious!) I wouldn't mind an accidental death overseas in the service of my country, would you?

CHAPTER 22

Ukungu ya Mlima
(Mountain Mist)

You will bring them in and plant them on your
own mountain—the place, O Lord, reserved for
your own dwelling,
the sanctuary, O Lord, that your hands have
established.
**New Living Translation (©2007) Exodus
15:17**

I WISH I KNEW MORE about the myths the Wadawida have about
their mountains. Every culture that becomes attracted to the high ground
invents mystical relationships with their mountain. I sometimes wonder
what makes the difference between high-land and flat-land dwellers like
the Wdawida and Maasai respectively. I definitely am one of the high land
dwellers. I have always been drawn to mountains, not to conquer them
but to draw strength from them. Take this scene from a mountain forest
looking over to Mt. Wesu. It conjures up leprechauns or Menehune.[233]

I don't know that the Wadawida had myths of little people, but they
certainly believed in the spirits of their deceased. And I am not sure that
all the Islam and Christianity in the world have driven those beliefs from
them completely.

The peaks of Taita Hills, such as Wesu, Vuria and Iyale[234] were more
than landmarks to the Wadawida; they were sentinels.

Mt. Wesu through the forest (above) http://picasaweb.google.com/sighinya/KughokaShigharo#5486696986028868866

Mt. Yale (below) is visible above children running to school in Kironge. (Both photos reproduced with permission of Tom Callens) http://www.panoramio.com/user/568365

It is believed that spirits of ancestors live on the mountain peaks Iyale and Vuria (…), which makes those the holiest places in the Taita Hills. These places have remained untouchable because of their holiness and also because the slopes of the mountains are too steep for cultivation.[235]

I can almost imagine Iyale looking down on me as I took that fateful turn around this very bend in the road, where I came face to face with Mayai (the bus). I could have been one of those Peace Corps fallen, but fate had another plan?

I myself, and to some extent, my own son, have a kind of mystical "belief." We think that my grandfather, Meritt, guides James in his career in the forest. Meritt himself having been a woodsman, I wonder if he doesn't take interest in James' great love of nature, and his work trying to protect forests from man. That is all I will say on the subject, because I have already promised to let James tell his own story. I will say that after 15 years moving from one Forest Region to the next, he has been assigned to the Freemont-Winema National Forest. Now, here is a twist of fate: the Freemont-Winema includes three regions, the Chiloquin, the Kalamath and the Chemult. Ring a bell? How about Shevlin-Hixon? That's right; James is assigned, probably permanently if he gets his degree in Forest Ecology, to the very region that his great grandfather logged in his youth. Remember that I lived with my Grandparents very near the town of Chemult.

I was born under the watchful eye of Mt. Hood, I was raised in the shadow of Mt. Shasta, I was educated under the imposing view of Mt.

Rainier, I spent summers on the road to Mt. St. Helens. I lived in the Hills of Taita looking over the plains to Mount Kilimanjaro, I have hiked in the Coast Range in Washington and California, I have measured trees and kept honeybees in the Cascade Range, and now I live on the slopes of an erupting volcano, Pu`u O`o. Even San Francisco is a city built on seven hills like the hills of Rome. The only place I ever lived that didn't have mountains in view was Oceanside, and even there the seminarians tried to walk 15 miles to scale a monadnock.

Living in Taita Hills was probably the closest I ever felt to being a mountain dweller. In most places that I lived I was always looking up at the mountain; in Taita I was looking down at the broad savanna below.[236]

View from **Mwachora Peak**, Taita Hills looking toward Mwatate. (Photo reproduced with permission of Tom Callens) http://www.panoramio.com/photo/13273353

Sirke Piireainen in a self-portrait sitting on **Vuria Mountain.** (Photo reproduced with permission of Sirke Piireainen.)

It gives one a very different perspective on life. Maybe there is a genetic element; I am not sure. Why did the Maasai (all over East Africa) decide mainly to stay in the open savanna? Sure the grazing is good for cattle, but the Wadawida also keep cattle. In fact, I will try to transcribe a very interesting story told by Michaeli Mwandighi about the continual feud between the Maasai and the Wadawida over cattle.

But first let me relate the story of a true flatlander, encountering the highest mountain she had ever climbed in her life. Bent Hansen's mother came to visit Taita Hills at Christmas time in 1970. You need to know that the highest "mountain" in Denmark is 400 meters (1300 ft.), and she had lived in Denmark all of her life. She was a healthy 60 year old; so much so that she wanted to dance at our Christmas party, but she couldn't get any of us clumsy bumpkins to dance with her. Bent might have spun her around the floor once, but in my tape recordings, I only mentioned that she was disappointed in our lack of social graces. Nevertheless, she liked me. I forget how Bent put it. He said I brought out her "mothering instinct". Bent had shown her all over the District, and had taken her to Mombasa, but there was one thing she wanted to do more than anything else. That was to climb Vuria.

Now consider that Vuria is 2209 m (7439 ft.) above sea level. Mgange is about 4000 ft., so the road up the mountain is a climb of 3439 ft. By then Bent had been issued a Land Rover and could have easily driven her up to the top of Vuria. She would not have it. She wanted to walk it, and so, the day after the party, we all climbed Vuria[237] on foot. She had to rest from time to time on the way up. I was grateful that she did, because it was a strenuous climb even for us young whippersnappers. It might have been Christmas or New Year's Day (we had had parties on both holidays), and a glorious day it was! Mrs. Hansen was very pleased with herself. I am sure it was a seminal event in her life; and we all reveled in the magnificence of nature. I believe you could actually see the curvature of the earth from Vuria. The life that the Wadawida led was generally simple. Most of them lived in very modest houses, which is still the case today. For example, this house in Kironge[238] looks very much like the house in which Michaeli Mwandighi, his daughter, and her family lived.

Typical Taita home (above). Typical hillside farm (below) bordering on Chawia forest. (Photos reproduced with permission of Tom Callens.)

I went to pick him up at his house one day early in the morning; when I arrived the whole family was out in the yard. The daughter had a fire torch and was brushing it along the ground.

The children were huddling off in one corner of the clearing. I finally realized that they had been invaded by *siafu* (safari ants) in the middle of the night. However, on Public Broadcasting Station's program NOVA, they said that siafu are good pest control for the local farmers. Maybe the siafu forgot which pests they were supposed to control? Well, you can't blame the *siafu*: they were used to invading the mud cities of the termites; the farmers built their houses with mud too. That's just another day in the life of the *Wadavida*.

The principle source of income in Taita is from agriculture and the farms are challenging, at best. The picture is of a fairly typical mountain farm, although the more advanced growers (such as those in Werugha) terrace their land more carefully than this one on the border of Ngangao Forest reserve.[239]

Of course, things are a bit more "upscale" in Wundanyi[240] now; you might not be able to distinguish it from a town in many areas of the developing world. From my prospective, Wundanyi has just about doubled in size since I was there in 1970. Still, from a distance, Wundanyi is barely visible tucked in among the hills of Taita.[241]

Two views of **Wundanyi**, Headquarters of Taita Taveta Distict. (Photos reproduced with permission of Tom Callens.)

And that is how mountain life felt, "tucked away", as if Taita was "the world." And in an earlier age, that was quite true for the Wadawida; it was their world, probably the only world that most of them would have known. There may have been the adventurous few who ventured out of the hills. But I suspect most were like me, wondering why anyone would want to go anywhere else.

I am trying to be somewhat philosophical about what it meant to

545

live in Taita Hills, or Sagalla or Kasigau. Not just for the indigenous
people but for outsiders, too. I just made contact with Tom Wolf, with
whom I had not communicated since he left Taita in 1970. He was so
taken with the Wadawida and Taita that he wrote his PhD. dissertation
about politics and culture in the Coast Province. Of course, that brought
him back to Taita, and, I am told, he lived in Mgange. To this day, he is
still in Kenya. Tom's friend, Shako, and he still communicate. I guess if
circumstances had been different, I would still be there myself. I certainly
have never forgotten Taita; it is not a place one easily forgets neither the
place nor the people.

Of course, I look at the satellite image and think that I would have
expected more development by now. But then I ask myself: why? What do
we in the overdeveloped West have that Wadawida don't have? I can think
of a long list, but to name a few: headaches, war, cancer, confusion, stress,
suspicion, lack of free time, lack of employment, lack of exercise... I could
go on. For their headaches, the Wadawida not only have Western medicine
(asperin), but they have *waganga* (medicine men). They have not been at war
since colonial times. When I was in Taita, I heard of only one case of cancer
(that may have changed with agricultural 'developments' like pesticides).
As to confusion, the only confused people I saw in Taita were the *wazi wazi*.
Most people had pretty level heads regarding what they needed to do to
bring in their crops and send their kids to school. I suppose the Wadawida
had their stresses, but it was much different than what causes heart failure
in America. Their stresses were real; lack of rain, illness, injury, the natural
events of life. Our stresses in the West are undefined, constant, eating away
at the heart with no safety valve. Even a husband might not be able to tell
his wife what pressures he bears every day; he might not even recognize
that he is stressed. In Taita, the people support each other, they listen, and
they help each other with *harambee*. If you have a field to plow, the local
chapter of *Maendeleo ya Wanawake* (Progress for Women) will help you
out. They will all come together, each with her *jembe*, and till the field with

song and good conversation. There will always be suspicions in any human society; what was once called sorcery. But whereas a Mdawida might be suspicious of his neighbor or a person from another village or tribe, we tend to be suspicious of whole ethnic or religious groups throughout the world. Perhaps our suspicions are well founded, but perhaps they are convenient for political purposes as well? After I just explained how much work there is to do in the subsistence-agriculture lifestyle, lack of free time seems like something that the Wadawida would also lack. Nevertheless, free time is what you make of it. We rush from our eight to ten hours-per-day job, spend 2 hours in traffic, pop a meal in the microwave and plop down in front of the boob tube; probably waking from an exhausted snooze and going to bed. For Wadawida, washing clothes is a social event, meals are prepared around a communal fire, and market day is another *mkutano* (meeting). Is it all work? I think not; I think the Wadawida know how to enjoy their daily routine... together! Lack of employment, in the sense of earning a wage, is something that the Wadawida have. But their lives are not turned from success to catastrophe because they lose their job. My own son-in-law is facing that catastrophe now; do you remember how I thought his family was doing so well. Talk about your ironies of life. He has lost his job as a process engineer at a computer manufacturing firm; his wife left him with their son and daughter; he is losing his house; and has no prospect for employment. In Taita, when a man comes back after being on a job in, say, Mombasa, he will be accepted by his family as part of the work force. He will be expected to work on the family farm, but he can be sure he will be fed if anyone else is. And as for lack of exercise, when you live in a mountainous region, going to the store is exercise. I doubt if they have a gym with exercise equipment in Wundanyi yet. I could be wrong, maybe they have "progressed" that far. They certainly do have cell phones, and, I hear, even computers. I wish them well! *Mwisho namlomba dikundane diwose wa Wadawida* (a blessing).

Let us part this chapter with a prospective from the hills of Ngangao forest to the "shining mountain", from where the Wadawida originated; Wachagga from the slopes of Kilimanjaro[242] found their own mountains where they could gaze back to how far they had come.

Kilimanjaro from Ngangao forest. (Photo reproduced with permission of Tom Callens)

CHAPTER 23

Hadithi ya Wazee
(History of the Elders)

These are the memoirs of Nehemiah son of
Hacaliah.
New Living Translation (©2007) Nehemiah 1:1

I WAS IN THE PROCESS of transcribing the stories of Michaeli
Mwandighi from Kiswahili to English. It is slow going from a 40 year
old magnetic tape. Actually, my recording technique left something to be
desired back then, before the auto-volume control, etc. I was surprised that
we still had a tape recorder whose drive mechanism has not been eaten
up by the sulfuric acid precipitating out of the air here on the slopes of an
active volcano. It would be a lot easier to just relate the gist of the story that
Mzee Michaeli tells, but I am trying to be faithful to his own words out of
respect for the now deceased[243] senior citizen that gave me the benefit of
his time, his knowledge and his friendship. I regret that I so totally ignored
any opportunity I had to maintain contact with those people that I knew
in Taita. One gets so wrapped up in one's own life when one is young.
Then one day you wake up and realize that you are old. All the people
and circumstances, that have made you what you are, have been forgotten,
lost, and disconnected from your life. It is not usually possible to reconnect
to them, so you try; but you accept that probably all you have left are the
tenuous memories. It is nice to find one or two people you knew, like Tom
Wolf and Charles Howe.

The reader may be wondering what importance this translation has for
my memoir.[244] Well, I have already explained that I am doing this out of

heshima (respect) for *Mzee* Mwandhigi, but more than that I am giving back to the people that I know from Taita, a picture of the life and history of a people that I learned to love. I am worried that I could only find one small reference to the life of Reverend Jeremiah Kiwinda on the internet. Perhaps he will appear in some scholarly journals which most young Wadawida will never read. Certainly the family of Wadawida that I brought to America will have only a marginal awareness (if any) of this important reverend in the history of Taita. Mzee Mwandighi was more important to Charity's immediate family than Jeremiah. He was a friend of the family; the children knew him, although they would probably not remember. Even though we have a tape of him relating the stories of Taita, they will mostly not be able to understand it, because they have lost their ear for the fluid Kiswahili of the Pwani (Coast). Edward Amon and Gertrude Tabu might remember *Mzee* Mwandighi.

If a family member looked for a book to help him/her learn Kidawida, such a book does not exist as far as I know. Charity's relatives in Taita suggested that she obtain a copy of the Kidawida Bible, which was the most scholarly study of the language done to that date. Having gathered together the elders of the Tribe, it is based on their skill and knowledge of the language. This is common in bible publication. There is even a Creole version of the New Testament produced in Hawaii. Called *Da Jesus Book*, it had input from 26 native speakers (fluent in Hawaiian Creole). There is also an older Hawaiian language version of the entire bible[245]

In spite of the interest of family members in Kidawida, the *Mzee*'s *hadithi* (story) was in Kiswahili. I like Will Roger's definition of a memoir (see endnote 243), but in all honesty, I am trying to be factual, for the sake of the family. I am including everything about my life that was unique, and the opportunity to hear Mzee recount Taita history was truly unique. So unlike Gore Vidal's concept of a memoir, this one involves some research, checking dates, etc. I hope this will be of some help to the Diaspora that I brought from Taita to America.

In the larger sense, what does this historical personal account of Mzee Mwandigi mean to most readers? Perhaps not much, in fact, one might want to skip this chapter altogether; be my guest to do so. But if you want to have a feeling for how the older Wadawida speak (albeit in translation), this chapter will give you a feeling for it. There is a lot of repetition and remonstrating about old rivalries and injustices. We westerners find this sort of banter boring. We do not have the feel for the cadence and reinforcing repetition of oral history. Perhaps it loses its poetic song-like quality in translation, but I could not help feeling I was sitting around a campfire listening to the elders when I was transcribing this soliloquy. Perhaps the story of the Taita from Mzee Mwandigi's mouth would only be of interest to anthropologist.

Mzee Michaeli Mwandigi (Author's personal photo taken at Wundanyi FTC Beekeeping course)

Michaeli Mwandighi was a political activist, so this tape contains many personal opinions and evocative statement, in addition to the somewhat historical retelling of stories that he had heard from tribal elders, whom he describes at the end of the story. Although Michaeli was a Mdawida, he was also fluent in Kiswahili because he had lived amongst the Chagga and the Pare for many years. Therefore he refers to the Wadawida by the Kiswahili name of Wataita. By the way, some believe that the word Taita was derived from a Kisagala word which means 'fierce', as they described the Wadawida to those coming from the Coast. Mwandigi's delivery style was crisp, but repetitive (in the story-telling mode of the Wadawida). He always refers to the 'Maasai' whether he is referring to one man or the whole tribe. The proper Kiswahili for Maasai would be {Kiswahili: Mmaasai, pl. Wamaasai}, but I am translating it as spoken on the tape recording. There are exceptions: Mwandighi keeps referring to the "Wakipare", and the "Wakisambara", and the "Wakichaga." I suspect that is an error on his part. Therefore, I have chosen to translate those terms as Mchage, pl. Wachaga; Mpare, pl. Wapare; Msambara. pl. Wasambara. If there is a reason why he combines the neuter form of the word with the gender form, I would appreciate being informed of the purpose.

There are a few places where the *Mzee* gets entirely too repetitive about excoriating the government officials for their complicity in the illegal cattle rustling, so I excerpted that repetitive part of the text (as indicated in brackets []).I have one more admonition to you the reader before you launch into this. Remember that you are not reading Hemingway!

Michaeli Mwandighi's account of the history of the people of Taita Hills
Translated from Kiswahili recording made in Mgange, Taita-Taveta
District, in 1971 by L. Michael Klungness (completed Sept 24 2010)

They [the Wadawida] would steal the cattle of the Maasai, because the manner of the bond of the Maasai was to say that cattle are their property only, not the property of other people. Even when their children would go to work here and there in many places, they would say the money that they earned and put in the banks had no meaning in Maasai culture... because this money that they use is the wealth of idiots. Let them pay the idiots there money. Useless people! (meaning, yes, the farmers whose money is their wealth). So they are useless people, let them have their cash. Therefore, get busy and steal cattle to return our wealth [to us, the Maasai]. All of the cattle that are with the farmers, who eat food, are our wealth. Return the cattle to us, don't pay for them. Pool resources to save money but go take the cattle. If you see that people want to stop you from taking the cattle, then use the money to buy them. The main thing, come back with the cattle. Use the money to build places to keep the cattle. But to <u>use</u> the money for these purposes, it has no purpose in our land. The thing the Maasai value the most is cattle. Therefore they will go looking for cattle everywhere. If you have to, pay the money for the cattle, if there is someone trying to stop you, someone powerful, a policeman or whomever, just give him the money and bring back the cattle.

Because other people value money, if you give them money [bribe], they will let you go with the cattle.

Cattle are indeed the wealth of the Maasai, even if a Maasai has money, he has no use for it; his need is cattle. So the young men, even if they have acquire a lot of money, they have no need to put it away, they follow the directives of their fathers, and buy cattle. The Maasai have knowledge of cattle more than any other tribe, because it is their [proprietary] secret. They do very well by their cattle, and they collected them from everywhere... even at night, they don't fear the lions. They just steal cattle and move them in darkness. They don't fear elephants, they don't fear rhinoceros... even if a rhino appears they don't care; they can throw spears at him to insure that they pass with their cattle. They see it as great *mapolu*[246]. When they go with their cattle and the young women see that cattle have been captured, they will go in *mapolu* and spend the night. Also, when they go to steal cattle they will have found a place that is adequate to hold the cattle.

Now when people organize to follow the Maasai, they will go to the East, and then they will turn around and return. The people are following them far ahead, and they have already turned around. They go back and forth like this, the pursuers go back, the Maasai move ahead; the pursuers go forward again, the Maasai go backwards. This way they go round and round in circles, and little by little they fetter the cattle in safe places. The Maasai of Kenya cooperate with the Maasai of Tanganyika to sequester the cattle so they cannot be arrested. When they come back to Kenya, they tell the police they don't know where the cattle went. One Maasai [raiding party] can travel from Tanzania to Nairobi and anywhere. This is the way they travel about with their cattle. The reason is that they all have one heart where ever they are, one by one they cooperate; it is one big union. If they go here, they are with their own, if they go there they are with their own. The cattle are moved great distances, but they know the cattle are the property of so-and-so. So the cattle of one Maasai can be separated, and the man will pay to have them transported by vehicle. Therefore the cattle are transported everywhere. Or perhaps, if people are wondering what is going on, the Maasai will trade cattle with their brothers in another country, sell the cattle, and go buy other cattle in their own territory. This is the way they work, just like that!

Likewise, the Maasai look out for problems. If one Maasai has no wealth, he will take his money and go to Maasai in another country, and they will give him money. The *Wazee* will give him cattle to use; 50, whatever number, even more than fifty. He will become the herdsman and will get his share. Those cattle, the Maasai manage like this, and they know the places to herd them. Every place that has good pasture, the Maasai know. The Maasai will pull some grass and chew on it, and then he will say whether it is good grass for the cattle or not. If he thinks the grass will not suit the cattle, he will move them; he will not stay in that place.

These people, when they eventually come to understand the value of money, and if they start to farm, we hear that they begin to exceed other people because they have many cattle. So they move their cattle and all at once they buy tractors and plows to farm. But now a few are beginning to understand, but mostly they prefer to herd cattle. So they are very shrewd people, and they are people with much skill for the lowlands. If the police try to catch the Maasai, they are greatly annoyed. But if they try very hard everywhere, if they put out sentries, and if they have airplanes, so that when they hear of a theft they can search from the air, then they can [Loud noise drowned out voice]. But before, it was very difficult, because some people really love money, and if a Maasai encountered a police officer, he might pull out 1000 KSh. to bribe him, and the officer will say "go ahead". Yeah, the officer might even give him information so that they would not be caught. If the Maasai offers 1000 KSh. any officer will give them permission to pass with their stolen goods. Thus you hear [news on the radio], the Maasai were not arrested, they were not apprehended. The thieves were seen, but the money talks, the police just want to get paid. In addition, some of the higher authorities, the Party Members, and the Inspectors are in the gang, they are the friends of the Maasai. That's how they are able to pass; the police don't "see them". For this reason it will be a very difficult job for the Maasai to be caught.

The Maasai still contend that all the cattle in the whole world belong to them. If a Maasai sees a farmer with a cow, he will say it was the farmer who's stolen his cow. This is the side [stance] of the Maasai. If the government undertakes a big program to assemble all of the forces to put everywhere, and I mean everywhere, they will be able to arrest them. But if things continue as they are, many times it will be a huge problem. People love money, and those Inspectors have the smarts to guard themselves, so that they will not be seen as having any violations. In order to make it look like they are doing their job, they go looking for the Maasai… they don't see them. They look for them and they look for them…. No! Not true! They know, for sure. But they go to great lengths to hide this lie from the government. It would be better if the inspectors did their jobs. It is they that give the Maasai permission to continue. Those big inspectors, many of them are the ones who are biggest swindlers. They have many secrets. If the government wanted to stop the cattle rustling, they should first go after the Inspectors (paraphrased).

It would be good, if cattle disappeared in the National Park, that the National Park be charged for the cattle lost there. In a short time, the National Park staff would work very hard to make sure the cattle were not stolen [paraphrased]. [Mwandighi repeats himself about the connection between the cattle rustling and the lax oversight by the staff of the National Parks and the police.]

The Maasai love cattle, and they know the places to go for good pasture. They will test the grass in their own mouths. In this land, the Taita Hills, in the past, in the *Kali* [literally translated: hot; means time of conflict], the Massai did not come here. Again, Maasai can be a very good person, and a true friend. If you become the friend of a Maasai, he will love you very much. Again, he will show respect and his children will also show respect, they are good children who love their fathers. However, in days gone by, the Maasai did not like to come near Taita. They did not like to meet up with Mtaita; if he encountered one, he would hide. The reason was that there was hatred between their two tribes from ancient times. The Wataita, when they would see a campfire in the lowlands, if they saw there was fire, they would blow their cow-horn signal, and in an instant the message would spread through Taita Hills. Taaa! Taaa! The signal would spread from Mwanda all the way to Sagalha, and Kaseghau, even all the way to Mbololo below all within a short time.

Now when people would hear this, and it is called the horn of war, they had their store of food that they kept for this purpose. They would put this food in their bags, and their weapon would be handy, too. Night or day they would pack their provisions and go. When they reached the area called Mwanda, the people of Mwanda would have commissioned others. "We saw there were fires in such-and-such place." Some of the Wataita would circle far around. They would take mafundo (knots, markers) with them, five or ten mafundo; these were their markers. Each night when they slept, they would leave a marker behind where they slept. Each day another marker. On the last day, when they would be ready to encounter those whom they came down to the lowlands to attack. When they would be ready for the attack, the party would receive backup from other Wataita who had followed the trail of markers. The Maasai would feel hungry and stop to eat. Just then the Wataita would descend on them from all around and kill all of the Maasai warriors, except one. This one they would spare. This is what we were told. They would cut off a part of his ear, and then they would slaughter one of the Maasai cattle and roast it. They would give the prisoner a part of the cow for his journey home, and then would send him to tell the other members of his tribe what the Wataita had done. That is the reason that the Maasai feared to come near the Wataita. [or so the Wataita believed].

The Wataita would kill every last one of the Massai raiding party. Even if there were women or children, the Wataita did not want to take them. They would not only kill the men and women, but even the children. The Wataita would not take a Maasai or their children, because, they would say, "if we bring them to live at our homes, what will we do to protect our cattle?" They killed them all, even the children. In spite of the fact that they might bring back women from other tribes like the Wakichanga, or the

Wakipare, or the Wakichaga or the Wakisambaa, these they would like. But the Maasai, they did not like. Therefore they [the tribes] would persecute each other constantly. Very far in the past they were friends [the Wataita and the Maasai]. [Charity adds that Wataita would say that if you adopted a Maasai, you would raise a thief] The Watiata did not like thieves. Even if you took a Maasai and he did not have any interest in theft, eventually he would become a thief. And [the Wataita] did not like thieves. But we here that in the distant past those two tribes were friendly and had markets where they traded with each other. The Maasai would buy oranges and fruit while the Wataita would buy meat. This was a time of friendship, until the Maasai started stealing cattle. They would form friendships, but at night they would steal cattle. If [the Maasai] would see a sheep, he would go at night and carry it off... this is how the war between the tribes started. Therefore, [the Maasai] were driven completely out of this land [Taita]. There was a place called Kiangache Mbele, which was called *mara ya wangenga*, which means "until they were enemies". It was there that they would have their market together in times past, but it is where the war started.

Therefore, when the Wataita would travel in Maasai land, they would say "I am not Mtaita", because that hatred is there until the current time. This is how bad blood came between them. And nowdays, the cattle rustlers all over East Africa are the Maasai, even in Tanzania. Again, to abolish it is very difficult. Another tribe called the Manati there near Singira who are like the Maasai in cattle rustling, but their rustlers are worse than the Maasai. This is because they kill people! In the territory of the Manati, if they find someone keeping cattle, they kill them. The Maasai, when they steal cattle, are not prone to kill the herdsmen; they leave them, or sometimes bind them only. The Manati, their job is to kill people. They are very much thieves but they have very hard hearts. Otherwise, the Maasai have a heart to mercy for human beings. But when it comes to cattle, if he wants to take a cow, he will be stricken with hunger until he gets it.

These words and these acts are the responsibility of the government to investigate, to determine how it will be in the National Parks. They need to know that the Maasai are moving cattle everywhere, but if they do take the initiative, without unforeseen surprises, or even to pay for the stolen cattle, the problem of cattle rustling will subside. If this doesn't happen, it will continue indefinitely. In Mwaktau [plains area in Taita-Taveta District] frequently cattle are stolen. When they are stolen there, they are moved through the brushy areas of the veld until they end up in the National Park. These days there are National Park police all over the Park, but if they see the Maasai moving cattle they don't try to stop them. Even if they [the Wataita] follow the Maasai into the Park, they themselves are halted, and are asked, "Where is your letter of permission to follow your cattle". The Park Department doesn't know what is going on? And the cattle are lost. We hear until this very day that the Wataita are complaining about their cattle being stolen. The calves that are left behind die [for lack of milk]. The police do nothing, the Wataita are not paid. So this evil comes from the hand of the National Park. The National Park knows. If one of them is exposed, he is transferred to another area, and replaced. And those that were brought before will be taken around with the Maasai; they will be rewarded, and are paid much money. [*Mzee* Mwandighi cannot abandon this argument, and goes on and on, over and over again, claiming that "the Maasai have driven the herdsmen to eat the dust of Mwaktau and are dying of poverty". I pass over this part for brevity, and concern about the veracity of it all.]…

There is no wealth in Kenya like the wild animals of the savannah. These are the greatest wealth of Kenya. They were the wealth in the past and they will be until the end. There is nothing like it, it is the wealth of the nation. First people came to look at the animals. To look, just to look at the animals. They would pay money to get licenses to observe the animals. And then came the pictures. Taking a picture is money. Taking pictures of the animals that were once game to be killed, is now big business. Big money is paid to photograph the game, but the cattle of the poor are passed through the park, and the poor are not paid. This is intentional, to make the poor even poorer. Those with wealth and education have not mercy on the poor herdsman who herds his cattle in the veld. But if the National Park was required to pay for the cattle lost to the poor herders, then the probably of the theft would subside.

I have traveled all over the country and Maasailand when I was young. I have never seen anyone who loves the wealth of having cattle like the Maasai. There are not any! The Maasai have no hatred, they love people very much. Except that they love people who have no need of cattle. But someone who really loves his cattle, the Maasai has no use for him. I have traveled a lot in Kenya and Tanzania, and I have many friends who are Wamaasai. But I fear them; if I am with them, I say I have not need of *Mfugo* (livestock), I have not need of cattle. Then he will be a true friend... I mean serious friend, he will kill a cow roast it and give it to you. And he will say, this is the wealth of the Maasai, you have no need of it, it is the possession of the Maasai. Your job is to farm. They love a man like that, so I was very well loved by the Maasai. Except that they did not know I was Mtaita. They thought that I was Mpare or Msabaa, because I had lived with those tribes and knew their language. I stayed there long enough to learn Kipare and Kisabaa, because I lived in Tanganyika more than 20 years. I would say I was Mpare or Msabaa. They [the Maasai] liked me a whole lot! The young ones and even the old ones liked me. But I understood that it is better if a person does not express interest in the cattle, because if you have cattle Maasai will ask for them back. [Mandighi is laughing here]. Therefore, even if you were raise from a child among the Maasai, it is better that child not express interest in cattle. The Maasai might think the child would do them wrong or report them to the police for stealing cattle. So, the Maasai are good people except that they have a great lust for cattle.

[I asked *Mzee* Mwandighi if he had cattle] Yes, I had my herd of cattle, but I did not tell the Maasai that I had any cattle. If I told them, they would be enemies. [Then he goes on about the Maasai realizing that the police are just people and can be bribed, so the Maasai pooled their resources to bribe the police]...

I don't have more to say. I am Michaeli Mwandighi. I was born here in Taita. My blood relations are more than 24 people. I am Michaeli, son of Mwandighi, son of Kuranda, son of Mpisha, son of Nyambu, son of Mwandigha, son Nyambu, son of Tutu, son of Chenga, son of Ilimba, son of Digha, son of Mur[h]asha, *Omo* Mandigi, son of Choke. Choke was the man who planted this tree in the mountains of Taita; he came from the west. [Mandighi laughs briefly, I think with pride, that he can recite his ancestors]. When he came here, he was the result of a man named Ngeti, who was the result of Mchana, and one was called Mwalimu. They were the result of a man named Mwaalu, who resulted from Maruma, who resulted from a man named Chase (and now they are called Kese). He resulted from Mlondo, and those people are called Wamlondo. They came here [to Taita] and they found people called Mwakamu. We don't know where they were from, but they lived in the area of Lushangoni. They were driven from there and returned here. Choke went through here and returned to Nika and Babacha; then he went to Shimbi and then Lushangoni; then he went to Wundanyi; then he went down to Kishamba. There in Kishamba he saw that his children were afflicted with sores. And those sores were Matanu [could not find definition]. He saw that this was a bad area, so they returned to Wundanyi. When they all reached Wundanyi, from Mbauru and all of that area up to [Mwandighi paused to think] Mkororo, and came to the area at Vurugu. This place had a stream which descended to Mbauro, and along this stream was the land of Wundanyi, and these people were the descendants of Choke. Some of the decedents stayed in the place now called Choke, and others descended to Lushangoni, but the people from that whole area were the descendants of Choke. The other family in [in the general area] was the family of Ngure. Another family was that of Nymabu. Ngure and Nyambu were brothers. [it is not clear what Mwandighi is saying but he is probably enumerating other families or decedents of Ngure and Nyambu] All of these people were descendent of one line, those who lived in this land. This which I am telling you was told to me by my elders in March 1937. I had gone to Mombasa to visit my sister. When I arrived there I lived there for a period; I was baptized there in October of 1936. In 1937 I had the chance to go home. I was with my Godfather, Stephan Mwatele. After I arrived I visited the old folks [*Mzee*, pl. *Wazee*), both women and men, in order to collect the histories of the ancestors. I went to one *Mzee*, whose name was Mwondo Wakimunda; he told me all these stories. He was an old man not less than 100 years old. Although he was old, he had his wits. He lived in Kidogwa, and he was from the family of Choke. Another *Mzee* who lived in Lushangoni, who was called Mkushwa [sp?] Magang[h]a, and he also retold these stories. Then I went to interview a woman who was very very old, but she still had her mind. She was called Mama Kidasi, or Mwanyange. She told me stories. Then I went to another *Mzee* whose name was Lombo Mwajondo; he was the one who told me many stories. This Lombo Mwajondo had a disability. His mark was that he has been burned by a spear in the battle of Kilimanjaro. He told me all of these stories about how he went to war, and how it was to be in battle. He told me that story of our family. Then I went to visit another woman named Mkandung[h]i, she was from the Mwakisha of Mganga. She told me her stories. Then I put the stories together, and my mother added her stories. Her name was Binti Nayambu. Then I compiled all these stories and whatever I could see was in agreement from the different stories, these are the things I have related. And this is how the story of my family came about as I have told you. Other *Wazee* that I interviewed, even those from my own family, were not able to remember the stories of the Wataita very well, so I took it upon myself to memorize what I had heard and to this day I remember things as I was told by those whom I have mentioned.

I was also told the traditional histories of the Maasai, and of the Wachaga, because the Wachaga and the Wataita had fought wars in the past. When [the Wataita fighters brought back women and children from] Wachaga to Taita, they did not stay, because the Wataita accused them of being thieves. The Wachaga were sold and sent to Mombasa. If [the Wataita] took slaves from among the Wapare, some would be sold, but others would stay here and there in Taita Hills. After the last war, there were so many Wapare brought to Taita that the [English Colonial] government intervened and sent all the Wapare to the mission in Bura. Eventually some of the Wapare returned to their homeland. That is how I came to hear the stories of a *Mzee* Mpare named Nyasi (Luwigo, daughter of Luwigo and her sister) in a mission called Kilomini there in Pare. Because Kilomini did not originally have a mission, those women would have to travel three days and sleep on the road to go to Kilimanjaro to hear Mass. They did this for two or three years until eventually the mission at Kilomini was built; and it was a big church. I met this woman [Nyasi] and I saw her children, some of whom were born in Taita. One son's name was Joakim and the other was Francis; these were the children born in Taita. [Nyasi] was captured and taken to Taita when she was a child. After her children [two sons] were born in Taita, she went back to live in that area [Kilomini] and she had other children there. It was she who brought the religion to that area. And it was she who told me how she was captured during the war when she was a small child.

Even in Sambara I was shown all the places where the Wataita had gone, and how far the Wataita went to secure wealth. If the encountered the children of the Wachaga, the Wapare or the Wasamba they would like them very much and take them and bring them to Taita. For this reason some of the residents of Chaga, Pare and Sambara had come from Taita Hills at one time. [in is not clear in Mzee Mwandighi's narration under what circumstances the children were taken, whether abducted or exchanged. In Hawaii the practice of Hanai was common, where one person or one relative would take a child from his parents and treat him/her as his own family. This might have been what Mwandighi was suggesting] The Wataita would ask some person, why are you called Mchali. The family is that of Mchali, If they would not leave, they would all be killed. They left with the name of Mchali and they traveled a great distance until they arrived in the land of Sambara. So they had completely migrated. And they continued to migrate and migrate again like that, and that is how they arrive in the land of Sambara.

And the Taita did not go to make war with the Wapare by themselves, but they were led there. It was people who came from that place, they would come [to Taita] with [their numbers?] and would lead the Wataita to the place where they would fight. Those people [leading the Wataita] would speak the Kipara language. When they would come together [with the Wapare] to do battle, the Wapare would think these were their own people. Kumbe! [shock, wow!] They were allied with the Wataita. Yes, that is the way the war went on, like this and in that way. But today and for a long time the Wapare and the Wataita have had great friendship because they have been told that they all come from one family.

They have a great friendship with the Wataita, right up to today. And later when the government builds a road between the Usambara and Taita... there is a big plain between the two tribal areas. If you look towards Sambara from Taita you will see their hills, and if you look from Sambara toward Taita you will see the Taita Hills. Between is a great basin (valley) in which you would have to sleep 3 or 4 nights to cross the expanse. And believe me, there is no water there! If the government would build a road between Sambara and Taita, it would be a very good thing for the Wasambara and the Wataita because there a many Wataita that live amongst the Wasambara. There are many Wataita that came in times past by way of Kasegau. Even I went to visit them, they know how to speak Kitaita, and they had a Chief who married an Mtaita... about the year 1942 I spent time in that area. Well! For this reason there are many Wataita, there are many Wasambara, but now they are called Wapare. So, in the future it will be that, once they come to know each other, the friendship between the tribes will grow. The Wapare have no hatred for the Wataita and the Wataita have not hatred for the Wapare. The same is true for the Wasamba.

But the hatred between the Maasai and the Wataita lives to this very day. Even now [Mwandighi chuckles] if the Wataita hear that a Maasai is being brought to tour Taita Hills, every person with come out to see him. There are many people in Taita who have never seen a Maasai. If he be brought to Taita to be toured around the Hills, ever person will close their business and go to see the Maasai. "Oh, so those are the people who used to annoy our fathers in the past" [Mwandighi cannot contain his amusement]. Well, that is the way it is. That's the way it is. [Mwandighi is like the African version of Walter Cronkite].

Now we will go forward, matters proceed slowly, that is all. In the end they will join together as friends when the cattle rustling stops. And the Maasai, when they obtain education, they will be wealthier than all the other tribes. This is because they had wealth in their cattle. If they become educated, their sons will buy tractors, and they will buy plows (the cattle drawn kind). In the end, they will become richer than all the other tribes. If they become educated, they will be first in the Nation. I saw in the past, that the Maasai had become members of the army. They would understand much from the Europeans, and would be educated. When they would get leave of one or two months to return home, some would go to purchase English pigs. Nevertheless, they would go to get their red dirt and cover their whole bodies with the fat and red dirt, even his hair would be red with this mixture. If you came to visit you would think him just an ordinary Maasai... Kumbe! [surprise!] this is a man that can speak very well and understands everything. At the end of his leave, he will wash completely, put on his uniform and return to his work as a soldier. [Mwandighi chuckles again] Kumbe! When he goes to stay with his clan he will be compelled to teach his fellows to steal cattle. He has only this one fault! But those people, when they become educated and learn how to farm, they will enrich themselves. They will be more successful than all the other tribes.

If all the tribes learn to like each other, and pull together there will be progress. But if there is not Unity, Hoooiii! Worthless! The Nation will continue to descend into poverty. But if people pull together, then we will rise up [like a bird] and go forward.

[I asked Mwandighi this question. I am told that within their tribe they have a rule that two friends share everything. If you want something from your friend, even his wife, he will give it/her to you. Is that true?] Yes, the nature of the Maasai is that they ask for much. If a Maasai sees something that you have that he wants, he will ask you for it. If he wants it, you cannot refuse him. He will have a great urgency to get that item from you. By the same token, if a Maasai sees that you like something of his, he will give it to you straight out. Whether it is cattle or anything else, he will give it to you. But he does not like to be denied what he wants from your things either. And he will give you whatever you want from him.

Well! We will discuss these things later at another time. Also, let us not forget one thing. The Maasai have a great deal of love for their fellow human beings. They love people a lot, but they have the problem of cattle rustling. Nevertheless, a Maasai does not like theft in others. He does not like someone who would go in your house and steal. The Maasai don't think of their cattle rustling as theft. They just believe the cattle are theirs. But a Maasai would not invite a person who is known to steal, inside his house. [Mwandighi goes on in this vein repeating the same thing over and over.] Nor do the Maasai like a liar. Someone with secrets is not liked by the Maasai. [Mwandighi laughs] The Maasai also know very well how to pray to God, they love God a great deal. They will ask for protection from God to protect them and their animals in the veld. They go into the veld by themselves with their animals and they depend on God to protect them. [Mwandighi goes on facetiously about the Maasai and God.]

The discussion went on for a few more minutes, but it was nothing of importance: just a discussion of the virtues and faults of people in general. In this recording I recall the spirit of the man who had helped me in Taita, and who was willing to share his knowledge of the people and their origins.

There are other stories that *Mzee* Mwandighi told that were not recorded. These were stories about the moral character of the Wadwaida and how it was maintained. How the sacred forests were so important for the Wadawida, some of which is documented in a paper by Nina Himberg in 2004.[247, 248]

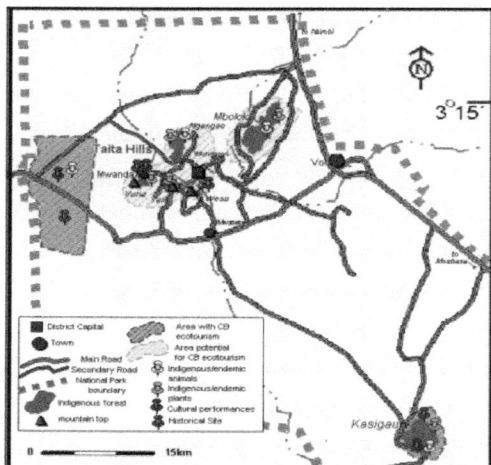

Taita Hills diagrammed to indicating the the indigenous forests or **figis**. (map of Nina Himberg in the public domain)

Three types of forests are found in the Taita Hills: planted forests, indigenous forests and sacred forests called *figis*. The sizes of the remaining indigenous forests are alarmingly small and they are partly disturbed. The size of the forest counts when ensuring the long-term survival of the flora and fauna (Bytebier 2001). The largest indigenous forest fragment in Taita Hills is Mbololo with 200 ha of quite undisturbed forest [see map]. Ngangao is the second largest fragment (92 ha). Other forests are small and disturbed by selective logging. On the top of the mountains Iyale, Wesu and Vuria (0.01 ha) are small remnants of forests and isolated trees. Only Mbololo and Ngangao may be viable forests in the long run (Wilder et al. 1998, Bytebier 2001:24). According to Brooks et al. (1998:191) Taita Hills contain three endemic and threatened birds, one snake, two amphibians and three butterflies. This generic endemism also characterizes the flora of these hills. The forest flora consists of over 400 species of plants of which at least 13 are endemic (Kenya Forests Working Group 2003). A crucial task is to preserve the remaining high altitude indigenous forests of the Taita Hills to prevent this uniqueness being lost forever.

The sacred forests are traditionally protected

The laws governing the forest resources and the strengthening of Christianity have changed the relations between local people and the forests during the history. Traditional land tenure system classified land as cultivated and uncultivated. Taita people had usage rights to the land (Maundu & Ogutu 1986:56-67). They set aside areas of forest, which they respected because those places are used in many traditional ceremonies. The Taita have their traditional religion called Wutasi, which was still strong by the early 1950's. The belief in a higher being called Mulungu and in ancestor spirits, played important part in the lives of the Taita (Maranga & Mathu 1986:43-46).

According to village elder Judah Mwanjumba (2004), the clans have their own places in the forests or caves for sacrificing to higher powers. Initiation training and rainmaking rituals are practiced in these sacred places. It is forbidden to cut trees or collect firewood from the holy forests. Indigenous plant and tree species can be found on the patches. These holy forests called *figis* have had many purposes. In former days they were considered crucial in protecting the community from bad-intentioned intruders. They acted as a gateway between homeland in the hills and lowland areas considered dangerous. In every social unit there was an elder responsible for rituals. Many important preparations concerning traditional laws and village governance took place in *figis*. For example certain plants found there could be used in making medicine for bringing love to the community if the situation seemed unsettled. The purification of the elder, and judging and sentencing wrong doers to death took place in a sacred forest as well. According to Ville (1994:24) the Taita ritual complex has been even something more than just protecting territory and bringing rain. The food chain was controlled by magical means to suit husbandry production and the agricultural timing was directed by the elders.

Indigenous forests are still important places for collecting plants for medicinal use in health care means, although their value has diminished due to the growing awareness about western medicine. The knowledge about traditional use of plants has been diminishing during past decades, as people seem to find it easier to buy the cure for an illness from a pharmacy and lack of proper knowledge about herbalism makes them unsure how to treat children especially. Even if these small forest patches are traditionally protected, they also have had to make way for agriculture. Some *figis* have been destroyed by fundamentally thinking Christians (Mwanjumba 2004).

It is believed that spirits of ancestors live on the mountain peaks Iyale and Vuria (Figure 3), which makes those the holiest places in the Taita Hills. These places have remained untouchable because of their holiness and also because the slopes of the mountains are too steep for cultivation. Traditionally Taita and Taveta people venerated the skulls of their ancestors one year or more after the burial in order to avoid bad things happening. The skulls were deposited in a holy lineage skull-depository, usually in a cave (Maranga & Mathu 1986:44-46). Some of these caves still exist even if most of them have been destroyed.

The traditional ceremonies have diminished among the Taita with the coming of Christianity and western education. Some of the old people still practice rituals, but most of the ritual experts like diviners, seers, defenders and rainmakers have died and have not been replaced. As most of the younger generation are Christians and have been educated in a "modern" way they are not interested to follow old traditions in a thorough way (Mwanjumba 2004). What has happened is that Wutasi has mixed with Christianity and certain old Wutasi traditions and values still rule. Traditions like name giving, circumcision of boys and funeral ceremonies are accepted in Christianity. Strong respect of older people and parents, high working morale and the spirit of harambee (cooperation) are also values that still lead the lives of Taita (Kapule & Soper 1986:13).[249]

The stories related to me by *Mzee* Mwandighi support the conclusions of this scholarly article. He confirmed that forests were very important areas for many ceremonies of the Wadawida. Important meetings of the elders were held in the forests. Initiation ceremonies and celebrations honoring the deeds of noteworthy people were held in the *figis*. These could be young people, old people or anyone whom the community considered worthy. This habit of the community had a sinister side, because the ceremony could be a judgment as well. The invited honoree of the event might not actually know why he/she was being invited into the woods. The elders of the community knew most everything about everyone's actions. A worthy honest person would have nothing to fear in the *mkutano figini* (meeting in the forest). However, a deceitful person, even if they thought their actions were not known, might find the *mkutano* his or her last. For example, theft was greatly despised amongst the Wadawida. As so many thieves are inclined to do, a *mwizi* (a robber) Mdawida might believe that no one knew of his/her transgression. This was not true. The Wadawida would take careful note of occasions of theft, and they would conspire to find the thief. Once identified, the thief would be watched covertly. Once three offenses could be documented by the observers, the thief would be invited to the *figi*. He would think he was being invited to be honored. *Kumbe!* ("Oh!" as they would say in Kiswahili), the meeting would be a trial. If the thief came up wanting, he would be escorted over the cliff! Of course, the punishment was the same for any serious crime, like murder or rape. It was a very effective method of maintaining civil order, and is probably the reason the Taita people were trusted for their integrity from early colonial times.

It is curious to compare these stories of the Wadawida in the past to the people of the current day. On average, the Wadawida tend to be educated, they are largely Christianized, and by East African standard might be considered quite modern. On the whole, their reputation among the tribes of Kenya is quite positive. When you compare that to Mzee Mwandighi's account of the wars, and taking slaves in ancient times, it seems very incongruous with modern Wadawida. Nevertheless, some of the virtues instilled by the ancient practices have proved useful in modern times (e.g. honesty, group cohesion and cooperation). Of this there is no doubt: the Wadawida consider themselves a unique people, a clan for which cohesion extends all over the world. There are Wadawida websites, like Wadawida. com, which requires that the participants be registered.[250]

> In order to login you must be registered. Registering takes only
> a few moments but gives you increased capabilities. The board

administrator may also grant additional permissions to registered users. Before you register please ensure you are familiar with our terms of use and related policies. Please ensure you read any forum rules as you navigate around the board.

I requested permission to use this website some time ago, but have not yet received confirmation. I guess Taita has dawned with the 21st century. Now there is a Facebook wall for the Wadavida!

CHAPTER 24

Kwaheri Kenya
(Goodbye Kenya)

So the Lord God banished them from the Garden
of Eden, and he sent Adam out to cultivate the
ground from which he had been made.
New Living Translation (©2007) Genesis 3:23

Panorama of Taita Hills (Photo reproduced with permission of Dr. Bartolomeo
Gorgoglione) http://commondatastorage.googleapis.com/static.panoramio.com/
photos/original/6674639.jpg

THE CIRCUMSTANCES BY WHICH I eventually departed from
Kenya were entirely out of my control. I was actually trying to extend when
our tour of duty ended. Frankly, I would have done a second tour with Peace
Corps if my mother had not had health problems and Uncle Sam had not
sent me notice to attend my induction physical… for the military. I will get
to that, but I needed to finish out my tour in Taita.

I have mentioned many of the people I met in Kenya, but not all. Some
were well known to me and others not so much. There was a teacher at
the Bura Girls' Secondary School who became very well known to Bent
Hansen. In fact, she became Mrs. Hansen. I am not sure of the details but I
believe they married after Bent left Kenya, or possibly when he moved back

to Kenya to work for the FAO (U.N. Food and Agriculture Organization). Kokila was her name, and I believe she was born and educated in Kenya. There was also a British woman volunteer at that High School, but I only met her once or twice. I have tried to find the Hansens on the internet in Denmark, but without success. The name Hansen is as common as Smith in America.

Another teacher who I met fairly frequently was Dolly Walker. Dolly was a teacher at the High School in Voi and she was part of the first group of African American Peace Corps teachers. The reason I got to know Dolly is because she very kindly put me up when I was in the low country around Voi. The school had provided her with a comfortable cottage, and it had a guest bedroom. I forget how I found out she worked there. I think it might have been the students at the High School that told me they had an American teacher. I took that as a suggestion that I should probably visit and introduce myself. Which I did, and she was very cordial. We had some good discussions about Kenya and what was going on at home in the USA. This was still a time of much racial unrest. I think she appreciated being able to talk to a fellow PCV, because she said that it was a bit harder for the African American volunteers, especially the women. This was because they encountered expectations from the locals that they did not themselves anticipate. Of course, most of the Kenyans would assume that the black PCVs were African until they had a chance to talk to them. Sometimes that involved a rude familiarity to which the women, in particular, were not accustomed. I think Dolly appreciated the fact that I was always very respectful of her, and tried to be a polite guest.

I was quite frank with Dolly, so since I was already involved with Charity and the family, I told her about them. I don't know exactly what she thought, but she did not seem to disapprove. In fact, at one point, when I was traveling through Voi with Charity, Dolly invited Charity to stay at her house, and I slept on the floor of the Agriculture Office in Voi. I remember sleeping in the office at Voi (which I did several times); how could I forget that cement floor? However, I did not remember this sleepover involving Dolly and Charity. It was one of the tape recording that reminded me. I don't know if Dolly was just being polite, or whether she genuinely enjoyed my visits. Her job kept her in Voi most of the time, and although I know she made trips out of Voi for vacation, she did not have much opportunity to move around Taita. I think she enjoyed hearing about the people and the life in the Hills. As far as I know, she never did make an effort to get up to the Hills to visit. That is not surprising because the Peace Corps did not provide the teachers with transportation. She had probably had enough experience of traveling "local-style" to know that she did not want to expose herself to the type of male chauvinism that she would meet on the mountain bus. She seemed a proper lady, and took her teaching duties quite seriously. I know the students were very curious about the red-headed long-haired hippy spending the night with their straight-laced teacher!

Dolly is another person that I have not been able to find since I started this project. Walker is a common name, and I have found Dolly Walkers, but none seem to fit the profile that I would expect. She might also have married and changed her name. Given what a revolutionary time it was in US social history, it would be very interesting to find out what Dolly had gone on to do. She was a pretty woman, and I think quite intelligent. I assume she would probably have done something very useful with her life. Well, as fate would have it, some people are just not to be found on the internet.

Speaking of the visits to Voi, I mention on the tape recording that I sometimes spent a week at a time away from the house in Mgange. I guess I would travel to Taveta and then to Sagalla. Having the Trekker (Thing) made that possible because I could carry overnight supplies and equipment. Of course, between Charles Howe, and the Catholic Church residence in Sagalla I had lodging in both places. This made it much easier to spend days walking the farms. Where there were roads, I was actually helping the AAs get to their farmers by providing transportation. In fact, one place on the tape I actually said "All the women agricultural staff are in love with me." Can you imagine the audacity of youth? In my defense, I will say I was very careful to keep the relationships with the agriculture staff professional, in spite of the many hours we spent on the farm visits.

I can't say that I was immune to temptation in my own home, however. It is ironic that I was so critical of the pastor of the Pentecostal Church in Ngerenyi, and yet I almost was guilty of the same transgression. At first Charity hired a young girl named Wakisha to help in the kitchen and around the house. She was probably just turning teenager, and I liked to tease her, sometime even resorting to tickling her. Charity did not approve of my actions, and she was not satisfied with Wakisha's inattention to her work. Therefore Charity was quick to remove her from our employ. The second girl that Charity hired was a little older, and probably would have been in high school except for the family finances. I will not name her for obvious reasons. She was a Catholic, and she was smart and efficient. Charity liked her, and depended on her a lot. I had offered to help her with some English lessons, so evenings we would spend time in my room studying. She was quite attractive, so I began to have fantasies about her. Once I accidentally entered the bathroom when she was showering; she did not act too surprised. Later I began to have her sit on my lap while we were studying, but I soon realized that it was getting out of hand. Charity even caught us kissing one evening, but she did not seem to react. Even though Charity herself was Christian, she knew Arabic culture, and she knew that men in Kenya are not always satisfied with one wife. I think Charity and I once discussed that inequity. However, I did react; I realized that this was a foolish thing that I was doing. Here was a girl from the very community and church in which I lived, worked and worshipped. To have an illicit relationship with a minor was a bridge too far, even for me who was living "in sin" with Charity. So I terminated the employment of the girl, which, to my surprise, did not make Charity happy. I guess she considered the girl a useful addition to the labor pool, and, in fact, liked her. Fr. Cook, on the other hand, very much approved of my action, and was relieved not to have to intervene in what could have been a distasteful public scandal. They say youth lacks discretion, but even youth can be tempered with good judgment.

I noted in my tape recording of January 31, 1971, that Edward Amon (named after his grandfather), the oldest son of Charity Mshoi, had come to live with us. I was rather strict about the conditions under which he was to stay with us. It probably seemed harsh at the time, but I think it was, in the long run, a benefit to him. He came to stay with us so that he could go to school in Mgange which was within easy walking distance. Apparently, the arrangement I made was that he was to pay room and board. On the tape I said $5 US per month. I wonder if it was not Kenya shillings, which would have been 35 Kshs. Whether he paid it or not, I am not sure. At least it would have come out of work that he did for us at the farm. He did not relate well to school, and was soon in difficulty. So I pulled him out of school and set up a program for him at home. He had to remain in his room for 4 hours every day (with bathroom breaks, of course), and I would give him reading material and assignments. He had a desk, and I provided writing tablets for his assignments. I did not have a library to loan him books, so much of the material was either things provided by the Peace Corps, or the occasional book which I might have acquired in Kenya. I think he did advance in English and I worked with him on Math problems.

Ed did not like this arrangement, either, but I think it was a smart move on my part. He eventually adapted to using his time wisely, and I think actually learned more than he would have in school. When he did go back to school, he buckled down and did what was necessary to graduate primary school with good enough scores to get into a secondary school. After I brought him to the USA, he went on to complete mechanics trade school and eventually earned a bachelor's degree. Of all of Charity's sons, Ed has always been the most ambitious, having run businesses and worked in corporate America. Perhaps holding Ed out of school for part of a year had a positive impact. A parent really never knows for sure.

Having Ed at home, and other people to look after the farm, freed Charity up to travel a bit, so she began to take some of the trips with me. I don't think we ever went to Sagalla, but we did go to Mombasa on at least two occasions. We went to Taveta together, and stayed with Charles Howe. Charity had a friend that she had been in school with in Taveta. On one of those trips, we visited a lake that I did not even know existed. As you are riding over the Tsavo, near to Taveta, there is a small hill, which from the road looks like any other dry hill in the plains. But looks are deceiving. In the middle of that hill is a beautiful fresh water lake about 1.66 square miles (4.2 Km^2) in area. Where does the water come from? Well, that is a long story in itself. I was certainly surprised when we drove the two and a half miles up the dirt road to the ridge of the hill, and found ourselves overlooking this crystal blue lake. The clarity of the water and the deep blue color told me that it was a very deep lake (like Crater Lake in Oregon). It is called Lake Chala[251],

Lake Chala is a beautiful crater lake in the middle of Tsavo's savanna on the boarder of Kenya and Tanganyika which is fed and drained by subterraneous lava tubes.(Photo reproduced with permission of Sarah blogspot.com) http://sarahwanderlust.blogspot.com/2011/06/lake-chala-tanzania.html

and, as I later discovered, it is fed through ancient lava tubes which formed this crater. I am told these tubes extend to the slopes of Kilimanjaro. So if the water is coming off the great mountain, why doesn't it overflow when the snow is melting and recedes during the dry season? Well, apparently the network of lava tubes also involves a drain that, at that time, had been reported to have its effluent in the Indian Ocean. More recent scholarship by Brian R. Pain made the following determination:

> Artificially injected tritium was used to estimate the water balance of Lake Chala, Kenya, which has no surface inflow or outflow. Over 5 years mean annual subsurface inflow and outflow are estimated to be $12.5 \times 10^6 m^3$ and $8.2 \times 10^6 m^3$ respectively. It is concluded that environmental tritium cannot be used for such balance estimation.
>
> The relation of the lake to springs in the area was studied on the basis of the deuterium and oxygen-18 content of the waters. The data indicate that none of the springs derives a major component of its discharge from the lake. Tritium concentrations of two springs point to a high probability of partial recharge by lake water. [252] [from Lake Chala]

So the jury is still out as to exactly what happens to the water flowing into Lake Chala from Kilimanjaro, but there is a large lake about 15 miles to the south by south east (SSE) of Lake Chala called Lake Jipe, which is a large body of water, on the north of which is marshland. Undoubtedly there is some connection underground. Lake Chala itself sits on the border of Tanzania and Kenya, whereas Lake Jipe is mostly within Kenyan territory.

Lake Chala has its own species of freshwater tilapia.[253] There was a bustling trade in dried tilapia when Charity and I were there; the fishermen had set up their drying racks and fires right on the shore. There were also hundreds of fresh water crabs, but the Kenyans have nothing to do with crustaceans because they consider them garbage collectors... which, of course, they are. The question is what will happen to Lake Chala as global warming proceeds. Kilimanjaro is already losing its year round snow cap.

Even though I was totally unaware that Lake Chala was there in the middle of the dry savanna, the whole subterranean water system is obviously vital to the all of the life forms found in that part of Africa. Kilimanjaro is the major source of that water. Millions of animals and people depend on that mountain for life. It makes you understand a little better the animistic religions of the indigenous people. They understood how necessary the mountain was to the life zones of East Africa.

What I did not know was why people do not swim in Lake Chala. There are many myths about monsters or evil spirits. It worried Charity, and she did not want to get too close to the water. I, of course, ignored all of that and went swimming! The water was clear and cold, and looked entirely safe to me. And it is free of bilharzia (liver flukes). However, in looking up information about Lake Chala I found out that a British teenager was badly mauled and killed by crocodiles in Lake Chala in 2002.[254] Apparently crocodiles have been in Lake Chala all along, although where they came from, God only knows. The only information that I can find about the crocodiles in the lake is this quotation:

> Peter Kimanthi, a Nairobi police spokesman, confirmed that crocodiles lived at the lake. They are thought to be Nile or Mamba crocodiles, reptiles that can grow to 23ft in length. [255]

Nevertheless, the article, in which Officer Kimanthi was quoted, reports that Lake Chala now receives as many at 100,000 tourist visitors per year. When I was there it was known only to the local people. Times have obviously changes a lot in Taita-Taveta. I am speculating that the crocodiles don't appear often because they have a plethora of tilapia and crabs to eat; unless the Kenyans have overfished the tilapia.

Perhaps this is a good time to recall the discussions I was having on tape about Charity and my uncertainty about what would be next. We had not really given careful consideration to what would happen when I had to leave. I was still somewhat ambivalent because of the advice I had received from Mr. Moon, and I suppose I was thinking out loud on the tapes to my mother. There was no doubt that Charity had been a great help to me in Taita. She showed me the local ways, and introduced me to people. She smoothed over the transition to Mgange, in that she got along with the Police Officer's family (the woodworkers). She knew some people in Mgange as well. They appreciated what she was doing for the local people by hiring workers and by demonstrating farming techniques and crops. She knew Mrs. Mjomba, who was the head government official in the *Maendelo ya Wanawake*. This was Kenya's version of the Womens' Progress League. It was the *Maendeleo* that cultivated the potato fields, which Bent had abandoned, for replanting.

An example of how Charity helped me was an invitation we received to visit the house of a school teacher in Mwanda. She was a friend of Charity, and this was unusual for us to be invited to visit locals in the Mgange area. Most people would be embarrassed to invite us because they believed Charity was my common-law wife. Of course, they were right. People visited us at the Mgange farm all the time. Some had business with me, some were just curious. Some were friends of Charity. When we visited the family in Mwanda, I was able to understand very little of what was being said, and the smoke from the fire in the middle of the thatched roof rondavel house[256] was killing my eyes. There were possibly 8 people sitting around the fire. They were of all ages, including an old man and an infant. At one point the old man asked to hold the baby. In Taita they do not use diapers, and the baby proceeded to urinate on the old man. The group chuckled as the old man explained that it was a blessing. When a child pees on you, it means he is comfortable with you and has no constriction of the urethra.

This always amazed me that the women seemed to know when to put the children on the ground to relieve themselves. The bond between a Taita mother and child is much closer than in the West. The child is carried around in a large cloth tied around the neck of the mother. This provides a kind of papoose for the child. The mother can swing the child around to the front to nurse, and then push the child around to her back so that she can work. I can confirm that I never saw a woman, or even a little girl, drop an infant from this form of carrier. This is part of the reason that the children seldom have crying spells. They are always moving around with the mother, even as she cultivates her crops, cooks meals, or pluck chickens. Their world is large and varied compared to a basinet or a crib. They are usually mesmerized with the vision of it all.

On the way back from the home of the teacher, Charity and I encountered a fight between two men. One man had an axe but at that point they were just exchanging blows with their fists. I tried to stop the fight, but they would not listen. The local Chief, who was also the police officer, had been called, and when he arrived, we started to leave. But looking back we could see that the men were not obeying the Chief, and the man with the axe was grappling with the Chief for control of the *slaa* (weapon). I hollered "*Wacha slaa yako* (Let him have it)!" to the pugilist. He finally released the axe into the hands of the Chief. I said in my tape-recorded description that "educated blacks harass white people but the older generation still has respect for the white." But in retrospect, I wonder if it wasn't the presence of Charity that kept the angry man from doing something he would have later regretted.

I myself had my periods of anger and frustration. I think Charity was most helpful to me as a sounding board, someone who would listen to my remonstrations. The other volunteers would get tired of me complaining about the locals all the time. But Charity understood my frustration. I said on the tape that without Charity, I might have had a nervous breakdown. I don't know if that is true, but the frustrations of the job, the uncertainty of what was to happen to the family if I left, was a lot to endure. Just the sheer sexual tension of being 23, working with lovely women, and being "adulated" by them, was disturbing. In fact, in all honesty, I told my mother and Fr. Carl that my biggest fear was that, if I stayed with Charity, I might not be faithful to her. My mother's advice was "Go to Nairobi and get it out of your system". My reply was that there were too many venereal diseases around to take that chance. Fortunately, I must have been there just before the outbreak of the Human Immunodeficiency Virus, because I tested negative when I married my second wife. Charity is in her eighties now, and apparently has escaped that curse, as well. It would prove that faithfulness to Charity would not, in the long run, be our problem.

In Charity's own words (in Kiswahili), on Feb. 19 1971, she commented to my mother on the tape recording. I translate it here but I don't know if I ever did that for my mother.

> Mike was in trouble but he changed. If he leaves the women alone, it will be ok. Mike is *ngumu* [tough, hard or difficult]. I help him a lot, but if he listens to me it will be ok. Thanks for the gifts. Greet the folks there and Mr. and Mrs. Moon. The weather here is very hot; no rain. We have many rabbits. Mike is motivated, he is not lazy. He does a great deal. I am happy with his work. It will be difficult when he leaves to go back to America. I am leaving it to God. My mother came to Mgange on Feb 14th [1971]. She only stayed one night, but she thinks that Mike is a good man. Sam was in traction for 6 months, so now he needs to be taught to walk again.

I got sick the week before we made this tape. I was running a temperature of 104 ° F, so Charity and I went to Nairobi so I could see the Peace Corps doctor. Charity had a cousin in Nairobi so we visited his family. I had to be careful about Charity being seen at the Peace Corps office. Not because they didn't know about her, but because I wasn't supposed to be carrying family around in a Peace Corps vehicle. In fact, the Agriculture Program Director, Dave Redgrave, and his wife had visited us in Mgange. The Director for Peace Corps Kenya, Ed White (who was himself African American) strongly discouraged me from trying to take the family to America, as did other staff members at Peace Corps. Dave and his wife, who were both from Texas and who had adopted a Cherokee and a Mexican to add to their brood of three, were less dogmatic. He said the decision was up to me, as long as Charity and I could get along together. But he said "I cannot do it for you". What he did eventually do for me, was to let me withdraw my readjustment allowance so I could buy a house and land for Charity, and he also agreed to let me extend my tour of duty. Only one of which actually happened, but I will get to that.

Before I discuss the circumstances in which Charity and I found ourselves at the end of my tour, I need to explain what was happening in the Ministry of Agriculture. After the successes of the previous year, I had expected that the DAO would begin the take notice of the 4K Clubs and start assigning youth training activities to the AAs. This did not happen, and in fact, whatever was accomplished that second year had more to do with the interest the AAs had in the program than Katingumu's support. He was far more interested in promoting the Potato Marketing program, that Bent had developed, and the Grade Milk cow program that was being pushed from high levels in government. Finding a farmer that had enough land and the resources to fence in a pasture for Jersey cattle was a tall order. I frankly think an inordinate amount of time was spent on it. Had the DAO taken as much interest in the OXFAM grant that we got to purchase high grade meat rabbits, and the market that I had developed in Mombasa and the tourist hotels in Tsavo, I think it would have brought more income to the District with less economic risk to the farmers. But it was just a "kid's project", and of marginal concern to the DAO.

As the year progressed I petitioned for more interest in Agricultural education. As part of my school lectures program I developed a test to check the knowledge of the students in the area of agriculture. I gave the test to students in primary and secondary school and even some of the teachers were willing to take the test. It demonstrated that there was a considerable gap in the extant knowledge of modern agriculture techniques among this farm-based population. I immediately sent it to every Ministry I could think of including Education, Agriculture, County Council, District Office, and the Peace Corps. It had some effect, and I think it started or contributed to a general movement in the direction of considering the importance of agriculture education in a country whose population was largely dependent on subsistence farming.

There is an peculiar fact that I must insert here. When I wrote this, I has just finished helping a student from Northwestern University (Chicago) complete a survey of the agricultural community here in Hawaii. In his survey the single most widely-held concern of the growers was the lack of agricultural knowledge among the general public and the youth. They all agreed that agriculture in Hawaii could not continue without 1) raising the level of understanding of the challenges of the grower, and 2) training young people to take over the farms. I did not develop this survey on our island, but I helped steer the student in that direction. Another non-profit actually funded it. Nevertheless, my experience in Kenya helped me organize surveys in this small project, and for my final USDA project on fruit fly suppression. Did the former lead to the latter, or is it all just happenstance?

There seemed to be some agreement about this same fact among the government and business people of Taita. Namely, that training of youth is necessary to sustaining agriculture. It was also part of a trend developing nationally throughout Kenya. The DAO in Taita continued to be distracted by other priorities. In the late spring there was a meeting between the agriculture officers and the other government officials in the county. The topic was how to proceed with the 1971 Agricultural Show. I spoke up and suggested that there should be more emphasis on youth training. There was some agreement, but I still was not getting a commitment of staff from the DAO. So I consulted the Agriculture Director at Peace Corps, and obtained permission to withdraw from my assignment if efforts were not made to transition my responsibilities to the Kenyan Agricultural staff. To make a long story short, the result was mixed. I resigned with a transitional period; Katingumu assigned several AAs to Youth Training responsibility with Moses being the AA in charge. I helped them as much as I could to get the transition started, but I was officially out of the Ministry of Agriculture.

Instead, I worked closely with Dr. M. V. Smith to survey Taita-Taveta

District for honeybee forage plants. Dr. Smith was from Guelf Univ. Ontario Canada, and was working in cooperation with Dr. Gordon Townsend on the Canadian International Development Agency's Beekeeping Development Project for Kenya. Smith was an expert on crops pollination and was highly familiar with techniques for monitoring pollination systems. He gave me a set of slides and materials to mount pollen collected from plants for which I also took herbarium samples so the plants could be identified. Inevitably, given the great number of indigenous species in Taita, I collected one that was an undiscovered species. There is an entry in the East African Herbarium at the University of Nairobi:

> "Taita Hills, Mgange Nyika, 1520 m, Klungness 2 (EA, K); Taita Hills, Ngerenyi", which is referenced in an article by Lukoba, C. W. and Paton, A. J. in the *Kew Bulletin* 58: 909-917 (2003) "A new species and new variety in *Plectranthus [caespitosus]* L'Her. (Labiatae) from East Africa."

I didn't even know until recently. I was doing a Google Search on my publications, when a link to The National Botanical Garden of Belgium popped up. Sure enough, I was listed as a collector. Looking further I found this citation of the paper which named the species that I collected. I don't remember how many pollen and plant samples that I collected, but it was a good opportunity to practice my training as a botanist.

Since I still had the Trekker, and could get around the district, I was able to keep other projects, which we had started, in play. We continued to support the beekeepers, purchasing *wishwa*, building Kenya hives and catching swarms. As I said, even Jared Babu (County Council Treasurer) bought a hive.

Purchasing rabbits from the 4K members, so we could market them in Mombasa, proved to be complicated. I was training an albino Mdawida who raised rabbits and expressed interest in getting involved in the marketing. While I had the vehicle, it was not too difficult. The first time, I took the rabbits to Mombasa live (on the hoof. so to speak in the same cage that transported the 4K exhibits to Mombasa for the Agricultural Show). The meat market had a crew of men to slaughter the rabbits. The problem, as I later learned, is that meat is not normally sold dry and then skinned. The weight of the meat is minimal. The next time, the albino and I slaughtered the rabbits, and put the washed carcasses in a barrel around which I placed wet burlap bags and topped the barrel off with water. One of the Peace Corps manuals illustrated that you can create a "refrigerator" by creating a cloth-covered frame where the cloth is draped in a pan of water. The manual suggested that the evapotranspiration of the water off the cloth would reduce the temperature by 10 °F. This is the same principle as the old canvass bags that Model A Fords carried on their fenders to keep the drinking water cool. It worked; we were able to get the rabbits to the meat market in the morning and they were still cool and fresh. More importantly, each carcass weighed considerably more, and therefore earned a higher price. I know it seems like cheating, but the butcher did not think so, because all meat is sold that way. In the USA carcasses of beef are sprayed with water in the freezers to "protect the meat". In reality it is just to increase the poundage, and only secondarily to prevent freezer burn.

This marketing scheme was working well. There was a demand, and we could hardly meet it. The problem came when I had to leave. I let the albino try to deliver the rabbits on his own by bus. I don't think the butcher turned him down, but it was not ideal, because the barrel was placed on the top of the bus and the delivery time varied. Later he worked out a deal with the same lorry that delivered my motorbike and me to Mombasa. If he could get the rabbits to Wundanyi early enough to catch the lorry, they would arrive in Mombasa before the mid-morning heat. I don't know whether he was able to keep up the marketing. It is so much easier for someone with a vehicle to take on those kinds of projects. But if the market was to be established, we had to use the available resources.

I was also in the process of trying to purchase a house on some land near Mwatate for Charity. We still did not know what was going to happen when my tour ended. I was looking into extending, but I had not found an assignment yet. I figured the best thing would be to assure that Charity and the *watoto* would have a place to live in case I had to leave. The property I had come across, on trips through the lowland, was just a mile or two out of Mwatate. It was a former graphite mine. The vein had been depleted in colonial times, but there was a three-room building that was made of cement block (the blocks had been formed with wood shavings mixed into the concrete). It had a metal roof, but it needed new door and window frames, which had been eaten by termites. I don't remember how many acres of land came with the building. It was deceptive because one end of the property went off into a swampy area.

If only I had known then what I know now. It was an ideal place for growing vegetables in the dry season. I had seen mounded planting terraces near the stream beds in Werugha, but I didn't know that the entire ancient Peruvian/Bolivian culture was built on raised bed agriculture:

Raised Fields in Peru and Bolivia

Traces of an impressive agricultural system referred to as raised fields (waru waru, suka kollus) are found throughout the Lake Titicaca region at 12,500 feet (3,810 m) in the Andes. Raised fields are large, elevated planting platforms constructed of earth taken from adjacent canals, which improve planting conditions by doubling topsoil, aerating the soil, and providing local drainage. In addition to irrigation, the deep canals capture, produce, and recycle nutrients in the form of organic matter, algae and green manure and act as a heat sink to protect fields from frosts. Although once a highly productive landscape, the ancient fields now lie abandoned and little agriculture is practiced here because of poor soils, seasonal inundation, and harsh frosts. A number of indigenous communities in the region have worked with two archaeological projects in the rehabilitation of raised fields. In 1981, raised fields were rebuilt for experimental purposes in Huatta using information recovered from excavations of ancient fields. The results were so impressive that a number of projects have begun to promote raised fields as a sustainable alternative to capital-based western models of agriculture being introduced into the region. An estimated 741 acres (300 ha) of fields have been put back into production and over fifty communities are participating in the rehabilitation projects. A similar raised-field rehabilitation project based on the study of ancient fields has begun with native communities in the Amazon region of Bolivia. Read more: Development, Economic - Raised Fields in Peru and Bolivia, Prehispanic Terracing in Peru, Desert Agriculture in the Negev.[257]

I suppose the whole piece of property was not 5 acres, but it had some large trees on it, so I hired the two lads from Mwanda to fell and saw the trees into boards we could use for the door and window frames. As it turned out the type of wood was difficult to work with because it had very solid heartwood. The boards tended to warp when they dried, but the heartwood was very durable, and I believe quite resistant to termites. Charity's brother Wilson built the framing for the doors and windows. They also built an adobe enclosure in front of the house where they had a kitchen and storage area. It was probably mud from the swampy ground that provided the plaster for the walls of this addition to the house. I also purchased window screen for Wilson to make screen frames on the windows because that low area was bad for malaria due to the swampy ground where mosquitoes could breed. It is ironic how the wetland provided both a blessing and a curse.

Looking at the Google map of that area, it looks like farmers have opened up the swamp area to a great extent. I suspect it is a lot drier their now because of the reduced rainfall resulting from climate change. The area is probably still subject to flooding in the event of heavy rains, but it is probably very productive at other times of year. The property was registered in the name of Charity Edith Mshoi and paid for with my readjustment allowance. All of the surrounding land was also assigned to individuals by land adjudication. In all, the reconstruction project continued at a good pace, and Wilson actually lived there while he was making the improvements.

Perhaps the Mshoi family provided an early example of how productive the wetlands could become.

I was hoping that I might be able to get assigned to the CIDA honeybee project, which already had the service of one of the PCVs in our group. Instead, our Director, David Redgrave, suggested that I check with the Director at the Mtwapa Research Station at the coast. One of the PCVs from our group was working on a project which was intent on developing a tree nursery to produce coconut and mango seedlings for distribution to growers throughout the Coast Province. That volunteer did not intend to continue in that position, and was, in fact, considering departing early, to use up his vacation (and readjustment allowance) traveling the world. I visited the Station, and met the young English Horticulturalist who was experimenting with the newly developed air-layering method of producing mango rootstock. This consisted of scoring a branch while still on the mother tree, and wrapping the wound with a foil wrap that was filled with potting soil and rooting hormone. Once the roots began to grow in the wrap, the stem was cut and the air-layered roots and stem were planted in pots. So this looked like a good project for me. I had not yet considered the possibility of where Charity and the watoto would live, but Mwatate was an option. It was less than 100 miles from Mtwapa to Mwatate, so I believed I could get back and forth until we made a final decision whether to move the whole tribe to the coast. Of course, Charity had lived at the coast so she was not concerned.

The preparation for the Agriculture Show drew closer, and the *sukuma* (push) that I had started began to get traction. According to my final Peace Corps performance review:

> In connection with the special rural development plan being developed by the Ministry of Economic Planning, Mr. Klungness researched and developed an educational plan which was accepted. It recommended that a fund of £20,000 (Kenyan) be administered under the District Development Committee for Education and

group projects aimed at production in the rural economy. For example a school would be financed to develop a potato field on school land. The project would be educational and financially beneficial to the school, and the original cost would be returned to the fund for reuse....

Mobilization: Because of Mr. Klungness' extensive report on the problems and needs of Youth Training, 10 Ministry of Agriculture staff members were assigned to Youth Training, the Chief of Werugha Location established a Youth Committee, and the District Commissioner is considering the appointment of a youth representative to the District Development Committee.

The concept of the school fund was developed during the visit of a consultant, who was from some international organization -- maybe the World Bank -- who had sent him out to do an evaluation and proposal for the District of Taita-Taveta. Because he boarded with us in Mgange, I was able to discuss concepts with him in great detail, and he in turn incorporated some of those suggestions about youth training in his proposal. Actually, I recently had a clarification on this matter from one of my fellow AgV Peace Corps volunteers, Larry Frank. In his own words:

Via email Saturday, August 06, 2011 5:55 AM

I ended up finding myself an assignment at Min of Ag HQ in Nairobi (I became an "Economic Planning Officer," of all things). That's when Dennis and I were housemates in Nairobi; I shared an office with a volunteer named Dan Boxer (Ag IV) -- Dan had an MBA from Harvard and got appointed the head of an official "working party for horticulture industry." We put together a development plan and talked the World Bank into giving us $20 million. When Dan left, I got put in charge of the project, and worked with a British VSO volunteer who took over after I left. I think I remember visiting you once in Taita when I was working on the horticulture plan, or maybe when I was shepherding around a UN ag expert who was touring Kenya.

I don't remember the VSO volunteer's because the fellow who visited me was American (probably the UN agricultural expert mentioned by Larry). He was an intelligent fellow, so he learned a lot about Taita in a short period of time. From one point of view, it is a crazy way to do development assessment. I mean, why send a perfect stranger with no concept of the place or the culture to try to devise an economic plan for a whole region? But from the UN's point of view, maybe it is better to send a complete neophyte with a sharp head and an understanding of economics to take a fresh, unbiased look at a situation. I don't know; the jury is still out on that one.

But then how much sense does it make to send a young college grad out to live in a foreign country for two years, as if he or she would be able to accomplish much within two years. Maybe the second year, but that is a leap of faith, too. I still believe that the principle benefit of the Peace Corps is to the USA. Maybe it generates some good will, but it certainly generates awareness in the PCV. And how that PCV approaches the rest of his or her life, will be largely influenced by what was learned in a two year tour in the Peace Corps It certainly changed the course of my life.

Some of these conceptual juggernauts would take time to make seaworthy, but the assignment of the Agricultural staff occurred rather quickly as the pressure to prepare for the 1971 Agricultural Shows mounted. While I tried to help the AAs in whatever way I could, I was more concerned with getting the ongoing projects on a firm basis. Mr. Moon had assisted me in submitting a grant request to OXFAM for a Freedom from Hunger grant to promote rabbit breeding in Taita. I was impatient, so I went to Nairobi and purchased thirteen huge New Zealand White rabbits that a breeding farm had developed over years of careful selection. I mean these rabbits were three and four times larger than the stock we had in Taita Hills. I personally delivered all 13 breeders to the best 4K members and leaders that I knew throughout Taita-Taveta District. Some went to Werugha, some went to Sagalla, and I think some went to Taveta. I don't remember who the recipients were now, but if I ever have the opportunity to go back to Taita, I will check to see if any of the rabbits are large white stock; you can bet on that!

Likewise, if I go back to Taita someday, I will have to make sure that the Top-bar hives are not still using my faulty plan. Hopefully someone will have taken advice from the Bee Project at Thika on the proper construction of a Kenya Top Bar hive. Maybe I can introduce my combined Langstroth-top bar hive concept. Harrison Kimbio, the AA from Dembwa who was so ambitious, was chosen for the Honeybee Project and transferred to the Ngonge research station in Nairobi. I am sure that he probably brought the proper technology back to his clan in Taita. Life is full of loose ends; sometime you just have to assume that someone will take up the slack.

So it was looking hopeful that the Mtwapa project would be my next job, and we were making progress on preparing the place near Mwatate for the family to live. It was a step down from the house in Mgange, because the climate was harsher, and there was only a nearby water tap for water. I intended to try to get permission to extend a pipe off the water line if I could. Still, it was a better situation than carrying water from over the cliff at Charity's family home.

Thinking about Mwatate reminded me that I wanted to relate a story about the "platoon ants". Bent and I were driving to Mwatate during the wet season, and we had to go through a deep stream of water across the road. After we passed through the water, Bent stopped the Land Rover, and let the engine idle to dry off the block. This was so that we would not suffer any electrical shorts as we started bouncing along the road again. This was a common problem for Land Rovers because the electric fuel pump was located low on the body.

While we were waiting we saw this most unusual "platoon" of ants. They were larger than any ants I had ever seen. I have recently checked the amazing world catalogue of ants[258], and I only find two genera as large as 8 mm in length: these are *Camponotus* and *Odontomachus*. But even these do not seem as large as I remember the platoon of ants. I thought they

591

looked easily 15 to 20 mm in length. The peculiar thing was that these ants were obviously migratory, because they were carrying their eggs with them, and the whole colony was not more than ~100 ants. I am sure the queen was in the platoon, although I did not spot her. Bent had apparently seen these ants before, and demonstrated their behavior by dropping a pebble in the middle of the column of ants. Like some prehistoric cavalry platoon they immediately dispersed into the undergrowth, leaving behind the huge soldier ants to ward of the invaders. The soldier ants stood their ground ready to sink their mandibles into any and all comers. When it was apparent to them that the danger had passed, the workers, carrying the eggs, emerged from the undergrowth, and like a well-disciplined military unit they reformed into a column several bodies wide, and headed off down the trail. I thought it ironic that nature mirrors itself from the lowliest life form to the pinnacle of evolution.

"Hey, who you calling pinnacle?" says the ant in my head. "We are far greater contributors to the earth's biomass than your soft and pudgy species. You may yet become our primary food source when we learn to herd you like aphids." Whoa! Where did that come from? Still, when you think about it… When I searched Google for these ants, I read an article in which they had reported that every acacia tree on the plains of Africa provides shelter for at least three species of ant.[259] And another article said that there is a species of ant that actually protects the acacia from the mega herbivores (like elephants).[260] They swarm the face of the animal feeding on the tree and drive them away. And that is only three of the 480 known species of ants in Kenya alone. The lowly ant?

While we are speaking of ants, I have to mention the introduction of the little fire ant to Hawaii. I first saw them in 2000 when I was conducting a survey of aphids and their parasitoids for a professor at Univ. of Hawaii. These ants were tiny but beautiful, like clear amber or gold. Little did I know then that they would become a major pest of fruit growers and beekeepers alike. They nest in trees, eat honeybee larvae, sting fruit pickers, and can actually cause blindness in pets by stinging their eyes. And yet these little golden wonders are all about the common good… of their own species.

Bent left for the Europe before I finished my tour. He went to take training in England, which would lead to his return to Kenya to work for the Food and Agriculture Organization of the United Nations. There was a new teacher volunteer in Werugha named Douglas, but I was so busy trying to tie up loose ends that we only met once or twice. Otherwise most of my volunteer contacts in Taita were now gone. I think Dolly stayed longer than I did, but again, I didn't have much time or reason to go to Voi.

The District Agriculture Show proceeded with the AA staff in charge. I think it went well but I was not able to attend the event; although I do not remember why. I can't remember whether I went to the Show in Nairobi, but I am sure I did not attend the Ag. Show in Mombasa. I did start to help move all of our belongings down to the house near Mwatate, although the rent in Mgange was paid up through the month of October.

It was about the beginning of October when I receive my induction notice from the U.S. Military. I was not required to appear before the end of my tour of duty, but I think I visited Nairobi to consult with Dave Redgrave on what I should do. Apparently I had the option of reporting for my induction physical in Italy, after which I could return to Kenya, if I was not inducted. We continued to operate on the assumption that I might be able to take the job in Mtwapa.

But then the letter came from my mother. She was having health problems again, and it sounded serious. It wasn't actually that serious, but I will not say that she did it to get me to come home. However, I felt obligated, so I told Dave that I would take my home leave in California, take my military physical in Oakland, California, and then come back to Kenya. I don't know if Ed White and Dave Redgrave expected I would be able to come back to Kenya, but they did leave my appointment open.

Although it looked like it would be a challenge to accomplish everything,

I was looking forward to making the trip. I had talked to Dr. Smith when I returned the pollen samples to him and he informed me that Dr. Townsend had invited me to visit the Guelf Bee Research Facility in Canada on my way home. It was not yet decided, but they were still considering having me work in cooperation with the CIDA project if I was going to be stationed in Mtwapa.

So we packed up the remainder of the possessions and I left Charity with the responsibility of cleaning the house before in was turned back to the owner at the end of October. I have no memory of the details of my departure, but I think I was letting the children know that I was just leaving temporarily, and that I would be back. I don't know if Charity believed it, but she was very stoic about it. I left all of my personal possessions except my clothes and some handcrafted items that I intended to give as gifts. The tape recorder, all of my tools, books, tapes, etc. were left behind. I think the Peace Corps manuals that I had in later years were probably shipped, but I was still limited to 90 lbs of luggage. It is strange to live for two years, and then leave with only the clothes on your back. Of course, I was sure I was coming back. How did I think I was going to get out of the military? I was going to apply for conscientious objector status; I guess I figured they would think two tours in the Peace Corps would fulfill my obligation to my country…. Foolish me!

In Nairobi, the Peace Corps did arrange for me to have some work done on my teeth. I can't remember if it was a root canal, but I didn't have time to have the final crown placed so I went home with a temporary filling. During the time I was there in Nairobi, I got word that the situation was improving markedly for the 4K Program and the orientation to youth training in general. I think I mentioned before that the Peace Corps was getting so concerned about the lack of response on the part of the Kenyan Government that, at one point, they had threatened to end the Teacher Volunteer Program. That did not happen, because the Kenya government ordered 100 additional teachers. Similarly, as I was reminded by the tape recording of March 31, 1971, there had been an increase in support for youth training. The PCVs in Nandi had gotten 6 agriculture staff to work the 4K farms, for which 12 breed milk cows had been acquired. He decided to extend to see the project through.

I was officially mustered out of the Peace Corps on October 16, 1971, with airline tickets to travel to England, layover 2 days, and fly to Toronto, Canada for a two-day layover. From Toronto, I was to fly to Chicago then disembark at Seattle, Washington.

I have no memory of the flight, but landing in London was interesting. I remember taking the airport shuttle to Victoria Station, where I booked a ticket to what, I believe, was Southend-on-Sea. But it isn't on the sea; it is on the Thames Estuary. I believe that is where Bent was studying. I might be wrong about the town, but it was up the Thames and not too far from London. By Google Map, Southend seems almost part of London, and much more densely populated than I remembered it. My memory of the place was that of a small sea village.

Before I departed for Southend-on-Sea, I had a hamburger at Wimpy's. Seated across from me in the fast food dining area was a family of American tourists. They were the quintessential "ugly Americans". I could tell by their complaints and bickering that they were having a "typical" American vacation. They seemed to have very little appreciation of the historic city in which they were. I also noticed that the clerks and waiters were rude to me, so I put two and two together. Even though I was dressed shabbily with my beat up logan and patched leather boots (they do patch shoes in Kenya), I had been speaking in an American accent. When I shifted to the Kenyan English accent, people were much more polite, and could actually understand what I was saying.

I had some time to wander around London before my bus left Victoria Station. I spent some time admiring St. Paul's and the Thames. I think I touched on Trafalgar Square, although I can't swear to that. I don't remember if I took the bus or walked; it is less than a mile from Victoria Station to Trafalgar Square but it is a long walk up the Thames to get to St. Paul's Cathedral. I would have passed Westminster and probably Buckingham Palace, but there is no longer even a residual blur in my mind.

My memories of the little sea town are more vivid. On the trip up there we passed by some farm land, but what surprised me was the fact that they were growing crops in the islands between the freeways. In fact the whole countryside was much manicured; not even a patch of wild or weedy ground. I arrived in the evening, and managed to find a bed and breakfast not far from the ocean. It was a quaint little row house, with a garden in the front, half of which was flowers and half vegetable garden. I called Bent and we got together that night at a local Pub that he recommended. I don't remember what we talked about, but we did come near to shutting the place down. I am sure I was bemoaning the impersonal nature of western society. He had to attend class the next day, but we exchanged impressions of our tours in Taita. I told him that I expected to go back to Kenya, and he also was leaning that direction. Kokila was still in Kenya, and I think he had pretty much decided he could not do without her. I don't remember when or where they did finally tie the knot, but I got one letter from him confirming the fact.

The next morning I had to put some coin in the electric heater to take the chill off the room. Then, after eating the breakfast provided at the door of the room, I decided to take a walk to the beach. There wasn't actually a sandy beach but there were a row of shops along the rock-walled street by the shore. I stopped in at one to see if they had any kidney pie (memories of Mrs. French's). They did not have that, but what they did have was gooseberry pie. Scrumptious with a cup of English tea! I returned to the B&B in time to check out, and get to the bus. I don't remember any of the return trip or Heathrow Airport. It is all like a dream to me now.

In Toronto I can't remember whether they sent a car from Guelph to pick me up or whether I took a bus. The university is over an hour away from Toronto so I am sure I did not pay for a taxi. When I arrived in Guelph, I was delivered to the home of Dr. Townsend. It being Sunday, I spent the night with him and his wife... I remember the wonderful peaches which

I had not eaten since departing the US two years before. The Townsends were very cordial, and I enjoyed the visit. The next day Gordon took me to the Bee Biology Lab and we discussed the Kenya project. They were interested in my cooperation if I returned to Kenya.

Since he was chair of the department, Gordon had commitments, so he turned me over to his chief technician to tour the honey processing facility. That is where I learned that Guelph had developed spun honey. Rape seed honey gets mixed with clover honey in that part of Ontario, and the Rape honey tends to crystalize. To prevent this they developed a refrigerated centrifuge which spins and chills the honey simultaneously. The result is that tiny crystals are formed and the honey will stay in that state of fine crystallization until the honey is heated or allowed to absorb moisture from the air. Hence, you have spun honey. Unfortunately that product is no longer available in the markets on Hawaii Island, but I just learned that kiawe (mesquite) honey is very much like spun honey. It crystalizes so fast that the crystals are microscopic. The color is white, and the flavor is exquisite.

They delivered me back to Toronto, and the flight into Chicago was brief. The thing I remember most is that when I stepped off the plane and into the terminal, "Amazing Grace" was playing on the loudspeakers. During the time of my tour, the Peace Corps mailed every volunteer the weekly *New York Times* as part of our volunteer perks. It wasn't always timely, but it kept us informed of changes at home. Of course, the times had been most turbulent. Before I left the shores of my homeland, there had been the assassination of Martin Luther King, Jr., Malcolm X and Bobby Kennedy, as well as subsequent riots in the ghettos. During my PC tour, Kent State, the interminable Vietnam War and near revolution transpired. Unfortunately, Nixon was still in office, and the war still raged by the time I left Kenya. To have this spiritual song playing on a public sound system was surprising. I was hoping it was a redemptive sign for the country?

These were the years that formed me, and whatever would come after that would reflect the powerful influences of my family upbringing, my Catholic education, my college years during the turbulent 1960s, and my escape to the wholly other world of Taita Hills in Kenya. Was there a plan? Not that I could discern. It did then, and does now, seem all a series of happenstances, fortuitous or otherwise. Now the question would be whether it had prepared me for the rest of my adult life.

ENDNOTES

[1] Each chapter will begin with **a biblical quote**, not because the chapter content is religious, but because the Bible covers every aspect of human behavior, proving yet again the words of Ecclesiastes 1:9 (New International Version) "What has been will be again, what has been done will be done again; there is nothing new under the sun."

[2] *Alfie* is seminal cult film first made in 1960's, which was remade in 2004. Michael Cane was Alfie in the first version and Jude Law in the second. https://www.imdb.com/title/tt0060086/

[3] **John D. Krumboltz,** "The Happenstance Learning Theory," by John D. Krumboltz. *Journal of Career Assessment* 17, no. 2 (2009) 135–154. What-you-should-be-when-you-grow-up need not and should not be planned in advance. Instead career counselors should teach their clients the importance of engaging in a variety of interesting and beneficial activities, ascertaining their reactions, remaining alert to alternative opportunities, and learning skills for succeeding in each new activity. Four propositions: (1) The goal of career counseling is to help clients learn to take actions to achieve more satisfying career and personal lives—not to make a single career decision. (2) Assessments are used to stimulate learning, not to match personal characteristics with occupational characteristics. (3) Clients learn to engage in exploratory actions as a way of generating beneficial unplanned events. (4) The success of counseling is assessed by what the client accomplishes in the real world outside the counseling session. http://journals.sagepub.com/doi/abs/10.1177/1069072708328861

[4] **Manditory Retirement** is required by law for judges in the state of Hawaii.

[5] *Father Knows Best* is an American radio and television comedy series which portrayed middle class family life in the Midwest. It was created by writer Ed James in the 1940s. Season 6 (1959-1960) it was #6 in the Neilson Ratings http://en.wikipedia.org/wiki/Father_Knows_Best

[6] *The Tao of Steve* is a 2000 romantic comedy film written by Duncan North, Greer Goodman, and Jenniphr Goodman, directed by Jennipher Goodman, and starring Donald Logue and Greer Goodman. The film was produced by Ted Hope and James Schamus' Good Machine production company and released

through Sony Pictures Classics. It won the 2000 Sundance Film Festival's Special Jury Prize for outstanding performance in a dramatic film and the film itself was nominated for the Grand Jury Prize. It was filmed in and around Santa Fe, New Mexico, where the story is set. "The Tao of Steve", Dex's own personal pseudophilosophy on seduction, combines a Taoist outlook with the qualities embodied by TV characters such as Steve Austin (The Six Million Dollar Man) and Steve McGarrett (Hawaii Five-O) and, above all, by the actor Steve McQueen. "We pursue that which retreats from us." https://en.wikipedia.org/wiki/The_Tao_of_Steve

[7] Title	:	"Will she come from the East? (East - North - West or South"
Alternate Titles	:	"Will she come from the East?"
	:	Music Box Revue 1922-23
	:	Four little crossroads lie before me, one of the four I must choose [FirstLine]
	:	Will she come from the East where the Broadway peaches grow [Chorus]
Creators	:	Berlin, Irving [composer] Grant, Chas. N. [arranger]
	:	

[8] There is a funny story that Meritt told me about his pack mule running off on him while he was shepherding. He said the only way he could get the mules' attention was to take a big stick and club him up side the head. Of course, he had to catch him first.

[9] **Lickety-split:** Meaning Headlong; at full speed.

This is an American phrase in origin, possibly with Scottish influences, and isn't commonly used in other countries. Lickety may be taken from lick, meaning speed - as in *going at quite a lick*. That usage is known by the early 19th century; for example, this piece from Thomas Donaldson's *Poems, chiefly in the Scottish dialect*, 1809: "Ere I get a pick, In comes young Nannie wi' a lick." It is variously spelled in early citations but, whatever the spelling, it is just as likely to be a nonsense word, not pertaining to anything in particular. The first record of it in print is in D. McKillop's *Poems*, 1817:

"I rattl'd owre the A, B, C, as fast as lickitie An' read like hickitie."

The *hiciktie* in that line may be a version of heck - itself a euphemism for hell. I can't find out anything about Mr. McKillop but I would guess he was a Scottish gentleman - Donaldson certainly was. Lickitie in that spelling certainly wouldn't look out of place in Scotland. The second word of the term is just an intensifier, and 'split' was settled on eventually. That is first cited in *American Speech*, 1848, as '*lickoty split*'. Lickety may have been imported into the USA via emigration from Scotland. Split seems to have been added in the USA. http://www.phrases.org. uk/meanings/lickety-split.html

[10] **Annie Dunn Spencer** was Grandma Seely's full name.

[11] **Meritt Ambrose Seely** enlisted in the Navy on September 24 1917.

[12] **Childhood Dreams** - *Career Answers: A Woman's Practical and Playful Guide to the Career Puzzle*

Thayer, Vicki, **Chaney, Marti** Published by Lifeworks Pr, 1991 ISBN 10: 0963071777ISBN 13: 9780963071774.

Imagine Loving Your Work: *A Woman's Practical and Playful Guide to the Career Puzzle*

Vicki Thayer; **Marti Chaney** Published by Ten Speed Press, 1995 ISBN 10: 0890877017ISBN 13: 9780890877012

[13] **Meritt Seely's joke** told to me on his deathbed: There was an old lady who lived in a village where she had been an active member of the local church. As she aged, she stopped attending services. By and by, the pastor and the church council noticed her absence, and decided to check on her. This was before phones, so they sent a note ahead. When they knocked at her door she was ready to invite them in. She had prepared tea. After everyone sat down and tea was poured, the pastor put a question to the old woman, "We have been concerned that we have not seen you in church. Don't you ever think of the Hereafter?" The old woman replied, "I do think of the hereafter all of the time. When I wake up in the morning, I think about the hereafter. When I go to the bathroom, I think about the hereafter. When I go to the kitchen, I think about the hereafter. When I go to the woodshed for wood, I think about the hereafter. When I build the fire, I think about the hereafter. When I go to the pump, I think about the hereafter. When I put the water on the stove, I think about the hereafter. When I go to the pantry, I think, what am I here after!"

[14] Hawaii's 1921 Territorial Legislature funds construction of the **Living Memorial** with its 100 X 40 meter saltwater swimming pool was built to honor 101 who died and the nearly 10,000 others who served in WWI from Hawaii with

$250,000. Opened on August 24, 1927, the birthday of Olympic Gold Medalist and godfather of modern surfing, Duke Kuhanamoku, who dives in for the first ceremonial swim before a cheering, capacity crowd. During its heyday, the **Natatorium** hosts celebrity swimmers including Esther Williams, Buster Crabbe and Johnny Weissmuller as well as some 34 members of the International Swimming Hall of Fame. It is later also used by the DOE for its mandatory elementary school Learn to Swim Program. Hawaii's last Olympic swimmer learned to swim at the Natatorium. Owned by the State but operated under and executive order by the City, the Natatorium is closed in 1979 due to thirty years of neglect. Prior to its closure in 1979, the last recorded public investment in capital maintenance was $100,000 in 1949. http://natatorium.org/history/

[15] **McCloud Soda Springs** In 2006 Nestlé began a negotiations process with the town of McCloud, CA to build one of the nation's largest bottled water plants and use a portion of the water flowing from the springs of Mt. Shasta. The contract process was protested by local special interest groups whose claims include that Nestle neglected to study the impact on the region's ground water and have overstated the potential economic benefits of the proposed plant. On May 13, 2008 AP Press reported that Nestle announced plans to reduce the size of the proposed McCloud Bottled Water plant to 350,000 sq ft (33,000 m2) from the originally-planned 1,000,000 sq ft (93,000 m2) proposal. Nestle also agreed to monitor the impact of the plant on the local watershed for two years. Nestle opened a different bottling plant in Sacramento, CA, in July 2009, and then in September 2009 Nestle announced they would no longer pursue any bottling operation in McCloud. Nestle plans to sell the property they had acquired for the bottling site, which was the site of the defunct McCloud lumber mill (closed by last mill owners Cal Cedar). https://en.wikipedia.org/wiki/McCloud,_California

[16] **Sad Sack** is an American comic strip and comic book character created by Sgt. George Baker during World War II. Set in the United States Army, Sad Sack depicted an otherwise unnamed, lowly private experiencing some of the absurdities and humiliations of military life. The title was a euphemistic shortening of the military slang "sad sack of shit", common during World War II. The phrase has come to mean "an inept person" or "inept soldier". https://en.wikipedia.org/wiki/Sad_Sack#cite_note-1

[17] **Abdominal adhesions** are bands of fibrous scar tissue that form on organs in the abdomen, causing the organs to stick to one another or to the wall of the abdomen. In people living in developed countries, this scar tissue most commonly

develops after abdominal surgery, in which organs are handled by the surgical team and are shifted temporarily from their normal positions. It can also form in people who develop peritonitis, an infection that has spread to the membrane that covers the abdominal organs. Peritonitis commonly occurs after appendicitis or another abdominal infection. Another cause of adhesions is endometriosis, an inflammatory condition that affects some women and may involve the abdomen and serious abdominal trauma. http://www.healthcentral.com/chronic-pain/guide-153911-75.html

[18] Goggle Map shows the street view of the rental house and **the Bornholt house**. The rental house is nicely kept with bright yellow paint and white trim. The current owners of the Bornholt house have cleared out all of the landscaping and erected a Cyclone fence around the bare yard. Somehow it doesn't seem to fit my memory of it.

[19] Jang, E. B., **L. M. Klungness** and G. T. McQuate, 2007. Extension of the use of Augmentoria for Sanitation in a Cropping System Susceptible to the Alien Tephritid Fruit Flies (Diptera: Tephritidae) in Hawaii. *J. Appl. Sci. Environ. Manage.* 11 (2) 239 – 248

Klungness, L. M., Eric B. Jang, Ronald, F. L. Mau, Roger Vargas, Jari S. Sugano, and Earl Fujitani. 2005, Approaches to Sanitation in a Cropping System Susceptible to the Alien Tephritid Fruit Flies (Diptera: Tephritidae) in Hawaii. *J. Applied Science and Environmental Management* 9: 2 5-14..

[20] What we did not realize until I started working at the **Pulp Mill** is that the hydrogen sulfide and the dehydrated lime from the mills were murder on paint and metal.

Table 1. Air Emissions from Pulp and PaperManufacturing (milligrams per normal cubic meter)

Parameter	Maximum value
PMa 100	for recovery furnace
Hydrogen sulfide	15 (for lime kilns)
Total sulfur emitted	
Sulfite mills	1.5 kg/t ADP
Kraft and other	1.0 kg/t ADP
Nitrogen oxides	2 kg/t ADP

a. Where achieving 100 mg/Nm3 is not cost-effective, an emissions level up to 150 mg/Nm3 is acceptable. Air emissions requirements are for dry gas, at 0°C and 1 atmosphere.

http://www.ifc.org/ifcext/enviro.nsf/AttachmentsByTitle/gui_pulp_WB/$FILE/pulp_PPAH.pdf

[21] **Obituary of Lyle Frank Shabram**

Carmel Valley- Lyle Frank Shabram, Sr. 90, died peacefully at his home in Carmel Valley, CA on October 3, 2012. Mr. Shabram was born February 23, 1922 in Tilden, Nebraska. He was a WWII Navy Veteran who volunteered to serve in the Aleutian Islands. He moved to the Monterey Peninsula in 1961. Mr. Shabram was a self-educated engineer and inventor with a brilliant scientific mind. He was the co-founder of several companies and his achievements include many patents in the packaging industry. These innovations have benefitted society for more than 60 years. His creative genius and fortitude of heart inspired many to follow his example. He continued to develop his ideas even at the age of 90. A loving father of 10, Mr. Shabram was a man humble in spirit who always put others before himself. He considered his proudest achievement to be his family. He was preceded in death by his son Mark and Iris, his devoted wife of 59 years. He is survived by 9 children: Sandra Plass of Shelton WA, Lyle Jr. of Carmel Valley CA, Joel of Monterey CA, Catherine Robertson and Mary Benedict of Salinas CA, Paul of Olivenhain CA, Kevin of Carmel CA, Jeffrey of Omaha NE and Stephen of Santa Maria CA. Mr. Shabram was the grandfather of 33 grandchildren and 31 great grandchildren. Mission Mortuary, 450 Camino El Estero Monterey, California https://missionmortuary.com/tribute/details/101677/Lyle-Shabram/obituary.html

[22] **The 1964 "Christmas" flood** followed the pattern familiar in Salem history: near- record snowfall followed by record amounts of rain. Snow and freezing temperatures early in the month gave way to warm temperatures and unrelenting rain - all within a 48-hour period, Salem received four inches of rain. Accumulated snow melted quickly and, with the rain, created heavy runoff which swelled the Willamette and its tributaries. By December 22nd, the Willamette was rising at the rate of three inches per hour at Salem. Basements in the City, including that of City Hall, were flooding, and storm drains were clogged with chunks of ice and snow. The pressure of the water rushing through the sewers sent "gushers" shooting out of manholes and drains. Shelton Ditch and Mill Creek overflowed their banks, and control dams on both were working at full capacity.

Salem's main source of water at Stayton Island was flooded, but auxiliary water supplies were holding up. Highways in and around the City, including

Inter-state 5, were closed in places by high water. Still, at this point, Salem's flooding was not considered serious.

The River was expected to crest at 27 feet, seven feet above flood stage, and recent dike work was expected to prevent flooding at Keizer, thought to be the area most vulnerable to high water.

All that changed on December 23rd. The Willamette crested at 30 feet and stayed there for about three hours before dropping off slightly. More than 300 Keizer homes were flooded by the raging Willamette, and the National Guard, crews of local firemen, and sheriff's deputies used helicopters, boats, and even amphibious vehicles to evacuate more than 1,000 residents from their sodden homes.

Compiled and written by Kathleen Clements Carlson http://www.salemhistory.net/natural_history/christmas_flood.htm

[23] **The Pulaski:** Forest Service folklore holds that the Pulaski firefighting tool was invented by Edward C. Pulaski, a hero of the Great Idaho Fire of 1910, who led his crew to safety when they became imperiled.

Pulaski was a ranger and tinker who struggled to solve equipment problems of the fledgling forestry profession. After firefighting became an important function of forestry agencies, foresters used commonly available tools, such as the shovel, ax, hoe, and rake. Seeking efficiency in their labors as well is transporting equipment via horseback, foresters began modifying common tools into combination tools. It's likely that working in a home workshops or blacksmith shops, the Pulaski, a combination ax and mattock, was born.

One version of events was that the "Pulaski" was developed as a tree-planting tool by other Forest Service employees (Joe Halm and Ed Holdomb), with a shovel as a third tool on the handle. The prototype was thought to be developed in Ed Pulaski's home blacksmith shop. Pulaski was fascinated by the potential of the tool, but abandoned the shovel and lengthened and reshaped the ax and mattock blade.

By 1920, the demand for the tool was so great that a commercial tool company was asked to take over production.

Whether or not Ed Pulaski, "invented" the tool is open to debate, but he did develop, improve, and popularize it.

In 1914, Pulaski inquired about a patent for the tool in hopes that royalties would defray his medical expenses incurred from injuries he received in the 1910 fire. He abandoned the idea, stating, "I do not see any use of proceeding, as I do not intend on spending the money necessary to procure the patent."

After his death in 1931, the idea of a patent resurfaced, shepherded by C.K. McHarg, regional forest inspector. But the hopes of royalties for Pulaski's widow were never realized. According to patent law, an inventor lost his or her right to patent any invention that had been in use for more than 2 years prior to application. But the patent office did suggest a statue under which the Pulaski might be patented. It pertained specifically to patents awarded government officers for inventions used in the public service. Pulaski had forfeited royalties by not acting in 1914, but this statute at least made it possible to put his name on the tool. Thus the Pulaski. http://web.archive.org/web/20060506173557/http://www.fs.fed.us/newcentury/pulaski.htm

[24] *Cytisus scoparius* (**Common Broom**; syn. *Sarothamnus scoparius*) is a perennial, leguminous shrub native to western and central Europe, where it is found in sunny sites, usually on dry, sandy soils at low altitudes. In some places outside of its native range it has become an ecologically damaging invasive species. It typically grows to 1-3 m tall, rarely 4 m, with main stems up to 5 cm thick, rarely 10 cm. It has green shoots with small deciduous trifoliate leaves 5-15 mm long, and in spring and summer is covered in profuse golden yellow flowers 20-30 mm from top to bottom and 15-20 mm wide. Flowering occurs after 50-80 growing degree days. In late summer, its legumes (seed pods) mature black, 2-3 cm long, 8 mm broad and 2-3 mm thick; they burst open, often with an audible crack, forcibly throwing seed from the parent plant. It is the hardiest species of broom, tolerating temperatures down to about -25°C. Description revised from botanical reference texts.

[25] **Richard McGiff** did reply, and it was indeed the same Rick I knew from McCloud. We have corresponded several times and find out that, not only did he follow his father into the Navy (for 33 years) but he is now an almonds farmer near Modesto CA. He provided the picture of his father, the fighter pilot that appears earlier in this book.

[26] Following her commissioning, *Nautilus* remained dockside for further construction and testing. At 11:00 hours on 17 January 1955 she put to sea for the first time and signaled her historic message: "Underway on nuclear power." On 10 May, she headed south for shakedown. Submerged throughout, she traveled 2,100 km (1,100 nautical miles) from New London to San Juan, Puerto Rico and covered 2,223 km (1,200 NM) in less than ninety hours. At the time this was the longest

submerged cruise by a submarine and at the highest sustained speed (for at least one hour) ever recorded.

From 1955 to 1957, *Nautilus* continued to be used to investigate the effects of increased submerged speeds and endurance. The improvements rendered the progress made in anti-submarine warfare during the Second World War virtually obsolete. Radar and anti-submarine aircraft, which had proved crucial in defeating submarines during the War, proved ineffective against a vessel able to move out of an area in record time, change depth quickly and stay submerged for very long periods.

Nautilus passes under the George Washington Bridge during a visit to New York Harbor in 1956.

On 4 February 1957, *Nautilus* logged her 60,000[th] nautical mile (111,120 km), matching the endurance of her namesake, the fictional *Nautilus* described in Jules Verne's novel *Twenty Thousand Leagues Under The Sea*. In May, she departed for the Pacific Coast to participate in coastal exercises and the fleet exercise, operation "Home Run," which acquainted units of the Pacific Fleet with the capabilities of nuclear submarines. http://en.wikipedia.org/wiki/USS Nautilus (SSN-571)

[27] The **Lewis and Clark Bridge** is a cantilever bridge that spans the Columbia River between Longview, Washington and Rainier, Oregon.

The bridge was open on March 29, 1930 as a privately owned bridge named the **Longview Bridge**. The $5.8 million cost was recovered by tolls, $1.00 for cars and $.10 for pedestrians. At the time it was the longest and highest cantilever bridge in the United States. The state of Washington purchased the bridge in 1947 and the tolls were removed in 1965 after the bridge was paid for. In 1980 the bridge was rededicated as the Lewis and Clark Bridge in honor of the Lewis and Clark Expedition. The deck was replaced in 2003–04 at a cost of $29.2 million.

The bridge is 8,288 ft (2.5 km) long with 210 ft (64 m) of vertical clearance. The main span is 1,200 ft (366 m) long and the top of the bridge is 340 ft (104 m) above the river. It was designed by Joseph Strauss, engineer of the Golden Gate Bridge. http://en.wikipedia.org/wiki/Lewis_and_Clark_Bridge_(Columbia_River)

[28] **Duck's Breath Mystery Theatre** is a comedy team best known for its radio sketches broadcast on National Public Radio. The group was formed in 1975 by University of Iowa students Bill Allard, Dan Coffey, Merle Kessler, Leon Martell, and Jim Turner. In 1976, the comedians moved to San Francisco. Starting in 1980, they

began performing short sketches on NPR's *All Things Considered*. The sketches became nationally popular, and three of the recurring characters – Dr. Science, <u>Ian Shoales</u>, and <u>Randee of the Redwoods</u> – became better known than the group. The Ducks toured throughout the United States during the 1980s, but went on to separate projects after 1990. They had a reunion performance in 2005, and several live performances in 2007. <u>http://en.wikipedia.org/wiki/Duck's Breath Mystery Theatre</u>

[29] ***The Music Man*** is a 1962 musical film starring Robert Preston as Harold Hill and Shirley Jones as Marian Paroo. The film is based on the 1957 Broadway musical of the same name by Meredith Willson. The film was one of the biggest hits of the year and highly acclaimed critically. In 2005, *The Music Man* was selected for preservation in the United States National Film Registry by the Library of Congress as being "culturally, historically, or aesthetically significant". <u>http://en.wikipedia.org/wiki/The Music Man (1962 film)</u>

[30] **Bandstand** began as a local program on WFIL-TV (now WPVI), Channel 6 in Philadelphia on October 7, 1952. Then it was hosted by Bob Horn and was called Bob Horn's Bandstand. On July 9 of 1956 the show got a new host, a clean-cut 26 year old named Dick Clark. When ABC picked the show up, it was renamed ***American Bandstand***, airing it's first national show on August 5, 1957. The show was moved to Los Angeles in 1964. From 1963 to 1987 Bandstand was on only once a week, on Saturday. Briefly it was part of the USA Network with new host David Hirsh but went off the air in 1989. <u>http://www.fiftiesweb.com/bandstnd.htm</u>

[31] **John Gnagy** class sessions can still be seen on YouTube, athough the artist died in 1971. <u>http://www.youtube.com/watch?v=lIGMQbF7Ayk&NR=1</u>

[32] **Lilias Folan**, known as the "First Lady of Yoga" since her groundbreaking 1972 PBS series *Lilia's! Yoga and You* and "Lilia's," shows you how to add more flexibility, energy and joy to your life in these four programs from that PBS series. <u>http://www.liliasyoga.com/</u>

[33] ***Our Mr. Sun*** is a 1956 television film directed by Frank Capra. It is a documentary that explains how the sun works and how it also plays a huge part in human life.

The film starred Frank Baxter as "Dr. Research", and Eddie Albert as the writer, the other recurring character in the The Bell Laboratory Science Series. Marvin Miller voiced the animated sun. Sterling Holloway voiced an animated version of chlorophyll. The film marked the last project of Lionel Barrymore, who played the voice of Father Time. (It has been claimed, however, that the voice was actually that of an actor imitating Lionel Barrymore's voice; Barrymore died in 1954, two years before *Our Mr. Sun* was first shown.)

    Our Mr. Sun, and a companion film *Hemo the Magnificent* (about blood circulation), were popular favorites for showing in school science classrooms. The film is currently packaged on DVD with companion film *The Strange Case of the Cosmic Rays (1957)*. http://en.wikipedia.org/wiki/Our_Mr._Sun

[34] This article describes **C-3 and C-4 photosynthesis** https://sciencing.com/key-differences-between-c3-c4-cam-photosynthesis-11383843.html

[35] **Hydrothermal vent** communities are able to sustain such vast amounts of life because vent organisms depend on chemosynthetic bacteria for food. The water that comes out of the hydrothermal vent is rich in dissolved minerals and supports a large population of chemo-autotrophic bacteria. These bacteria use sulfur compounds, particularly hydrogen sulfide, a chemical highly toxic to most known organisms, to produce organic material through the process of chemosynthesis. The ecosystem so formed is reliant upon the continued existence of the hydrothermal vent field as the primary source of energy, which differs from most surface life on Earth which is based on solar energy. However, although it is often said that these communities exist independently of the sun, some of the organisms are actually dependent upon oxygen produced by photosynthetic organisms. Others are anaerobic as was the earliest life. http://en.wikipedia.org/wiki/Hydrothermal_vent#Biological_communities

[36] I knew from the Northness dairy farm that there is a channel that runs behind the cows in a milking barn so that the unpredictable discharge of manure from the milking cows can be hosed into the gutter and away from the milking machines.

[37] **The Munchers:** Proto-claymation goes awry with talking teeth and a demonic tooth decay character. A food group hoe-down highlights the importance of good nutrition to help maintain healthy teeth. http://www.archive.org/details/munchers

[38] A **skid row** or **skid road** is a run-down or dilapidated urban area with a large, impoverished population. The term originally referred literally to a path along which workingmen skidded logs. Its current sense appears to have originated in the Pacific Northwest. http://en.wikipedia.org/wiki/Skid_row

[39] **Powell's Books** is a chain of bookstores in the Portland [Oregon] metropolitan area. Powell's headquarters, dubbed **Powell's City of Books**, claims to be the largest independent new and used bookstore in the world. Powell's City of Books is located in the Pearl District on the edge of downtown, and occupies a full city

block, between NW 10th and 11th Avenues and between W. Burnside and NW Couch Streets. It contains over 68,000 square feet (6,300 m[2]), about 1.6 acres of retail floor space. The inventory for its retail and online sales is over four million new, used, rare, and out-of-print books. Powell's buys around 3000 used books a day. http://en.wikipedia.org/wiki/Powell%27s_Books

[40] Xerox was founded in 1906 in Rochester as "The Haloid Photographic Company", which originally manufactured photographic paper and equipment. The company subsequently changed its name to "Haloid Xerox" in 1958 and then simply "Xerox" in 1961. The company came to prominence in 1959 with the introduction of the **Xerox 914**, the first plain paper photocopier using the process of Electro-photography. http://en.wikipedia.org/wiki/Xerox

[41] *Black Like Me* is a non-fiction book by journalist John Howard Griffin first published in 1961. Griffin was a white native of Mansfield, Texas and the book describes his six-week experience travelling on **Greyhound buses** (occasionally hitchhiking) throughout the racially segregated states of Louisiana, Mississippi, Alabama and Georgia passing as a black man. *Sepia Magazine* financed the project in exchange for the right to print the account first as a series of articles. Griffin kept a journal of his experiences; the 188-page diary was the genesis of the book. In 1959, at the time of the book's writing, race relations were particularly strained in America; Griffin's aim was to explain the difficulties facing black people in certain areas. John Howard Griffin (2009). *Black Like Me*. Souvenir Press. ISBN 978-0-285-63857-0 http://en.wikipedia.org/wiki/Black_Like_Me

[42] **Jeanine Deckers** (17 October 1933(1933-10-17) – 29 March 1985), better known in English as **The Singing Nun**, was a Belgian nun, and a member (as **Sister Luc Gabriel**) of the Dominican Fichermont Convent in Belgium. She became internationally famous in 1963 as *Sœur Sourire* (Sister Smile) when she scored a hit with the song "Dominique". In the English language world, she is mostly referred to as "The Singing Nun". http://en.wikipedia.org/wiki/The_Singing_Nun

[43] Joe Barecca's website http://mapmet.com/

[44] Gretchen was interviewed by the FBI when they were doing the security clearance on me to go into the Peace Corps. She told the agent that the only problem she could see was that I had a certain amount of missionary zeal.

[45] The program in the Philippines is the second oldest in the **Peace Corps**. It began with the arrival of 123 education Volunteers in October 1961. Since then, more than 8,000 Volunteers have served in the Philippines. In June 1990, the program was suspended because of a threat from Communist rebels; it resumed in 1992.

Currently, Volunteers are addressing the country's development priorities through projects in youth, education, environment and business development. http://www.peacecorpswiki.org/Philippines#Peace_Corps_History

[46] Two researchers take More at his word. It is quite possible, they argue, that he did meet an explorer who had encountered or heard about a pre-Columbian society in the Americas that served More as a prototype for Utopia. Arthur E. Morgan, an engineer who was chairman of the Tennessee Valley Authority in the 1930s, takes the Inca Empire as the prototype (*Nowhere was Somewhere: How History Makes Utopias and How Utopias Make History*, University of North Carolina Press 1946), while the anthropologist Lorainne Stobbart identifies the Utopians with the Maya of the Yucatan Peninsula in present-day Mexico (*Utopia: Fact or Fiction? The Evidence from the Americas*, Alan Sutton 1992). http://www.whatissocialism.net/thinkers/utopias/11-was-nowhere-somewhere-more-s-utopia-and-the-meaning-of-socialism

[47] The **stencil duplicator** or **mimeograph machine** (often abbreviated to **mimeo**) is a low-cost printing press that works by forcing ink through a stencil onto paper. Along with spirit duplicators and hectographs, mimeographs were for many decades used to print short-run office work, classroom materials, and church bulletins. They also were critical to the development of early fanzines because their low cost and availability enabled publication of amateur writings. These technologies began to be supplanted by photocopying and cheap offset printing in the late 1960s. http://en.wikipedia.org/wiki/Mimeograph

[48] **pan (n.)** O.E. *panne*, earlier *ponne* (Mercian), from W.Gmc. **panna* (cf. O.N. *panna*, O.Fris. *panne*, O.L.G. *panna*, O.H.G. *phanna*, Ger. *pfanne*), probably an early borrowing (4c. or 5c.) from V.L. **patna*, from L. *patina* "shallow, pan, dish," from Gk. *patane* "plate, dish," from PIE base **pet-* "to spread." Ir. *panna* probably is from English, and Lith. *pana* is from German (n.) http://www.etymonline.com/index.php?search=pan&searchmode=none

[49] Copper frying pans were used in ancient Mesopotamia. Frying pans were also known in ancient Greece (where they were called *téganon*) and Rome (where they were called *patella* or *sartaginem*). *Pan* derives from the Old English *panna*. *http://en.wikipedia.org/wiki/Frying_pan#History*

[50] The Middle English word *Pancake* appears in an English culinary manuscript from 1430. http://en.wikipedia.org/wiki/Pancake#Etymology

[51] The **White Elephant** was a "vintage" school bus. I suspect it was pre-WWII, probably 1936-39. The seminary also had a smaller, mid-fifties GMC school bus,

but it was not big enough to hold the whole student body. The White Elephant actually served the seminary longer than its younger partner, because somebody sabotaged the GMC by pouring sugar in the gas tank. We were actually rescued by the White Elephant because we were on a field trip when the engine froze.

[52] October 13, 1995: **Dr. Francis Patrick Purcell**, professor emeritus of social work at San Francisco State University, died of cardiac arrest Sunday in the city. He was 71. Professor Purcell, former director of the department of social work education at the university, specialized in research on poverty and low-income groups. He was on the S.F. State faculty for more than two decades. Before coming to the city, Professor Purcell was on the faculty at the University of Louisville, the University of Illinois and Rutgers University. He was also on the staff of the Mobilization for Youth organization in New York City. http://articles.sfgate.com/1995-10-13/ news/17818291 1 social-work-rutgers-university-work-education

[53] A *missionary companionship*, consisting of two (or occasionally, three) missionaries, is the smallest organizational unit of a mission [in the Church of the Latter Day Saints]. Every missionary is assigned by the mission president to be another missionary's *companion*. Missionary companionships are generally maintained for months at a time and most missionaries will have served with multiple companions by the end of their mission. These companions rarely have prior acquaintance outside of the mission. Companionships are always of the same gender, with the exception of married couples, who serve as a companionship for the entirety of their mission… Single missionaries are prohibited from dating or courting while serving missions. The policy of companionships staying together at all times serves to discourage these activities. While missionaries may interact with members of the opposite sex, they may never be alone with them or engage in any kind of intimate physical or emotional activity (e.g., kissing, hugging, holding hands, flirting). http://en.wikipedia.org/wiki/Missionary (LDS Church)#Romantic relationships

[54] **QWERTY** (pronounced /ˈkwɜrti/) is the most used modern-day keyboard layout on English-language computer and typewriter keyboards. It takes its name from the first six characters seen in the far left of the keyboard's top row of letters. The QWERTY design is based on a layout designed by Christopher Latham Sholes in 1874 for the Sholes and Glidden typewriter and sold to Remington in the same year, when it first appeared in typewriters. It was designed to minimize typebar clashes, became popular with the success of the Remington No. 2 and No. 3 and No. 389 of 1878, and remains in use on electronic keyboards due to the network

effect of a standard layout and the failure of alternatives to prove very significant advantages. http://en.wikipedia.org/wiki/QWERTY

[55] **Airstreamers** are a group of RV-ers who share a community spirit because of their mutual love of the trailers. In the early 1950s, Airstream company founder Wally Byam began leading groups of owners on travels to many portions of the world, where the towed trailers were quite remarkable. Photos taken of the trailers in front of many famous tourist sites were common. This promoted a mystique which surrounded Airstreams and persists to this day.

The Wally Byam Caravan Club was formed during the 1955 rally in Kentville, Nova Scotia, Canada. Later, the word "International" was added to the club name, resulting in the acronym "WBCCI" and more commonly known as the "Wally Club". On August 17, 2005, a commemorative plaque was dedicated on the site. Club members join together for one large International Rally each summer (which by club rules always includes the dates of July 1 and July 4), and hundreds of smaller local rallies are held coast-to-coast by "units" (chapters). Airstreams are more popular than ever, and restoration of older models is a passion shared by many. http://en.wikipedia.org/wiki/Airstream

[56] The basic form of **confession** has not changed for centuries, although at one time confessions were made publicly. In theological terms, the priest acts *in persona Christi* and receives from the Church the power of jurisdiction over the penitent. Typically the penitent begins the confession by saying, "Bless me Father, for I have sinned. It has been [time period] since my last confession." The penitent then must confess mortal sins in order to restore his/her connection to God's grace and not to merit Hell. The sinner may also confess venial sins; this is especially recommended if the penitent has no mortal sins to confess. http://en.wikipedia. org/wiki/Confession#Catholicism

[57] One of a **tender conscience** is exact in observing any deviation from the word of God, whether in thought, or word, or work; and immediately feels remorse and self-condemnation for it. And the constant cry of his soul is,

O that my tender soul may fly the first abhorr'd approach of ill,

Quick as the apple of an eye the slightest touch of sin to feel!

By Patrick Abur, CEO at 8D Imaging and CEO & Founder at Timber Villa https://www.facebook.com/TimberVilla/posts/christian-consciencein-this-message-find-out1-what-is-the-conscience2-four-types/273916339398617/

[58] Brady published a play version of Richard Connell's short story **Brother Orchid**, which became a staple of the Samuel French catalog and inspired Hollywood

to adapt the story for a film starring Edward G. Robinson. (Brady received no credit.) In collaboration with Walter Kerr, he wrote *Yankee Doodle Boy*, a musical about the life of Broadway showman George M. Cohan, which debuted to great success in Washington and received national media exposure along with the endorsement of Cohan himself. Again, Hollywood lifted this idea whole cloth without giving the authors credit, and subsequently released the film version, *Yankee Doodle Dandy*, starring James Cagney. Brady received his first major New York credit as the coauthor (again with Kerr) of a 1942 Broadway musical revue called *Count Me In*. After serving in World War II, where he continued creating as a writer and radio producer for the Army Recruitment Service, Brady returned to civilian life as a drama teacher at his alma mater. For a brief time he wrote film criticism for the *Washington Post*, while teaching, doing some acting and also beginning his career as a stage director. http://en.wikipedia.org/wiki/Leo_Brady

[59] ***Great Ceasar's Ghost*:** The play described is not what we performed at SFS. It must have been freely adapted by our director, because the synopsis does not allude to a Roman ghost, but an Incan. "Synopsis:

How would you like to have a pet ghost? A nice, tame one that would be easy to take care of, sleep in your closet, do your work, or frighten people out of their wits – whichever you preferred? It sounds strange, but amusingly different, doesn't it? And that's why "Great Caesar's Ghost!" is one of the funniest, most unusual farces ever written for the amateur stage. When Phineas Farthingale comes to visit his niece, Helen Maxwell, he brings with him the fun-loving, temperamental protective ghost of an Inca Chief whom Phineas once befriended on a trip to South America..." GREAT CAESAR'S GHOST - Author: William D. Fisher, Heuer Publishing, ISBN: 978-1-61588-060-7 https://www.hitplays.com/default.aspx?pg=sd&st=GREAT+CAESAR%27S+GHOST.

[60] The **Milgram experiment** on obedience to authority figures was a series of social psychology experiments conducted by Yale University psychologist Stanley Milgram, which measured the willingness of study participants to obey an authority figure who instructed them to perform acts that conflicted with their personal conscience. Milgram first described his research in 1963 in an article published in the Journal of Abnormal and Social Psychology, and later discussed his findings in greater depth in his 1974 book, Obedience to Authority: An Experimental View. The experiments began in July 1961, three months after the start of the trial of German Nazi war criminal Adolf Eichmann in Jerusalem. Milgram devised his psychological study to answer the question: "Was it that

Eichmann and his accomplices in the Holocaust had mutual intent, in at least with regard to the goals of the Holocaust?" In other words, "Was there a mutual sense of morality among those involved?" Milgram's testing suggested that it could have been that the millions of accomplices were merely following orders, despite violating their deepest moral beliefs. http://en.wikipedia.org/wiki/Milgram experiment

[61] The U.S. context of the word **Cholo/Chola** originated in Los Angeles and can be a derogatory term meaning Chicanogangster or pandillero or marero. They are born in the U.S. and favor Spanglish. They might refer to any Latino unlike them as pocho, or white-washed. http://www.urbandictionary.com/define.php?term=cholo

[62] Seeger found inspiration for the song in October 1955, while on a plane bound for a concert in Ohio. Leafing through his notebook he saw the passage, "**Where are the flowers**, the girls have plucked them. Where are the girls, they've all taken husbands. Where are the men, they're all in the army."[4] These lines were taken from the traditional Ukrainian folk song "Tovchu, tovchu mak", referenced in the Mikhail Sholokhov novel And Quiet Flows the Don (1934), which Seeger had read "at least a year or two before".

Seeger adapted it to a tune, possibly a pre-existing folk song. With only three verses, he recorded it once in a medley on a Rainbow Quest album (Folkways LP FA 2454) and forgot about it. Joe Hickerson later added verses one, four and five, in May 1960 in Bloomington. The original Koloda Duda was published in Sing Out! in 1962. In 2010, the New Statesman listed it as one of the "Top 20 Political Songs". http://en.wikipedia.org/wiki/Where Have All the Flowers Gone%3F

[63] "**The Ballad of Barbara Allen**", also known as "Barbara Ellen," "Barbara Allan," "Barb'ry Allen," "Barbriallen," etc., is a folk song known in dozens of versions. It has been classified as Child Ballad 84 and Roud 54. The author is unknown, but the song may have originated in England, Ireland, or Scotland. The earliest known mention of the song is in Samuel Pepys' diary for January 2. 1666 (ed. Robert Latham & William Matthews, Vol. vii, London: [1972], p. 1.) where he refers to the "little Scotch song of '**Barbary Allen**'". http://en.wikipedia.org/wiki/Barbara Allen (song)

[64] "**Frog Went A-Courtin'**" (Roud 16, see alternative titles) is an English language folk song. Its first known appearance is in Wedderburn's Complaynt of Scotland (1548) under the name "The frog came to the myl dur", though this in Scots

rather than English. There is a reference in the London Company of Stationer's Register of 1580 to "A Moste Strange Weddinge of the Frogge and the Mouse." There are many texts of the ballad, however the oldest known musical version is in Thomas Ravenscroft's Melismata in 1611. http://en.wikipedia.org/wiki/Frog_Went_A-Courting

[65] The **Columbus Day Storm** of 1962 (otherwise known as the Big Blow, which began as Typhoon Freda) was an extratropical cyclone that ranked among the most intense to strike the United States Pacific Northwest since at least 1948, likely since the January 9, 1880 "Great Gale" and snowstorm. On a larger scale, the Columbus Day Storm of 1962 is a contender for the title of most powerful extratropical cyclone recorded in the U.S. in the 20th century; with respect to wind velocity, it is unmatched by the March 1993 "Storm of the Century" and the "1991 Halloween Nor'easter" (aka "The Perfect Storm"). In the eastern United States, only hurricanes of Category 3 or higher have brought winds of the magnitude witnessed in Oregon and Washington on Columbus Day, October 12, 1962. Portland, Oregon's major metropolitan area, measured wind gusts reached 116 mph (187 km/h) at the Morrison Street Bridge. http://en.wikipedia.org/wiki/Columbus_Day_Storm_of_1962

[66] **Revielle** is the traditional wake up bugle call of the armed forces. http://www.youtube.com/watch?v=SGnZxcS7VKA

[67] A **Dutch oven** is a thick-walled (usually cast iron) cooking pot with a tight-fitting lid. Dutch ovens have been used as cooking vessels for hundreds of years. Dutch ovens are commonly referred to as cocottes in French, and as 'casserole dishes' in British English. They are similar to both the Japanese tetsunabe and the Sač IPA: [satʃ], a traditional Balkan cast-iron oven, and are related to the South African Potjie and the Australian Bedourie oven. A camping, cowboy, or chuckwagon Dutch oven has three legs, a wire bail handle, and a slightly concave, rimmed lid so that coals from the cooking fire can be placed on top as well as below. This provides more uniform internal heat and lets the inside act as an oven. https://en.wikipedia.org/wiki/Dutch_oven

[68] *The Picture [Portrait] of Dorian Gray* (Oscar Wilde) is considered a work of classic gothic horror fiction with a strong Faustian theme. http://en.wikipedia.org/wiki/The_Picture_of_Dorian_Gray

[69] **The Betrothed** (orig. Italian: *I Promessi Sposi*) is an Italian historical novel by Alessandro Manzoni, first published in 1827, in three volumes. It has been called the most famous and widely read novel of the Italian language. Set in

northern Italy in 1628, during the terrible, oppressive years under Spanish rule, it is sometimes seen as a veiled attack on Austria, which controlled the region at the time the novel was written. (The definitive version was published in 1842). It is also noted for the extraordinary description of the plague that struck Milan around 1630. http://en.wikipedia.org/wiki/Promessi_sposi

[70] Martin [**Arrowsmith**] 's wife, Leora, is the steadying, sensible, self-abnegating anchor of his life. When Leora dies of the plague that Martin is sent to study and exterminate, he seems to lose all sense of himself and of his principles. The novel comes full circle at the end as Arrowsmith deserts his wealthy second wife and the high-powered directorship of a research institute to pursue his dream of an independent scientific career in backwoods Vermont. *Arrowsmith* by Lewis, Sinclair, ISBN: 0451530861.

http://en.wikipedia.org/wiki/Arrowsmith_(novel)

[71] From **Donatus, *de tropis*,** text prepared by Jim Marchand. **https://faculty. georgetown.edu/jod/texts/donatus.3.html**

[72] **Jesus freak**, a pejorative term for those involved in the Jesus movement of the late 1960s and early 1970s, was quickly embraced by them and soon broadened to describe a Christian subculture throughout the hippie and back-to-the-land movements that focused on universal love and pacifism, and relished the radical nature of Jesus' message. Jesus freaks often carried and distributed copies of the *Good News for Modern Man*, a 1966 translation of the Bible that fit the bill by including only the New Testament in its initial editions, and by being in modern English.

[73] In 1202 the Assisi nobility who had taken refuge in Perugia confronted the people of Assisi. **Francis took part in the battle of Collestrada**, in which the Assisi forces were captured and taken prisoners. Francis spent one year in prison, and he was lucky enough to be ransomed by his rich father. His frail health had taken its toll upon him in prison, and he had to spend much of 1204 in bed. Excerpted from The *Saint and the Sinner* Chapter One:Outfitted to Kill by Paul Moses, © 2009, RandomHouse, Inc ISBN 978-0-385-52370-7. https://www.penguinrandomhouse.ca/books/117902/the-saint-and-the-sultan-by-paul-moses/9780385523707/excerpt

[74] During the same occasion [During the Chapter of 1217] **Francis decided to leave for Acre and Damiata, in Egypt,** where the fifth crusade was trying to conquer Egypt. During the autumn of 1219 Francis arrived at Damiata and requested permission from the papal legate to enter the saracen camp at his own risk.

Together with frate Illuminato he went into the saracen camp and even spoke to the sultan Melek-el-Kamel. The sultan listened willingly to Francis, and it seems that he also gave Francis permission to visit the Holy Land. After the crusades conquered Damiata in 1220 Francis went to Acre, probably after having had the occasion to see the Christian sanctuaries of the Holy Land, then in the hands of the saracens. Francis and his followers have remained in the Holy Land ever since. The historical facts of Francis' journey to the orient are documented also in a letter written by Jacques de Vitry, from Diamata in 1220. IBID.

[75] Excert from Christopher M. Parry, Alfrun Erkner, and Johannes le Coutre. Divergence of T2R chemosensory receptor families in humans, bonobos, and chimpanzees. PNAS 2004 101 (41) 14830-14834.

"To test this hypothesis and also to identify T2Rs that possibly function beyond bitter taste, we compared all human T2R genes with those of the closely related primate species *Pan paniscus* (bonobo) and *Pan troglodytes* (chimpanzee). The differences identified range from large sequence alterations to nonsynonymous and synonymous changes of single base pairs. In contrast to olfactory receptors, no human-specific loss of the amount of functional genes was observed. Taken together, the results indicate ongoing evolutionary diversification of T2R receptors and a role for T2Rs in dietary adaptation and personalized food uptake." http://www.pnas.org/content/101/41/14830.full#abstract-1

[76] The expression **"while away the time"** is the only surviving context for a very old use of "while" as a verb meaning "to spend time." Many people substitute "wile," but to wile people is to lure or trick them into doing something—quite different from simply idling away the time. Even though dictionaries accept "wile away" as an alternative, it makes more sense to stick with the original expression. http://www.wsu.edu/~brians/errors/wile.html

[77] **Avalon** (probably from the Welsh word afal, meaning apple; see Etymology below) is a legendary island featured in the Arthurian legend, famous for its beautiful apples. It first appears in Geoffrey of Monmouth's 1136 pseudohistorical account Historia Regum Britanniae ("The History of the Kings of Britain") as the place where King Arthur's sword Caliburn (Excalibur) was forged and later where Arthur is taken to recover from his wounds after the Battle of Camlann. As an "Isle of the Blessed" Avalon has parallels elsewhere in Indo-European mythology, in particular the Irish Tír na nÓg and the Greek Hesperides, also noted for its apples. Avalon was associated from an early date with immortal beings such as Morgan le Fay. http://en.wikipedia.org/wiki/Avalon

[78] As we commemorate the 50th anniversary of the Cuban Missile Crisis, *SECRETS OF THE DEAD* chronicles how the actions of one man, during arguably the most dangerous moment of the Cold War, averted nuclear war. "The Man Who Saved The World" tells the unsung story of Soviet naval officer Vasili Arkhipov, the Brigade Chief of Staff on submarine B-59, who refused to fire a nuclear missile and saved the world from World War III and nuclear disaster. By Jennifer Robinson, first aired on PBS Tuesday, July 29, 2014. https://www.kpbs.org/news/2012/oct/19/secrets-dead-man-who-saved-world/

[79] *Anabasis* (Ἀνάβασις - Greek for "going up") is the most famous work of the Greek professional soldier and writer Xenophon. The journey it narrates is his best known accomplishment and "one of the great adventures in human history," as Will Durant expressed the common assessment.

[80] *The War* is a 2007 American seven-part documentary television mini-series about World War II from the perspective of the United States that premiered on September 23, 2007. The program was produced by American filmmakers Ken Burns and Lynn Novick and narrated primarily by Keith David. http://en.wikipedia.org/wiki/The_War_(documentary)

[81] **~ The Gift Outright ~**

The land was ours before we were the land's.

She was our land more than a hundred years

Before we were her people. She was ours

In Massachusetts, in Virginia.

But we were England's, still colonials,

Possessing what we still were unpossessed by,

Possessed by what we now no more possessed.

Something we were withholding made us weak.

Until we found out that it was ourselves

We were withholding from our land of living,

And forthwith found salvation in surrender.

Such as we were we gave ourselves outright

(The deed of gift was many deeds of war)

To the land vaguely realizing westward,

But still unstoried, artless, unenhanced,

Such as she was, such as she would become.

~ Robert Frost; 1874-1963 ~

[82] **Francis Patrick Purcell** (1924-1995) was Professor of Social Work and former Director of the Department of Social Work Education at San Francisco State University. He specialized in research on poverty in low-income groups. Previously he had been on the faculties of the University of Louisville and Rutgers University, and was a staff member of the Mobilization for Youth organization in New York City.

[83] **Robert Meredith Willson** (May 18, 1902 – June 15, 1984) was an American composer, songwriter, conductor and playwright best known for writing the book, music and lyrics for the hit Broadway musical *The Music Man*, which won the Tony Award for Best Musical in 1958. The cast recording of *The Music Man* won the first Grammy Award given for best cast album, and its 1962 film adaptation was a success.

Starting in the 1920s as a member of John Philip Sousa's band and then the New York Philharmonic Orchestra, Willson became a radio music director in the 1930s. He then worked on films and was nominated for two Academy Awards; in 1940 (Best Original Score for *The Great Dictator*) and in 1941 (Best Music Score of a Dramatic Picture for *The Little Foxes*). After more radio work during World War II, he worked on the Burns and Allen and Jack Benny radio programs, among others. Willson's second Broadway musical, *The Unsinkable Molly Brown*, was a success in 1960. He also composed symphonies and a number of popular songs. Paraphrased from https://en.wikipedia.org/wiki/Meredith_Willson

[84] **"Oh, Pretty Woman"** is a song, released in 1964, which was a worldwide success for Roy Orbison. Recorded on the Monument Records label in Nashville, Tennessee, it was written by Roy Orbison and Bill Dees. The song spent three weeks at number one on the Billboard Hot 100. The best-known guitar performance was by Wayne Moss later of Barefoot Jerry. Although the official recording appeared in 1964, the Beatles recalled Orbison's having written and performed the song during a mid-1963 tour of the UK which included both acts. http://en.wikipedia.org/wiki/Oh,_Pretty_Woman

[85] In 1940, **Brando** had to repeat the second year, prompting the deep anger of his father. Later he was sent to Shattuck Military Academy in Fairbault (Minnesota)... At the Academy, however, his pranks took turns with Marlon's insufficient grades, until one day something changed: the young man finally showed interest for a task, namely acting... His first role was in the comedy drama *A message from kufu* and was so good that in the middle of the show all the other students stood and applauded. Immediately after this success, Marlon spoke for the first time with his mother to become an actor, she immediately revealed her pride and

admiration. But interest in acting was not enough to keep the eighteen [year old] at Shattuck and within a year he was expelled. [translated from Italian] at http://www.filmscoop.it/cgi-bin/attori/MARLONBRANDO/MARLONBRANDO.asp

[86] The play **The Million Dollar Saint**, written in the mid-1950s, portrays Saint Francis of Assisi returning to earth at a Jesuit university and recommending that they "throw away all books" because intellectual pursuits were proud and led to all kinds of evil. Unfortunately the playwright misunderstood the saint who actually welcomed eminent theologians to his humble fraternity. Danny Devito played St. Francis in that comedy in high school. https://www.emmys.com/news/interviews-archive/archive-danny-devito

[87] After I attended University of California, Davis, I did manage to find a contact email for Tim McDaniels, who was, at that time, a Prison Councelor. Tim never contacted me back, but his son did. The later was attending U. C. Davis.

[88] **Saint Christopher:** Pope Paul VI removed his feast day from the Roman Catholic calendar of saints in his 1969 *motu proprio Mysterii Paschalis*. At that time the church declared that this commemoration was not of Roman tradition, in view of the relatively late date (about 1550) and limited manner in which it was accepted into the Roman calendar but his feast is still observed locally. http://en.wikipedia.org/wiki/Saint_Christopher

[89] I actually did find all of our group of **Troubadours** that were still alive, but Kurt Seippel had died of cancer a number of years before. The Troubadours reunited at a SFS alumni reunion on January 15 2011. They were Dan Vandyke, Daniel Larry Landry, FR. Chris and me plus Joe Barreca on the wash tub bass, and Len Ricky on guitar…but that is the stuff of another book!

[90] Actually, after the drafting of this book in 2012, I found out more about the friends I had lost. Fr. Christian lived to the ripe old age of 93, and was an active priest and banjo player right up to the end in May of 2018. Charlie Beegle went on to be a lifelong musician and piano tuner. He died in Custer South Dakota in 2019at the age of 74. The two Dans, Joe, Len and I are all still kicking as of 2021.

[91] **Lead** was probably one of the first metals to be smelted by man, being known since 3500 B.C., in agreement with archaeological discoveries done in Egypt. The oldest lead piece is in the British Museum and dates from 3800 A.D. http://nautilus.fis.uc.pt/st2.5/scenes-e/elem/e08210.html

[92] The **Deepwater Horizon** oil spill (also referred to as the BP oil spill, the Gulf of Mexico oil spill, the BP oil disaster or the Macondo blowout) is a massive oil

spill in the Gulf of Mexico that is the largest offshore spill in U.S. history. Some estimates placed it by late May or early June 2010, as among the largest oil spills in history with hundreds of millions of gallons spilled to date. The spill stems from a sea floor oil gusher that resulted from the April 20, 2010 Deepwater Horizon drilling rig explosion. The explosion killed 11 platform workers and injured 17 others. On July 15, 2010, BP said the leak had been stopped by capping the gushing oil wellhead, though there is a risk that a significant pressure shift could create a new leak on the sea floor. The drilling of relief wells to permanently close the well is ongoing. http://en.wikipedia.org/wiki/Deepwater_Horizon_oil_spill

[93] The zoo became world famous in 1962 when the Asian elephant "Packy" was born. He was the first elephant born in the Western Hemisphere in 44 years and is (as of 2006) the largest Asian elephant in the United States at 10.5 ft (3.2 m) tall and 13,500 lbs (6,100 kg). A total of 27 more calves have been born at the **Oregon Zoo**, including 7 sired by Packy, making it the most successful zoo elephant breeding program in the world. https://www.oregonencyclopedia.org/articles/packy_the_elephant_1962_/#.YQ3X5cpKjDc

[94] **Mariam Makeba** (4 March 1932 - 10 November 2008) was a South African singer and civil rights activist. The Grammy Award winning artist is often referred to as **Mama Afrika**. In 1959, she performed in the musical King Kong alongside Hugh Masekela, her future husband. Though she was a successful recording artist, she was only receiving a few dollars for each recording session and no provisional royalties, and was keen to go to the United States. Her break came when she had a short guest appearance in the anti-apartheid documentary Come Back, Africa in 1959 by independent filmmaker Lionel Rogosin. The short cameo made an enormous impression on the viewers and Lionel Rogosin managed to organize a visa for her to leave South Africa and to attend the première of the film at the Venice Film Festival. Makeba then travelled to London where she met Harry Belafonte, who assisted her in gaining entry to and fame in the United States. She released many of her most famous hits there including "Pata Pata", "The Click Song" ("Qongqothwane" in Xhosa), and "Malaika". In 1966, Makeba received the Grammy Award for Best Folk Recording together with Harry Belafonte for An Evening With Belafonte/Makeba. The album dealt with the political plight of black South Africans under apartheid. She discovered that her South African passport was revoked when she tried to return there in 1960 for her mother's funeral. In 1963, after testifying against apartheid before the United Nations, her South African citizenship and her right to return to the country

were revoked. She has had nine passports, and was granted honorary citizenship of ten countries. http://en.wikipedia.org/wiki/Miriam_Makeba

[95] **Odetta Holmes**, (December 31, 1930 – December 2, 2008) known as Odetta, was an American singer, actress, guitarist, songwriter, and a human rights activist, often referred to as "The Voice of the Civil Rights Movement". Her musical repertoire consisted largely of American folk music, blues, jazz, and spirituals. An important figure in the American folk music revival of the 1950s and 1960s, she was influential musically and ideologically to many of the key figures of the folk-revival of that time, including Bob Dylan, Joan Baez, Mavis Staples, and Janis Joplin. http://en.wikipedia.org/wiki/Odetta

[96] **Mary Virginia Martin** (December 1, 1913 – November 3, 1990) was an American actress and singer. She originated many roles over her career including Nellie Forbush in South Pacific and Maria in The Sound of Music. She was named a Kennedy Center Honoree in 1989. http://en.wikipedia.org/wiki/Mary_Martin

[97] **Captain Edwin Ellsworth Peabody** (February 19, 1902 - November 7, 1970) was an American musical entertainer. His career spanned five decades and he was perhaps the most famous plectrum (4 string) banjo player ever. He was also known professionally as "Little Eddie", "King of the Banjo", and "Happiness Boy". He developed, with the Vega Banjo Company of Boston, a new type of "deep resonator" for the four-stringed banjo called the Vegavox, based on the zither banjo. The Vegavox has been produced mainly in four-stringed plectrum (22 frets) and tenor (19 frets) models; however, some five-stringed models were created and sold as special orders. Eddie also developed a special type of electric guitar, first with the Fender Company and then with Rickenbacker, called the Banjoline. This instrument is tuned as a plectrum banjo but with the 3 and 4 string doubled in octaves, similar to the way a 12 string guitar is strung. The Banjoline is now a very rare and highly-priced collector's item, although very seldom used today in live performances. At some point in the 1920s, a music critic nicknamed Peabody "The King of the Banjo" because of his frenetic playing style which involved fast triplets and cross-picking, made some listeners think he was playing two banjos at once. The nickname "King of the banjo" stuck for the rest of his life.

Eddie Peabody served in the U.S. Navy during WWII as a Lt. Commander in charge of the music/band department at the Great Lakes Training Station near Chicago, Illinois. During his career Eddie played not only shows for paying concert customers, servicemen etc. but also for kings, queens, potentates, dukes, duchesses, one dictator and presidents. http://en.wikipedia.org/wiki/Eddie Peabody

[98] After World War II, and the building of the Interstate Highway System beginning in 1956, automobile ownership and travel became a preferred mode of travel in the United States. Along with a similar downward trend in public transportation in general, ridership on **Greyhound** and Trailways bus routes began a long decline.

For many young people from Europe, Greyhound was the way they got to know America because of a special unlimited mileage offer: "99 days for $99" or, in other words, a dollar a day, anytime, anyplace, and anywhere. However, young African-Americans faced segregated buses and facilities in the South, as well as intolerant bus drivers. Prior to the Civil Rights reforms of the sixties, black passengers were often forced to give up their seats to white riders and stand by until a seat became available in the back of the bus. In 1961, Freedom Riders boarded Greyhound and Trailways buses to test court-ordered desegregation of buses, trains and planes, because previous Interstate Commerce Commission (ICC) rulings and Presidential mandates to integrate interstate travel had been largely ignored by southern carriers. Black and white integration activists faced persecution and violence, and buses which attempted to conform to the new rulings were, in some cases, burned by pro-segregationist mobs. http://en.wikipedia.org/wiki/Greyhound_Lines

[99] An **arroyo** (literally brook in Spanish), also called a wash, is usually a dry creek bed or gulch that temporarily fills with water after a heavy rain, or seasonally. As such, the term is similar to the word wadi. Arroyos can be natural or man-made. The term usually applies to a mountainous desert environment. In many rural communities, arroyos are the principal roads, and in many urban communities they are important multi-use trails for recreation, pedestrian and equestrian travel. http://en.wikipedia.org/wiki/Arroyo_(creek)

[100] **St. Anthony's Seminary** was established in 1896 by the Franciscan friars as a boarding school for young men exploring the Franciscan way of life and the Franciscan priesthood. The school was started at Mission Santa Barbara and was originally known as St. Anthony's College. It was moved to 2300 Garden Street in 1900 and was renamed St. Anthony's Seraphic Seminary. The community included the Franciscan friars, young men from around the world, lay faculty and the greater community of Santa Barbara. Saint Anthony's Seminary closed its doors in 1987 and was sold in 2005. Under new ownership the school reopened that same year as San Roque High School. http://www.sasarchive.org/?q=node/3

[101] The **Texas prickly pear cactus** is the *Opuntia lindheimeri*. The broad leaves, called pads or nopalitos, produce pretty yellow to red flowers in spring, which in turn produce red to purple fruit in fall. Both the pads and fruit are edible, but both have tufts of spines protecting them. The spines can be long and large on the pads, but those on the fruit are usually extremely small but just as painful. The peeled fruit has an aroma similar to watermelon. The fruit is the part of the cactus from which wine can be made. Description revised from botanical reference texts.

[102] In Mexican cuisine, **cabeza** (lit. 'head') is the meat from a roasted head of an animal, served as taco or burrito fillings. Typically, the whole head is placed on a steamer or grill, and customers may ask for particular parts of the body meats they favor, such as ojo (eye), oreja (ear), cachete (cheek), lengua (tongue), or labios (lips). https://en.wikipedia.org/wiki/Cabeza

[103] **Reverend Valentine John Healy**, O. F. M., was born in Oakland, California. He entered the Novitiate of the Order of Friars Minor, Mission San Miguel, California in 1945. He received his A. B. at San Luis Rey College in 1949, and until 1953 undertook Theological studies at Mission Santa Barbara.

In 1952 he was ordained to the Priesthood and the following year was Lector of History and Government at San Luis Rey College. Between 1955 and 1961 he studied at Saint Louis University where he received his A. M., and his doctorate of Philosophy in history.

Since 1957 Reverend Healy has served as President of San Luis Rey College. He has published in the Historical Bulletin, Pacific Philosophy Forum, Catholic Historical Review and Way -- Catholic Viewpoints. His paper on "Father O'Keefe, Rebuilder of Mission San Luis Rey" was read at the First Annual San Diego County Historical Convention held in San Diego in March, 1965. Journal of the San Diego History Park, Balboa Center, San Diego, California. https://www.sandiegohistory.org/journal

[104] *Reader's Digest* is a monthly general-interest family magazine co-founded in 1922 by Lila Bell Wallace and DeWitt Wallace, and based in Chappaqua, New York, United States. For many years, Reader's Digest was the best-selling consumer magazine in the United States, losing that distinction in 2009 to Better Homes and Gardens. According to Mediamark Research, Reader's Digest reaches more readers with household incomes of $100,000+ than Fortune, The Wall Street Journal, Business Week and Inc. combined. Global editions of Reader's Digest reach an additional 40 million people in more than 70 countries, with 50 editions in 21 languages. It has a global circulation of 17 million, making it the largest

paid circulation magazine in the world. It is also published in braille, digital, audio, and a version in large type called Reader's Digest Large Print. http://en.wikipedia.org/wiki/Reader's_Digest

[105] *Look* was a bi-weekly, general-interest magazine published in Des Moines, Iowa from 1937 to 1971, with more of an emphasis on photographs than articles. A large-size magazine of 11 by 14 inches, it was generally considered the also-ran to Life magazine, which began publication only months earlier and ended in 1972. It is known for helping launch the career of film director Stanley Kubrick, who was a staff photographer. http://en.wikipedia.org/wiki/Look_(American_magazine)

[106] *Harper's Magazine* (also called Harper's) is a monthly, left-leaning, general-interest magazine of literature, politics, culture, finance, and the arts. It is the second-oldest, continuously-published monthly magazine (Scientific American is the oldest) in the U.S.; current circulation is more than 220,000 issues. The current editor is Ellen Rosenbush, who replaced Roger Hodge in January 2010. Harper's Magazine has won many National Magazine Awards. http://en.wikipedia.org/wiki/Harper's_Magazine

[107] *The Atlantic* is an American magazine founded (as *The Atlantic Monthly*) in Boston, Massachusetts, in 1857. It was created as a literary and cultural commentary magazine. Though based in Boston, it quickly achieved a national reputation, which it held for more than a century. It was important for recognizing and publishing new writers and poets, and encouraging major careers. It published leading writers' commentary on abolition, education, and other major issues in contemporary political affairs. http://en.wikipedia.org/wiki/The_Atlantic

[108] *La strada* (English: The Road) is a 1954 Italian neorealist drama directed by Federico Fellini in which a naive young woman (Giulietta Masina) is sold to a brutish man (Anthony Quinn) and goes on the road as a part of his itinerant show. La strada won the Academy Award for Best Foreign Language Film in 1956. http://en.wikipedia.org/wiki/La_strada

[109] **The Santa Ana winds** are strong, extremely dry offshore winds that characteristically sweep through Southern California and northern Baja California in late fall and winter. They can range from hot to cold, depending on the prevailing temperatures in the source regions, the Great Basin and upper Mojave Desert. The winds are known for the hot dry weather (often the hottest of the year) that they bring in the fall, and are infamous for fanning regional wildfires. http://en.wikipedia.org/wiki/Santa_Ana_winds

[110] An aerated lagoon (or **aerated pond**) is a simple wastewater treatment system consisting of a pond with artificial aeration to promote the biological oxidation of wastewaters.

There are many other aerobic biological processes for treatment of wastewaters, for example activated sludge, trickling filters, rotating biological contactors and biofilters. They all have in common the use of oxygen (or air) and microbial action to reduce the pollutants in wastewaters. https://en.wikipedia.org/wiki/Aerated_lagoon

[111] **Udall** served as Secretary of the Interior under Presidents John F. Kennedy and Lyndon B. Johnson from 1961 to 1969. Under his leadership, the Interior Department aggressively promoted an expansion of federal public lands and assisted with the enactment of major environmental legislation. Among his accomplishments, Udall oversaw the addition of four parks, six national monuments, eight seashores and lakeshores, nine recreation areas, 20 historic sites and 56 wildlife refuges to the National Park system, including Canyonlands National Park in Utah, North Cascades National Park in Washington, Redwood National Park in California, and the Appalachian National Scenic Trail stretching from Georgia to Maine. http://en.wikipedia.org/wiki/Stewart_Udall

[112] **Samuel Pepys** FRS, MP, JP, (pronounced /ˈpiːps/ "peeps") (23 February 1633 – 26 May 1703) was an English naval administrator and Member of Parliament, who is now most famous for the diary he kept for a decade while still a relatively young man. Although Pepys had no maritime experience, he rose by patronage, hard work and his talent for administration, to be the Chief Secretary to the Admiralty under both King Charles II and subsequently King James II. His influence and reforms at the Admiralty were important in the early professionalization of the Royal Navy. The detailed private diary Pepys kept from 1660 until 1669 was first published in the nineteenth century, and is one of the most important primary sources for the English Restoration period. It provides a combination of personal revelation and eyewitness accounts of great events, such as the Great Plague of London, the Second Dutch War and the Great Fire of London. http://en.wikipedia.org/wiki/Samuel_Pepys

[113] **Amurka** (America) I use as a derogatory term, referring to a segment of the American society that seem to mispronounce the name of their own country. It tends to be prevalent among members of an anti-intellectual movement that distrusts government and educated people. On such critical issue as facing a pandemic, this group refused to be vaccinated for COVID19. There are so many sources of information on the internet, that these people seem to gravitate to irrational purveyors of erroneous information.

Urban Dictionary defines it as Amurka: The way to say 'America' when you are being comical in the sense of acting redneck.

Although the word is heard often, I can find only one reference to it on Google: *Amerka!* In a documentary short by Sara Goldblat (writer and director)

[114] **Sophism** can mean two very different things: In the modern definition (from Plato), a sophism is a specious argument used for deceiving someone. In Ancient Greece, the *sophists* were a category of teachers who specialized in using the tools of philosophy and rhetoric for the purpose of teaching aretê — excellence, or virtue — predominately to young statesmen and nobility. The practice of charging money for education, and providing wisdom only to those who can pay, led to the condemnations made by Plato in regard to their profession itself being 'specious' or 'deceptive', hence the modern usage of the term. http://en.wikipedia.org/wiki/Sophism

[115] The proverb is of French origin and was used by the French novelist Alphonse Karr (1808-90). It also appears in George Bernard Shaw's 'Revolutionist's Handbook' (1903). Listed in the 1946 'Macmillan (Home) Book of Proverbs, Maxims and Familiar Phrases' by Burton Stevenson and in the 1992 'Dictionary of American Proverbs' by Wolfgang Mieder et al." From "Random House Dictionary of Popular Proverbs and Sayings" by Gregory Y. Titelman (Random House, New York, 1996). http://www.phrases.org.uk/bulletin_board

[116] **St. Gertrude**, Virgin (Patroness of the West Indies) Feastday-November 16 St. Gertrude was born at Eisleben in Saxony. At the age of five, she was placed in the care of the Benedictine nuns at Rodalsdorf and later became a nun in the same monastery, of which she was elected Abbess in 1251. The following year she was obliged to take charge of the monastery at Helfta, to which she moved with her nuns.

St. Gertrude had enjoyed a good education. She wrote and composed in Latin, and was versed in Sacred Literature. The life of this saint, though not replete with stirring events and striking actions, was one of great mental activity. It was the mystic life of the cloister, a life hidden with Christ in God. She was characterized by great devotion to the Sacred Humanity of Our Lord in His Passion and in the Blessed Eucharist, and by a tender love for the Blessed Virgin. She died in 1302. http://www.catholic.org/saints/saint.php?saint_id=281

[117] **Chichester Psalms** was Bernstein's first composition after his Third Symphony (Kaddish). They are his two most overtly Jewish works. While both works have a chorus singing texts in Hebrew, the Kaddish Symphony has been described as a work often at the edge of despair, while Chichester Psalms is affirmative and at times serene.

The Psalms and the first movement in particular are noted among performers for their musical difficulty, with the opening section of the first movement often considered one of the hardest passages for choral tenors ever written, owing to the range of the piece, its rhythmic complexity and the consistent presence of the strange and difficult-to-maintain interval of a minor 7th between the tenor and bass parts (see illustration). The seventh interval figures prominently due to its numerological importance in the Judeo-Christian tradition; also the first movement is written in the 7/4 meter, and the third in 10/4 (separated into half-bars of 5/4). http://en.wikipedia.org/wiki/Chichester_Psalms

[118] *Chichester Psalms* Leonard Bernstein, composer and conductor. https://youtu.be/7Yhnml4DW9g?t=804

[119] Author **Tageson, C. William** published *Humanistic psychology: a synthesis* Homewood, Ill.: Dorsey Press, 1982. xv, 286 p.; 25 cm.
ISBN 0256027420 Series The Dorsey series in psychology
Bibliography: p. 259-276.

[120] **Liberation theology** is a movement in Christian theology which construes the teachings of Jesus Christ in terms of liberation from unjust economic, political, or social conditions. It has been described by proponents as "an interpretation of Christian faith through the poor's suffering, their struggle and hope, and a critique of society and the Catholic faith and Christianity through the eyes of the poor", and by detractors as Christianity perverted by Marxism and Communism.

Although liberation theology has grown into an international and inter-denominational movement, it began as a movement within the Roman Catholic church in Latin America in the 1950s - 1960s. It arose principally as a moral reaction to the poverty caused by social injustice in that region. It achieved prominence in the 1970s and 1980s. The term was coined by the Peruvian priest Gustavo Gutiérrez, who wrote one of the movement's most famous books, A Theology of Liberation (1971). Other noted exponents are Leonardo Boff of Brazil, Jon Sobrino of El Salvador, and Juan Luis Segundo of Uruguay.

The influence of liberation theology diminished after proponents using Marxist concepts were admonished by the Vatican's Congregation for the Doctrine of the Faith (CDF) in 1984 and 1986. The Vatican documents criticize certain strains of Liberation Theology for focusing on institutional dimensions of sin to the exclusion of the individual; and for supposedly inaccurately identifying the church hierarchy as members of the privileged class. http://en.wikipedia.org/wiki/Liberation_theology

[121] **Arthur Livingstone**, author of this 1930's reproduction of *Little Flowers*, characterizes this text as a masterful work of folk literatures from the Middle Ages. The phrase "little flowers" refers to "notabilia," or a collection of noteworthy events in the lives of St. Francis and his followers. These stories were originally collected and compiled by Brother Ugolino during the early 1300's. Ugolino attempted to draw out similarities between Jesus and St. Francis, since both leaders taught their disciples to deny the things of this world and to instead seek humility and holiness. Ugolino's original Latin text was lost, but by consulting a variety of sources, scholars have worked to reconstruct Little Flowers into both Italian and English translations. Livingstone advises readers to enjoy Little Flowers with a sense of humor, as the contents of several stories contain much irony and amusement. http://www.ccel.org/ccel/ugolino/flowers.html

[122] **Blessed Pope John XXIII** (Latin: Ioannes PP. XXIII; Italian: Giovanni XXIII), born Angelo Giuseppe Roncalli (25 November 1881 – 3 June 1963), known as Blessed John XXIII since his beatification, was elected as the 261st Pope of the Catholic Church and Sovereign of Vatican City on 28 October 1958.

He called the Second Vatican Council (1962–1965) but did not live to see it to completion, dying on 3 June 1963, two months after the completion of his final encyclical, Pacem in Terris. He was beatified on 3 September 2000, along with Pope Pius IX...

After the long pontificate of Pope Pius XII, the cardinals chose a man who, it was presumed because of his advanced age, would be a short-term or "stop-gap" pope. In John XXIII's first consistory, Montini was raised to the rank of cardinal; and in time he became John's successor, Pope Paul VI. John XXIII's personal warmth, good humor and kindness captured the world's affections in a way his predecessor, for all his learning, had failed to do...

Far from being a mere "stop gap" Pope, to great excitement John called an ecumenical council fewer than ninety years after the Vatican Council. Cardinal Montini remarked to a friend that "this holy old boy doesn't realize what a hornet's nest he's stirring up". From the Second Vatican Council came changes that reshaped the face of Catholicism: a comprehensively revised liturgy, a stronger emphasis on ecumenism, and a new approach to the world. http://en.wikipedia.org/wiki/Pope_John_XXIII

[123] The body of Blessed John XXIII, the pope best known for the reform of the Catholic Church during the Second Vatican Council (1962-65), was removed

from the crypt of St Peter's Basilica on June 3 and transferred in a glass coffin to the interior of the church.

He is only the third pope to be given this honor. Millions of Catholics are expected to visit the basilica to pay homage to John XXIII, one of the most respected pontiffs of the 20ᵗʰ century.

The embalmed body of Blessed John XXIII, who died on Pentecost Sunday, June 3, 1963, had since his death been in the crypt, alongside the remains of dozens of other popes. The remains of many other popes are buried in the interior of the basilica.

The only other popes in glass coffins for public viewing are Blessed Innocent XI (who died in 1689, and was beatified by Pius XII in 1956) and St Pius X (who died in 1914, was beatified in 1951 and canonized in 1954 by Pius XII).

When John XXIII's coffin was opened 38 years after his death, his body was practically intact. "A miracle," some Italians declared, but without support from the Vatican authorities.

Gennaro Goglia, who in 1963 was a professor of anatomy at the Catholic University of the Sacred Heart in Rome, also rejected suggestions that there had been a miracle.

Dr Goglia told the daily newspaper Famiglia Cristiana that he injected Pope John's body with a "special liquid" to preserve human remains which had been developed by Professor Winkler of the University of Lausanne (Switzerland), an "authority in this field."

Before Sunday's ceremony, Blessed John's body was clothed in pontifical vestments and placed in a 450-kilogram bronze-and-glass coffin. On Pentecost Sunday, June 3, the coffin was carried in procession to St Peter's Square, where Pope John Paul II pronounced a solemn liturgy before thousands of Catholics.

After the ceremony, the coffin was carried to the interior of the basilica and placed temporarily before an altar under a huge dome painted by Michelangelo. The coffin's final resting place will be under the altar of St Jerome, in the basilica's central nave. By Luigi Sandri, in *Christianity Today*, June 1 2001. http://www.christianitytoday.com/ct/2001/juneweb-only/6-11-13.0.html

¹²⁴ The word **paranoia** comes from the Greek "παράνοια" (*paranoia*), "madness"[1] and that from "παρά" (*para*), "beside, by"[2] + "νόος" (*noos*), "mind"[3]. The term was used to describe a mental illness in which a delusional belief is the sole or most prominent feature. In original attempt at classifying different forms of mental illness, Kraepelin used the term *pure paranoia* to describe a condition where

a delusion was present, but without any apparent deterioration in intellectual abilities and without any of the other features of dementia praecox, the condition later renamed "schizophrenia". Notably, in his definition, the belief does not have to be persecutory to be classified as paranoid, so any number of delusional beliefs can be classified as paranoia. For example, a person who has the sole delusional belief that he is an important religious figure would be classified by Kraepelin as having 'pure paranoia'. Even at the present time, a delusion need not be suspicious or fearful to be classified as paranoid. A person might be diagnosed as a paranoid schizophrenic without delusions of persecution, simply because their delusions refer mainly to themselves, such as believing that they are a CIA agent or a famous member of royalty. http://en.wikipedia.org/wiki/Paranoia

[125] **Interstate 5** spans the West Coast, originating at the nation's busiest international border crossing at San Ysidro (San Diego), California, and culminating at Blaine, Washington. This freeway connects all of the major population centers of the western seaboard, including San Diego, Santa Ana, Anaheim, Los Angeles, Sacramento, Portland, and Seattle. Via Interstates 580 and 505, Interstate 5 provides freeway connections to the populous San Francisco Bay Area. Most of the route was constructed in the 1960s and 1970s, with Oregon's section opening in October 1966.

Interstate 5 in Oregon was completed and open to traffic as a four-lane highway by October 1966. Two segments were completed at that time to finish the route in Oregon: (1) the Marquam Bridge over the Willamette River in Portland (between the Baldock Expressway and East Bank Freeway) opened on October 18, 1966, and (2) a segment south of Canyonville near Douglas County was opened second, on October 22, 1966. The new freeway was dedicated in a ceremony held at the Cow Creek Rest Area. http://www.interstate-guide.com/i-005.html

[126] **Juliet Anne Prowse** (September 25, 1936 – September 14, 1996) was a South African dancer, whose four decade career included stage, television and film but dancing remained her true love. She was known for her striking beauty, sultry smile and famous long legs. It was during the filming of "Can-Can" in 1959 that she captured the international spotlight. Soviet leader Nikita Khrushchev visited the set of the film and after Prowse performed a rather saucy can-can for the Russian leader, he proclaimed her dance "immoral". Little did Khrushchev know that he was a great press agent, because the publicity brought Prowse considerable attention in the United States. From there, her career took off. Throughout

the mid 1980s and 1990s, Prowse hosted the Championship Ballroom Dance Competition on PBS. In 1994, Prowse was diagnosed with pancreatic cancer. In 1995, she went into remission and was well enough to tour with Mickey Rooney in Sugar Babies. The cancer subsequently returned and she succumbed to the disease on September 14, 1996, two weeks before her sixtieth birthday. http://en.wikipedia.org/wiki/Juliet_Prowse

[127] The [**Amish**]**couple's** first night together is spent at the bride's home because they must get up early the next day to help clean the house. Their honeymoon is spent visiting all their new relatives on the weekends throughout the winter months ahead. This is when they collect the majority of their wedding gifts. Usually, they receive useful items such as dishware, cookware, canned food, tools and household items. Typically, when the newlyweds go visiting, they will go to one place Friday night and stay overnight for breakfast the following day. They'll visit a second place in the afternoon and stay for the noon meal and go to a third place for supper. Saturday night is spent at a fourth place, where they have Sunday breakfast. A fifth place is visited for Sunday dinner and a sixth for Sunday supper before they return to the bride's parents home. The couple lives at the home of the bride's parents until they can set up their own home the following spring. Excerpted from PancasterPA.com produced by Action Video, Inc.
Lancaster, PA https://lancasterpa.com/amish/amish-weddings/

[128] "**Lara's Theme**" is the generic name given to a leitmotif written for the film *Doctor Zhivago* (1965) by composer Maurice Jarre. Soon afterward, it became the basis of the song "Somewhere My Love." http://en.wikipedia.org/wiki/Lara's_Theme

[129] **The Quiet Man** is a 1952 American romantic drama film directed by John Ford and starring John Wayne, Maureen O'Hara, Victor McLaglen and Barry Fitzgerald. It was based on a 1933 Saturday Evening Post short story by Maurice Walsh. The film is notable for its lush photography of the Irish countryside and the long, climactic, semi-comic fist fight between Wayne and McLaglen. http://en.wikipedia.org/wiki/The_Quiet_Man

[130] **Objections to Roman Catholicism**" by Kenelm Foster, O. P.1965 New in *Blackfriars* Vol. 46, No. 535 (January 1965), pp. 234-237, published by Wiley https://www.jstor.org/stable/43243829

[131] **Lillian Eugenia Smith** (December 12, 1897 – September 28, 1966) was a writer and social critic of the Southern United States, known best for her best-selling novel *Strange Fruit* (1944). A white woman who openly embraced controversial positions on matters of race and gender equality, she was a southern liberal

unafraid to criticize segregation and work toward the dismantling of Jim Crow laws, at a time when such actions almost guaranteed social ostracism. http:// en.wikipedia.org/wiki/Lillian_Smith_(author)

[132] Count **Michael Anthony Maurice de la Bédoyère** (1900 – 1973) was an author, editor and journalist. He was educated at Stonyhurst College, Lancashire, and took a first in Modern Greats at Campion Hall, Oxford University. His initial plans to become a Jesuit priest were abandoned. In 1930-1931 he lectured at the University of Minnesota. In 1934 he became editor of the *Catholic Herald*, a post he held until 1962. During this time he transformed it from one of limited regional appeal into a more challenging and intellectual newspaper, which often brought it into conflict with the more conservative members of the Roman Catholic Church. Circulation increased to six figures. After he left, he founded the magazine *Search*. During these years he wrote a number of books, mainly biographies such as those of *Lafayette* (1932), *George Washington* (1935), *St Francis of Assisi* (1962), as well as theological works such as Christianity in the Market Place (1943). http://en.wikipedia.org/wiki/Michael_de_la_B%C3%A9doy%C3%A8re

[133] This ["**Valediction**"] is a "classic" Donne poem. In it, he shows off his vast knowledge of everything from alchemy to astronomy, and puts his most famous technique, the conceit, to great use. There is a rumor that this poem was written by Donne to his wife, before he went away on a long holiday with his friends, leaving her at home... Donne's basic argument was that most people's relationships are built on purely sensual things - if they are not together at all times, the relationship breaks down. Donne asserts that the love between him and his wife is different - it is not a purely sensual relationship, but something deeper, a "love of the mind" rather than a "love of the body". This love, he says, can endure even though sometimes the lovers cannot be close to each other at all times... Donne is then very disparaging of the love of the rest of the population. The wails and screams and tears that "ordinary" lovers display when they must part is shown to be simply an act, with no real emotion in it. The lovers are then likened to planetary bodies. In such a way, Donne places them above the "mortal earth". Unlike natural disasters, which are unpredictable and chaotic, the movement of the planets is peaceful and calm, even though the planets move much further. Donne's most famous conceit is then introduced. The two lovers are likened to the two points of a compass. At first this seems ridiculous, but Donne shows how it makes sense. The idea of the wife staying and minding the house while the husband

goes away is old-fashioned now, but we can still comprehend it. http://lardcave. net/hsc/2eng-donne-valediction-comments.html

[134] *Diary of a Country* **Priest** (original French title: *Journal d'un curé de campagne*) is a 1951 French film directed by Robert Bresson, and starring Claude Laydu. It was closely based on the novel of the same name by Georges Bernanos. Published in 1937, the novel received the Grand prix du roman de l'Académie française. It tells the story of a young, sickly priest, who has just arrived in his first parish, a village in northern France based on *The Diary of a Country Priest*, 1936 by Georges Bernanos. The novel has been translated to English by Pamela Morris and was published the same year as the French original. http://en.wikipedia.org/wiki/ Diary_of_a_Country_Priest

[135] **The Suicide of Thomas Merton:** Moral Narcissism, Contemplative Prayer, and the Religion of Humor by Joseph M. Kramp, Volume 55, Number 5 / May, 2007, 619-635. Abstract: In this third and final of three successive essays, the author argues that Thomas Merton suffered from narcissistic personality disorder in conjunction with his melancholic condition. The author argues that contemplative prayer disabled Merton from working through his melancholic condition. Finally, the author argues that Merton's melancholia, coupled with his heightened identity conflicts lead him to kill himself.

[136] The earliest known version of the ***Romeo and Juliet*** tale akin to Shakespeare's play is the story of Mariotto and Gianozza by Masuccio Salernitano, in the 33rd novel of his Il Novellino published in 1476. Salernitano sets the story in Siena and insists its events took place in his own lifetime. His version of the story includes the secret marriage, the colluding friar, the fray where a prominent citizen is killed, Mariotto's exile, Gianozza's forced marriage, the potion plot, and the crucial message that goes astray. In this version, Mariotto is caught and beheaded and Gianozza dies of grief. One of the earliest references to the names Montague and Capulet is from Dante's Divine Comedy, who mentions the Montecchi (Montagues) and the Cappelletti (Capulets) in canto six of *Purgatorio*. http://en.wikipedia.org/wiki/Romeo_and_Juliet#Sources

[137] *The Flowers of St. Francis* (in Italian, *Francesco, giullare di Dio*, or "Francis, God's Jester") is a 1950 film directed by Roberto Rossellini and co-written by Federico Fellini. The film consists of a series of modest vignettes, based on the 14th century book Little Flowers of St. Francis, which relate the life and work of St. Francis and the early Franciscans, all of whom are portrayed by actual monks (a total of thirteen in the cast); with the exception of Aldo Fabrizi in a small supporting role,

the entire cast is non-professional. http://en.wikipedia.org/wiki/The_Flowers_of_St._Francis

[138] *Brother Sun, Sister Moon* (Italian: *Fratello Sole, Sorella Luna*) is a 1972 film directed by Franco Zeffirelli and starring Graham Faulkner and Judi Bowker. The film is a biopic of Saint Francis of Assisi. http://en.wikipedia.org/wiki/Brother_Sun,_Sister_Moon

[139] The **Anchor Bible project**, consisting of a Commentary Series, Bible Dictionary, and Reference Library, is a scholarly and commercial co-venture begun in 1956, when individual volumes in the commentary series began production. Having initiated a new era of cooperation among scholars in biblical research, over 1,000 scholars—representing Jewish, Catholic, Protestant, Muslim, secular, and other traditions—have now contributed to the project. Their works offer discussions that reflect a range of viewpoints across a wide theological spectrum. The Anchor Bible project continues to produce volumes that keep readers current on recent scholarship and are grounded in analysis. The works bring advances in science and technology to bear on biblical materials, making historical and linguistic knowledge related to the interpretation of the biblical record available to experts and students alike. As of 2005, more than 120 volumes had been published, each edited by David Noel Freedman, General Editor and published by Doubleday (part of Random House, Inc.). In 2007, Yale University Press purchased the Anchor Bible Series. Yale now publishes backlist titles and new titles as the Anchor Yale Bible Series. http://en.wikipedia.org/wiki/Anchor_Bible_Series

[140] A **monadnock** or inselberg is an isolated rock hill, knob, ridge, or small mountain that rises abruptly from a gently sloping or virtually level surrounding plain. The term "monadnock" is usually used in the United States, whereas "inselberg" is the more common international term. In southern and southern-central Africa, a similar formation of granite is known as a kopje, a Dutch word from the Afrikaans word: koppie. http://en.wikipedia.org/wiki/Monadnock

[141] **4-F** Registrant not acceptable for military service. To be eligible for Class 4-F, a registrant must have been found not qualified for service in the Armed Forces by a Military Entrance Processing Station (MEPS) under the established physical, mental, or moral standards. The standards of physical fitness that would be used in a future draft would come from AR 40-501. http://en.wikipedia.org/wiki/4F_(military_conscription)#Classifications

[142] In fact, I never was able to speak to Fr. Alberic again because he died shortly thereafter:

Father Alberic Smith, OFM, 84, a member of the Franciscan Friars for 65 years, died at his residence, the friary of St. Francis of Assisi Church, Spokane, WA, May 31, 2016. His religious career included teaching history, math, science, chemistry and English courses at seminaries in Santa Barbara, Troutdale, OR, and San Luis Rey, CA. He also taught for four years an "English As A Second Language" program in Los Angeles for Latin Americans interested in entering the Franciscan order. He spent three summers in the Philippines teaching science and geography at Our Lady of the Angels seminary in Manila. From 1991 to 1997 he was administrator at St. Anthony's Seminary, Santa Barbara. He served three years -- 1997-2000 -- as pastor of Mission San Xavier del Bac, Tucson, AR, then became administrator and religious superior at Old Mission Santa Barbara. At the time of his death, he was associate pastor at St. Francis of Assisi church in Spokane, and chaplain for the Poor Clare monastery in Spokane. Excerpted from Catholic Funeral and Cemetery Services of Spokane 7200 N Wall Street. https://www.legacy.com/us/obituaries/spokesman/name/alberic-smith-ofm-obituary?pid=180216171

[143] It is, as someone has already mentioned, the opening lines of "**A Tale of Two Cities.**" It is one of the most famous openings in English literature, in fact, in all literature. The author is Charles Dickens. The two cities are London and Paris. And it is--also mentioned--during the time of the French Revolution, just 15--20 years after our [America] Revolution, which deeply inspired and influenced the French. https://en.wikipedia.org/wiki/A_Tale_of_Two_Cities

[144] **Excommunication** is a legal process in the Catholic Church. At least one form of excommunication is automatic, namely taking a second spouse while the first is still alive. It bars the offender from partaking in the spiritual life of the Church, particularly the Mass. Some extenuating circumstances are allowed, such as renouncing sexual intercourse with the second spouse, all of which has to be documented by a complex procedure of canon law.

[145] *Casablanca* is a 1942 film about an American expatriate owner of an upscale club and gambling den in the Moroccan city of Casablanca who meets a former lover, with unforeseen complications. http://en.wikiquote.org/wiki/Casablanca

[146] **The Chevrolet Corvair** is a compact automobile produced by the Chevrolet division of General Motors for model years 1960-1969 — the only American-made, mass-produced passenger car to feature a rear-mounted engine. Initially marketed as a six passenger four-door sedan, the platform subsequently gave rise to coupe, convertible and station wagon models. The Monza, a five-passenger coupe with

bucket seats was introduced mid-1960, inspiring Ford to produce the Mustang three years later. http://en.wikipedia.org/wiki/Chevrolet_Corvair

[147] **Fr. Christian** (deceased) said in his letter to me: "I was transferred to Serra High School in Salem and served there until it closed two years later. Then I went to Mt Angel College where I joined the Education Dept. as assistant professor and campus minister. The Fall of that year (1969) I was named president and served until the college also closed (1974)." The complete story is contained in this memoir at a website made in his honor: BIO: FR. CHRISTIAN MONDOR, OFM (1925 – 2018)

Fr. Christian Mondor, OFM, (aka "The Surfing Padre") was the vicar emeritus at Ss. Simon and Jude Church, Huntington Beach, CA. The world experienced a great loss when he passed away during open-heart surgery in May 2018. He was involved in parish ministry as well as in civic affairs, was a member of the Board of Trustees for the Huntington Beach Council on Aging and served as president of the Greater Huntington Beach Interfaith Council.

He was a member of the Bishop's Commission on Ecumenical and Interreligious Affairs for the Diocese of Orange. He holds a B.A. from the Franciscan School of Philosophy at Mission San Luis Rey, an M.A. in theology from the Santa Barbara Theological Seminary, an M.A. in education from the University of San Francisco, and a Ph.D. from the University of Portland in Oregon.

Over his sixty-three years as a priest, Fr. Christian was involved in high school, college and graduate level teaching, campus ministry, retreat and parish work. His first assignment in 1952 was to teach English and Religion at St Mary's High School in Phoenix, Arizona. Two years later he was asked to help found the new Serra Catholic High School in Salem, Oregon. In 1958, while continuing as vice-principal and teacher there, he was appointed pastor of St. Mary's Church in Shaw, Oregon and administrator of St. Patrick's Church in Independence, Oregon.

As administrator of the latter parish, he was ex-officio Campus Minister of the nearby Oregon College of Education (later Western Oregon University) In 1961 he joined the faculty at St. Francis Seminary in Troutdale, Oregon, where for six years he taught English and American Literature, speech and drama. In 1967 he returned as Vice Principal at Serra High School until its closure two years later. In the fall of 1969 he was offered a position a Mt. Angel College in Oregon. There he served first as campus minister and assistant professor in the education department and then as president during the tumultuous years of rapid change in the church and society, and the political unrest of the Vietnam war.

On a sabbatical in Canada, he taught in the school system of the Province of Quebec and wrote commentaries on the Sunday scripture readings for the Archdiocese of Montreal in their weekly publication Discover the Bible. After returning from Canada he was engaged in full-time retreat work at Serra Retreat in Malibu.

In 1980 he was appointed religious superior at the Franciscan School of Theology in Berkeley, CA. While there he served as a member of the faculty and supervised students fn field education and conducted doctoral seminars in Religion and Education for the Graduate Theological Union. During that time he also conducted retreats every weekend at St. Clare's Retreat in Santa Cruz. In 1984 while on a six month's sabbatical in England, he served as lecturer and confessor for priests and religious at a recovery center near Gloucester.

Returning to Franciscan formation ministry in 1985, he joined the novitiate team in Los Angeles for three years, followed by two years as one of the directors of the pre-novitiate formation program in Portland, Oregon. In 1990 Fr. Christian was named parochial vicar at Sts. Simon and Jude parish in Huntington Beach, where he remains active after his formal retirement in 2005. He has traveled widely in western and central Europe, including Russia and the Middle East, on high school and university-sponsored study tours.

He also assisted in several scripture-based retreats in the Holy Land. During his term as president of the Greater Huntington Beach Interfaith Council, he chaired the committee that planned the first city-wide interfaith Procession of Light service of prayer and song at the Huntington Beach Pier Plaza to commemorate the beginning of the new century.

The event, held annually for many years, invited people of all faiths to come and pray together for a better community and a better world. Recipient of the Interfaith Council's annual Peacemaker Award, Fr. Christian was also honored, along with the Rev. Dr. Peggy Price of the Church of Religious Science and Rabbi Steven Einstein of Congregation B'nai Tzedek in recognition for their work in promoting better understanding and mutual respect in the midst of cultural and religious diversity. After the terrorist attack of September 11, he helped organize a city-wide, interfaith response to the tragedy. In 2012, he was named Community Grand Marshal for the annual Fourth of July Parade in Huntington Beach.

For many years, usually on the weekend of the Feast of St. Francis of Assisi, at the Huntington Beach Pier Fr. Christian helped coordinate the annual interfaith Blessing of the Waves originally sponsored by the Diocese of Orange (currently by the local Interfaith Council). The event has attracted surfers and others from all faiths and all walks of life to a service of prayer and song in thanksgiving for the gift of the ocean and for raising the consciousness of our shared responsibility toward this great natural resource.

In 2013 he was named a lifetime member of the H. B. Longboard Crew and in the summer of the same year, he was inducted into the Surfing Walk of Fame honor roll with his name on the sidewalk in downtown Huntington Beach. A swimmer and body-surfer all his life, he took up longboard surfing and competitive swimming only after coming to Sts. Simon and Jude parish. For many years he participated in the annual Huntington Beach Pier Swim and the one mile Rough Water Swim at La Jolla, CA and competed regularly in local and regional U.S. Masters swim meets.

He took part in the National Senior Olympics swimming events in Baton Rouge, Orlando and San Antonio. He has also competed in the International Masters Swim Meets in Palo Alto, Melbourne, Australia where he won a silver medal in the 50-meter backstroke, and in Edmonton, Alberta, Canada where he won a gold in his age group in the 1000 meter open water swim.

While teaching at St. Francis Seminary in Oregon in the 1960's, Fr. Christian provided an opportunity for the seminarians to ski at Mount Hood during the long winter months. He also took up the banjo and formed a folk-singing group called The Troubadours of St. Francis that performed around the Pacific Northwest to promote interest in the seminary. He loved playing the banjo and his role as chaplain to the Fretted Instrument Guild of America at their annual conventions. He is sorely missed but his spirit and mission from God lives on through the SURFINGPADRE foundation, Excerpted from SURFINGPADRE. ORG(501c3) Marina California.. https://surfingpadre.org/bio/

[148] **Shorthand** was used more widely in the past, before the invention of recording and dictation machines. Until recently, shorthand was considered an essential part of secretarial training as well as being useful for journalists. Although the primary use of shorthand has been to record oral dictation or discourse, some systems are used for compact expression. For example, health-care professionals may use shorthand notes in medical charts and correspondence. Shorthand notes are typically temporary, intended either for immediate use or for later

transcription to longhand, although longer term uses do exist, diaries (like that of the famous Samuel Pepys) being a common example. http://en.wikipedia.org/wiki/Shorthand

[149] **Hardware Specialty Co.** is the sort of place where you would expect to find the ark of the covenant. A big, dusty warehouse piled to the ceiling with various sorts of electrical and mechanical equipment. It is a great place to go to get a good deal on wire and industrial electronic equipment. A lot of their stuff is dusty old stock. If you are building something on the cheap, try here. Best to remain flexible in your needs because while the may not have exactly what you want, they will most likely have something that will work. 2009 User Rating: 4 out of 5 stars by Brian. *Yahoo.com* URL may no longer applicable; Robert Unger's company may no longer exist.

[150] **George Stanley McGovern** (born July 19, 1922) is a historian, former United States Representative, Senator, and Democratic presidential nominee. McGovern lost the 1972 presidential election in a landslide to Richard Nixon. As a decorated World War II combat veteran, McGovern was known for his opposition to the Vietnam War.

Appointed in 1961 by U.S. President John F. Kennedy as the worldwide director of the Food for Peace program, he remained a longtime leader in ensuring nutrition and food security as a means to fight poverty and political instability. McGovern was appointed United Nations Ambassador on World Hunger in 2001. In 2008, he and Senator Bob Dole were named the 2008 World Food Prize Laureates for their work to promote school-feeding programs globally. http://en.wikipedia.org/wiki/George_McGovern

[151] http://en.wikipedia.org/wiki/Vietnam_War_casualties

[152] The **Tet Offensive** was a military campaign during the Vietnam War that began on January 31, 1968. Forces of the National Liberation Front for South Vietnam (NLF, or Viet Cong), and the People's Army of Vietnam (the North Vietnamese army), fought against the forces of the Republic of Vietnam (South Vietnam), the United States, and their allies. The purpose of the offensive was to strike military and civilian command and control centers throughout South Vietnam and to spark a general uprising among the population that would then topple the Saigon government, thus ending the war in a single blow. http://en.wikipedia.org/wiki/Tet_Offensive

[153] While "Just the facts, ma'am" has come to be known as *Dragnet's* catchphrase, it was never actually uttered by Joe Friday. The closest lines were, "All we want are the

facts, ma'am" and "All we know are the facts, ma'am". On the flip side of the popular Stan Freberg parody St. George and the Dragonet, is another Dragnet parody entitled Little Blue Riding Hood. The recording contains the line "I just want to get the facts, ma'am"... **Dragnet**, syndicated as **Badge 714**, is a radio and television crime drama about the cases of a dedicated Los Angeles police detective, Sergeant Joe Friday, and his partners. http://en.wikipedia.org/wiki/Dragnet_(series)

[154] Construction of the liberal arts quadrangle, known to students as **"The Quad,"** began in 1916 and continued in stages until 1939. The first two wings of Suzzallo Library, considered the architectural centerpiece of the University [of Washington], were built in 1926 and 1935, respectively. Further growth came with the end of World War II and passage of the G.I. Bill. Among the most important developments of this period was the opening of the medical school in 1946. http://en.wikipedia.org/wiki/University_of_Washington

[155] **Masekela** was born in Witbank, South Africa. He began singing and playing piano as a child. At age 14, after seeing the film Young Man With a Horn (in which Kirk Douglas plays a character modeled after American jazz trumpeter Bix Beiderbecke), he took up playing the trumpet. His first trumpet was given to him by Archbishop Trevor Huddleston, the anti-apartheid chaplain at St. Peter's Secondary School.

Huddleston asked the leader of the then Johannesburg "Native" Municipal Brass Band, Uncle Sauda, to teach Masekela the rudiments of trumpet playing. Masekela quickly mastered the instrument. Soon, some of Masekela's schoolmates also became interested in playing instruments, leading to the formation of the Huddleston Jazz Band, South Africa's first youth orchestra. By 1956, after leading other ensembles, Masekela joined Alfred Herbert's African Jazz Revue.

Since 1954, Masekela played music that closely reflected his life experience. The agony, conflict, and exploitation South Africa faced during 1950's and 1960's, inspired and influenced him to make music. He was an artist who in his music vividly portrayed the struggles and sorrows, as well as the joys and passions of his country. His music protested about apartheid, slavery, government; the hardships individuals were living. Masekela reached a large population of people that also felt oppressed due to the country situation.

Following a Manhattan Brothers tour of South Africa in 1958, Masekela wound up in the orchestra for the musical King Kong, written by Todd Matshikiza. King Kong was South Africa's first blockbuster theatrical success, touring the country for a sold-out year with Miriam Makeba and the Manhattan

Brothers' Nathan Mdledle in the lead. The musical later went to London's West End for two years. He had hits in the United States with the pop jazz tunes "Up, Up and Away" and the number one smash "Grazin' in the Grass" (1968), which sold four million copies. He also appeared at the Monterey Pop Festival in 1967, and was subsequently featured in the film Monterey Pop by D. A. Pennebaker. http://en.wikipedia.org/wiki/Hugh_Masekela

[156] **Cherry Blossoms in the Quad** The early days of the Quad - as it is commonly called - reach back almost to the very beginnings of the Alaska-Yukon-Pacific Exposition campus itself. Although the completed work that is the Quad wasn't finished until 1950, its layout had been all but set in stone as early as 1915 by its designers, early University President, Henry Suzzallo and distinguished architect, Carl Gould, whose works include the basic campus plan and 28 of its buildings. https://www.dailyuw.com/news/article_3435de14-a8ec-5fee-b0d2-169e860ceea8.html

[157] **Denny Hall** is the oldest--and was originally the only--building on campus. It contained laboratories, a teaching museum for natural sciences, classrooms, 10 recital halls, faculty and regents rooms, the president's office, and a 736 seat assembly hall. The building, designed in the French Renaissance style with round turrets and candle-snuffer roofs, was built of Tenino sandstone and pressed brick. Students and faculty used it for the first time in September 1895. It was named for Arthur Denny, the pioneer who donated 8 2/3 acres of the University's original 10-acre downtown tract. Denny Hall is now home to the Departments of Anthropology, Classics, Germanics, Near Eastern Languages and Civilization, and the Language Learning Center. Crowning Denny Hall is the belfry containing "Varsity Bell," which was brought around the Horn of South America in the winter of 1861-62 for installation in the original Territorial University building. In its years at the downtown site the bell pealed for weddings, tolled for funerals, guided ships to safe harbor in foggy weather, warned of the anti-Chinese riots of 1886, and signaled the start of the great Seattle fire of 1889. Today, it is rung at Homecoming, on weekdays at 8:20 a.m. and for special events. https://www.lib.washington.edu/specialcollections/collections/exhibits/site/bldgs

[158] **Washington state's broad prohibition** on Sunday business activity was repealed by the initiative process in 1966. The state's Liquor Control Board authorized Sunday liquor sales on a restricted basis in 1967, and in 1976 expanded the hours for those sales to the same as for other days of the week. http://en.wikipedia.org/wiki/Blue_law#Washington

¹⁵⁹ On October 12, 1885, the little brick Catholic Church of **St. Christopher's** was built and dedicated in Galt at the corner of 3rd and F Streets. St. Christopher's Catholic church in Galt, California made the four promised churches, each on a corner of the original town grid.

As it happened, the day of the dedication of St. Christopher's Church was also the 393rd anniversary of the discovery of America by Christopher Columbus, so the members of the congregation chose the patron saint of travelers, Saint Christopher, as the name of the church.

The Galt Weekly Gazette of October 10, 1895, reported that the Italian man-of-war, Christopher Columbus, was lying at anchor in San Francisco Bay, ready to fire an honorary salute at the precise hour of the dedication of the Galt Church. Present for the dedication ceremony was Governor George Stoneman and Patrick Riordan, Archbishop of San Francisco Diocese.

At first the church had no pastor and the pastoral duties were performed by the priest from Jackson. In 1919, St. Christopher's became an independent parish with Father James Grealy as pastor and remained until 1927. The first baptism recorded in St. Christopher's Parish Register, is that of Angleina Batchelder, and the first marriage was that of Mary McEnerney and August James Beakey. Other pioneer families known to be a part to the Galt church history are Kenefick, Rae, Valensin, Lippi, Denevi, McCauley, McEnerney and Marengo.

On October 12, 1985, St. Christopher's celebrated its 100th birthday. Its Etruscan spire was refurbished and some cement decorations removed for safety. A new handicap ramp and brick stairway replaced the old cement stairs, but the body of the church and its stained glass window over the altar are still original. In 2001, a new church was built and dedicated to meet the needs of a growing congregation.

The old St. Christopher's Church is still in use as a Catholic Community Center. http://www.galthistory.org/history/churches/index.htm

¹⁶⁰ **The Hitchcock Years** (1937-1972): Many years prior to 1937, the Botany Department's collections of vascular plants were either given or loaned to the Washington State Museum (now the Thomas Burke Memorial Washington State Museum). In the fall of 1937, under the leadership of C.L. Hitchcock, the herbarium was returned to Botany. It was first housed in small cubicles between rooms 301 and 302 Johnson, but was soon expanded into those rooms.

In 1938 Hitchcock initiated exchanges with several other herbaria of the Pacific Northwest, and for several years departmental collecting was done chiefly in connection with field trips under the summer school program. The trips lasted for nine weeks and enrolled an average of 30 students. As a result of this activity, the vascular plant collection grew to about 50,000 specimens between 1937 and 1942....

In the vascular plant collection, little collecting was done during 1942-43 and little material was incorporated into the Herbarium. However, in 1943 Mr. J.W. Thompson, one of the best field botanists in the western United States, and the owner of the best private herbarium and botanical library in the Pacific Northwest, gave both his herbarium and library to the Department of Botany. A token payment of $1,500 was made to him. The herbarium is particularly rich in topotypes, since Thompson made a consistent effort to visit type localities of as many northwest taxa as he could. His collection also includes much type material from such early Pacific Northwestern collectors as Cusick, Leiberg, Elmer, Heller, Howell, Flett, Abrams, Blankinship, Macbride, Sandberg, and Aven Nelson, as well as more recent collectors such as St. John, Peck, Maguire, Eyerdam, English, Ownbey, Cronquist, Holmgren, Constance, and Detling.

The next twelve years saw a very active collecting program by C. Leo Hitchcock and C.V. Muhlick, mainly in Idaho and Montana, but also in Oregon, Washington, and southern British Columbia. J.W. Thompson did much of the work involved in getting the material ready for exchange, and did all the mounting, stamping, and filing of an average of the 15,000 numbers added to the Herbarium in each of these years. The first duplicate set of the huge Suksdorf collection, mainly from Klickitat County, was received through exchange with Washington State University during this period.

In 1948 a wing was added to Johnson Hall and the vascular plant and bryophyte collections were moved to room 345. In the 1950s and 60s, Hitchcock, Muhlick, and A.R. Kruckeberg concentrated their field work less on general collecting and more on field studies of particular families or genera, such as Sidalcea, Lathyrus, Astragalus, Delphinium, Sisyrinchium, Streptanthus, and many genera of grasses that were undergoing study for treatment in the monumental work Vascular Plants of the Pacific Northwest. During the writing of this work, the medium of communication between several authors was mainly by reference to collections made by Hitchcock and Muhlick or by J.W. Thompson, such collections being cited frequently. Consequently, the University of Washington Herbarium became very important to persons interested in the Flora of the Pacific Northwest. The five-volume illustrated flora was published over a span of 15 years; volume 5 appeared in 1955 and the series culminated in 1969 with volume 1. The abridged one-volume *Flora of the Pacific Northwest* was published in 1973. ...

During the Hitchcock years, the vascular plant Herbarium maintained an active exchange with 56 other herbaria. By 1973, the vascular plant herbarium contained about 280,000 sheets. Most were housed in wooden cases made by the University of Washington's Buildings and Grounds Department.

Unfortunately, the above history, that was available on the Herbarium's website, was erased from university history when the Burk Museum was developed to consolidate all of the natural history collections into one museum. There is, in fact, no remaining reference the UW Botany department's herbarium collection. A search of C.L. Hitchcock in this website returns no results. As a graduate of the Botany Department, I am incensed. http://www.washington. edu/burkemuseum/collections

[161] **Students for a Democratic Society (SDS)** was a national student activist organization in the United States that was one of the main representations of the New Left. Founded in 1960, the organization developed and expanded rapidly in the mid-1960s, with over 300 chapters recorded nationwide by its last convention in 196 (SDS) was a national student activist organization in the United States that was one of the main representations of the New Left. Founded in 1960, the organization developed and expanded rapidly in the mid-1960s, with over 300 chapters recorded nationwide by its last convention in 1969. https://en.wikipedia. org/wiki/Students_for_a_Democratic_Society

[162] **Swizzle** was an inexpensive wine similar to Ripple. Both appeared on the market at about the same time, in about 1968 or 1969. Like Ripple, Swizzle was sweet and fruit flavored and came in 12 oz. bottles. Their popularity came from the effect wine has on women. (If you plan on getting layed - what other reason is there?, you have to be careful that they don't get sick and pass out.) About a year later, Boone's Farm and **Annie Green Springs** appeared on the market in one liter bottles along with a less well known wine drink called Ariba, which was 20% alcohol. The latter had a reputation as a "sneaky Pete" because you could slip them to a date who could normally guzzle the 11% beverages all night while keeping her mouth running and her knees together. http://www.urbandictionary. com/define.php?term=annie+green+springs

[163] We are excited about our plans for July; it is a key month in our parish's Jubilee Year. Saturday July 31st will be a Seattle city-wide celebration at Overlake Christian

Church in Redmond WA. We will be celebrating the 50th anniversary of the Charismatic Renewal led by Fr. Dennis Bennett. http://stlukesseattle.org/

[164] **Dennis J. Bennett** (October 28, 1917 – November 1, 1991) was an American Episcopal priest, who, starting in 1960, testified that he had received the Baptism of the Holy Spirit. Born in England but raised in California, Bennett was a seminal figure in the Charismatic Movement within the Christian church. After proclaiming on April 3, 1960 from the pulpit that he had been baptized in the Holy Spirit, he was asked to resign at St. Mark's Episcopal Church, a 2600-member congregation in Van Nuys, California. Bennett was featured in articles in both Newsweek and Time magazines and rather than subjecting his church to media frenzy, he did resign his pastorate. He continued his ministry at St. Luke's Episcopal Church in Seattle, Washington until 1981 when he left the parish to found and lead the Christian Renewal Association with his wife Rita. He was also instrumental in the 1973 founding of Episcopal Renewal Ministries (now named Acts 29 ministry). https://en.wikipedia.org/wiki/Dennis_Bennett_(priest)

Eric Pryne wrote in the Seattle times:The Rev. Dennis Bennett, who transformed a dying Episcopal church in Ballard into a center of the charismatic renewal movement in the 1960s, died Friday night at his home in Edmonds. He was 74. His wife, Rita Bennett, said he had had heart trouble for years and apparently suffered a heart attack. He served 20 years as rector of St. Luke's Episcopal Church, where his emphasis on the practice of speaking in tongues brought him followers, fame and controversy. The church's Friday-night prayer services drew hundreds and changed the lives of many.

"He turned the world upside down for a while," said Ruth Gothenquist, former youth director at St. Luke's. https://archive.seattletimes.com/archive/?date=19911103&slug=1314867

[165] **Schistosomiasis** (also known as **bilharzia**, bilharziosis or snail fever) is a parasitic disease caused by several species of tremotodes ("flukes"), a parasitic worm of the genus Schistosoma.

Although it has a low mortality rate, schistosomiasis often is a chronic illness that can damage internal organs and, in children, impair growth and cognitive development. The urinary form of schistosomiasis is associated with increased risks for bladder cancer in adults. Schistosomiasis is the second most socioeconomically devastating parasitic disease after malaria.

This disease is most commonly found in Asia, Africa, and South America, especially in areas where the water contains numerous freshwater snails, which may carry the parasite.

The disease affects many people in developing countries, particularly children who may acquire the disease by swimming or playing in infected water. http://en.wikipedia.org/wiki/Schistosomiasis

[166] Creeping speedwell (*Veronica filiformis*) is a low growing perennial that prefers shade, moist soils, good fertility and a low mowing height. Creeping speedwell is also sold as an ornamental ground cover and is available and many greenhouses. Many times the speedwell will escape from the landscape beds into the lawn. Creeping speedwell spreads by stolons much like ground ivy and displays its blue-violet flowers in the spring. http://www.msuturfweeds.net/details/ /creeping_ speedwell 2/

[167] Jewel bearings were invented in 1704 for use in watches by Nicolas Fatio de Duillier, Peter Debaufre, and Jacob Debaufre, who received an English patent for the idea. Originally natural jewels were used, such as sapphire, ruby, and garnet. In 1902, a process to make synthetic sapphire and ruby (crystalline aluminum oxide, also known as corundum) was invented by Auguste Verneuil, making jewelled bearings much less expensive. Today most jewelled bearings are synthetic ruby or sapphire.

The advantages of jewel bearings include high accuracy, very small size and weight, low and predictable friction, including good temperature stability, and the ability to operate without lubrication and in corrosive environments. They are known for their low static friction and highly consistent dynamic friction. The static coefficient of friction of brass-on-steel is 0.35, while that of sapphire-on-steel is 0.10–0.15. Sapphire surfaces are very hard and durable, with Mohs hardness of 9 and Knoop hardness of 2000, and can maintain smoothness over decades of use, thus reducing friction variability. Disadvantages include brittleness and fragility, limited availability/applicability in medium and large bearing sizes and capacities, and friction variations if the load is not axial. http://en.wikipedia.org/ wiki/Jewel bearing

[168] Shaw University, founded in 1865, is the oldest historically black college of the south. Shaw is a private, coeducational, liberal arts university affiliated with the Baptist Church. The University awards degrees at the undergraduate and graduate levels. (picture is from same citation) http://www.campusexplorer.com/ colleges/9CA0DF41/North-Carolina/Raleigh/Shaw-University/

[169] Kittrell College was a two-year historically black college located in Kittrell, North Carolina from about 1886 until 1975. It was associated with the African Methodist Episcopal Church.

After the college closed, many of its facilities became the Kittrell Job Corps Center campus. About 400 students learn trades or better themselves by working toward going to college. Many trades are taught there including furniture making, culinary, and electronics. Each quarter many students graduate and take on a trade or go onto college. http://en.wikipedia.org/wiki/Kittrell_College

170 A **moon landing** is the arrival of a spacecraft on the surface of the Moon. This includes both manned and unmanned (robotic) missions. The first human-made object to reach the surface of the Moon was the Soviet Union's Luna 2 mission on September 13, 1959. The United States's Apollo 11 was the first manned mission to land on the Moon on July 20, 1969. http://en.wikipedia.org/wiki/Moon_landing

171 The earliest reference to this old African American spiritual was attributed to Charles Albert Tindley, 1851-1933 Arr. by F.A. Clark https://youtu.be/-ahKtKxUAP8

172 "**Mother Popcorn** (You Got to Have a Mother for Me)", is a song recorded by James Brown and released as a two-part single in 1969. A #1 R&B and #11 Pop hit. It was the highest-charting of a series of recordings inspired by the popular dance The Popcorn which Brown made that year. Other entries included "Let a Man Come In and Do the Popcorn" and an album of instrumentals, The Popcorn.

1969 video recording of James Brown performing "Mother Popcorn" at https://youtu.be/5eoSXpNZD9o

173 The **ocarina** (/ˌɒkəˈriːnə/) is an ancient flute-like wind instrument. While variations exist, a typical ocarina is an oval-shaped enclosed space with four to twelve finger holes and a mouthpiece that projects from the body. It is often ceramic, but other materials, such as plastic, wood, glass, and metal may also be used. https://en.wikipedia.org/wiki/Ocarina

174 The English Flute or **recorder**[1] is a woodwind musical instrument of the family known as fipple flutes or internal duct flutes — whistle-like instruments which include the tin whistle and ocarina. The recorder is end-blown and the mouth of the instrument is constricted by a wooden plug, known as a block or fipple.[2] It is distinguished from other members of the family by having holes for seven fingers (the lower one or two often doubled to facilitate the production of semitones) and one for the thumb of the uppermost hand. The bore of the recorder is tapered slightly, being widest at the mouthpiece end and narrowest at the top on Baroque recorders, or flared almost like a trumpet at the bottom on Renaissance instruments. https://en.wikipedia.org/wiki/Recorder_(musical_instrument)

[175] **SNL Season 3 Episode I:**

    77k: Robert Klein / Bonnie Raitt

    "Olympia Café"

    Female Customer.....Jane Curtin

    Male Customer.....Garrett Morris

    Pete Dionasopolis.....John Belushi

    George Dionasopolis.....Dan Aykroyd

    Sandy Dionasopolis.....Laraine Newman

    Nico Dionasopolis.....Bill Murray

    Female Customer #2.....Gilda Radner

    Male Customer #2.....Robert Klein

    Female Customer: I'll have a tuna salad sandwich, and an order of French fries, please.

    Pete Dionasopolis: No. No tuna.

    Female Customer: You're out of tuna?

    Pete Dionasopolis: No tuna. Cheeseburger? Come on, come on, come on! I don't have all day, we gotta have turnover, turnover. [turns to Male Customer] What are you gonna have?

    Male Customer: Uh.. I think I'll have grilled cheese and a Coke.

    Pete Dionasopolis: Uh.. [turns to kitchen] Grilled cheese?

    George Dionasopolis: No grilled cheese.

    Male Customer: No grilled cheese.

    Male Customer: Uh.. cheeseburger and a Coke.

    Pete Dionasopolis: Uh, no Coke - Pepsi.

    Male Customer: Okay, uh.. Pepsi, and french fries.

    Pete Dionasopolis: No fries - chips.

    Male Customer: Okay, chips.

    Pete Dionasopolis: [to kitchen] One cheeseburger, one Pepsi, one chip!

    George Dionasopolis: Cheeseburger!

    http://snltranscripts.jt.org/77/77jolympia.phtml

[176] **Washington Square Park** is one of the best-known of New York City's 1,900 public parks. At 9.75 acres (39,500 m2), it is a landmark in the Manhattan neighborhood of Greenwich Village, as well as a meeting place and center for cultural activity. It is operated by the New York City Department of Parks and Recreation.

An open space with a tradition of nonconformity, the park's fountain area has long been one of the city's popular spots for residents and tourists. Most of the buildings surrounding the park now belong to New York University. Some of the buildings have been built by NYU, others have been converted from their former uses into academic and residential buildings. The university rents the park for its graduation ceremonies, and uses the Arch as a symbol. Although NYU considers the park to be the quad of the school's campus, Washington Square remains a public park.Since the late 1970s, the central part of NYU has been its Washington Square campus in the heart of Greenwich Village. http://en.wikipedia.org/wiki/Washington_Square_Park Despite being public property the **Washington Square Arch** is the unofficial symbol of NYU. Until 2007, NYU had held its commencement ceremonies in Washington Square Park, but moved the ceremonies to Yankee Stadium in 2008 because of renovations to Washington Square.

[177] **Historical references about Thomas [the Apostle]**

Many early Christian writings, which belong to centuries immediately following the first Ecumenical Council of 325, exist about Thomas' mission. The Acts of Thomas, sometimes called by its full name The Acts of Judas Thomas: 2nd/3rd century (c. 180-230) Gist of the testimony: The Apostles cast lots as to where they should go, and to Thomas, twin brother of Jesus, fell India. Thomas was taken to king Gondophares the ruler of Indo-Parthian Kingdom as an architect and carpenter by Habban. The journey to India is described in detail.

After a long residence in the court at Taxila he ordained leaders for the Church, and left in a chariot for the kingdom of Mazdei. According to the Acts of St. Thomas the Kingdom of Mazdai, in the Western India, Indus Valley, was ruled by King Misdeus. Parts of the Indus Valley, was then ruled by Persians called the Indo-Parthian Kingdom. Some Greeks Satraps, the descendants of Alexander the Great, were vassals to the Indo-Parthian Kingdom. The king Misdeus was infuriated when St.Thomas converted the Queen Tertia, son Juzanes, sister-in-law princess Mygdonia(a province of Mesopotamia) and her friend Markia. The King Misdeus led St. Thomas outside the city and ordered four soldiers to take him to the nearby hill where the soldiers speared St. Thomas and killed him.

Syphorus was elected the first presbyter by the brethren after the death of St. Thomas while Juzanes the prince became the deacon. The names of the King Misdeus, Tertia, Juzanes, Syphorus, Markia and Mygdonia suggest Greek descent or Hellenised Persian descent. Thereafter performing many miracles, he dies a martyr. During the rule of Vasudeva I, the Kushan emperor, the bones of St. Thomas were transferred from the Indus Valley to Edessa. These are generally rejected by various Christian religions as either apocryphal or heretical. The two centuries that lapsed between the life of the apostle and recording this work, casts doubt on their authenticity. http://en.wikipedia.org/wiki/Thomas_the_Apostle

[178] **Krishna** (in Devanagari, kṛṣṇa in IAST, pronounced [ˈkr̩ʂɳə] in classical Sanskrit, literally "the dark one") is a deity worshipped across many traditions in Hinduism in a variety of perspectives. While many Vaishnava groups recognize Krishna as an avatar of Vishnu, other traditions within Krishnaism consider him to be svayam bhagavan, or the Supreme Being.

Krishna is often depicted as an infant or young boy playing a flute as in the Bhagavata Purana, or as a youthful prince giving direction and guidance as in the Bhagavad Gita. The stories of Krishna appear across a broad spectrum of Hindu philosophical and theological traditions. They portray him in various perspectives: a god-child, a prankster, a model lover, a divine hero and the Supreme Being. The principal scriptures discussing Krishna's story are the Mahabharata, the Harivamsa, the Bhagavata Purana and the Vishnu Purana....

The various traditions dedicated to different manifestations of Krishna, such as Vasudeva, Bala Krishna and Gopala, existed as early as 4th century BC. The Krishna-bhakti movement spread to southern India by the 9th century AD, while in northern India Krishnaism schools were well established by 11th century AD. From the 10th century AD, with the growing bhakti movement, Krishna became a favorite subject in performing arts and regional traditions of devotion developed for forms of Krishna such as Jagannatha in Orissa, Vithoba in Maharashtra and Shrinathji in Rajasthan.

Since 1966, the Krishna-bhakti movement has also spread outside India. This is largely due to the Hare Krishna movement, the largest part of which is the International Society for Krishna Consciousness (ISKCON)...

"Krishnology" is a term coined to highlight parallels between Krishnaism in Vaishnava theology and Christological dogma in Christianity. Krishna worship or reverence has been adopted by several new religious movements since the 19th century, and he is sometimes a member of an eclectic pantheon in occult texts, along with Greek, Buddhist, Biblical and even historical figures. For instance, Édouard Schuré, an influential figure in perennial philosophy and occult movements, considered Krishna a Great Initiate; while Theosophists

652

regard Krishna as an incarnation of Maitreya (one of the Masters of the Ancient Wisdom), the most important spiritual teacher for humanity after Buddha. Krishna was canonized by Aleister Crowley and is recognized as a saint in the Gnostic Mass of Ordo Templi Orientis. Reviewers linked the imagery of the blue-skinned Na'vi in James Cameron's Avatar film to Krishna as one of possible conceptual prototypes for the film's Hindu theme. http://en.wikipedia.org/wiki/Krishna

[179] Patti LaBelle (born Patricia Louise Holte; May 24, 1944) is an American singer and actress. She fronted two groups, **Patti LaBelle and the Bluebelles**, which received minor success on the pop charts in the 1960s, and Labelle, which received acclaim and a mainstream breakthrough in 1974 with their song "Lady Marmalade". She went on to have a solo recording career, earning another U.S. #1 single in 1986 with "On My Own", a duet with Michael McDonald. http://en.wikipedia.org/wiki/Patti_LaBelle

[180] **The Supremes,** an American female singing group, were the premier act of Motown Records during the 1960s.

Originally founded as The Primettes in Detroit, Michigan, in 1959, The Supremes' repertoire included doo-wop, pop, soul, Broadway show tunes, psychedelic soul, and disco. They were the most commercially successful of Motown's acts and are, to date, America's most successful vocal group with 12 number one singles on the Billboard Hot 100. Most of these hits were written and produced by Motown's main songwriting and production team, Holland–Dozier–Holland. At their peak in the mid-1960s, The Supremes rivaled The Beatles in worldwide popularity, and their success made it possible for future African-American R&B and soul musicians to find mainstream success.

Founding members Florence Ballard, Mary Wilson, Diana Ross, and Betty McGlown, all from the Brewster-Douglass public housing project in Detroit, formed The Primettes as the sister act to The Primes (with Paul Williams and Eddie Kendricks, who would go on to form The Temptations). Barbara Martin replaced McGlown in 1960, and the group signed with Motown the following year as The Supremes. Martin left the act in early 1962, and Ross, Ballard, and Wilson carried on as a trio.

During the mid-1960s, The Supremes achieved mainstream success with Ross as lead singer. In 1967, Motown president Berry Gordy renamed the group Diana Ross & the Supremes, and replaced Ballard with Cindy Birdsong. Ross left to pursue a solo career in 1970 and was replaced by Jean Terrell, at which point the group's name reverted to The Supremes. After 1972, the lineup changed more frequently; Lynda Laurence, Scherrie Payne, and Susaye Greene all became members of the group during the mid-1970s. The Supremes disbanded in 1977 after an 18-year run. http://en.wikipedia.org/wiki/The_Supremes

[181] **Diana Ross in Central Park** http://www.youtube.com/watch?v=3cK--Ha9fSI

[182] **Topsoil and civilization**. 1974. Vernon Gill Carter and Tom Dale. rev. ed. Norman, University of Oklahoma Press. A more thorough discussion of man's relationship to topsoil. Originally published in 1955.

[183] **Roman Agriculture** describes the farming practices of ancient Rome, during a period of over 1000 years. From humble beginnings, the Roman Republic (509 BCE to 27 BCE) and empire (27 BCE to 476 CE) expanded to rule much of Europe, northern Africa, and the Middle East and thus comprised many agricultural environments of which the Mediterranean climate of dry, hot summers and cool, rainy winters was the most common. Within the Mediterranean area, a triad of crops were most important: grains, olives, and grapes.

The great majority of the people ruled by Rome were engaged in agriculture. From a beginning of small, largely self-sufficient landowners, rural society became dominated by latifundium, large estates owned by the wealthy and utilizing mostly slave labor. The growth in the urban population, especially of the city of Rome, required the development of commercial markets and long-distance trade in agricultural products, especially grain, to supply the people in the cities with food. https://en.wikipedia.org/wiki/Agriculture_in_ancient_Rome

[184] The town of **Marsabit** is an outpost of urban civilization in the vast desert of northern Kenya. The town is situated on an isolated extinct volcano, Mount Marsabit, which rises almost a kilometer above the sea of desert. The hills here are heavily forested, in contrast to the desert beyond, with their own "insular" eco-system.

The town is inhabited by the Nilotic Samburu and Turkana, as well as the Cushitic-speaking Gabbra, Burji, Borana and Rendille. It is also home to some Somali traders and migrants.

In addition, Marsabit has an airstrip and a mountain peak (Mount Marsabit), with "singing" wells just outside the town. Elephants can also often be seen in the local wildlife refuge that surrounds the town, occasionally breaking down fences and causing damage to local farmers crop beds.

The town's name is from the Amharic word 'Marsa bet' (Meaning Marsa's home/house) is believed to have been named after a farmer named 'Marsa' (ethnically Burji) who was brought to Marsabit from Mega (in Ethiopia) by the Consul to assist in consolidation of farming and permanent settlement on the slopes of Mount Marsabit. http://en.wikipedia.org/wiki/Marsabit

[185] **Mount Kenya** is the highest mountain in Kenya and the second-highest in Africa, after Kilimanjaro. The highest peaks of the mountain are Batian (5,199 metres (17,057 ft)), Nelion (5,188 metres (17,021 ft)) and Point Lenana (4,985 metres (16,355 ft)). Mount Kenya is located in central Kenya, just south of the equator, around (150 kilometres (93 mi)) north-northeast of the capital Nairobi. Mount Kenya is the source of the name of the Republic of Kenya. http://en.wikipedia. org/wiki/Mount_Kenya

[186] The term **White Highlands** describes an area in the central uplands of Kenya, so-called because, during the period of British Colonialism, white immigrants settled there in considerable numbers. The main motivation was to take advantage of the good soils and growing conditions, as well as the cool climate. The British East Africa colony, founded in 1905, encouraged British immigration. By the time the Kenya Colony came into being in 1920, about 10,000 British had settled in the area. Settlers got 999 year leases over about 25% of the good land in Kenya. The original occupants of the land were predominantly from the Kalenjin, Maasai and Kikuyu tribes. Later, the Kikuyu and allied tribes, the Embu and Meru, collectively known as G.e.m.a., mounted a bloody campaign against the British occupation of their land in central Kenya in an uprising known as the Mau Mau. http://en.wikipedia.org/wiki/White_Highlands

[187] Whatever their early origins, it is generally accepted that starting from around the **16th century, the ancestors of the Kikuyu**, Meru (including the Igembe and Tigania), Kamba, Embu and Chuka, began moving south into the richer foothills of Mount Kenya. By the early 17th century, they were concentrated at Ithanga, 80 km southeast of the mountain's peaks at the confluence of the Thika and Sagana rivers. As Ithanga's population increased, oral traditions of all the tribes agree that the people began to fan out in different directions, eventually becoming the separate and independent tribes that exist today. The theory that the Chuka, Embu, Mbeere, Gicugu and Ndia 'broke away' from the main Kikuyu group before arriving at Ithanga is plausible, but is contradicted by the oral traditions of various tribes, many of which include Ithanga in their histories. The Kikuyu themselves moved west to a place near present-day Murang'a, from where the Kikuyu creation myth picks up the story. http://en.wikipedia.org/wiki/Kikuyu#Origins

[188] **Irony**: "condition opposite to what might be expected; contradictory circumstances; apparent mockery of natural or expected consequences" from Etymology.org. synonyms: paradoxical, absurd, contradictory, puzzling.

[189] **Ugali** is an East African dish (also sometimes called sima, sembe, or posho) of maize flour (cornmeal) cooked with water to a porridge- or dough-like consistency. It is the most common staple starch of much of Eastern and Southern Africa. When ugali is made from another starch, it is usually given a specific regional name. This food is considered of relatively low nutritional value. http://en.wikipedia. org/wiki/Ugali

[190] The origin of the word **matatu** is ascribed to different sources. One attribution is that it is derived from the Kenyan tatu, meaning three ten cent coins. When matatus made their first appearance in the late 1960s, the standard fare for a trip was three coins worth thirty Kenyan cents. Matatu are sometimes known as 'ma3' as the swahili word for "three" is tatu, normally used in text messaging and more recently, as 'mats' in Sheng, Kenya's creolised swahili language. Matatus are mostly Isuzu minibuses; other popular models include the Nissan Caravan and Toyota Hiace. http://en.wikipedia.org/wiki/Share_taxi

[191] Swahili (or **Kiswahili**) is a Bantu language spoken by various ethnic groups that inhabit several large stretches of the Indian Ocean coastline from northern Kenya to northern Mozambique, including the Comoros Islands. Although only 5–10 million people speak it as their native language. Swahili is a national, or official language, of four nations, namely Tanzania, Kenya, Uganda and the Democratic Republic of the Congo. Within the Congo, as in much of East Africa, it often acts as a lingua franca. It is the only language historically African in origin among the official working languages of the African Union.

Swahili is a Bantu language that serves as a second language to various groups traditionally inhabiting parts of the East African coast. About 35% of the Swahili vocabulary derives from the Arabic language, gained through more than twelve centuries of contact with Arabic-speaking inhabitants of the coast of Zanj. It also has incorporated Persian, German, Portuguese, English and French words into its vocabulary through contact during the last five centuries. Swahili has become a second language spoken by tens of millions in three countries, Tanzania, Kenya, and Congo (DRC), where it is an official or national language. The neighboring nation of Uganda made Swahili a required subject in primary schools in 1992—although this mandate has not been well implemented—and declared it an official language in 2005 in preparation for the East African

Federation. Swahili, or other closely related languages, is spoken by nearly the entire population of the Comoros and by relatively small numbers of people in Burundi, Rwanda, northern Zambia, Malawi, and Mozambique and the language was still understood in the southern ports of the Red Sea and along the coasts of southern Arabia and the Persian Gulf in the twentieth century. http://en.wikipedia.org/wiki/Swahili_language

[192] *Phytophthora infestans* is an oomycete or water mold that causes the serious potato disease known as late blight or potato blight. (Early blight, caused by Alternaria solani, is also often called "potato blight"). Late blight was a major culprit in the 1840s European, the 1845 Irish and 1846 Highland potato famines. The organism can also infect tomatoes and some other members of the Solanaceae. http://en.wikipedia.org/wiki/Phytophthora_infestans

[193] The Maasai (also **Masai**) are a Nilotic ethnic group of semi-nomadic people located in Kenya and northern Tanzania. Due to their distinctive customs and dress and residence near the many game parks of East Africa, they are among the most well-known of African ethnic groups. They speak Maa, a member of the Nilo-Saharan language family that is related to Dinka and Nuer, and are also educated in the official languages of Kenya and Tanzania: Swahili and English. The Maasai population has been variously estimated as 377,089 from the 1989 Census or as 453,000 Maa language speakers in Kenya in 1994 and 430,000 in Tanzania in 1993 with a total estimated as "approaching 900,000" Estimates of the respective Maasai populations in both countries are complicated by the remote locations of many villages, and their semi-nomadic nature. http://en.wikipedia.org/wiki/Maasai_people

[194] **Amboseli National Park**, formerly Maasai Amboseli Game Reserve, is in Kajiado District, Rift Valley Province in Kenya. The park is 39,206 hectares (392 km2; 151 sq mi) in size at the core of an 8,000 square kilometres (3,100 sq mi) ecosystem that spreads across the Kenya-Tanzania border. The local people are mainly Maasai, but people from other parts of the country have settled there attracted by the successful tourist-driven economy and intensive agriculture along the system of swamps that makes this low-rainfall area (average 350 mm (14 in)) one of the best wildlife-viewing experiences in the world. The park protects two of the five main swamps, and includes a dried-up Pleistocene lake and semi-arid vegetation. One hundred fourty kilometres (87 mi) South of the capital city Nairobi, Amboseli National Park is the second most popular national park

in Kenya after Maasai Mara National Reserve. http://en.wikipedia.org/wiki/Amboseli_National_Park

[195] *Out of Africa* is a memoir by Isak Dinesen, a nom de plume used by the Danish author **Baroness Karen von Blixen-Finecke**. The book, first published in 1937, recounts events of the seventeen years when Blixen made her home in Kenya, then British East Africa. The book is a lyrical meditation on Blixen's life on her coffee plantation, as well as a tribute to some of the people who touched her life there. It is also a vivid snapshot of African colonial life in the last decades of the British Empire. Blixen wrote the book in English and then translated it into Danish. http://en.wikipedia.org/wiki/Out_of_Africa

[196] **Out of Africa** is a film released in 1985. The story based loosely on the autobiographical book *Out of Africa* written by Isak Dinesen (the pseudonym of the author Karen Blixen), which was published in 1937, with additional material from Dinesen's book Shadows on the Grass and other sources. This film received 28 film awards, including seven Academy Awards. https://en.wikipedia.org/wiki/Out_of_Africa_(film)

[197] **The Ghost and the Darkness** is a 1996 Oscar-winning thriller starring Michael Douglas and Val Kilmer set in Africa at the end of the 19th century. It was directed by Stephen Hopkins and based on a screenplay by Academy Award-winner William Goldman. The film tells a fictionalised account about the two lions that attacked and killed workers at Tsavo, Kenya during the building of the African Uganda-Mombasa Railway in 1898. http://en.wikipedia.org/wiki/The_Ghost_and_the_Darkness

[198] **Lake Baringo** is, after Lake Turkana, the most northern of the Great Rift Valley lakes of Kenya, with a surface area of about 130 km² and an elevation of about 970 m. The lake is fed by several rivers, El Molo, Perkerra and Ol Arabel, and has no obvious outlet; the waters are assumed to seep through lake sediments into the faulted volcanic bedrock. It is one of the two freshwater lakes in the Rift Valley in Kenya, the other being Lake Naivasha. It lies off the beaten track in a hot and dusty setting and over 470 species of birds have been recorded there, occasionally including migrating flamingos. A Goliath Heronry is located on a rocky islet in the lake known as Gibraltar. http://en.wikipedia.org/wiki/Lake_Baringo

[199] **Murram** is a gravelly lateritic material, often used to surface minor roads in parts of Africa https://www.collinsdictionary.com/us/dictionary/english/murram
They are good material for building huts and paths, as they can be compacted easily to form hard surfaces.

[200] **The Makonde** is an ethnic group in southeast Tanzania and northern Mozambique. The Makonde developed their culture on the Mueda Plateau in Mozambique. At present they live throughout Tanzania and Mozambique and have a small presence in Kenya. The Makonde population in Tanzania was estimated in 2001 to be 1,140,000, and the 1997 census in Mozambique put the Makonde population in that country at 233,358, for a total estimate of 1,373,358.

The Makonde successfully resisted predation by African, Arab, and European slavers. They did not fall under colonial power until the 1920s. During the 1960s the revolution which drove the Portuguese out of Mozambique was launched from the Makonde homeland of the Mueda Plateau. At one period this revolutionary movement known as 'Frelimo' derived a part of its financial support from the sale of Makonde carvings. The Makonde are best known for their wood carvings and their observances of puberty rites. They speak Makonde, also known as ChiMakonde, a Central Bantu language closely related to Yao. Many speak other languages such as English in Tanzania, Portuguese in Mozambique, and Swahili and Makua in both countries. The Makonde are traditionally a matrilineal society where children and inheritances belong to women, and husbands move into the village of their wives. Their traditional religion is an animistic form of ancestor worship and still continues, although Makonde of Tanzania are nominally Muslim and those of Mozambique are Catholic or Muslim. In Makonde rituals, when a girl becomes a woman, Muidini is the best dancer out of the group of girls undergoing the rituals. http://en.wikipedia.org/wiki/Makonde_people

[201] When Mzee Simon Muthoka Ngila presented a **flywhisk** and a wand to Kenyatta in 1961, little did he know that the man was set to be the first president of Kenya and that the flywhisk was to be Kenyatta's symbol of authority.

"I had followed the trials of Kenyatta in the hands of the British rule with a lot of bitterness," recounts Ngila who adds that in Kenyattta, he had seen a strong visionary who could lead the country into independence. "When he (Kenyatta) was finally released, I decided to give him something that would scare away the oppressive colonialists who were masking his leadership that would lead his people out of the chains of colonialism". http://www.somalilandtimes.net/sl/2005/225/19.shtml (picture of Kenyatta is also from this website).

[202] **Newcastle disease** is a contagious bird disease affecting many domestic and wild avian species. Its effects are most notable in domestic poultry due to their high

susceptibility and the potential for severe impacts of an epidemic on the poultry industries. It is endemic to many countries.

Newcastle Disease was discovered in Newcastle upon Tyne, England in 1926 (Doyle), but also at this time slightly different strains were found in other parts of the world.

Exposure of humans to infected birds (for example in poultry processing plants) can cause mild conjunctivitis and influenza-like symptoms, but the Newcastle disease virus (NDV) otherwise poses no hazard to human health. Interest in the use of NDV as an anticancer agent has arisen from the ability of NDV to selectively kill human tumour cells with limited toxicity to normal cells.

No treatment for NDV exists, but the use of prophylactic vaccines and sanitary measures reduces the likelihood of outbreaks. Description revised from Veterinary Literature. https://www.merckvetmanual. com/poultry/newcastle-disease-and-other-paramyxovirus-infections/ newcastle-disease-in-poultry

[203] **The Kent State shootings** – also known as the May 4 massacre or Kent State massacre – occurred at Kent State University in the city of Kent, Ohio, and involved the shooting of unarmed college students by members of the Ohio National Guard on Monday, May 4, 1970. The guardsmen fired 67 rounds over a period of 13 seconds, killing four students and wounding nine others, one of whom suffered permanent paralysis.

Some of the students who were shot had been protesting against the American invasion of Cambodia, which President Richard Nixon announced in a television address on April 30. Other students who were shot had been walking nearby or observing the protest from a distance.

There was a significant national response to the shootings: hundreds of universities, colleges, and high schools closed throughout the United States due to a student strike of four million students, and the event further affected the public opinion – at an already socially contentious time – over the role of the United States in the Vietnam War. http://en.wikipedia.org/wiki/Kent_State_shootings

[204] **Priscilla Mshoi:** In 2019 Priscilla and subsequent children are still alive, but Mawuganga had recently died. He had married and had a son, but his wife died and he followed not long after.

[205] In general, traditional East African cultures do not favor the use of juices. Juice made from ripe banana (*umutobe*) is commonly served in Rwanda, and a hot

drink and juice made from *karkade* (*Hibiscus sabdariffa*) are common in Sudan, but these are exceptions. However, a great variety of alcoholic drinks are made in the region. *Muratina* is a common weak beer served in rural parts of Kenya. In Tanzania it is called dengelwa (local sugar cane beer). [probably the source of the name *denge* in Kidwada] It is prepared from honey, sugar, or sugar cane and is named after the fermenting agent, the sausage tree fruit (*Kigelia africana*). The Maasai use aloe root (*osuguroi*) in place of sausage tree fruit for fermentation. http://www.enotes.com/food-encyclopedia/east-africa

[206] The **absorption refrigerator** is a refrigerator that uses a heat source (e.g., solar, kerosene-fueled flame) to provide the energy needed to drive the cooling system. Absorption refrigerators are a popular alternative to regular compressor refrigerators where electricity is unreliable, costly, or unavailable, where noise from the compressor is problematic, or where surplus heat is available (e.g., from turbine exhausts or industrial processes). Absorption refrigerators powered by heat from the combustion of liquefied petroleum gas are often used for food storage in recreational vehicles.

Both absorption and compressor refrigerators use a refrigerant with a very low (less than 0 °F/−18 °C) boiling point. In both types, when this refrigerant evaporates or boils, it takes some heat away with it, providing the cooling effect. The main difference between the two types is the way the refrigerant is changed from a gas back into a liquid so that the cycle can repeat. A compressor refrigerator uses an electrically-powered compressor to increase the pressure on the gas, and then condenses the hot high pressure gas back to a liquid by heat exchange with a coolant (usually air). Once the high pressure gas has cooled, it passes through a pressure release valve which drops the refrigerant temperature to below freezing. An absorption refrigerator changes the gas back into a liquid using a different method that needs only heat, and has no moving parts. The other difference between the two types is the refrigerant used. Compressor refrigerators typically use an HCFC, while absorption refrigerators typically use ammonia. http://en.wikipedia.org/wiki/Absorption_refrigerator

[207] **Paloma Hot Water Heater:** When you turn on the tap in your bathroom, it's as if you turned the key of your ignition system on your car. The movement of the water in the unit tells your Paloma that it's time to get started making hot water. This kicks off a series of events inside the heater. The gas valve opens, allowing gas to enter the combustion chamber in the middle of the heater. Then the electronic ignition system starts combustion in the chamber. (Our Legacy series uses a standing pilot light.) Water is then routed through the heater in copper

tubes with fins extending into the combustion chamber. At this point, inside the Paloma there is a very efficient exchange of heat energy from the gas flame to the water. http://www. http://besttanklesswater.com/copyright.html

[208] The Kenya Ceramic *Jiko* [pl *vijiko*, diminutive *kijiko*] is a portable charcoal stove which, with proper use and maintenance, can reduce fuel consumption by 30-50%, saving the consumer money, reducing toxic gas and particulate matter, and resulting in better overall heath for the user. The stove is now used in over 50% of all urban homes and 16% of rural homes in Kenya and is spreading to neighboring African countries. http://other90.cooperhewitt.org/design/kenya-ceramic-jiko

[209] Secondary schools in Kenya fall into three categories - government funded, harambee and private. Government funded schools are divided into national, provincial and district levels. **Harambee schools** do not receive full funding from the government and private schools are run by private organizations or individuals. After taking the primary school leaving exam and successfully passing, government funded schools select students in order of scores. Students with the highest scores gain admission into national schools while those with average scores are selected into provincial and district schools. Harambee schools accept students with low scores. Students who fail examinations either repeat the final school year or pursue technical training opportunities. A number of students also drop out of school by choice due to poor scores. http://en.wikipedia. org/wiki/Education_in_Kenya

[210] **Greek top-bar hive** with movable comb, described in 1682. Top-bar hives have a long history as the concept is believed to be several thousand years old. The earliest hives are believed to be baskets with sticks lain across the top as bars. Most modern top-bar hives are found in Africa. Owing to the low cost and ease of construction these are especially appropriate for use in non-industrialized and impoverished locations.

The two basic forms of top-bar hives (named after their countries of origin) are the Kenyan (KTBH, with sloped sides) and the Tanzanian ("Tanz", with vertical sides). The Tanzanian is easier to construct, while it is suggested that bees in a Kenyan hive will have much less tendency to adhere comb to the sides of the hive. Once adhered comb is freed from the side (leaving a beespace) the bees tend to not rejoin the comb, so this is not a significant problem for either hive. It is important in either type that end access or some free space without comb is available so adhered comb may be freed. http://en.wikipedia.org/wiki/Top-bar_hive

[211] **Warwick Estevam Kerr** (b. September 9, 1922, Santana do Parnaíba, São Paulo, Brazil) is a Brazilian agricultural engineer, geneticist, entomologist, professor and scientific leader, notable for his discoveries in the genetics and sex determination of bees. He was also responsible for the release in 1957 of experimental, Africanized bee queens, also called killer bees, a hazard to human beings. Africanized bees are hybrids of European and African honey bees. These queens were eventually responsible for the spread of the Africanized bee to continental areas that were previously dominated by the more docile European bee. Kerr became well known for his research on the hybridization of the African bee and the Italian bee (Apis mellifera ligustica), which initially created a national and international stir when several African bee queens escaped inadvertently from Kerr's research apiary in Rio Claro, and colonies of African bees, which are much more aggressive than its European cousin, spread throughout the whole continent, in the process causing many attack and stinging accidents (and a few deaths), until it was thoroughly intermixed with the local bee populations; the descendants are now known as Africanized bees. http://en.wikipedia.org/wiki/Warwick_Estevam_Kerr

[212] *Varroa destructor* is an external parasitic mite that attacks honey bees Apis cerana and Apis mellifera. The disease caused by the mites is called varroatosis. *Varroa destructor* can only replicate in a honey bee colony. It attaches at the body of the bee and weakens the bee by sucking hemolymph. In this process the mite spreads RNA viruses like deformed wing virus (DWV) to the bee. A significant mite infestation will lead to the death of a honey bee colony, usually in the late autumn through early spring. The Varroa mite is the parasite with the most pronounced economic impact on the beekeeping industry. It may be a contributing factor to colony collapse disorder (CCD), as research shows it is the main factor for collapsed colonies in Ontario, Canada.

[213] **Norman Ernest Borlaug** (March 25, 1914 – September 12, 2009) was an American agronomist, humanitarian, and Nobel laureate who has been called "the father of the Green Revolution". Borlaug was one of only six people to have won the Nobel Peace Prize, the Presidential Medal of Freedom and the Congressional Gold Medal. He was also a recipient of the Padma Vibhushan, India's second highest civilian honor. http://en.wikipedia.org/wiki/Norman_Borlaug

[214] **Gung ho** is a term used to mean "enthusiastic" or "dedicated." The term was picked up by United States Marine Corps Major Evans Carlson from his New Zealand friend, Rewi Alley, one of the founders of the Chinese Industrial Cooperatives. Carlson explained in a 1943 interview: "I was trying to build up the same sort of

working spirit I had seen in China where all the soldiers dedicated themselves to one idea and worked together to put that idea over. I told the boys about it again and again. I told them of the motto of the Chinese Cooperatives, Gung Ho. It means Work Together-Work in Harmony...." https://en.wikipedia.org/wiki/Gung_ho

[215] The **Langstroth bee hive** is the standard beehive used in many parts of the world for bee keeping. The advantage of the Langstroth hive over hives previous to its invention on October 30, 1851, is that the bees build honeycomb into frames, which can be moved with little trouble because the frames are designed so that the bees do not attach wax honeycomb between the frames or to the walls of the hive, and do not cement the frames to the side of the box using a resinous substance called propolis. This ability to move the frames allows the beekeeper to manage the bees in a way that had previously been impossible.

[216] When **John S. Harbison**, with his partner, Mr. R. G. Clark, arrived in San Diego aboard the "Orizaba" with one hundred and ten colonies of bees on November 28, 1869, he had long been recognized as California's leading beekeeper. His appearance in San Diego County was the beginning of a chapter in his life that was destined, within seven years time, to make him the largest producer of honey in the world. His success in capitalizing on the vast honey potential of San Diego County, along with his extensive campaign of selling bees to the residents of the county was the major force in making San Diego County the greatest honey producing county in California by 1874. The State of California at that time became and has remained the leading honey producing state of the Union. His was a rare genius that combined theory with practice. During the great explosive development of modern beekeeping in the latter half of the nineteenth century America, he made several important basic contributions to apicultural industry, especially with his "section honey box," which was an intregal part of his patented "California Hive," developed during the winter of 1857-58. His hive, soon to be known to all as the "**Harbison Hive**," was described and illustrated in great detail in his book, *The Beekeeper's Directory, Or The Theory And Practice Of Bee Culture*, published by H. H. Bancroft and Co. in San Francisco, April, 1861. He also published a number of papers on beekeeping and was the leading figure in organizing The Pacific Apiarian Society in 1860, the first beekeepers association west of the Mississippi River. In San Diego History Journal 1969 fall issue https://sandiegohistory.org/login

[217] **Tanzanian beehive.** https://grossmannsbees.wordpress.com/2014/11/13/hive-what-is-the-tanzanian-top-bar-hive/

[218] G. F. Townsend. 1998. **Beehive designs for the Tropics.** Echo Technical Note. University of Guelph.

[219] **Taita Hills forestry beekeeping project.** *Eastern Arc Mountain Information Source* The Bugwood Network - The University of Georgia, College of Agricultural and Environmental Sciences and Warnell School of Forest Resources, Copyright 2004. All rights reserved. Page last modified: Wednesday, August 8, 2001 article is no longer available at the website http://www.easternarc.org/pub/taita_hills_forests_.html

[220] **Elephants and Bees Project: Save the Elephants.** http://elephantsandbees.com/beehive-fence/

[221] **Colony Collapse Disorder** (CCD) or sometimes honey bee depopulation syndrome (HBDS) is a phenomenon in which worker bees from a beehive or European honey bee colony abruptly disappear. While such disappearances have occurred throughout the history of apiculture, the term colony collapse disorder was first applied to a drastic rise in the number of disappearances of Western honey bee colonies in North America in late 2006. Colony collapse is economically significant because many agricultural crops worldwide are pollinated by bees.

European beekeepers observed similar phenomena in Belgium, France, the Netherlands, Greece, Italy, Portugal, and Spain, and initial reports have also come in from Switzerland and Germany, albeit to a lesser degree while the Northern Ireland Assembly received reports of a decline greater than 50%. Possible cases of CCD have also been reported in Taiwan since April 2007.

The cause or causes of the syndrome are not yet fully understood, although many authorities attribute the problem to biotic factors such as Varroa mites and insect diseases (i.e., pathogens including *Nosema apis* and Israel acute paralysis virus). Other proposed causes include environmental change-related stresses, malnutrition and pesticides (e.g. neonicotinoids such as imidacloprid), and migratory beekeeping. More speculative possibilities have included both cell phone radiation (e.g.) and genetically modified (GM) crops with pest control characteristics, though no evidence exists for either assertion. It has also been suggested that it may be due to a combination of many factors and that no single factor is the cause. Revised from Apicultural literature. https://en.wikipedia.org/wiki/Colony_collapse_disorder

[222] **Madaraka Day**, 1 June, commemorates the day that Kenya attained internal self-rule in 1963, preceding full independence from the United Kingdom on 12 December 1963.

[223] I did hear back from **Charles Howe III** and it was the same guy. His answer to my question was: "After returning home and completing construction of my own log home. I've always had the strong desire to keep in agricultural production of any kind. On what was basically a dairy farm, my father also produced honey, maple syrup, beef, and vegetables for our own consumption. With CT's tax structure and rocky land there are very few areas of profitable production." He has lived in Goshen since he returned to the USA, and only married when he was 55. Now he is 64 and taking care of foster children (ages 1 and 3). He is retired from his job, but it doesn't stop him from working. He figures if he lives as long as his parents did, he'll have "twenty more years to work."

[224] A **dik-dik**, pronounced "dĭk' dĭk", is a small antelope of the Genus *Madoqua* that lives in the bush of East Africa, Angola and Namibia. Dik-diks stand 30–40 cm (approx. 12–16 inches) at the shoulder, are 50–70 cm (approx. 20-28 inches) long, weigh 3–6 kg (approx. 7-16 pounds) and can live for up to 10 years. Dik-diks are named for the alarm calls of the females, which make a dik-dik, or zik-zik sound. In addition to the female's alarm call, both the male and female make a shrill whistling sound. These calls often alert a variety of other animals to any disturbance in the area. Consequently, hunters regard dik-diks as a nuisance and have killed great numbers in the past in order to prevent them from scaring away game animals. The picture is also from this website. http://en.wikipedia.org/wiki/Dik-dik

[225] **Sky King** was an American radio and television series. Its lead character was Arizona rancher and aircraft pilot Schuyler "Sky" King. The series may have been based on a true-life personality of the 1930s, Jack Cones, known as the "Flying Constable" of Twentynine Palms in San Bernardino County, California, although this notion is unverified. https://en.wikipedia.org/wiki/Sky_King

[226] 1969: **"Thing"** is unveiled at the Frankfurt Auto Show. http://www.dastank.com/VW-History-1931-1999 The Volkswagen Type 181 "Kurierwagen", popularly known in the United Kingdom as the Trekker, in the United States as the Thing, and in Mexico as the Safari, was a small military vehicle produced by Volkswagen from 1969 to 1983, although civilian sales stopped in 1980. It was based in part on 1969 The Volkswagen's Type 1 (Beetle), and was a continuation and improvement over the Kübelwagen, which had been used by the German military during World War II. The name Kübelwagen is an abbreviation of

Kübelsitzwagen, meaning "bucket-seat car". http://en.wikipedia.org/wiki/Volkswagen_181 The picture of the Thing is from http://www.thesamba.com/vw/forum/viewtopic.php?t=376382

[227] The Taita people (the Wataita or Wadawida) are a Kenyan ethnic group located in the Taita-Taveta District. They speak Taita/Kidawida which belongs to the Bantu languages. The West-Bantu moved to the area of the Taita-Taveta District first approximately in 1000-1300 A.D.

The Taita people migrated to Kenya through Tanzania. They migrated to Kenya in five group each settling at different places of the present Taita Taveta district in Kenya. While settling in these areas the taita speaking people interacted with other communities or tribes particularly the Taveta, the Pare of Tanzania, the borana, the wakamba and the maasai.

There are sub-groups or subtribes of Taita. They can be divided into Wadawida who traditionally lived around the Dawida, the **Wasagalla** who lived around the Sagalla and the Wakasigau who lived around the Kasigau massif of the Taita Hills. The Saghalla people speak Kisaghalla which is much closer to the Kigiriama or Mijikenda (nine tribes who speak almost same language). The Kasighau are more closer to the pare and chagga of Tanzania but are Taita (Kidawida) speaking people. http://en.wikipedia.org/wiki/Taita_people

[228] *The Gods Must Be Crazy* is a 1980 film, written and directed by Jamie Uys. The film is the first in The *Gods Must Be Crazy* series of films. Set in Botswana and South Africa, it tells the story of Xi, a Sho of the Kalahari Desert (played by Namibian San farmer N!xau) whose band has no knowledge of the world beyond. http://en.wikipedia.org/wiki/The_Gods_Must_Be_Crazy

[229] A **two-man saw** is a saw designed for use by two sawyers. While some modern chainsaws are so large that they require two persons to control, two-man saws were primarily important when human power was used. Such a saw would typically be 4 to 12 feet long (approximately 1.2 to 3.6 meters), and sometimes up to 16 feet (4.9 meters), with a handle at each end. In some cases, such as when felling Giant Sequoias, sawblades could be brazed together end-to-end in order to create longer saws. http://en.wikipedia.org/wiki/Two-man_saw

[230] The "**kudus**" are two species of antelope: Lesser Kudu, "*Tragelaphus imberbis*", Greater Kudu, "*Tragelaphus strepsiceros*". The name of the animal was imported into English in the 18th century from isiXhosa iqudu, via Afrikaans koedoe. Lesser Kudus come from the savannas near acacia and *commiphora* shrubs. They have

to rely on thickets for protection, so they are hardly ever seen in the open. Their drab brown and striped pelts help them disappear in scrub environments. http://en.wikipedia.org/wiki/Kudu The picture of the male Great Kudu camouflaged in acacia bush is taken from the same URL.

[231] The death of David Bogenschneider Dayton Daily News http://www.daytondailynews.com/project/content/project/peacecorps/daily/1029peacelist.html

[232] **Peace Corps** statistics from *Dayton Daily News*, Dayton, Ohio. http://www.daytondailynews.com is still on the internet, but the article reference (/project/content/project/peacecorps/daily/1029peacelist) has been removed.

[233] In Hawaiian mythology, the **Menehune** [pronounced meh-neh-HOO-neh] are said to be a people, sometimes described as dwarfs in size, who live in the deep forests and hidden valleys of the Hawaiian Islands, far from the eyes of normal humans. http://en.wikipedia.org/wiki/Menehune

[234] **Children** running to school in Kironge. Picture by Tom Callens

[235] Himburg, N., Community-based ecotourism as a sustainable development option in Taita Taveta, KenyaIn: Pellikka, P., J. Ylhäisi & B. Clark (eds.) Taita Hills and Kenya, 2004 – seminar, reports and journal of a field excursion to Kenya. Expedition reports of the Department of Geography, University of Helsinki 40, 87-95.

[236] View from **Mwachora Peak**, Taita Hills looking toward Mwatate. Picture by Tom Callens

[237] Sirke Piirainen on top of Mt. Vuria http://seipii.vuodatus.net/blog/category/Tapahtumat

Sometimes I kick myself for not taking more pictures back then, but that was in the days of celluloid, it was hard to get film developed, and most of the pictures I did take have long since been lost. I didn't learn to do my own film developing until after I came back from Kenya and went to work for Weyerhaeuser Co. But thankfully, other people have recorded the Taita Hills and made them available through the internet. Like this one posted by Ms. Piirainen.

[238] Taita farm house in Kironge. Picture by Tom Callens.

[239] Taita farm next to Ngangao rain forest. Picture by Tom Callens.

[240] Wundanyi. Picture by Tom Callens.

[241] Yale (left) Wundanyi (center). Picture by Tom Callens.

[242] - The name Kilimanjaro has no certain origin, but one of the most popular theories is that it came from KILMA NJARO meaning "shining mountain" in Swahili. The shiny snow on the peak led nearby residents to believe that evil spirits guarded

the mountain. This myth could also explain why some referred to NJARO as a demon that caused cold. http://www.journeys.travel/portal/kilimanjaro/kili_facts.html

Pictures are by Tom Callens:

Kilimanjaro from Ngongao Forest. Photo curtesy of Tom Callens

Kilimanjaro from from Chawia Forest. Photo curtesy of Tom Callens

[243] Tom Wolf and Shako confirmed that **Michaeli Mwandighi** had passed away, although he did not have details.

[244] As a literary genre, a **memoir** (from the French: mémoire from the Latin memoria, meaning "memory", or a reminiscence), forms a subclass of autobiography – although the terms 'memoir' and 'autobiography' are almost interchangeable in modern parlance. Memoir is autobiographical writing, but not all autobiographical writing follows the criteria for memoir, as listed here. The author of a memoir may be referred to as a memoirist.

Memoirs are structured differently from formal autobiographies which tend to encompass the writer's entire life span, focusing on the development of his or her personality. The chronological scope of a memoir is determined by the work's context and is therefore more focused and flexible than the traditional arc of birth to childhood to old age as found in an autobiography.

Memoirs tended to be written by politicians or people in court society, later joined by military leaders and businessmen, and often dealt exclusively with the writer's careers rather than their private life. Historically, memoirs have dealt with public matters, rather than personal. Many older memoirs contain little or no information about the writer, and are almost entirely concerned with other people. Modern expectations have changed this, even for heads of government. Like most autobiographies, memoirs are generally written from the first person point of view.

Gore Vidal, in his own memoir *Palimpsest*, gave a personal definition: "a memoir is how one remembers one's own life, while an autobiography is history, requiring research, dates, facts double-checked." It is more about what can be gleaned from a section of one's life than about the outcome of the life as a whole.

Humorist Will Rogers put it a little more pithily: "Memoirs means when you put down the good things you ought to have done and leave out the bad ones you did do."

Contemporary practices of writing memoirs for recreational, family or therapeutic purposes are sometimes referred to as legacy writing or personal history. Such products may be assisted by professional or amateur genealogists, or by ghostwriters. http://en.wikipedia.org/wiki/Memoir

245 A Hawaiian language translation was completed by New England Christian missionaries including Reverends Hiram Bingham, Asa Thurston, Lorrin Andrews, and Sheldon Dibble from 1800-1850. The Gospels (Matthew, Mark, Luke, and John) were translated in 1828. The rest of the New Testament was translated in 1832, the Old Testament was translated in 1839, and the translation was revised in 1868. https://en.wikipedia.org/wiki/Bible_translations_into_Hawaiian

246 I have consulted three Kiswahili dictionaries (*Kamusi.org*). One includes 'mapolu' but does not have a definition or a translation.

247 In: Pellikka, P., J. Ylhäisi & B. Clark (eds.) Taita Hills and Kenya, 2004 – seminar, reports and journal of a field excursion to Kenya. Expedition reports of the Department of Geography, University of Helsinki 40, 87-95. Helsinki 2004, ISBN 952-10-2077-6, 148 pp.

248 Map of the forests of Taita Hills. In: Pellikka, P., J. Ylhäisi & B. Clark (eds.) Taita Hills and Kenya, 2004 – seminar, reports and journal of a field excursion to Kenya. Expedition reports of the Department of Geography, University of Helsinki 40, 87-95. Helsinki 2004, ISBN 952-10-2077-6, 148 pp.

249 In: Pellikka, P., J. Ylhäisi & B. Clark (eds.) Taita Hills and Kenya, 2004 – seminar, reports and journal of a field excursion to Kenya. Expedition reports of the Department of Geography, University of Helsinki 40, 87-95. Helsinki 2004, ISBN 952-10-2077-6, 148 pp.

250 **Wadawida.com** The meeting point for all Taitas in Kenya and outside Kenya https://www.facebook.com/Wadawidacom-115533391901867/

251 **Lake Chala** is now a tourist destination complete with a tourist lodge. https://www.tanzania-experience.com/blog/lake-chala-crater-in-shadow-of-kili/

252 **Pain, B. R. 1970.** Water balance of Lake Chala and its relation to groundwater from tritium and stable isotope data. *Journal of Hydrology* 11:1 47-58

253 The **Lake Chala tilapia** (*Oreochromis hunteri*) is a species of fish in the Cichlidae family. It is endemic to Kenya. Its natural habitat is freshwater lakes. http://en.wikipedia.org/wiki/Lake_Chala_tilapia

254 By Adrian Blomfield in Nairobi and Richard Alleyne in *The Telegraph* UK. http://www.telegraph.co.uk/news/worldnews/africaandindianocean/kenya/1387432/Crocodile-girl-told-that-lake-was-safe-to-swim-in.html

255 Same reference as footnote 247.

[256] A rondavel is a traditional African-style house. The rondavel is usually round or oval in shape and is traditionally made with materials that can be locally found in raw form. Its walls are often constructed from stones. The mortar may consist of sand, soil, or combinations of these, mixed with cow dung or cement. The floor of a "traditional" rondavel is finished with a dung mixture to make it hard and smooth. The main roofing elements of a rondavel are spars or poles taken from tree limbs (called "gumpoles" these days), which have been harvested and cut to length. The roof covering is of thatch that is sewn to the poles with grass rope. The process of completing the thatch can take as little as one weekend or up to a year if made by a skilled artisan, as it must be sewn in one section at a time, starting from the bottom working towards the top. As each section is sewn, it may be weathered and aged to form a complete weatherproof seal. http://en.wikipedia.org/wiki/Rondavel

[257] Terracing swamp land in Bolivia. L. excerpted from Erickson.Clark "Raised Field Agriculture in the Lake Titicaca Basin" *Expedition Magazine* 30. (1988): n. pag. *Expedition Magazine*. Penn Museum, 1988 Web. 07 Aug 2021 http://www.penn.museum/sites/expedition/?p=2314

[258] The **Ants of Kenya** (Hymenoptera: Formicidae)—Faunal Overview, First Species Checklist, Bibliography, Accounts for All Genera, and Discussion on Taxonomy and Zoogeography Author(s): Francisco Hita Garcia, Eva Wiesel, Georg Fischer
Source: *Journal of East African Natural History*, 101(2):127-222. 2013.
Published By: Nature Kenya/East African Natural History Society
DOI: http://dx.doi.org/10.2982/028.101.0201
URL: http://www.bioone.org/doi/full/10.2982/028.101.0201

[259] Hellmuth, S. M., Chalmers, P. N., Kemp, M. T., Lapin, H. E. and Marino, P. A. 2004 Local abundances of three acacia-ant species, *Pseudomyrmex flavicornis*, *P. nigrocincta*, ... response among the three ant species Dartmouth Studies in Tropical Ecology 1-3. www.dartmouth.edu/~biofsp/pdf04/p1fsp04.pdf

[260] Goheen, Jacob R. AU - Palmer, Todd M. T1 - Defensive Plant-Ants Stabilize Megaherbivore-Driven Landscape Change in an African Savanna Y1 - 2010 JF - Current biology: CB JO - Current biology: CB JA - Curr Biol VL - IS - SP - EP - PB - Cell Press SN - 0960-9822 http://linkinghub.elsevier.com/retrieve/pii/S0960982210010055 http://www.cell.com/current-biology/abstract/S0960-9822(10)01005-5

Made in the USA
Las Vegas, NV
12 February 2022